A BELFAST CHRONICLE
1789

High Street, Belfast, 1786. Painted in 1786 by John Nixon: engraved in the 1880s.

For my mother and to the memory of my father

We are very grateful to the Belfast Central Library for
giving permission to use their original copies of the
Belfast Newsletter of 1789.

The Friar's Bush Press
24 College Park Avenue
Belfast BT7 1LR
Published 1989
© Copyright reserved of introduction

ISBN 0946872 28 7

Cover designed by Rodney Miller Associates, Belfast.
Printed by W. & G. Baird, Antrim.

A BELFAST CHRONICLE 1789

a compilation from the
Belfast Newsletter

compiled and introduced by James McAllister

FRIAR'S BUSH PRESS

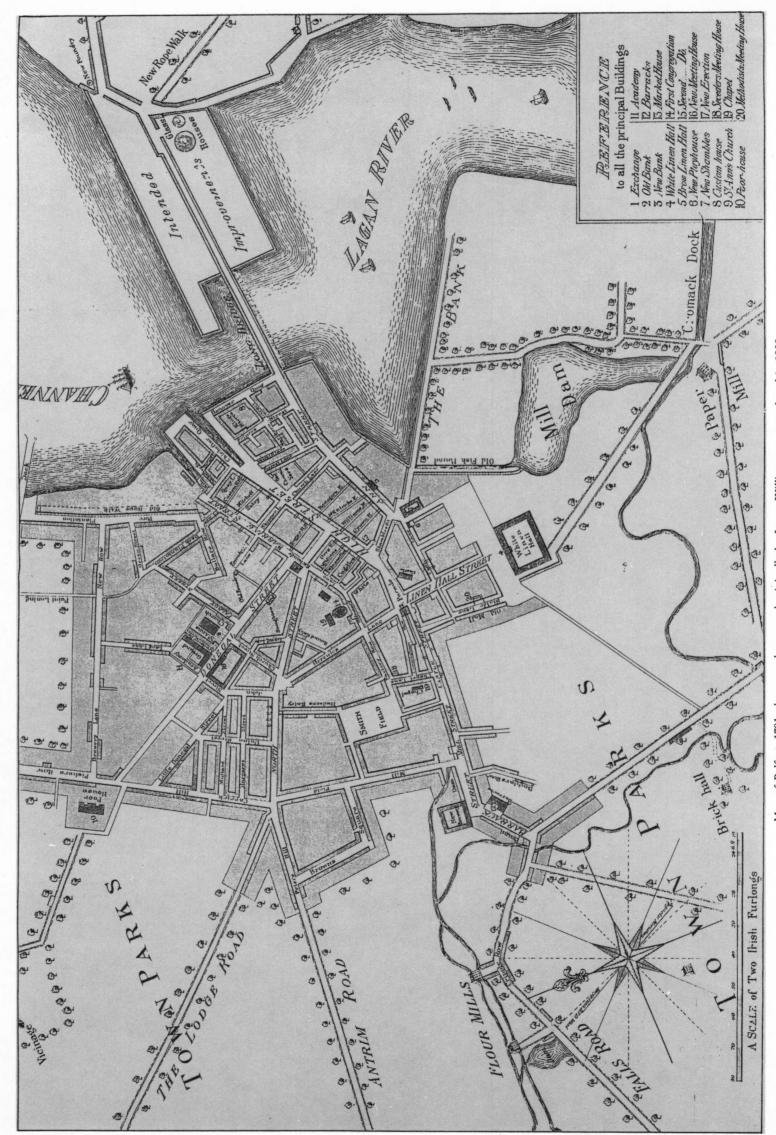

Map of Belfast, 1791, drawn and engraved originally by James Williamson, reproduced in 1888.

Belfast Two Hundred Years Ago:

Introduction

The *Belfast Newsletter* is a truly unique, yet under-used, source not only of local but British, European and, indeed, world history. Founded in 1737 the paper is the oldest surviving newsheet in Europe. During 1789, already a mature 52 year old institution, the *Newsletter* appeared twice every week on Tuesday and Friday. Each issue contained four large, tightly packed pages of advertisements, news, parliamentary reports, poetry, letters, comment and scandal. To modern eyes the paper is difficult to read, it would win few prizes for graphic design. Each page consisted of a jumble of dates and snippets of news (often totally unrelated to each other) under each by-line and straight lines were virtually non-existent. Despite such weaknesses, the archaic language and sardonic humour still appeal greatly to a modern reader. If, as the cliche claimed, every society received the press it deserved, Belfast readers were very well served by Henry Joy's rag. Reading through a single year helps recreate a fascinating glimpse into a forgotten world stretching from central Belfast westwards to America and eastwards through Britain and Europe to India and Australia. As a bonus the year 1789 also proved of pivotal significance for both domestic and world events.

Belfast in 1789 was still a relatively small town of approximately 18,000 souls located on the Co. Antrim bank of the river Lagan. In Co. Down, across the bridge, Ballymacarrett now developed as a thriving industrial village largely out of sight and out of mind. Even historians often forget that Belfast's rapid demographic and economic growth only really took off well into the nineteenth century. This expansion relied upon metal ships, engineering, tobacco processing and linen production. Yet if still modest in size, Belfast in 1789 was a hive of economic and social activity. From the *Newsletter* we obtain the clear impression of a well developed, diversified regional economy. Belfast's population, or at least the richer members of it, also enjoyed a varied social life.

Clearly the port of Belfast stimulated the whole local economy. Students of British commercial history write about a "commercial revolution" taking place between 1650 and 1750 when new trade routes and novel commodities became well established. Certainly we can detect considerable evidence in support of this thesis; in 1789 Belfast trade across the Atlantic to Jamaica, New York, the southern states and through Europe was commonplace. Clearly Belfast shipping and merchants were already well integrated into a genuine 'Atlantic Economy'. Migrants seeking greater economic opportunities moved westwards while American produce, tobacco, cotton, wood ashes, were transported eastwards. Several Belfast merchants imported bales of cotton to supply the nascent cotton spinning factories. Cotton production began in Belfast's Poor House during 1778 when pauper children learnt handspinning. Nicholas Grimshaw, a committee member, generously donated a carding machine and spinning wheel to this employment experiment. In 1779 Robert Joy and Thomas McCabe installed machinery and a section of the poor house, now employing 90 labourers, became Belfast's first spinning mill. By 1789 several cotton factories operated but still on a modest scale. Despite these very promising cotton experiments, in 1789, linen still dominated the local economy. Increased exports of linen to Dublin and overseas created pressures for the erection of a handsome new White Linen Hall. Built with a £10,000 public subscription this opened in 1785. Throughout the year we read about opportunists stealing linens from bleach fields, advertisements for suitable workers and the location of bleaching sites, e.g. Whitehouse, are often noted. Linen exports also called for comment. Certainly linen production pervaded life in Belfast and along the Lagan Valley; the *Newsletter's* advertisements and comments provide valuable insights into this crucial industry.

Foreign trade also enriched individuals' lives through the provision of new commodities from distant and exotic places. The richer Belfast citizen clearly enjoyed a wide range of imported products: wines (including vintage champagnes) and spirits, tobacco, fruit, especially figs (a useful laxative), and

pottery. This sophisticated range of consumer goods reflected both growing trade and rising incomes among many local groups, including professional men, land owners, merchants and industrial employers. In late eighteenth century Belfast some people, at least, enjoyed a consumer revolution. The advertisements here reproduced provide a unique illustration of this whole process in operation, showing the goods and services available to consumers in Belfast society.

While the foreign trade sector remained important agriculture, land, and property were also central to local life. Again the *Newsletter* provided literally hundreds of advertisements from virtually all over Ulster offering land, houses and shops for rent or sale. From this we may identify new areas of development, e.g. Peter's Hill where building went on apace through 1789. The location of shops and houses help historians recreate eighteenth century Belfast. Farm size, methods of land measurement and lease agreements all appeared in abundance. While neither a truly random sample nor a systematic data base this detailed information is still extremely valuable to local historians.

Often advertisements provide useful insights into almost forgotten activities: ads for Crown Glass and the 'New Foundry' awaken interest. Before 1776 most glass used in Belfast was imported from Britain. In that year Benjamin Edwards, a glass master from Bristol, introduced the technique at Bridge-End. John Smylie built a second, larger, glass works close by in 1785 with a 120 foot cone – the largest in Ireland. Perhaps, after all, Ballymacarrett was not out of sight. Edwards also established a 'New Foundry' in 1783 at the junction of the Newtownards Road and Foundry Street where he produced moulds and machinery for his glass works, boilers for bleachers and a vast range of domestic pots and pans. These advertisements for Crown Glass and the New Foundry remind modern readers about the wide, and growing, range of goods and services now available from *within* the local economy. As domestic production increased, imports from England or elsewhere became less important. This represented considerable economic progress.

From these pages we learn much about society and social activities. Without much exaggeration we can detect the faint stirrings of a 'leisure revolution' in Ulster society. For richer people at least a considerable range of outdoor and indoor activities became available. Seabathing was considered efficacious, promoting health and long life. George III's periodic visits to Weymouth and Prince George's entourage at Brighton created fashionable seabathing centres in England. Ulster could claim nothing quite so grand, a cottage at Cultra was hardly comparable. Yet such advertisements provided faint glimmers of what would become a holiday revolution a century later with north Down at its centre.

Bloodsports, especially cockfighting, hare chasing and bear baiting were still taken for granted in this society. Social historians detect a repudiation of such cruel activities after 1700 among elites in Britain and Europe. In Ulster the 'middling groups' advertised, indulged in and clearly still relished these plebeian pleasures.

Society was not a cultureless desert; throughout long winter months plays and concerts were well advertised by a series of actor/entrepreneurs. The *Newsletter* is an important source for names and programmes on offer. Admittedly some events proved less commercial than others as several performances never opened. A series of Assemblies met in Belfast and elsewhere for dancing and social intercourse. As in England these social occasions often encouraged marriage by providing an acceptable meeting place for unattached individuals. After one Assembly, in Newtownards, someone liberated four spoons. Human nature never changes! Political meetings, business deals, gossip and serious drinking were also conducted in numerous, well advertised, inns throughout the province.

Modern economists insist that education is an important investment in human capital. Advertisements for tutors and schools were well represented in the *Newsletter*. Most schools, e.g. Belfast Academy, provided a traditional, classical education of little use in a work-a-day world. Similar criticisms were often made of English public and American private schools. Belfast, like eighteenth century Boston, produced at least one school, Mawhinney's in Pottinger's Entry, which taught the 3 'R's along with book-keeping. These were essential skills for any commercial community bent upon making profits.

Belfast citizenry have long enjoyed (if that is the *mot juste)* an unenviable reputation as worshippers of mammon. In every issue, on virtually every page

High Street, Belfast, 1831, drawn by T. M. Baynes and engraved by J. Davies.

of the *Newsletter*, advertisers sought loans or investments on good security. Also Magee's and Nicholson's lavishly advertised lotteries, like modern football pools, proffered untold wealth for investors in the Irish or British lotteries. In late eighteenth century Belfast an impersonal capital market with banks and stock exchange hardly existed. Personal reputation, good security and an appeal for funds through the columns of the *Newsletter* achieved more than bank loans. Unfortunately, we never discover where these funds went. Often, one suspects, they sustained personal consumption and enjoyment of life rather than promoted sound investment in the local economy.

"Love of money is the root of all evil." St. Paul and many Christian apologists repeated the message over the centuries – but none did in this year's *Newsletter*. Surprisingly, in an alleged "age of faith", religion contributed little to the *Newsletter's* stories. Certainly no minister of religion condemned money grubbing. Raising cash for Down Cathedral (a perennial problem), internecine squabbles among Presbyterians, conversion to Anglicanism for squalid personal motives, accounts of lodges attending church and repeated celebrations of King George's recovery were among topics covered in varying detail. References to the religious and marching activities of several already well established Loyal Orange "Lodges" are especially interesting because they predate the beginnings of Orangeism by six years. Were they really Masonic lodges or some form of Orange club rather than a genuine Orange Lodge?

Finally, Ulstermen, if these advertisements reflected reality, were exceedingly careless: watches and wives become misplaced with gay abandon. Pickpockets or sheer carelessness after drink account for the frequent loss of fob watches in Belfast streets and elsewhere. In a society where divorce required an expensive act of parliament an ill-treated woman could only desert her matrimonial home. Elopement meant forfeiting any dowry brought to the marriage. Unless eloping with a 'friend' life could become very hard. Divorce by migration was an important, but overlooked, part of early modern society throughout Britain and Ireland.

Ulster society was but one aspect of the *Newsletter's* concern throughout 1789. Readers enjoyed an extensive coverage of important events in Ireland, Britain, Europe, America and beyond. Several factors help explain the remarkably eclectic range of news stories jostling side by side on virtually every page. Before investigative journalism, editors found it exceedingly difficult to fill pages of tightly printed newspaper. Henry Joy, like his contemporaries elsewhere, employed only a few editorial staff. He was forced to rely on, and publish, virtually every scrap of news which came his way. Belfast in 1789, still a small peripheral town, generated little real news, certainly too little for eight large pages each and every week of the year. Every issue necessarily contained considerable out of town news, some stolen from English papers – with or without attribution – some came through overseas correspondents and even extracts from recent books.

Legal cases and parliamentary procedures from Dublin and London also provided an important backbone to the paper.

During 1789 three major news stories meandered through Joy's paper: George III's unstable mental health, Farmer Washington's progress as American president and, of course, the French Revolution. During early 1789 King George's health almost precipitated a constitutional crisis as his estranged son prepared for Regency. Once the King recovered prayers ascended Godwards, householders lit lamps and celebration balls were enjoyed without any thought of expense. In time the king, his queen and family proceeded to Weymouth for rest and recuperation. Public concern tended to decline. Despite a conscious republicanism in parts of Belfast society then, as now, royal stories helped fill and sell newspapers.

The continued interest in General Washington and his newly created nation is also easily understood. Throughout the eighteenth century, especially after 1720 when rents increased, Scotch-Irish migrated westwards from Ulster to America. Emotional links between the province and north America remained strong, indeed many Ulstermen, from general to private, served in Washington's revolutionary army. Both Washington and the newly independent United States of America were mainly portrayed with naive goodwill looking for, and reporting, mainly positive achievements in America.

French financing of a revolutionary war in America against England helped bankrupt Louis XVI's administration and so ultimately released revolution in France and Europe. Ironically throughout January 1789 interest in things French centred on fashion rather than bloody revolution. Then, as now, Paris was the European centre for *haute couture*. However fashion soon took second place as French society underwent political and then economic and social revolution. The detailed coverage of French affairs was very impressive, at one point news took only 36 hours to arrive from Paris. Or, was this claim in fact hollow? Certainly accounts about the Bastille and events in Paris proved very comprehensive. Revolutionary spirit effected not just France but spread from the Parisian epicentre to Belgium and Germany as these regions revolted from their own *ancien régimes*.

Historians all too commonly overstate the importance of both their sources and the thesis they wish to propound. Such human frailty is understandable simply because closeness lends an impression of importance to the subject under scrutiny and no-one wishes to be accused of studying trivia. I would repeat my earlier contention that the *Newsletter* provides a truly unique source for the study of local affairs to history on a world stage. While some sources, e.g. British parliamentary reports, remain accessible elsewhere, others exist only within the *Newsletter's* pages. Letters and comments from Dublin, London, Paris, America exist nowhere else. Only here are they captured, and displayed, like flies in amber. To claim that the *Newsletter* in 1789 (and other years too) is unique and important is no overstatement.

Finally a short comment must be made about method. All selections of material for such an edition are necessarily highly selective, reflecting the concerns of an individual compiler. As an economic and social, rather than political or constitutional, historian I plead guilty to perhaps overrepresenting my particular specialism. Yet there was some method in my madness. As this book reproduced approximately one tenth of the *Newsletter* a draconian approach to editing was necessary. I omitted reams of extremely tedious parliamentary business, most of which was still available elsewhere. Also by excluding duplicated items, especially advertisements inserted issue after issue, this limited selection still permitted the inclusion of a wide range of material. In my selection I included the maximum amount of relevant information about Belfast and Ulster. This remained my prime priority within this project. In some weeks local news proved thin indeed – a few brief lines in a total of eight pages – at other times such reports provided a rich vein of fascinating detail. Also I tried to include a wide, but necessarily brief, selection of national and international reports which both placed local life and events within a context and reminded the reader about the many wider issues of life in the world at large. This melding of local with national and international newsreporting also contributes much to the interest of this selection of 1789's *Belfast Newsletter*.

James McAllister

Anno 1789.] Printed by HENRY JOY, Senr. and Junr. BELFAST.

The BELFAST NEWS LETTER.

TUESDAY December 30, FRIDAY January 2, 1789.

For LONDON,

THE LONDON PACKET, JAMES GLASS, Master, (a constant Trader and now in Port ready to load) will sail the 10th January next, wind and weather permitting.——For Freight apply to
ARCH. TAYLOR.

Newry, 15th Dec. 1788.

For Charlestown,

The ANN, of LARNE.

ANTHONY SINCLAIR requests all who wish to take a passage on board the ANN, of LARNE, for Charlestown, will meet him at Ballymena on the first Tuesday of February next, to settle on the time (most convenient for the Passengers) for the sailing of said Vessel.

Larne, 23d Dec. 1788.

Fresh Teas, Dantzig Ashes, &c.

GEORGE LANGTRY

HAS just received a large assortment of each.——He has also for sale, First and Second Clayed and Scale Sugars of a remarkable fine quality; in consequence of a late fall on that article will be sold remarkably cheap to close sales.

Belfast, 1st December, 1788.

The Publick are respectfully informed,

THAT THOMAS NEILSON, & CO. have just compleated their

WINTER ASSORTMENT

of *Woollen Drapery, Hosiery, New Buttons*, and all the other Articles which they usually sell.

*** LADIES Gilt, spangled, Plate, and Lace HATBANDS, of the most elegant Patterns.

NEAT PATENT HATS, at 8s. 8d. each, with Livery and other LACES of various Breadths and Patterns.

Belfast, 23d December, 1788.

Wholesale Woollen Warehouse, Belfast.

BROWN, GAW, & Co. have received their Winter Assortment of Broad Cloths, Forests, Plains, Coatings, Stuffs, &c. &c. which they are selling cheap for cash or bills in course.

24thNovember, 1788.

New Fruit.

WILLIAM HENDREN, has just arrived a Quantity; consisting of Figs—Tar, Box, and Cask Raisins, Jordan and Valencia Almonds, Lemons and Oranges—all in choice condition, which, with a general Assortment of Groceries, he is determined to sell on the most moderate terms, at the Shop formerly occupied by Mr. James Mooney, *who hath resigned the Grocery Business* in Favour of said Hendren.

Said Hendren has a House to Let, consisting of three stories, back Yard, and other conveniencies, in Harp Entry:——Also a first Floor genteelly furnished, and Stabling if required.—Enquire at the Shop of William Hendren. 22d December, 1788.

New Warehouse, Rosmary-Lane.

FORSYTH, SHAW, and Co. beg leave to inform their Friends, they have got home their Winter Assortment of Woollens, Fustians, Stuffs, &c. which will be sold on very low terms for cash or bills in course.

Belfast, 8th Dec. 1788.

Taylor, Maxwell & Co. Grocers,

BEG leave to inform their Friends, that they have laid in from the best Markets, a general Assortment of Goods in the above Line, at their Shop in the lower End of North-street.

As their chief Study shall be the Interest of their Correspondents, they hope to merit their approbation and that of the Publick in general.

Belfast, 27th Nov. 1788.

Wanted immediately,

THE Sum of Two Hundred Pounds, for which the very best Security will be given.——Apply to Mr. Henry Joy. Belfast, November 24, 1788.

Hu. and Wm. Johnson

HAVE received their winter assortment of superfine, broad, and narrow Cloths, Cassameres, Coatings, Elastic Cloths, new Waistcoating, new Buttons, Florentines, Lutherines, Thicksets, Mullinetts, Marseilles quilting, furniture and garment Cottons, Callicoes and Dimities, Damascus, Ticking, Counterpanes, Marseilles quilts, &c. &c. Belfast, 1st December, 1788.

N. B. They shortly expect Moreens.

Robert Getty

HAS received per the Charlotte, from London, a large supply of new Teas, which will be sold on the most reasonable terms for ready money or good bills.

He has at present for sale

New Dantzig, } Ashes,	Gum Senegal,
1st American, }	Aleppo Galls,
Pot and Pearl }	Italian Cream Tartar,
Refined Saltpetre,	Carolina Rice,
Kentish Bag Hops,	French Barley,
Black Pepper,	Leaf Tobacco.

Wanted a few tons barley, for which the highest price will be given.

Belfast, 1st Dec. 1788.

FLOUR, *first, second, third*, and *fourth*, Prestonpans Vitriol, best White Pearl Ashes, and Galway Kelp. A cargo of each is just landed by

Clements Gillespie,

who is as usual largely supplied with best Allicant and Carthagena Barilla, blue Pearl ashes, and No. 4 Smalts. He has just received a cargo of American Pot Ash of the first mark, and daily expects an assortment of Weed Ashes from Dantzig, of different brands, with Timber and Lathwood. He has also received his fresh Teas from the last India Sales;—all which will be sold at his Stores in Canal-street on the most reasonable terms.

Newry, 1st Nov. 1788.

New Fruit, *&c.*

ROBERT GETTY has just received from Malaga a Cargo of New Fruit—which are in very fine order, and consist of Figs in casks, Sun Bloom and Muscatel Raisins in casks and boxes, Jordan and Valencia Almonds, Lemons and Sweet and Sour Oranges.—This Cargo will be sold on very reasonable terms, and every encouragement given to Wholesale Purchasers.

He has received per same opportunity, a parcel of best Spanish Shumach. Belfast, 25th Nov. 1788.

Strong JAMAICA RUM, fine SCALE SUGAR, St. DOMINGO COTTON, &c.

ROBERT SCOTT has just imported per the Snow Mary, Captain Corry, from Jamaica,—A Cargo of strong well flavoured Rum, very fine Scale Sugar, St. Domingo and Jamaica Cotton, Logwood, white Ginger, Pimento, and a few Logs of Mahogany of a very good quality.

He is also well supplied with variety of TEAS from the last Sales, and daily expects the arrival of a parcel of New HOPS.

Belfast, 1st November, 1788.

To be let and entered on immediately, Two commodious new-built Houses, on Chichester-Quay: They are elegantly finished with marble chimney-pieces, grates, locks, &c. and each House accommodated with a backyard, and office-houses suitable.

Also two large Stores fronting the Lime-kiln Dock For particulars enquire of said Robert Scott.

Narcissus Batt,

IS now landing out of the Brig John, from Malaga, a Quantity of Mountain Wine, Raisins in Boxes and Casks, Figs, Almonds and Green Grapes, which, with the following Articles, he will dispose of on the most reasonable Terms, at his Stores in Linenhall-street:

Claret,	In Wood & Bottle,	Old Spirit,
Madeira,		Cherry Juice,
Port,		American Pot Ashes of 1st and 2d quality,
Sherry,		American Pearl do.
Canary,		Oil of Vitriol,
Mountain,		Carolina Indigo,
Frontigniac,		Essence of Spruce,
Vin de Grave,		Bergen Deals,
Brandy,		Yellow Cotton Wool.
Geneva,		
Rum,		

November 7th, 1788.

Advertisement.

TO be set for the term of thirty one years from the first of November next, the following lands; (part of the estate of Amos Stretell, Esq;) situated in the barony of Kilconway, and county of Antrim, viz. the town land of Carelinty, containing 253 acres arable and pasture, lying within five miles of Ballymena; the Half Town of Galdinah, containing 275 acres arable and pasture, situated on the great road leading from Ballymena to Ballymoney, within four miles of the latter—also the farm of Eglish, within a quarter of a mile of the town of Clough, containing 58A. 3R. 20P. arable and pasture, together with the customs of said town. The above lands are well situated for Fire and Water, and also persons carrying on the Linen Manufacture. Application to be made to Mr. James Edmonston, junr. Dunbought near Ballymena; who will receive proposals from any persons disposed to treat for said lands. Dated Sept. 12th, 1788.

MARY CONNOR,

Milliner and Haberdasher,

INFORMS the Publick she has opened Shop in High-street, next door to Mr. Bellew's, Jeweller, and is assorted with the most fashionable Goods in that Line, of the best quality, which she is enabled, (from her having purchased for ready money from the Manufacturers) and determined to sell on the most moderate terms.

The punctuality with which she is determined to execute the commands of those who are pleased to favour her in the Millinery Department, added to the knowledge, which she flatters herself she has acquired of the business by several years experience in Dublin; emboldens her to look up to the Ladies of Belfast and its vicinity, for their countenance and protection.

Belfast, Dec. 24th, 1788.

JOHN GETTY,

CABINET-MAKER, a few Doors above the Brown Linen-Hall, Donegall-street, Belfast,

RETURNS his sincere thanks for the very flattering encouragement he has received since his commencement in Business; and hopes by his reasonable Charges, neat Workmanship, and good Materials, to merit a continuance of public favour.

He has MAHOGANY for Sale in all Scantlings from whole Logs down to Quarter Inch Board; also OAK of a very good quality.——ORDERS from the Country executed with Care, Punctuality and Dispatch.

GETTY has lately received for the inspection of his Customers, a Pattern-Book of the most Fashionable Furniture used at present in London.

January 1st, 1789.

To be Sold by Auction,

AT the Market-House in Belfast, at twelve o'clock on Monday 19th day January next, that tenement late Mr. George Mitchell's, situate on the North side lower end of High-Street, Belfast, held under lease from the Earl of Donegall for 99 years and three lives, from 1st May, 1767, at the yearly rent of 7l. 4s. (including fees.) On the premisses are two dwelling houses in front, one of which is set, during the term, to Mr. John Mitchell;—and in the rear extending down Mitchell's Entry, are four new built houses, three stories high, and three two stories high, yielding a profit rent of 81l. 1s. per annum.—To be set up together or by separate houses agreeable to the bidders.

A tenement on the West side of North-Street, opposite Mr. Thomas Scott's, held under lease from Alexander Legg, Esq; for 91 years and three lives from 1st May, 1771, at the yearly rent of 4l. 10s. 6d. which produces a profit rent of 9l. 4s. 7d. h. per year. On the front is a dwelling house set to Wm. Duncan for 3 lives or 61 years, from 1st November, 1779;—and on the rear on one side of the lane leading from North-Street to Hercules-Lane, are seven cabbins set to tenants at will.

Also the lease of two fields adjoining Humphry Dillon's garden, held under William Mussenden, Esq; three years of which unexpired at November last, and set to a tenant at will for two guineas profit rent. For further information apply to Mr. John Mitchell who will shew the premisses.

The Executors of the late Mr. George Mitchell request that all persons who have not yet discharged their accounts may immediately do so to Mr. George Munro, or they will be put into the hands of an attorney to recover them.

Stewart Beaty, } Executors.
Chr. Hudson }

Belfast, 9th Dec. 1788.

Boot and Shoe Manufactory.

GEORGE Monro who acted in the capacity of a Foreman to the late Mr. George Mitchell, deceased, for the space of eight years last past, humbly requests the protection and favour of said Mr. Mitchell's customers, whose particular study it always was to merit their countenance.

ALEXANDER ARMSTRONG requests that all those who are indebted to him above six months, may discharge their respective accounts, otherwise he will be under the disagreeable necessity of putting them into the hands of a proper person, in order to recover them.

Belfast, 1st January, 1789.

THE Master, Wardens, and Brethren of Lodge, No. 599, and of the other Lodges who accompanied them this day to Church, return their grateful thanks to the Revd. Geo. Galbraith, for his excellent Discourse delivered to them on that occasion.

Signed by Order,
J. M. Secretary.

Aughnacloy, 27th Dec. 1788.

NEW FRENCH DRESSES.

BALL DRESS.

The habit is a long-sleeved robe and petticoat of white sattin; the fore part of the robe, down to the waist, and the skirt of the petticoat, are trimmed with a furbelow of gauze, cut in points; above which runs a garland of rose ribband, flounced, and interlaced with artificial oak-leaves, made of geren satin.

Under the robe is a *corset* of rose satin, the skirts of which are edged with white ribband.

The head-dress is only a garland, of the same kind as that on the robe.

The hair is dressed in detached curls, four of which fall on the bosom—behind is a waving *chignon*.

On the neck is a large *fichu*, very projecting, and open; its ends go round the waist, and are tied in the middle of the back.

At the girdle hang two golden chains, belonging to two watches, in two little fobs.

The shoes are of green satin, trimmed with broad fringe of white silk.

D U B L I N, DEC. 30.

It is now asserted, and that with much confidence, that the M———s will undoubtedly meet Parliament on the 20th of January.

When the Irish Parliament meet, the Viceroy will declare from the throne the situation of the Sovereign, and recommend to Parliament to ascertain the facts—this cannot be done otherwise than in England, by the examination of the State Physicians, who must personally inspect the King's condition.

By direction of the Irish Parliament, the State Physicians will visit his Majesty at Kew, and their report will determine the measure of a Regent for Ireland.

The physicians journey will require some time, and it is not improbable, in the intermediate time, that Parliament may adjourn.

The M———s piques himself no little on this arrangement, as by this mode he affects to preserve the independence of Ireland pure and unsullied.

There is now a very general scramble for the many good things vacated by the death of Sir Wm. Montgomery. The snug place of Inspector of Permits, with 1000l. per annum, is already given away to Capt. Stephen Freemantle, who is married to the Attorney General's niece.

Capt. T. Burgh has secured the agency of the artillery and Drogheda's light horse.

Not less than 26 regimental agencies were held by Sir William. The candidates for these are numerous —Mr. H. Stuart—Major Cane—Mr. Ormsby—Mr. Frazer—Mr. Wybrant—Major Read—Mr. Burgh, &c. &c.

On Sunday the 7th instant, the following persons embraced the Protestant religion in the church of Tarbert, before the Rev. Ralph Wall and a full congregation, viz. Francis Kelly, John Ware, John Fitzgerald, Michael Fitzgerald, Charles Connor, Jane Rea, Ann Ware, and Winifred Cunningham.

A letter from Monaghan, dated December 26, says, "Yesterday the following persons renounced the errors of the Church of Rome and embraced the Protestant religion, before the Rev. Dr. Warren; Francis Moynagh, Terence Duffy, and Peter M'Attee."

Last week a dreadful fire broke out in the house of Mr. Stanley, farmer, at Cookstown, in the county of Wicklow, which in a few hours consumed every valuable article therein, to the amount of upwards of one thousand pounds; the fruits of the unremitting industry of that worthy man, who by this catastrophe is with his family, reduced the greatest distress. The house of Mr. Henry Strong, which joins that of Mr. Stanley's, was happily rescued to from sharing the same fate by a fortunate change in the wind.

Yesterday a young gentleman skaiting on one of the ponds in the Park, was unfortunately drowned.

In ancient times it was not the custom in Russia to deposit in the earth the remains of such people as died in the winter until the return of mild weather, as appears from the following account by Phineas Fletcher, Ambassador from Queen Elizabeth to Russia: "In winter time, when all is covered with snow, so many as die are piled up in a hovel in the suburbs, like billets on a woodstack; they are as hard with the frost as a very stone, till the spring-tide come and dissolve the frost; when every man taketh his dead friend, and committeth him to the ground."

BANKRUPT. James M'Cleery, of Portaferry, co. Down, merchant, to surrender on the 10th and 12th of January, and 10th of February next.

Belfast, *January* 2.

In the present struggle in England beveen the two great parties of the state, we have endeavured to hold as equal a hand as we possibly could; conning ourselves chiefly to the DEBATES IN PARLIAMENT, hich we have not given entire from the Papers devoteo any party, but have selected from the different Printthe best account of each persons speech, and followe thoſe papers where we found the *reasoning* of the respeive speakers exhibited in the most favourable and ampleanner.

Money wanted.

SIX HUNDRED POUNDS wanted immediately on a Mortgage of Lands in the county of Antrim, held by lease renewable;—also £ 600 on personal security, three in a bond.——Apply to Mr. Arthur, Attorney, Belfast.

29th December, 1788.

To be Lent,

EIGHT HUNDRED POUNDS upon real Security. Application to be made to Daniel Moore Echlin, Attorney.

Newtown-Ards, 2d Jan. 1789.

WHEREAS there was a Black Mare left in my Stable on the 21st November last, by a Man who called himself Cronie; and as said Mare has never since been called for, I give this public notice, that unless she is taken away before the tenth of January next, she will be sold for her keeping. Given under my hand in Moneymore this 29th December, 1788.

THOs. Mc. CORRY, junr.

This to be inserted three times.

THE Sale of Goods advertised to be sold at the Custom House, Downe, on Saturday the 10th January, is postponed till Saturday 17th of same month.

Downe, December 29th, 1788.

L I N E N S,

WILL be taken in to bleach by JAMES MACKEY, (who conducted the Bleaching Business formerly for Simpson and Maxwell) at the extensive Bleachyard lately occupied by Thomas Simpson, Esq; Ballyards, near Armagh.

December 27th, 1788.

Tenements in Perpetuity.

THE House and Garden occupied by the late widow Brown, with the Tenements adjoining, at the east end of Holywood, in Ballykeel—to be let for ever to a solvent tenant, who may be accommodated with a few acres of ground near the premisses. The situation would answer well for lodgings in the bathing season, as it lies near the sea side. Written proposals will be received by John Kennedy, Esq; Cultra, and the tenant declared the first of February next. January 1st, 1789.

Donegall-Street.

TO be sold by Auction, at the Broker's Office, Belfast, on Monday next the 5th January instant,——The LEASE of two Dwelling Houses on the East Side of Donegall-Street, at present set to Mrs. Armstrong and Mr. Lemon, Upholder. The Premisses yield a profit rent of 13l. 16s. per annum.

For further particulars apply to JOHN TISDALL, in whose hands the lease may be seen.

Belfast, 1st January, 1789.

The old Rock Harriers,

DINE at Mrs. Blaney's, Carrickfergus, on Tuesday the 6th January next.———A full Meeting is requested, as there is particular business.——Dinner to be on the table at 4 o'clock.

C. Fergus, 29th Dec. 1788.

MARRIOTT DALWAY, Esq; President.

A Parcel of PEAR and APPLE TREES, to be sold at Mr. Greg's Garden, on Friday next, at twelve o'clock.

Belfast, 29th December, 1788.

The Lurgan Club,

DINE at the BLACK BULL INN, on Monday the 5th of January next.——Dinner on the Table at four o'Clock.——26th December, 1788.

By Order,
H. Mc. VEAGH, Secretary

To be Let,

From the first of February next,

THAT House in Castle-Street, at present occupied by Mrs. Byrtt.——Apply to Mrs. Clark.

Belfast, 29th December, 1788.

To be continued twice.

To be Sold by Auction,

On Wednesday the 14th Day of January next, on the Premisses, at Noon,

A Farm of Land, containing 41A. 2R. 25P. statute measure, held from the Earl of Hertford for one life, at the yearly rent of 8l 18s. 6d Sterl. duty and fees included, in either one, two, or three lots, as may be most agreeable to the bidders then present.——The above Farm is situated in upper Ballinderry, and on the new road from Lisburn to Glenavy, and only three and half miles from the former; it is conveniently calculated for a linen manufacturer or manufacturers, being within a few perches of the moss, and having a river running through the center of the farm: The greatest part of this land has been limed and grazed these 12 years past, and is now in the greatest perfection for tillage.—Any person wishing to become a purchaser will be informed fully by applying to Edward H. Murray at Killulta, near Lisburn, in whose hands the title-deeds are.——The purchaser or purchasers may hold the money at legal interest in their hands on proper security.

December 26th, 1788.

The Stock of Goods on Hand,

consisting of Sattins, Lustrings, Tabbinets, Calicoes, Muslinets, Modes, Laces, Ribbons, &c. with a large assortment of Muslins of all breadths; Jaconet, Book, and Decca Handkerchiefs; also Carpets and Carpetines of the most modern Patterns which have been lately imported, will be sold off much under the usual Prices, for ready Money only.

Belfast, 1st January, 1789.

ROBERT WILSON respectfully informs the Publick that he intends, on the expiration of the Partnership, to resume the Business in the same extensive Manner as formerly.

A Meeting of the Belfast Annuity Company,

WILL be held in the Market-House of Belfast, on very particular Business, on Saturday the 10th day of January next, precisely at 11 o'clock forenoon.

Belfast, 23d December, 1788.

HUGH CRAWFORD, Secretary.

Dissolution of Partnership.

WHEREAS the Partnership in the Grocery Business between James Maxwell and William Maculllough of Armagh is, by mutual consent, dissolved; it is requested all persons indebted to said Partnership will immediately pay off their respective debts to William Macullough, who is empowered to receive them; and all debts due by said Partnership to be furnished to William Macullough, who will discharge the same.

Armagh, Dec. 22, 1788.

Wanted,

A COOK and HOUSEKEEPER, who can be well recommended.——Apply to Mr. Ewing at the Bank.

Belfast, 22d December, 1788.

Advertisement.

THOMAS Mc. CAN, Land Surveyor, in Ballinderry, near Lisburn, begs leave to inform the Nobility and Gentry of the North of Ireland, that he Surveys and Maps Lands as usual, upon the shortest notice; and hopes that his extensive practice in that line, together with minute returns, which his critical knowledge of calculation enables him to give in, will procure him the approbation of all those who will please to favor him with their commands.

Dated Ballinderry, near Lisburn, Dec. 23d, 1788.

Comber Fair,

FORMERLY held on the 5th of January, will be held on Thursday the 8th, being the Market-day.

Comber, 29th Dec. 1788.

AT a Meeting of a very considerable number of Gentlemen in the Linen Trade at the New Inn at Toome, upon Monday the 22d of December, 1788, for the purpose of taking into consideration the idea of holding a Linen Market at Toome once a month, the following Resolutions were unanimously agreed to:

1st. Resolved, That we conceive it highly proper and eligible that a monthly Market be held at Toome, and that it is our present intention to promote the same to the utmost of our abilities.

2dly, That said Market be held upon the 20th day of each month, except where the same shall fall upon Sunday; in which case, the said Market shall be held upon the 19th.

3dly, That it is our wish to have Toome Market considered as a place PRINCIPALLY for the sale of SEVEN-EIGHTH-WIDES.

4thly, That the Market of Toome shall commence upon Friday the 20th of March next, and that we will attend said Market accordingly.

Given under our hands at Toome the twenty-second December, 1788.

Wm. Holmes, jun.	Charles Hill	James Stein
Stafford Gorman	John Birnie	John & Jas. Cook
John Ridgway	Ken. Henderson	Jervis Wier
Samuel Hill	Adam Dickey	Robert Crawford
James Davison	Sam. Thompson	Arthur Tracy
Adam Duffin	Js. Dickey	Mitch. Woods
John Davison	Wm. Swan, junr.	David Birnie
HughGlenholme	And. Crawford	Robert Swan
David Wier	Charles Dickey	James Mc. Adam
James Wier	John Millar	Hugh Walker
John Glenholme	Nath, Maxwell	John Thomson
Sam. Crawford	James Watt	James Ferguson
Hugh Crawford	John Barnett	Charles Adair
Benjamin Adair	George Matthews	William Lyons.

THE following Lands, in the County of Antrim, the Estate of Mr. Leslie, are to be let from the first of November next, for 3 lives or 31 years.——Proposals will be received by John Bell, at Leslie-Hill, near Ballimoney:

	A.	R.	P.
Ballyaghmore—one mile and a half from Ballymoney, containing - - - -	110	2	15
The four Ballyoghloughs, within three miles of the sea—six miles from Ballymoney,	581	0	0

All the above Lands are in the highest State of Improvement—the Ballyoghloughs are inclosed and divided into fields with stone and lime walls.

August 25th, 1788.

Anno 1789.]   Printed by HENRY JOY, Senr. and Junr. BELFAST.

The BELFAST NEWS-LETTER.

TUESDAY January 6,   FRIDAY January 9. 1789.

OCCASIONAL ANTHEM,

PERFORMED AT THE CATHEDRAL OF ARMAGH.

The words selected from the Pfalms of David, and set to mufic by Richard Langdon, M. B. Organift, &c. of that Church.

LESSED is the man, that feareth the Lord: he hath great delight in his Commandments.

His feed fhall be mighty upon earth: the generation of the faithful fhall be blessed.

The eyes of the Lord are over the righteous: and his ears are open unto their prayers; for the Lord is full of compaffion and mercy; long fuffering and of great goodnefs.

He will not always be chiding: neither keepeth he his anger for ever.

The righteous cry, and the Lord heareth them: and delivereth them out of all their troubles.

The Lord preferveth thofe that are broken in heart: and giveth medicine to heal their ficknefs.

Behold, O God, our defender: and look upon the face of thine annointed.

Comfort him, O God, when he lieth fick upon his bed; make thou alfo his bed in his ficknefs.

The Lord preferve him, and keep him alive, that he may be bleffed upon earth.

So we, that are thy people, and fheep of thy pafture, fhall give thee thanks for ever.

And let all the people fay, Amen.

LONDON, Dec. 31.

Yefterday his Royal Highnefs the Prince of Wales dined with Mrs. Fitzherbert, at her houfe in Pall Mall.

Laft night, after the Houfe of Lords adjourned, his Royal Highnefs the Duke of York had a conference with the Lord Chancellor in one of the chambers of Parliament.

Yefterday the Lord Chancellor and Mr. Sheridan had a long conference with his Royal Highnefs the Prince of Wales, at Carleton-houfe.

The PRINCE has been for thefe laft ten days engaged in ftudying all the exifting treaties with the various European powers; together with all our commercial regulations at prefent in force.

The firft reading of the Regency Bill was expected yefterday in the Houfe of Commons accompanied by an opening from the Minifter, of his purpofed limitations; —it was deferred by agreement, as it was more formal to wait until the Report of the Committee on the Refolutions had been agreed to by the Houfe of Peers.

Immediately after the confultation of the faculty was over, yefterday morning, and the King dreffed, her Majefty was introduced into the apartment by Dr. Willis, and fpent the better part of an hour with the King.

We are happy to fay, and we do it from undoubted authority, that his Majefty's diforder bears the moft promifing appearance of an approaching return of health. It is now five days fince the diforder fhewed any very ftrong marks of violence and vigour, and the phyficians about his Royal perfon augur from the prefent fymptoms very favourably.

DUBLIN, Jan. 6.

The Two Brothers, Captain Geddes, arrived in the river, on Saturday evening laft from Philadelphia, after a fine paffage of only 29 days.

By letters received from Philadelphia, per the Two Brothers, Captain Geddes, we are informed, that the New Foederal Government is to take place in the different American States, on the firft day of March next; and that the next meeting of Congrefs will be held in the city of New York.

The crops this feafon in the different parts of America have been exceedingly abundant; and a very confiderable quantity of wheat and flour was exported in the months of September and October laft from Philadelphia and New York, for the Neutral Iflands, and alfo for the iflands of Martinique and Guadaloupe.

Middling and high priced linens are in tolerable demand in the American market; but there is fcarcely any call whatever for the coarfe or low priced linens; and what have been fold of the latter defcription generally fold at a lofs of eight or ten per cent.

Several manufactures of corduroys, thickfets and jeans, are now eftablifhed in different parts of America, and promifes in a little time, to be fully fufficient for the home confumption.

The Right Hon. Denis Daly is to be one of the members of the new Adminiftration. Talents fuperior to thofe poffeffed by Mr. Daly, are feldom the portion of humanity—to thefe he unites a delicacy, which is his peculiar characteriftic. Whenever he fpeaks in public, it is with fuch manlinefs and decifion, as to win the heart—and in private life his opennefs and amicability conciliate unbounded efteem.

The interior Council in this kingdom, we underftand will confift of the Right Hon. Mr. Grattan, Rt. Hon. Mr. Conolly, Right Hon. Mr. O'Neill,

---

Lord Chief Baron Yelverton, Mr. Forbes, and the Crown-lawyers—Lord Charlemont, Right Hon. Mr. Rowley, Right Hon. Mr. Brownlow, and feveral other refpected characters will be invited to attend—fo that there is every profpect of an Adminiftration truly *popular.*

Who our new Lord Lieutenant will be, is not yet known to a certainty, or is kept a profound fecret—but the Right Hon. Mr. Pelham, who was here in the fame capacity under Lord Northington, will certainly come over as Secretary.

Though the period from the meeting of our Houfes of Parliament, (the 20th of this month) to the expiration of the money-bills, is fo fhort as fcarcely to admit the leaft delay in the progrefs of the new ones, yet as it is now nearly afcertained that it is improbable the nomination of a Regent will not be made, and the new adminiftration fettled before the time, it is determined that on the day of meeting a week's adjournment, at leaft, will take place; and the fupply bufinefs be tranfacted afterwards with double celerity.

The dearth of bread corn in feveral of the inland parts of France is fo great, that famine may be faid already to ftare the miferable inhabitants in the face; we learn by a letter from Poitiers, dated December 15, that bread was then fold in that city at fix fols (three pence fterling) per pound. An enormous price in any country, but more than in any other, in France, where, for want of any fuccedaneum, the peafantry live almoft entirely on bread.—The quantities of wheat and flour now fhipping in England and Ireland for the French ports, will, we hope for the fake of humanity, prevent fo dreadful a calamity in that populous nation.

Some few days ago a duel was fought at Skibbereen in the county of Cork, by two Gentlemen of the moft fingular furnames that ever met upon the fod to decide a point of honour;—Henry Pickle, and John Whiffle, Efqrs.—Mr. Whiffle had the misfortune of being wounded in the thigh, but not dangeroufly.

LONDON-DERRY, Jan. 6.

At a large meeting of the Mayor, Aldermen, &c. of our Corporation, the freedom of this City was voted to the Right Hon. Wm. Pitt.

The fhip Eleanor, Capt. Kearney, belonging to Belfaft, bound from Guernfey to North Bergen, laden with rum and tobacco, is now in Lough Swilly under the feizure of R. Cannon, Efq.

Belfaft, January 9.

PORT NEWS.

ARRIVED.

Jan. 2. Peggy, M'Ilroy, Liverpool.
 5. Falmoth, M'Donnell, Rotterdam, geneva, &c.
 7. Neptune, Miskelly, Bourdeaux, brandy, &c.
   Chance, Beatton, Jamaica, rum, fugar, &c.
   Betty, Duncan, Glafgow and Greenock, fugar.

CLEARED OUT.

Jan. 2. Charles and Margaret, Atkinfon, Jamaica.
   Oroonoko, Fletcher, do.
 3. Nancy, Lamont, Greenock.
 7. Two Sifters, Greigg, Greenock, ballaft.

COTERIE.

There will be a Coterie at Newtown-Ards on Thurfday next, Lady's to pay 3s. 3d. Gentlemen, 8s. 1d. h.

January the 8th, 1789.

Wanted,

On the firft of FEBRUARY next,

A Houfe Servant or Footman, who can be recommended for honefty, fobriety, and knowledge in his bufinefs; he will have his choice of wearing his own cloaths or livery. Apply to the printers hereof.

January 8th, 1789.

Wanted,

ON real Security, Two THOUSAND POUNDS.—For further Particulars apply to Thomas L. Stewart, Attorney, Belfaft.

January 8th, 1789.

Final Clofe.

John Kenley, a Bankrupt. } EXACTLY at twelve o'Clock, on Tuefday next, the 13th inft. at faid Bankrupt's Houfe and Timber-Yard, in Lifburn, will be fold by Auction, about fixty Hampers of excellent ENGLISH CYDER, a Quantity of fquare Timber, and fome Deal-Boards, in fuch Lots as may be agreeable to the Bidders who attend.

Money to be paid down for every Article.

Tobacco Preffes.

TO be fold in publick Sale, to the higheft bidder, for ready money, at the Yard adjoining the Dwelling-Houfe of Jofeph T. Senhoufe, Efq; at the higher end of Lowther-ftreet in Whitehaven, on Wednefday the 28th day of January, 1789, at ten o'clock in the forenoon, feveral large TOBACCO PRESSES in complete Order, (fuitable for Irifh Roll) formerly the property of the late Robert Watters, Efq;

HUDDLESTON & PEEL, Brokers.

Anno 1789.]   Printed by HENRY JOY, Senr. and Junr. BELFAST.

The BELFAST NEWS-LETTER.

TUESDAY January 13,   FRIDAY January 16, 1789.

MAGEE's LOTTERY OFFICE

ENGLISH STATE LOTTERY, 1788,
Begins Drawing February 16, 1789.

In which are 1 of 30000l. 1 of 25,000l. 1 of 20,000l.
1 of 15,000l. 2 of 10,000l. 5 of 5,0.0l. 10 of 2,000l.
26 of 1,000l. 30 of 500l. 103 of 100l. &c. &c.

WHOLE TICKETS, HALVES, FOURTHS, EIGHTHS,
and SIXTEENTHS, are now selling at the

Belfast Licensed Lottery-Office,

No. 9. BRIDGE-STREET.

WILLIAM MAGEE, truly sensible of the very general public Patronage he experienced last Lottery—presents his grateful acknowledgements—and, being desirous to give his friends every advantage that can possibly be offered; he will allow the full amount for all Prizes or Shares of Prizes in the late Irish Lottery, in exchange for English Tickets or Shares—same time engaging them on as low terms, as they can be had at any Office of repute in the kingdom.

☞ MAGEE trusts he will not give offence, by declining to give Tickets in future, to any person whatever, but for ready Money.

Genuine Patent Medicines.

GREENOUGH's LOZENGES of TOLU, so justly celebrated for their superior Efficacy in immediately removing all Coughs, Hoarsenesses, Sore Throats, Shortness of Breath, Defluxions upon the Lungs, Soreness of the Breast, &c. price 1s. 4d.

TWO TINCTURES; the one for Cleansing and preserving the TEETH, and effectually Curing the Scurvy in the Gums; preventing the Teeth from further Decay, and rendering the Breath perfectly sweet—the other for the TOOTH-ACH, which seldom fails giving immediate Ease, without injuring the Teeth or Gums, price 1s. 4d. each Bottle.

Curious ISSUE PLAISTER, to stick without filleting, which in neatness and agreeableness of scent, as well as in being less troublesome and more efficacious far exceed all others yet made use of, price 1s. 7d. h. each Box, with directions.

ORANGE ISSUE PEAS, 6d. per dozen.
QUINTESSENCE of PEPPERMINT, 1s. 4d. per Bottle.

The above Articles have been held in the highest Esteem for thirty years past; but as the great benefit to be derived from them can only be secured by having them genuine, every purchaser is requested to observe that R. HAYWARD, No. 10, Ludgate-Hill, is printed on each Label; all others are counterfeits.

Sold by Mr. Hayward's appointment at MAGEE's Stationery, and Patent Medicine Warehouse, Belfast.

A BALL.

MR. HULL respectfully informs the Ladies and Gentlemen of Down and its Vicinity, that his Scholars BALL will be held in the Market-House, on Wednesday 21st inst. to open at Seven o'Clock Afternoon.——Tickets to be had at Mr. Sharrock's, 2s. 2d. h. each.——Mr. Hull returns his benefactors in general most unfeigned and hearty thanks for the past distinguished marks of their civilities and support, which he hopes he has and will yet further study to merit, by the most unremitting attention to the duties of his profession.

N. B. Mr. Hull if encouraged, will engage another School.——Letters directed to Mr Sharrock, Downe, or Mr. Rickards, Hillsborough, will be attended to.

Downpatrick, 7th Jan. 1789.

FIVE POUNDS,

TO be run for on the Gallows-Green, near Carrickfergus, on Monday the 19th instant, by any Horse, Mare, or Gelding that never started for, or won Two Pounds, carrying ten stone, the best of three heats.

On Tuesday, THREE POUNDS, for any Horse, Mare, or Gelding, that never started for Six-pence, catch weight, the best of three heats.

Same Day, A SADDLE to be run for, free for any Thing.

Horses to be entered on the day of running before ten o'clock with John Shannon.

Carrickfergus, Jan. 1st, 1789.

BARILLA.

TO be sold by Auction, on Friday the 16th instant, at one o'Clock, at the Stores of Hugh Montgomery, Ann-street, Fifty Bales of BARILLA. As they are to close the Sale of a large Parcel, they will be sold without reserve.——Approved bills at six months will be taken in payment.

Belfast, 8th January, 1789

Wanted,

A Person to instruct a few Boys in a private Family in English Grammar, Writing, Arithmetic, &c. being able to teach Latin would be an additional recommendation. A married man could be accommodated with House, &c.——For particulars apply to Mr. Welch, Stationer, Armagh.——Letters (post-paid) will be attended to early.

24th December, 1788.

NOTICE.

THE several persons who stand indebted to the late William Cluff of Cookstown, by bond, note, or book account, are desired immediately to pay the same to James Richardson of Bloom-Hill, Esq; his Executor, otherwise they will be sued for the same as the law directs.

Dated this 3d day of January, 1789.

Wanted,

On the first of FEBRUARY next, A House Servant or Footman, who can be recommended for honesty, sobriety, and knowledge in his business; he will have his choice of wearing his own cloaths or livery. Apply to the printers hereof.

January 8th, 1789.

Wanted immediately,

AN APPRENTICE to the Apothecary Business, by David Mc. Anally, Surgeon

Market-Hill, Dec. 30th, 1788.

To be Sold by Auction,

ON Friday the 16th instant, on the Premisses in Mill-street, next Entry to Mr. Samuel Ferguson's, where the new Street is to be opened into Smithfield, a Lease of 41 years from November 1787, of two New HOUSES, one of which is let for eleven pounds per annum, and the other fit for the immediate reception of a tenant;—ground rent of both only 7l. per annum.

Belfast, 8th Jan. 1789.

To be Let,

And entered on immediately,

A Neat House and Shop, with Counter, Shelves, and Drawers, with every necessary Fixture, fit for the Grocery or Cloth Business.——Enquire at Richard Barnett.

High-street, Belfast, 10th Nov. 1789.

TO BE LET,

From first May next,

THE House, Garden and Office-Houses, at present occupied by the Revd. William Bryson, (with or without a few acres of Land, or Sums Grass) all in good tenantable order, situated within one mile of Antrim, on the road leading to Templepatrick.——Application to be made to

ALEXANDER LEDLIE.

Antrim, 8th of Jan. 1789.

NOTICE.

JOSEPH TURBETT, of LURGAN, BEGS Leave to inform his Friends and the Publick, that he has declined the Grocery Business; and requests that those who are indebted to him will pay the same without delay; and those who have any demands on him, are requested to apply for payment.

January 12th, 1789.

Wanted,

ON the twentieth of February, A POSTILION, who understands his Business. None need apply that cannot bring certificates of their honesty and sobriety.—This to be continued three times.—— Apply to the Printers hereof.

January 15th, 1789.

Wanted,

A MILLER to a Mill in the vicinity of Coleraine, to which are annexed a considerable succon, and several other desirable circumstances.—Application to be made to Mr. Joseph Wardin, Publican, Coleraine.

10th January, 1789.

None need apply who do not bring Certificates of good character and professional knowledge.

For Bordeaux,

THE Brigantine NEPTUNE, WILLIAM MISKELLY, Master, a constant Trader, will be clear to sail in ten days.——For Freight apply to Jones, Tomb, Joy, and Co

Belfast, 12th January, 1789.

Samuel & Andrew Mc. Clean,

HAVE lately received a large Quantity of excellent RUM, which they will dispose of on very moderate terms, for Cash or good Bills.——They are, as usual, well supplied with all other Kinds of Liquors, in Spirit and reduced; also Wines, Porter, &c.

Belfast, 1st January, 1789.

WRITING SCHOOL.

J. WALKER respectfully returns his sincere thanks to the Ladies and Gentlemen of Belfast and its Vicinity; for the flattering deference he has experienced for some years past, and assures them that the most punctual care will ever be observed on his part to merit their countenance, by an unremitting attention to the Tuition of the Pupils committed to his care.

School hours from 10 o'clock to 12—from 12 to 2—and from 3 to 5.

Pottinger's-Entry, Belfast, Jan. 12th, 1789.

Samuel Brown, & Co.

ARE now landing out of the Neptune, from Bordeaux, a Quantity of Brandy in Pipes and Hogsheads, and a parcel of Cane Reeds, which, with the following Articles, they will dispose of on very moderate terms:

Jamaica Rum,		Single and Congou Teas,
Antigua do.		New Muscatell and Cask
Barbadoes do.		Raisins,
Claret,		Kentish Bag Hops,
Red & White	Wines in	Bristol Window Glass,
Port,	Wood and	French Vinegar in tierces,
Sherry, and	Bottle.	Scotch Vitriol, and
Mountain		Pearl Ashes.

☞ They want a Quantity of White Boiling Pease.

Belfast, 12th January, 1789.

Robt. and Alex. Gordon,

HAVE just received from Rheims, a large Quantity of Burgundy and Champaigne—the latter is Silery-White and Still Wine Vintage 1781, the former a first Growth of 1784.

They have a general assortment of Wines in wood—Sherry, Calcavella, Lisbon, Port, and French Whitewines in bottle,

13th January, 1789.

Belfast Assembly.

AN ASSEMBLY will be held at the Exchange-Rooms, on Tuesday the 20th instant: It is requested that all those who wish that the Assembly should be continued, will attend and subscribe on that Night.

Belfast, 12th Jan 1789.

Boarding-School, Belfast.

MRS. WARE begs leave to inform the Publick her School commences after the Christmas Holidays, on Tuesday 20th instant.——Young Ladies are taught English, French, Musick, Dancing, Drawing, Writing, and Accounts, Tambour, Embroidery, Fillegree, and other Work.

Deal-Boards.

HENRY WELSH is selling six and nine feet Deals under the usual Prices, for ready Money.

He is at present largely supplied with Rum, Brandy, Geneva, Spirit of Whiskey, Red and White Wines, Window Glass by the Side, Flour and Bran: With a regular assortment in the Grocery Line.

Lisburn, January 10th, 1789.

NEW FRUIT.

THOMAS PARKINSON has lately landed a large Parcel of New Malaga RAISINS, which he is enabled to dispose of at Dublin Prices in any Quantity not less than a cask.

He wants a small Cargo of Wheat, which he will receive at Killileagh, and for which the highest Market Price will be given; it must be of a good quality, and well dressed. He will attend on Tuesdays and Fridays at Killileagh to receive and pay for it. Application to be made at all times to Mr. James Mc. Connel there.

Downpatrick, 8th Jan. 1789.

DECLARATION of RIGHTS.

The following is the Declaration of Rights, agreed on by the STATE of NORTH CAROLINA in Convention.

1ft. That there are certain natural rights of which men, when they form a focial compact, cannot deprive or divest their posterity; among which are the enjoyment of life and liberty, with the means of acquiring, possessing, and protecting property, and pursuing and obtaining happiness and safety.

2d. That all power is naturally vested in, and consequently derived from the people; that magistrates therefore are their trustees and agents, and at all times amenable to them.

3d. That Government ought to be instituted for the common benefit, protection, and security of the people: and that the doctrine of non-resistance against arbitrary power and oppression is absurd, slavish, and destructive to the good and happiness of mankind.

4th. That no man or set of men are entitled to exclusive or separate public emoluments or privileges from the community, but in consideration of public services; which not being descendible, neither ought the offices of magistrate, legislator, or judge, or any other public office, to be hereditary.

5th. That the legislative, executive, and judiciary powers of government should be separate and distinct; and that the members of the two first may be restrained from oppression, by feeling and participating the public burthens, they should at fixed periods be reduced to a private station, return into the mass of the people, and the vacancies be supplied by certain and regular elections in which all or any part of the former members to be eligible or ineligible, as the rules of the constitution of government, and the laws shall direct.

LONDON, Jan. 7.

Kew, Jan. 6. His Majesty was quiet yesterday during the greatest part of the day, became a little disturbed towards the evening, has had a good night, and is calm this morning.

Kew Palace, Jan. 7. His Majesty has had a good night—and is calm this morning.—Signed by the Physicians

Yesterday morning Mr. Fox had a long conference with the Prince of Wales at Carleton-House.

On Monday night there was a Cabinet Council held at the Lord Chancellor's private Chamber at the House of Lords, which was attended by most of the Ministers; the Council sat two hours; and yesterday morning, at half an hour past eight o'clock, the Right Hon. Mr. Pitt set off from his House in Downing-street, to Kew Palace, where he laid the result of the Council before Her Majesty.

PITT.

How far the Character of WILLIAM PITT, lately EARL OF CHATHAM, corresponds with that of the WILLIAM PITT of the present day, the reader will judge from the following:

" The Secretary of the late King stood alone.—Modern degeneracy had not reached him—Original and unaccommodating, the features of his character had the hardihood of antiquity.—No State chicanery—no narrow system of vicious politics—no idle contest for ministerial victories, sunk him to the vulgar level of the great: but overbearing, persuasive, and impracticable—his object was England—his ambition was fame.

" Without dividing he destroyed party—without corrupting, he made a venal age unanimous. France sunk beneath him—with one hand he smote the House of Bourbon, and wielded in the other the democracy of England. The SIGHT of his mind was infinite, and his schemes were to affect not England but posterity. Wonderful were the means by which this was accomplished, always seasonable—always adequate—the suggestion of an understanding animated by ardour, and enlightened by prophecy.

" The ordinary feelings which make life amiable and indolent—those sensations which soften and allure and vulgarize, were unknown to him. No domestic difficulties—no domestic weakness reached him; but aloof from the sordid occurrences of life, and unsullied by its intercourse he came occasionally into our system to council and to decide.

" A character so exalted—so strenuous—so authoritative—so serious astonished a corrupt age, and the Treasury trembled at the name of Pitt thro' all her classes of venality.

" Upon the whole there was something in the man that could create, subvert or reform——an understanding, a spirit, and an eloquence to summon mankind to society, or to break the bonds of slavery asunder, and to rule the wilderness of free minds with unbounded authority—something that would establish or overwhelm empire, and strike a blow in the world that should resound through the universe."

" Corruption indeed imagined she had found defects in this statesman, and talked much of the inconsistency of his glory, and much of the ruin of his victories, but the history of his country, and the calamities of our common enemy, answered and refuted her.

By R. CUMBERLAND, ESQ.

From "ARUNDEL," A NOVEL, lately published.

" O SOLITUDE! to whose serene abode
" The Hermit flies to commune with his God,
" Where buried in some deep and silent glen
" Shuddering he quits the guilty haunts of men.
" With thee and the dear partner of my life,
" Far, far from mad ambition's strife,
" Here let me dwell a fond and faithful wife.

" Nobility, thou empty, borrowed name,
" I leave thee for substantial, self-earn'd fame;
" And ye, that on the painted wing
" Flutter awhile, then fix the sting,
" Ye insect tribe of pleasures gay,
" I brush your flimsy forms away,
" Be gone, impertinents! you've had your day.

" Thou Solitude, art Contemplation's friend,
" On thee the rational delights attend;
" No gilded chariot haunts thy door,
" No flambeaus blaze, no drunkards roar,
" No rattling dice, no clashing swords,
" No squand'ring fool, no wretch that hoards,
" No lordly beggars and no beggar'd lords.

" And, O deceitful world! too well I know
" How little worth is all thou can'st bestow
" The reputation of a day,
" Which the next morning takes away,
" The flattery that beguiles the ear,
" The hypocrite's fictitious tear,
" These thou can'st give, this semblance thou can'st wear.

" Temperance shall spread my rural feast,
" Content shall be my welcome guest,
" No guilty thoughts that shun the light,
" No conscious dreams to terrify the night;
" Here in my peaceful rustic cell
" With thee, calm Solitude, I'll dwell;
" Hail, nature's offspring! sons of art, farewell!

" At noon I'll walk beneath these spreading trees,
" Where honied woodbines scent the passing breeze.
" At eve, what time the flocks go forth to graze,
" I'll follow where yon silver current strays,
" And as it flows, Behold! I'll cry,
" Pleasure's fleet emblem passes by;
" Pass on, false friend!—we part without a sigh.

" Come then, thou pure and sainted youth,
" Holy interpreter of truth.
" Friend of my soul, my bosom's wedded Lord,
" Impart those treasures which thy mind hath stor'd;
" By the soft link of nuptial love
" Lead me the way that I should move,
" And wed me to that bliss which reigns above."

DUBLIN.

An eminent Lawyer, whose posting is so much the subject of conversation, refused fighting the Officer in consequence of the unanimous request of the Bench and Bar at Cork, at the last assizes, who suspected that a challenge might be sent to the Lawyer as soon as the Officer should be liberated from confinement; and we hear that agreeable to the request of the same persons he means to prosecute the Officer at common law for sending him a challenge.

On investigation into the affairs of the late Sir William Montgomery, personal property, independent of his estate, to the amount of 64,000l. has, it is said, already been discovered. This, as he has died intestate, and left eight surviving children behind him, will be equally shared among them, and will give to each 8,000l. Mrs. Gardiner, his eldest daughter, being dead, no part of his personal property will devolve to Mr. Gardiner; but his estate in the North, which came to him by his first wife, Mrs. Gardiner's mother, will be equally divided between Mr. Gardiner, Mrs. Beresford and the Marchioness Townshend; the two last of whom are her only surviving issue, her son having died in America in the late war.

Last week, the temple of Marino, belonging to that worthy Nobleman the Earl of Charlemont, was stripped of about 1,500lb. of lead and several other articles, by a set of nefarious villains, after which the strictest search is making, which we hope will lead to a discovery.

A letter from Philadelphia, dated the 1st of October, says, that Congress, by a resolution of the 16th of the preceding month, had recommended to the several states to pass proper laws for preventing the transportation of convicted malefactors from foreign countries into the United States. The same letter adds, that the Assembly of Connecticut had passed such a law, and another to prevent negro traffick.

The popularity of Hamilton Rowan, Esq. daily encreases in consideration of his manly, humane and disinterested conduct on behalf of the injured child Mary Neil.—He has been already complimented with the freedom of the Guilds of Merchants, Goldsmiths, and Sadlers—and many others are preparing to testify their approbation of his conduct in a similar manner. —This is a just tribute of patriotic gratitude to the protector of infant innocence oppressed.

Belfast, January 16.

PORT NEWS.

ARRIVED.

Jan. 14. Liberty, M'Roberts, Liverpool, tobacco, bale goods, &c.
8 Colliers.

CLEARED OUT.

Jan. 14. New Draper, M'Nillage, Liverpool, linen cloth and butter.
1 Collier.

PRICES in this Market Yesterday.

OATMEAL,	-	09 80 to 10 00 per cwt.
WHEAT,	-	08 08 — 09 00 per cwt.
OATS,	-	04 04 — 05 2½

STATE of the WEATHER for the year 1788, taken about 2 miles S. of Belfast.

	Rain.	Showers.	Snow, hail, or sleet.	Fair.
January	12	6	0	13
February	17	0	0	12
March	13	3	3	12
April	9	8	1	12
May	4	3	0	24
June	6	0	0	24
July	12	15	0	4
August	15	5	0	11
September	15	9	0	6
October	5	4	0	22
November	5	7	1	17
December	3	2	8	18
	116	62	13	175

N. B. 21 days of heavy rain.

We are favoured with a Diary of the Weather kept in the town of Belfast, which states;

Fair Days -	156
Showery -	192
Wet -	18
	366
Frost -	45
Snow -	14
	59

It is be observed that tho' there was snow fourteen times, there were but three heavy falls of it in the year. The Autumnal Equinox was very severe.

Anno 1789.] Printed by HENRY JOY, Senr. and Junr. BELFAST.

The BELFAST NEWS-LETTER.

TUESDAY January 20,   FRIDAY January 23, 1789.

For *LONDON*.

BY Order of the Shippers, the Sailing of the LONDON PACKET, James Glafs, Mafter, is poftponed till the firft February.

Newry, 19th January, 1789.
ARCH. TAYLOR.

For the Benefit of Mrs. Hoskin.

ON Wednefday 29th of January, will be prefented a favourite COMEDY, call'd,

The Chapter of Accidents.

With Shakefpear's celebrated Entertainment of

The JUBILEE.

Tickets to be had of Mrs. Hofkin, at Capt. Englifh's, Princes-Street.

For the Benefit of Mr. Chalmers,

ON Monday Night, the 26th inftant, will be prefented the COMEDY of

The Trip to Scarborough.

Lord Foppington, Mr. CHALMERS.
And Mifs Hoyden, Mrs CHALMERS.

To which will be added the PANTOMIME of

PROMOTHEUS; or, HAREQUIN's ANIMATION,

With Alterations and Additions.
The Character of Harlequin, by Mr. CHALMERS.
In which (by particular Defire) he will introduce

The DYING SCENE; and a Leap through a
BRILLIANT SUN
Of VARIEGATED FIRE,
And Difplay of FIRE-WORKS.

Tickets and Places to be had of Mr. Chalmers, at Mr. Dawfon's on the Quay.

ROBERT HILL.

HAS juft received (by the Mary, Capt. Corry, from Jamaica), at his ftores in Ann-ftreet, oppofite the New Bank; a quantity of Jamaica Rum, that with fome excellent old fpirit and other articles in that line, he hopes will anfwer his cuftomers expectations.

Belfaft, 23d. Jan. 1789.

Cheap Scale Sugars.

STEWARTS, THOMSON, and Co. continue to fell remarkably fine Scale Sugar, at 8s. per Stone. Fine ditto at 7s. 6d. and common ditto at 6s. 6d.; and they are (as ufual) amply fupplied with all kinds of Refined Sugars, and with Molofles.

Belfaft, 23d January, 1789.

£ 3,000 for Two Guineas.

BRITISH STATE LOTTERY,

COMMENCES drawing on Monday the 16th of February, including

Seventy-feven Capital Prizes,
From 30,000l. down to 500l.
BRITISH TICKETS and SHARES
are now felling as ufual, at

MAGEE's Licenfed Lottery-Office, Bridge-Street, Belfaft,

In the greateft diverfity of Thoufands: As alfo,
TWO GUINEA TICKETS,

by which the following unexampled Benefits, may be obtained, viz.

3,000	if a Prize of	30,000	
2,500	—— ——	25,000	
2,000	—— ——	20,000	This Ticket partakes of an equal proportion of every Prize the Lottery, and the value of Prizes is to be paid in Britifh Money.
1,500	—— ——	15,000	
1,000	—— ——	10,000	
500	—— ——	5,000	
200	—— ——	2,000	
100	—— ——	1,000	
50	—— ——	500	
10	—— ——	100	
1 16	—— ——	18	

The Originals of all Tickets and Shares fold at MAGEE's, are lodged in the *Bank of Ireland*, therefore equally fecure as whole Tickets.

Mufical Inftruments, Prints, &c.

JAMES and WILLIAM MAGEE,

Printers, Bookfellers and Stationers, Bridge-ftreet, Belfait, have lately imported from London,

GRAND, PATENT, and COMMON PIANO FORTES, the manufacture of the firft Houfe in the Mufical line in that Capital, and which will be fold on as low terms as they can poffibly be imported, duty and other expences confidered.

Elegant Patent PIANO FORTE GUITTARS, poffeffing a ftrength and fweetnefs of tone far fuperior to thofe on the common conftruction.

Clarionets, tipt or plain—Reeds for ditto:
Violins, from one Guinea price to five.
German Flutes, Box, Cocoa and Ebony, tipt or plain.
Harpfichord, Piano Forte, Guittar and Violin Strings.
Englifh Flutes, Fifes, Mufic for the Piano Forte, Violin, Flute, &c.—fingle Songs at a reduced price, Mufic Paper, blank Mufic Books, Tutors for moft Inftruments, Mouth Pieces for German Flutes, Harpfichord Hammers, Violin Cafes, with many other things in the mufical line.

The largeft and moft elegant Collection of fine PRINTS to be met with on fale any where in Ireland, the Capital only excepted—they will be fold at the loweft *London Prices*, and confift of fquare, oval and circle of various fizes, defigned or engraved by Cippriani, Bartalozzi, Bunbury, Angelica Kauffman, &c—which may be had either with or without rich Gold burnifhed Frames—to accommodate Ladies and Gentlemen who are in poffeffion of Prints unframed, the Frames may be had feparate.

A very great variety of fancy and droll METZOTINTO PRINTS and cheap Views for fhew-boxes or Furniture, plain or coloured—elegant japanned Prints for Fire Screens, Pictures for Children, Drawing-books, Camel Hair, and fitch pointed Pencils, Boxes of Colours, Paints, Indian Ink, Indian Rubber, Fillagree, India and painted Paper, Maps, Charts, &c

Ladies and Gentlemens JAPAN DRESSING BOXES, Gentlemens Mohogany and Leather Travelling Cafes, Mahogany portable Defks, Tea Caddies of elegant workmanfhip, Pocket Brufhes with or without glaffes—the greateft choice of fafhionable Silk Purfes, of peculiar brilliancy of colour and firmnefs of texture—Balloon Purfes, Ladies and Gentlemens Pocket-Books, Thread Cafes, Slides for the Hair, Ebony, Inlaid and Pewter Inkftands, and curious cut fmelling Botties in the moft elegant variety.

SMYTH's and other Lavender Water, Warren's Milk of Rofes, Rufpini's, Hemet's, Delafcotte's and Bailey's Tooth Powder, Vine Root and other Tooth Brufhes of the beft kind.

WINDSOR, Italian, Naples, Palm and Bailey's Soap, Almond Pafte, Face Powder, Liquid Rouge, Pearl Powder, Liquid Bloom of the Eaft, and Carmine—Liquid to change red hair to black—Hudfon's Compofition for removing fuperfluous hairs—Bergamotte and Hungary Water, and Effences of various kinds.

ORANGE, Citron, Rofe and Jafmin Pomatum in rolls or pots, plain and brown Hair Powder, Marechall and Oeillet ditto—Swan, Down and Silk Powder Puffs, Powder Knives and Mafks.

GODBOLD's VEGETABLE BALSAM, fo wonderfully efficacious in the cure of Confumptions, Effence of Spruce, Antiacid, Peppermint, and Tolu Lozenges, Dalby's Carminative, moft effectual in the cure of cholicky and other complaints in the bowels fo fatal to children, Anodyne Necklaces, excellent for children when teething, Hooper's Female Pills, Balfam of Honey, Balfam of Liquorice—with almoft all the PATENT MEDICINES of repute, as well as a great variety of other curious Articles, not to be met with at any other Place in the NORTH.

They are always fupplied with PAPER HANGINGS for Rooms, and Borderings of the moft fafhionable patterns —beft and common Playing Cards, Wax Candles of different fizes, Wax Taper and Flambeaux—Infide and Outfide Lapping Paper, blue Stripes for white Webs, on which a confiderable abatement will be made, when ten quires and upwards are taken, ready money—Marking Ink for brown Webs, Marking Ink and Letters for Linen, &c.——The greateft choice of blank Accompt Books fit for the Merchant, Shopkeeper, &c. in various rulings and bindings, or made as befpoke to any pattern.

Fine Writing Parchment, STAMPS on Paper or Parchment, ftamped Bonds, Indentures, and Leafes for years and Lives of the moft approved forms—Magazines, Reviews, new Plays, new Publications, the different kinds of Englifh, Latin, Greek, and French School Books—with almoft every thing in the BOOK-SELLING and STATIONARY Line, wholefale, retail, and for exportation, on terms moft reafonable.

☞ A few very fine GUITTARS on the common conftruction, to be difpofed of at or under firft coft.

THE Brigantine SUCCESS,

THE Brigantine SUCCESS, James Watfon, Mafter, is arrived at Larne from Alicante, and expected here in a few days, with a Cargo of New BARILLA, and Spanifh CANES for Reedmakers—which will be fold on the moft reafonable Terms, by JONES, TOMB, JOY, and Co.

Be'faft, 19th Jan. 1789.

Roll Tobacco.

SAMUEL EADDY begs leave to inform his Friends That he is (as ufual) well fupplied with Roll Tobacco of his own Manufacture, which he can affure them is of the very beft quality, and will be fold on the very loweft terms.

Church-Lane, Belfaft, 19th Jan. 1789.

John Bafhford,

IS landing out of the Chance from Jamaica, a large Parcel ftrong Rum in Puncheons, which, with the following Articles, will be fold on the loweft Terms for Cafh or good Bills:

Swedifh Iron, well afforted,	St. Domingo Cotton Wool,
Ruffia ditto,	German and Blifter Steel,
Kieve Hoops,	Roll'd Iron,
Swedifh Plank,	Pan Plates.

Belfaft, 20th Jan. 1789.

Roll Tobacco.

HUGH HYNDMAN has now ready for Sale, A large Quantity of fine Roll Tobacco, of exceeding fine Quality, which with other Articles in that Line, he will fell cheap for Cafh or good Bills.

Belfaft, 19th January, 1789

DRUGS.

JOHN BANKHEAD, informs his Friends and the Publick, that he continues to be a Druggift and Apothecary on his own Account; and is at prefent fupplied with a confiderable quantity of moft of the Medicines now in Ufe; he hopes for a continuation of that favour already experienced—for which he feels himfelf truly fenfible.

Belfaft, 19th January, 1789.

BLEACHING.

LINENS, CAMBRICKS, and COTTONS, will be taken to bleach at White-Abbey Green; where they will be as well done, and at as low a price as at any Green in this Country.

ALSO TO BE LET,

WHITE-ABBEY Houfe and Gardens, with or without the Farm; a defcription of this place is confidered ufelefs, it being well known there are few places in this kingdom fo well calculated or fo pleafingly fituated for a Linen Draper or private Gentleman. For further particulars enquire at   THOs. Mc. CABE.

Belfaft, 8th Jan. 1789.

James Scott, of Armagh,

HAS this day got home from North-Britain, a large Affortment of Carpets and Carpetteens of the neweft Patterns; alfo Muflins and Muflin Handkerchiefs, Cambricks, Lenos, Spa Gauzes, black and white Silk Gauzes, Scotch Thread, which will be fold on the moft reafonable terms.

January 14th, 1788.

Premiums for fpinning fine Yarn.

I Will attend to adjudge the Claims at Lurgan, on Friday 23d January. Lifburn, on Tuefday 27th, and Hillfborough, on Wednefday the 28th, of which all concerned are defired to take Notice.
JOHN GREER, Infpector General Ulfter.

Amicable Annuity Company of Newry,

WILL be held at M'Clatchy's Tavern, on Wednefday the 4th day of February next, to tranfact the bufinefs of the Company and dine together. All perfons wifhing to become Members, are defired to apply to the Regifter 14 days previous to, and appear at the meeting, otherwife they cannot be ballotted for.

The capital ftock of the Company, for which there is approved real fecurity, is now upwards of 10,000l. which can never be leffened, and muft increafe very confiderably annually, and the Widows of the prefent and future Members will, by the laws of the Company, receive their refpective proportions of the entire intereft of the capital ftock, until the fame fhall exceed 60l. annuity to each Widow.

JAMES SEARIGHT, Regifter.
Newry, 5th January, 1789.

PRICE OF STOCKS.

Bank Stock 170	4 per Cent. Conſ. 93 ⅛
3 per Cent. Red. 73 ⅛ ¼	Lottery Tickets 16l. 0s. 6d.
3 per Cent. Conſ. 72 ½	

SLAVERY.

The Slave Laws of Jamaica have been reviſed, and ſeveral regulations made in favour of the negroes.—The Aſſembly have paſſed an act which contains the following reforms:

1. Every poſſeſſor of a ſlave is prohibited from turning him away when incapacitated by age or ſickneſs, but muſt provide for him wholeſome neceſſaries of life, under a penalty of 10l. for every offence.

2. Every perſon who mutilates a ſlave ſhall pay a fine not exceeding 100l. and be impriſoned not exceeding 12 months, and in very atrocious caſes the ſlaves may be declared free.

3. Any perſon wantonly or bloody-mindedly killing a ſlave ſhall ſuffer death.

4. Any perſon whipping, bruiſing, wounding, or impriſoning a ſlave not his property, nor under his care, ſhall ſuffer fine and impriſonment.

5. A parochial tax to be raiſed for the ſupport of negroes diſabled by ſickneſs and old age, having no owners.

The legiſlature of Grenada, it is ſaid, will ſhortly inveſtigate the above ſubject.

TEARS OF LOYALTY;

OR PORTRAIT OF A PRINCE.

Ye too, whoſe fine etherial nerves are ſtrung,
To thrill at ev'ry tone of Sorrow's tongue,
Who, cautious to alarm, conceal your ſmart,
And throw the tear-drop back upon the heart---
Far ſhall you haſten from th' illuſive maze,
Where FOLLY ſhouts, and painted PLEASURE ſtrays,
To ſeek the willowy wood, the fountain-fall,
When twilight ſpreads around her ſhadowy pall,
And pauſe to hear the diſtant HAMLET's bell,
With ſolemn cadence toll the poor man's knell,
There think, how ſmall the difference between
The Regal Palace, and the Cottage Green!
And as Reflection's loyal pangs prevail,
Catch the low languiſh of the ſuff'ring dale,
While all that Honour, all that Beauty gave,
BENDS O'ER A WORSE AFFLICTION---THAN THE GRAVE.

Kew Palace, Jan. 13.

"His Majeſty has had ſeven hours and a half of continued ſleep, and is not unquiet this morning.

G. BAKER, F. GISBORNE."

Kew Palace, Jan. 14.

"His Majeſty has had three hours ſleep in the night at intervals, and is not unquiet this morning.

R. WARREN, J. R. REYNOLDS, F. WILLIS."

LONDON, JAN. 12—13—14.

The mode of proceeding upon the ſubject of the Regency in Ireland, will of neceſſity be different from that which has been adopted here. Copies of the reports of the examinations of his Majeſty's phyſicians before the Houſes of Lords and Commons, and of the reports of the Committees appointed to ſearch for precedents, are now making out, and after being regularly and formerly atteſted by the principal officers of the two Houſes, will be tranſmitted to the Lord Lieutenant of Ireland, in order to be laid before the Parliament of that kingdom, when it aſſembles.

On Saturday laſt, his Royal Highneſs the Prince of Wales gave a grand dinner, at which many of the nobility, and ſeveral of the Iriſh members were preſent; amongſt whom were the Duke of Devonſhire, Lords Spencer and Claremont, Mr. Grattan, Mr. Forbes, Mr. Ogilvie, Mr. Yelverton, Mr. Pelham, Mr. Burke, Mr. Sheridan, and many other very diſtinguiſhed characters.

The meeting of the Whig Club yeſterday was highly reſpectable. In the abſence of Lord Fitzwilliam, Lord William Ruſſel took the chair, and the day was ſpent in the utmoſt conviviality. The club is now full, and no new members can be admitted. It conſiſts of 500 gentlemen, and this body comprehends the moſt reſpectable names in this country for illuſtrious deſcent, ſplendid talents, and opulent fortune.

Monday his Majeſty was, by the advice of his phyſicians, taken out in a coach to have the benefit of the air.

The Phyſicians have lately permitted every branch of the Royal Family, except the three younger daughters, to viſit his Majeſty, in order to try the effect that it would have.

For *LONDON*.

BY Order of the Shippers, the Sailing of the LONDON PACKET, James Glaſs, Maſter, is poſtponed till the firſt February.

IRELAND.

News-paper printed in Dublin every morning.

Saunders's News-Letter.	1
Mornings of Tueſday, Thurſday and Saturday. Dublin Gazette—Dublin Journal—Freeman's Journal—Morning Poſt.	4
Evenings of ditto, (General Poſt Nights.) Dublin Evening Poſt—Dublin Chronicle—Dublin Evening Packet.	3

In the provinces of Ulſter and Munſter the Dublin Chronicle has the greateſt circulation of any newspaper; and the Dublin Evening Poſt the next greateſt circulation.

In the provinces of Lienſter and Conaught the Dublin Evening Poſt has the greateſt circulation, and the Dublin Chronicle the next greateſt circulation.

Mornings of Monday, Wedneſday and Friday. Hibernian Journal.	1
Evenings of ditto.—Evening Herald.	1
Mornings of Tueſday and Saturday. Pue's Occurrences.	1
Weekly Papers on Saturday Morning.	2

Country News-papers, viz.

Athlone	1	Mullingar	1
Belfaſt	1	Monaghan	1
Cork	3	Newry	1
Clonmel	1	Sligo	1
Drogheda	1	Tralee	2
Ennis	1	Tuam	1
Galway	2	Waterford	1
Kilkenny	1	Wexford	1
Limerick	3		
Londonderry	1	Total	24

Total News-papers printed in Ireland, 37.

WHEREAS on the night of Saturday the third day of January inſtant, A Turf Stack, the property of Thomas Potter of Ballybregagh, in the county of Down, was maliciouſly and feloniouſly ſet on Fire by ſome perſon or perſons unknown, which had it not been providentially diſcovered, muſt in a ſhort time have deſtroyed his Dwelling-houſe, Offices, Corn, Hay, &c. and endangered the lives of the whole Family.

NOW we the undernamed Perſons, having a juſt abhorrence, and holding in deteſtation ſuch horrid crimes, and with a view of bringing the perpetrators of ſuch villanous acts to condign puniſhment, do promiſe to pay the ſeveral ſums to our names annexed, to any perſon who will within ſix calendar months from the date hereof, diſcover on and proſecute to conviction the perſon or perſons concerned in ſetting fire to ſaid Turf Stack; and we hereby pledge ourſelves that if any perſon concerned in ſaid Felony, (except the perſon who actually ſet fire to the turf) will diſcover on and proſecute to conviction his, her or their accomplice or accomplices, he or ſhe will not only be entitled to the above reward, but application ſhall be made to Government for his Majeſty's Pardon. Dated 7th January, 1789.

	l.	s.	d.		l.	s.	d.
Rt. Hon. Robt. Stewart	22	15	0	Rev. Jas. Clewlow	5	13	9
Hon. Edward Ward	22	15	0	John Gordon, Eſq.	5	13	9
Hon. George Rawdon	5	13	9	Jn. Crawford, Eſq.	5	13	9
Sir John Blackwood, Bart.	22	15	0	Jas. Crawford, Eſq	5	13	9
Gn. Hamilton, Eſq.	22	15	0	Fras. Turnly, Eſq;	5	13	9
Rev. Ham. Trail	11	7	6	R. Johnſton, Eſq;	5	13	9
John Knox, Eſq.	11	7	6	Hen. Savage, Eſq.	5	13	9
James Bailie, Eſq.	11	7	6	Revd. Robert Mortimer	5	13	9
Fras. Price, Eſq.	5	13	9	Sam. Stone, Eſq.	5	13	9
Mat. Ford, Eſq.	5	13	9	H. Montgomery, Eſq.	5	13	9
Pat. Savage, Eſq.	5	13	9	H. Gilleſpie, Eſq.	5	13	9
Alex. Stewart, Eſq,	5	13	9	Mr. John M'Cully	3	8	3
Nichs. Price, Eſq.	5	13	9	Mr. John Riddle	3	8	3
Eld Pottinger, Eſq.	5	13	9	Mr. Robt. R. Reid	3	8	3
T. Dowglaſs, Eſq.	5	13	9	Mr. Mich. Rankin	3	8	3
Rev. H. Montgomery	5	13	9	Mr. Thos. Orr	2	5	6
Rev. Jas. Ham. Clewlow	5	13	9	Mr. R. Montgomery	2	5	6
				Mr. Thos. Stewart	22	11	6
				Thomas Potter	56	17	6

Amounting in all to £ 1137 16 5

Reverend George M'Ewen, 11l. 7s. 6d.——☞ The Names of the Subſcribers in the united Pariſhes of Killinchy, Tollynakill, and Killmud, are ſo numerous that they cannot be inſerted; the original is in the hands of Mr. M'Ewen; the total amount thereof is 660l. 1s. 5d. Doctor Little 5l. 13s. 9d. The names of the Subſcribers in the pariſh of Killileagh are alſo ſo numerous that they cannot be inſerted. The Original in the hands of Mr. James Mc. Connel amounted to 118l. 6s.

N. B. I will give a further Sum of Twenty Guineas (excluſive of the Sum to my Name annexed) to any perſon who will give ſuch private information as will lead to a diſcovery of the perſon or perſons who committed the above Felony.

THOMAS POTTER.

Belfaſt.

His Excellency the Lord Lieutenant of Ireland has been pleaſed to appoint James Watſon Hull, of Belvidere, Eſq. High Sheriff of the County Down for the enſuing year.

James Watſon Hull, Eſq. High Sheriff of the County of Down, has appointed Robert Stewart, of Belfaſt, in the County of Antrim, Gent. his Under Sheriff.

DIED on Tueſday laſt, HENRY JOY, SENIOR, one of the Proprietors of this Paper.

Died on Tueſday laſt, Margaret Smith, of Carmoney, aged 94 years: what is remarkable in her life-time, ſhe was never known to complain of any bodily infirmity theſe 60 years paſt, and five hours before her diſſolution ſhe was in her uſual health.

THREE BRITISH PACKETS DUE.

PORT NEWS.

ARRIVED.

Jan. 22. Friends, Ferguſon, Baltimore, flax-ſeed, &c. Three colliers.

A correſpondent remarks with regret that the ſeveral premiums offered by the Right Hon. the TRUSTEES OF THE LINEN MANUFACTURES, and their general regulations for the ſtaple trade of Ireland, are ſeldom if ever to be found in the NORTHERN PRINTS, tho' the Manufacture and the Manufacturers of Linen are only to be found in the North; the conſequence of which frequently is, that the moſt judicious regulations and well-judged offers of reward are often unheard of in the North, and conſequently paſs by without their intended effect. It is humbly ſubmitted as a queſtion worth an anſwer,—whether the regulations of a great and reſpectable Board, would not have additional effect, by publication in the province to which the Staple Trade is confined?

At the requeſt of a reader the following remarks are inſerted.

On Friday night laſt, the Comedy of *She Stoops to Conquer*, or the *Miſtakes of a Night*, with the Pantomime of *Prometheus*, were performed at this Theatre to a crowded audience.

In the comedy, a Young Lady, whoſe name (we are informed) is *Bradbury*, made her firſt appearance in the character of Miſs HARDCASTLE—and was very flatteringly received by the Houſe.

Her ſtature is rather low; but ſhe has youth, beauty, and a ſtriking countenance. Her voice is full and harmonious, and her action, though it has not the eaſe and poliſh of the higher circles of life, yet gives that promiſe of future improvement, which deſerves indulgence in a young performer.

The ſcenery in the Pantomime does great credit to the Manager, particularly that of the Church Yard and the laſt ſcene, a Temple of Hymen.

MARRIED.] Lately at Belfaſt, Mr. Thomas Ludford Stewart to Miſs Boyd, daughter of Ezekiel Davis Boyd, Eſq; formerly of Ballycaſtle.

DIED.] At Dromore, after a few days illneſs, on Thurſday the 5th inſt. in the ſeventy-ſecond year of his age, Mr. David Sweeney, who kept an Engliſh School in that town near fifty years paſt.

To be Let,

From the 25th of March next, for ſuch Term as may be agreed upon,

THE Houſe at preſent occupied by Mr. Lyle, in the New Row, Colerain.——For further particulars apply to Mr. Lyle on the premiſſes.

Colerain, Jan. 16th, 1789.

WHEREAS on Friday the 9th inſt. an advertiſement appeared in this paper, ſetting forth in the moſt ſcurrilous language, that Robert Dixon of Moy-begg, had on the 27th or 28th of April laſt, extorted from John Mullan of Coolcoſchran, a promiſſary note for the ſum of thirty-eight pounds, ten ſhillings ſterl. for which note Mullan ſays he never received any value.

Now in order to convince the publick, that the afore-mentioned advertiſement was intended as a malicious aſperſion on the character of Robert Dickſon:

Thomas Hanna of Moyheland, pariſh of Ballymaſcreen and county of London-derry, came this day before me, Arthur Tracy, one of his Majeſty's Juſtices of the Peace for the afore-mentioned county, and made oath, that on the 28th day of laſt April, he ſaw the aforeſaid John Mullan perfect a note to Robert Dickſon for 38l. 10s. ſterl.—in lieu of which note Dickſon gave Mullan up a proteſted bill, which amounted, with expences, to 38l. 10s.—and as Mullan could not then conveniently pay the amount of the proteſted bill, he freely, and without any compulſion whatever, gave his note to Robert Dickſon payable four days after date for the aforeſaid ſum, to which note I am a witneſs,

THOMAS HANNA.

Sworn before me at Maghrafelt, this 12th day of January, 1789.

ARTHUR TRACY.

Anno 1789.] Printed by HENRY JOY, Senr. and Junr. BELFAST.

The BELFAST NEWS-LETTER.

TUESDAY January 27, FRIDAY January 30, 1789.

For *LONDON*,

THE FRIENDS ENCREASE, P. Nevin, Master, eighty tons burthen, now ready to load, has one half of her Cargo engaged, and will be ready to fail the 8th day of February next.

This a remarkab'e fine Veffel, not more than two years old, and is set up at the particular defire of fome of the principal Shippers in Newry who have had an opportunity of inspecting her.———For Freight apply to JOHN NEVILL,

Newry, 26th Jan. 1789.

Auction of Tobacco.

NINETY-NINE Hogfheads of a fuperior quality, to be fold in the Town-Hall, by Dickfon Coningham, on Tuefday 3d February next, at the hour of eleven o'clock.———Approved bills on Dublin at four months date from the fale, will be taken, or 6d. per pound difcount allowed for cafh ;———and on Monday 26th inft, will be fold in the Town-hall, at the hour of one o'clock, the fine Brig Richmond, as fhe now lies fitted out, Britifh built, 200 Guineas depofite down, and an approved bill on Dublin at three months date for the remainder, otherwife fhe will be fold over again fame day at three o'clock.

L. Derry, 20th January, 1789.

PURSUANT to an order of the Houfe of Commons, Notice is hereby given, that an application will be made by George Hamilton, Efq; and Mr. Samuel Norris to Parliament, the enfuing Seffion, for a fum of money for improving the harbour of Strangford, in the barony of Lecale and county of Down, by building a Pier. December 1, 1788

A HUNTER, rifing eight years old, perfectly well trained, able to carry fixteen ftone—no horfe leaps better—he is found, cool and fteady :

Alfo another excellent Hanter, found and able to carry thirteen ftone with any hounds. A Gentleman may have any reafonable trial.———Apply to Mr. James Ruffel, Tyrella, Downe. Letters (poft paid) will be anfwered.

Mr. ATKINS,

WITH the greateft refpect informs the Ladies and Gentlemen of Belfaft, that his Benefit is fix'd on Friday the 30th inftant, when will be performed the COMEDY of

The HIPPOCRITE,

With Variety of Entertainments.
And the FARCE of

Three Weeks after Marriage.

Tickets and Places in the Boxes to be taken by Mr. Atkins, in Ann-ftreet.

For the Benefit of Mr. King,

ON Monday next, February 2d, 1789, will be prefented a favourite Comedy and Farce, and Variety of Entertainments.

Tickets and Places for the Boxes to be taken of Mr. King, at the Theatre.

THE feveral perfons indebted to the late Partnerfhip of William Potter and Company, are requefted immediately to difcharge their refpective accounts to Mr. Alexander Armftrong, who is duly authorized to receive the fame, otherwife they will be put into the hands of an Attorney for a more immediate recovery thereof.

Belfaft, 26th January, 1789.

WILLIAM POTTER.

BALLYCLARE.

IN a very fhort time Waddell Cunningham, James Holmes, & Co. will fell by public Auction, the Grand Leafe from Lord Donegall to Nath. Wilfon, of the Town and Lands of Ballyclare, yielding a profit rent of upwards of 5ll. per annum. all well fecured, befides the Cuftoms, which are valuable, with the Cloghan Mofs, Flow Mofs, and Black Mofs, which are not let to under tenants.———The particulars will be given in a future Paper by

WADDELL CUNNINGHAM,
JAMES HOLMES, & Co.

Belfaft, 26th Jan. 1789.

To be Sold,

A BAY MARE, fix years old, a good hunter, and able to carry twelve ftone after the fleeteft hounds; has been in conftant practice this feafon :—Alfo a good Hack

The above are the property of a Gentleman gone abroad, which is the only reafon of their being fold—to be feen at Downpatrick by applying to Mr. Samuel Holliday. January 26th, 1789.

To be inferted three times.

BALLYCLARE.

ON Friday the fixth day of February, Robert Bradfhaw will fell by public Auction, in the Market-Houfe, Belfaft, at twelve o'clock, that Lot of the Lands of Ballyclare which he purchafed at the firft day's fale. viz.—Lot No. 6, which Lot for the convenience of Buyers he will divide into four fhares as under, for which Meffrs. Waddell Cunningham, James Holmes & Co. have confented to give to the Buyers four feparate leafes, one for each fhare—all to commence from laft November, and to continue for 58 years and 11 months, at the rents under-mentioned :

No. 1. Alexander Mc. Allefter's holding of 8A. 2R. 0P. at the yearly rent of 3l. 12s. 6d.

No. 2. George Craig's Holding of 15A. 2R. 0P. at the yearly rent of 6l. 12s. 6d.

No. 3. The Holding of John Quin, Pat. Marphy, and Widow Robinfon, containing 8A. 0R. 20P. at the yearly rent of 3l. 9s. 4d.

No. 4. John Wilfon's Holding of 12A. 2R. 16P. at the yearly rent of 5l. 7s. 8d.

TERMS of SALE the fame as thofe under which the lands of Ballyclare were lately fold by Meffrs. Wad. Cunningham, James Holmes, & Co.

Belfaft, 24th Jan. 1789.

ROBERT BRADSHAW.

New Garden Seeds.

THOMAS WRIGHT, of Monaghan, begs leave to inform his Friends, that he has imported his entire Quantity of Garden Seeds—Flowers—Peas—Beans, and Clover Seeds, for the prefent year—and which his correfpondents in London and Holland engage to be of excellent Quality.

Thofe who fow quantities of Onion will find their account in applying to him : He has likewife Garden Tools on the neateft conftruction—Fruit and Foreft Trees—feedlings—Thorn Quicks, &c. &c. and is well fupplied with frefh Teas—and Groceries of every fort : Alfo a Collection of well-chofen Ironmonger Goods, &c. &c. Monaghan, 21ft Jan. 1789.

Hugh Montgomery,

HAS juft imported a few hogfheads of James's River Wrappery Tobacco, of the very beft quality, which, with the following Articles, he has for Sale at his Stores in Ann-ftreet :

Kentifh Bag Hops,	Antigua Rum,
Barrilla,	American Barrel and Hhd.
American Pot Afh,	Staves,
Dantzig ditto,	Tierce and Barrel Hoops,
Black Soap,	Bergen Deals,
Oil of Vitriol,	Rofin,
Dutch Starch,	Sherry in wood & bottle,
Firft, fecond and third	Red and White Port do.
Smalts,	Yellow Cotton Wool.

N. B. The Brigantine Walters, Walter Stevens, Mafter, is arrived at Larne, from Alicant, with a quantity of new Barrilla, which fhe expects round in a few days.

Belfaft, 27th January, 1789.

James Hamill,

HAS received per the Neptune, Captain Mifkelly, Mafter, from Bordeaux, French Plumbs, Prunes, Walnuts, Almonds.———And has on hand FRESH TEAS, confifting of Hyfon, Bloom, Sufong, Congou, Green and Bohea ; which, with Mace, Cloves, Cinnamon, Nutmegs, white and Black Pepper, Ginger, Alfpice, Ifinglafs, Lemons and fweet Oranges, Dublin Glue, Figs, Box, Jar and Cafk Raifins, Currants, Brufhes of different forts, Dyeftuffs, Anchovies, Capers, Liquorice Ball, Glauber Salts, Starch, Blue, Hair Powder, Miferable, Scotch and common Barley, Rice, beft French Indigo, Saltpetre, Gunpowder, Shot, beft Whitewine Vinegar, and Dantzig Afhes of different brands ;— All which, with a general Affortment of Groceries, he will fell on moderate Terms.

Belfaft, 26th Jan. 1789.

N. B. He is well fupplied with fine and common Scale Sugars, which will be fold remarkably cheap.

Advertisement.

TO be Sold by Auction, on Monday the 9th of February next, at the Houfe of Archibald Mc. Clure, North-ftreet, Belfaft, at 12 o'clock at noon :—

The Houfe and Offices now in the poffeffion of Thomas Doody in Shamble-ftreet, Belfaft; 61 years of the leafe to come from May next, chief-rent and fees 9l. 10s. a year.———Terms to be declared at Sale.

Dated this 24th January. 1789.

To be Lent,

EIGHT HUNDRED POUNDS upon real Security; alfo FIVE HUNDRED POUNDS upon perfonal fecurity. Application to be made to Daniel Moore Echlin, Attorney.

Mrs. Freeman,

(With the moft grateful Recollection of paft Favours) BEGS leave to inform the Ladies and Gentlemen of Belfaft, that her BENEFIT is fixed for Wednefday 4th of February, when will be performed the COMEDY of

The HEIRESS.

During the Evening, an Entertainment, call'd, The SCHOOL of HARMONY ; In which will be introduced the following favourite SONGS :

" To the GREENWOOD GANG."
" BRIGHT PHOEBUS."
" The SOLDIER TIR'D—And
" HOW SWEET the LOVE."
To which will be added,
A FAVOURITE FARCE.

Any Commands for Boxes, or Tickets, which Mrs. Freeman fhall be honour'd with, will be carefully attended to, at Mr. Victor Coats's, Caftle-ftreet.

Dungannon School.

THE Revd Dr. WILLIAM MURRAY, has removed to his new School-Houfe, near Dungannon, which is peculiarly convenient for the accommodation of Boarders, as it affords a fingle bed for each ; it has alfo a large enclofed Yard, together with a field for play-ground immediately under the parlour windows, which give every opportunity for air and exercife, without removing the boys from the Mafter's infpection.

His Terms are, for Boarding and Tuition 20 Guineas yearly, and five Guineas entrance ; for wafhing, firing for the School, &c. Half-a-Guinea quarterly ; for Writing and Arithmetic, Paper, Pens and Ink, Half-a-Guinea quarterly, and Half-a-Guinea Entrance ; Dancing and French upon the moft reafonable Terms. He does not now, nor will in future employ as an Ufher (except in the very loweft Grammar Departments) any perfon who has not had public opportunity, at the Irifh, or at one of the Englifh Univerfities, of fhewing his merit, and who is not recommended to him by the Fellows of the College in which he was educated as a proper perfon to affift him. January 24th, 1789.

Archibald Bankhead,

HAS juft received by the Falmouth, Capt. Mc. Donnell, from Rotterdam, Barbary Gum, Sugar of Lead, Black Soap, and Linfeed Oil—which he will fell on reafonable Terms.

Belfaft, Jan. 19th 1789.

BLEACHING.

LINENS, CAMBRICKS, and COTTONS, will be taken to bleach at White-Abbey Green ; where they will be as well done, and at as low a price as at any Green in this Country.

ALSO TO BE LET,

WHITE-ABBEY Houfe and Gardens, with or without the Farm ; a defcription of this place is confidered ufelefs, it being well known there are few places in this kingdom fo well calculated or fo pleafingly fituated for a Linen Draper or private Gentleman. For further particulars enquire at THOs. Mc. CABE.

Belfaft, 8th Jan. 1789.

George Langtry,

Has juft imported for Sale,

Remarkable fine and fecond	New Prunes,
Clay'd Sugars,	Walnuts,
Scale ditto,	Shell Almonds,
French Plumbs,	Bordeaux Vinegar.

The above, with a general Affortment of Dyeftuffs, Teas, Dantzig Afhes, &c. will be fold on reafonable terms. Belfaft, 26th Jan. 1789.

Diffolution of Partnerfhip.

JOHN HASLETT, and Co. finding that many of their Friends have overlooked the Requifition formerly made in this Paper—are under the neceffity of reminding them, that the time of diffolving their Partnerfhip draws near (the firft of February next)—before which they muft infift on being paid every account due them longer than three months.

They likewife requeft their feveral Friends to obferve, that a Perfon from their Houfe will fet out in a few days for the purpofe of fettling all depending accounts, and receiving the amount of fuch as come under the above defcription.

Belfaft, 23d December, 1788.

Cheap Scale Sugars.

STEWARTS, THOMSON, and Co. continue to fell remarkably fine Scale Sugar, at 8s. per Stone.

Vienna, December 31.

THEY write from Constantinople, that the Divan, to excite the greater courage in the soldiers, have had a new coin struck, with the following inscription in Arabic:

"There is one God: there in one prophet, Mahomet is his name. The true victories come from God, who is our King, and with whom Mahomet is our advocate: he teaches us to pray, to believe, and conquer. The God of Mahomet is our God; the prophets of God are Mahomet, Abubekir, Omar, and Ali. O Mahomet, sole matter of riches and victory, let the blood spilt in battles against miscreants be dear and sacred to thee!"

Paris, Jan. 2. History does not afford us an example of so long and cold a winter as the present. The frost began to shew itself on the 24th of November with a North-east wind, and continued increasing day and night till the 25th of December, when a temporary thaw came, which lasted two days, after which the frost returned as strong as before, and has continued ever since. The Seine is frozen over entirely, and more compleatly than in 1776, and the snow from the 5th to the 6th of December was five inches deep, and remained so untill the 16th, when there fell two inches and a half more, and on the 27th it was nine inches deep.

LONDON, JAN. 22.

The Royal apartment at Kew, during the time of coercion, is wholly dark. This, and the being confined down in bed, make up the whole of the practice; which, however, has never been resorted to but on two or three occasions, when the paroxysms were uncommonly violent.

The King was so well on Saturday last, as to play at *Piquet* with the Queen, and he played with as much recollection as at any former period of his life. This being an undoubted fact, he will certainly recover.

On Monday, at four o'clock in the afternoon, the King, accompanied by Doctors Baker, Gisborne, Willis and son, and General Lascelles, Groom of the Chamber, walked round Kew-gardens, but on their return his Majesty seemed very unquiet.

It is not a principle in law or in reason in any case, still less in the present, that a father and his son are the same; but it is a legal principle that a husband and wife are considered as one person in the contemplation of law. Hence the necessity of vesting this power over the Houshold in the Royal Consort; no expediency, however pressing or deceptive in the State, should urge a great country and a generous people to an act of injustice.

The King is extremely thin. His pulse varies from 68 to 126.

It is curious, says a correspondent, that, in the year 1481, King John of Denmark, one of the best Princes that kingdom ever had, was afflicted with lunacy for a considerable time, and a regency was appointed; but the King afterwards perfectly recovered, and reigned happily for nineteen years.

At the beginning of the late reign, the Viceroys of Ireland had a similar power and patronage with that of their Sovereigns in this country; but since 1729 the donation of bishopricks, military commissions, and patent places, and the signature of their commissions, are reserved to his Majesty. Lord Carteret, the late Earl Granville, was the last Lord Lieutenant who enjoyed this plenitude of Vice-regal power.

There are no Conge d'Elires in Ireland as in England, consequently the Bishops there are appointed by the Crown, and their patents granted as Lords of Parliament, without any commission to their Deans and Chapters.

The Acts of the Irish Parliament obtain the Royal assent in the following manner, since the alteration of Poyning's Law in 1780:—A copy of any Act which has passed the two Houses in Ireland is certified under the Great Seal of Ireland to the Council of England, and a warrant under the Great Seal of Great Britain is annexed to the copy which is returned to Ireland, and enables the Lord Lieutenant to pass the bill, and personally to give the Royal assent. Hence no alterations can now be made in the Councils of either kingdom in Irish bills, because the roll or original record of a bill which has passed the two Houses, remains in the office of the Lords in Ireland.

BRITISH HOUSE OF COMMONS.

Tuesday, January 20.

Mr. Wilberforce having, in consequence of the resolutions of the preceding night, waited on the House of Lords, with a number of gentlemen of the House of Commons, for the purpose of desiring a conference with their Lordships; the same being agreed to, Mr Wilberforce returned and intimated the same to the house.

The order of the day for Thursday next, to call over the house, was moved by Mr. Pitt to be discharged, and deferred to Monday next.

PRINCE OF WALES AND MR. PITT.

Copy of a letter from a great Personage to Mr. Pitt, in answer to Mr. Pitt's letter, containing the proposed restrictions on the intended Regency, which was so much called for in the House of Commons last Monday.

"The Prince of Wales learns from Mr. Pitt's letter, that the proceedings in Parliament are now in a train which enable Mr. Pitt, according to the intimation in his former letter, to communicate to the Prince the outlines of the plan which his Majesty's confidential servants conceive to be proper to be proposed in the present circumstances. Concerning the steps already taken by Mr. Pitt, the Prince is silent—nothing done by the two houses of Parliament can be a proper subject of his animadversion; but, when previously to any discussion in Parliament, the outline of a scheme of Government is sent for his consideration, in which, it is proposed that he shall be personally and particularly concerned, and by which the Royal authority, and the public welfare, may be deeply affected—The Prince would be unjustifiable, were he to withhold an explicit declaration of his sentiments; his silence might be construed into a previous approbation of a plan, the accomplishment of which, every motive of duty to his Father and Sovereign, as well as of regard to the public interest, obliges him to consider as injurious to both.

"In the state of deep distress in which the Prince and the whole Royal Family were involved by the heavy calamity which has fallen upon the King: and at the moment when Government, deprived of its chief energy and support, seemed peculiarly to need the cordial and united aid of all descriptions of good subjects, it was not expected by the Prince that a plan should be offered to his consideration, by which government was to be rendered difficult if not impracticable, in the hands of any person intended to represent the King's authority, much less in the hands of his eldest son, the Heir Apparent of his kingdom, and the person most bound to the maintenance of his Majesty's just prerogatives and authority, as well as most interested in the happiness, the prosperity, and the glory of his people.

Postscript.

Extract from the last Packet, published in London on Wednesday evening last.

The following are some of the principal arrangements that will certainly take place immediately after passing the Regency Bill:

The Duke of York to be the Commander in Chief.
Earl Fitzwilliam first Lord of the Admiralty, assisted by Lord Rodney and Admiral Pigott.
Mr. Fox and Lord Stormont, Secretaries of State.
Mr. Sheridan, Treasurer of the Navy, with the Head of the Board of Controul.
Lord John Cavendish, Chancellor of the Exchequer.
Dr. Pare is to be the Master of Trinity College, Cambridge.

It is positively asserted at the West end of the town, that the Prince of Wales will not accept of the Regency under the proposed restrictions.

Belfast, January 27.

SINCE OUR LAST ARRIVED SIX B. PACKETS.

** The advertisement of the Bellaghey Association, with several others, are unavoidably omitted till next publication, on account of the extraordinary length of the Physicians Examination and the Debates in the British Parliament.

Some ill inclined, or intoxicated persons, broke a number of LAMPS and WINDOWS on Sunday evening. Such wanton folly, deserves every punishment that the law will permit.

On Monday the Sovereign committed two men to the county goal (as they could not produce security) for an imposition, which they attempted by filling three canvas bags partly with sawdust and sand, and a small quantity of raw sugar on the surface; which they sold and were paid for as being entirely sugar. They called themselves Pat. Nooner and Wm. Trodden.

The Sale of Dr. Crawford's Farm (advertised in the last page of this paper) is postponed to the 20th of February next.

James Watson Hull, Esq. High Sheriff of the County of Down, has appointed Robert Stewart, of Belfast, in the County of Antrim, Gent. his Under Sheriff.

Married, on Thursday the 15th inst. Thomas Legg, Esq. to Miss Hull, both of Carrickfergus.

Died at Bath the 17th inst. Samuel Bristow, Esq. a gentleman of truly respectable character.—Also at Belfast, Mr. Francis Hamilton, of Donegall-street, deservedly regretted.

Belfast, January 30.

The Lord Chancellor and Judges of his Majesty's Courts of King's Bench, Common Pleas, and Exchequer, have been pleased to appoint Patrick Connor, of Belfast, Gent. a Master Extraordinary and Commissioner for taking affidavits for the said courts in the co. Antrim.

His Excellency the Lord Lieutenant of Ireland has been pleased to appoint James Watson Hull, of Bel-

---

videre, Esq. High Sheriff of the County Down for the ensuing year.

Died, at Carrickfergus, on Sunday last, Mrs. Sampson, widow of the late Rev. Arthur Sampson.

Anno 1789.] Printed by HENRY JOY, and Co. BELFAST.

The BELFAST NEWS LETTER.

TUESDAY February 3, FRIDAY February 6, 1789.

For LONDON,

THE FRIENDS ENCREASE, P. NEVIN, Master, eighty tons burthen now ready to load, has one half of her Cargo engaged, and will be ready to sail the 8th day of February next.

This a remarkable fine Vessel, not more than two years old, and is set up at the particular desire of some of the principal Shippers in Newry who have had an opportunity of inspecting her.——For Freight apply to JOHN NEVILL,

Newry, 26th Jan 1789

For LONDON,

THE Brig ROYAL OAK, 90 tons burthen, GEORGE CUNNINGHAM, Master, now in the Canal, will be clear to sail the 10th February next——For Freight apply to JOHN BLACK.

Newry, 23th Jan. 1789.

N. B. The principal part of the Cargo is engaged, the Master well acquainted with the London Trade, having been several years Mate of the New Draper, Capt. Hughes, from this Port.

Oats and Oatmeal.

A Quantity of good Oats and Oatmeal wanted by WM. SEED, and Co. at their Stores adjoining the Weigh-house, for which a fair market price will be given.

WHEAT.

Constant attendance is given at their Mills, Beer's-Bridge, for the receiving of Wheat.

FLOUR.

They are largely supplied with all Kinds of Flour, from their Mills at Beer's-bridge, which they are selling on the lowest terms, at their Stores, Weigh-house-lane. Belfast, 30th Jan. 1789.

BRAN to be had at their Stores in Town.

Rum by Auction.

FORTY Puncheons choice good JAMAICA RUM, to be sold by Auction for Account of the Shippers, at the

Stores of Robert Scott on Chichester-Quay,

on Wednesday the 4th of February next, at *one o'Clock.*—To be set up in Lots of Five Puncheons each, and paid for by approved Bills on Dublin or Belfast at three months date, or two per cent. discount for cash.

Also to be sold at same Time and Place,

Sixteen Planks of Mohogany,

of a remarkable good quality and scantling—to be set up in Lots of four Planks each, and paid for by bills at three months, or two per cent. discount for cash.

Belfast, 28th Jan. 1789.

Auction of Tobacco.

NINETY-NINE Hogsheads of a superior quality, to be sold in the Town-Hall, by Dickson Coningham, on Tuesday 3d February next, at the hour of eleven o'clock.—Approved bills on Dublin at four months date from the sale, will be taken, or 6d. per pound discount allowed for cash.—And on same day, at the hour of one o'clock, in the Town-Hall, will be sold the fine Brig Richmond, as the now lies, British built; 200 Guineas deposit down, and an approved bill on Dublin at three months date for the remainder, otherwise she will be sold over again same day at three o'clock.

L. Derry, 27th January, 1789.

History of the City and County of Derry.

A NUMBER of curious and interesting Papers, relating to the City and County of Derry, has been collected for the purpose of publication. Upon a review of these papers, and upon further consideration, it is proposed to extend the first idea, and to publish "*An Essay towards an History of the City and County of Derry.*"

To enable the Undertakers of this Work to make it worthy of the attention of the Public, it is requested, that such gentlemen as have in their possession any Manuscripts, Papers, Books, Pamphlets, Maps, or other Publications, either Civil, Military, or Ecclesiastical, relating to the City and County of *Derry*, or the Counties of *Donegall* or *Tyrone*, will be so good as to communicate them to the Mr. Henry Joy, Belfast, or to Mr. G. Douglas, Bookseller, Derry.—Any Papers, or Books, intrusted to their care, will be thankfully received and faithfully returned, Derry, Jan. 1789.

New Alicant & Carthagena Barilla.

TWO Cargoes just arrived to JOHN ROCHE and ANDREW GEEHAN, at No. 34, Bachelors-Walk, per the Hero, Capt. Tapley, and the Asia, Capt. Hall—the quality is remarkable good, and 500 bales were shipped at Alicant, and 420 at Carthagena.

Mrs. Freeman,

IMPRESSED by the profoundest respect and gratitude for the very distinguished favours wherewith she was last night honoured at her *Benefit*—intreats permission to express her sincerest thanks to the *Ladies* and *Gentlemen* of *Belfast* for so auspicious a test of the flattering estimation in which they have the goodness to hold her efforts for their entertainment.——Patronage at once so honourable, and so liberal, while it exalts, will also perpetuate her respect and gratitude to the *Belfast* audience.

Belfast, 5th Feb. 1789.

For the Benefit of Mrs. Chalmers,

ON Wednesday February 11th, will be presented the COMEDY of

Much ado about Nothing.

The Part of Benedick and Beatrice, by Mr. and Mrs. CHALMERS.

To which will be added a FARCE as will be expressed in the Bills of the Day.

With a Pantomimic Afterlude, call'd,

HARLEQUIN GARD'NER.

Preceding which Mr. CHALMERS will speak HARLEQUIN'S PROLOGUE.

With a Leap through FIRE and WATER.

Harlequin, Mr. Chalmers.

And Colombine, (for that Night) Mrs. Chalmers.

The Whole to conclude with a Front Leap

Through a BRILLIANT SUN of Variegated FIRE, And Grand Display of FIRE-WORKS.

Tickets and places to be had of Mrs. Chalmers, at Mr. Dawson's on the Quay.

Hillsborough Fair,

WILL be holden on Wednesday the 18th instant, when the very extensive Premiums, the same as at the last Fair, will be given by the Sovereign.

MICHAEL THOMSON, Clerk of the Market.

Hillsborough, Feb. 4th, 1789.

The Belfast Coterie,

WILL be held, (as usual) at the Exchange-Rooms on Tuesday next, the 10th instant.

February 6th, 1789.

The Union Assembly,

WILL be held at the ROOMS, on Thursday next the 12th February, 1789.

February 5th, 1789.

Mc. Tear and Henderson.

RESPECTFULLY inform their Friends and Customers, that they have removed a few doors further up High-street:——Where they are largely supplied with Bleachers and second Soap, mold and dipp'd Candles, and a few tons exceeding good dry Kelp, the quality of which they can recommend.

As they will endeavour always to have the several Articles in their line of business of the best qualities, they hope for a continuance of the publick favour, which they thankfully acknowledge to have already received.

The Shop they formerly occupied to be let, or the interest for eight years and a half in the lease, with two Dwelling Houses adjoining, to be sold.——Apply as above.

☞ An Apprentice wanted.

Blea Flax.

JOHN WIGHTMAN has lately arrived by the Falmouth, from Rotterdam, a Parcel of Blea Flax, remarkably fine; there is a quantity of it dressed, so as to answer the fine Cambrick Manufactory.

His present Stock of Old Spirit, Rum as imported and reduced, Cherry and other Brandy, Gin, Red Port, French bottled and other Clarets, Madeira, Sherry, Lisbon and Mountain Wines, will (as usual) be sold on the lowest terms.

Lisburn, 2d February, 1789.

Fair of Connor.

FROM the inclemency of the weather the fair of Connor, which was to be on the first instant, being held on Monday the second, but, from the bad day, no business could be transacted;—therefore there will be a Fair held on Friday the 13th inst. at Connor, custom free, and the day following, being the 14th instant, will be set up a neat Hunting Saddle to be run for with sweep-stakes. All horses admitted to run who never, at any one time, won above twenty pounds.

Connor, 4th Feb. 1789.

To be continued Twice.

Robert Getty,

MOST respectfully informs his numerous friends and customers, that he has removed from Bridge-street, to the House in North-street, immediately above Mr. Hugh Crawford's; where he continues to carry on his usual line of trade, in the same extensive manner as heretofore.

He has just received New French Plumbs, Pruens and Zant Currants, best Italian Liquorice Ball, Walnuts, new Bag Hops, Miserable, Aleppo Galls, and Bordeaux Vinegar. And is at present very largely supplied with Congou, Singlo, and Bohea Teas, which will be sold by the chest on the most reasonable terms.

January, 21, 1789.

In the Matter of John Kenly, a Bankrupt. } TO be sold by publick Auction, on Tuesday third February next, at the house of John Shaw, in Lisburn, All said Bankrupt's right, title and interest in and to the following Tenements in said Town:

No. 1. A large extensive house, ware houses and garden, at present occupied by said Kenly and under tenants, situate in the South side of the Corn-market, and well calculated for carrying on business; part of said concerns are at present let to tenants at Will, being a lease of lives renewable for ever, at the yearly rent of two pounds some odd shillings annually, besides an annuity of nine pounds per annum.

No. 2. Hugh O'Hara's house at the Mill-race, set at Will for 7l. per annum, being a lease of lives renewable for ever, and subject to the yearly rent of 4s. 2d. including pipe water and receivers fees.

No. 3. Thomas Greer's house and garden near the Mill-Race, at present let at will at six guineas per annum, and subject to 4s. 2d. chief rent, pipe water and Receiver's fees, being a lease renewable for ever.

No. 4. William Neill and Arthur Carson's two houses and gardens, adjoining the Linen Hall, at present let at will at 8l. per annum, being a lease of lives renewable for ever, and sold free of chief rent, pipe water, &c.

No. 5. A large Garden in the rere of the Tenements at the Linen hall, being a lease of lives renewable for ever, and sold free of rent;——the whole to be entered upon the first day of May next.——Ten Guineas to be paid as a deposit on the sale of each lot, and the remainder on perfecting the conveyances.

Belfast, 22d Jan. 1789.

WAD. CUNNINGHAM, Mortgagee.
JOHN CUNNINGHAM, } Assignees.
HUGH CRAWFORD, }

Bellaghey Association.

AT a Meeting of the Gentlemen of Bellaghey and its Vicinity, on Tuesday the 20th day of January, 1789, convened for the purpose of taking into consideration the disorderly and unlawful behaviour of a set of people in the neighbourhood thereof, who, without respect to persons or property, daily commit the most wanton excesses; (in particular, numberless depredations upon Lord Bristol's property; and their nocturnal meetings at Claudy, where, by violent force and threats, they have lately obliged two families to abandon their homes) and who, by a total defiance to the civil power, have hitherto evaded the punishment annexed by the laws to such offences.

Resolved, That in order to bring all such offenders to punishment, We do hereby pledge ourselves to each other, and the public, that we will upon the shortest notice, turn out, whenever called on by the civil power, to apprehend them.

2dly, That for the better carrying our intentions into effect, We will at our own expence, prosecute any person who shall within twelve months from the date hereof, be guilty of any assault in the town of Bellaghey, or who shall cause or excite a riot in the neighbourhood thereof within said time.

3dly. That the following Gentlemen be, and hereby are appointed a Committee to this Association, Mr. Spotswood, Mr. Archdeacon Sodon, Mr. Hill, Mr. Mc. Neill, and the Revd. John Ballour.

4thly. That Mr. John Hill be requested to act as Treasurer and Secretary, for the purpose of collecting Subscriptions, and conducting any prosecutions that the said Committee may think proper to commence.

5thly. That a Subscription be kept open by our Treasurer, that such Gentlemen as approve of our intentions, may contribute to the carrying them into effect.

6thly. That no person be admitted a Member of this Association, without the unanimous approbation of said Committee.

7thly. That the thanks of this association be given those Gentlemen of Maghera, who, on a late occasion so readily turned out to escort a notorious offender to the county gaol.

8thly. That these Resolutions be published in the Belfast News-Letter.

Signed by Order,
JOHN HILL, Secretary.

LONDON, Jan. 30.

KEW PALACE, *Jan.* 29.

His Majesty passed yesterday without irritation, has had a very good night, and is in a calm state this morning.

Jan. 30. His Majesty has had a restless night, and is not so quiet this morning as he was yesterday.

Signed by the Physicians.

The Duke of Gloucester, who is a thoughtful character, does not participate in the new administration.

The Duke of Northumberland, in his spirited oration of Wednesday, touched upon a point that creates an universal alarm. It is no less than making the Regency annually elective!

His Grace affirmed, that a very respectable person has pledged himself to introduce it in another place!

Mr. Fox, who is gone to Bath for the benefit of his health, is not expected to return till the completion of the Regency.

DUBLIN, Feb. 3.

On Saturday last there was a most respectable meeting at Lord Charlemont's in Rutland-square.—Mr. Grattan—Mr. Rowley——Mr. Conolly——Lord R. Fitzgerald—Mr. Stuart, of Killymoon—Mr. Montgomery, &c. &c. were of the assembly.——The object was, the arrangement for supporting an address to the Prince to take upon himself the Regency during the indisposition and incapacity of his Majesty.

The motion for an address to the Prince, in the Lower House, will be most powerfully supported, and from every concurring circumstance it scarce admits a doubt of being carried with a majority of *two to one*.

We may certainly expect his Grace of Northumberland, or Lord Spencer, to be the Marquis's successor in the Vice-regal throne—but it is a duty that Reason, aided by fatal experience, imposes on the people of Ireland, not to be *too eager* in demonstrating joy, on the arrival of the Great Personage deputed to reign over us, lest, instead of a friend to the kingdom, they should find to their cost, a second volume of the edition of December the 16th, 1787. Let them suspend their opinion, until they see whether a Charlemont, a Conolly, a Grattan, a Forbes, a Rowley, an O'Neill, and a Hardy, be the advisers in the cabinet—the instant that patriotic selection takes place, the signal for universal joy should be given, but in the interim, Prudence whispers indifference.

BANKRUPT. Robert Bleakly, of Greenvale, in the county of Armagh, merchant, to surrender on the 14th and 16th days of February, and on the 17th day of March next, at the Tholsel, Dublin.

INUNDATION AT CORK,

Cork, Jan. 19. From Friday noon until Saturday noon, we had a most incessant heavy rain, which overflowed all the low grounds about this city and suburbs, and succeeding the very great fall of snow from Sunday night until Tuesday morning, which it dissolved, —there came such a flood into the city as never was remembered by the oldest person living.—It appeared on Saturday morning, when all the flat ground, and low situations were covered, which, with the going out of the tide was expected to subside; but about noon such an inconceivable torrent came down the river as to cause the passages to Grattan-street, Henry-street, Mardyke, Globe-lane, Cross's-lane, Batchelor's-quay, &c. &c. to be totally stopped; and then furiously made its way from the North to South Gate about three o'clock P. M. which obliged the citizens to shut up their shops and remove what goods they could. It is much easier to feel this inconvenience than describe it, at a time when most people expected the waters to have been carried off by the tide. At four o'clock it was very unsafe, from the great increase of the flood for horsemen to pass the Exchange, and continued rising until five o'clock, when many houses had from three to nine feet water in them according to their elevations.

About twelve o'clock at night the water was perceivable lessened, and totally gone before five yesterday morning.—During this melancholy scene several boats plied in different streets and lanes, and many persons in carriages, and horsemen, would have been lost after night-fall had it not been obviated by the vigilance of the citizens who held out lights to them, and cautioned them of the impending danger. The situation of the numberless sufferers is inconceivable, many cabbins carried off by the rapidity of the current, with cattle, hay-ricks, corn, furniture, &c.—and the loss sustained by the merchants, grocers, brewers, linen-drapers, and all other shopkeepers, must amount to at least fifty thousand pounds. Notwithstanding this melancholy catastrophe, we do not hear of any lives being lost, except Mr. N. Mann, house-carpenter, in endavouring to get into his house in French-church-street, fell into the channel close by it and was unfortunately suffocated.

At six o'clock on Saturday morning an old brig lying at Pope's-quay, without any person on board, broke from her moorings, ran against the new bridge, and threw down the centre arch now building, and soon after, the other arch came down. The current of water being so great that at the commencement of Merchant's-quay, Baldwin's cornerwas washed away, and in consequence Mr. James Coppinger's house came down; but we are happy to announce, that from the expected current the family and furniture were removed before the house fell. On the North Abbey a merchant's store fell down, and a small house in Globe-lane, occasioned by their foundations being sapped from the increase of flood in the tide.

The houses on Merchant's and Lavit's-quay, Morrison's Island, and Dunscombe's-marsh, happily escaped the ill effects of the inundation.

The miseries of the poor sufferers on this lamentable occasion is unequalled; without bedding, fire, food, &c. their all being carried off and destroyed.

LONDON-DERRY, Feb. 3.

In the late stormy weather, a vessel bound from the Westward to Port Glasgow, was forced into one of the bays on the coast of Donegal.—We are extremely sorry to hear, that the people on the shore, instead of affording relief to the distressed crew, by force and violence, proceeded to the plundering of the cargo, and carried off nearly the whole of it.

A few nights ago, the prisoners formed a plan to break the gaol, by cutting the bars of one of the windows: accordingly four men and a woman made their escape, and the whole might have got off, but for the timely discovery of the centinel.—Indeed, our gaol is in such bad order, and so very unfit for the purpose, that the wonder is, how any felons are detained in it.

Last Tuesday morning, a young lad, a sailor, stepping from one vessel to another at the quay, missed his footing, fell into the river, and was drowned. His body is not yet found.

To the PRINTERS of the BELFAST N. LETTER.

GENTLEMEN,

TO you as men, free from the influence of party, or the bias of partiality, I offer the following letter: if deserving of publication, let it speedily meet the eye of the public; if not, treat it with that contempt, consign it to that oblivion, which it merits.

The hint to Ireland, which so lately made its appearance in the Belfast News-Letter, has very much attracted the attention of the people; the elegance of its dress has procured it a number of admirers. Many, heedless of the dangers which environ its opinions, give it implicit faith on account of its novelty, whilst others, equally inattentive, allow their judgments to be warped by the beauties of its phraseology: be it my part to point out the fallacy of its doctrines, to strip the figure of that garniture with which it had been so artfully decorated, and to shew to the public how the dæmon of discord had assumed the habiliments of independence.

We are free, says this insinuating pretender to patriotism, we are independent; and to prove that we are so, let us in the present perplexed state of affairs, take up that side of the question which Britain is averse to; let us gainsay whatever she wishes for—let us oppose whatever she advises;—by this mode of acting the two countries will be eminently distinguished from each other—by this the independence of Ireland will not only be acknowledged by lips, but asserted by deeds—by this a precedent will be afforded to prevent in future the exactions of the one country, or requests of the other.—Such are the principles laid down in the paper alluded to—such was the embryo as first engendered by its author, as yet uncovered with the swadling clothes of art, and unattired with the ornaments of imagery.

Will the system here stated bear the scrutinizing eye of impartiality?——let us examine it:—we have independence; that every nation must acknowledge;—Ireland with a manly firmness demanded it as a right, and Britain, with a generous frankness, admitted the justice of her demand;—why then attempt to prove what no person has dared to deny?—why bring evidence to the world of our freedom, when all the world is already conscious that we are free?—The virtue which unassailed, offers a defence, always incurs suspicion:—the stability of the edifice is suspected when the over-cautious architect props the side-wall.

If, therefore, this proof of our independence is in itself unnecessary, what plea could we set up in justification of our procedure?——None.—State necessity is out of the question,—and we overleap gratitude, generosity, and honour, for a pitiful affectation of shew, which can neither add consequence to us as a nation, nor dignity to us as men.

The inhabitants of Britain are seldom wrong in their political opinions, nor is it probable that in the present instance, they will lose sight of the paths of rectitude; shall therefore the Irish deviate from the right, merely to avoid the foot-path which their judicious neighbours had pointed out to them?—No, the idea is too ridiculous to be dwelt on;—Irishmen would not allow to be recorded in their annals such a stigma on their liberality.

PHILANTHROPOS.

Belfast, *February* 3.

☞ The SOVEREIGN requests a full Meeting of the Burgesses and principal Inhabitants of the Town of *Belfast*, at the Town-House, on this Day, TUESDAY, the 3d of February, at TWELVE o'Clock, —to consider of the proper Measures to be taken with respect to the Persons who broke the Public Lamps on the 26th of January last.

Belfast, February 3d, 1789.

The Commissioners of his Majesty's Revenue have received a letter from John Lees, Esq. Secretary to the Post Master General of Ireland, inclosing the copy of an information from Mr. William Kerr, of the General Post Office, at Edinburgh, giving an account that the small Light House, lately erected at Portpatrick, has been entirely destroyed by fire.—This public notice is given for the sake of the shipping, which may otherwise suffer, until the said Light House shall be rebuilt.

The Linen Hall, Hugh Dickson, master for London, put into Milford the 25th ult. Captain Dickson writes that he had very severe weather which split his sails, but hopes his cargo has not suffered much damage.

The Charlotte, William Campbell, master for London, is still detained here by contrary winds.

The Lord Chancellor has been pleased to appoint George Birch, Esq. of Ballybeen, a Magistrate for the county Down.

Married, on Saturday last, Mr. Charles Clark of Dublin, merchant, to Miss Grace Thomson, of Newtown-Ards.

⁂ PHILANTHROPOS, in reply to A HINT TO IRELAND, that lately appeared in this paper, shall be inserted as soon as possible; also IMPARTIAL, on the same subject.

Belfast, *February* 6.

Tho' it is not to be supposed that the frequenters of the Theatre will readily forget the many occasions on which they derived excellent entertainment, from the old theatrical favourite of this town, ROWE, we think there are many who will be obliged by our reminding them that his benefit is to be on Monday next, when they will have a good opportunity of giving him substantial proof of their own taste, and of their esteem for so enable a performer.

The poem signed *Libertas*, offered to the Committee, appointed in *Derry*, to judge of the poetic merit or demerit, of the pieces written on the Siege, is immediately to be published at the particular request of the friends of the author.

James Watson Hull, Esq. High Sheriff of the county Down, has appointed Thomas Merry, junr. of Newtown-Ards, in said county, Gent. to issue and grant Replivins in and for said county.

Died, suddenly on the 28th of January last, Mr. Thomas Corry, junr. of Moneymore. His moral character was unsullied; he was an affectionate husband and a tender parent. He was an early member of Lodge, No. 531, which with twelve other respectable bodies (in solemn procession) accompanied his remains to the place of interment.

Anno 1789.]   Printed by HENRY JOY, and Co. BELFAST.

The BELFAST NEWS-LETTER.

TUESDAY February 10,   FRIDAY February 13, 1789.

By Auction.

On Friday the 13th inst. at one o'Clock, where she now lies at the Chichester-Quay, will be sold by public Auction,

 THE LIGHTER DOROTHY, with all her Materials. She is about three years old, will carry forty tons and upwards on an easy draft of water, and answers remarkably well for going up the Lagan.——Terms of payment will be declared at Sale.

Belfast, Feb. 9th, 1789.

A Gamekeeper,

For the Parishes of HOLYWOOD and DUN-DONALD.

NOTICE is hereby given, that Hugh Mc. Leroth of Ballymascaw, is employed and sworn to lodge informations against all poachers he shall see going in said parishes with dogs, guns, &c. in search of Game, in order that they may be prosecuted according to the Game Laws.

February 9th, 1789.

ON Saturday the 14th day of February, will be sold at the Custom-House in Down, by Inch of Candle, about three Tons of good Tobacco, and a considerable quantity of Brandy.

29th January, 1789.

At same Time will be sold four Tobacco Tables and Wheels.

Jones, Tomb, Joy & Co.

ARE landing out of the Success from ALICANT, a Cargo of choice New BARRILLA and Spanish CANE for Reedmakers, which, with the following Articles, will be sold on reasonable Terms :

Claret in wood and bottles,	Smalts, Vitriol,
Red and white Port,	Black Soap,
Sherry, Lisbon,	French Cane,
Mountain,	Dantzig & Memel Timber,
Calcavella,	Oak Timber,
Tent, Hock,	Oak and Fir Plank,
Paxoretta,	Dronton Deals,
Champaigne,	Oak Staves for Wheel-wrights,
Burgundy,	Laths, Oars,
Scale Sugar,	Beech Logs, Spars,
Teas of different kinds,	Milled Sheet Lead,
American Pot Ashes,	Bristol Window Glass.
Dantzig Do.	

Belfast, 9th February, 1789.

Thomas Mc. Cabe,

INFORMS his Friends and the Publick, that he has formed a Partnership with James Hunter of Dublin, Watchmaker, and the Watch Business will be carried on at their Shop, opposite the Exchange.

Mc. CABE and HUNTER purpose always to have ready for Sale, Horizontal, Seconds, and Plain Watches, in Enamel, Gold, Silver and Metal. From the experience of said Hunter in the first line of business in Dublin for twelve years, they venture to hope the above business will be conducted in such a manner as to give perfect satisfaction to all who are pleased to favour them with Orders.

Belfast, 8th Feb. 1789.

Miss VALOIS,

RESPECTFULLY informs the Ladies and Gentlemen of Belfast, that her Benefit is fixed on Monday next, when will be performed the COMEDY of

The HEIRESS.

End of Act III An ALLEMANDE, by Miss Valois and Mr. Lynch.

End of the Play, a DOUBLE HORNPIPE, by Miss Valois and Mr. Lynch, for that Night only With a FARCE as will be expressed in the Bills.

Tickets and Places to be taken of Miss Valois, at Mr. Huggard's, Mill street.

Mr. TYRRELL

BEGS leave to inform the Ladies and Gentlemen of Belfast and its Neighbourhood, that his Benefit is fix'd for Friday the 13th instant, at which Time will be performed the favourite COMEDY of

The Clandestine Marriage.

To which will be added a New FARCE, (never performed here) call'd,

TIT for TAT; or, MUTUAL DECEPTION.

Tickets to be had at the Coffee-house, and of Mr. Tyrrell, at Mr. Steele's, Hercules-lane, where places in the Boxes may be taken.

Carrickfergus Assembly,

Will be held on THURSDAY the 12th instant.
Monday, 9th Feb. 1789.

Classical School, in Lisburn.

ON Monday and Tuesday the 2d and 3d inst. was held the Quarterly Examination; at the conclusion of which the following young Gentlemen obtained Premiums :—Campbell, Wilson, Clarke, T. Fulton, Marmion, senr. Boyd, Jas. Fulton, Garner, senr. and junr.

Mr. Foley felt himself much honoured by the approbation of the Ladies and Gentlemen who attended ; and he assures the public, that his endeavours to merit their further notice shall be unremitting His terms and accommodation for Boarders being frequently mentioned, need not be particularly insisted on.

Lisburn, Feb. 5, 1789.

£600

WANTED to borrow, on unexceptionable Security, the Sum of Six Hundred Pounds.——Apply to Mr. Henry Joy.

Belfast, 9th February, 1789.

Linen-Board.

TUESDAY, FEB. 3, 1789.

RESOLVED,

THAT an Advertisement be published in the several public Papers in this Kingdom, desiring all persons who have any demands on this Board of any kind whatever, on the 25th of March last, to make application for payment of the same ; and that all sums claimed to be due on the said day, and which shall not be demanded on or before the first day of May next, be cancelled.

By Order of the Trustees,
JAMES CORRY.

Theatre.

MR. PYE most respectfully begs leave to inform his Friends and the Public, that his Benefit is fix'd for WEDNESDAY the 18th instant, on which Evening will be performed the COMEDY of

The BROTHERS.

With the FARCE of

The Devil to Pay.

Tickets to be had, and places in the Boxes taken of Mr. Pye, at Mr. Mc. Master's, Shugborough, North-street.

THE sovereign requests a full Meeting of the Burgesses and principal Inhabitants of Belfast, at the Market-House, on Saturday next, the 14th instant, precisely at Noon, to receive the Report of the Committee appointed at the last Town Meeting.

Thursday, Feb. 12th, 1789.

Samuel and James Hewitt,

RESPECTFULLY inform their Friends and the Publick, that they have commenced Business in the Spirit Line, next door to Mr. Thomas Brown's, Waring-street ; and are well supplied with common Rum, Rum-D, old Spirit, Brandy, Cherry do. Gineva, Vinegar, sweet Mountain and Port Wines ; all of which they are determined to sell at the most reduced Prices.

Belfast, 8th Feb. 1789.

Train Oil and Leaf Tobacco.

HUGH CRAWFORD has just imported a Cargo of Train Oil and Leaf Tobacco that will be sold cheap, particularly the Oil ; such as are in want will find it their interest to apply to him.

He is well supplied with Alicant and Carthagena Barilla, American Pot and Pearl Ashes, (best sort) a variety of Dantzig Ashes, with all other Articles for the use of bleachers—together with a large and extensive assortment of Goods for Country Grocers, which he can sell on the lowest Terms.

Belfast, 12th Feb. 1789.

A few Puncheons of strong Jamaica Rum, Scale Sugar in Barrels to be sold cheap to close sales ; also Brazil and Jamaica Cotton Wool in small bags.

To be sold by public Auction,

FOR Account of the Shippers, at the King's Stores, in Linen Hall-Street, on Monday 16th inst. precisely at 12 o'Clock,

12 Buts of Sherry,

150 Quarter Casks of Mountain Wine.

To be set up in Lots as most agreeable to the Purchasers. Approved bills or notes at three months date will be taken in payment, or one and 3-qrs. per cent. discount allowed for cash.

A Dog Thief.

STOLEN, on Sunday the first of this month, a large red and white Pointer Dog—answers to the name of NERO, with a brass collar round his neck, and John Sinclaire, Belfast, engraven thereon :—The very day he was miss'd a fellow was seen leading him on the Malone road—he had also with him a little white Cocking Bitch, which he had no doubt for the purpose of decoying him out of town—This vagabond wore a grey coat, with dark short hair, tied.——I request any Gentleman to whom this Dog may be offered for sale, will give me information ; and I will pay five Guineas to any one who will prosecute the Thief to conviction

JOHN SINCLAIRE

Belfast, 12th Feb. 1789.

A Meeting of the Belfast Insurance Company,

WILL be held at the Donegall-Arms, at twelve o'clock on Tuesday the 17th instant :—Gentlemen who wish to become Members of said Company, are requested to send in their names previous to that day, in order to their being balloted for, to Mr. Robert Bradshaw, or Robert Ewing.

Belfast, 10th Feb. 1789.

The Belfast Assembly,

WILL be held at the EXCHANGE-ROOMS, on Tuesday next, 17th instant.

Belfast, 12th February, 1789.

THOMAS SEED informs the Public, that he found a Boat near Garmoil, with three Oars and two Rudders.——Whoever proves property, and pays expences, may have her on applying to said Seed on the Quay.

Belfast, Feb. 13th, 1789.

Hugh Montgomery,

IS just landing a Quantity of New BARRILLA out of the Brigantine Walters, Capt. Mun, from Alicant, which his Customers may rely on are of the very first Quality.

Belfast, 13th February, 1789.

New Almanacks.

This Day is published by J. and W. MAGEE, Belfast, printed on good Paper, and entire New Type, with a neat Map of Ireland,

STEWART's IRISH MERLIN, for 1789 :—Containing besides what is found in such compilations—A compleat Gardeners Directory—A Schedule of Stamp Duties—Extracts from the Acts of last session—Dublin Society's Premiums—State of the Linen Markets of Ulster, &c. &c. Price 1s. 1d.

DITTO, with the UNIVERSAL REGISTRY for Ireland, England, Scotland and America, enlarged and improved—containing with the usual Matter—an Irish Chronological Table—Abstract of Net Duties on Imports and Exports—List of Barristers, &c. Price 2s. 2d.

Magee's Belfast Almanack—Price 4d.
Magee's Universal Sheet Almanack.

No Time to be lost !—as

The ENGLISH STATE LOTTERY,

COMMENCES drawing, Monday, 16th February instant ; in which no less than seventy-seven capital Prizes, from £30,000 down to £500.

WILLIAM MAGEE,

At the Belfast Licensed Office,

Is selling in a Diversity of Numbers, and at Dublin Prices,

Whole English Tickets—also

HALVES,	EIGHTHS, and
QUARTERS,	SIXTEENTHS.

Also incomparable TWO GUINEA TICKETS, Which include every Prize, and by which the following extraordinary Benefits may be obtained,

3,000l. British, if 30,000l.	1,000l. British, if 10,000l.
2,500 - - 25,000	500 - - 5,000
2,000 - - 20,000	200 - - 2,000
1,500 - - 15,000	100 - - 1,000

And a proportional part of every other Prize in the Wheel

Present Prices of TICKETS and SHARES :

A Whole Ticket, may gain £30,000

Half,	-	9 10 0	-	15,000
Quarter,	-	5 0 0	-	7,500
Eighth,	-	2 12 6	-	3,750
Sixteenth,	-	1 7 1	-	1,875

To the PRINTERS of the BELFAST N. LETTER.

GENTLEMEN,

NOTHING, in my opinion, more clearly evidences the political spirit of Great Britain which exists in America, than the great predilection its citizens have for News-Papers, and their love of governmental disquisitions. There the liberty of declamation and censure is as unlimited as the wind;—every tavern (and taverns are very numerous in America) has its knot of politicians, some one of which, like an oracle, never fails to disclose the misfortunes of the State, the cause of their poverty, (for want of money is the universal theme of the vulgar) and the downfal of liberty. The man of unsullied reputation who was but yesterday elected to the offices of government, is to day cried down as a peculator or fool. The private citizen, who passes his time in domestic affairs, may enjoy a life of repose, but as soon as he becomes a Majistrate or a Ruler, he is sure to be hunted like a tyger. Too great an equality among the citizens renders the lower orders turbulent;——every man is for being a governor, and none will submit to be governed;—hence free governments are the most restless; their revolutions are not frequent, but their insurrections are numerous; and their greatest evil, from whence all their others arise, is want of energy and coercion.

In their great superfluity of News Papers, an account of which I have subjoined, daily proofs may be found of what I have advanced.—News-Papers are like straws, says Doctor Franklin, but yet they serve to shew what way the wind blows.

NEWS PAPERS printed in NORTH AMERICA.

In Vermont and the four New England States, viz. New Hampshire, Massachuset's Bay, Connecticut, and Rhode Island	12
State of New York—at Albany and Poughkupsee	2
City of New York—Daily Advertiser—New York Journal—New York Packet—Independent Journal—New York Gazette—Daily Evening Post—New York Morning Post	7
New Jersey—at Trenton, Elizabeth-town and New Brunswick	3
Pennsylvania—at Carlisle, German-town, and Fort Pitt	3
In the city of Philadelphia.—Pennsylvania Gazette—Pennsylvania Journal—Pennsylvania Packet—Independent Journal—Freeman's Journal—Pennsylvan a Mercury—Pennsylvania Herald—Pennsylvania Evening Post—and a Paper printed in the German Language	9
Delaware	2
Maryland—at Baltimore, Anappolis, and Frederick-town	6
Virginia—at Richmond, Alexandria, Winchester, Norfolk and Williamsburgh	7
North Carolina	1
South Carolina	4
Georgia	1
In all	57

The Pennsylvania Gazette, the oldest paper in the State of Pennsylvania, was purchased from its original founder, subscribers and all, by the great Dr. Franklin, for *thirty shillings*, and was the first foundation of his fortune and greatness. It was in that paper, and an almanack which he annually published, that the superiority of his genius burst forth from the humility of his situation in life, and displayed talents which have astonished the world.

Of the above papers five are published daily, viz three in New-York and two in Philadelphia; and of the whole, not more than six deserve the name of News-Papers, viz. one in N: England, printed under the title of a *Magazine* to evade the duty on *News-Papers*——one printed under a similar title at New Haven, near New York——The Daily Advertiser at New York——The Pennsylvania Packet and Herald at Philadelphia——and The Columbian Herald printed in Charlestown. All the rest contain little else than the twentieth or thirtieth edition of paragraphs and pieces from the other papers.

A CITIZEN of the WORLD.

To the PRINTER.

SIR,

WHILE some of the papers are running riot in praise of Mr. Fox, and others as strenuously supporting the cause of Mr. Pitt, it is a matter of difficulty for a plain man to have his sentiments laid before the public, if he does not profess a blind attachment to one or other of those leaders.

I have therefore, Sir, chosen the medium of your paper, long established in its character of honest moderation, and I trust you will not refuse to assist me in offering some thoughts to the public.

First, then, Sir, I desire to assert, that Ireland has nothing whatsoever to do with English parties—for an hundred years we laboured under the most cruel oppression—'tis true, Mr. Pitt was not then in political existence;—but, after the brave and virtuous citizens of Ireland had roused themselves to arms, and secured their freedom, Mr. Fox was the very last man who acceded to the principles of Irish liberty, and even then—with a reservation of England's retaining a power of legislating for us externally.

Secondly, I desire to assert—that no Governor nor Government should ever be suffered to erect themselves upon the basis of unconstitutional submission on the part of the people.—When a King of England is crowned, he is bound by a solemn oath to govern in justice and mercy, according to the laws of the realm. Not satisfied with this general severity, the English have thought proper to subject the Regent, or substitute for a Monarch, to still great restraints; but those who pretend to be patriots in Ireland, propose to leave the Regent at liberty to act as he thinks proper, and assert, that it would imply a suspicion—be an affront to his dignity, were he to be restrained. Now, this, I profess, I cannot comprehend—for, if it be no affront to the King of England and Ireland, mounting the throne with the general approbation of all his subjects, to be obliged to swear that he will govern in justice and mercy, according to law, how can it be an affront to a Regent, or imply any suspicion of his conduct—to guard him from the solicitations of insidious friends, and by proper restrictions, prevent him from injuring the common weal, and at the same time provide for the return of his Majesty to the enjoyment of his throne?

England is a great and powerful country—we she to allow the Regent to assume the reins of Government, without any condition,—yet has she strength and energy sufficient to check any abuse, to restrain any excess of power, and even to remove a Regent who should abuse his trust!—Yet England, in her wisdom, does not yield at discretion, but conditions for the preservation of what she deems essential to her own honour and prosperity, and to facilitate the return of our beloved Sovereign to the enjoyment of his right.

But Ireland has much stronger reasons for a prudent and guarded conduct—were she to appoint a Regent with unrestrained authority, how should she check any abuse of his power, when she should behold all her profitable and sinecure employments bestowed upon the hungry followers of Mr. Fox;—when she should see her Pension List swelled to an enormous degree to bribe British majorities—when she should feel her taxes accumulated, and her honours debased by the admission of an host of English and Scotch adventurers into her House of Peers—*gamblers*, and *fellows of no mark or likelihood*;—then she might, indeed, vent her sorrow and and vexation in unavailing complaints, and find, too late, that England had acted with wisdom in conditioning to preserve her rights;—but that we had debased ourselves, and yielded up all the glorious acquirements of our virtuous Volunteers, by submitting at discretion.——Therefore BEWARE!

DUBLIN, FEB. 4.

The Lord Chancellor has been pleased to appoint John Darcus of the city of Londonderry, Esq; to be a Justice of the Peace for the county of Donegall.

We hear that John White, of Salt Bridge, co. Wexford, died, last week, in consequence of a bite he received from a mad cat.

By letters received per the Dublin Packet, Capt. Smith, arrived here on Saturday last from Philadelphia, we are informed that Congress had it in contemplation to appoint a Consul to reside in this city, for the care and protection of the trade of the different States of America.

Since its foundation our University has not been so crowded with students. At the examination in the College Hall, which ended on Thursday last, no less than 462 young gentlemen answered the examinations; a greater number than ever appeared in the Hall on a similar occasion since the College existed.

SKETCHES of the CHARACTERS of the PRINCIPAL MEMBERS of the HOUSE of COMMONS.

Right Hon. HENRY GRATTAN, Esq;

THE emancipators of nations, and the deliverers of their native land from political thraldom, are justly entitled to the warmest retributions of gratitude which the liberality of mankind can pay, both on account of the importance of the benefit, and the general difficulty of its atchievement. To rouse the languid, to inflame the cold, and to inspire the spiritless, is not the work of common talents or inferior souls—but of transcendant abilities, emulous of distinction by deathless deeds, and of superior genius invigorated by genuine patriotism. To perceive the happy moment for rendering their exertions effectual, and to seize on the fortunate opportunity which the revolution of time and of accidents has produced, for giving decisive efficacy to their efforts, are instances of sagacity and foresight, of opportune resolution and vigorous determination in the highest degree laudable; which may be extolled, but cannot be exaggerated. So many concurrent circumstances are requisite to shake off the yoke of long-confirmed usurpation, to infuse a contempt of threatened menaces without infringing fraternal affection, and to elevate a people from the meanness of obsequious servility to all the dignity of independence, that to combine these circumstances, to direct their operation, and to moderate their energy are marks of such merit as deservedly claims the amplest and richest civic meed that can recompence the worthy citizen.

Mr. GRATTAN is certainly one of the most conspicious ornaments of the Irish Senate. To his manly and persevering exertions do we owe an independant Legislature, and the gratitude of the nation for the boon, though testified with a munificence becoming its spirit, by no means exceeded the measure of his deserts.

As a public speaker, Mr. GRATTAN's voice is thin, sharp, and far from powerful; not devoid of a variety of tones, but these neither rich nor mellow; and though not harsh, its want of an harmonious modulation is often striking. Unequal to impassioned energy it is shrill when it should be commanding, and in its lower notes, is sometimes scarcely audible, from its hollowness of sound. His management of it, is but ill adapted to remedy its natural defects or to supply its deficiencies, as he allows it to spatiate at large, unrestrained by any curb from rule; now raising it to an elevation that it cannot bear, and then sinking it to a depth where its distant murmurs can be barely guessed at. His language is lofty, magnificent, copious, and peculiarly his own. Not tricked out with the guady dress of poetic phrases, nor fatiguing the attention with pompous terms, high-sounding but unmeaning, but familiarly combining strength with beauty, conciseness with ornament, and sublimity with elegance. Adapted to the exigence of the occasion it is now a wide-spreading conflagration, and anon a concentered fire; now abundant and splendid, then brief and pointed; equally fitted to instruct, delight, or agitate; to soothe the soul to peace, or to awaken and arouse all its exalted and elevated energies. His delivery admirably accords with the style of his oratory; never languid, or insipid, or cold, but always possessing a pleasing warmth, expressive of feeling and imparting spirit: whilst his pronunciation, generally correct, though frequently rapid, is never crowded or redundant, but distinct and articulate, leaving ample space for strength and propriety of emphasis. In his manner, life, animation and ardour predominate, and that to such a degree that they fascinate the prejudiced and invigorate the torpid. From their impulse Prostitution forgets for a moment the voice of the Minister, and the influence of place, pension and peerage have but an enfeebled hold on the half-revived carcase. All are conscious of a new-born spark of patriotic fire, that with the rapidity of the electric shock, and alas! too with its short-lived duration, darts from breast to breast. With comprehensive intelligence embracing a great object, not catching at its parts by detail, he takes in the whole at one glance, and sees instantly the pivot whereon it turns with almost intuitive acuteness. In argument he is strong, pointed, close, and conclusive, never deviating from his subject, never straying in search of extraneous matter, but explaining with success what he understands with facility.—He conducts not the mind to the conclusion he aims at by a long chain of abstruse disquisition, but guides it with seeming ease through the pleasing path of natural illustration. Every man thinks he could reason like him, but when attempted it is found to be the bow of Ulysses. In the refutation of his opponents he puts forth all his might and accumulates his force to overwhelm and oppress them; but his superior greatness is most apparent when he enforces what cannot be denied; when he defends the rights of a nation; when he pourtrays the hopes, the fears, the expectations of a magnanimous people; when he threatens the vicious and appals the proud: when he pronounces the panegyric of departed excellence; then, indeed, he is magnificent, sublime, and pathetic.

Belfast, *February* 10.

The Charlotte, William Campbell master, for London is still detained here, by contrary winds.

Joseph Wright, of this town, Gent. (who served his apprenticeship to Geo. Gordon Carson, Esq; a Gentleman very eminent in his profession) was on Friday last admitted and sworn an Attorney of his Majesty's Court of King's-Bench in this kingdom.

Charles Crymble Esq; High-Sheriff of the county of Antrim, hath appointed Mr. Joseph Fulton of Lisburn, his Under-Sheriff.

Belfast, *February* 13.

The Charlotte, William Campbell, master, for London, sailed the 11th instant.

The Lord Chancellor has been pleased to appoint James Watson, Esq; of Brookhill, a Magistrate for the county of Antrim.

Anno 1789.]   Printed by HENRY JOY, and Co. BELFAST.

The BELFAST NEWS-LETTER.

TUESDAY February 17,   FRIDAY February 20, 1789.

Drawing began this Day (in *London*.)

MAGEE's LOTTERY OFFICE

W. MAGEE, intreats those who mean to adventure this Lottery, may purchase immediately, as the first Day's Drawing is expected on *Saturday*—and Tickets will certainly advance in price, should any remain unsold

He has now ready for the inspection of his Friends, Whole Tickets, Halves, Fourths, Eighths, Sixteenths, and Two Guinea Tickets; in a Variety of Numbers, all which partake of every Prize in the Wheel.

Prizes in the late and preceding Irish Lotteries will be taken in Payment, *without any Discount whatever*.

Belfast, Feb. 16th, 1789.

HUGH HERRON,

BEING the only Person in Banbridge, appointed by Messrs. A. and S. Law of Castlewellan, to dispose of their Whiskey by wholesale—begs leave to inform his Friends and the Public, that he is at present largely supplied with the genuine Spirit so much esteemed by private Families;—also Spirits reduced to different Prices—Publicans will find it their interest to deal with him, on account of its superior flavour to any distilled in this kingdom; which he will sell at Castlewellan Prices, for ready Money, at the house of the late James Mc. William, next door to Geo. Crozier, Esq.

Banbridge, 13th Feb. 1789.

THE Sovereign gives this Notice to those who bring Horses and Cows to the Market of Belfast for Sale—that they must drive their Cattle to Smithfield, the place appointed for that purpose, as he will not permit them to expose them to sale in any of the Streets or Lanes of the Town.

February 16th, 1789.

For NEWCASTLE and NEW-YORK, in AMERICA,

THE fine new Ship St. JAMES, burthen 500 tons, Mark Collins, Commander, is daily expected, and will be ready to sail from Belfast the 15th April next for Newcastle and New-York, in America.——This Vessel is high and roomy between decks, sails remarkably fast, and will be fitted out in the best manner with plenty of provisions.

Such persons as choose to embrace this favourable opportunity will meet with good treatment, Captain Collins being a man of experience and highly esteemed.

For Freight or Passage apply to Mr. Alex. Mitchell, Ballymena; Mr. Joseph Dickson, Cullybackey; Mr. Robert Elder, Portna; Mr. Thos. Prentice, Armagh; or Jones, Tomb, Joy & Co. Belfast.

Belfast, 16th February, 1789.

N. B. As there are frequently Vessels from Newcastle not only to Philadelphia but Charlestown in South-Carolina, Persons intending for either, would do well to go by the St. James.

Leaf Tobacco.

PATTERSON and FLETCHER are landing seventy Hogsheads of very fine fresh WRAPPERY TOBACCO; which they will sell on the most reasonable Terms.

L. Perry, 26th Jan. 1789.

ABEL HADSKIS,

HAS for Sale, a Quantity of Kiln Tiles, and Ribs for ditto, and a Quantity of large Fire Brick of different Sizes—all which he will sell on moderate terms, and of the best quality.

Belfast, Feb. 16th, 1789.

TO BE LET,

From the first of May next,

THAT large and convenient House in Donegall-street, where the late Mr. Francis Hamilton lived. For particulars apply to William Thompson, junr.

Belfast, 18th Feb. 1789.

JAMES Mc. CLEAN, WATCH-MAKER,

HAS taken the Shop next door to the Donegall-Arms; where he will thankfully receive and execute the Commands of those who are pleased to employ him.

Belfast, 19th February, 1789.

The Coterie,

WILL be held (as usual) at the Donegall-Arms, on Tuesday the 24th instant.

Belfast, Feb. 19th, 1789.

Mr. *LYNCH*,

RESPECTFULLY informs the Ladies and Gentlemen of Belfast, that his Benefit is fix'd for Friday 20th instant, when will be performed the COMEDY, (not acted this Season) call'd,

All in the Wrong.

After the Play, (by particular Desire) and for the last Time this Season, An

Allemande, and Double Hornpipe,

By Miss VALOIS and Mr. LYNCH.

With a FARCE as will be expres'd in the Bills.

Tickets to be had and Places in the Boxes taken of Mr. Lynch, at Mr. Mc. Master's, Snugborough, North-Street.

Miss *HOSKIN*,

BEGS leave to inform the Ladies and Gentlemen of Belfast and its Neighbourhood, that her Benefit is fixed for Monday February 23d, at which time will be performed a Play, Farce, and Entertainments.

Tickets to be had and Places in the Boxes to be taken of Miss Hoskin, at Capt. English's, Princes-street.

House---near Loughbrickland.

To be Set, for such Term as may be agreed on, and entered upon immediately,

A Very neat Lodge and Offices, in perfect good repair, and only lately built, with about twenty acres of land in high condition, and most part in meadow. There is every necessary Office whatever inclosed in a Court-yard to the rere of the house. Corn, Hay and Potatoes on the premises for the accommodation of a tenant. Application to be made to John Whyte, Esq; 47, Dorset-street, Dublin, or to Mr. James Scott, Loughbrickland.

New Alicant Barilla.

JOHN BOYLE, and Co. are just landing from on board the Brigantine Walters from Alicant, a parcel of very best quality, which with American Pot, Pearl and Dantzig Weed Ash, Smalts, Oil of Vitriol, &c. they will dispose of on reasonable terms.

They are also landing from on board the Brigantine Lord Bangor, a Cargo of remarkably fine St. Domingo Mahogany, which they will sell cheap for cash or approved bills.——A commodious new Dwelling-House, with a convenient Back yard, &c. adjoining Hercules-Lane, to be let and entered upon immediately.

Belfast, 11th Feb. 1789.

Herrings for Sale on board the Jenny of Greenock,

JUST arrived at the Old Quay, a Cargo of White Herring, well saved, and will be sold for ready Money, on the lowest Terms.

Belfast, February 16th, 1789.

Houses and Lands for ever.

TO be Sold by Auction, at the Market-House of Antrim, on Thursday the fifth day of March next, two large Houses lately built, situated in said town; with ten acres of town parks, held by lease of lives renewable for ever under Lord Massereene; yearly rent four pounds, with fees. One hundred Pounds to be deposited at the time of sale, and the remainder by approved bills or notes at two and four months date.—The Title-deeds may be seen by applying to Mr. Robert Young.

February 18th, 1789.

N. B. The houses will be sold separately, with an equal proportion of Land, if found most agreeable to the Purchaser.

Wholesale Scotch Ware-house, Lurgan,

BERNARD COILE informs his Friends and the Public, that he has just received from the principal manufacturing towns in Scotland, a general assortment of Goods in the Millinery Line, viz. Kenting, Cambrick, Lenaus, Spaw Gauzes; Catguts, Silk Gauze, Muslins of all kinds, Scotch Threads, with many other articles too tedious to mention: He has a large assortment of Carpets and Carpeteens.

He (as usual) manufactures chequed, striped and plain Lawns; those, with his other assortment of Goods, he is enabled and determined to sell on the most moderate terms.

Feb. 19th, 1789.

An Apprentice

WANTED immediately to the Cabinet Business—Apply at this Office.

Belfast, Feb. 19th, 1789.

☞ To be inserted three times.

NOTICE

IS hereby given, that the proposed *Belfast Insurance Company*, for the Insurance of Goods, Merchandize and Vessels at Sea—yet want to compleat their Number a few Members.

Such as wish to become Members, are requested to give in their names on or before Wednesday next, the 24th inst. to Messrs. Robert Ewing, Robert Bradshaw, Hugh Montgomery, or John Cunningham, on which day a full Meeting is requested at the Donegall-Arms, at 12 o'clock, as the final settlement of the Company will then take place.

Feb. 18th, 1789.

Just published, and to be sold by the Booksellers in Belfast, Price 6d. h.

APPENDIX to WALKER's HIBERNIAN MAGAZINE, or, Compendium of Entertaining Knowledge, for the Year 1788.

Illustrated with the following Copper-plates, elegantly engraved by Irish Artists: I. An emblematic Frontispiece. II. An elegant Title and Vignette. III. A beautiful Portrait of Sigifmunda. And IV. A striking Likeness in Profile of Tancred, Tete-a-Tete. V. An elegant Pattern for Painting and Needle Work. VI. Down Top Gallants. VII. A Quick March. VIII. A favourite Country Dance, set to Music.

DROPP'D,

ON Thursday 11th February, in Ballynahinch Fair, A SILVER WATCH of Emond's making, No. 885.——Whoever brings it to Mc. Cabe and Hunter, Watchmakers, Belfast, or James Armstrong, Innkeeper, Ballynahinch, shall receive half a Guinea reward.

Belfast, Feb. 12, 1789.

☞ If offered for Sale, it is requested it will be stopp'd, and the person detained.

STOLEN at different times in the latter part of last season and beginning of this, out of my Bleach-yard near Lurgan, eighteen Pieces of the following denominations—the letter G and number, marked with liquid, on one end, and length on the other end of each Piece.

Pieces	wide	
2	7-8 wide	Diaper.
3	8-4	do.
10	10-4	do.
1	5-4	Sheeting, sett a 14 hundred.
1	6-4	do. sett a 13 do.
1	4-4	Ticken, sett a 13 do.

18 Pieces all finished, or nearly so.

I hereby promise a Reward of *Twenty Guineas*, exclusive of the above One Hundred Pounds, to any person or persons who shall give me the most private information such as may lead to a discovery and conviction of thief or thieves concerned in said robbery. Given under my hand this 9th day of 2d mo. 1789

JAMES GREER

Sycamore Beetling Beams,

TO be disposed of by JOHN HERVEY of Armagh. Linen Merchants may depend upon their being of an excellent Quality. February 10th, 1789.

To be peremptorily sold by Auction,

IN the Town-Hall, on Monday the 30th instant, at one o'clock, thirty-three Hogsheads best Virginia Tobacco.——Approved Bills on Dublin at 61 days sight will be taken in payment, or 6d. per pound discount allowed for cash.

HEADS of the REGENCY BILL.

On account of, and during his majesty's indisposition, the Prince of Wales is appointed Regent. Before he enters on his office, the following oath is to be taken by him, before the Privy Council:

" I do solemnly promise and swear, that I will
" truly and faithfully execute the office of Re-
" gent of the kingdom of Great-Britain, accord-
" ing to an Act of parliament passed in the
" twenty-ninth year of the reign of his Majesty
" King George the Third, intituled, 'an act
"
"
" and that I will administer, according to law,
" the power and authority vested in me by virtue
" of the said act, and will in all things, to the utmost
" of my power and ability, consult and maintain
" the safety, honour, and dignity of his Majesty,
" and the welfare of his people.
" So help me God."

It is also enacted, " That if his Royal Highness George Agustus Frederick, Prince of Wales, shall not continue to be resident in Great-Britain, or shall at any time marry a Papist, all the powers and authorities vested in his Royal Highness, by virtue of this act, shall cease and determine."

The Regent to grant no Peerages, except to those of the Royal Family who may have attained to the age of twenty-one.

With no power to alienate any part of his Majesty's Personal Property.

The Civil List to be paid, as formerly, at the receipt of the Exchequer.

DUBLIN, Feb. 12.

On Saturday, as his Excellency the Lord Lieutenant was passing through Castle-street, from Kilmainham to the Castle, a brick fell from the top of one of the Houses, and striking against the front glass of his chariot broke it to pieces, and hit his Excellency on the knee. Fortunately he received no manner of hurt from it.

His Excellency the Lord Lieutenant has been pleased to appoint the following Gentlemen to be High Sheriffs for the present year:

Co. Limerick. Crosbie Morgell, of Rathkeal, Esq;
Co. Fermanagh. Ambrose Upton, of Gledstown, Esq;
Co. Tyrone. Sir William Richardson, of Augher, Bart.
Co. Antrim. Charles Crymble, of Ballyclare, Esq;
Co. Donegall. Wybrants Olphers, of Ballyconnel, Esq;
Co. Louth. Turner Camac, of Greenmount-lodge, Esq;

On Sunday a number of members of the House of Commons were magnificently entertained at dinner by the Duke of Leinster at Leinster House. We hear it is his Graces's intention to give a round of dinners, to which he means to invite all the members who composed the majority on Friday night last, by eighteen or twenty at a time.

The parish of Killyleagh, in the county of Down, now vacant and in the gift of the University, has been refused by all the junior Fellows of the College. This marks pretty strongly the value of a junior Fellowship, when it is preferred to a living of 400l. a year.

DUBLIN, Feb. 17.

A correspondent observes, that while the restrictions proposed on the Regent have been agitated in the newspapers, and in every circle, the RESTRICTIONS on the PRESS of Ireland, by too heavy a tax on communication by Advertisements, have been altogether unnoticed.—These restrictions, however, if duly considered, are of infinitely greater moment to this kingdom than those which regard the Heir Apparent: They interest, or should do so (because they materially affect) almost every useful and active member of society. That spirit of vengeance, flowing from private resentment, in which the last additional duties was conceived, has extended its baneful influence so far as very particularly to injure the general line of printing throughout the kingdom, by preventing booksellers from announcing their new and old publications, unless at an expence which the present duty renders it too expensive to bear. The consequences are obvious -- they become averse to print what they cannot with prudence advertise---they import new publications, and the evil reaches not only to the paper-making business, but to many other branches dependant on printing.

It is hoped the new Administration will alleviate the more severe and injurious parts of the stamp-act, and render it, where the interests of manufacture and trade are concerned, less onerous, particularly in advertisements of length; thereby to reconcile it to the abilities of the nation, to justice, and to the example of Britain, and not annihilate the infant fine-paper manufacture, or preclude the community from instruction, who cannot generally know what books are published, except through the shop catalogues of the venders.

About twelve years since, no less than fifteen hundred stuff weavers, including apprentices, were employed in the stuff weaving branch, in the Liberty parts of this city—At present, from the report of their own committee, there are but four hundred and fifty, in which number apprentices are also comprehended, and the complaint is, that they do not find one half employment—surely if the Manufacturers made up their goods upon the same principles as those of England, and sold to shop-keepers and others upon reasonable prices, the work-men would not be left much longer, in their present unhappy predicament.

DIED.] At his house on the North Strand, Mr. William Sleater, senior, of Dame street, printer and bookseller, deservedly lamented. In Ormond Market, Mr. Samuel Leathly, printer.

DIED.] Lately, at Antwerp, Philip Coets, at the age of 104 years. He was a soldier from his youth, and served in all the campaigns of Prince Eugene against the Turks. In 1717, he was at the capture of Belgrade. At 40 years old he married, and lived with his first wife 12 years, by whom he had six children and ten grand-children. At 60 years of age he married again, and had eight children, from whence spring 30 grand-children. He was so strong, that at 73 years of age, he lifted a butt of beer from a cart without the least trouble. Having lost his second wife at 92 he married again, but had no children; he was always in health, and preserved all his senses, except his hearing, till his death.

Belfast, February 17.

. We are unavoidably obliged to omit several new Advertisements till next publication.

The importance of the proceedings in the Irish Parliament, relative to the appointment of THE PRINCE to an UNLIMITED REGENCY in this Kingdom, induces the Editor to supply the deficiency, so obvious in the best accounts that are to be found in any ONE paper, and the want of COINCIDENCE so frequently observable—by forming out of them ALL as perfect a sketch of the argument on each side of this great question as the case admits of.—Local situation giving the advantage of a general comparison of all the papers published in the Capital, before this one appears, it is hoped that the readers of the Belfast News-Letter will find the mode pointed out, well calculated to effect the proposed purpose. [For the Debate on Wednesday last, formed in this manner, see the first and second page.]

DIED.] At Lisburn, Mr. William Rogers;——being in health to appearance the 9th, was taken ill same night, and departed this life next morning, much regretted by a great number of friends.—On Tuesday the 10th instant, at Portaferry, Mrs. Hamilton, widow of the late James Hamilton, Esq; of this town. She was in the 72d year of her age——her remains were interred here on Thursday last.

Belfast, February 20.

The turn which the matter of the Regency has taken in our Houses of Lords and Commons, so diametrically opposite to the proceedings of the British Parliament on the same subject—has, we trust, ere this brought to the recollection of our Readers, with honour to its Author, the "HINT TO IRELAND," an original Production, published in this Paper on the 25th ult.—The precise idea of that ingenious publication, is the same of that on which Mr. Grattan at the head of one branch of the Parliament of this Kingdom seems at present to act. A quotation from the Paper itself will best prove this assertion.

" Ireland is now for the first time called upon to act as a sovereign and independent nation. If there be yet remaining any of that hibernicism of heart, which lately produced one luminous lustrum in the blank of our history, you will seize the present precious opportunity to think and act for yourselves. It is a groveling glory, a sneaking ambition, for a great country to be always dodging at the heels of a British Faction. It is not so much the right of the Regent as the rights of this Nation, which are involved in the decision of this question. These rights will become matters of Fact; your independence will be realized by varying from the measures adopted in BRITAIN, as far as such variation is consistent with the preservation of the connection between the two countries. In this important alternative, when the arguments on each side are almost equally persuasive, you ought to take the part which will best illustrate your independence. Precedents from the most savage times may be laboriously sought for by the senators of Britain, but the History of Ireland is only beginning, and she is not to search for precedents, but to create them; she is not to copy what is set before her with scrupulous and servile uniformity; but to act with that insulated independence which will point out her character as a nation. This, in short, is the season for her assuming and putting in practice that sovereignty which is her clear and indisputable right."

The Lord Chancellor and the Judges of his Majesty's courts of King's Bench, Common Pleas, and Exchequer, have been pleased to appoint Samuel M'Tier of Belfast, in the county of Antrim, a Commissioner for taking affidavits in the said courts, in and for the said county, also, a Master Extraordinary for taking affidavits in his Majesty's High Court of Chancery.

Anno 1789.]   Printed by HENRY JOY, and Co. BELFAST.

The BELFAST NEWS-LETTER.

TUESDAY February 24,   FRIDAY February 27, 1789.

The Lord Donegall,

JAMES Mc. ROBERTS Master,

For *LONDON*,

WILL clear out the 28th next Month, and fail very first fair wind after.

Belfast, 22d Feb. 1788.

Samuel Hyde,	Jacob Hancock,
Robert Thomson,	David Wilson,
Samuel Brown,	Val. Smith,
William Sinclaire,	James Stevenson.
Robert Bradshaw,	

Mr. KING,

WITH the greatest respect acquaints the Ladies and Gentlemen of Belfast, that his Benefit is fixed for Wednesday March the 4th, 1789, when will be presented a favourite Comedy, Farce, and Variety of Entertainments.

Tickets to be had, and Places for the Boxes to be taken of Mr. King, at Mr. Myles's, Caddel's-Entry, and at the Theatre.——Tickets delivered for the second February will be admitted.

Robbery of Tan-yards.

WE the undersigned, do promise to pay to Messrs. Robt. & Wm. Simms, the several sums annexed to our names, for the purpose of discovering and prosecuting any person or persons who may be guilty of stealing Leather from any of our Tan-yards until the first of May 1790.

	l. s. d.		l. s. d.
Robert & Wm. Simms	11 7 6	John Harper	2 5 6
		David Dunn	7 19 3
James Wier	7 19 3	Joseph M'Cammon	2 5 6
Thomas Major	5 13 9		
Chr. Hudson	5 13 9	Francis Wilson	2 5 6
Wm. Mc. Cleery	4 11 0	John M'Cammon	2 5 6
		Sam. Ferguson	6 16 6
Samuel Law	5 13 9	Harris Beck	3 8 3
John Brown	5 13 9	Joseph Smyth	3 8 3
John Ferguson	5 13 9	James Martin	5 13 9

WHEREAS on the night of the 18th inst. the Tan-yard Gate of John Brown of North-street was broke open, and a Hide of tanned Leather carried away :

WE do hereby offer a reward of Fifty Pounds to any person who will discover and prosecute to conviction the person or persons guilty of said robbery ; and we will also amply reward any private information that may lead to a discovery of the same.

ROBT. & WM. SIMMS.

Belfast, 25th Feb. 1789.

Oats Wanted,

JOHN BOYLE & Co. are wanting a few Tons of good OATS, for which they are giving Market Prices.   Belfast, 23d February, 1789.

Best Champagne.

JAMES T. KENNEDY has just received from Rheims a few Hampers of best sparkling Champagne, which will be sold cheap.——He is also largely supplied with the following Articles, at his Stores in Rosemary-Lane, viz.

Antigua and Jamaica Rum, as imported and reduced.

Cognac and Bordeaux Brandy	ditto.
Holland Gineva	ditto.

Best old Antigua Spirit.

Red Port in Pipes, Hogsheads, Quarter Casks and Bottle, of the first Quality.

Clarets at different Prices in Wood and Bottle.

Frontiniac	ditto.	
Lisbon in Pipes, Quarter Casks, and Bottle.		
Calcavella	ditto.	ditto.
Sherry	ditto.	ditto.
Mountain	ditto.	ditto.

Belfast, 26th Feb. 1789.

ON Thursday, the 12th March next, HUGH O'HANLON, will sell by Auction,

One hundred Bales best Carthagena Barilla.

TERMS:

For 5 Bales, approved Bills on Dublin at 3 months.

10   do.   do.   6 months.

& for 20 or upwards,   9 months.

As they are the remainder of a larger parcel, the Sales of which he is desirous closing, THEY will be sold WITHOUT RESERVE.   Newry, 25th February, 1789.

For the Benefit of Mr. FREEMAN,

ON Monday second March, will be presented a COMEDY, (not perform'd here these five years) call'd,

The Inconstant; or, The Way to win him.

The following favourite Songs by Mrs. Freeman,

" Hoot awa ye Loon,"——" A new Hunting Cantata."—— " Let Fame sound the Trumpet,"—and " The new Highland Laddie."

With a Musical FARCE, call'd,

The DESERTER.

To which will be added an Afterlude, call'd,

The POOR SOLDIER.

Patt, the Poor Soldier, by Mrs. Freeman.

The whole to conclude with An Occasional Address to the Town, written, and to be spoken by Mrs FREEMAN.

Mr. *Remington,*

RESPECTFULLY begs leave to inform the Ladies and Gentlemen of Belfast, and its Vicinity, that his Benefit is fix'd for Friday the 27th instant, on which Night will be performed the COMEDY of

Such Things Are.

With the FARCE of

The CRITIC.

Tickets to be had, and Places in the Boxes to be taken of Mr. Remington, at Mr. Brown's on the Quay.

Belfast, 25d Feb. 1789.

Lottery Tickets,

(Warranted undrawn)

WILL continue on Sale for a few Days only,——at MAGEE's LOTTERY-OFFICE, Bridge-Street, Belfast.

Cash for Prizes soon as drawn, or taken in Exchange at their utmost Value.

Tickets sold at the Belfast Licensed Office examined gratis—those purchased elsewhere must be paid for each examination.

Monday, 23d February, 1789.

Swedish Iron.

A Cargo of well-assorted Swedish Iron is just arrived to ANDREW and HUGH CARLILE of Newry, and THOS. PRENTICE of Armagh.—They will sell it on reasonable terms for cash or bills at a short date.

Newry, 16th February, 1789.

TO BE LET,

From the first of May next,

A Small convenient House in Thomas-street, Armagh :—Also a Shop and Room in Scotch-street. Apply to Thomas Prentice.

Armagh, 19th February, 1789.

Bleach-Green---Lease for ever.

TO be Set, lease of lives renewable for ever, of the Bleach-Green and Farm of 23 acres and half of Land in Gleno—lately occupied by Messrs. Lee.—The Green in its present state is capable of finishing 4500 pieces linen, and may be greatly improved—the Land is in high condition.——Apply to James Holmes.

Belfast, 24th Feb. 1789.

A VESTRY

WILL be held in the Parish Church of Belfast, on Monday the second day of March—to receive the Treasurer's accounts of the money expended last year in lighting and paving the town ; and also to determine, what sum may be necessary for the same purpose, for the present year.

Belfast, Feb. 23d, 1789.

THE DROMORE FORRESTERS meet at Dromore on Monday the second day of March.

Belfast, Feb. 23d, 1789.

To be Let,

FROM the first day of March or May next, for such term as may be agreed on, the House in which the late Mr. John Deeryn lived, in Enniskillen. The house is large and commodious, with a large shop compleatly fitted with counters, shelves, and drawers ; cellars, store-houses, and every necessary office, all in complete order, with a large yard and excellent garden, all inclosed with stone-walls.

The situation the most desirable of carrying on the Mercantile Business extensively ; being vastly superior to any in the town ; a tenant can be accommodated with some choice meadow fields very convenient to the town. Proposals in writing to be made to Mrs. Deeryn.

Enniskillen, Feb. 27, 1789.

Variety of Carpets and Carpetings, Scotch Plaids, &c.

JAMES GRAHAM has just received a very elegant Assortment of Carpets, Carpetings, and Scotch Plaids, of the very newest and most fashionable Patterns ;—also English, Scotch, and Lambeg Blankets, at manufacturers prices, Oil Cloth for stairs and floors, Paper for rooms in a variety of patterns, plain and Sattin Hair Cloth for chairs, with Furniture Cottons, Check and Damascus, Tickens, Horse Cloth, straining and girth webs, and many other articles in the Cabinetmakers and Upholsterers way ;—almost every article in the Millinery, Hosiery and Haberdashery Line ; plain, check'd and stripe Muslins ; also a beautiful assortment of the very newest fashioned

Gilt Pier Looking-glasses and Gerandoles,

square and oval, variety of plain do. of all sizes, dressing do. with and without drawers, a large parcel of choice English ground Skins for Breeches-makers and Glovers, with a general assortment of Gloves—all sorts of Pins at Pin-makers Price, on which the largest discounts will be allowed, Flannels, Plaids and Serges, Sattinets, Lastings, Callimancoes and Stuffs, Drogheda and other Linens, Worsted and other Tapes and Garters, Sewing Silks, No. and coloured sewing Threads, Shirt Buttons, Silk Purses, Hair Powder and Powder Puffs, and best playing Cards,

Silk and Stuff Petticoats,

Silk, Cotton and Linen Handkerchiefs for neck and pocket ;—all which will be sold (by wholesale and retail) at the most reduced Dublin prices.

N. B. A Parcel of printed Cottons and Linens to be sold under first cost.

Belfast, February 20th, 1789.

Races, at Ballyholme, near Bangor.

On TUESDAY the 10th March, 1789,

THREE Pounds to be run for by any Horse, &c. which never won the value of the same as a given Prize.

On WEDNESDAY,

Five Pounds, to be run for by any Horse, &c. which never won the value of said Prize.

On THURSDAY,

Two Pounds, &c. for any Horse, &c. which never won the value of said Prize.

On FRIDAY,

A Purse of Thirty Shillings for beaten Cattle.

On SATURDAY,

A Saddle for any Horse, &c. which never won 1l. 2s. 9d. the best of three four-mile heats.

All the above Matches catch weight. No crossing nor jostling. Cattle to be entered with Hugh Brown the evening before running ; 1s. 1d. entrance, or 2s. 8d. half. at the post.——Judges to be appointed at the Course on the first day for the running.

Rathgill, 19th Feb. 1789.

ALEX. Mc. CULLOCH.

Take Notice,

THAT a Sessions of the Peace will be held at Downpatrick, on Tuesday the third day of March next, that those Freeholders, who have not registered, may have an opportunity of doing it.

February 23d, 1789.

Forest-Trees, Deciduous and Evergreens, &c. &c.

FOR Sale by THOMAS TAYLOR, at his Nursery in the Townland of Cattogs, near Comber. They have been raised in a very exposed situation, and poor soil ; within one hundred yards of where the tide constantly flows, which renders them equal if not superior to most Plants in the kingdom. He returns grateful thanks to the Publick who have honoured him with their commands ; and hopes by moderate charges to merit a continuance of their favour.

N. B. He has a large quantity of Scotch Fir or Pine and Larch, greatly reduced in Price.

February 23d, 1789.

Thomas Seed,

INFORMS the Publick, that he found a Boat near Garmoile, with three Oars and three Rudders.—— Whoever proves property, and pays expences, may have her on applying to said Seed on the Quay.

Belfast, February 23d, 1789.

Money wanted.

FROM Five to Eight Hundred Pounds, for which good personal Security will be given, and if required a Mortgage on Land in the county of Antrim, valued at six hundred Pounds ; the borrower would repay the money in the course of eighteen months or two years, as most agreeable to the lender.——For particulars apply to Mr. D. Gordon, Attorney

ORIGINAL POETRY.

FOR THE BELFAST NEWS LETTER.

TO MY GENIUS.

O! Genius what a wretch art thou,
That can'st not keep a mare nor cow,
With all thy compliment of wit so frisky;
While dullness, as a mill horse blind,
Beside his compter gold can find,
And Sunday sports a strumpet and a whisky.

PETER PINDAR.

DEAR Genius, if thou art my friend,
For once thy vot'ry's call attend;
Thou who hast oft, while youth was warm,
Supply'd each fond delightful charm;
Who cheer'd my fancy with thy lore,
And spread thy gay successive store,
Ere yet my tongue could lisp thy name,
And fir'd me with the hopes of fame:
Why did'st thou give a haughty mind,
By *Prudence* not to be confin'd?
Why didst thou tell me *Fortune's* smiles
Were but a syren's artful wiles?
Why with philosophy and rhyme
Didst thou delude my youthful prime?
Why didst thou bid me leave the road
Where *Comfort* all her treasures strew'd!
And why should dunces live in state,
Without the talents to be great,
While I scarce share a meal a day,
And when I write, receive—no pay?

"My friend, my pupil, and my child,"
Thus Genius spoke and sweetly smil'd,
"I gave thee honest pride to bear
"Each adverse turn, and scorn despair:
"The gifts of Fortune I despise,
"But for a richer, greater prize;
"What Fortune gives she takes again,
"And makes her vassals heirs of pain:
"I bade thee court immortal fame,
"And shew'd her under virtue's name;
"To mitigate thy pains and toils,
"I shew'd thee Fortune and her spoils,—
"Shew'd her a ready slavish friend,
"A second means to work thy end.
"If thou hast err'd the fault's not mine,
"Thou'st taken Folly's for my shrine;
"The world has flatter'd thee astray—
"Remember this and go thy way;
"Go, and begin the world once more,
"Thy talents will afford thee store.
"Thou seest the way that Dunces thrive,
"And so may'st thou—but only strive;
"Get gold to keep and give away,
"And get the name of *ready pay:*
"When thus equipp'd, devote thy time
"To Prose, Philosophy and Rhyme.
"Fame and her handmaids then will deign
"To let thee join their gala train;
"For if thou'rt rich, thy wit is good,
"If poor, not read nor understood;
"But be thy station what it will,
"Be firmly independent still."

A. B.

Belfast, Feb. 20th, 1789.

ANECDOTES.

Lord Chancellor Cowper, when at the bar, was wont to say of Lord Chief Justice Holt, that "He had but little wit, but then he had it always about him."

WHIMSICAL CHARACTER.

Last week died at Linton, in Northumberland, aged 81, Richard Jewitt, Esq.—The whimsicallities of this venerable gentleman may be conceived by his making use of the coffin, in which he was buried, as a corner cupboard, in his bed-chamber, depositing therein bread and cheese, wines, spirits, &c. with the pictures of Adam and Eve at the head, and Darby and Joan at the feet.

BOXING.

London, Dec. 17.

Yesterday the long expected Battle between Johnson and Ryan, took place in a gravel-pit, within a quarter of a mile of the town of Rickmansworth, in Hertfordshire, and after a contest of 32 minutes and a half, victory was declared in favour of Johnson.

The spot on which the stage was erected, was certainly the best calculated of any ever known, as although upwards of 6000 spectators were present, yet no one person could claim a superiority of situation. The seat of contest was in a gravel-pit of great depth, sloaping gradually, and in the bottom of it, the stage of 21 feet square was erected.

The door money, which was to be divided equally between Johnson and Ryan, amounted to five hundred and twelve pounds—The report was given out, that the contest was to take place in the yard of the Bell inn; but when about four thousand people had subscribed guineas, half guineas and crowns, the stage which had been deposited in the yard, was carried to the spot above mentioned, were all ranks might equally be gratified.

At half past two o'clock, Johnson mounted the stage, with Humphreys as his second, and in about two minutes after Ryan appeared, with a Master Baker as his second.—As soon as they were on the stage, Major Hanger appeared, and presented a hat to those who had not subscribed.—When he had collected about thirty guineas, the stage was cleared.

When the combatants stripped, the odds were two to one in favour of Johnson, though Ryan certainly appeared the largest man.

The set-to was prodigiously fine; and after a few *feints* on each side, Ryan put in the first blow in the chest of his opponent, and brought him down. When the *time* was *up*, and each were on their guard, Johnson returned the compliment, by a severe blow on the left eye of Ryan, who, before the end of the battle, was nearly blind of that eye. Although there were about *thirty rounds*, yet, excepting three times, they were always in favour of Johnson.

As soon as Ryan gave in, Johnson was crowned with a hat ornamented with blue ribbons, and the pigeons were let loose.

Many Amateurs were present, amongst whom we saw on the stage, the Duke of Hamilton, Mr. Bradyll, Col. Tarleton, and Mr. Harvey Aston. All the profession of noted bruisers were present.

The stage was extremely slippery, owing to snow and rain, of which there fell a great quantity.

L O N D O N.

Continuation of the PACKET of February 18.

SATURDAY afternoon a person of genteel appearance shot himself in Greenwich Park, by discharging two horse pistols through his head. He had previous to his committing the rash action, distributed near 20 guineas to whoever came in his way. He was dressed in a black coat and breeches, and black silk waistcoat with small fringe, a pair of stone knee-buckles and boots, his hair queued, and a ruffled shirt; a letter wrote in French was found in his pocket, which was addressed to no particular person, desiring the privilege of interment, and intimating his aversion to existence. He is supposed to be a French person of some distinction, and had come from town in one of the stages.

Belfast, *February* 24.

The Treasurer of the Belfast Charitable Society acknowledges the receipt of Ten Guineas for the benefit of the Charity, from the Lord Bishop of Down and Connor.

James Fulton, of Lisburn, in the county of Antrim, Gent. was last term admitted, and sworn an Attorney of his Majesty's Courts of Kings Bench, and Common Pleas, in this kingdom.

The Linen Hall, Hugh Dickson, master, for London, arrived safe in the Downs the 15th inst.

The London Packet, Glass, from Newry for London, arrived safe in the Downs the 14th inst. after a passage of only 84 hours.

Died, on Wednesday last, in the 62d year of his age, Mr. George Joyce, of Knockbridge, in the county of Armagh, his death is much regretted by his friends and a numerous acquaintance.

Belfast, *February* 27.

☞ THREE BRITISH PACKETS DUE.

The present state of the great road leading hence to Lisburn, deserves immediate attention. It is in such bad repair that the *Mail Coach* which is shortly to run on it, will receive more injury in passing over a few miles of that road than on all the rest of the line to Dublin.

On Friday se'nnight the carrier of this paper, from Tynon to Augher, (in the county Tyrone) was set on by some villains near Caledon bridge, and inhumanly abused and robbed.—Any person who will prosecute to conviction shall be very liberally rewarded.

A petition to Parliament from the Governors of the Foundling Hospital and Work-house of the city of Dublin, sets forth, that on the 25th of December there were supported by the charity 5482 children, of which number 506 were in the hospital, aged eight years and upwards; infants in the foundling nursery 29, and at nurse in the country 4947; that the children of eight years and upwards are taught to read and write, and employed in several useful manufactures and gardening, and are fully instructed in the principles of the Christian religion.

DIED.] In this town the 18th inst. Mrs. Mary Orr, relict of the late Revd. James Orr, of Loughgall, county Armagh, in the eighty-second year of her age—a bright example of the power and purity of the doctrines of christianity, by which she professed and appeared to be actuated in every station and relation, through so long a life, in the constant exercise of piety towards God and Righteousness towards men.

LENT ASSIZES for 1789.

North East Circuit.

Co. Meath, at Trim, Wednesday March 11.
Louth, at Dundalk, Monday 16.
Down, at Downpatrick, Thursday 19.
Antrim, at Carrickfergus, Thursday 26.
Town of Carrickfergus, at Carrickfergus, same day.
Armagh, at Armagh, April 1.
Monaghan, at Monaghan, Wednesday April 8.
Town of Drogheda, at Drogheda, Wednesday 15.

The Hon. Mr. Baron Power, }
The Hon. Mr. Justice Hellen, } Justices.

Richard Evans, Esq. Aungier-street, }
Michael Harris, Esq; Golden-lane, } Registers.

The Grand Jury of Louth will be sworn and the Records proceeded on immediately after the reading of the King's Commission, and the Records in the other Towns will be called on the morning after the commission days.

WHEREAS on Monday night the 23d inst about ten o'clock, several persons yet unknown, two of which had their faces blackened, (being assisted, as supposed, by a number without) entered the house of Robert Smith of the parish Drumbo, county of Down, Farmer; and after knocking him down, by which he received several wounds on the head, they barbarously stabbed him with a bayonet, and then tied him and three other persons belonging to the family, and afterward proceeded to plunder the house, and feloniously took and carried away two hundred and thirty pounds in cash, above one hundred spangles of linen yarn, a gun, some sheeting, and other linen to a considerable amount.

WE whose names are hereunto subscribed, in order to bring said offenders to justice, do promise to pay the several sums annexed to our names, to the first person who shall within six calendar months from the date hereof, discover and prosecution to conviction one or more of said felons.

February 24th, 1789.

Lands of Ballyclare.

WHEREAS EDWARD MOORE and ALEXANDER DUBOIS, the purchasers of Lots, No. 24 and 25, have not paid their deposits agreeable to the terms of sale, those two Lots will be again sold by public auction without reserve, at the Market House Belfast, exactly at twelve o'clock on Friday the 6th day of March next, to the highest bidder, and subject to the same terms of sale as before.

No. 24. A Lease for 54 years and 11 months, from Nov. 1792, at the yearly rent of 3l. 0s. 4d. and 1s. 8d. duties, of those houses and gardens in Ballyclare and fields behind them, containing together 7 A. held by Alexander M'Alester by lease for 20 years from November 1772, at the yearly rent of 13l. 13s. which 13l. 13s. the buyer shall receive during the 4 years unexpired, he paying to the sellers for said term 3l. 2s. yearly.

No. 25. A Lease for 55 years and 5 months, from May 1792, at the yearly rent of 10l. 8s. and 2s. duties, of that Farm lying between the road to Ballyeaston and Ballyclare Moss, containing 26A. held by Alexander Duboys by lease for 18 years from May 1774, at the yearly rent of 22l. 15s.—The Purchaser shall receive the said rent from Duboys for the 3 and half years unexpired, paying the sellers for said time 10l. 10s. yearly.

And whereas several purchasers of other Lots who have paid their deposits, have hitherto neglected to give security for the other three fourths of the purchase money agreeable to the terms of sale, and to get out their Leases, all such are desired to take notice that unless they come in and settle before the fourth of March next, their Lots will be sold again on that day by public auction, and they will forfeit their deposits.——The grand Lease of the Town and Lands of Ballyclare from Lord Donegall to Nath. Wilson, will be sold immediately after those matters are settled, that is as soon as a perfect Rentall can be made out.

Belfast, 20th Feb. 1789.

W. CUNNINGHAM.
JAMES HOLMES & Co.

THERE is to be sold by ROBERT Mc. MECKIN at Belvidere, near Lisburn, a large Quantity of remarkably good Seedling Beeches, which he proposes to sell at 6s. 6d. per 1200; the poorness of the ground that they grow in, is an additional advantage.—This to be inserted three times.

February 23d, 1789.

Anno 1789.] Printed by HENRY JOY, and Co. BELFAST.

The BELFAST NEWS-LETTER.

TUESDAY March 3, FRIDAY March 6, 1789.

For *PHILADELPHIA*,

THE fine ship COMMERCE, Preserved Seston, Master, (arrived here from New York, to Henry Ogle, with a cargo of Flaxseed and Staves), will sail for the port of Philadelphia aforesaid the 14th of March next, wind and weather permitting, with such Goods and Passengers as may offer. —This ship's accommodation for Passengers is *excellent*, being lofty between decks, is a remarkable sailor, and the Captain perfectly acquainted with the Passenger Trade. ——For freight or passage apply to the Captain at Warrenpoint, or to Henry Ogle.

Newry, 26th February, 1789.

Strayed or Stolen,

ON the night of the 26th last month, a black Mare, big with foal, about 12 years old, 14½ hands high, strong made, part of one hind foot white, her mane had been hogged but now grown bushey, and what is very remarkable she had a large lump on the top of her forehead, occasioned by the kick of a horse. If stolen, whoever secures Mare and thief and prosecutes to conviction shall receive five guineas, and for the Mare shall be handsomely rewarded by applying to Joshua Ridgway near Lurgan, or Dan. Delacherois, Esq. Donaghadee.

2d March, 1789.

The Belfast Coterie,

WILL be held (as usual) at the Exchange-Rooms, on Tuesday next the 10th instant.

March 6th, 1789.

Colerain District.

THE Licence Offices of this Collection will be held on the days and at the places under-mentioned, for the ease and convenience of the people in obtaining their Licences for the year commencing the 26th instant.

And as the new regulations have multiplied the licence business with numerous books and voluminous papers very inconvenient to be carried abroad, it is expected that the whole Licence Duty will be paid and done away at the Offices hereby appointed, for afterwards there will not be a Licence granted at any of the out Offices of the District during the course of the year.

Ballcastle, on Monday 30th March.
Ballymoney, Wednesday 1st April.
Coleraine, Friday the 3d.
Maghrafelt, Monday 6th.
Maghera, Wednesday 8th.

Custom-House, Colerain, 6th March, 1789.
SAM. BRISTOW, Collector.

Snug Hall House

WITH about 25 acres of land, to be set from Nov. last:—It is pleasantly situated for sea bathing, within about a mile of the Giants Causway, there is a fine prospect from it of sea port and Mr. Leslies improve ments. Proposals to be received by Mr. Richard Lloyd near Dunganon, and Mr. James Haslett, Colerain. Dan. Corkedel who takes care of the house, will shew it and the land. Dated this 28th of Feb. 1789.

LIVERPOOL,

HAMILTON GRAHAM, acting partner of the late Firm Geoghegan and Graham, respectfully informs his friends and the public, he carries on the Commission business with forwarding Consignments as usual, is thankful for past favors, and hopes to merit a continuance by assiduity and attention. Stores No. 4, Parke-lane attiguous to the Old Dock.

To be Sold by public Auction,

AT the Donegall-Arms, in the Town of Belfast, on Wednesday the 11th day of March instant, exactly at 12 o'clock at noon, by John Banks of Strandmillis, Farmer,—All that Tenement or Parcel of Land, being part of the Lands called the Course, containing by admeasurement 12A. 1R. 30P. or thereabouts, plantation measure, at the yearly rent of 10l. 10s. held by lease under the Right Hon. Arthur Earl of Donegall, of which there are to come and unexpired two years from the first of May 1789. For further particulars apply to said John Banks on the premisses, or to Robert Stewart of Belfast, Gent.

Dated this 5th day of March, 1789.

GRAZING.

THE Demesne of Portavo, will be grazed this Season from the 12th May to the 12th November—Cows at one Guinea and a half—no broken Sums will be taken.

The Copland Island will be grazed as usual. The Publick are desired to take notice, that great care has been taken of the Grass.——Apply to Alexander Martin at Portavo

March 4th, 1789.

An extensive Tan-yard

TO be Set, from May next, in the Town of Portaferry, capable of containing upwards of 2,000 Hides; complete and commodious in all its parts; and every part in excellent order and repair.—To enumerate all its advantages and conveniencies is unnecessary in an advertisement, as the premisses may, at any time, be viewed, and will bear the strictest inspection. Proposals will be received by Mr. William Galway, the Proprietor.

Portaferry, 3d March, 1789.

TO BE LET,

A Farm of Land in the Townland of Bush, containing 67A. 0R. 20P. arable and pasture, for three lives or thirty-one years from the first of November last. The said Lands lie within a mile of the town of Antrim.——Apply to Mr. Arthur, Belfast.

Dated 5th March, 1789.

To be Sold by private Contract,

AN Article of a neat House in Castle-street, for nine years from November last, next door to the Bank, with a Stable and two lofts over, and a pump in the yard ——For farther particulars enquire at Victor Coats on the premisses.

N. B. A House in Ann-street to be let. Enquire as above.

Belfast, 6th March, 1789.

Wanted,

A Man properly qualified to take care of a pair of Horses, and attend on a single Gentleman, he must be very well recommended for sobriety, honesty and a knowledge of his Business, as a very strict scrutity will be made: such a person will hear of a very advantageous place by applying to the Collector of Armagh, either by letter or in person.

A Turnpike Board of the second and third Division of the Road from Banbridge to Belfast—will be held on Tuesday the 10th instant, at 12 o'clock, at Hastings' in Lisburn.

Lisburn, 3d March, 1787. By Order, WILL. YOUNGHUSBAND, Register.

A School-Master Wanted,

BY the Inhabitants of Dungannon, who is qualified to teach Writing, Arithmetick, and the English Language Grammatically.—Application to be made to Chas. Duffin of Dungannon. None need apply who can not produce undoubted proofs of their sobriety and good character.——To be inserted four times.

Dungannon, Feb. 28th, 1789.

Stolen,

OUT of the stable of James Chambers of Glengormley, parish of Carmoney, and county of Antrim, on the night of the 28th of February, a black Mare rising 6 years old, about 14 or 15 hands high, the far hind foot white, a few white hairs on her forehead, saddle mark'd on the back, a bushey tail rumped but not set. The person who returns said Mare to Mr. David Thoburn of Belfast, or to Mr. Wm. Russell of Cowlinward, or to the said James Chambers, shall receive one guinea reward, or whoever returns said Mare and lodges the thief or thieves in any of his Majesty's goals in this kingdom, shall receive two guineas upon prosecuting him or them to conviction.

Glengormley, March 2d, 1789.

MONEY.

THREE HUNDRED POUNDS wanted on undeniable Security in the Town of Belfast.—— Apply to Mr. Joy.

Belfast, March 2d, 1789.

WHEREAS on Monday night the 23d inst about ten o'clock, several persons yet unknown, two of which had their faces blackened, (being assisted, as supposed, by a number without) entered the house of Robert Smith of the parish Drumbo, county of Down, Farmer; and after knocking him down, by which he received several wounds on the head they barbarously stabbed him with a bayonet, and then tied him and three other persons belonging to the family, and afterwards proceeded to plunder the house, and feloniously took and carried away two hundred and thirty pounds in cash, above one hundred spangles of linen yarn, a gun, some sheeting, and other linen to a considerable amount.

WE whose names are hereunto subscribed, do promise to pay the several sums to our names annexed, to any person who will discover and prosecute to conviction the person or persons concerned in the above felony.

☞ The original Paper, with the Subscriptions, amounting to £ 172l. 6s. 7d. is in the hands of the Printers hereof. February 24th, 1789.

Irish Crown Glass.

JOHN SMYLIE & CO. of Belfast, beg leave to acquaint their Countymen, that they are now manufacturing and have ready for sale, at their Glass-Works, CROWN-GLASS, which they will dispose of either by the Side, or Cut into any sizes that may be wanted) at a much lower rate than any which can be imported.

They embrace this opportunity of offering their most grateful thanks to the Public for their kind patronage and support to this their Manufacture ever since its commencement, even when thro' some unavoidable circumstances, (which generally attend the establishment of a new manufacture in a country) it was impossible for them to bring their Glass *at once* to that state of perfection they could have wished; but they have the satisfaction of being *now* able to produce Irish Crown-Glass, *superior in every respect to any imported from Bristol*, and which they will sell by the Side at least 14 per cent. cheaper; and when cut into Squares at least 50 per cent.

They would have declined saying even this much for their Manufacture,—as well foreseeing that the fair and judicious eye of a discerning Public would soon have made the observation, were it not that an importation of Window-Glass from Bristol, at this very time, puts it in their power to prove their assertion by a comparison, which they wish much to have made by any number of skilful and impartial persons.

Belfast, 2d March, 1789.

A VESTRY will be held by adjournment, in the Parish Church of Belfast, on Monday the 9th instant, to receive the report of a Committee appointed at the last Vestry, to examine the state of the pavement in the different quarters of the town.

Belfast, March 5th, 1789.

For the Benefit of Miss Valois,

ON Monday the 9th March, 1789, will be presented a favourite COMEDY, call'd,

The HEIRESS.

Between the Acts (for this night only) the following Entertainments:

End of the third Act, An ALLAMONDE, by Mr. LYNCH and Miss VALOIS

End of the Play, A DOUBLE HORNPIPE, by Mr. LYNCH and Miss VALOIS.

And a FARCE as will be expressed in the Bills.

For the Benefit of Mrs. Remington,

WHO having unfortunately failed in her former Attempt, solicits the patronage and support of the Ladies and Gentlemen of Belfast, and its Vicinity, on this occasion, which she will ever most gratefully remember.

On Friday March the 6th, will be presented, a Play, Farce, and Entertainments, as will be expressed in a future Advertisement.

Tickets to be had, and Places in the Boxes to be taken of Mrs. Remington, at Mr. Brown's on the Quay.

Belfast, 2d March, 1789.

Linen Cloth stolen.

OUT of the Bleachyard of Joshua Ridgway of Milltown, near Lurgan, the middle of last season, two pieces of Diaper; and the latter part of the same, five pieces of Cambrick, all marked H. and the number. The Cambrick had been taken about ten days before the remainder of the parcel were blued; so that it is apprehended they had been finished at some other Bleachyard. I hereby promise a reward of Twenty Pounds Sterl. exclusive of the above sum of 100l. subscription, to any person or persons who will prosecute to conviction the persons concerned; or to any person who will give information that may lead to the same, and their names shall be kept a profound secret if required.

And whereas in the month of September last my late Watchman Samuel Williamson run away from my service on my getting information of his stealing my Pot Ashes and Turf, and selling them to his son John, who resold them again; on a warrant being granted by Richard Magenis, Esq; against said Williamson, he fled as I understood to Scotland; and from this circumstance am apprehensive the said Williamson or his accomplices have stolen the said Diaper or Cambrick, as I heard lately he has been seen lurking about Killileagh or the lower part of this county: This is therefore to caution all persons from being deceived by so artful a rogue, or employing or harbouring him; and I hereby offer a Reward of Five Pounds Sterl. to any person or persons who will lodge the said Williamson in any of his Majesty's Gaols in this kingdom.—He is a low, set, strong-made fellow, wore his own hair, very active, above fifty years of age; had on a grey ratteen coat when runaway.——Milltown, 2d March, 1789.

JOSHUA RIDGWAY.

NEW DRESSES at PARIS.

The length of the Carnival this year, affords room for fancy to ſport many elegant dreſſes. Two have appeared worthy of particular deſcription.

The firſt is a CARACO, with a long train of white ſattin, gathered on the ſides, and fixed with ſilver flowers—long ſkirts obove the train, cut of ſtripped ſattin, blue and white—aud the ſame for the breaſts and ſhoulders——the back is of white ſattin, as are the ſleeves, which reach only 10 the elbows.

The petticoat is of blue ſattin, very long—cut at the bottom—trimmed in different places, with large roſes of white ſattin, and with a cut garland of the ſame, inſtead of a fur below.

On the neck, a *fichu* of gauze, very projecting, the ends of which go under the ſtomacher.

Round the waiſt, a broad girdle of black velvet, with two large medallions.

The hair in buckles, bound with a garland of blue cut ribband, a *bouquet* of artificial flowers on the left ſide, and four large feathers on the brow.

The ſecond is very ſimilar, excepting that it has only a long train gathered on the ſides with knots, and gold and ſilver taſſels. What appears like ſkirts over the train, is only the handkerchief, the ends of which, after going under the ſtomacher, come out at the ſides through ſlits made on purpoſe, and are tied behind, above the girdle.

The head-dreſs is a *Bonnet-chapeau*, the *pappillons* of which are gauze trimmed with lace, and the crown preciſely like the hats *a to Tarrare*, of roſe and white ſtripped ſattin. A *bouquet* of artifical flowers is before, and an *aigrette* of feathers ſtained green.

MASQUERADE.

London, Dec. 18.

The Pantheon has not had ſo numerous a company at a maſqued ball for ſeveral years as on Monday night. The rotunda was crowded even to inconvenience by one o'clock, and the joſtling multitude continued without much decreaſe till five in the morning.

The elegant ſcene was graced by faſhion as well as beauty. The Ducheſs of Devonſhire and Lady Duncannon, as *Religieuſes*, were highly faſcinating. Their party was large, and they were joined by the Prince of Wales and the Duke of York. Miſs Fortune was a good maſk—her gown, of white linen, is covered with *blank* lottery tickets; and under her cloak of Succeſs, decked out in different colours, are the *prizes*. A beaver hat, trimmed to reſemble the wheel of Fortune, ornamented with a bunch of feathers and windmills; in the front a device of boys blowing bubbles; and the crown bound round with a row of lottery tickets. A girdle, inſcribed in front, *indiſcretion*; and on the ends behind, are theſe words, *diſtreſs and reflection*. She rolls a wheel, in which each adventurous fool puts his, or her hand, and draws a lable, or ticket, which generally proves perfectly applicable to the peculiar folly of the drawer.

Mr. P—n, one of the talleſt and moſt corpulent men in the metropolis, came as a *baby*, and Mrs. P. as his nurſe. A very elegant woman alſo was in the ſame character of an *infant* in leading ſtrings, whom many an amorous ſpark was anxious to lead aſtray. There were ſeveral well dreſt Indians, and of the female characters the beſt fancied was a *Lady of the laſt Century*, in a robe, and in every point the perfect faſhion of the old ſchool.

The Prince and the Duke of York, with ſome others of the Nobilty, appeared unmaſked, during a ſhort ſtay in the rooms, and beſtowed the ſmile of complacency on every one round them.

The exhibition of beauty was abundant, and the fair were dreſt in all the captivations of elegant fancy. The transformations of ſex were as uſual numerous and diſguſting.

The company kept together till very late, and the ſaloon was not quite cleared at eight o'clock in the morning.

DUBLIN.

Laſt night the Caſtle and almoſt every houſe in this city was illuminated, on hearing the joyful news of his Majeſty's recovery. The Theatre and Aſtley's were in one continued blaze; the latter had prepared a firework, which alternately changed to the following words, internal, "*He is recovered*, huzza!"—external, "LONG LIVE THE KING, huzza!"—Both had an amazing effect on the ſpectators, particularly ſo, as the Band accompanied the fireworks with "*God ſave the King!*"

The petition delivered into the Houſe of Commons Tueſday ſe'nnight, from the corporation inſtitued for the relief of the poor in the city of Dublin, contains, among other allegations, "That from the 8th of November, 1773, when the Houſe of Induſtry was opened, to the 25th of December, 1788, the number of perſons received into the houſe amounted to 39,994: That there are actually in the houſe 1622, the expence of maintaining whom, (on the average number, which was 1540) amounted, together with the officers ſalaries and other expences, to the yearly ſum of 10,188, that notwithſtanding the utmoſt attention and frugality the corporation was actually in debt to the Treaſurer, John Latouche, Eſq. 133l.

Though the accounts of the imports and exports delivered into Parliament, are not brought up nearer than the year ending the 25th of March laſt, (now almoſt twelve months) yet they contain ſome particulars that muſt give pleaſure to thoſe who have the welfare of this country at heart. We mean the exportation of articles of produce or manufacture, which have encreaſed comparatively with the quantity in the preceding year, as in the following ſtatement of the exports of the two years may be ſeen.

Exported.		1787.	1788.
Bacon, Flitches,		16,525	29,587
Butter,	Cwt.	330,866	341,599
New Drapery,	Yards,	206,849	315,111
Herrings,	Barrels,	11,366	16,855
Flannels,	Yards,	17,251	61,000
Fuſtians,	Ditto,	2,170	16,803
Frize,	Ditto,	3,000	4,000
Linen, plain,	Ditto,	30,728,728	35,487,691
Pork,	Barrels,	101,859	111,000
Shoes,	lbs. wt.	10,983	12,602

Though the Engliſh, from the happy circumſtance of ſuperior wealth, have been able to carry their manufactures to an high degree of perfection, they owe more to the genius of Iriſh artiſts than they are diſpoſed in many caſes to acknowledge. The firſt idea of printing linen with copper-plates, which has proved ſo lucrative a branch of manufacture, originated in Ireland, and the buſineſs was actually begun at Drumcondra; but after ſome trials it was given up, from a want of encouragement and ſufficient capital. The artiſt, however, migrating to England, was there countenanced, and laid the foundation of that branch which has been ſo extenſively as well as beneficially carried on in the ſiſter country.

Another inſtance occurs wherein a native of Dublin, named Fry, diſtinguiſhed himſelf as chief in a china manufactory (the firſt attempted in England) at Bow, and from the ruins of which aroſe thoſe of Chelſea and Worceſter. After fifteen years cloſe application this manufacture was brought to ſuch perfection that in tranſparency it nearly equalled, and in deſign and painting infinitely exceeded, the productions of the Eaſt. Fry being an excellent painter; the only defect appears to be the inferior degree of glazing. An high duty having been laid on the white clay uſed, which was brought from South Carolina, the price of the manufacture became enhanced, and in conſequence declined; but when domeſtic clays were found, it was again taken up, and is now advantageouſly carried on in many parts of England.

It is imagined the heavy tax on newſpaper advertiſements, ſo very burdenſome on retail traders in this country, will undergo a modification in the preſent ſeſſion, which will render it at once more productive to government, leſs oppreſſive to traders and encouraging to the printers of newſpapers, who ſtand reſponſible with conſiderable properties at ſtake. In England newſpapers are conſidered by government as grand ſources of commercial information, and conſequently the cement of national wealth, and they are therefore encouraged by government, who have given orders at the General Poſt-office to co-operate with the Stamp-office, in extending at once the purpoſes of general information, the intereſts of advertiſers, and the benefit of the revenue; but in this country the ſyſtem of taxation on newſpapers, and the advertiſements contained therein, ſeems rather intended to cramp the circulation, and fruſtrate the purpoſes of thoſe vehicles, than to forward the intereſts of the revenue.—But ſurely whatever prohibitory ſteps might have been warranted by the licentiouſneſs of former printers, it is hard the ſin ſhould be viſited on the high taxed traders of this country, the intereſts of ſubſequent and unoffending printers, or the vehicles of public information.

DIED.] At Kilmainham, Miſs Kane, aged nineteen;—and we are ſorry to add, that as ſoon as Mrs. Kane entered the room where her daughter lay waking ſhe dropped on the floor and inſtantly expired, leaving ten children behind her.

Belfaſt, *March* 3.

Extract of a Letter from Dublin, dated Feb. 28.

"On Tueſday our H. of C. will come out with a volley of Reſolutions on the ſubject of the late refuſal reſpecting the Addreſſes;—and immediately will be brought forward a—*Penſion Bill—Revenue—and Police Bill.*"

Private letters of the firſt authority, received in this town from London, declare the certainty of the re-eſtabliſhment of the King's health—and that no Regency Bill will now take place.

It is with much pleaſure that we can, from the beſt authority, inform the Public, that Iriſh Crown Glaſs is now manufactured, and ſelling, at our New Glaſs-houſe, of *ſuperior* quality, and cheaper than any imported from Briſtol.

On Saturday laſt Patrick Magee, pavior of the Town of Belfaſt, was committed to jail by the Sovereign, for ſtealing a porter caſk, the property of John Magarrahy, of Church-lane.

Died on Wedneſday laſt, Mr. James Cowan, ſon to Mr. Wm. Cowan, of Larch-hill near Dromore, in the 24th year of his age, greatly regretted by a numerous acquaintance.

Belfaſt, *March* 6.

Extract of a Letter from Hillſborough, dated March 4, 1789, ten o'clock at night.

"The very much wiſhed for and joyful intelligence of the reſtoration of our good and much beloved Monarch's health having arrived this day, we are all in a frenzy of joy on the occaſion; the bells (which conſiſt of an excellent peal of eight) have been ringing all day, every houſe in town is illuminated, drink given to the populace, bonfires, fire-works, &c. the Warders of the Fort paraded and fired a feu-de-joy, and never was ſincere loyalty more conſpicuous than by the teſtimony of his Majeſty's moſt faithful ſubjects of this town."

We think it our duty to inform the public, that ſeveral forgeries have been committed on the Bank of Ayr—and that many of the forged notes are now in circulation in the counties of Down and Antrim.

The Treaſurer of the Belfaſt Charitable Society acknowledges to have received from the Rev. Wm. Briſtow and Val. Jones, Eſq. executors of the late Mrs. Barbara Collyer, two hundred and twenty-ſeven pounds, ten ſhillings, ſterl. being a legacy bequeathed by her to the Belfaſt Incorporated Charitable Society for the uſe of the Poor-houſe and Infirmary.

MR. LYNCH having failed in his firſt attempt, begs leave to inform his Friends, that his ſecond is fixed for WEDNESDAY the 11th March, inſt. at which time he hopes for their countenance and protection—when will be preſented the celebrated Comedy of the BROTHERS, and the muſical Farce of the FARMER. Tickets to be had, and places for the boxes to be taken, of Mr. Lynch, at Mr. M'Maſter's, Snugborough, North-ſtreet.

The UNION ASSEMBLY will be held at the Rooms, as uſual, on Thurſday next 12th inſt.

The ſale of the ſeveral Tenements in Church-lane, &c. advertiſed in the 4th page of this paper, the property of Mr Henry Bamber, is poſtponed till Monday the 16th March, inſt.

WHEREAS on the 17th of January, 1789, I had the misfortune to be ſtranded near this place, (in the bay of Dundrum) on my voyage from Roſs for Dublin, being in a diſtreſſed ſituation, and a ſtranger; upon which occaſion Francis Savage, Eſq; jun. moſt humanely afforded me relief, by ordering the revenue officers here, and attending himſelf, to give every aſſiſtance for my preſervation, at the ſame time refuſing to accept of any manner of compenſation, though my chief preſerver—I am therefore in duty bound to return him this my publick thanks—and further to recommend his goodneſs to all diſtreſſed ſeamen like me.

JOSEPH CROOKS, Maſter of the Mary Ann Brig of Whitehaven.
MIRAS TRAULY, Mate.

To be Let,

FROM the firſt of May next, or the intereſt in the Leaſe ſold—the Houſe in Bridge-Street at preſent occupied by Joſeph Stevenſon;—it is held by leaſe from the Earl of Donegall for 99 years, from the firſt of May, 1767, and three lives, all in being, at the yearly ground rent of 6l.—and 2s. 6d. fees.—The ſituation for buſineſs requires no comment, being confeſſedly among the firſt in town. The purchaſer or taker of this Houſe may be accommodated with ſtabling for four horſes, and a ſtand for a cow in a very convenient ſituation.—Any perſon wiſhing to treat for ſaid premiſſes, are requeſted to ſend in their propoſals as above.

Belfaſt, 5th March, 1789.

To be Sold by Auction,

ON Tueſday the 10th inſt. and the following days, at the Brown Bear, High-Street, Belfaſt, the genuine Houſehold Furniture of a gentleman in the country, removed for convenience of ſale, conſiſting of four poſt bedſteds and hangings, field do. mahogany Northumberland tables, do. dining and card tables, mahogany chairs, painted and oak chairs, a ſide-board table, a handſome pier glaſs burniſhed gold frame, oval and ſquare dreſſing glaſſes, a lady's gold watch, a pair ſilver candleſticks, a pair ſilver tumblers, a pair ſilver ſervers, a large ſilver do. twelve ſilver tea-ſpoons, all ſterling, ſilver handled knives and forks, and plated candleſticks, an eight day clock, a ſilver watch, a ſet of tea china 46 pieces, do. 40 pieces, a breakfaſt ſet do. nankeen, mahogany deſk and bookcaſe, do deſk, oak preſs bedſted, a deal wardrobe and book-caſe, a lady's ſide-ſaddle, a ſofa, five tablecloths, cotton counterpane, four feather beds with blankets, a large copper boiler, with many other articles too numerous to mention.

The ſale to begin each day at eleven o'clock and continue till all is ſold, by JOHN PARROCK Upholder and Auctioneer.

TO BE LET,

AT May next, the Corner Houſe at the Head of Ann-ſtreet, fronting the new-intended ſtreet leading to the White Linen-Hall.—It conſiſts of a variety of good warm and convenient Rooms, with ſeveral neceſſary fixtures, and locks and grates compleat, at preſent occupied by Mr. Hugh Lynden; if the tenant chuſes he may have a ſtable fit for five or ſix horſes.

There is alſo to be let in the ſame neighbourhood, a ſmall Dwelling-Houſe, containing a kitchen, parlour, and two rooms above ſtairs.——For further particulars enquire at the proprietor William Irwin.

Belfaſt, 4th March, 1789.

Anno 1789.] Printed by HENRY JOY, and Co. BELFAST.

The BELFAST NEWS-LETTER.

TUESDAY March 10, FRIDAY March 13, 1789.

For Newcaſtle, Wilmington and Philadelphia.

THE Brig Brothers, about 200 tons burthen, captain James Jeffers, will be clear to ſail for ſaid ports by the 12th April next.—For freight or paſſage apply to Meſſrs. Daniel and John Murry, Lurgan; Mr James Duffey, merchant, Stewartſtown; Mr. William Small, merchant, Dungannon; Mr. George Pentleton, Liſburn; Mr Moſes Bodle, merchant, Dromore; Mr. John Luke, merchant, Belfaſt; or the captain on board, who will agree with them on the moſt reaſonable terms.

This veſſel is very ſtrong and well found, and ſails faſt: Thoſe who wiſh to embrace this favourable opportunity, may depend the greateſt care will be taken to have plenty of the beſt proviſions and water for the voyage, and on meeting with the beſt of treatment by applying as above.

Belfaſt, 7th March, 1789.

N. B. Above one half of the paſſengers are already engaged for ſaid veſſel, which will induce her to ſail at the day appointed.

We the Manufacturers of Tobacco in the Town of Belfaſt,

REQUEST a Meeting of the Licenſed Manufacturers of Tobacco in the North of Ireland, or as many of them as can conveniently attend, at the Donegall Arms, in the Town of Belfaſt, on Monday the 16th inſtant, preciſely at 12 o'clock, on buſineſs of the greateſt importance to the Trade.

Belfaſt, 9th March, 1789.

Thompſon & Oakman, William Henderſon,
William Emerſon, Samuel Eaddy,
Conway Carleton, James Suffern.

New Teas and Scale Sugar, and Flour,

ROBERT KNOX, has juſt arrived from London, a compleat aſſortment of Teas; and lately from Liverpool, a quantity of fine Scale Sugar, which with a variety of articles in the Grocery line, will be ſold on moderate terms.

N. B. A conſtant ſupply of ſuperfine, firſt, ſecond, and third Flour from the mills, to be ſold by ſaid R. KNOX. Belfaſt, 10th March, 1789.

New Garden, Graſs & Flower Seeds.

SAMUEL ROBINSON, Seedſman, Waring-ſtreet,

HAS juſt received from London and Holland, his annual Aſſortment of Garden and Flower Seeds and Roots, early Peas and Beans, whole and ſplit boiling Peas, Engliſh White Graſs Seed, broad red Clover Seed, Flour of Muſtard, Hempſeed, &c. &c.——Truly grateful for the very great encouragement he has received, and the unuſual demand laſt ſeaſon, he has conſiderably enlarged his Aſſortment; and can with confidence aſſure thoſe Gentlemen who ſhall be ſo kind as to favour him with their Orders this ſeaſon, that the quality of his Seeds is equal if not ſuperior to any he ever imported.

Catalogues of the different Articles may be had at his Shop.

☞ Large Baſs Mats for covering Hotbeds, Garden Lines, Hoes, Rakes, &c. with a Quantity of double and ſingle Glo'ſter Cheeſe. Belfaſt, 9th March, 1789.

Jones, Tomb, Joy & Co.

ARE landing out of the Lord Donegall, Captain Mc. Roberts, from London, a parcel of Hyſon, Singlo, and Congo Teas; alſo a few bags of Pepper, which will be ſold on the moſt reaſonable terms.

Belfaſt, 9th March, 1789.

Roger O'Donnell,

Nurſery and Seedſman, Salt-water Bridge, near Belfaſt,

BEGS leave to inform his Friends and the Public, that he has juſt imported from London, per the Lord Donegall, Capt. M'Roberts, a large collection of Garden and Flower Seeds, Peas, Beans, &c. which he will diſpoſe of at his Nurſery, where he has an opportunity of trying their quality, and giving inſtructions reſpecting their culture. He has alſo a variety of good Green-houſe plants;—and continues to lay out and execute improvements in the modern taſte; likewiſe Hot-houſes, Green-houſes, and Vine-houſes, with ſeveral uſeful additions.—Any commands for him will be duly attended to.

NEW SEEDS.

THOMAS PRENTICE, Armagh, has juſt received from England and Holland, an extenſive Aſſortment of *Garden Seeds, Red and White Clover*, Dutch *Flaxſeed, Smalts, Starch, Madder, Spaniſh Indigo*, &c. which, with every Article in the Grocery Line, he will ſell on the loweſt terms.

Armagh, 6th March, 1789.

Armagh Brewery.

JOHN Mc CAN, of the City of Armagh, returns his moſt reſpectful thanks to his numerous friends and cuſtomers who have favoured him with their commands ſince his commencement in the Brewing Buſineſs; informs them that he has now at his Brewery, a Stock of excellent Ale, fit for immediate uſe, which he can recommend for quality and flavour, and will ſell at all times on the loweſt terms poſſible; would wiſh his old Cuſtomers would make trial of the Ale at preſent on hand, and informs his cuſtomers that no Ale or Small Beer ſhall leave his Stores that are not perfectly ſound and good; and that he will not receive any Ale or Small Beer, after it leaves his Stores, nor will he be accountable for the miſmanagement of carriers or ſervants: He requeſts that all empty veſſels be forthwith returned—many of them are in the counties of Tyrone, Monaghan and Down, where there was not one ſixth part of the value of the veſſels profit on the Beer ſold; and if this is not complied with, muſt take the ſpeedieſt method to recover the value of his veſſels; and informs his cuſtomers with whom he keeps accounts, that it is not in his power to give more than ſix months credit, as it was his misfortune to have ſome dealings with ſome of thoſe faſhionable people called *Bankrupts*. He requeſts that thoſe who are indebted to him for Ale or Small Beer, will pay off their accounts immediately, as he cannot give longer forbearance.

N. B. A Brewer is wanted, whoſe ſkill in that profeſſion, and his morals, will bear the ſtricteſt enquiry. None need apply but thoſe that can bring proper certificates of their characters.

Armagh, 3d March, 1789.

To be continued ſix times.

New Garden and Flower Seeds, &c.

THOMPSON and OAKMAN have juſt received per the Lord Donegall, captain M'Roberts, from London, a general and extenſive aſſortment of new garden and flower ſeeds, early peas and beans, red and white clover, hemp, rape, and Canary ſeed, &c. all of which their friends may reſt aſſured is of the very firſt quality, and will be ſold on as low terms as they can be had elſewhere.

Belfaſt, 9th March, 1789.

Juſt arrived to Wm. RAMSEY,

NEW GARDEN and FLOWER SEEDS, Garden Peas and Beans, whole and ſplit boiling Peas, Hemp, Rape and Canary Seed, Whin and Broom Seed, &c. &c.

Belfaſt, March 9th, 1789.

New Garden and Clover Seeds, Teas, &c.

GEORGE LANGTRY has juſt arrived per the Lord Donegall, from London, a general Aſſortment of the above;—alſo early Peas and Beans, boiling and ſplit Peas, and Hempſeed——All of which his Friends may rely on being freſh, and will be ſold on as good terms as they will be got elſewhere.

Belfaſt, 7th March, 1789.

New Garden Seeds, &c.

M'KEDY and STEVENSON have juſt imported per the Lord Donegall, James M'Roberts, maſter, from London, a very extenſive aſſortment of garden and flower ſeeds, garden peas and beans, ſplit and whole boiling peas, hemp, rape, and Canary ſeeds, which, with their general extenſive aſſortment of groceries, they will ſell cheap. Belfaſt, 9th March, 1789.

New Garden Seeds.

WILLIAM EMERSON is now landing from London, his annual aſſortment of Garden and Clover Seeds, Garden Peas, Beans, &c. which his Friends may rely on being of the beſt quality;—alſo from Briſtol, a parcel of Crown and Quarry Glaſs of a very ſuperior quality, and equal to the niceſt taſte of any Gentleman; with Tobacco Pipes in boxes, double and ſingle Glo'ſter Cheeſe, which, with every article in the Grocery Line, will be diſpoſed of on the loweſt terms, for ready money. Belfaſt, March 9th, 1789.

N. B. He is well ſupplied with Roll Tobacco of his own manufacture in prime order.

Freſh Porter.

JAMES CUNNINGHAM, High-Street, Belfaſt, is juſt now landing out of the Lord Donegall, from London, a parcel of Whitbread's Porter in hogſheads.—He has a Stock of the ſame Porter four months in bottle, juſt beginning to be fit for uſe. He alſo ſells common Rum, Rum-D, old Spirit, (of the fineſt flavour) Brandy, Gineva, Spaniſh Wine, and Vinegar of the firſt Quality.——Said Cunningham hopes the quality of his Porter and Liquors will procure him a ſhare of the publick favour, as he is determined to ſell on the very loweſt terms, for ready money.

Belfaſt, 7th March, 1788.

WHEREAS one Samuel Hyndman, was taken into cuſtody at Donaghadee, on Wedneſday laſt the 4th inſt. on ſuſpicion of being concerned in a forgery, committed on the AYR BANK.——Hyndman, on being examined by the Collector of Donaghadee, acknowledged having received eight Notes, of Air Bank, knowing them to be forged, and had iſſued them on the road betwixt Air and Portpatrick, two he had iſſued at Portpatrick were ſworn to be received from him, before the Magiſtrate at Donaghadee, and his perſon ſworn to. Samuel Hyndman is about 28 years of age, born at or near Ballymena, county of Antrim, by a certificate found in his pocket-book, dated 3d October, 1787; it appears he has been about ſix years at Air, in Scotland, ſometime employed as a Clerk, but for near a year paſt was a petty Grocer, he is ſlender made, flat cheſted, about 5 feet eight inches high, his face from the eyes upwards rather flatiſh, brownith hair which he wore queued, had on black clothes, and without boots or ſhoes when he made his eſcape out of a window, on Saturday the 7th inſt. —Such perſon or perſons who ſhall diſcover on and proſecute to conviction the before deſcribed Samuel Hyndman, ſhall be entitled to One Hundred Guineas reward. Or for apprehending and lodging him in any of his Majeſty's jails in this kingdom twenty Guineas will be paid by Meſſrs. Ewing, Holmes and Co. in Belfaſt.

Belfaſt, March 10th, 1789.

William Hendren,

HAS juſt got in a large quantity of Lemons and Oranges in excellent order; and is at preſent well ſupplied with the following Articles,—Rum, Brandy, Geneva and Whiskey in Spirit and reduced, Raſberry and Cherry Juice, Bordeaux Vinegar, French Pomatums, Mareſchal and other Hair Powders, fine Eſſences and ſcented Waters, Brandy Fruit, Olives, Capers, Anchovies, Capilaire, Lavender and Seltzer Waters, Truffles in Oil Pickles, red Herrings, &c. &c. which, together with a regular and general aſſortment of Groceries, will be ſold wholeſale and retail, on very moderate terms, at his Shop, near the Market-Houſe, High-ſtreet, Belfaſt.

March 6th, 1789.

N. B. To be let, a firſt floor, genteelly furniſhed, and ſtabling if required. Alſo to be let, or the intereſt in the leaſe will be ſold, 67 years to come from November laſt, a large houſe three ſtories high, completely finiſhed, good garrets, back-yard and other conveniencies, ſituated the ſecond in Harp-entry. Enquire as above.

Tobacco Pipe Manufacture, Belfaſt.

JOHN EDWARDS moſt reſpectfully informs the Publick, that he has commenced the above buſineſs adjoining his Father's Flint Glaſs-Houſe, Bridge-End; where he has ready for ſale, Tobacco Pipes of all kinds, which he is ſelling by the Box remarkably cheap, much lower than they can be imported, duty conſidered; and having employed one of the firſt workmen in England as foreman, he flatters himſelf, from the quality of his Goods, moderate charges, and attention to buſineſs, to merit the confidence and ſupport of the Publick.

Glaſs-Houſe, 8th March, 1789.

Welch Slates, and Briſtol Window Glaſs.

NARCISSUS BATT is now landing a quantity of each, which, with the following Articles, he will diſpoſe of on the moſt reaſonable terms, at his Stores in Linenhall-ſtreet. March 7th, 1789.

Wines in Wood & Bottle.	
Burgundy,	Old Spirit, Rum,
Champagne,	Brandy, Geneva,
Madeira,	American Pot and Pearl Aſhes,
Canary,	Oil of Vitriol,
Claret,	Bergen Deals,
Frontigniac,	New Figs and Raiſins in caſks,
Hock,	A few Hogſheads of Guernſey Cyder,
Port,	Yellow Cotton Wool,
Sherry,	Eſſence of Spruce.
Vin de Grave,	
Mountain	

Belfaſt, 9th March, 1789.

New Teas, Kentiſh Bag Hops, Black Pepper, &c.

SAMUEL GIBSON has received for ſale a parcel of freſh Teas, imported from laſt India Sales in London: They conſiſt of Hyſons, fine and common Congous and Singlos—alſo a few bags Kentiſh Hops of a very fine quality—and black Pepper.—He is (as uſual) well ſupplied with Scale Sugars of different qualities, which he ſells cheap—and daily expects the arrival of a parcel of New Red Clover Seed, Madder, and Black Soap from Rotterdam—all of which will be ſold at very reduced prices for good payments.

North-ſtreet, Belfaſt, 12th March, 1789.

GENERAL ILLUMINATIONS.

The brilliancy and ſplendor diſplayed on this joyful occaſion, exhibit a convincing proof that loyalty and freedom live together.

The Earl of Hopetoun's was incomparably the beſt. The whole front of his ſuperb houſe was covered. The tranſparencies, only, coſt him 800l. The whole was not lighted, nor the ſcaffolding removed, till near one o'clock in the morning.

Drury-Lane and Covent-Garden were next in taſte and brilliancy. The diſpoſition was extremely ingenious, and the colours brilliant.

St James's-ſtreet was a blaze. The gaming-houſes vying with each other. Brookes's had the palm in taſte—White's in abundance.

Marlborough-ſtreet.——Lord Heathfield, who has a right to be fond of gunpowder, filled the ſtreet with fireworks.—His houſe had theſe three tranſparencies :—

"King George"——"Queen Charlotte"——"Happy Britons, and they know it."

Bloomſbury-ſquare.—The Duke of Bedford covered his wall with flambeaux ; Mr. Bootle was very ſplendid.

Gower-ſtreet.—Colman, Mrs. Siddons, Mr. Andrews, Mrs. Jordan ; indeed, every houſe in the ſtreet, flamed away from top to bottom.——Kemble, in the adjoining ſtreet, was as laviſh in his loyalty.

His Royal Highneſs the Prince of Wales evinced his happineſs on the re-eſtabliſhment of his Royal Father's health, by an elegant diſpoſition of flambeaux in the front of Carlton-houſe.

The houſes of the Dukes of York, Cumberland, and Glouceſter, were illuminated in the ſame manner.

Lane's Public Library, Leadenhall-ſtreet, was diſtinguiſhed by tranſparencies, which were neatly painted ; the Crown, emblazoned by the words, "Long live the King ;" underneath, richly ornamented, was wrote "Reſtored to his ſubjects," on each ſide the G. R. the upper parts relieved by lights, the whole forming a pleaſing appearance.

The ſtreets every where preſented a moſt ſingular picture. The train of carriages at one time extended from Oxford-ſtreet to the end of Pall-Mall ; from Charing-croſs to St. Paul's ; and from thence to the Exchange, and were at intervals ſo wedged in, as to be unable to move. The multitudes of people on each ſide in Bond-ſtreet, St. James's-ſtreet, and Pall Mall, were ſo numerous, that thoſe who got in, found ſome difficulty in getting out again.

Various parties were ſinging "God ſave the King!" Marrow bones and cleavers, and muſical bells were in rude ſerenade in various parts. Every child in London ſeemed out of doors ; and thoſe who could not walk were in the arms of their mothers. The bells in every church ſounded, and often in exploſions, ſuch as we have never heard before. Ordnance in various parts were diſcharging.

The Duke of Norfolk diſplayed the loyalty of his ſentiments in an eminent degree, by the brilliant appearance of his houſe in St. James's-ſquare.

Sir Joſeph Banks, in Soho-ſquare, had a moſt exquiſite painting, from the hand of *Hamilton*, of the King again receiving his crown! The likeneſs and finiſhing of the whole picture moſt perfect. The motto under it, in truth, moſt appoſite—"Redeunt Saturnia Regna."

Sir Sampſon Gideon's houſe in Arlington-ſtreet exceeded every thing of the kind ; the whole front of the houſe towards the Green Park was grand beyond conception ; above five hundred lamps of different colours diſplayed his MAJESTY's Arms, with LONG LIVE THE KING, in large capital letters ; and at the top the crown was formed with great taſte, of a vaſt variety of beautiful coloured lamps : the whole had a ſtriking and noble appearance from the Green Park and Piccadilly.

Martindale's Houſe in St. James's ſtreet cut a moſt brilliant appearance. The other public Coffee-Houſes in St. James's ſtreet were more or leſs brilliant.

Mr. Brodie, of Carey-ſtreet, placed in the opening before his houſe a large ſhip-ſtove, on a curious conſtruction, which roaſted, boiled, and baked at the ſame time. The funnel was decorated with variegated lamps, and made to repreſent a Chineſe pagoda : the novelty attracted an immenſe number of perſons to the ſpot, who liberally received roaſted and boiled beef, with plumb-pudding, dreſſed in this ſingular machine ; plenty of porter, was likewiſe diſtributed.

LONDON-DERRY, Feb. 24.

Since our laſt, arrived the ſhip Sally, Captain Miller, from Philadelphia ; the brig Keziah, Captain Brown, in 26 days, from Wilmington ; alſo the brig Maria, Capt. Fort, from do.

TOBACCO.——Within theſe few months, there have been landed in this port, from America, 356 hhds. of tobacco, making 377,915 lb. which at the duty of 1s. per lb. will be ſeen to produce an handſome revenue to Government, and ought not to paſs unnoticed in the Houſe of Commons, where certain perſons ſeem to be fond of ſpeaking diſreſpectfully of the city of Derry.——Beſide the above, there were 79,168 lbs. of tobacco ſold by inch of candle in the Cuſtom-houſe.

On the 12th inſt. a man of the name of O'Brien was murdered near Ballybofey. The murderer, who is ſaid to be an Edward Briſland, has made his eſcape ; he was born in Glenfin, aged 45 years, about 5 feet 7 inches high, freſh complexion and ſtrong made.

Married, the Rev. Mr. M'Kay, Preſbyterian Miniſter of Brigh, near Stewartſtown, to Miſs Elizabeth Neſbit of Rathmelton.

Died, Miſs Shannon, eldeſt daughter of Mr. John Shannon, organiſt of St. Columb's Cathedral.

Belfaſt.

At the requeſt of a CORRESPONDENT we inſert the following.

To the PRINTER of the NEWRY CHRONICLE

SIR,

I HOPE ſome of your engenious and learned Readers will conſider the following, and let me ſee a Grammatical Anſwer to the ſame, in your entertaining Paper as ſoon as poſſible.

Quere—whether the Engliſh Adjective Participle (Situate) can with propriety, according to the nature of the Engliſh, be uſed in a paſſive ſignification, though we have many examples in good Authors ; as, a houſe pleaſantly ſituate : the eye is artificially compoſed, and commodiouſly ſituate.

IGNORAMUS.

To the PRINTER of the NEWRY CHRONICLE.

SIR,

YOUR obliging condeſcenſion in publiſhing for Ignoramus a Query, too inſignificant for the notice of the *Learned*, induces me to hope you will, through the ſame channel of uſeful intelligence, preſent the *engenious* Queriſt with the following anſwer.

——" *Cadentque*
Quæ nunc ſunt in honore vocabula, ſi volet uſus,
Quem penes arbitrium eſt, et jus, et norma loquendi."

——" And ſhall words preſume
To hold their honours and immortal bloom ?
Many ſhall riſe, which now forgotten lie ;
Others, in preſent credit, ſoon ſhall die,
If cuſtom will ; whoſe arbitrary ſway,
Words, and the forms of language, muſt obey."

Ancient Authors of the higheſt rank have uſed participial adjectives, ſuch as *ſituate*, incorporate, elate, in the place of paſſive participles ;—but modern writers, poets excepted, who claim a peculiar licence to themſelves, reject, as obſolete, ſuch a mode of expreſſion. *Dr. Lowth* admits it may be uſed in common diſcourſe ; yet, with becoming deference to ſuch great authority, I ſhall venture to aſſert, that the uſe of the term muſt at preſent appear pedantic in poetry, affected in proſe, and vulgar in converſation.

Newry, 22d Feb. 1789. DISCIPULUS.

Diſcipulus is received, and when he pleaſes to ſend a grammatical anſwer to Ignoramus, (who requires only a grammatical anſwer) it ſhall appear in this paper.——Newry Chronicle.

Whether the Anſwer to Ignoramus be too ungrammatical for the NEWRY CHRONICLE, Diſcipulus humbly appeals to the unbiaſſed judgment of the candid Public.

LENT ASIZES.
NORTH-WEST CIRCUIT.

Co. Weſtmeath, at Mullingar, March 16.
Longford, at Longford, Thurſday 19.
Cavan, at Cavan, Monday 23.
Fermanagh, at Enniſkillen, Friday 27.
Tyrone, at Omagh, Wedneſday April 1.
Donegall, at Liſford, Friday 10.
And City of Derry, at Derry, Thurſday 16.

Lord Chief Baron Yelverton, Hon. Juſtice Henn, } Juſtices.
John Naſh, Eſq; Bride-ſtreet, Wm. Harriſon, Eſq; Exchequer-ſtreet, } Regiſters.

The Grand Juries of the counties of Weſtmeath and Cavan will be ſworn at ten o'clock in the morning on each of their reſpective Commiſſion Days, and the Records in each of the counties will be proceeded on the next morning after the Commiſſion Days.

MARKET-HOUSE, BELFAST, 7th March, 1789.

AT a Meeting of the Belfaſt Firſt Volunteer Company, Mr. DAVID DINSMORE in the Chair, Reſolved Unanimouſly, that this Company will turn out in full uniform on Tueſday the 17th inſtant, at 12 o'clock, in order to celebrate our *Eleventh* Anniverſary, and to elect Officers for the enſuing year.

Signed by order
DAVID DINSMORE, Chairman.

MARCH 9. 1789.

AT a Meeting of Deputies appointed by the three Volunteer Corps of Belfaſt—the following Requiſition was unanimouſly agreed to :

There having been no Aſſembly of Delegates at the concluſion of the Belfaſt Review of 1788—A Meeting of Repreſentatives from ſuch Corps as think proper, is with much deference requeſted, on Tueſday the 17th inſtant, at the Donegall-Arms, for the purpoſe of collecting the ſenſe of the neighbouring Companies and Troops on the ſubject of Reviews for the preſent year.

Signed by Order of the ſeveral Deputies of the Belfaſt Corps.

WAD. CUNNINGHAM, for the Belfaſt 1ſt Co.
WILLIAM BROWN, for the Belfaſt Vol. Co.
CHARLES RANKEN, for the Belfaſt Troop of Dragoons.

The ſhip, Iriſh Volunteer, John Johnſton, maſter, from Larne with paſſengers, arrived at Charleſtown the 1ſt December, after a pleaſant paſſage of ſeven weeks and five days.

Died, on the 4th inſtant, at his ſeat in Thomaſtown, in the county of Down, John Echlin, Eſq. a gentleman whoſe benignity of temper, and goodneſs of heart, in every ſituation and relation of life, moſt juſtly endear him to all who had the pleaſure of knowing him.—Alſo, at Bmena, near Holywood, univerſally regretted by his acquaintances, JAMES HAMILTON, Eſq.

The Lord Chancellor has been pleaſed to appoint James Falls, of Aughnacloy, in the county of Tyrone, merchant, a Maſter Extraordinary for taking affidavits in the High Court of Chancery.

A General Board of the Belfaſt Incorporated Charitable Society, will be held at the Poor Houſe, on Wedneſday the 11th inſt. at 12 o'clock at noon.

Belfaſt, March 9th, 1789. WILLIAM BRISTOW, V. Preſident.

MR. LYNCH having failed in his firſt attempt, begs leave to inform his Friends, that his ſecond is fixed for WEDNESDAY the 11th March, inſt. at which time he hopes for their countenance and protection—when will be preſented the celebrated Comedy of the BROTHERS, and the muſical Farce of the FARMER. Tickets to be had, and places for the boxes to be taken, of M. Lynch, at Mr. M'Maſter's, Snugborough, North-ſtreet.

MISS HOSKIN, begs leave to inform the Ladies and Gentlemen of Belfaſt, and its vicinity, that her Benefit is fixed for FRIDAY the 13th Inſt. at which time will be performed the Play of MUCH ADO ABOUT NOTHING, with the Farce of the HOTEL.

Tickets to be had and places for the Boxes, to be taken of Miſs Hoſkin, at Captain Engliſh's, Princes-ſtreet. Belfaſt, March 9th, 1789.

*** *By very particular deſire*—For the BENEFIT of MR. CHALMERS—on Wedneſday, March 18th, will be performed the BEGGAR's OPERA—the part of Capt. Macheath by Mrs. Chalmers.—End of the Play, *Bucks have at ye All*—(for the firſt time) by Mrs. Chalmers—To which will be added the Farce of *The Way to keep Him*.—The whole to conclude with a Pantomimical Venture, call'd, *Neck or Nothing* ; or, *Harlequin's Flight from the Gods*.—Harlequin by MR. CHALMERS—in which character he will riſe from the back of the Stage to the top of the Theatre over the Gallery, and return head foremoſt over the Pit to the back of the Stage.

Chalmers, apprehenſive his taking a ſecond Benefit, (though at the requeſt of ſome particular Friends,) might by the Public in general be conſidered an intruſion ; begs permiſſion to inform them, his emoluments from the Theatre are the ſame and no more than pertains to any other member of the Company, for both Actor and Harlequin. In conſideration of the latter therefore, he ventures to comply with the wiſhes of his Friends, and ſolicits the patronage of the Public on the above occaſion, whoſe favours will be ever moſt gratefully acknowledged and remembered.

Mr. BYRNE reſpectfully informs his friends and the public, that his Benefit is fix'd for Monday next, when will be preſented the Comedy of DUPLICITY.——With the Farce of the INTRIGUING FOOTMAN.

☞ *A well circumſtanced Eſtate, Leaſehold Intereſt, Houſe and Furniture——to be SOLD BY AUCTION*—by the Aſſignees of James Maxwell, a bankrupt, on Thurſday the ſecond day of April next, at the houſe of the ſaid James Maxwell in the town of Armagh, all the ſaid bankrupt's eſtate and intereſt in the lands of Roſebrook near ſaid town, being an eſtate for ever, ſubject to neither quit or crown rent or tythes, part of which is ſet for 71l. a year, and the part to ſet is worth and would ſet for 50l. a year to a ſolvent tenant. It is unneceſſary to deſcribe it further, as its ſituation is ſo well known.—Alſo will be ſold, ſaid bankrupt's intereſt in the lands of Ballyduff and Tamlettee, in the county of Armagh, being a term for years renewable, held under the See of Armagh, ſubject to about 81 a year. Alſo ſaid bankrupt's intereſt in the lands of Cammon, in the county of Tyrone, ſituate within three miles of Omagh, held for three lives, two of whom are in being, and which lands now produce a profit rent of 21l. 6s.—Alſo ſaid bankrupt's intereſt in a well ſecured profit rent of 12l. a year in the town of Newry, for bankrupt's life.—At ſame time will be ſold, the intereſt in the houſe wherein the ſaid James Maxwell now reſides in Armagh, of which there are about 16 years to come, and ſubject only to 20l. a year, and for which ſaid Maxwell paid a large fine. As alſo all the ſaid James Maxwell's houſehold furniture, &c.—The particulars relating to ſaid premiſſes will be explained at the time of ſale ; and in the mean time, any information deſired will be given by applying to the ſaid James Maxwell, at Armagh, to his Aſſignees Mr. John Lyndſey of Jervis-ſtreet, and Mr. Barth. Maziere of Mary's-Abbey, or Mr. Wm. Coſgrave Capel-ſtreet, Agent to the Commiſſion, in Dublin. And all perſons who have any lien or demand againſt any of ſaid premiſſes are required to furniſh an account thereof to the ſaid Aſſignees, on or before the 20th of March next, and all perſons indebted to the eſtate of the ſaid James Maxwell are requeſted to pay their reſpective debts to the Aſſignees, or to Mr. Thomas Prentice, Mr. James Lowry, or Mr. Samuel Brown of Armagh, aforeſaid, who are empowered by the Aſſignees to receive the ſame. 27th Feb. 1789.

London Porter.

SAMUEL and ANDREW Mc. CLEAN, have juft received per the Lord Donegall, a few Hogfheads Whitbread's beft Porter, which will be fold on reafonable terms.——They are (as ufual) well fupplied with every Article in the Spirit Line;—alfo with Port, Claret, Sherry, Frontiniac, Sweet Mountain, and Porter in bottles.——Belfaft, 16th March, 1789.

☞ The Houfe and Shop at prefent occupied by Mr. Mooney, next to Mr. Patterfon's, in High-ftreet, (juftly efteemed among the firft fituations in this Town for Bufinefs) to be let, either together or feparately, from the firft of May next. Apply as above.

Thorn Quicks.

ROBERT SMITH, No. 32, Bridge-ftreet, had advice this day from Dublin, that a frefh fupply of Thorn Quicks for him left that place on Wednefday laft, and may reafonably be expected—To-morrow or Wednefday next at fartheft.

Belfaft, 16th March, 1789.

N B. In a few days afterwards he will receive a quantity of fine large three Year-olds.

The Ship St. James, Mark Collins, Commander,

IS arrived from New-York with Flaxfeed, Pot Afhes of the firft Quality, and Staves, which will be fold on reafonable Terms, by

JONES, TOMB, JOY & Co.

Belfaft, 16th March, 1789.

The Belfast Hunt,

DINE at the Donegall-Arms, on St. Patrick's-Day. Dinner on the Table at five o'clock.

JAMES HOLMES, Prefident.

Belfaft, 14th March, 1789.

Elopement.

THIS is to give notice that my wife Jean Sample, otherwife M'Leane, hath eloped from me without any lawful caufe;—I therefore affure the public that I will not pay any thing fhe may contract from this date.—— Given under my hand this 8th day of March, 1789.—Caftledawfon.

JAMES M'LEANE.

WHEREAS my wife Jane Johnfton, alias Gamble, hath eloped from me without any caufe given by me, and carried off money and goods to a confiderable amount: This is to caution the publick not to credit her on my account, as I will not pay any debts fhe may hereafter contract.

Dated at Iflandreagh, 14th March, 1789.

ROBERT GAMBLE.

I TAKE this method requefting the public will not credit Rofe Wiley, otherwife Adams my wife, as we are parted for very fufficient reafon, and am determined not to pay any debts fhe may contract

Ballymacaret near Belfaft, March 16th, 1789.

County of Armagh.} AT a numerous meeting of refpectable Freeholders, at a full county court held in the Court-houfe of Armagh, purfuant to notice thereof, on Tuefday the 10th day of February laft, for the purpofe of electing a Coroner for faid county in the room of Robert Livingfton, Efq; refigned and fuperfeded at his own requeft; I am authorized and requefted by the Freeholders then and there prefent, as well as many others who could not attend, to return their fincere thanks to the faid Robert Livingfton, for his very upright and impartial conduct as a Coroner during the time he continued in faid Office.

And at the fame time Mr. John Johnfton of New-ftreet, in the city of Armagh, being put in nomination, he was unanimoufly elected a Coroner of faid county, in the room of the faid Robert Livingfton, Efq, and was then and there in open court fworn into office accordingly.

Dated March 2d, 1789.

STOLEN,

ON Monday the 9th inft. out of the Stable of Patrick O'Mullan of Loughgeel, near Ballymoney, A Black MARE in Foal, with a ftar and fnip, cut tail not fet, about fourteen hands high. Any perfon who will return faid Mare to Mr. Mc. Guckan, Ballymoney, fhall receive one Guinea Reward, or for Mare and Thief, three Guineas, on profecuting the Thief to conviction.

Loughgeel, March 12th, 1789.

Royal Sport of Cockfighting.

THERE will be a Main of thirty-one Cocks, and fifteen Byes, fhewn in the Town of Newtown-Ards the 4th day of April, and fought the week following, between the Gentlemen of the county of Down and Antrim,—For Fifty Guineas the Main or odd Battle.

To be Let from the 1ft of May next, A large NEW STORE:

IT confifts of three Floors, and is fituated at the End of Johnfton's Entry, oppofite the New Bank, in Ann-ftreet.——Application to be made to the Proprietors, H. Joy & Co.

Belfaft, March 20th, 1789.

THE Sovereign requefts a Meeting of the Burgeffes and principal Inhabitants, on Saturday next, in the Town-houfe, exactly at 12 o'clock—to confider of a congratulatory Addrefs to his Majefty on the joyful event of his recovery.

Belfaft, March 19, 1789.

James Hutcheson, Colerain,

HAS juft received his general Affortment of New Garden Seeds, early Peas and Beans, &c. which, with his ufual Affortment of Groceries, he will fell cheap for ready Money.

14th March, 1789.

J. WILLIAMSON, Land Surveyor and Draughtfman,

WILL attend at Carrickfergus during the Affizes, for the purpofe of receiving any Commands he may be favoured with in the line of his profeffion, for the enfuing feafon.

Ballymena, 16th March, 1789.

To be Sold by Inch of Candle,

AT the Cuftom-Houfe, Downpatrick, on Saturday the 28th inftant, upwards of one Ton of very good Tobacco, and ten Ankers of excellent Brandy.

Newcaftle, dated 18th March, 1789.

To be lent on landed Security,

TWO THOUSAND POUNDS fterling upon the firft day of June next.——Application to be made to David Gordon, Attorney at Law, or to Mr. Patrick Connor, at his Office, Belfaft.

18th March, 1789.

THE Sale of BARILLA, (advertifed in our laft) for the 24th inft. at Killough in the County Down, is put off till further Notice.

Belfaft, March 20th, 1789.

DROPP'D,

ON Tuefday the 17th inft. in the Fair of Down, A SILVER WATCH, of Goulding's make, London, No. 323.——Whoever brings it to N. F. Hull, Watchmaker, Downe, fhall receive half a Guinea Reward.

Downe, 18th March, 1789.

If offered for fale, it is requefted it may be ftopp'd, and the perfon detained.

To be Sold,

A Leafe for ever of a good Houfe and Offices, and thirty acres of Land, pleafantly fituated on the fea fhore, within half a mile of the Giants-Caufway. Application to be made to Mr. Lyle, Colerain:

March 10th, 1789.

To be Sold,

AT the Corporation-Arms, Hillfborough, exceeding good well-won HAY; alfo very good white HAY SEED, for Ready Money only.

March 19th, 1789.

Malting Coals.

A Small Cargo to be fold at the Salt-Works, from the Riccarton Pits near Kilmarnock:—This Coal is found to anfwer better for drying malt or grain than any hitherto found in Scotland.

Belfaft, 19th March, 1789.

District of Londonderry.} TO be fold by Inch of Candle, at the Cuftom-houfe of Londonderry, on Monday the 30th day of March inftant, at eleven of the clock in the forenoon, forty-five Hogfheads of Leaf Tobacco of a good quality.

Dated this 17th March, 1789.

ALEX. CUDDY, Regifter of Informations and Seizures.

Flax Premiums, 1789.

THE Truftees for the Linen and Hempen Manufactures having appropriated a Sum of Money to encourage the Growth of Flax and Hemp; and alfo a Sum of Money for promoting the Yarn Trade in the Province of Ulfter: Notice is hereby given, that the different Schemes of Premiums (when printed) will be diftributed by the County Infpectors, and Abftracts thereof publifhed in the Belfaft News-Letter.

J. GREER, Infpector General Ulfter.

Cotton Manufacture.

JAMES HOLMES & Co. at the Warehoufe in Waring-ftreet, late Nath Wilfon's, continue to receive every week frefh fupplies of the following Articles, viz.

All Cotton and Linen Thickfet—King and Queen's Corderoy, twill'd and plain—Sattinets, Denims, Pillow Fuftians, Jeans, and other plain Goods—printed Calicoes and Cottons of the neweft and moft fashionable pattern—Dimities, Muflinets, Muflins both chequed and ftriped—Cambrick and Kenting Handkerchiefs, and thick Cambrick.—All which they are determined to fell on lower terms than any Goods of equal quality in the kingdom.——They have a very large Stock of Machinery on hand, particularly Spinning Jennies—Looms and Harnefs—Roving Billies, &c. &c. which, as they have no farther occafion for them, they will fell on terms exceffively low.

Cafh or Bills at a fhort fight will always command fuch extra encouragement to the buyer as to make it an object well worth attention to come fo provided.

JAMES HOLMES & Co.

Belfaft, 13th March, 1789.

Advertifement.

THE Contractors for conveying his Majefty's Mails between Dublin and Belfaft, will run an elegant Poft Coach for reception of four infide and two outfide paffengers, only two days in every week, between Newry and Belfaft both ways, untill they take up the Mail, of which the public fhall have due notice, when a Coach will run feven times in every week between Dublin and Belfaft both ways; fare between Belfaft and Newry twelve fhillings and fix-pence Englifh. The Coach will fet out from Meffrs. M'Kean and Sheridan's, New-Inn, in Belfaft, (where places are to be taken) at eight o'clock in the morning on Tuefdays and Saturdays, and from the Globe-Inn, in Newry, (where places are alfo to be taken) at fame hour, on Sundays and Thurfdays.—The running to commence from Newry on Thurfday the 19th inft. and from Belfaft on Saturday the 21ft inftant.

Belfaft, 15th March, 1789.

N. B. Outfide paffengers to pay half fare—and paffengers travelling fhort of the whole way, (in cafe of room in the carriage) to pay five pence halfpenny per mile.

WE the underfigned Magiftrates, give this Notice to the Victuallers, and perfons keeping Inns and publick Houfes, within the Town and Liberties of Belfaft, that we will attend at the Sovereign's Office, adjoining the Market-houfe, on every Tuefday and Friday until the firft day of April, at 12 o'clock, for the purpofe of granting Certificates to entitle them to Licenfes from the Excife-Office.—They who apply for fuch Certificates muft be prepared with fufficient fureties, (if required) and authentick teftimonials of a fair character; as we are determined to give a preference to thofe perfons whofe paft conduct has met with the approbation of their neighbours, and who fhall be able to procure the beft fecurity, for maintaining peace and regularity in their houfes.

And to accomplifh fo defirable a work, as the fuppreffion of thofe publick houfes which are known to be diforderly; we moft earneftly call upon the principal inhabitants in every diftrict of the town; and particularly we charge all Peace Officers to make a candid reprefentation to us, as foon as poffible, of thofe houfes in particular which are not conducted in a regular and orderly manner;—and therefore do not merit a renewal of their Licence.

WILLIAM BRISTOW, Sovn. of Belfaft.
STEWART BANKS.
EZ. D. BOYD.

N. B. No Certificates will be figned but in the Sovereign's Office, at the days above-mentioned.

Belfaft, March 14th, 1789.

WE the Prifoners confined in the gaol of Down, acknowledge to have received from David Kerr, Efq. (by the hands of the Rev. John Dickfon and Dr. Macara) at different diftributions, the fum of Ten Guineas, for which humane and feafonable relief we beg to return him our moft grateful thanks.—At fame time give us leave to return our grateful thanks to the Rev. Mr. Dickfon and Dr. Macara for their very judicious diftributions of the above charitable donation.

Signed by order of the Prifoners,

JOSEPH ROBINSON, Gaoler.

TO BE LET,

AT May next, the Corner Houfe at the Head of Ann-ftreet, fronting the new-intended ftreet leading to the White Linen-Hall.—It confifts of a variety of good warm and convenient Rooms, with feveral neceffary fixtures, and locks and grates compleat, at prefent occupied by Mr. Hugh Lynden; if the tenant chufes he may have a ftable fit for five or fix horfes.

There is alfo to be let in the fame neighbourhood, a fmall Dwelling-Houfe, containing a kitchen, parlour, and two rooms above ftairs.——For further particulars enquire at the proprietor William Irwin.

SONG.

By Peter Pindar, Esq.

SINCE, Cynthia has left us how dark is our sky,
The hill and the vale how forlorn;
At her absence poor Zephyr moves on with a sigh,
And the Linnet sits mute on the thorn.

At morn when I wake, ah! unblest by repose,
And the dew on the herbage appears;
I think that the pastures partake in my woes,
That all Nature is covered with tears.

Now sunk on the grass, of the fair one I dream—
Now I muse by the riv'let alone:
Where methinks thus I hear the lorn voice of the stream,
" The pride of our valleys is gone."

Ah, say when will Nature her lustre resume,
And rapture return to each swain?—
When she who alone can enliven the gloom,
Shall visit those valleys again.

DUBLIN.

The petition of the bleachers and linen manufacturers of the counties of Armagh, Down, Antrim, Derry and Tyrone, which was presented to the House of Commons, 23d. ult. sets forth, that they have now the satisfaction to acquaint the house that they have every reason to believe that in consequence of the encouragement already afforded to the Tyrone collieries, the proprietors are thereby enabled to raise a sufficiency of coal for the supply of the bleachers and linen manufacturers in a great part of the counties of Armagh, Down, Antrim, Derry and Tyrone; that they cannot avail themselves of the great advantages that might be derived to their manufacture therefrom, from the want of an easy and ready communication between said collieries and the navigation; that turf, which has hitherto been the common firing of the country, is grown scarce and dear, and the bogs in many places so exhausted as to reduce the inhabitants already to use English sea coal, the price of which is too high for the manufacture; that fuel is used in large quantities in the linen business, particularly in the bleaching, and will be more so should the manufacture so far extend itself as that recourse must be had to steam engines for working their mills; that the price of turf is rising every year, and they express with great concern their apprehensions, that if an easy communication from the coal-pits to the navigation be not made before the bogs are exhausted, or the price of fuel so raised as to render it impossible for the manufacturers to purchase it, the manufacturers will quit that part of the country where the linen business is now fully established, and if once they quit it the petitioners need not state their apprehensions that it will be very difficult if not impossible to re-establish it there, and therefore praying relief.

The petition of John Staples and James Caulfield, Esqrs. which was presented to the House of Commons on Monday 23d. ult. sets forth, that they are proprietors of the collieries of Drumglass, near Dungannon, in the county Tyrone, that they have compleated their fire engine at the expence of more than 2000l. above the sum granted them by Parliament, and have the satisfaction to assure the house that it answers every purpose intended by it, they being thereby enabled to furnish the public with coals to any amount, and of a quality superior to any imported; that the petitioners have now on bank a very large quantity of coal, the advantage of which they cannot avail themselves of, for the want of an easy and cheap conveyance of them to the head of the Newry navigation, the present communication being tedious, difficult, and of course very expensive; that they conceive that the most certain and cheap mode of communication between Drumglass and said navigation would be by means of a road framed with timber, or a good gravel road, that they from the great expenses they have hitherto incurred, are not in a capacity to make such a communication; and therefore prayed the aid of the house in an undertaking in which the public utility; and particularly the linen manufacture of the north of Ireland. is so much interested.

DUBLIN, March 17.

Last night was exhibited, at Stephen's-green, in honour of his Majesty's recovery, the most extensive fire-works. They commenced about a quarter past eight o'clock, and continued until ten. Before the display of fire-works commenced, a Royal salute of 21 guns was fired by the train of artillery, and succeeded by three vollies, in running firing, by the regiments from the garrison, who formed a large square in the Green. When several devices of the fire-works had been played off, the regiments on a signal by a sky rocket, again gave three vollies.—The fire-works then continued, and terminated with the exhibition of a most beautiful transparency (amidst a radiant blaze of stars, festoons, sky rockets, &c.) of our gracious Monarch, rising from his chair under a canopy, and standing between two figures of Britannia and Hibernia. At this moment the regiments fired three more vollies, and was succeeded, as the conclusion of the whole, by another Royal salute from the artillery. On a moderate computation not less than fifty thousand spectators attended, on this joyful occasion, and who testified their heartfelt satisfaction, by acclamations that reverberated, to the sky. Every window in Stephen's-green appeared to be crowded with people of the first fashion and respect.

We are sorry to inform our readers, that Mr. Booth, who suffered under the merciless hands of the villain Cooper, as stated in a former paper, died yesterday morning in consequence of his wound. The retreat of the atrocious perpetrator of the deed remains still undiscovered, but it is earnestly to be wished may not long continue so.

Last Saturday night three villains stopped a gentleman in Townshend-street, and the alarm being given the Police were called, who instantly pursued the robbers, when one of them turning about, pulled out a pistol and shot a policeman dead. The culprits afterwards effected their escape.

LONDON-DERRY, March 17.

It is with the sincerest pleasure we inform the public, that in consequence of the laudable exertions of the Corporation to forward the erection of a Bridge over the River Foyle, Mr. Thompson and Mr. Cox, of Boston in New England, arrived in this city yesterday. They are strongly recommended for their knowledge of bridge building; and, we understand that they entertain not the smallest doubt of being able to construct a Bridge over our River upon the same plan of that which they lately erected near Boston.

The long-depending cause between the Co-heiresses of the late Counsellor Hamilton of Castlesin, and Rich. Cowan, late of Lifford, and John Cowan of London, his son, has been at length determined by the Lord Chancellor.—It was a bill filed in the year 1775 on behalf of the plaintiffs, who were minors, to set aside a purchase made by the defendant Richard, from the plaintiff's father. After the fullest investigation, which took up six days, the Lord Chancellor was pleased to set aside the sale, and to order that the defendant shall account for the profits which might have been made out of the estate during the time that the same has been out of lease.—The Attorney General, Prime Serjeant, Mr. Boyd, Mr. Burston, Mr. Stewart, and Mr. Warren were Counsel for the plaintiffs, and Mr. Galbraith their Agent; the Solicitor General, Mr. Duquery, Mr. Hutchinson, and Mr. Cantwell, were Council for the defendants, and Mr. Thomas Cowan their Agent.

The brig Sophia, which had been some time ago condemned by the Sub-Commissioners in Derry, has been lately cleared by the unanimous sentence of the Commissioners of Appeal in Dublin, and ordered to be restored to her owners.

A few days ago, the brig Washington, burthen 200 tons, and carrying 14 guns, was taken off the coast of Donegal, after a chase of three days, by the Beresford, Bushe, and Townshend revenue cruizers.—The above vessel is said to have been commanded by a Capt. Murphy of Drogheda, who was also the owner.—In the chace, the Washinton's main-mast went by the board, which was the cause of her being taken.

Died.] At the Mill of Convoy, Mr. Samuel Hayes.—In Derry, Mrs. Alexander, relict of the late Mr. Peter Alexander—Mr. Robert Fisher.

Belfast, March 20.

On Wednesday last the Belfast First Volunteer Company, with their Artillery Corps, assembled to make the annual election of Officers, and to celebrate the ELEVENTH Anniversary since their formation. After firing 19 guns by the Artillery, and three vollies by the small arms, they spent the day in festivity, and drank the following toasts:

Patrickmasday 1778, the Birth of this Company, and of the Volunteers of Ireland.—The King: may his reign be long, happy, and prosperous. [*three cheers*.]—Her Majesty: may she long be a living example of the domestic virtues, and an ornament to the throne.—The Prince of Wales and the rest of the Royal Family.—Lord Charlemont, the virtuous and illustrious head of the army of the people.—The Duke of Leinster and the other Irish Commissioners.—Mr. Grattan: and the virtuous part of the Parliament of Ireland.—Mr. Flood: a speedy restoration of his health.—Mr. Forbes: may the enormous pension list no longer be a satire on government, a shameful prostitution of the public purse, and an intolerable burthen on the nation.—The friends of Ireland in the British Parliament.—General, now Farmer Washington.—Mr. Pitt.—Equal liberty to all mankind.—The glorious Revolution of 1688; and may the spirit of our ancestors never cease to animate their descendants.—May the voice of the people prevail.—May the Volunteers of Ireland, when the rights of their country shall be at stake, appear with redoubled lustre, their numbers trebled, and discipline not impaired.—Short Parliaments, and a more equal representation of the people of Great Britain and Ireland.—Colonel Irwin and the Dungannon meeting of 1782.—The few surviving members of the Belfast Volunteer Company of 1745.—May the crowns of England and Ireland be long united by the only tie that can hold them—that of equal liberty.—The memory of our deceased members.—Colonel Banks and the Belfast Battalion.—Capt. Brown and the Belfast Volunteer Company.—Capt. Ranken and the Belfast Troop of Light Dragoons.—Messrs. Rowley and O'Neill, the faithful Knights of this Shire.—Messrs. Sharman and Jones.—Mr. Brownlow.—A speedy abolition of Slavery in the British West India Islands and all over the World.

We hear that a vessel is lost about the Maiden Rocks, near Larne, and all on board perished. It is apprehended she is from America, several barrels of apples and billets of hiccory-wood having drifted on shore.

With the illiberality that too often disgraces some Britons, a cariacature print is in circulation through London of the six Irish Commissioners. Our surprise is somewhat diminished when we recollect that the Sovereign of an empire, in the most afflicting malady to which humanity is liable, was in a similar manner deem'd a proper subject of ridicule.

In consequence of excessive intoxication, on account of the King's recovery, a young man was found suffocated in his bed on Tuesday morning.

We hear from Lisburn, that on Wednesday last, there was a general rejoicing on account of the happy recovery of his Majesty; the joy of the inhabitants was expressed by illuminations, bonfires and every other testimony of loyalty and affection to our Sovereign.

In a paragraph inserted in last paper, it was mentioned that the 15th regiment fired in consequence of an order from Government. We since find that that mark of their loyaly was not the consequence of any order from Government, but proceeded from their own wish to testify their happiness at the joyful event of his Majesty's recovery.

One of Mr. Grimshaw's apprentices to the printing business, was committed to the house of correction yesterday by the Sovereign of Belfast, for refusing obedience to *the orders* of his master.

Extract of a Letter from Banbridge, March 18.

" Yesterday in consequence of intelligence arriving here of the complete restoration of his Majesty's health, the most sincere joy was visible in every countenance. In the evening the Volunteer Company, commanded by Captain Law, paraded and fired three vollies;—a general illumination succeeded, which, from the situation of the town, had a most pleasing effect; and every other testimony of satisfaction was added, which could manifest the feelings of a loyal and affectionate people. In short, we may affirm, that, on no occasion have the zeal and attachment of faithful subjects been more conspicuous, than in the interest which all persons in this neighbourhood have taken in the indisposition and happy recovery of our beloved Sovereign."

Extract of a letter from Lough-Brickland, March 18.

" Last night the town of Lough-Brickland was illuminated, and a number of bonfires made on account of the happy recovery of his Majesty;—every denomination of people joined in the most sincere expressions of pleasure on this joyful occasion, and a number of the principal Gentlemen of the neighbourhood, after parading the town, adjourned to the tavern where the King, the Prince of Wales, the Queen and Royal Family, Lord Hillsborough, Lord Kilwarlin, Mr. Pitt, and many other loyal and patriotic toasts were drank."

In consequence of the joyful news of his Majesty's complete recovery and resuming the reins of government, the inhabitants of Newtown-ards, actuated by that loyalty and patriotic spirit which warms the hearts of a free and happy people, displayed their united gratitude for the restoration of their Sovereign's health, by a general illumination, bonfires, &c.——Among other devices which appeared in the windows, one particularly arrested the attention, viz. the Arms of Ireland, Hibernia on one side, the Harp on the other, the Crown on the top and the Union Flag waving below—alluding to the happy and inseparable connection of the two kingdoms under the same beloved Sovereign.—On many other windows there were mottos characteristic of the joys of the night, and of the spirit and loyal affection of the inhabitants.

The following notice from the Castle was sent to the Rev. Dr. Dunn of Dublin, and transmitted to the Rev. Dr. Crombie of Belfast, for the information of the public.

" Mr. Fitzherbert presents his compliments to Doctor
" Dunn, and has the honour to acquaint him that the
" prayers for his Majesty's recovery are in future to be
" discontinued in the established Church, and in lieu
" thereof, a thanksgiving is to be offered up for the pre-
" sent happy state of his Majesty's health; and Mr. Fitz-
" herbert is directed by the Lord Lieutenant to express
" his Excellency's confidence, that all his Majesty's sub-
" jects will joyfully concur in testifying their thankful-
" ness on this happy occasion. Dublin Castle, March
" 6th, 1789."

To save---is to gain !

MAGEE grateful for the many favours conferred on him by the Public, begs to acquaint them that they now have an Opportunity of supplying themselves with every Article in the

Stationary Bufiness,

Of the beft Quality, and on truly advantageous Terms, for ready Money, at the Warehoufe of

J. and W. MAGEE,

No. 9, BRIDGE-STREET, BELFAST.

That the Public of the Province of Ulfter may judge of the Advantages to be derived from a Wholefale and Retail Paper Warehoufe, eftablifhed upon the fame Principle of thofe found fo generally ufeful in the Capitals of this and the Sifter Kingdom—the following Prices are fubmitted to their Confideration :

LETTER PAPERS.	PLAIN. Qu.	Ream.	GILT. Qu.	Rea.	Superfine Red or Black Blazing SealingWax, hard or foft, 12 fticks to the lb. 10s. od. or 1s. 1d. per.
	s. d.	s. d	s. d.	s. d	
London Parliament	1 1	19 0	1 1	32 0	
Double Parliament	1 7	27 0	3	54 0	or 1s. 1d. per.
Dutch Demy	1 0	16 0	1 8	26 8	Superfine Wafers at 5s. 5d. per
London Thick Poft	0 11	16 0	1 8	25 0	lb. or 6d. per oz.
Dutch Thick Poft	0 9	13 0	1 6	22 9	
London Thin Poft	0 8½	11 11	1 4	17 0	Prime, Second
Beft Irifh Thin Poft	0 6½	9 0	1 0	15 0	and Flag Dutchified Quills and
Thick Lined Poft	1 1	18 0	2 0	32 0	Pens at various
Extra Thick Poft	1 1	19 0	2 0	32 0	Prices.
Extra Thin Poft	0 11	16 6	1 8	25 0	
FOLIO PAPERS.					Pruffian Blue Paper fo-
London Parliament	2 2	37 6			White Linen, &c. with
Dutch Demy	1 10	31 0			every fpecies of PAPER
London Thick Poft	1 10	31 6			BOOKS in various Ru-
Dutch Thick Poft	1 0	25 0			lings and Bindings, or
London Thin Poft	1 5	23 0			made to any Pattern at
Irifh Thin Poft	1 0	15 0			fhort Notice.
Superfi.Lon.Propa.	1 4	22 9			They have now for fale a
Lond. Britifh Arms	1 0	15 0			great Variety of ufeful
Irifh Propatria	1 0	15 0			and uncommon Writing,
8d. Propatria	0 8	10 0			Fillagree, and India Pa-
Fine 8d. Paper	0 8	10 0			pers, with feveral Arti-
Beft 6d. Paper	0 6	7 0			cles of Stationary not
Kitchen Paper	0 6	8 0			hitherto on Sale here.

☞ Not lefs than TEN Quires fold at Ream Price.

March 26th, 1789.

THERE will be a BALL, at the Market-Houfe in Carrickfergus, on Friday the 27th inftant, for the Benefit of fome Perfons in Diftrefs.

Carrickfergus, March 18th, 1789.

An Auction at Newry,

WILL commence on Thurfday, 26th day of March, 1789, by order of the Affignees of JOHN ANDERSON, a Bankrupt.

For the immediate Sale of a very extenfive Stock in Trade of faid Bankrupt, confifting of the following Goods, viz.

140 Pieces fuperfine, refine, and Livery Broad Cloths, from 5 to 25 yards in each.

150 Pieces Foreft Cloth, from 5 to 30 yards each.

60 Pieces Coating and Bath Rugg, from 5 to 40 yards

50 Pieces Wolton, from 10 to 30 yards.   [each.

700 Yards Flannel, and 500 yards Chequer.

56 Pieces Thickfets and Corduroy.

15 Pieces printed Velverets.

50 Pieces of Serge, and 6 Pieces of Jean.

30 Pieces of Welboar Stuff.

50 Pieces Durants.

25 Pieces Callimancoes.

300 Yards Bed Ticken.

70 Pieces printed Cotton and Linen.

15 Dozen Silk Handkerchiefs.

700 Groce Metal Buttons.

with feveral other articles too numerous to infert ; and at fame time will be fold, the Bankrupt's houfehold furniture—alfo, his intereft in two houfes and a tenement, all in the town of Newry ; the particulars of which will be fet forth in hand bills.

PAT. DUFFIN, Parliament-ftreet, Dublin.

N. B. Approved bills on Dublin will be taken for 20l. or upwards.

The Lurgan Whift Club,

DINE at the Black Bull Inn, on Monday the 30th inftant.——Dinner on the Table at five o'clock.

20th March, 1789.

WM. BROWNLOW, junr. in the Chair.

Signed by Order,

JOS. DESVAEUX, Sec.

LOST,

BETWEEN Belfaft and Antrim, (Templepatrick Road) A fmall Cafe, containing a miniature Picture. Any perfon who has found, on returning it at Mr. Joy's Office, fhall receive two Guineas Reward.

Lisburn Diftrict.

ALL Retailers of Ale, Wine, Dealers in Spirits, Manufacturers of Tobacco, Soap or Candies, Grocers, Tanners, Spirit Factors, Makers or Sellers of Gold and Silver Plate, Hawkers, Pedlars, and all defcriptions of perfons in the faid diftrict who are by law directed to pay for Licences to carry on their trades or occupations, are defired to obferve, that Offices will be held on the days and at the places undermentioned, for the purpofe of collecting the duties on licences for the year commencing the 26th March inftant.

And as the new regulations have multiplied the Licence bufinefs with numerous books and voluminous papers, very inconvenient to be carried abroad ; it is expected that the whole licence duty will be paid and done away at the offices hereby appointed, for afterwards there will not be a Licence granted at any of the out offices of the diftrict during the courfe of the year.

Carrickfergus and Templepatrick,	At Carrickfergus, on Friday 3d April.
Belfaft,	Thurfday the 2d. Saturday the 4th. Monday & Tuefday 6th & 7th Ap.
Dromore, Moira, & Hillfborough,	At Hillfborough, Thurfday the 9th.
Lifburn,	At Lifburn, on Saturday 11th.
Loughbrickland and Banbridge,	At Banbridge, Monday 13th.

Excife-Office, Hillfborough, March 25th, 1789.

JOHN SLADE, Collector.

Eafter Plate.

TO be run for over the Maze, on Eafter Tuefday next, TEN POUNDS, given by the Earl of Hillfborough for Three-years-old, bred in the County of Down, the beft of three two-mile heats.—Colts 8ft. Fillies 7ft. 11lb. Non-fubfcribers to pay five Guineas entrance—all to go to the winner ; to ftart at one o'clock.

NICHOLAS PRICE, Governor.

March 23d, 1789.

TO BE LET,

FROM the firft day of May next, for fuch term of years as may be agreed upon, an excellent Houfe in Glenarm Town, with a good Garden and Offices, now occupied by David Mc. Killip, Efq;——Propofals to be received (in writing only) by Phill. Gibbons, at Carnlaugh.   23d March, 1789.

GEORGE BRADFORD,
At the Poft-Office,

TAKES the liberty of informing his friends and the public, that he intends removing to the Houfe next door to where he now lives, formerly poffeffed by the late Mrs. Collyer ;—where he will be conftantly fupplied with an extenfive and elegant affortment of Rich, Cut, and Plain GLASS ; alfo the neweft and moft fafhionable Patterns of China, Delft, &c.—all which he is enabled and determined to fell on the very loweft terms.

N. B. The Shop he now lives in, with counters, fhelves, &c. and ftores adjoining, to be fet from the firft of May, for the term of eight years from the firft of Auguft next.

For particulars apply to faid Bradford.

Belfaft, 22d April, 1789.

For the Benefit of Mifs VALOIS,

ON Wednefday the 25th of March, (by particular Defire) will be performed, the Comic Opera of

INKLE and YARICO,

With Entertainments of Dancing, by Mr. Lynch and Mifs Valois.

To which will be added the favourite Farce of the

SON-IN-LAW.

Tickets to be had and places in the Boxes taken of Mifs Valois, at Mr. Huggard's, Mill-ftreet.

Belfaft, 23d March, 1789.

Mifs HOSKIN,

BEGS leave to inform the Ladies and Gentlemen of Belfaft and its Neighbourhood, that her Benefit is deferr'd till Monday the 30th inftant, when will be performed a Play, Farce, and Entertainments as will be expreffed in the Bills—when fhe hopes for their patronage and protection, which will ever be moft gratefully acknowledged and remembered.

Belfaft, March 23d, 1789.

THE Election of a Steward and Houfekeeper for the Poor-Houfe, is poftponed until the General Board of the Charitable Society, which will be held in May next—of which notice will be given in this Paper.

Poor-Houfe, March 18th, 1789.

By Defire of the Prefidents,

THE BELFAST COTERIE will be held at the Exchange-Rooms, on Monday next the 30th inftant.

March 27th, 1789.

Old Cotton Manufactory.

FRANCIS JOY, and CO. have for Sale, at their Ware-houfe in Rofemary-lane, a large Affortment of the following Goods, Viz.

Printed Cottons and Calicoes,	Mock do.
Shawls and Handkerchiefs,	Dimities, Muflinets,
Printed Linens,	Lining, Jeans, & Fuftians,
Marfeilles Quilting,	Cotton Wrappers, &c &c.

As the ftricteft attention is given to the manufacturing and printing, they are enabled to fell the above Goods as cheap as any other Ware-houfe in the kingdom. Every encouragement will be given to thofe who buy with cafh or approved bills at fhort date.

Belfaft, 27th March, 1789.

Wanted,

A Middle aged Man as Poftillion on the 1ft of May next——Apply to Mr. Ranken, Richmond-lodge.

March, 27th 1789.

Wheat Straw.

A Quantity of Wheat Straw to be fold by Robert Johnfton of Derriaghy, at 13d. per Thrave.

March 25th, 1789.

Wanted immediately,

AN APPRENTICE to the Apothecary Bufinefs.—— Apply to Rober Chambers, Downpatrick.

Downe, 25th March, 1789.

Money Matters.

TWENTY Thoufand Pounds ready to be advanced in different Sums on Freehold Land.——Any part of the above fum not lefs than 200l. will be advanced on the fecurity of infurance ; the borrower to have his life infured, and the policy to be lodged with the lender.

Any perfon that applies on the fecurity of infurance, muft mention age, line of life, and refidence.—Inviolable fecrecy will be obferved if requefted—no agent or any perfon but the principal will be treated with. Perfons under age, heirs to eftates or property, may be accommodated.——Direct, poft paid, to G. W. Hankey, Efq; near Clapham, Surry.

GRAZING,

AT BALLYNAFOY, either for Horfes or Cows, to be immediately let.——Application to be made to Henry Joy & Co.

Belfaft, 23d March, 1789.

William Auchinleck,

HAVING been admitted a Notary Publick, and appointed to grant Replevins for the county of Antrim,—begs leave to affure his friends and the publick, that he will duly attend to the duties of thefe Offices ; and that he continues to draw up wills, affidavits, claims on bankrupts, deeds of partnerfhip, affignments, and fuch other inftruments in writing as he may find himfelf equal to ; that he will attend the infpecting of tobacco as ufual, and execute commiffions in that line.—With the moft heart-felt gratitude he embraces this opportunity of returning his unfeigned thanks, for the kind attention of his friends, and for the encouragement he has met with from the publick, whofe further favour he folicits, and hopes by his care to merit.

Belfaft, 19th March, 1789.

To be Sold by Auction,

ON Wednefday the 1ft of April, and the following days, at the Brown Bear, High-ftreet, Belfaft—A great variety of houfehold furniture, confifting of four-poft and field bedfteads, a fet of mahogany Northumberland tables, ditto card and round tables, ditto a fideboard table, three handfome defks, double and fingle chefts of drawers, bafon ftands, fpider-leg tables, tea boards and tea chefts, looking glaffes in burnifhed gold frames, ditto oval and fquare ditto, filver candlefticks and fervers, ditto tumblers, ditto table and tea fpoons, all fterl. filver handled knives and forks, two pair of plated candlefticks, two pair of handfome cut glafs decanters, two dozen of wine glaffes, feveral fets of India china, a fowling piece, an eight day clock, a jack and weights, a great affortment of chairs, and many other articles too numerous to mention. The fale to begin at 11 o'clock at noon, and continue till all are fold, by

JOHN PARROCK, Auctioneer.

LONDON, March 19—20.

ST. PATRICK'S DAY.

THURSDAY, a numerous and splendid meeting of Irish Nobility and Gentry, assembled at the London Tavern, Bishopsgate-street, to commemorate the festival of their Patron Saint. About six o'clock his Royal Highness the Duke of York honoured the company with his presence, and an elegant dinner was served up. Among those present, were Lords Rawdon (Chairman) Barrymore, Corke, Dungarvan; Mess. Burke, Sheridan, St. Leger, Captain O'Brien, &c. After dinner, the following toasts were given:

The King, and may his restoration be long remembered by a grateful people.

The Queen and Royal Family.

His Royal Highness the Prince of Wales.

(This being received with marked approbation, the Duke of York rose, and expressed, in his Brother's name, "that the *signal marks* of *affection* he had received from the Irish nation were such as never could be effaced.)

His Royal Highness the (Duke of York) Earl of Ulster, was then given, which he politely returned, by drinking the Benevolent Society.

The Irish Commissioners.

The City of London.

The Land we live in.

The united Trade of Great Britain and Ireland,—and many other constitutional toasts.

Afterwards the children supported by the Charity, were brought up, and a collection made by Lord Dungarvan, &c. to the amount of 750l. above 200l. more than at any former meeting. In the course of the evening several excellent songs were given by Kelly, Dignum, Sedgwick, and Robinson. Old Macklin sung, and was much attended to, and a song on the institution was given by Mr. O'Reilly. At half past nine his Royal Highness withdrew, 'midst the warmest acclamations for the honour he conferred; and the evening concluded with the greatest harmony and festivity.

The Duke of York accepted of the President's Chair for the ensuing anniversary, and Messrs. Burke and Sheridan are among the Stewards elect.

This day se'nnight her Majesty will appear at St. James's. His Majesty has expressed wishes to take a jaunt to Hanover in the summer, thinking the change of air will be conducive to the compleat restoration of his strength.

It is confidently said, that a match is in agitation, and will be proposed by his Majesty to the Prince of Wales. The Lady is unexceptionable in point of youth, beauty, mental accomplishment and royal rank in Europe.

His Royal Highness is grown amazingly corpulent, his exercise not being now near so great or regular as it was last summer. He seems well pleased that he escaped being Regent; for he was under such promises when in power, that he would have found it a difficult matter to keep his party together.

The preparations for building the new bridge across the river Liffey, from Aston's-quay to the Batchelor's-walk, are going forward: A piece of ground is enclosed on the north side, for the mason's yard. This bridge, we hear, it is proposed to open for the public passage, on the first of May, 1790.

On an authentic account of the King's recovery having arrived at Monaghan, a part of the Monaghan Rangers dined together, and displayed their flag in testimony of their joy on the happy occasion, and in the evening gave a bonfire and beer to the populace.

Died yesterday morning at 4 o'clock, the Right Hon. Owen Wynne, representative in Parliament for the borough of Sligo—governor of the county, custos rotulorum of the country Leitrim, a trustee of the linen-board, &c. The amiability of his manners, and the sincerity of his disposition endeared him to an extensive circle of acquaintance. His family towards the close of the last century, settl:d in the co. Sligo, and almost all the improvements that have been made in that quarter, were the effects of their influence. Besides two members for the borough of Sligo, he generally returned one member for the county; and his interest generally preponderated in the same manner in the co. Leitrim.

Owen Wynn, Esq; his eldest son, a deserving young gentleman, succeeds to the estate, which is between five and six thousand a year.

DOWN ASSIZES.

At the Assizes held for the county of Down, Patrick Campbell was found guilty of picking the pocket of James Smyth in Newry of 1l. 14s. 8d. and sentenced to be hanged the 9th of May next.

At the above assizes, addresses to his Majesty and the Lord Lieutenant were agreed to, in the name of the Nobility, Clergy, High Sheriff, Grand Jury and Gentry of the County of Down.

There is to be built for the County of Down, a Goal, with a *bath*, a *stove*, and other requisites, ordered by the late act of Parliament, agreeable to the ideas of Mr. Howard. This humane plan will be carried into effect without encreasing the burthen of taxes on the county.

Extract of a letter from Carrickfergus, dated the 19th instant.

"On Tuesday last the news of his Majesty's happy recovery having reached this place, the inhabitants assembled in the evening, to testify their joy on that occasion, attended by Sir William Kirk the Mayor, who ordered abundance of ale and spirits to be distributed among the populace. The evening concluded with bonfires and illuminations, expressive of the sincere pleasure which every member of this ancient and loyal corporation feel on that happy event."

For the information of Gentlemen in the Linen Manufacture, and others who use Kelp, we insert the following:

Extract of a Letter from Downpatrick, dated 18th March, 1789.

"In consequence of the very desirable news of his Majesty's recovery being announced from authority, there was a general Illumination of this Town on Monday evening last—A Ball at the Market-house, and every demonstration of joy suitable to the occasion. In the course of the day three companies of the 61st regiment quartered at Killough, marched in and joined five companies of the same regiment quartered here, and fired three vollies on the same occasion.——It is but justice to say they made as fine an appearance as any troops in his Majesty's service, being exceedingly well appointed, and great attention paid to discipline and behaviour by their Officers.——The Volunteer Company of the Town also turned out, and fired three vollies."

We hear from Clough (a small estate belonging to David Ker, Esq. in the county of Down) that, during the inclemency of the winter season, that gentleman ordered the sum of 20l. 9s. 5d. to be divided by the Clergy of the different denominations of christians in that neighbourhood, amongst the poor of their respective flocks. When such instances of benevolent attention occur, to conceal would be injurious to the influence of laudable example, and robbing the philanthrophist of merited praise.

At the last Assizes at Downpatrick, an action was tried before Mr. Justice Hellen, wherein James Ripton was plaintiff and the Glass-house Company of this town defendants. It appeared that Ripton had sold to the defendants a quantity of Kelp made by him, and on trial it was found to be adulterated so much, that it would not answer the purpose of common Kelp; in consequence of which they offered to return it.—The plaintiff proceeded to recover payment by law: samples of the Kelp were produced in court, also 9½lb. *wt. of gravel and sand*, which was mixed in 30lb. of Kelp. The process was dismissed on the merits.

We are informed the defendants are resolved to sue for the penalty incurred by those who adulterate Kelp with sand, gravel or stones, which is 3l. per Cwt.

If purchasers of Kelp would be attentive in detecting frauds practised by the manufacturers of it in this country, it would be a mean of improving the quality of that useful article, at present so shamefully neglected—so much so, that it is often brought here from the remotest parts in the Highlands of Scotland, and sold at an advanced price.

A correspondent requests we may remind the importers, venders and retailers of spirits, that the 25th of March is past, and of course they have no time to lose in making their returns to the Collector.

The complete recovery of our amiable and much beloved Sovereign, was celebrated in Magherafelt on the evening of Thursday the 19th inst. by general illuminations, bonfires, and three vollies of the Volunteers in conjunction with the regulars quartered there; after which the principal gentlemen of the town adjourned to an Inn, where they concluded the evening with great harmony and festivity, and with many loyal and patriotic toasts.

LONDON-DERRY, March 24.

Yesterday the Corporation of this city resolved to present a loyal and affectionate Address to his Majesty, on his providential recovery and re-assumption of his Royal functions.

In consequence of the death of our Chief Magistrate, the rejoicings on account of his Majesty's happy recovery were postponed—but they are to take place to-morrow evening, when it is expected, that the illuminations will be general and brilliant.—On thursday evening, there will be a ball and supper for the Ladies.

Since our last arrived the brig Abigal, Capt. Hamis, from New-York, with flaxseed.

Since our last, the Engineers who lately arrived here from America, have founded the river across at the Ferry-quay, and we have authority in saying, that it is their decided opinion, a wooden bridge, on the construction of those lately erected near Boston, is very practicable at said place.

Died.] In London, Frederick Gregg, Esq; of this city.—At Rochester, in England, Henry Hart, Esq; late Major in the Army, and Lieutenant Governor of Sheerness Fort, by whose death a fortune of 2,000l. per ann. devolves to the Rev. Edw. Hart of Kilderry.

Died.] On Friday the 20th inst. sincerely and universally regretted, Squire Lecky, Esq; Mayor of this city; he had before, in the years 85 and 86, filled the important office of chief Magistrate with the highest honour to himself and with the fullest approbation of his fellow-citizens—his conduct having been distinguished by the most inflexible integrity, the most unremitting attention, and the most unbounded hospitality.—The painful anxiety shewn by all ranks of people during his illness, as well as the total suspension of every kind of amusement, strongly evinced the esteem and affection in which he was held—every friend and intimate knew and valued his *private* worth; every citizen felt and acknowledged his public virtue.

The annals of the corporation of Derry afford but one other instance of a person dying during the course of his Mayoralty—and 'tis remarkable, that that person was the great grandfather of our deceased chief Magistrate, Wm. Squire, Esq; who died suddenly on the 5th of Feb. 1693, just three days after his entrance into office.

On Saturday the corporation met, and, agreeably to the injunctions of the Charter, proceeded to the election of a Mayor: Thomas Bateson, Esq; was accordingly chosen to serve for the remainder of the year, and (as the Charter enjoins) immediately took the usual oaths—The many substantial virtues that mark the character of this gentleman, afford us every reason to expect, that, by a punctual discharge of his Magisterial duties, he will do honour to himself and give solid consolation to his fellow-citizens for that melancholy event which has occasioned his call into office.

TO THE MERCHANTS OF BELFAST.

Gentlemen,

SUPPOSE a man signs his name to a blank bill, which he desires another to fill up with whatever sum an invoice of goods which he had purchased might amount to, and accept,—but when the goods were delivered and examined, it appeared that they were of a very inferior quality to what had been purchased,—by what means can the acceptor avoid paying that bill?—Will the valuation of two respectable intelligent men, who swear the goods were not worth half the sum charged, together with an order from the drawer not to pay it, be sufficient?

MERCATOR.

Belfast, *March 24.*

At a respectable meeting of the Burgesses and principal Inhabitants of Belfast, convened by the Sovereign, at the Town House on Saturday, a loyal and dutiful address of congratulation to his Majesty on his happy recovery, was unanimously agreed to, and was sent to his Excellency the Lord Lieutenant for transmission.——An address to her Majesty on the same occasion, was also unanimously agreed to.

The following ships were spoken with at sea by the Christee of Greenock, Captain Johnston, from Jamaica on the 9th inst. bound to Belfast.——The Mally's, of and from London, Capt. Stevenson, the Symon of and from London Captain Gordon, long. 16. 50 W. lat. 50. 11. bound to St. David's Straits, all well.

It is with very particular pleasure that we inform the public of the arrival at London of the *Charlotte*, William Campbell master, with a valuable cargo of linens. She sailed from Belfast on the 12th ulto. and the account of her arrival did not reach this till Monday, 23d inst—so that there was no account of her for 5 weeks and 3 days—in such a series of bad weather that very little hopes were entertained of her safety.

A vessel from Sligo for Liverpool with oats, was lately lost on the Burbo Bank, near the Rock of Liverpool, all on board perished. Also, a vessel from Newry for Liverpool, laden with wheat, is on shore and full of water in Chester water—cargo damaged.

Extract of a letter from Newry, March 21.

"Last night the town and quay of Rostrevor were elegantly illuminated, as was also the town of Warrenpoint and its vicinity, when the inhabitants expressed the sincerest satisfaction on account of his Majesty's happy recovery. No person testifyed greater loyalty on the occasion than the Rev. George Rogers, who a second time illuminated his beautiful seat at Marli,—on the 6th inst. when he first received the joyful intelligence of his Majesty's returning health,—and again last night with the rest of the neighbourhood, when the whole country was in a blaze of joy.

At the instance of a Correspondent we insert the following.

The opposition to the payment of Tythes in the parish of Kilrea and county of London-Derry, which for some time had unfortunately prevailed, hath, through the spirit and humane disposition of Alexander Stuart Esq; the proprietor of that proportion, been happily and effectually subdued.

Equally predetermined to support his tenants if aggrieved—and the rights of the Rector if unjustly attacked—he entered upon an investigation of their complaints, with the steadiness, candour and benevolence of a man—and with all the condescension and politeness of a Gentleman.

But in the progress of the enquiry instead of oppression—behold lenity and indulgence!——and instead of extortion—moderation and generosity in the extreme!——Satisfied of this and of the fair and honourable conduct of the Rector, he generously became *his* advocate, and by a spirited mediation, effected a reconciliation with the people, and restored peace and harmony to the country. A noble example!—and worthy the imitation of every land-lord of rank, fortune and influence throughout the kingdom.

Married, on Saturday last, at the Revd. Mr. Lang's of Broughshane, James Lendrick of Shanes-Castle Esq. to Miss Alder of Dublin.

Died, at Belfast, Miss Rea.—At Spring-hill, Moneymore in the county of Londonderry, David Conyngham, Esq. late of Belfast.—Mrs. M'Kibben of this town.—At Tullycarnet, Miss Katherine Montgomery.

"Early, bright, transient, chaste as morning Dew—
"She sparkled, was exhal'd and went to Heav'n."

Young.

*** Several accounts of rejoicings at Downpatrick, Carrickfergus, &c. unavoidably postponed till next day.

Anno 1789.]   Printed by HENRY JOY, and Co. BELFAST.

The BELFAST NEWS-LETTER.

TUESDAY March 31,   FRIDAY April 3, 1789.

NOTICE

TO all Paſſengers that intend going in the Brig Coningham, Robert Coningham, Maſter, to New-Caſtle in America, to be on board the 15th April inſt. as ſhe will ſail firſt fair wind after that day.

L: Derry, 3d April, 1789.

Wines for Sale.

ROBERT GOUDY has for ſale, forty hogſheads Claret, a principal part of which is of vintage, 1784, with upwards of four hundred dozen French bottled in caſes, as imported, containing 50 bottles each, a chief part of theſe Wines was imported 18 months ago. As it his intention to withdraw from the ſale of this articles, this aſſortment of Clarets is well worth the attention of country Gentlemen; they will be ſold cheap for Money or good Bills at three Months.

He is well ſupplied with red and white Port, Sherry, Frontinac, Vin de grave Wines, French white wine Vinegar, in Tierces, Porter in Hogſheads, Briſtol Cider in Hampers.

Belfaſt, 30th March, 1789.

Jamaica Rum by Auction.

TO be ſold by Auction, at the King's Stores in Linen-Hall-Street, on Thurſday next 2d April—ſeventy puncheons of Jamaica rum, in lots of five puncheons each;—the purchaſer ſubject to pay the duties on taking ſame away;—to be delivered at the cuſtom-houſe guage.

At ſame time to cloſe ſales, for account of the ſhippers, fifty quarter caſks of Mountain wine, and one butt of Sherry. Approved bills or notes at three months date, will be taken in payment or 1¼ per cent. diſcount allowed for caſh.

Belfaſt, 30th March, 1789.

Strayed or Stolen,

ON Monday the 30th April laſt, between the hours of ſeven and eight o'clock in the morning, from High-Street, in the town of Belfaſt—a reddiſh coloured Cow, white rigged, the top of her tail white, wide between the horns, her far hind leg white, a ſtripper in low condition, about 9 or 10 years old. If ſtrayed, whoever has found and returns her ſhall be rewarded, and if ſtolen, five guineas reward to whoever will proſecute the thief to conviction to be paid by Mr. James Patterſon.

Belfaſt, 2d April, 1789.

A handſome Black Draft Mare,

PERFECTLY ſound, full mane and tail, ſeven years old, fifteen and half hands high, to be ſold at Birch-Hill, near Antrim.—Alſo a good ſtrong ſecond-hand Coach and Coachman's Box belonging to it.

March 31ſt, 1789.

The late David Conyngham, Eſqrs. Sale.

TO be ſold by Auction, at Spring-hill in the county of Londonderry, on Monday the 6th day of April next, and the ſucceeding days,—Six fat Bullocks, five draft do. one remarkably large high-bred three years old Bull, ſeveral milch and ſtripper Cows, and Cows with calf, a number of young Bullocks and Heifers of different ages, thirty-two Sheep, ſix black carriage Horſes, ſeveral work Horſes, four Mules, and two Swine, a handſome faſhionable Coach almoſt new, with full-mounted plated harneſs for four horſes, a Poſt-Chaiſe with braſs-mounted harneſs for four horſes, a very neat four-wheel'd crane neck'd low Capriole, a neat jaunting Car, a number of farming and brewing Utenſils, a large quantity of Oatmeal, Barley, Oats, Potatoes, &c.

Springhill, March 28th, 1789.

Herrings.

JUST arrived per the Fortitude, at the Chicheſter-Quay, a Cargo of large well ſaved HERRINGS, which will be ſold on reaſonable terms; alſo on board ſame Veſſel, a quantity of COD and LING FISH.

Belfaſt, March 30th, 1789.

TO BE SOLD,

HENRY ATKINSON's Intereſt in a Piece of Land, near Portadown, held for three lives under Michael Obins, Eſq; yielding a profit rent of about 3l. 10s. Propoſals will be received by the Revd. George Maunſell, Drumcree, near Portadown; Doctor Woolſey, Portadown; or by John Atkinſon, Attorney, 134, Abbey-ſtreet, Dublin.—A perſon attends to ſhew the Lands.

White-abbey Houſe & Gardens,

TO be let during the ſeaſon with a few Acres of Land if required.—Apply to Thomas M'Cabe, alſo a few tons of excellent Hay to be diſpoſed of.—A Houſe to be let oppoſite the Academy, enquire as above.

BY AUCTION.

ON Wedneſday next, the 8th inſt. at 12 o'clock, will be Sold in the Brick yard, a quantity of laſt years Brick together with two horſes, a cart, cars, and utenſils for Brick making, &c. being the property of the late partnerſhip which ſubſiſted between George Mitchell deceaſed and Richard Simpſon.

Belfaſt, 2d April, 1789.

N. B. Thoſe who are indebted to ſaid partnerſhip, are requeſted to pay off their accounts to ſaid Simpſon immediately, to enable him to make a final ſettlement with the Executors.

Wanted,

A Young Man thoroughly bred to the Linen Buſineſs, who can give every requiſite attention to a Green.—Such a perſon properly recommended, will be directed by Mr. Joy where to apply by letter poſt paid.

30th March, 1789.

Money Wanted.

THE Sum of Eight Hundred Pounds on a mortgage of a valuable Leaſe held under the Earl of Donegall, for three lives, all in being, or 41 years.—Apply to Alex. Arthur, Attorney, Belfaſt.

2d April, 1789.

WHEREAS on the morning of Saturday the twenty-eighth of March inſt. between the hours of one and two o'clock, a Gang of Ruffians ſurrounded the Houſe of Mr. Roger Magenis of Bally, county Down, who after firing divers ſhots into the room where Mr. and Mrs. Magenis lay, to the imminent danger of their lives; they proceeded to break and demoliſh the windows both in front and rere, through which numbers of them burglariouſly entered, armed with guns and bayonets, &c. threatening to ſet fire to the houſe, to the great terror of the family, putting them in fear of their lives; and in the moſt wanton and daring manner broke open the inner doors, ranſacking the whole houſe, with intent (as they ſaid) to take and carry away arms, &c. which they alledged were in Mr. Magenis's poſſeſſion; but finding none they diſperſed, threatening in the moſt alarming manner to pay a ſecond viſit.

NOW, we whoſe names are hereunto ſubſcribed, having a juſt abhorrence, and holding in deteſtation ſuch horrid crimes; do hereby promiſe to pay the ſeveral ſums to our names annexed, to any perſon who will within ſix months from date hereof, diſcover and proſecute to conviction any of the aforeſaid Gang, (who ſtile themſelves Break of Day Men) or that will give the moſt private information that may lead to a diſcovery and conviction. AND we do hereby pledge ourſelves, that if any perſon or perſons concerned, will diſcover and proſecute to conviction his or their accomplice or accomplices, he or they will not only be entitled to the above reward, but application will be made to Government for his Majeſty's pardon.

Dated 30th March, 1789.

	l.	s.	d.			l.	s.	d.
Hance Fairly	5	13	9	T. Tighe, Rector				
Stewart Blacker	5	13	9	Drumgooland	5	13	9
Robt. Dowglaſs	11	7	6	Chas. Leſlie, Vicar				
John C. Gordon	5	13	9	of Clanduff	5	13	9
John Knox	22	15	0	Wm. Beers	5	13	9
Matt. Forde, junr.	5	13	9	Robt. Roſs Rowan	5	13	9
Eldred Pottinger	5	13	9	Samuel Murphy	5	13	9
Thos. Dowglaſs	5	13	9	John Carr	5	13	9
Chas. Matthews	5	13	9	John Ingram	5	13	9
Francis Price	5	13	9	Joſ. Murphy	5	13	9
Nichs. Price	5	13	9	Henry Wallace	5	13	9
Roger Magenis	100	0	0	George Crozer	5	13	9
Jas. M'Clelland	11	7	6	John Murphy	3	8	3
James Law	11	7	6	John Swan	3	8	3
James Lowry	11	7	6	James Chriſtian	3	8	3
Joſeph Magenis	11	7	6	Matthew Caplin	3	8	3
James Mc. Key	5	13	9	David Lindſay	3	8	3
Wm. Harriſon	3	8	3	Henry S. Willock	3	8	3
Wm. Sampſon	3	8	3	William Law	3	8	3
Wm. Cowan	5	13	9	John Bradford	3	8	3
John Cowan	5	13	9	James Fleming	3	8	3
Patt. Ruſſell	5	13	9	Wm. Crawford	3	8	3
Hu. Savage	5	13	9	Philip Graham	3	8	3
Thos. Johnſton	5	13	9	Alex. Mecredy	2	5	6
Samuel Holmes	5	13	9	Patt. M'Donnell	2	5	6
Oſborne Sheil	3	8	3	Henry Gilmor	2	5	6
Thos. Crafford	2	5	6	Robt. Scot	2	5	6
Thos. D. Laurence	11	7	6	John Birch	2	5	6
Edward Trevor	11	7	6	Arch. Lowry	2	5	6
Wm. Sturrock	11	7	6	Thomas Corbet	1	2	9
				Robt. Brown	1	2	9

Wanted;

TO attend a ſingle Gentleman, a Servant who can dreſs hair, take care of horſes, and be well recommended; very particular enquiry will be made. Enquire at the Office of Mr. Joy.

April 2d, 1789.

To be Sold;

AN Article of two new Houſes, Offices, and a large Garden, in Ballyronan, near Magherafelt, for twenty-eight years from November laſt.—Application to be made to Alexander Hull on the premiſes; if not ſold before the 22d day of April next, it will be ſold by Auction at noon on ſaid day, at Ballyronan aforeſaid.

Dated the 30th March, 1789.

Sicily Aſhes and Cork Tallow—a Cargo of each juſt arrived to THOMPSON & GORDON,

WHO have alſo juſt landed ſome Cargoes of Flaxſeed, Barilla, American Pot and Pearl Aſhes, and Virginia Leaf Tobacco, which with their uſual aſſortment of Goods, they will ſell on moderate terms.

Newry, 30th March, 1789.

Larne Diſtrict.

NOTICE is hereby given to all Retailers of Wine, Ale, and Spirits, Manufacturers of Tobacco, Grocers, Tanners and Chandlers, and all deſcriptions of perſons reſiding in the ſaid Diſtrict, who are ſubject to the Licence Duty, that Offices will be held for granting them for the current year at the places and on the days undermentioned, viz.

At Antrim, for that Walk and Randalſtown, on Monday the 13th of April next.

At Ballymena, for that Walk, Ahoghill and Broughſhane, on Tueſday the 14th April.

At Larne, for that Walk and Glenarm, on Thurſday the 16th April.

It is hoped that all perſons concerned will without fail, pay their Licence Duties on thoſe days, and thereby avoid the penalties they will otherwiſe incur.

Cuſtom-Houſe, Larne, 30th March, 1789.

THOMAS LEA, Collector.

Warehouſe to be let.

TWO Lofts of a Warehouſe on Chicheſter-Quay, to be let by the week, month, or year.—Apply to James Holmes.

Belfaſt, 1ſt April, 1789.

WE the Mayor, Corporation and Inhabitants of the Town of Coleraine, truly ſenſible of the very correct, and exemplary conduct of the detachment of the 15th Regiment quartered here; take this publick method of returning our moſt ſincere thanks to Captain Dougla's and the Officers under his command, for their conſtant attention to the preſervation of good order and harmony, and have now only to regret their approaching departure.

Coleraine, 31ſt March, 1789.

To James Douglaſs, Eſq.
Commanding Officer, 15th Regt. Coleraine.

To be Sold by Auction,

ON Saturday the fourth day of April next, at the Houſe of Francis Dickſon, Ballymena, the right, title, and intereſt of a Leaſe of 22 years unexpired from November laſt,—Iſland Bann Farm, lying within one mile of the town Ballymena, on the road to Cregbilly; containing about 26 Iriſh acres: The land is in good condition and of the firſt quality, ſix acres of meadow, and plenty of firing on the premiſes; houſe and offices newly built, at a low yearly rent, tythe free. The purchaſer to commence from November laſt, to pay ten guineas at the time of ſale, the remainder on perfecting the deeds. David Gillmore will ſhew the lands.

27th March, 1789.

A Hog Swine,

FOUND the 20th of laſt month ſtanding on a rock within the ſea mark, was brought to John Mackee's. Any perſon proving their property, and paying equitable expences, may have the ſaid Swine by applying to John Mackee.—If no ſuch claimant appears, the Swine will be ſold by Auction the 15th of this month to defray the expences, and the reſidue of the price to be given to the poor of the pariſh of Holywood.

Craigavade, April 1ſt, 1789.

COCKING.

TO commence on Monday the 13th day of April, A Cock-Main, in the Town of Glenavy, between Down and Antrim, for one hundred Guineas the Main. And likewiſe, a Stag Main for ſaid Sum, in the town of Maralin, between ſame Gentlemen, on the firſt Monday of June.—Dated this 30th day of March, 1789.

Mc. CULLY and BROWN, } Feeders.

TO BE LET,

From the firſt of May next,

A HOUSE, next door to Mrs. Douglaſs; and, from the firſt November next, two Houſes in Linenhall-ſtreet. Apply to Waddell Cunningham or John Boyle.

EXPEDITION to BOTANY-BAY.

The two ships of war, named the Sirins and Supply, with the transports, under the command of Commodore Phillips, have made good their voyage to Botany Bay: Of this important arrival, intelligence has been brought by the Prince of Wales, Moore, one of the transports which carried out the convicts. The Prince of Wales buried only one convict. The dispatches for Government are not yet arrived, as the Borrowdale transport, by which Commodore Phillips sent them, as well as a third transport in company, have not reached England.

On the arrival of this squadron at Botany Bay, the destined spot was found not to have water sufficient for the supply of the new settlement: A council was in consequence held, and the ships weighing anchor stood away for Jackson's Bay, where Nature's gifts appeared equal to all their wishes: The verdure strong and rich, and the springs of the best water: The face of the country too possessing great variety, and well clothed with wood.

The moment Commodore Phillips had made good the landing of the Marines, and some lines of limitation were marked out, the convicts were put on shore; and the artizans among them, with those belonging to the ships, proceeded to cut down wood to form their habitations. This task continued for some time during the hours of day, and in the evening the workmen and others returned on board the shipping, leaving only the Marines, and a detachment of the seamen, to guard the works as they advanced towards completion. The natives, when they discovered the preparations on foot, and that their visitors were likely to become stationary, appeared so dissatisfied, that several pieces of ordnance were mounted on the lines to awe them; they however kept at a distance, and though they did not provoke a fire, they declined all communication.

Of the convicts and others, from the departure of the squadron from Portsmouth, to the time the ship which brings the advice left Jackson's Bay, only 40 appear to have died; and to compensate for this loss, 42 infants were born.

Three of the convicts were induced to try their fortunes among the natives, where they hoped to have a favourable reception: two of these were in this expedition killed and eaten; and the third, after subsisting on roots for some time in the woods, returned, almost perished through hunger. This operated to deter further adventures of a like nature.

F R A N C E.

March 17, 1789.

IT is easy to see that France is advancing very rapidly towards a Revolution in its Government. The various pamphlets which every day appear in Paris, all tend to the same object. Among these, that which seems the best written, is a piece entitled. "Instructions to the Duke of Orlean's Representatives in his respective Bailiwicks, &c." The first part of this work is composed of sixteen articles, which form the basis of the piece. As these will shew not only his Highness's plan of conduct which he proposes to hold at the ensuing Assembly of the States, but will also give an idea of the general disposition of the French in the present conjuncture, we shall present them to our readers, omitting only those parts which relates merely to matter of form.

Art. I. That the Deputies to the States General shall co-operate to have the liberty of individuals secured to every French subject. This consists, in the first place, in being at liberty to live where one likes, to go, return, and dwell wherever one pleases, without any obstacle or difficulty, either in or out of the kingdom, and without any necessity to obtain permissions, passports, certificates, or other formalities, tending to obstruct the liberty of the citizens; 2dly, That none should be in danger of being arrested, or sent to prison, but in virtue of a warrant issued by the ordinary Judges; 3dly, That in case the States General should think proper to adjudge imprisonments necessary, all persons thus arrested shall be delivered within twenty-four hours into the hands of his natural judges; 4thly, That no officer, soldier, or other persons in office, shall ever attempt to deprive any of the citizens of their liberty, except those appointed by the laws, under pain of death, or, at least, of corporal punishment, as shall be decided by the Grand General Assembly; 5thly, That whoever shall issue such unlawful orders, or countenance the execution of them, shall be amenable to justice, and not only be sued for damages, &c. but liable to suffer corporal punishment, as the States shall think proper.

Art. II. The freedom of publishing one's thoughts and opinions, being part of the liberty of individuals (since man cannot be free, when his thoughts are confined) shall be insisted upon, without any reserve whatever, except those restrictions the States-General shall think proper to appoint and decree.

Art. III. The strictest regard and most sacred respect shall be paid to every letter entrusted to the Post-office, and proper care shall be taken to prevent the iniquitous practice of opening letters.

Art. IV. All rights of property shall be sacred and inviolate, and no individual be deprived of them, not even for the public good, except on requital at the highest price, and without the least delay.

Art. V. No imposts, or tax, shall pass for legal, or be collected, but what shall have obtained the consentment and sanction of the nation in the Assembly of the States General; and they shall agree to them for a limited time only, viz. till the next meeting of the States;

L O N D O N, MARCH 25, 26, and 27.

Orders are given by the Bishop of London, for St. Paul's church to be properly matted, and the necessary preparations to be made, in order to accommodate their Majesties on the 23d of next month, being the day fixed on for certain, for their Majesties to attend Divine Service at that Cathedral.

D U B L I N, MARCH 26 and 28.

Yesterday, during the sitting of the Recorder at the Tholsel, ten of the prisoners in the men's side of the boarded enclosure, where they are kept on being brought up from the gaol till called to trial, and to which those found guilty are also remanded, contrived means to raise a loose flag at the bottom of the enclosure, and let themselves down through the apperture into the Tholsel kitchen, from whence eight most desperate offenders made their escape before any alarm was given. But Mr. William Shea (who acts as an assistant to Mr. Cox, the new gaoler) observing one of those desperadoes coming out through one of the kitchen windows, on Nicholas-street side, immediately seized him, and brought him back into the Tholsel, and on searching the kitchen, another prisoner, a young boy, was discovered coiled up in one of the stew-holes.

The names of the eight prisoners who effected their escape were, Michael Delany, Patrick Hughes, Francis Magenis, Francis Gore, John Hackett, Thomas Carroll, Wm. Tracy, and John Paine, alias Neal. The first two, Delany and Hughes, had been cast for transportation some time ago, and were brought up to trial for robberies committed by them in the prison, of which however they were acquitted. The two last, Tracy and Paine, alias Neal, had been also under rule of transportation some time ago, and were brought up as witnesses in the behalf of Delany, Hughes, and others, charged with the above-mentioned robberies. The other four who escaped were tried yesterday, and received sentence to be transported for seven years: As all the eight were most daring villains, it is hoped they may be speedily apprehended.

Tuesday a deputation from the Protestant Dissenters of Dublin waited on his Exellency with a congratulatory Address, in consequence of the happy restoration of his Majesty's health. the deputation was received very graciously, and his Excellency returned them his thanks for their loyalty and public spirit on the occasion.

We hear, that Mr. Grattan will defer his tythe bill until the next session of Parliament.

Mr. Grattan, we understand, intends to move for an account of the several examinations sworn against police-men for breaches of the peace.—We can assure the public, strange as it may appear, that they are more numerous than those sworn against all the inhabitants of the Metropolis besides.——Excellent peace-makers!

On Wednesday night a gentleman was attacked at the corner of Montague-street, Camden-street, by four ruffians, who knocked him down, snapped a pistol, which missed fire, and struck him on the head in a most violent and brutal manner, but were prevented robbing him by the approach of the police guard. We are sorry to add, those villains, though pursued, effected their escape through Long-lane, owing to the darkness of the night, and the total want of lamps in that part of the town.

The clergy and communion of the Roman Catholic religion of Waterford, exhibited their loyalty and attachment to the present government, on the happy recovery of our most gracious Monarch, on Monday night last, in a particular manner:—They not only illuminated their own houses elegantly, but beautifully the Chapel; and during his Majesty's indisposition, prayers were daily offered up to the Almighty, for the restoration of his health.

His Majesty has appointed Dr. Cleaver to the vacant see of Cork.—[Saunders's News-Letter.]

ANTRIM ASSIZES.

At the Assizes for the County of Antrim, held at Carrickfergus, John M'Culloch was found guilty of perjury in giving evidence—sentenced to be whipped through the town of Carrickfergus on the 4th of April and 2d of May next.

Joseph Curran, found guilty of felony to the value of ten-pence, to be whipped as above.

Thomas Fairies, of Belfast, charged with counterfeiting two bills of exchange of the sum of 90l. 16s 6d. each —also with altering a third bill from the sum of 9l. 16s. 6d. to the sum of 90l. 16s. 6d.—and, on a second indictment, for altering two promissary notes from the sum of 20l. to the sum of 90l. each—was acquitted on both indictments.

The Lord Donegall, James M'Roberts master for London, is detained here by contrary winds.

James Watson Hull, Esq. High Sheriff for the county of Down, hath appointed John Heyland of Dromore, to issue and grant Replevins in and for said county.

LIST of High Constables appointed by the Grand Jury of the County of Down, at Lent Assizes 1789.

Upper Iveagh,	Upper half,	Andrew Potts of Cappy.
	Lower half,	Sam. Swan of Gralahgreenan
Lower Iveagh	Upper half,	Geo. Brush of Willowbrook.
	Lower half,	Wm. Archer of Toughblane.
Castlereagh.	Upper half,	Arch. M'Roberts of Lisowen
	Lower half,	John Kennedy, Knocknagony
Lecale.	Upper half,	Alex. Craig of Downpatrick.
	Lower half,	Robt. Craig of Ballyrolly.
Ards.	Upper half,	John Allen of Nuns Quarter.
	Lower half,	John M'Cully, Newtonards.

Belfast, *March 31.*

The following are copies of Addresses presented on the 24th instant. The deputation was headed by Dr. CAMPBELL, by whom the addresses were read, and accompanied by the eight Presbyterian Ministers of Dublin.

To the KING's Most Excellent Majesty.

The humble Address of the Protestant Dissenters of Ireland of the Presbyterian persuasion.

May it please your Majesty,

Graciously to accept the dutiful and affectionate congratulations of the Protestant Dissenters of Ireland, on the re-establishment of your Majesty's health; and to be assured, that as no class of your Majesty's subjects have offered up more early and earnest supplications, so none pour forth more fervent thanksgivings to the King of Kings, for that favourable dispensation of Providence.

Educated in the principles of the glorious Revolution, and exulting in the settlement of the illustrious house of Hanover on the throne of these kingdoms, as the security of our invaluable privileges, civil and religious,—We chearfully embrace this opportunity of expressing our inviolable attachment to your Royal Person, Family, and Government,—our unalterable resolution to support the dignity of your Majesty's crown, and our anxious desire to promote the strength, prosperity and glory of these nations.

Signed in the name of the Protestant Dissenters of Ireland. Dublin, March 24, 1789.

To his Excellency George Grenville Nugent Temple, Marquis of Buckingham, Lord Lieutenant, &c. of Ireland:

May it please your Excellency,

We, a deputation of the Protestant Dissenters of this kingdom, humbly pray your Excellency to transmit to our most gracious Sovereign the Address herewith presented; and presume to hope, that the Protestant Dissenters of Ireland, will at all times be honoured by your Excellency with a favourable representation to his Majesty.

Signed, &c. Dublin, March 24, 1789.

The Lord Lieutenant's Answer.

Gentlemen,

I will immediately transmit your dutiful and loyal Address to be laid before the King.

The Protestant Dissenters of Ireland may be assured, that I shall at all times be happy to make that favourable representation of them to his Majesty, which their loyalty and attachment to his person and government so justly merit.

The William and Mary, Simon Roche master, from Newry, loaded with linen cloth, arrived in London the 22d inst. after a passage of eight days, all well.

We hear from Armagh, that Monday the 9th inst. was there appointed for public rejoicings on the most happy event of his Majesty's entire recovery. The bells of the Cathedral rang several peals, and in the evening the city was universally illuminated, which standing on a hill, the houses rising one above another, afforded a most pleasing spectacle. The Lord Primate's Palace, the Deanery-house, and the barrack, which stand on eminences very near the city, being spendidly illuminated, added greatly to the beauty of the scene.

Extract of a Letter from Kircubbin, March 27th 1789.

"The recovery of our good and dearly beloved King, was celebrated here last night with heart-felt pleasure; bonfires and illuminations prevailed all the evening, and the blaze of joy was seen on every countenance from the oldest to the youngest, in that great concourse of loyal subjects who attended from all parts to celebrate the happy tidings. On the above occasion the Revd. Dr. Fraser's house was conspicuosly distinguished by transparencies, &c. &c."

Extract of a Letter from Armagh.

"On account of the King's recovery, Wood Park house presented to the neighbouring counties of Derry, Tyrone, Monaghan, and Cavan a very brilliant illumination of the four Gothic fronts of that building. The loyal proprietor gave drink to his tenantry and others assembled round two bonfires—and gave a splendid entertainment to the neighbouring gentlemen.

Married, on Thursday, the 26th inst. Stafford Gorman, Esq. to Miss Margaret Kirkpatrick, daughter of Alexander Kirkpatrick, Esq. of Drumcondra, near Dublin.

Died, on Sunday, Mr. William Eccles, long a teacher of writing in this town.

GRAND LEASE OF BALLYCLARE.

All who have any thoughts of buying said lease, are requested to take notice, that FRIDAY next, the 3d of April, is the day of sale—exactly at twelve o'clock in the Market-house of Belfast.

P O R T N E W S.

ARRIVED.

March 24. Mary, Malcom, Greenock, Rum, &c,
Christy, Johnson, Jamaica, Rum and Sugar.
16 Colliers.

CLEARED-OUT.

March, 23. Brothers, English, Alicant, linen cloth.
28. Success, Watson, Newfoundland, do.

Anno 1789.]   Printed by HENRY JOY, and Co. BELFAST.

The BELFAST NEWS-LETTER.

TUESDAY April 7,   FRIDAY April 10, 1789.

The FRIENDSHIP,

DALWAY LEPPER,

For LONDON,

WILL be clear to sail the fifth of next Month, and sail first fair wind after.
Belfast, 8th April, 1789.

Samuel Hyde,   David Wilson,
Robert Thomson,   Jacob Hancock,
Samuel Brown,   Val. Smith,
William Sinclaire,   James Stevenson.
Robert Bradshaw,

Post-Coach.

THE Contractors for conveying his Majesty's Mails between Dublin and Belfast, will run an elegant POST-COACH, with stout well trained Horses and skilful Coachmen, for reception of four inside and two outside Passengers *only*, three days in every week between Dublin and Belfast.

FARE { Between Dublin and Belfast, 1l. 16s. 3d. h.
{ Between Dublin and Newry, 1l. 2s 9d.
{ Between Newry and Belfast, 0l. 13s. 6d. h.

Passengers travelling short of the above places to pay 5d. halfp. per mile, and outside passengers half fare; 20lb. luggage to each passenger, and one penny per pound for extra luggage.
The running will commence on Monday the 13th instant, on which day, at six o'clock in the morning, a Coach will set out from the Belfast Hotel, Capel-street, where places are to be taken; and on same day, at same hour, a Coach will set out from Messrs. M'Kean's and Sheridan's New Inn, Belfast, where seats are also to be taken; and will continue to set out from each place on every Wednesday, Friday, and Monday following, until they take up the Mail, of which the public shall have due notice, when Coaches will run every day between Dublin and Belfast.
Belfast, 4th April, 1789.

Advertisement.

WE, JOHNSTON and ALEX. HENRY, do hereby give notice to all persons whatsoever, not to cut any turf in any part of our mosses in Culduff or Garryduff, (save what is necessary for firing for the occupiers of said premisses) as a bill is now preparing to prevent a continuance of the waste heretofore committed on the premisses; so that if any person attempts to cut turf therein, contrary to this notice, they will be prevented from taking them away.
Dated 6th April, 1789.

JOHNSTON HENRY,
ALEX. HENRY.

Wanted,

A POSTILION on the first of May next, who can be recommended for honesty and sobriety. Such a person will hear of a good place by applying at the Office of Mr. Joy.
This to be continued three times.

THE Officers of the detachment of the 15th Regiment lately quartered in Coleraine, deeply impressed with a due sense of the honor conferr'd on them by the Mayor, Corporation, and Inhabitants of that Town, by the publick and gracious manner with which they have been pleased to communicate to them their approbation of their conduct, beg leave through the same channel to return their warmest and best thanks; and to assure the Mayor, Corporation, and Inhabitants, that they must ever equally regret their departure from a place where they experienced so much happiness and hospitality.
Belfast, April 6th, 1789.
To the Mayor, Corporation, and
Inhabitants of Coleraine.

FELONY.

ON Wednesday night, the first of April instant, the stable door of Robert Gilmer of Dunamoy, parish of Ballyeaston and county of Antrim, was broke open and thereout feloniously stolen, a black Highland MARE, rising six years old, tolerably large, having mane and tail remarkably long, no white hairs on her but a few on the near shoulder at the saddle flap. Whoever gives information so as the Mare may be found, shall have one guinea reward; otherwise five guineas for apprehending and prosecuting the thief to conviction.
Dunamoy, 1st April, 1789.

ROBERT GILMORE.

Boarding School, Belfast.

YOUNG LADIES are educated at Mrs. Ware's School, in Donegall-Street, in English, French, Embroidery, Tambour, Phillagree Work, &c. &c. on the following Terms:
For Boarding and Tuition 22 guineas per annum.—3 do. Entrance, and a pair of Sheets.—Washing, 3l.
DAY SCHOLARS.

At the rate of 6 } { 1 do.
Music. 8 } Guineas { 1 do.
Dancing, 6 } per annum. { 1 do. } Entrance
Drawing, 4 } { ½ do.
Writing, 2 } { ½ do.

Stationary, 10s. 10d. per annum.
The House being large and in a good situation, she can now accommodate a number of young Ladies.
Belfast, 9th April, 1789.

The Belfast Assembly,

WILL be held at the Exchange-Rooms, on Tuesday next the 14th instant.
Belfast, 8th April, 1789.

Barilla Ashes, Clover Seed, &c.

THE following Articles are just arrived to BROWN and OAKMAN, and will be sold on very moderate Terms, Viz.
New Alicante Barilla Ashes,
Do. Broad Red Clover Seed } from Rotterdam.
Linseed Oil in Aums,
Belfast, 9th April, 1789.

New Broad Red Clover Seed, Madder, and Black Soap.

SAMUEL GIBSON has received per the Industry, Capt. Sharp, from Rotterdam, a quantity of the above Articles, all of the very best quality, which he will dispose of on very moderate terms.
North-street, Belfast, 9th April, 1789.

Fresh Drugs.

JOSEPH WALKER has just received from Dublin, a large and general assortment of the best Medicine, and a quantity of fine Florence Oil in Flasks.
☞ He wants an Apprentice to the Apothecary Business, who may have good opportunities of instruction None need apply who has not received a tolerable education.
Ballymoney, 8th April, 1789.

JANE LINN,

BEGS leave to inform her Friends, that she has removed from Skippers-Lane to the house formerly the White-Cross Inn, within a few doors of the Donegall-Arms;—where she has received from the last sales, great variety of Muslins; is also well supplied with every article in the Haberdashery Line, which she is determined to sell on the most reasonable terms.——She embraces this opportunity of returning her most grateful thanks for the very flattering encouragement she has met with since her commencement in business.
Belfast, 9th April, 1789.

Wanted,

AT May next, a good House Servant; also a Servant who can dress Hair and attend a single Gentleman.
Belfast, 9th April, 1789.

Linen Stolen,

ON the night of 5th inst. the Bleach Green of John Barclay of Lambeg, was robbed of two pieces of yard wide Linen, which were nearly fit for rubbing: Whoever will give such information as may lead to a discovery and conviction shall receive TWENTY GUINEAS, besides the reward of ONE HUNDRED GUINEAS, offered by the Association for prosecuting Linen Thieves.
Lambeg, April 8th, 1789.   JOHN BARCLAY.

Woollen Cloths on Commission

JUST arrived to John Hunter in Church-lane, a neat assortment of broad and forrest cloths of the newest patterns from his employer in England, which will be sold on good terms; a large discount to be given for ready money.
The said John Hunter has a good House to set in Prince's-street, with cellars and a back yard well finished, and in good order. He has some fine Hay to dispose of.
Belfast, 7th April, 1789

Samuel Ferguson,

HAS for sale at his stores in Mill-Street, a quantity of good Philadelphia flaxseed, this year's importation; also a few bags of broad red clover-seed, which he will sell for cash or good bills on the lowest terms.
Belfast, 6th April, 1789.

Thomas Mullan,

Next door to the Brokers-Office,

BEGS leave to acquaint his friends and the public, that he has received from France, a fresh assortment of prunes, and French plumbs, dried and liquid sweetmeats, in boxes and pots, anchovies, olives, capers, virgin oil and cordials, in bottles; Mareschal powder, perfumed hair ditto, scented waters, white wine vinegar, with a general assortment of perfumed, soft and hard pomatum, in pots and sticks. He has also received from Dublin, a large assortment of silk handkerchiefs, a variety of the newest fashioned ribbands, laces, and a quantity of fresh lemons and oranges, which he will sell by the box or retail. He is supplied as usual with every article in the grocery and haberdashery line, all which he is determined to sell on the lowest terms.
Belfast, 10th April, 1789.

Advertisement.

WILLIAM BLEAKLY, of Drum, having got his affairs settled, is now ready to take in cloth to bleach for the country.——Any person that chooses to favour him with their Linens, may depend on having them done in the best and safest manner.
Dated the 7th day of April, 1789.

HAY.

A Few Tons remarkably good, to be sold.——Enquire at Mrs. Ferguson's, Waring-street.
Belfast, 6th April, 1789

A New Boat.

TO be sold at Gray-abby, a new Boat on the stocks, ready for launching, 27 feet keel, and 12 feet 6 inches beam, burthen about 20 tuns, stout and strong built in every particular, the bottom being entirely of the best elm;—any person inclining to purchase said boat, may apply to Samuel Beck in Gray-abbey, who will treat with them for the same. If not sold by private contract before the 4th of May next, she will on that day be sold by public auction.
Terms of sale——ready money or an approved bill.
Gray-abby, 8th April, 1789.

Lagan Navigation.

WHEREAS some evil minded person or persons, did on the night of Thursday the second instant, cut through a bank made across the canal of the Lagan Navigation, near to the great Reservoir in Friar's Glenn, by which means a great deal of the water was let off, and which in its consequences might have rendered the Canal not navigable during the ensuing summer, had it not been timely discovered and repaired.
Now in order to prevent such pernicious practices so detrimental to the country in general, and to bring such wicked perpetrators to punishment: We the undertakers of the Lagan Navigation, do hereby promise a reward of Fifty Pounds sterl. to any person who will in three months discover and prosecute to conviction the person or persons who have been guilty of cutting the bank as aforesaid.
Belfast, 6th April, 1789.

For the Benefit of Mrs. LYNCH and Mr. REMINGTON,

ON Monday Evening, April 13th, 1789, will be performed a much admired and celebrated Tragedy, call'd,

The London Merchant; or, the History of GEORGE BARNWELL.

The Part of Maria, (by particular Desire) by the young Lady who performed Miss Hardcastle, (Being her second Appearance on any Stage.)
With the following Entertainments:
An Hornpipe, *blindfold, over twelve Eggs*, by Mr. LYNCH.
A Lilliputian Dance, in which the Characters will change from *Men of three feet high*, to *Women of six!!!* by Messrs. Remington and Lynch.
A Dance, composed by Signior Placido, and the little Devil, call'd,
LA FRICASSE.

CROMABOO,

WILL stand this season at Downpatrick, and be let to Mares at one Guinea each, and half a Crown to the Groom. The get of this horse prove him to be one of the best stallions that for a long time has appeared in this country; they are large sized and strong, perform well on the road, field and turf, and sell for high prices.——Good grass for mares.
Down, 6th April, 1789.

BOTANY BAY EXPEDITION.

(Supplementary to our last.)

LONDON, March 27.

EARLY on Thursday morning Lieut. Maxwell, of the Marines, arrived at the Admiralty with dispatches for Government; these are not very copious, as the principal packet is now on its way in the Alexander transport. From the accounts brought by the Prince of Wales and Borrowdale, we are enabled to lay the following particulars before our readers.

Commodore Phillips having made the Cape of Good-Hope, with the ships of war, transports, and victuallers, used the most unremitting diligence to supply the squadron with provisions and water; live stock for the ships use; and cattle, sheep, and hogs, for the benefit of the intended Colony. To these we may reckon a large quantity of poultry, in addition to some which was carried from England.

On the 16th of November 1787, the signal was given, and the squadron got under way, and continued their course for a time, with favourable winds, for New Holland; some short tempests interrupting their course, Commodore Phillips removed to the Supply, and proposed going a-head to prepare a reception for the rest of the fleet, at the place of destination: Three transports, the Friendship, Alexander, and Scarborough sailed in company, but retarded the Commodore's course so much, that he did not come in sight of land till the 14th of January 1788. Three days after, he made Botany Bay, and on the 18th of January landed with Lieutenant King. The natives, who had in small bodies witnessed their approach, appeared in great consternation, on seeing these officers on their territory, and after setting up a yell, fled to the woods. They returned soon after more composed, and from the signs made by Captain Phillips, were prevailed on to receive some presents of beads, necklaces, and other trifles; but they were deposited on the ground, and the Captain withdrawn to a distance, before they would venture to take them. After this, they appeared so friendly as to conduct, by signs, the officers to a rivulet, where they found some excellent water, though not in a very abundant supply. In the evening the Commodore, with his party, returned on board; and the next day the three transports, which he had outsailed, came to an anchor; on which the Commodore went again on shore, principally to cut grass for the use of the cattle and sheep; the hay on board being nearly all exhausted. On the dawn of the day following, the Sirius, Captain Hunter, with the remainder of the transports under his convoy, appeared in sight, and three hours after brought to and anchored in the Bay.

Captain Hunter immediately waited on the Commodore; and these Gentlemen, with a small party of officers and men, went on shore again towards the South Coast of Botany Bay, the former visits having been made to the North of the Bay. Here, as in most of the early interviews with the natives, Commodore Phillips usually laid his musquet on the ground, and advancing before it, held out presents. A green bough held aloft, or their lances thrown down, were like signs of amity in them. It was a practice with the seamen, in these intercourses, to dress up the inhabitants with shreds of cloth, and tags of coloured paper; and when they surveyed each other, they would burst in loud laughter, and run hollowing to the woods. The marines one day forming before them, they appeared to like the fife; but fled at the sound of the drum, and never more would venture near it.

Animals.—The kanguroo is as large as a sheep:—The head, neck, and shoulders are very small in proportion to the other parts of the body; the tail is long, but thick near the rump, and tapering towards the end: the fore legs in general measure only eight inches in length, and the hind legs twenty two;—the progress is by successive leaps or hops of a considerable length, in an erect posture; the fore legs are kept bent close to the breast, and seemed to be of use only for digging:—The skin is covered with short fur of a dark mouse or grey colour, excepting the head and ears, which bears a slight resemblance to those of the hare. One of these animals, of uncommon magnitude, is on board the Prince of Wales; a live dog from New Holland is also brought to England; and besides these annimals there are no other to be noticed except the Oposum and the Polecat.

Queen's Gala at Windsor.

The recovery of the best of Monarchs was on Thursday celebrated at Windsor, in all that splendor and magnificence so applicable to the occasion. The banquet was the most luxurious of any given at Windsor during the present reign. The day should likewise be particularly noticed as being the first time of his Majesty's appearance in public since his recovery. The congratulations of the Company were, as might be supposed, unbounded and loyal.

The effect of this Gala was fully equal to the preparations that had been made for it. It was a shew of exultation and magnificence, and the entertainments were such as might be expected from so noble an hostess.

At seven o'clock the Drawing Room began. Their Majesties were seated under a canopy. The King was in a full dress uniform of blue and gold, and looked remarkably well. The Queen had a most superb bandeau in her head-dress, with letters in diamonds of "Long live the King."

DUBLIN, *April 7.*

At a most numerous and respectable meeting of the National Committee of Roman Catholics, held at their Committee-room, on Thursday last, a most loyal and dutiful Address of Congratulation to his Majesty, on his happy recovery from his late severe indisposition, was unanimously resolved on; and a deputation appointed, consisting of Lord Kenmare, Lord Killeen and Baron Hussey, to present the same to his Excellency the Lord Lieutenant, in order for transmittal to his Majesty.

The port of Drogheda has been shut for these some days past from the export of corn and flour with bounty, the average price of wheat at that market being at 28s. 7d. the barrel.

Yesterday morning a duel was fought in the Phœnix-park between two officers of the regiments now in the Barracks, in consequence of a dispute the night before at Menzie's coffee-house. Though five shots were fired by each of the gentlemen, no life was lost: one of the parties only was wounded, and that not dangerously.

Extract of letter from Cashel, March 23.

"The following persons were tried and found guilty at the assizes of Clonmel:—Edmond Duggan, otherwise Crooskeen, for poisoning Catherine Gueray, to be hanged, quartered, and beheaded on Saturday the 28th instant. Alice Daniel, otherwise Duggan his wife, for the like offence, to be strangled and burned to ashes the same day. James Keane, for a burglary, committed at Golden-bridge, to be hanged the same day. Philip Murray, for horse stealing, to be hanged on the 4th of April next. William Walpole, for a felony committed at the church of Cashel, and other misdemeanors to be transported for seven years. James Ryan, for felony, to the vasue of 4s. 11d, to be transported for seven years. Catherine Edwards, for felony, to the value of one shilling, to be imprisoned six months, and to be twice privately whipped in goal. Elizabeth dillon, for receiving stolen goods, to be imprisoned nine months, and to be twice privately whipped in goal. William Barton, for manslaughter at large, was burned in the hand. Thomas Dawson, for different misdemeanors, to be imprisoned four years, whipped on the first Saturday in May, and first Saturday in November next, fined 1s. 6d. and give security for his good behaviour during life. Richard Hardy, for rescue, to be imprisoned six months, and fined 40l. James M'Guin, for an assult to be imprisoned six months and fined 5l."

Limerick, March 25. This day came on to be tried in the city court, before the Hon. Baron Hamilton and a special jury, (and as crowded a court as was ever known) a cause wherein the King, at the prosecution of Lieutenant Peacocke, of the 50th regiment, was plaintiff, and Mr. Andrew Watson, printer of the Limerick Chronicle, defendant, for a supposed libel, alleged to have been published in said paper in August, 1787.—The trial lasted four hours, when the Judge gave a most impartial charge to the Jury, and in a few minutes they honourably acquitted Mr. Watson. This was not merely the cause of a private citizen, it was the cause of the public. Council for the plaintiff, Messrs. Dwyer, Sankey, Stackpoole, Paterson, O'Callaghan, Casey, Monsell; agent, Mr. Finncane.—Counsel for the defendant, Messrs. Hacket, Wm. Lloyd, Duhigg, D. Esterre, Grady, Marsden, Lysaght; agent, Mr. Lysaght.

The importation of flax-seed this season from America has very considerably decreased; for the whole of what has been already imported, and what is yet expected, will not amount to more than 10,000 hogsheads; and last year the quantity imported was 18,460 hogsheads —so that there is a difference between the quantity imported last year and the present season, of 8,460 hogsheads.

Flax-seed can be imported much cheaper immediately from Russia than through Holland; and the Russia seed is generally imported from Archangel and Petersburgh to Holland in chaff, which is a safe way of preserving it, and it would tend very much to the advantage of our linen manufacture, if the law was so far altered as to allow of Russia seed being entered and cleaned for use in this kingdom after importation;—it is now imported clean through Holland under the name of Dutch seed, at double and treble the first cost in Russia.

LONDON-DERRY, March 31.

The Bridge.——Mess. Cox and Thompson having made every necessary examination concerning the depth and bed of the river between the quays where the ferry-boats ply, and having given it as their decided opinion, That a Wooden Bridge can be erected there, on Thursday last, they presented to the Corporation, in common council assembled, an estimate of the expence, which amounts to only 10,000l. British money.—The Corporation, with a spirit and promptitude, which should ever endear them to their fellow-citizens, unanimously resolved to accept the estimate, and to compleat the plan.

A letter from Nn-Limavady mentions, that on the night of Monday the 23d inst. that place was illuminated on account of his Majesty's recovery, and that the inhabitants and the neighbouring gentry testified every mark of joy on the happy occasion.

LONDON-DERRY, April 7.

On Tuesday last, Stephen Bennett, Esq; was unanimously elected to be an Alderman of the Corporation of this City, in the room of Alderman Squire Lecky, dec.

Last week, at Omagh assizes, Tho. Hughes was found guilty of being concerned in the cruel murder of Bryan and Edw. Harvey, near Ballygawly, for which the O'Donnelly's and M'Gough's were condemned and executed last year.—John M'Afee and Mary Wier were also found guilty of house breaking.

At Ennitkillen, one Magee was convicted of picking pockets.

Tuesday last, a man of the name of M'Gaughy, after having been missing for three or four days, was found hanged in a wood near Cumber-Claudy, co. Derry.—The occasion of this rash action it is thought was an attachment to a young woman; and tho' he never declared his passion to her, yet, on any of his comrades taking the least notice of this girl, he appeared in the greatest disorder, and which at last became so insupportable, that he plunged himself into eternity, without having the resolution to come to an explanation with the object of his affections!

Belfast, *April* 10.

A Sloop is ashore in Dundrum Bay, all the hands lost; she was bound from Dublin for Belfast or Derry.—Her name the Jennet or Jesset.

The inhabitants of Scotland have for some time distinguished themselves by the encouragement which they hold forth to gersons engaged in agriculture. Their annual rewards, even to those who plough the best furrow, are incitements that create a love for the profession among the lower classes engaged in its offices, which it is perceivable has excellent consequences. By a late determination it is intended that a new professorship for agricultural studies and lectures should be endowed in the University of Edinburgh, with the same salary as those of Latin, Greek, Logic, and Natural History; this will still farther tend to give respectability to a study, which, above all others, conduces to the benefit of mankind in general.

On Saturday last M'Culloch, for Perjury, was whipped through Carrickfergus according to his sentence.

Married.] Mr. Thomas Black of Newry, surgeon, to Miss Hale of Drumnevadey.

QUARTERS of the INFANTRY for the YEAR 1789.

13th regiment,—10 companies, Dublin,
40th ditto,—9 companies Dublin, 1 Naas.
61st ditto,—10 companies Dublin,
64th ditto,—9 companies Dublin, 1 Bray.
70th ditto,—8 companies Dublin, 2 Drogheda.
1st ditto,—8 companies Charles Fort, 1 Skibbereen, 1 Bantry.
15th regt.—2 companies Tralee, 2 Dingle, 2 Castle Island, 3 Ross-Castle and Killarney, 1 Nedeen.
16th regt.—6 companies Kilkenny, 2 Cashel, 2 Clonmel.
27th regt.—5 companies Wexford, 2 Waterford, 2 Arklow, 1 Wicklow.
28th regt.—5 companies Londonderry, 1 Strabane, 1 Killibegs, 1 Letterkenny, 1 Rutland, 1 Donegal.
39th regt.—8 companies Belfast, 2 Colerain.
41st regt —9 comp. Kinsale, 1 Clonakiltey.
43d regt.—2 companies Ballyshannon, 2 Enniskillen, 1 Cavan, 2 Carrick-on-Sh. 2 Granard, 1 Mullingar.
46th regt.—3 companies Dundalk, 3 Killough, 3 Newry, 1 Carrickmacross.
47th regt.—6 companies Cork, 3 Cove, 1 Millstreet.
51st regt.—10 companies Cork.
56th regt —3 companies Galway, 1 Athenry, 2 Ballinrobe, 1 Westport, 1 Tuam, 1 Banagher, 1 Newport.
58th regt.—8 companies Limerick, 2 Clare Castle.
62d regt.—7 companies Youghal, 1 Middleton, 1 Kilworth, 1 Dungarvan.
63d regt.—10 companies Galway.
69th regt.—8 companies Armagh, 1 Monaghan, 1 Omagh.

Note. The 39th and 41st are hourly expect to arrive from Great-Britain. to replace the 21st and 24th under orders of embarkation at Cork, for America.

PORT NEWS.

ARRIVED.

April 1. Alexander and Hugh, Cowan, Liverpool, bale-goods.
4. Peggy, M'Laughlin, Greenock, flax-seed.
Nancy, Lamout, ditto, ditto.
Four colliers.

Cleared-Out.

April 4. Mary, Malcolm, Antigua, linen cloth.

The Lord Donegall, Captain M'Roberts, for London, is still here detained only by contrary winds.

We are favoured with an account from Stewartstown of the mode of inoculation practised by a Gentleman who is not of the medical profession; which he wishes to have inserted with the worthy motive of removing prejudices still to be found in this country against inoculating for the small pox. As medical advice can easily be obtained, and as every day's experience has a tendency to correct the prejudice complained of,—we are tempted to decline, for the present, insertion of the paper alluded to.

MISS BRADBERRY,

With the greatest respect, begs leave to inform the Ladies and Gentlemen of Belfast, that her Benefit is fixed for WEDNESDAY April 15th, at which time will be presented, not acted here this season, the Comedy of the FOUNDLING, with a FARCE and a variety of Entertainments as will be expressed in the Bills. Tickets to be had and places in the Boxes to be taken of Miss Bradberry at the golden figure of Time, High-street, Belfast.

Anno 1789.] Printed by HENRY JOY, and Co. BELFAST.

The BELFAST NEWS-LETTER.

TUESDAY April 14, FRIDAY April 17, 1789.

Belfast Academy.

A Meeting of the Subscribers to said Institution will be held at the Publick-Hall within the Academy, on Thursday next the 16th instant;—when will be laid before them, a letter lately received by the Trustees from Lord Donegall's Law Agent, whereby they are required to compleat the building of houses on the front next to Donegall-street, conformable to a clause in the lease to that purport; as it must be determined by the Subscribers, whether they shall erect said buildings at their own expence, or let the ground on building leases; it is earnestly requested that there may be a full meeting.—Belfast, 11th April, 1789.

WADD. CUNNINGHAM,
JOHN EWING, } Trustees.
JOHN HOLMES.

A small Dwelling-House.

THE Lease of that Dwelling-House, in Skippers-lane, at present occupied by the Misses Maziere, will be sold at the Market-House, on Friday the 24th instant, at noon, by public Auction—there are five years and a half unexpired from 1st May next, and the rent is 9l. 2s. per annum. The purchaser will get immediate possession.—A snug Dwelling-house, opposite the Old Sugar-house; to be let from 1st May next—This is to be only once inserted.—Enquire of

ROBERT THOMSON.
Belfast, 10th April, 1789.

THE Assignees of Henry Haslett, a Bankrupt, will sell by public auction (on the premises) on Monday the 27th instant, all said Bankrupt's right, title, and interest in two dwelling houses, situate in Rosemary-lane, in the town of Belfast, held by lease for 31 years from 1st May 1786, at the yearly rent of 27l. One of said houses is let to a tenant at will for 6l. 16s 6d. per ann. the other is at present occupied by Mr. Haslett, and is in perfect repair, a large sum of money having been expended in improvements within these two years: The purchaser to have possession on the 1st day of May next.—Immediately after, will commence the sale of said Bankrupt's houshold furniture, and will be continued until the whole is disposed of. Any person desirous of purchasing said houses will be shewn the premises, and informed of further particulars by applying to Henry Haslett.

Belfast, 13th April, 1789.
WADDELL CUNNINGHAM
JOHN BOYLE } Assignees.
WILLIAM TENNENT

A Tanner wanted,

WHO can be well recommended.—Apply to Robert Magill at Annahavil, near Moneymore.
13th April, 1789.

To be Sold at Barnhill,

NEAR CUMBER, a Quantity of well-saved FLAX-SEED, the Produce of Dutch Seed.
April 12th, 1789.

Dancing-School, Downe.

MR. HULL respectfully informs the Ladies and Gentlemen of Down, that he has returned and will open his School for the Summer half Year in Downe, on Monday the 20th instant; in Strangford and Portaferry, on Wednesday the 22d; and will teach on Fridays and Saturdays if encouraged in Hillsborough or Dromore.
8th April, 1789.

Oat-meal & Wheat for Sale.

TO be sold by Auction at Strangford, on Thursday the 16th instant, (for ready money) for account of the Under-writers, between thirty and forty tons of Oat-meal; and three tons of Wheat, of a very fine and choice quality, saved out of the cargo of the Sloop Betsey, Richard Smith, Master, lately stranded on the shore of this district.—Apply to Mr. Vere Ward at Strangford.—Dated this 9th of April, 1789.

To be Sold,

THE Lease of a Farm in the sixteen Towns of Antrim, containing fifty-six acres, lying on the road to Ballymena, about a mile from Antrim, inclosed into small Parks with quickset ditches, and most of it lately limed, on which is a Farm-house lately built ——Said Farm is held under the Earl of Massereene, at the yearly rent of five pounds eight shillings, for three lives renewable for ever, paying a year's rent at the fall of each life; the whole is out of lease only ten acres, which are let for some time. Mr. Macay of Antrim will shew the premises, and treat for the same; and Mr. Young will satisfy as to the title:—If the premises are not sold by private sale before the 28th day of May next, they will be sold on that day by publick auction in the Market-house in Antrim.

Dated 10th April, 1789.

Pins at Dublin Prices.

And ten per cent Discount:

HUGH WARRIN, Bookseller New Buildings, High-Street, BELFAST, having formed extensive connections with some of the first Houses in the Pin Trade in this Kingdom, is enabled to sell the best PINS of all KINDS at the usual Prices; and also allow 7 and half per cent. on all sums under five Pounds, and on that sum and upwards 10 per cent. for Cash or Bills.
Belfast, 10th April. 1789.

The Union Assembly,

WILL be held at the ROOMS, on Thursday the sixteenth instant.
April 9th, 1789.

The Belfast Assembly,

WILL be held at the Exchange-Rooms, on Tuesday next the 14th instant.
Belfast, 8th April, 1789.

Samuel Robinson,
Seedsman, in Waring-Street,

ACQUAINTS his Friends and the Publick, that from the very great demand he has had for Seeds this Season, he has been induced to import a second Quantity, which is now landing out of the Friendship, Capt. Lepper, consisting of GARDEN SEEDS, Broad Red CLOVER, White Ditto;—also Lucerne, Burnet, and Saintfoine, double and single Glo'ster Cheese; with a few Bottles of the very best English Catsup.
Belfast, 16th April, 1789.

New Flaxseed.

JONES, TOMB, JOY, and Co. have for Sale a Parcel of best New-York and Philadelphia Flaxseed, which they are selling on reasonable Terms. They will take a few Redemptioners for the Ship St. James, Captain Collins, bound to Newcastle and New-York, but they must be persons of good character.
Belfast, 15th April. 1789.

New Alicant Barrilla.

HUGH CRAWFORD has just imported per the Sally, Capt. Giles, from Alicant, very best Barrilla Ashes—He is largely supplied with American Pot and Pearl Ashes first sort, Cross Arrow, and other Dantzig Ashes, best and second Smalts, best and second Starch, Vitriol, and every other Article for the use of Bleachers—the whole he will sell on the lowest terms.
Belfast, 14th April, 1789.

DANCING.

MR. DUMONT respectfully informs the Ladies and Gentlemen of Belfast and its Vicinity, that his days of teaching at the Publick school, are on Friday Evening, and Saturday all Day—He teaches the various Minuets with the English and French graces; also, Gavotte—Petticotee—Cotillons—Hornpipe, with the much admired Meddley, &c. &c.
N. B. Private Tuition on moderate terms.

Mr. ROWE,

WITH every degree of gratitude, returns his most sincere thanks to the Ladies and Gentlemen of Belfast and its Vicinity, for their countenance and support these twelve years past; begs leave to inform them that he is encouraged by some particular friends to take a second Benefit this season, which, he humbly hopes, will meet with their approbation: Should he be so happy as to succeed in this attempt, it will add considerably to the many obligations they have already conferr'd upon him.

On Monday Evening, April 20th, will be performed Mr. Cumberland's new Comedy of the

IMPOSTORS,

which has been received with universal and uncommon Applause in London and Dublin.

With a FARCE, &c. &c.

Tickets and places in the Boxes to be taken of Mr Rowe, Snugborough, North-street.
Belfast, 17th April, 1789.

By Desire of several Ladies and Gentlemen,

ON Wednesday next, the 22d instant, (being the last Night of performing this Season) will be performed a Play, Farce, and Entertainment,

For the Benefit of Mr. ATKINS,

Tickets and Places in the Boxes to be taken in Ann Street.
Belfast, 17th April, 1789.

Strolling Beggars.

THE Inhabitants of the Parish of Bangor give Notice, that from the date hereof, they are determined to support their own Poor, and give no Alms to strolling Beggars.
April 17th, 1789.

ONE THOUSAND POUNDS to be lent on personal Security, three joined in a Bond; the lender desires application to be made to Mr. Brett in Downe, and that this advertisement be continued three Tuesdays.
Downe, 7th April, 1789.

To be Sold by Auction,

ON Saturday the 25th of April instant, at the house of James Mc. Donnell of Tanderagee, Innkeeper, the Bleach-green and Mills, with the Dwelling-house, Office-houses, and Lands of Banvale, situate near Gilford in the county of Down, and lately occupied by John Mc. Creight.—The Mills are in thorough repair and capable of finishing in the course of a season 10,000 pieces of linen, having the entire command of the river Bann.—The Land, which consists of forty acres, is very highly improved, thirty-five acres whereof are held by lease under Lord Clanwilliam for 41 years, renewable for ever, at the yearly rent of six pounds; the remaining five acres are held by lease for three lives in being, renewable for ever, under Sir Richard Johnston, Bart. The Dwelling house is in good repair, and fit for the immediate reception of a tenant;—the situation is very central to the linen markets. The purchaser may hold the one half of the purchase-money at interest on securing same by mortgage on the lands; the other half to be paid on the deeds being executed: There are also four acres of turf-bog contiguous to the premises, which will be sold with the Bleach-green. For further particulars apply to Andrew Mc. Creight, Gilford.
14th April, 1789.

TO BE LET,

AT Dromore, near Ballymena,—A small Cotton Factory, containing a few Jennies and Carding Machine: There are apartments to dwell in; a stove; and every necessary convenience, all in good order—the demand for yarn cannot at present be supplied; and one disposed to manufacture may have looms, and all the apparatus for dyeing, finishing, &c. A quantity of cotton wool will be given at a valuation, and time allowed for payment; turf-bog convenient, and any land or grazing that may be required;—a Store is much wanted here, and a person qualified may find his account in carrying on both, as the country is good, place very publick, and opened with roads to every quarter. Apply to the Revd. James Mc. Cay, who has also two small Farms to let, which are good land, and well circumstanced in every respect.
April 14th, 1789.

New Teas, &c.

THOMPSON and OAKMAN have just received per the Friendship, Capt. Lepper, a parcel of fresh Hyson, Bloom, common Green, fine and common Congou Teas, French and Spanish Indigo; also new Broad Red Clover Seed—all of which they will sell on very moderate terms for cash or bills in course.
Belfast, 13th April, 1789.

Town Parks
TO BE LET.

SIX or eight Acres of TOWN PARKS, near the Lodge Road, to be let immediately.—Apply to JOHN KNOX, Watchmaker, in High-street.
☞ To be inserted twice only.
Belfast, 14th April, 1789

Robert Getty,

IS at present landing a Parcel of NEW ENGLISH RED CLOVER SEED, of very superior quality;—also first and second Spanish and French Indigoes, and Ombro Madders.
Belfast, 9th April, 1789.

Dutch Flaxseed.

CUNNINGHAM GREG has for Sale a few Hogsheads of last year's importation, which he will dispose of on reasonable terms.
Belfast, 13th April, 1789.

New red & white Clover Seed,

OF the very best Quality, is now landing, and to be sold on the lowest Terms, by
HUGH CRAWFORD.
Belfast, 13th April, 1789.
FLAXSEED, warranted new, to be sold.—Apply as above.

DUBLIN, April 14.

We are now on the eve of a general election—the people should keep a watchful eye on their representatives conduct—they will by this means be able to distinguish those honest delegates, whose faithful attention to their duty claim their future support.

Yesterday messages in form were again sent to the P——bys and Lord S———n; they were offered an entire re—in—statement——they insist on all their friends being included——for the present here rests the negociation.

The first bishopric that drops, certainly goes to the Speaker's brother.

Dr. Little had strong hopes—he will however be gratified by the accession of Mr. Foster's living, on his translation.

The Bishop of Ferns, who was given over by his physicians, is mending.

Mr. Burton is removed from his employment, as Paymaster of the Irish Army, on foreign service;—computed at a snug thousand per ann.

This morning the Castle runners (we suppose pursuant to orders) openly declared in all public places that the Marquis was certain of a majority of twenty-six in the House of Commons, on the first trial of strength.

Yesterday evening, about five o'clock, as a number of journeymen taylors were sitting in a house in Michael's-lane, at a customary annual entertainment given on Easter Mondays, a quarrel arose among some of them, who went out to decide the difference by boxing in the street. Soon after the fight, which was attended with no other ill consequences than a few black eyes, bloody noses, and torn clothes, a police serjeant being sent for, and having received information that there was a dangerous riot and desperate affray, came at the head of a party of police guards, armed with muskets and fixed bayonets, and laying hold of two or three persons, whom by their conduct, and from circumstances, appeared to be concerned in the affray, was escorting them to the guard house; upon which a mob assembled, suddenly attacked the police, disarmed them, and liberated the prisoners. In the course of the contest two police-men were killed, and another so dangerously wounded, that it is thought he cannot survive. All the muskets belonging to the policemen were broken by the mob, who appeared uncommonly outrageous and desperate.

The corps of Independent Dublin Volunteers paraded at eight o'clock Sunday morning, at the Royal Exchange, fully accoutred, from whence they marched to the Canal Harbour in James's-street, where they embarked on board one of the Canal passage boats for Sallins, where they were to land, and from thence to proceed to Rathcoffey, the country seat of Archibald Hamilton Rowan, Esq. where they are to spend the holidays, by invitation from that gentleman, he having been lately elected Major of the Dublin Independents.

Rathcoffey, the country residence of Archibald Hamilton Rowan, Esq. is about five miles distant from Sallins.

Bankrupt. Alexander Sutherland, of Belfast, in the county Antrim, merchant, to surrender the 27th and 29th days of April inst. and 16th May next.

SPORTING INTELLIGENCE.

CURRAGH, SPRING MEETING.

Monday, April 6th—50 Guineas, Craven weight and distance.

Mr. Conolly's Shot, by Richmond, -	5
Mr. A. Daly's Tinker, by Wellbred, -	6
Mr. Hamilton's King David, by Highflier,	2
Mr. Kirwan's Hippomenes, by Gamahoe,	7
Mr. Lumm's Trifle, by Justice, - -	1
Mr. Eyre's Oberon, - - - - -	3
Mr. Dennis's Kildare, by Cromahoo, -	4
Mr. Smith's b. m. by Mambrino, -	8

Same day; Mr. Dennis's Kildare, by Cromahoo, beat Mr. Daly's Louisa, by Friar, 8st. 7lb. each, for 100 Gs. each, h. f. from the Red Post home.

Same day, Mr. Lumm's Honest Tom, by King Fergus, beat Mr. A. Daly's Tinker, by Wellbred, 8st. for 100 Gs. each, from Sir Ralph's Post home.

Same day, Mr. Nesbitt's gr. two year old filly, by Fryar, 8st. 7lb. for 100 Gs each, h. f.——Conolly's mile.

Mr. Nesbitt's filly beat Mr. Dowling's filly.

LONDON-DERRY, April 14.

On Saturday last, came on at Lifford, before Lord Chief Baron Yelverton, and a special jury, composed of the principal gentlemen of the county of Donegall, the great cause of Bedford and Boyd.—It was an action brought by the Rev. Dr. Bedford against William Boyd, Esq. Collector of Ballyraine, for having maliciously preferred and prosecuted several informations against the plaintiff under the malt law, and for different other alleged frauds against the revenue laws. The Rev. gentleman laid his damages at 5,000l.

The case was stated for the plaintiff by Mr. Curran, with infinite ability—We are sorry that the confined limits of a paper will not allow us to give our readers an adequate idea of his beautiful speech, in the course of which he pathetically described the hardship which the plaintiff underwent during his persecution; particularly that scene in which his house was surrounded by an army brought in all the parade of military array to storm the plaintiff's castle, which was defended by only two servants fast asleep!—And then the old gentleman, in the 87th year of his age, dragged 17 miles in chains more heavy than those of a Baron Trenck, because more disgraceful, to the kitchen of the defendant, and there tried and condemned by his dependants!—" for (said the eloquent advocate) I cannot be said to abuse a culinary metaphor, when I compare the understrappers of the revenue to the domestics of their superior, where the plaintiff was convicted without the benefit of such assistance as the laws of the country allow to the vilest culprit!—But, such judgements cannot stand; they defeat themselves; and this one fell in a Court where law and justice alone can be obtained in revenue cases."

Mr. Jamison, for the defendant, moved the Court that the plaintiff be non-suited, in as much as the action was for "a malicious prosecution," and, in point of law, the malice was done away, by the judgment of the Sub-Commissioners.—This point was argued with great ability on both sides, and the Lord Chief Baron being of opinion that the point was founded, non-suited the plaintiff; "but by no means precluding himself from changing that opinion when it should be argued before him in full Court; and he was happy the plaintiff was a man of that fortune and disposition which could not be hurt by having the law settled on that point."—The Counsel for the plaintiff were, Mr. Curran and Mr. Burston, brought specially; Mr. Stewart, Mr. Warren, Mr. O'Farrel, Mr. Fox, Mr. Ball, and Mr. Mahaffy; Agent, Mr. Galbraith.—Counsel for the defendant, Mr. Jamison, Mr. Stewart, Mr. Hill, Mr. Scott, Mr. Alexander, and Mr. Curry; Agent, Mr. Boyd.

Same day, a cause was tried, wherein Ralph Johnston, Esq. was plaintiff, and his own uncle, John Johnston, Esq. was defendant, on an issue from the Equity side of the Court of Exchequer, to try whether the defendant had actual notice of the settlement executed on the marriage of the plaintiff's father and mother, previous to his purchasing the settled estate of plaintiff's father in the year 1750; after a full investigation of the matter, the jury (a special one) gave a verdict for the plaintiff.

Last Friday, the following Revenue trial was decided before the Sub-Commissioners of Strabane:—In the year 1785, an information had been exhibited against Robert Cochran of Strabane, for having knowingly harboured, &c. a quantity of tobacco, whereby he forfeited the sum of 148l. being treble the value of the goods seized. It appeared that this trial came on before the Sub-Commissioners in June 1788, at which time the defendant desired to put off his defence by affidavit until he could have a material evidence summoned from another district; but the Court refused to take his affidavit, and fined him in the above sum.—Mr. Cochran then brought his cause before the Court of Appeals, which being satisfied that the defendant tendered the affidavit before-mentioned agreeable to law, remanded back the proceedings for a re-hearing.—Accordingly the Sub-Commissioners, after a full hearing, discharged the information.—We hear that it has cost the defendant upwards of 100l. and that he means to bring an action against the prosecutor.——Counsel for the prosecution Mr. Hill; for the defendant Messrs. Jamison, and Fox.

At Omagh assizes, the following persons received sentence, viz. T. Hughes for murder, and John M'Afee for house-breaking, to be executed the 23d inst.—Pat Nugent, for a rape on the body of Mrs. Moor, to be executed the 23d of June; and, David Hog, for robbery, on the 30th of the same month.—Mary Wier, for theft, to be transported.

Since our last arrived two vessels at Derry, from America, one of them from New-York, the other from Salem; they are both loaded with flaxseed.

Married, Mr. Alexander Major, to Miss Penelope Reynolds.

Died, in Bishop-street, Miss Scott, sister to Alex. Scott, Esq.—The wife of Mr. Alexander, inn-keeper.—Mr. Alex. Thompson, taylor.

Belfast, *April* 14.

"We hear, a new and necessary regulation will shortly "take place in the Post-office, relative to the forwarding of newspapers. The want of punctuality in their "customers—is the cause assigned—debts have accumulated to a surprizing amount—on one road there is "an arrear of near 3,000l.——The Leinster road will "take the lead—from the first of May, we are confidently assured, that no newspapers will be sent to "the country, that are not paid for in advance."——[*D. E. Post.*]

In hopes that the preceding Article, copied from the Dublin Prints, may evince the absolute necessity for a regular discharge of Newspaper debts,—we take the liberty of inserting it.—To those who in consideration of the present enormous Stamp Duties paid *in advance*,—the extraordinary expence almost peculiar to *The BELFAST NEWS-LETTER* in distributing it by special Carriers thro' this Province,—and in personal application to each Subscriber for payment,—are so kind as to be regular in the settlement of accounts, every acknowledgment of gratitude is due.

The obvious advantages enjoyed by the Proprietors of Papers in the Capital, over those of the Country, in receiving payment for the papers in advance,—and in not giving credit on Advertisements,—will, we hope, induce the great body of our readers to assist us at this season of the year by an obliging attention to this Hint.

The Sovereign has received a letter from the Secretary of State, by command of the Lord Lieutenant, informing him that the congratulatory Address to his Majesty from the Town of Belfast, was most graciously received; and that the congratulatory Address to her Majesty had been presented to the Queen by Lord Ailesbury, her Chamberlain, and most graciously received.

The London Gazette of April 4, acknowledges the receipt of Addresses to their Majesties from the Protestant Dissenters of Ireland; the Inhabitants of Belfast; and the Grand Jury of the County of Lowth.

We understand that Mr. Rowe, who has for twelve years been deservedly held in esteem by the inhabitants of Belfast, intends to have a Benefit on Monday next. In addition to his confessed merits as a just Comedian, the present state of his health will no doubt operate in his favour on this occasion.

Several accounts of rejoicings in different towns in the North of Ireland, on account of his Majesty's recovery, come now too late for insertion.

Saturday morning last a weaver returning from Lurgan market, was found suffocated on the road leading to Rathfryland, a few perches from Banbridge. He had a wife and four children.

The Lord Donegall, James M'Roberts, master, for London, sailed the 12th inst. with a very fair wind, which has since continued.

At the request of a great number of Passengers, the sailing of the brothers for Philadelphia, &c. is put off to Saturday the 25th inst. when she will be ready to receive the passengers on board, and will sail with the first favourable wind.

Married, on Thursday last, James Law, Esq. to Miss Sarah Crawford, both of Banbridge.

Died, on Tuesday last, Mr. Matthew Brown, publican. At Banbridge, after a few hours illness, of a severe vomiting of blood, Mr. Henry Harrison.

MISS BRADBERRY,

With the greatest respect, begs leave to inform the Ladies and Gentlemen of Belfast, that her Benefit is fixed for WEDNESDAY April 15th, at which time will be presented, not acted here this season, the Comedy of the FOUNDLING, with a FARCE and a variety of Entertainments as will be expressed in the Bills. Tickets to be had and places in the Boxes to be taken of Miss Bradberry at the golden figure of Time, High-street, Belfast.

Belfast, *April* 17.

Cards seem of late years to have considerably augmented their influence over the fashionable world. The following opinion of the late Dr. Johnson, on this species of diversion, if generally known, may perhaps, in some degree, tend to the cultivation of more rational amusements: "This odious fashion is produced by a conspiracy of the old, the ugly, and the ignorant, against the young and beautiful, the witty and the gay; as a contrivance to level all distinctions of nature and of art, to confound the world in a chaos of folly, to take from those who could outshine them all the advantages of mind and body; to withhold youth from its natural pleasures, deprive wit of its influence, and beauty of its charms; to fix their hearts upon money, to which love has hitherto been entitled, to sink life into a tedious uniformity, and to allow it no other hopes or fears but those of robbing and being robbed." He says also on this subject, that "if those who have minds capable of nobler sentiments were to unite in vindication of their pleasures and prerogatives, they might fix a time at which cards should cease to be in fashion, or be left only to those who have neither beauty to be loved, nor spirit to be feared, neither knowledge to teach, nor modesty to learn, and who having passed their youth in vice, are justly condemned to spend their age in folly."

On Sunday evening last, died at Downpatrick, very much and very deservedly lamented, Mr. William Kean, woollen-draper; his death was occasioned by a fall from his horse the preceding Monday.—At Armagh, Richard Olphert, Esq. of Armagh.

TO BE LET,

From the first of May next, for such Term as may be agreed on,

TWO Houses in the town of Carrickfergus, at present in possession of Mr. WILLIAM FINLAY, situated in the Main-street leading from the Market-place to the Quay, adjoining the old Court-house of the county of Antrim. One of them a large Dwelling-house of two stories high, slated; consisting of a Kitchen and two rooms on the ground floor, with three rooms on the second floor; the lower part of the other house is now employed as a store room, the upper part in that of a lapping-room, with an inclosed yard, stable, and large garden in the rere.

Those houses are most agreeably situated, being nigh the Market-place, and having a most extensive view of the sea.——Proposals will be received by Alexander Gunning the Proprietor.

Carrickfergus, 11th April, 1789.

TO BE LET,

For such Term as may be agreed on,

THE House, Offices, Garden, and Meadow in the rere of the same, at present possessed by John Brown, Esq; in Peters-hill, in the Town of Belfast. The House consists of a parlour, drawing-room, five bed-chambers, a kitchen, office, &c.—there is stabling for eight horses, a coach-house, and lofts which will contain a sufficient quantity of hay for the season. The Garden is well stock'd with Fruit Trees, &c. in full bearing. Application to be made to Mr. Thoburn.

Belfast, July 21st, 1788.

Anno 1789.]   Printed by HENRY JOY, and Co. BELFAST.

The BELFAST NEWS-LETTER.

TUESDAY April 21,   FRIDAY April 24, 1789.

For Oporto and back to Belfast,

THE fine Sloop MARCELLA, burthen 100 Tons, William Cargy, junior, Master, is now clear for sea, and will bring any Goods for Belfast at the low Freight of forty Shillings Irish per Ton; as her Cargo is mostly engaged, any Orders given immediately will be forwarded by Narcissus Batt.

Belfast, 18th April, 1789.

Sea Bathing.

GOOD Accommodations for Ladies and Gentlemen at Portstewart near Coleraine, and Stabling for Horses. The House will be opened the first May next. Apply to Mr. Samuel Mc. Donnell, Coleraine.

15th April, 1789.

Thomas Humpries, Stay-maker,

IMPREST with the liveliest sense of gratitude for past favours; begs leave to return his most sincere thanks to the Ladies of Belfast and its vicinity for their manifold favours; he thinks it his duty to acquaint them that he has received a large assortment of the newest fashions from London, and being constantly supplied with the best Workmen the kingdom can afford, hopes from his attention to business, and assiduity to please, to merit their future commands.

N. B. A few Journeymen of sober character and distinguished abilities, will meet with good encouragement.

Royal Sport of Cock-fighting.

TO be shewn in Ballymoney on Saturday the 2d day of May next, and fought the week following, between the Gentlemen of the counties of Derry and Antrim. A Main of 31 Cocks and 15 Byes for One Hundred Guineas the Main or odd battle.

Ballymoney, 17th April, 1789.

To be Let,

SEVERAL large and convenient Houses lately built in English-street Armagh, which from their proximity to Market-street, are in a situation extremely eligible for every kind of business. Application to be made to Miss Mary Boyd, Armagh.

April, 19th, 1789.

Boarding-School

THE Miss THOMPSONs present their grateful acknowledgments to the Public, but particularly to the Ladies of Newry, for the encouragement they have met with since they opened School in this Town. They teach Tambour, Embroidery, artificial Flowers, raised and plain Phillagree, Reading, &c. &c.

They have accommodations for a few more Boarders. —Terms for these, twenty Guineas a year, and two do. entrance, with a pair of Sheets; for Day-pupils 16s. 3d. per quarter, and half a guinea entrance.—Proper Masters attend.   Newry, 18th April, 1789.

New-York Flaxseed.

WILLIAM Mc. CONCHY has for Sale a Quantity of New York Flaxseed of a remarkably fine Quality, certified new; also for sale, strong Jamaica Rum, Coniac and Bourdeaux Brandy, old Cherry Brandy, Gin"eva, Red Port, Malaga Wine, French bottled Clarets of the vintage 1784.

Antrim, 18th April, 1789.

Welch Slates.

CUNNINGHAM GREG is just landing a Cargo, which he will dispose of on reasonable terms.

Belfast, 20th April, 1789.

Woollen Warehouse, Belfast.

BROWN, GAW, & CO. are this day landing their Spring Assortment, which is extensive and compleat.—As those Goods have been purchased by one of their Partners at the best Markets, for ready Money, have no doubt of their giving satisfaction to those who are pleased to favour them with their commands.

20th April, 1789.

A Brewer wanted.

SUCH a Person, properly qualified, and well recommended, may apply to William Osborne, N. Lemavady, the 6th April, 1789.
To be continued six times.

Wants a Place,

A Middle-aged Woman, well qualified to act as Housekeeper in a Gentleman's Family, whose character will bear the strictest scrutiny.——Enquire at the Office of Mr. Joy.

Antrim Quarter Sessions.

THE next General Quarter Sessions of the Peace for the county of Antrim, will be held at Antrim on Thursday the 23d instant, when the attendance of the Coroners, Seneschals, and High Constables will be required as usual. Dated the 17th April, 1789.

CHARLES CRYMBLE, Sheriff.

Robert & Alexander Gordon

HAVE for sale the following Wines which they believe to be of equal quality to any in the kingdom, viz. Claret and Hermitage in wood, Sillery Champaign, and Burgundy of different growths in bottle, Malmsey and dry Madeira, remarkable old Hock, Sherry, Lunel, Calcavella, Frontiniac, Barsac, Vin de Grave, Lisbon, Port, Beziers, and Mountain in wood and Bottle.

The Madeira is London particular Wine, and they are assured by one of the first houses (in the London trade) at Madeira, that better Wine had never left that island.

Belfast, 21st April, 1789.

Young Slapdash,

STANDS this season at Cloughy near Portaferry, and will cover Mares, at one Guinea for a Foal, and half a crown to the Groom.——He is a beautiful bay, English bred, is very fruitful and his foals are large and strong, he is now five years old, full blooded.——He will attend the Markets of Newtownards and Portaferry. His pedigree in the hands of his Groom.

Cloughy, 20th April, 1789.

To be continued six times.

ACCOUNT-OFFICE,
17th April, 1789.

THE Commissioners of Account having in the last year issued precepts to divers persons who had received money by warrants from the late Corporation for promoting and carrying on Inland Navigation, to which very few returns have been made, give this public notice, that they intend to report finally to Parliament upon this subject with as little delay as the nature of the business will admit.

By order of the Commissioners,
ALLAN MAC LEAN, Secretary.

Household Furniture.

TO be Sold by Auction, on Tuesday 19th May next, by John Bailie, Auctioneer and sworn Appraiser, at the house of Mr. Thomas Hunter, Lisburn.—All his Household Furniture, consisting of feather beds and bedsteads, mahogany hair-bottomed and other chairs, a large Northumberland table, card, voidore and dressing-tables, pier and dressing-glasses, girandoles, carpets and carpeting for stairs, &c. a large mahogany wardrobe, a very handsome book-case with drawers, some paintings on glass and other pictures, a walnut desk, an oak do. a very good clock, table and tea china, delft-ware of various kinds, a great variety of kitchen furniture, &c. &c. cloth-presses and lapping-tables, a car and tacklings, two excellent ladders, one about 70 the other 30 feet long, a large beam and scales and some weights, with several other articles too numerous to insert.—The sale to begin at 11 o'clock, and continue from day to day till all are sold.

N. B. Said Bailie has for sale a very serviceable postchaise and harness, which will be sold remarkably cheap by applying to him at his house in Belfast.

April 23d. 1789.

The Ballymena Hunt,

MEET and Dine at their Club-Room, on Wednesday the 22d instant. It is requested the Members will all attend, as the Treasurer's accounts, and other business of consequence, are to be settled.—The hounds will be unkennell'd precisely at seven o'clock.

April 16th, 1789.

A General Half-Yearly Meeting of the Belfast Annuity Company, will be held at the Market-House in Belfast, on Friday the 1st of May next, precisely as eleven strikes, to pay the half Year's Subscription then due, and to ballot for the Gentlemen who have proposed themselves to become Members of this Company.

Belfast, 14th
April, 1789.

HUGH CRAWFORD,
Secretary.

Books by Auction.

ON MONDAY EVENING next, the 20th April instant, will begin to be peremptorily sold by Auction, at No. 13, Bridge-street, Belfast,

A large Consignment of Books,

In all the various Branches of useful, polite and entertaining Literature.—As these Books were not purchased with a view of being sold by auction, they will be engaged por[ss], unless otherwise declared at the time of sale.

Catalogues to be had gratis at the place of sale, at 12 o'clock on Monday next.

J. KNOX, Watchmaker, &c.

At the GOLD WATCH, High-Street,
(Licensed to buy and sell Gold and Silver Ware)

RESPECTFULLY informs his Friends, that he has at all times ready for Sale, a variety of Watches in Gold, Silver, and Metal Cases, on the newest Constructions;—Clocks and every other Article in the above Line.

Belfast, 18th April, 1789.

New Woollen Warehouse,
(Waring-Street)

HASLETT, STRONG, & CO. have this day received per the Hillsborough, a fresh supply of Woollen and Cotton Goods:—Those who wish to purchase on the lowest Terms, for Cash or Bills, will find their present Assortment worth Notice.

Belfast, 18th April, 1789.

Irish Woollen Warehouse,
Belfast.

SAMUEL NEILSON, & CO. are just receiving their Spring and Summer Assortment of Irish Manufactures, which will be sold at reduced Prices for good Bills on Dublin or Belfast not exceeding three months, or a proportionable discount allowed for cash.

☞ They continue to sell the very best Pins, and to give the same discount that is usually allowed in Dublin.

21st April, 1789.

This Day is published,
(Inscribed to the Earl of CHARLEMONT)

THE PATRIOT SOLDIER; or, IRISH VOLUNTEER. A POEM.

By a Member of the Belfast 1st Volunteer Company.

☞ Subscribers are requested to send for their Copies, as there are but a few more printed than what are subscribed for.—To be had at the different Booksellers, Price 1s. 1d.

Wanted,

A Lad of good Character, and unmarried, who can attend Table.——Apply to Mr. Joy.

April 20, 1789.

Hu. & Wm. Johnson,

HAVE received their Assortment of superfine Broad and narrow Cloths, New Fancy Waistcoating and Buttons, Cassimeres, Florentines, Lutherines, Thicksets, Worsted and Cotton Cords, Dimities, Muslinets, Marseilles Quilting, Marseilles Quilts, Counterpanes, Damascus, Moreens, &c. &c.

Belfast, 24th April, 1789.

An Apprentice

TO the Apothecary Business wanted immediately by James Jackson of Newtownards.

April, 23d 1789.

(The last Night of performing this Season.)

For the Benefit of Mr. ATKINS,

On Monday next, will be performed the new Comedy of the

IMPOSTORS,

With the
TRUE-BORN IRISHMAN.

Tickets and Places to be taken of Mr. Atkins.

Belfast, 23d April, 1789.

Post-Coach.

FOR the better accommodation of Passengers going from Belfast to Dublin, the Coach will leave the Donegall-Arms at 12 o'clock at noon, instead of six in the morning on the same days, as usual.

ANECDOTES.

A preacher in this metropolis conſtantly offers up a few libations to Bacchus, in the neighbourhood of the pariſh church, immediately before ſervice-time. The blunders he commits on theſe occaſions are truly laughable. He has been known to pray for the Princeſs Amelia, when ſhe had been dead, the Lord knows how long; and to ſupplicate the Divinity for rain, when almoſt a complete deluge had been poured upon us. A ſhort time ago, after committing ſeveral of theſe blunders, he proceeded to the ſermon, of which, when he had delivered eight or ten lines, the fumes of the hot punch overpowered him ſo effectually, that he fell ſprawling in the puplit. On getting up, he thus addreſſed his hearers: "My good friends, I don't know whether you have had enough, but I am ſure that *I have*.—farewell."

CONTRAST.

GOOD-FRIDAY.

THEN.	NOW.
A day appointed for the ſolemn commemoration of the death of our Saviour.	A holiday for ſervants and others, exempt from buſineſs of every kind.
A day of faſting and mortification.	A day of feaſting and gluttony.
The moſt punctual attendance on all the ſacred duties of the churches and chapels.	The moſt punctual engagements at taverns, inns, and ordinaries, in the country.
Faſting in moſt houſes for the whole day, or only fiſh permitted.	Every delicacy of the ſeaſon on our tables, not excepting fiſh.
No perſon went abroad on this day, but confined their employments to acts of devotion at home.	Nobody at home, but thoſe who receive large parties—and no acts but thoſe connected with good eating and drinking.
No employment for horſes or carriages on this day.	Not a horſe to be procured for love or money, unleſs beſpoke a week before.
Dinner regularly on the table, if any dinner at all, at one o'clock, that time might be allowed for the afternoon ſervice.	Dinner on the table, if not later, at four o'clock, that time may be allowed for a morning ride, and to dreſs in the afternoon.
Shops of all kinds cloſe ſhut on this day, from the voluntary and devout motives of the proprietors.	Many ſhops open, and thoſe ſhut, ſhut by compulſion, or from motives of holiday making.
Churches crowded, and taverns and all ſuch places ſhut, and prohibited from receiving viſitors.	Churches nearly empty, and taverns carrying on the uſual buſineſs, with large parties.
No money ſpent on this day, the neceſſaries having been procured the day preceding.	More money ſpent than in all the week beſides, Sunday excepted, and expended chiefly in luxuries, not forgetting *wager money!*
People retired to reſt with hearts filled with gratitude, on remembering the great merits of this day.	People carried to bed, their heads filled with wine, and d—ning the hearts of thoſe who enforced the great *bumpers* of the day.
SUCH THINGS WERE.	SUCH THINGS ARE.

AMERICAN NEWS.

New-York, Feb. 20. The Minerva, Captain Alexander Law, from Hudſon to Belfaſt, with a cargo of fiſh oil, pot-aſh, flax-ſeed, &c. is on ſhore near Æſopus, in the North River, and muſt unlade part of the cargo before ſhe can proceed.

The following is an extract of a letter from a gentleman at Stradford, in Connecticut, to his friend in this city, dated Feb. 14.

"In anſwer to your inquiries reſpecting our Duck Manufactory, it is with pleaſure I can inform you it greatly exceeds our expectations. We have made in the courſe of the fall and winter upwards of 200 bolts, which judges ſay are ſuperior to the Ruſſian Duck. I am perſuaded it will in a ſhort time be one of the firſt and moſt profitable manufactories in the United States. Our ſituation (on the Sound and Eaſt River,) and our flax, which has ever been admired for its ſuperior quality and fineneſs, are circumſtances ſo favourable to the buſineſs, that nothing but a want of ſpirit in the inhabitants can prevent it from flouriſhing agreeably to their wiſhes; and from what I have ſeen of them, I have no reaſon to ſuppoſe this will ever be the caſe, for they are not only ſenſible of the advantages ariſing from it, but are remarkably induſtrious."

New-York, Feb. 25. In moſt of the United States, the gentry and people have caught the flame for manufacturing for themſelves, and entered into combinations to uſe or wear no foreign article which their own country can produce or make: Separate States too are giving public aid to infant manufactures. Their working of iron in all branches is very fully eſtabliſhed; potteries for delft, hats, &c. &c. are alſo in great forwardneſs; but what ſeems to hit the appetite moſt, at the preſent criſis, is the cotton manufacture in all its branches. One under great patronage, and of large capital, is doing well at Philadelphia; another alike great, is began at Richmond, Virginia, and a third at Wilmington, on the Delaware. A glaſs houſe at Baltimore is alſo flouriſhing very much, and in every part the greateſt encouragemeut is given to artiſts.

Our worthy Governor, Clinton, has not only effected a treaty of amity, peace and commerce with the weſtern Indian tribes, but done eſſential benefit to the State, by purchaſe from the Mohawk and the Lake Indians, of a vaſt tract of as fine land as any on the continent for the ſum of four hundered dollars down, and as many more annual ly for twenty-one years. He has added to the State of New York above three millions of acres of land, chiefly on the Mohawk river and borders.

LONDON, April 18.

A meſſage from his Majeſty to both Houſes of Parliament, is now forming, and will be delivered the week after the of day public thankſgiving: the ſubject is ſaid to be on the King's intention of going to Germany.

The Earl Fitzwilliam has 30,000 acres of land in Ireland, in a chain within a reaſonable diſtance from the ſea, and conſequently augmenting in value every hour.

SPORTING INTELLIGENCE.

CURRAGH—SECOND SPRING MEETING.

Saturday, April 18.

Mr. D. B. Daly's ſealed up h. Mr. Denis's ſealed up h. and Mr. Savage's ſealed up h. Cup weights and diſtance, 4 miles.

Mr. Denis's Morgan, 7ſt. 11lb.	-	1
Mr. Savage's Douglas, 8ſt. 13lb.	-	2
Mr. D. B. Daly m. Louiſa, 8ſt. 8lb.		3

At ſtarting Louiſa the favourite, on the Long Hill 4 to 1 againſt her, even betting on the Flat between Morgan and Douglas, at the mile poſt 2 to 1 Morgan won.

Same day—Mr. D. B. Daly's Peeping Tom, carrying 7ſt. 13lb. beat Mr. Denis's Cherokee, carrying 8ſt. 1lb. for 200gs. each, h. ſt. one 4-mile heat. At ſtarting 3 to 2 on Cherokee: on the Flat even betting.

Monday, April 20.

Colonel Lumm's b. colt, Honeſt Tom—Mr. Denis's g. mare, Kitty—and Mr. Daly's Seducer—were to have ſtarted for two hundred guineas each—but Mr. Daly paid half forfeit—and Honeſt Tom, and Kitty ſtarted—two to one on Honeſt Tom, who carried 7ſt. 11lb.—giving Kitty 7lb.—over the King's Plate courſe, 4 miles. Honeſt Tom took the lead, and kept it the whole race—Kitty made a puſh coming acroſs the flat; after which, five to one againſt her.——Tom won by about half a length—but he pulled up, and waited for her to come in.

Mr. Daly's Louiſa was matched againſt Mr. Denis's Morgan, for two hundred guineas—and the gold cup; one four-mile heat—play or pay—but Mr. Daly paid forfeit—and Morgan walked over the courſe. The motive for drawing Louiſa was, that ſhe has a match to run on Saturday with Cherokee.

The meeting is tolerably full—little betting took place this day, as very few could be found to go againſt Honeſt Tom. The odds on the match between Morgan and Louiſa, were ſix to four againſt Louiſa—all the play or pay bets, were loſt by Morgan.

IRISH HOUSE OF COMMONS.

The houſe then reſolved itſelf into a committee for the application of the tillage duties, in which the following grants were made:

Barrow Navigation	20,000
Shannon ditto	83,000
Grand Canal	57,000
Ditto for the branch of the junction to the river Liffey	10,000
Navigation from Dublin to the Shannon	66,000
Boyne Navigation	12,500
Newry Canal	4,000
County Kildare Canal from Oſberſtown to Naas	33,000
Lough Erne Navigation	5,100

Being one third of the ſums ſpecified in the eſtimations in the reſpective petitions, agreeable to the principles laid down by the Chancellor of the Exchequer, in his preliminary on the application of the tillage duties in the buſineſs of yeſterday.

LONDON-DERRY, April 21.

At Lifford aſſizes, which concluded on Thurſday laſt' John and James Thomas, for feloniouſly breaking into the dwelling houſe of Wm. Logan, and thereout taking a ſum of money, &c. received ſentence to be hanged the 5th of May next.—And, Tonar, for horſe-ſtealing, to be hanged the 30th of May.—M. Farren, O. Farren, and M. M'Colgan, for burning a parcel of unthreſhed oats, the property of Wm. Porter, to be impriſoned 3 months, and fined 5 marks each.

At Lifford aſſizes, came on to be tried before the Right Hon. the Chief Baron Yelverton and a reſpectable jury, an action wherein the Revd. James Taylor, Diſſenting Miniſter of Convoy, was Plaintiff, and Mr. Andrew M'Clure was Defendant; the action was brought for calling the Plaintiff "a Liar, a Traitor, a Judas, and ſower of Sedition."—After a trial which laſted ſeveral hours, and a moſt learned charge from the Chief Baron, the jury retired, and brought in a verdict for the Plaintiff, with damages and coſts.

On Thurſday laſt, the hon. Juſtice Henn arrived in this city, as did Lord Chief Baron Yelverton on Friday, for the purpoſe of holding the Spring Aſſizes for this city and county.

On Friday, came on to be tried before Mr. Juſtice Henn, and a ſpecial Jury, a cauſe in which Meſſrs. Samuel and John King, in prohibition, were the Plaintiffs, and the Rev. Edmond Hamilton was the Defendant: the cauſe was, whether a Modus of ſix-pence in value in lieu of the tythes of each pariſhioner's potatoes, and of ſixpence in lieu of the tythes of each pariſhioner's flax, exiſted in the Defendant's pariſh, or not? When, after a trial which laſted nearly three hours, and an impartial charge in favour of the Modus, being given to the jury by the learned Judge, the jury retired, but finding it impoſſible to agree in their verdict, a juror was withdrawn by conſent of the Attornies concerned, whereby the event of this cauſe remains undetermined until the next aſſizes, when, we are aſſured, it will again be tried.

On Tueſday the 14th inſt. came on before the Sub-Commiſſioners of the Diſtrict of Ballyrain, the trial of the ſhip Eleanor, on board of which were 40 puncheons of rum, and a quantity of tobacco, lately ſeized in Lough Swily by Mr. Cannon. The veſſel and cargo were condemned.—Council for the Crown, Mr. Hill; Agents, Mr. Kerr and Mr. Murray.—Counſel for the Claimants, Mr. Dunn and Mr. A. Stewart; Agents, Meſſrs Stewart and Gordon.

Belfaſt, *April* 21.

As Thurſday next is the day appointed by Proclamation for a General Thankſgiving for his Majeſty's happy recovery, it is expected that it will be obſerved with the reverence and reſpect due by every loyal ſubject.

Friday laſt two men were whipped thro' this town for picking pockets.

Monday evening laſt, a ſet of lawleſs ruffians threatening diſturbance to ſome of the peaceful inhabitants of Banbridge, the drum beat to arms, and in a few minutes the Volunteer Company aſſembled, whoſe ſpirited appearance and well known reſolution of puniſhing, without reſpect to perſon or party, all ſuch violators of the law, ſoon left them in quiet poſſeſſion of the town, without any further trouble. An example not unworthy of imitation by ſome of the neighbouring towns on ſimilar occaſions.

Thurſday laſt being the anniverſary of the battle of Culloden, the Banbridge Volunteer Company paraded in uniform and fired three vollies.

A journeyman chandler a few days ago, drowned himſelf in the river Lagan at Liſburn.

CERTIFICATE TO BE GRANTED. 'James Murphy, of Belfaſt, in the county of Antrim, merchant, on the 5th day of May next.

PORT NEWS.

ARRIVED.

April 15—Sally, Giles, Alicant, aſhes.
17—Hillſborough, M'Donnell, Liverpool bale-goods.

Six Colliers.

CLEARED OUT.

April 15—Experiment, Donning, St. Vincents, cloth, pork, &c.
17—Induſtry, Hay, Boſton, cloth.
Chriſty, Johnſton, Dominico, do. pork, herrings
18—New Loyalty, Brown, Liverpool, do. and flour.

Belfaſt, *April* 24.

The wetneſs of Wedneſday night having occaſioned Rowe's benefit-play to be poſtponed till Friday (this Evening);—the entertainment that every perſon who attends the Theatre has repeatedly experienced in his performance, will, no doubt, be remembered on this occaſion, and bring him a full houſe, as a mark of the taſte of the town and its regard for a good actor.

The petition of Bartholomew O'Donnoghue, John Anderſon and Henry Forteſcue, of the city of Cork, merchants, preſented to the houſe on Wedneſday laſt, ſets forth, that the petitioners have entered into a contract for the conveyance of his Majeſty's mail between Dublin and Cork on a plan ſimilar to that lately adopted in England, and in order to carry the ſame into affect have gone to a very conſiderable expenſe in providing coaches, horſes, and other neceſſaries; that the petitioners intended to commence running ſaid coaches on the 5th of April, in full hope that, by that time, the truſtees of the different turnpike roads would, in compliance with his Excellency the Lord Lieutenant's circular letters to the different High Sheriffs, iſſued laſt ſummer, have cauſed the roads to be completely repaired; that upon a late minute inſpection of the roads, particulary between Kilkenny and Clogheen, the petitioners are much diſappointed to find the neceſſary repairs have been neglected, and in many inſtances they continue ſo bad and ſo extremely narrow as to render it impoſſible for two carriages to paſs even by day-light, without the utmoſt danger of one or both being overſet into the deep trenches on either ſide;

To be Let,

From the firſt of November, or May next,

THE HOUSE of CANDLEFORT, near Carrickmacroſs, with any quantity of Land from 20 to 75 acres, Iriſh plantation meaſure.—The Houſe conſiſts of two ſmall parlours, a good kitchen, and five ſmall bedchambers: The Offices—a Coach-houſe for two carriages, and ſtabling for eight horſes, lofted. The Land is well incloſed and planted, and in excellent condition, very near the whole of which has been highly marled within theſe five years, and well circumſtanced as to meadow and firing:—Its ſituation is within five miles of Carrickmacroſs and ſeven of Dundalk, both daily poſt and excellent market towns, and 43 from Dublin: It is alſo within a quarter of a mile of a church and chapel, and in a good ſporting country. Application to be made to Norman Steele, Eſq. at Candlefort, who will grant any term moſt convenient to the tenant, and who, for the ſake of inſuring the keeping up ſome neat planting about the houſe, will let the ſmaller number of acres on the ſame terms of the whole.—He promiſes that 10s. an acre of the rent ſhall be fined down.

Candlefort, 17th April, 1789.

Ship St. James,

MARK COLLINS, Master, for NEWCASTLE and NEW-RORK.

NOTICE is hereby given, that all Passengers intending to go by this favourable opportunity, are requested to be on board said Vessel on Monday the 11th May next, as she will sail the first fair wind after.——For freight or passage apply to Captain Collins, at Mrs. Moore's, or
JONES, TOMB, JOY, & Co.
Belfast, 23d April, 1789.

Surgeon and Man-midwife

JOHN CARMICHAEL, lately returned from London, where he studied for a number of years under the best Masters—begs leave to inform his friends and the public, that he has opened an Apothecary Shop in Castledawson, and laid in a general Assortment of Medicines of the first quality : He hopes, from his knowledge in his profession, and care and attention to those who are pleased to employ him, to merit their favour and approbation.
Castledawson, April 25th, 1789.

Wanted immediately,

THE Sum of 500l. upon an Assignment of the only Mortgage affecting a real Estate of upwards of £ 500 a Year in the County of Armagh.——Application to be made to John Shepard, attorney at law, Dublin, in term, and Lisburn in vacation.
27th April, 1789.

To be Sold,

AT the Whitehouse, a PIKE of good HAY, that did not get any rain in the making—Enquire at Magnus Prince.   May 1st, 1789.
This to be continued two times.

Robert Callwell and Co.

Are at present well stocked with
PORTER
Completely up in bottle—which in quality is such as they can with confidence recommend for strength—flavour and purity. They are always supplied with
WINES & SPIRITS
Of almost every kind—best WHITE WINE VINEGAR, HAMS and ENGLISH CHEESE of various sorts.
No. 11. Bridge-street, Belfast 1st May, 1789.
PORTER wired on the shortest notice for sea or exportation.

Hungarian Pearl Ashes, Jamaica Rum, and SCALE SUGAR.

ROBERT SCOTT has for sale a Parcel of White and Sky Blue Pearl Ashes, of the very first qualities—Also a quantity of strong Jamaica Rum, and first and second Scale Sugar—which he will sell by the Package as imported on reasonable terms.
Belfast, 29th April, 1789.
N. B. He has also for sale a few Pockets of St. Domingo and Jamaica Cotton.

Mount-Pottinger

HOUSE, Gardens, and Fields belonging thereto, to be let altogether or separately for one year or more.——Proposals may be left with the person in the house, who will communicate the same to Mr. Slade.
May 1st, 1789.

Partnership dissolved.

RENKIN and TAGGART, of Newtown-Ards, having dissolved Partnership, they take this opportunity of returning their sincere thanks to their friends and the publick, for the great encouragement they met with since their commencement in business; and, in order to enable them to settle the partnership accounts, they request that all those who now stand indebted to them, may speedily pay in the same to Francis Taggart, who will regularly discharge all demands against the Company.

Said Taggart begs leave to inform all those whose favours he has already experienced, and the publick in general, that he intends carrying on the Manufacture of Tobacco and Snuff on his own account, and hopes to give perfect satisfaction in that line to all who are pleased to favour him with their commands.—He is also licenced to sell Spirits wholesale, which with all sorts of white, tar'd Ropes, and Cordage, as usual, will be sold at his House on the most moderate terms, for ready money or good bills.
Newtown-Ards, April 20th, 1789.

Sale by Adjournment

THE sale of a Farm in Tullyverry near Killileagh, formerly advertised in this paper, is adjourned until Friday the 8th of May next, when it will peremptorily be sold at the house of Mr. Hamilton Lowry of Killileagh aforesaid.
Dated this 29th of April, 1789.
The sale will commence exactly at 2 o'clock.

Advertisement.

YOUNG SAILOR, a remarkable strong and fruitful Horse, just rising five years; stands this season at Mr. Patt Smyth's Raholp, at so low a rate as Half-a-Guinea for a Foal, and a Shilling to the Groom. His heighth full sixteen hands.
April, 28th 1789.

Money wanted.

THREE HUNDRED POUNDS on a Mortgage.—Apply to Mr. Joy.
Belfast, 1st May, 1789.

To be lent on approved Security,

THE Sum of SIX HUNDRED POUNDS, the property of the Bachelors Annuity Company of Belfast.——Apply to the Secretary Hugh Allen.
Belfast, May 1. 1789.

County Armagh.

SPRING ASSIZES, 1789.
To MEREDYTH WORKMAN, Esq;
SIR,

WE the High Sheriff and Grand Jury of the county of Armagh, take the opportunity of your non-attendance as a Grand Juror, to return you our sincere acknowledgments; and think it our duty thus publicly to testify our approbation of your general conduct, and faithful discharge of the duties of a Magistrate of this county, but more especially for your strenuous exertions on many occasions, in suppressing every illegal and disorderly rising of the inhabitants, so dangerous to society and the prosperity of a manufacturing county, and also for your firm and manly perseverance in bringing offenders to justice.

James Verner, Sheriff.	James Johnston
Alex. Thomas Stewart, Foreman.	Thos. M'Can
	Thos. Clarke
Wm. Richardson	Fras. Obre
Ar. Acheson	Jas Forde
Wm. Brownlow	Jacob Turner
John Reilly	Jas. Ashmur
Walter Synot	Arthur Noble
Edward Tipping	Robt. Livingston
M. Close	John Eastwood
Thomas Ball	Arth. Irwine
J. Greer	Jonath. Seaver.

To the High Sheriff and Grand Jury of the County of Armagh, assembled at Lent Assizes, 1789.
Gentlemen,
The approbation which you have been pleased to express of my conduct as a magistrate, most amply repays my feeble endeavours to preserve the peace of this county, and must prove the strongest incentive to a perseverance in that line of duty, which has procured me the esteem of so respectable a body.
I am, Gentlemen,
with the utmost gratitude,
your most obedient humble servant,
MEREDYTH WORKMAN.

[It was intended that this Advertisement should earlier have appeared in this Paper, but by mistake it was not received.]

AT an ASSIZES held at the City of Derry for said City and County, the 16th of April 1789.
WE, the Grand Jury of said City and County, give our warmest thanks to Geo. Ash, Esq; a Magistrate of said county, for his spirited exertions in suppressing different riots, which, from appearance, threatened the public peace, by extending a lawless spirit through the county, to the great annoyance of the peaceable inhabitants; and, at the same time, we take the opportunity of expressing our approbation of his humanity (when he had brought these rioters to a proper sense of their error) by using his best endeavours to prevent the rigour of the law being extended to them.
Conolly M'Causland, Foreman.

And. Knox,	Wm. Lecky,
John Hart,	Cha. Richardson,
Dan. Patterson,	Jackson Wray,
Wm. Ross,	Mar. M'Causland,
David Ross,	John Ferguson,
Hugh Lyle,	Laug. Heyland,
Tho. Fanning,	John Spotswood,
John Darcus,	Dom. M'Causland,
Sam. Curry,	Geo. Lenox,
John Gamble;	James Paterson.

LAWRENCE,

HAIR-DRESSER, from LONDON, West side of the Market-House, BELFAST,

BEGS leave to inform the Ladies that he prepares and sells all sorts of Tupees of the most fashionable make, which, for lightness and elegance, cannot be excelled—fine long Braids, curled do. silk and hair Cushions of all patterns—
Fine Hungary and Lavender Waters, Essence of Burgomot and Lemon.
⁂ Ladies Hair cut and dressed on the shortest notice.

New Cloths, Buttons & Waistcoats.

THOMAS NEILSON, & Co. have just received their Spring Assortment of the above Articles, which with CASSIMERS, Genuine NANKEENS, HOSIERY, PATENT HATS, Gold and Silver Laces, Florentines, Lutherines, Fustians, Sattinets, Lastings, &c. they will sell very cheap for money.
☞ Ladies Gold and Silver Hatbands, Spangles, Foil, Purl, and Threads.
Belfast, 30th April, 1789.

Telfair's School,

For Writing, Arithmetic, and Book keeping,
PUBLIC Class from 10 'till 12, and from 3 'till 5 o'clock.
Private Class from 12 till 2 o'clock.
The following young Ladies and Gentlemen of his School obtained SILVER MEDALS, as a reward for examplary conduct and diligence; and for excelling in the above branches of education, from the 1st January last, viz.
On the 1st of Jan. Master William Clark of Maghera.
1st of February, Master James Brown of Belfast.
1st of March, Miss Jane Spencer of do.
1st of April, Mr. Thos. Stewart of the Falls of Belfast.
1st of May, Master Henry Cashnaghan of Malone.
High-street, Belfast 1st of May, 1789.

Grand Lease at Ballygalloch.

TO be sold by public auction on Friday the 29th of May next, at the Market-house Belfast, exactly at twelve o'clock, by Wad. Cunningham, James Holmes, and John Hamilton, the Lease from Lord Donegall to Nath. Wilson deceased, of part of the Lands of Ballygalloch, containing 88A. 2R. 21P. Plantation measure, subject to a yearly rent of 25l. and a herriot of 20s. 0d. for sixty-one years from November 1786. A rental may be seen; and every information had, by applying to Robert Thomson Belfast.—As this Lease will be absolutely sold for whatever it may bring without reserve, and without any adjournment—Persons desirous to purchase will do well to attend exactly at the hour.
Belfast, 27th April, 1789.

JAMES MOONEY,

LATE of the old Post-Office, High-street, Belfast, begs leave to inform his Friends and the Publick, that he is removed nearly opposite, to the House where Messrs. Jameson and Auchinleck carried on their business.——Mooney being truly sensible of the many favours conferred on him since his commencement in business—humbly solicits a continuance of their friendship
He is largely supplied with a general assortment of Groceries, which can be relied on to be fresh and well chosen—and daily expects the arrival of French apples, powders and pomatums, pickling vinegar, lemons, and China oranges ; is at present supplied with brandy fruit, pickled walnuts and cucumbers, box raisins, French plumbs, large figs, China oranges, white candy, barley sugar and refined liquorice, cocoa nuts, miserable and chocolate.—N. B. A large dining-room and two bed-chambers on a first floor, genteelly furnished, to be let. Enquire as above.——Belfast, 1st May, 1789.

WILLIAM HENDREN,

HAS got in a fresh assortment of Lemons & Oranges in excellent order ; and is at present well supplied with the following articles :—Rum, brandy, gineva and whiskey in spirit and reduced, rasberry and cherry juice, Bordeaux vinegar, French pomatums hard and soft, mareschal and other hair powder, fine essences and scented waters, brandy fruits, olives, capers, anchovies, capilaire, lavender and seltzer waters, truffles in oil, pickles, vermicelli, macarony nutmegs, mace, cloves, cinnamon, black and white cayan and long pepper, allspice and white ginger, and a large quantity of sweetmeats in pots preserved of different kinds of fruits, almonds and muscatel raisins, red herrings, &c. which together with a general assortment of groceries, which he sold on very moderate terms, at his Shop near the Market-house, High-street.   Belfast, 1st May, 1789.
N. B. Said Hendren has a first Floor, genteelly furnished, to let, and stabling if required. Enquire as above

TRIAL OF WARREN HASTINGS, ESQ. WESTMINSTER-HALL.

MR. BURKE, in causing the papers to be read, wished to draw Mr. Hastings's own opinion into evidence against him. This opinion stated, that a man in the capacity of Chief Governor could, in the course of three years, acting honestly, and without any the smallest degree of rapacity, realize a noble fortune. Mr. Hastings's opinions contained sentiments of astonishment, that any person could have a recourse to improper means to obtain that which was to be got by not violating the laws of honour or justice. These, says Mr. Burke, are the sentiments of the prisoner, in the early stages of inexperience; but see how his noble mind is expanded! He has reigned the tyrant of India for thirteen years, and employed every means that peculation could devise, or avarice accomplish, and now declares that he is little better than a bankrupt!

Owing to the ceremony of re-chusing the Managers and Lawyers, the former did not come into the Hall till a quarter before twelve o'clock. In less than half an hour, the Lords came in with the same ceremony as was observed last year; that is to say, after the twelve Judges, the junior Baron entered first, and the Lord Chancellor closed the procession.

The Crier having proclaimed silence, and given notice, that Warren Hastings, late Governor General of Bengal, was to be tried for high crimes and misdemeanours;——

Mr. Burke rose, and, adverting to the solemn thanksgiving about to take place for his Majesty's recovery, observed, that we ought not to be thankful with our mouths only, but with our hearts——that whilst we were offering our prayers to the Almighty for his mercies, we should recollect that mercy was to be done to others, and that justice called upon us to revenge the wrongs and cruelties exercised upon the unhappy subjects of Bengal, by the late Governor General.——Mr. Burke said, that complaints had been made to their Lordships of an unnecessary protraction of the trial, and that it had already cost Mr. Hastings the sum of thirty thousand pounds; after remarking on the impossibility of this being the case, he considered it as a business which had no relation to the trial, and said that Mr. Hastings, whilst he pleaded poverty, had received, with his own hands, as he, Mr. Burke could prove, immense bribes; amongst others, one from a Raja whose name we could not distinctly hear.—He then proceeded by saying, that in opposition to what was usually observed in trials, he should beg to read to their Lordships certain certificates of Mr Hastings' good and honourable conduct in India, from some of his subjects there.

It was common in the Old Bailey to have such testimonials produced—" that the deponent has known the prisoner from his childhood, that he had been a good boy, and was in every respect a good fellow;" after which came GUILTY DEATH. The testimonials, Mr. Burke said, teeming with eloquence and fine language, had been first translated into the English, then into the Persian, and lastly into the English again.——After reading them he observed, that he could bring one of these very people who bore testimony, to prove that Mr. Hastings had taken large bribes, and that he had exercised the most unheard of cruelties amongst the natives.—Mr. Burke reminded their Lordships, that in the late scrutiny for Colchester, the High Bailiff *(a Miller)* had been convicted of having taken petty bribes; but of what consequence were these bribes when compared with those of the late Governor General.

SECOND DAY.

In consequence of a sudden and violent indisposition of Mr. BRUKE, the Court adjourned till Friday next; and we have some ground when we give it as our opinion, that a further Adjournment will then take place, till the beginning of the ensuing week.

On Wednesday Major Scott presented a petition to the House of Commons, from Mr. Hastings. It stated that Mr. Hastings had been impeached, and certain articles given in against him; to which he had replied, and was now in the second year of the trial; that the Managers had pledged themselves not to utter a word which they would not prove, and had repeatedly affirmed, that they spoke as they were instructed by the House of Commons; that various allegations were contained in the speeches of Mr. Burke, totally foreign to any one article of charge; that in particular, the petitioner was accused of being an accomplice in a plot to assassinate the Rhazada; of being an accomplice in the death of Meeran Adish, son of Meer Jaffier, and in various acts of oppression and savage cruelty, said to have been practised by Dely Sons; that on Tuesday Mr. Burke had accused him of having murdered Nundcomar, by the hands of Sir Elijah Impey; that these charges were utterly false and unfounded; and he confided in the justice of the house, to frame them into specific articles, so that he might be enabled to refute them in the same public manner in which they had been made. After some conversation, it was agreed to be taken into consideration on Monday next.

PROCESSION TO ST. PAUL's.

Thursday exhibited a striking proof, that genuine Loyalty is the daughter of Freedom, and that those only are capable of gratitude to their rulers, who know that the measures of Government are founded on public good.

An immense croud of spectators, many of whom had come from the most distant provinces of this kingdom, and not a few from the Continent itself, waited, their breasts throbbing with loyal expectation for the arrival of a Monarch whom Heaven had at length restored to the fervent wishes of a loyal people.

HIS MAJESTY AND THE QUEEN,

attended by the Ladies Holdernesse and Egremont, in a carriage, drawn by eight cream-coloured horses decorated with blue ribbands.

Party of the Horse Guards.

Ladies attendants on the Princesses.

Party of the Horse Guards.

The Princesses Royal, Augusta, and Elizabeth, in a coach and six, attended by one of the Ladies of Honour.

Another party of Horse Guards closed the procession into the City.

The Corporation received the King, at St. Paul's, where their Majesties arrived at twelve o'clock.

At the West door, the Peers in their Robes, attended by the King at Arms, and other Officers, met their Majesties, the Gentlemen Pensioners being all in waiting.

The Sword of State was carried before the King and Queen into the Choir, where, under a canopy, their Majesties seated themselves on the Throne of State, near the West end of the Choir, opposite the Altar.

Upon their Majesties entering St. Paul's, the 100th Psalm was sung by the Charity Children; and upon their leaving the Church, the Children sung the 104th. Their Majesties paid great attention to them.

The Prayers were read by the Rev. Mr. Moore, Minor Canon of St. Paul's. The Bishop of Lincoln read the first part of the Communion. Dr. Jefferys read the Epistle. The Bishop of Bristol the Gospel.

The Sermon was preached by the Bishop of London, from the following text in the psalms: " O tarry Thou the Lord's Leisure—Be strong, and He shall establish thy Heart."

As soon as their Majesties entered the Cathedral, a rocket was fired from the statue of Queen Anne, as a signal for the Tower, when the guns upon the wharf were immediately fired, and answered by those in St. James's Park. The same signal was repeated upon their Majesties leaving the Cathedral.

When their Majesties were seated in their Carriage, and waiting for their attendants, their Royal Highnesses the Prince of Wales and the Duke of York came to the Carriage, and conversed with their Majesties till the Procession moved.

At a quarter past three, the Procession reached Temple-bar on its return; the order of it, however, was *inverted*; for those who closed it, going to St. Paul's, headed it when it came back.

All the Royal Family returned together, except the Princess Sophia of Gloucester, who did not stay above an hour in the Cathedral.

Amongst the most extraordinary things of the day, may be reckoned the following respectable personages being at church—

The Earl of Sandwich,
Right. Hon. Charles Fox,
Mr. Wilkes,
Mr. Sheridan,
Mr. Gibbon, and
George Hanger.

OBSERVATIONS.

DRESSES.

His Majesty wore the full-dress Windsor uniform.

Her Majesty and the Princesses in garter blue, richly trimmed with gold fringe, and bandeaus in their head-dresses, with the motto of " God save the King!"

The Prince of Wales, the Duke of York, Gloucester, and Cumberland, in full dress Windsor uniforms, with insignia's of their several Orders of Knighthood.

The Ladies were all in full dress, complimentarily similar to that of the Queen. Mr. Pitt and many other of the King's particular friends were in the Windsor uniform.

The Lord Mayor in purple velvet, richly trimmed with gold. A rich crimson velvet robe embroidered with gold, hung across his shoulders.

All the Royal Liveries were made up new for the occasion.

THE DAY

Was at first unpromising, but, as if the all-watching and all directing eye of that Providence which had led us happily on so far, was determined not to leave the blessed work unfinished, no sooner were their Majesties and the Royal Family seated, than the radiant sun, bursting forth in all his splendour, seemed anxious to join in the devotions they were about to pay to the Supreme Being, who had vouchsafed to listen to the prayers of a loyal and affectionate people.

WINDOWS AND SCAFFOLDINGS

Displayed more beauty and loyalty than could have been concentrated in any other city in the world; and the earnestness of our fair country-women, to evince their feelings when the Royal Family passed, gave a new bloom to their countenances.

THE STREETS

Were filled at each side with generally speaking, a tractable, quiet, and loyal mob. There were some few renegants to good order, but fewer far than we could have expected.

THE MILITARY,

In Westminster, conducted themselves to admiration; and we cannot speak too highly of the officers of the Guards, who, whenever they saw a poor devil driven into the centre of the street, condescended, themselves, to conduct him to a good situation amongst the croud. In all of them we saw the soldier and gentleman happily blended.

Belfast, *April* 28.

Thursday last being the day appointed as a thanksgiving for the recovery of his Majesty, the same was observed with much decency by all ranks of people, and by a general cessation from business. In the parish church, the several dissenting meeting houses, and at the Roman Catholic chapel, there was public worship and excellent sermons suitable to the occasion.

The Artillery division of the Belfast First Company paraded on Thursday last, and marched to Holywood, where they attended public worship, and heard an excellent discourse, by the Rev. George Portis, on the subject of the King's happy recovery.

Extract of a letter from Stewartstown.

" At the assizes of Omagh, which ended on Friday the 10th inst. Mr. George Griffith, guager of Stewartstown, was most honourably acquitted, by a very respectable jury, of a groundless and malicious charge exhibited against him, of having, in the month of July last, grossly assaulted and beaten Robert Black, of Doons, in the county of Tyrone, an *alibi* having been proved to the entire satisfaction of the court. Said Black has carried on the business of a private distiller for several years past."

DIED. At Clifden near Bristol, George Bateson, Esq; late of Farmhill near Holywood.

Belfast, *May* 1.

Extract of a letter from Dublin, April 28.

" At ten o'clock this morning, died, at his Lordship's house in Sackville-street, in the 76th year of his age, the Right Hon. JAMES HEWIT, Viscount and Baron Lifford, Lord Chancellor of Ireland, and one of his Majesty's most Hon. Privy Counsel.—A nobleman whose professional and private character during an official residence for twenty-two years, was strictly unblemished and justly revered.

" His Lordship is succeeded in his estate and title, by his eldest son, the Hon. JOSEPH HEWIT, one of his Majesty's Serjeants at law, and Member of Parliament for Belfast."

Houses to be Sold in *Larne*.

TO be sold by private sale, two new Houses adjoining each other, two stories high, well finished and slated; one 29 feet front, the other 15 feet, and 24 feet wide each in the clear, situated in the new town of Larne, with a well inclosed back yard, two good back houses, a good spring well in the garden, which garden extends 156 feet backwards, up to which the tide flows—held by lease under the Right Hon. the Earl of Antrim for 3 lives renewable for ever, at the yearly rent of 30s. 3d. and half a year's rent at the fall of each life. If not sold before the 6th July next, they will then be sold by public auction on the spot to the highest bidder.—Fifty guineas to be immediately deposited by the purchaser, and the remainder on perfecting the deeds.—For particulars apply to the proprietor Samuel Hamilton, who lives in one of the houses.

Larne, 29th April, 1789.

To be Let or Sold,

THE Lease of a neat commodious House in Waring's-steet, at present occupied by James T. Kennedy, of which there are 44 years unexpired from the first of May next, at Twenty Guineas per annum.——There is a large stable and back-yard belonging to it, and the whole is in compleat order and may be entered upon immediately.

Belfast, 29th April, 1789.

To be Sold by Auction,

AT the Market-House of Belfast, on Friday the 11th day of September next, at 12 o'clock at noon, the Dwelling-House, Offices, Bleach-Green and Farm of Drumadaragh, in the possession of Mr. John Barklie: the house and Offices are in thorough repair, and fit for the reception of a genteel family; the Green is well supplied with spring and other water, and capable of bleaching 5000 pieces yearly, and the Farm contains about sixty Irish acres, is well inclosed and planted and in good condition, and convenient to firing: These lands are held under the Earl of Donegall for three lives, all in being, or 41 years from May 1768, and subject to the yearly rent of 20l. and are within 12 miles of Belfast, ten of Ballymena, and seven of Antrim, all good market towns; the purchaser to commence from November next——For particulars apply to Mr. Hugh Allen, Belfast, Mr. Robert Johnston, Derriaghy, or Mr. Arthur Allen, Rashee, who will shew the premisses.

2 th April, 1789.

To be Let,

FROM the first of May next, or the interest in the Lease sold—the House in Bridge-Street at present occupied by Joseph Stevenson;—it is held by lease from the Earl of Donegall for 99 years, from the first of May, 1767, and three lives, all in being, at the yearly ground rent of 6l.—and 2s. 6d. fees.—The situation for business requires no comment, being confessedly among the first in town. The purchaser or taker of this House may be accommodated with stabling for four horses, and a stand for a cow in a very convenient situation.—Any person wishing to treat for said premisses, are requested to send in their proposals as above.

Anno 1789.]   Printed by HENRY JOY, and Co. BELFAST.

The BELFAST NEWS-LETTER.

TUESDAY May 5,   FRIDAY May 8, 1789.

For the Cities of Philadelphia, New-York, and Albany,

THE Brig Havanna, Thomas Suter, master, a constant trader with a Mediterranean pass, has good accommodations for passengers, and will sail for the ports aforesaid the first week in May next. For freight or passage apply to Thos. Bunker, Coot-hill, Mr. John M'Clay, Monaghan, Mr. James Falls, Aughnacloy, Mr. Thos. Prentice, Armagh, Mr. George Caruth, Coal Island, the Captain on board, or at Michael Thumboce, Warren-point, or to Henry Ogle.

To be Let, in Bangor,

DURING the Summer Season, or any time that may be agreed upon,—A neat commodious Dwelling-House, or any part thereof: It is conveniently situated for Sea Bathing, and fit for the immediate reception of a genteel family.—For particulars apply to Robt. Goudy, Belfast, or Samuel Lyon's, Bangor, who will give every necessary information relative to the same.
Bangor, 7th May, 1789.

SEIZED, the 29th of April, in a garden buried under ground, adjoining the town of Newry, 26 cakes of Leaf Tobacco, weight 3,431 suttle pounds, with the assistance of Mr. Thompson, Walking Officer, and two other Revenue Officers, and lodged the same in his Majesty's Stores.
Newry, 3d   ALEX. LAUGHLIN,
May, 1789.   Revenue Officer.

Sweet William

TO be let to Mares at one Guinea for a foal, and one Shilling to the Groom; a strong handsome Horse, got by Cromaboo on an English mare. Apply to William Magie at Castleward. Good Grass at 6d. per night   April 13th, 1789.

Young Slapdash,

STANDS this season at Cloughy near Portaferry, and will cover Mares, at one Guinea for a Foal, and half a crown to the Groom.——He is a beautiful bay, English bred, is very fruitful and his foals are large and strong, he is now five years old, full blooded.——He will attend the Markets of Newtownards and Portaferry. His pedigree in the hands of his Groom.
Cloughy, 20th April, 1789.
To be continued six times.

Sailor,

WILL stand this season at Mount-Ross, within two miles of Portaferry, and be let to Mares at one Guinea, and half a Crown to the Groom. Any mares that miss to him will be covered gratis next year.
27th April, 1789.

Flaxseed by Auction.

TO be sold by Auction at the Stores of Samuel Brown and Co. on Friday next the 8th inst. at twelve o'clock at noon, Sixty Hogsheads American Flaxseed, this year's importation.
Belfast, 4th May 1789.

London Porter, Bristol and Guernsey Cyder.
Samuel and Andrew M'Clean,

HAVE lately received a fresh Parcel of Whitbread's Porter, in hogsheads and barrels; also, a few hampers and casks of the very best Bristol and Guernsey Cyder. The hampers contain from TWO to FIVE dozen each, and will be sold remarkably cheap.
Belfast, 4th May, 1789.

New Woollen Warehouse,
BELFAST.

HASLETT STRONG and CO. have this day received, per the Peggy, (from the several places of manufacture in England) a fresh Assortment of Woollen, Cotton and Haberdashery Goods for the Summer trade—which they persuade themselves, will meet the approbation of their Friends and Customers.
May 2d, 1789.

Fine English Butter-Salt.

HENRY WELSH has just received a quantity which he is selling by wholesale and retail upon low terms. He also informs his friends and the public, that he is largely supplied with rum, brandy, geneva and whiskey; red and white wines; fine and coarse flour; bran and pollard; nine and six feet deals, with a regular assortment in the grocery line as usual.

J Wilson, Portrait Painter,

BEGS Leave to inform the Ladies and Gentlemen of Belfast and its Vicinity, that though he expects to be employed in the country during the ensuing summer, yet any commands left for him at his house in Castle-Street, (opposite Mrs. Mc. Tiers) will be punctually and gratefully obeyed.
Belfast, 7th May, 1789.

To be Let,

DURING the summer season, from this to November, a snug Cabbin in good repair, at Cuitra, near Holywood, containing three rooms, a kitchen, a closet, three good garrets, a small orchard, half a kitchen garden, grass for a cow if wanted, and a stable for two or three horses. It is beautifully situated and very convenient for bathing. Application to be made to Capt. Scott, at the Crown Tavern, Belfast, who will treat for the same.
Belfast, May 2, 1789.

For Consumptions, Asthmas, &c.
Godbold's Vegetable Balsam,

At only ONE GUINEA the PINT Bottle,
Hitherto sold in Dublin at *a Guinea and a half.*

THE afflicted in the above Complaints are informed, they have now an opportunity of supplying themselves with a *fresh* Parcel of this invaluable Medicine, just imported from LONDON, in the Friendship, Captain Lepper, by

William Magee,

At the STATIONARY and PATENT MEDICINE WAREHOUSE, No. 9, Bridge-street, Belfast.

Wholesale Woollen Warehouse.

CULLY and CAMPBELL have this day received per the Loyalty from Liverpool, and the Grizzey from Bristol, a large Parcel of Woollen and Cotton Goods, which, with their usual Assortment, they are disposing of on low terms, for ready money or short bills.
Newry, 7th May, 1789.

Hillsborough Fair,

WILL be holden on Wednesday the 20th instant, when the very extensive Premiums; the same as at the last Fair, (Potatoes excepted) will be given.
MICHAEL THOMSON,
Clerk of the Market.
Hillsborough, May
6th, 1789.
N. B. Any Article sold after six o'clock in the afternoon, will not be entitled to the Premium.

For *LONDON,*

THE NEWRY, John Wilson, Master, (a constant Trader) will sail for London the 12th instant.——For Freight apply to   ARCH. TAYLOR.
Newry, 5th May, 1789.

N. B. The sailing of this Vessel is put off to the above day, at the desire of several principal gentlemen in the linen trade.

To be sold by Auction,

OPPOSITE the Donegall-Arms, on Friday the 15th instant, at 12 o'clock:
A second hand POST-CHAISE, in good repair, with Harness compleat.
8th May, 1789.

City and County of Derry.

AT an Assizes held at London-Derry, in and for said City and County, the 16th day of April 1789, the following persons were appointed High and Sub-Constables in and for said City and County, by the Grand Jury, and confirmed by the Court:
HIGH CONSTABLES.

City and Liberties London Derry }	John Clark of said City.
Half Barony Tyrkeeran }	David Larimer of Clony.
Barony Kennahgt. }	Thomas M'Cleland of Drumgaveny.
Town and Liberties Coleraine. }	John Johnson of said Town.
Half Barony Coleraine }	Hugh Blair of Aughadowy.
Barony Loughinsholton }	William Bunton, Magherafelt.

NOTICE.

THE Public are requested not to credit Susannah Mc. Glathry, otherwise Mc. Alexander, my wife, as I will not pay any debt she may contract. Given under my hand at Craighrogan near Templepatrick, 4th May, 1789.
JOSEPH Mc. GLATHRY.

Books by Auction,

At Lamont's Auction Room, in Wilson's Court, High-Street, Belfast,

THIS present evening, Tuesday 5th May, inst. at half past 7 o'clock (and the following evenings till all are sold) a large collection of Books in all the different branches of literature. Every book will be engaged perfect, unless otherwise declared at the time of sale. Catalogues may be had gratis at the place of sale.

WHEREAS the peace of the country, within the parishes of Larne, Glynn, Magrhemorne, Island Magee, Broad Island, and Kilroot, has lately been much disturbed by sheep-stealing, robbing of hen-roosts and other petty larcenies.
Now we the undersigned Landholders, Magistrates, and Inhabitants of said Parishes, having in utter abhorrence such illicit practices, and conceiving that these evils arise principally from Cock-fighting, petty Horse-racing, Gaming and other lawless and tumultuous meetings, whereby the morals of the lower orders of the people are very much hurt, do pledge ourselves to the publick and to each other, that we will on no account countenance, or renew a Lease to any person, who shall breed or feed any Game Cock for the purpose of fighting either for themselves or any other person, or is known to attend any of the above meetings—and such of us as are Magistrates declare we will not certify for any Innholder or Publican, who shall entertain at their houses, persons assembled together for said purposes, and that we will represent to the Honourable Commissioners of the Revenue, the reasons why their present licences ought to be withdrawn.
And we call upon all peaceable inhabitants of said parishes, for their own security, to unite with us in suppressing such disorders, and preserving the peace and tranquility of the country.
April 23d, 1789.

Conway Richd. Dobbs	Wm. Montgomery
Richd. Gervas Ker	Robt. Sinclair
G. A. M'Cleverty	John Montgomery.
Marriott Dalway	Edward Brice
Thomas Lea	Edward Kingsmill
Wm. Cleverty	Edward Jones Agnew

Wants a Place,

A Man from England (with an undeniable character) who understands husbandry—takes the liberty of informing the Gentlemen of this kingdom, that he was regularly bred from his infancy to the knowledge of all kinds of husbandry, ditching, draining, &c. &c. Application to be made at the Office of Mr. Joy.

THE Creditors of David Goodlatte of Derrygally, formerly of Castlecaulfield, co. Tyrone, Esq. are requested to furnish their several accounts to Mr. Thos. Richardson near Dungannon, in order that they may be put in the speediest method of payment.
April 30, 1789.

Rum, Brandy and Geneva,
BY RETAIL,

JAMES WOODBURN has opened a retail Cellar for the above articles opposite to the old Sugar House in Rosemary Lane, where those who want to purchase by the cag or gallon will find it their interest to make a trial.

John Walker,

IS now landing a cargo of Scotch Malting Coal, which on trial proves good—also, Coke for drying Malt, Swansey Coals for Smiths—which, with every article in in the Bleach Stuff line, he has for sale at his Stores on the Bason.
Newry, 3d May, 1789.

Classical School in Lisburn

ON Friday and Saturday last was held the Quarterly Examination. A most respectable number of ladies and gentlemen attended; before whom the following young gentlemen appeared most deserving in their respective classes. Wilson, Latin and writing a premium—Marmion, sen. English speech, a premium—Andrew Fulton, English speech and writing, a premium—James Fulton, English speech, a premium—Thos. Garner, critical English examination, a premium—Thomas Fulton, English, a premium—Clarke, French speech and translation and writing—Campbell, Latin speech and translation.
May 2, 1789.

AMERICAN NEWS.

NEW-YORK, MARCH 4.

OUR Fœderal Government commences this day, an event of great joy to the people. The morning was ushered in with the firing of cannon, ringing of bells, and every demonstration of joy. General Washington is chosen President, and Mr. Adams Vice-President; and the convention will sit in a few days; when, from the chosen characters that will compose the body, there is no doubt of such a code of laws being established as will diffuse the happiest consequences to this country. The first object to be taken up is the establishing of measures for raising a revenue to discharge the arrears of interest due on our debt; and it is expected there will be a thorough change in commercial regulations. A ship of 500 tons is arrived at Philadelphia, from Battavia, laden with pepper and divers other goods, and makes a great voyage; four more are expected there and here in the month of May from different parts of India.

LONDON, April 30, and May 1.

It is the genral opinion that his Royal Highness the Duke of Gloucester will be appointed Commander in Chief, before his Majesty goes to Hanover.

The charter of the East India Company is so near its expiration, that it must be very shortly brought before Parliament. The principal difficulty which will occur in this case, arises from the claims of the people of Ireland. In this kingdom, the public at large receives, by compact, a beneficial return for the monopoly; but the Irish contend, that they are excluded from the advantages of the trade; not only without a resulting benefit, but without an existing right.

By latest accounts from Vienna, we are assured that the report of the Emperor being dead, is without the least foundation.

It is said to be under consideration to stop in future the importation of American wheat from any of the Thirteen United States, even when the ports are open, the landed interest having been more hurt by importations from thence than from all other parts. The very low price of wheat in America makes their needy adventurers ship such quantities for Britain, when there is a prospect of the ports being opened, as fill the country for months after.

DUBLIN, April 30.—May 2.

There is a strong surmise that the existence of the present session of Parliament will terminate within ten days—as the money bills, which were the grand impediments with government to the measure of prorogation, will be passed this night in the Commons.

The late Viscount Lifford was born near Coventry England, in the year 1715, and applied himself early to the study of the law. After his admission to the bar, he went through the several ranks of King's Council and King's Serjeant, and was appointed one of the Judges of the Court of King's Bench in England, from whence he arrived in this kingdom on the 8th of January, 1768, and on the succeeding day being appointed one of his Majesty's most Hon. Privy Council, created a Peer with the title of Lord Baron Lifford, was appointed one of the Lords Justices of this kingdom.

The late Lord Chancellor was in apparent good health, the most part of last week, and on Thursday gave a sumptuous entertainment to a number of his friends—The whole of his illness, which did not amount to quite five days, arose from a cold he had received in the House of Lords, and not being much attended to in the beginning, it terminated in a malignant sore throat, which occasioned his death.

The Chancellor had long been haggling about terms—these were a pension for years—a Judge's place for one son—a Bishoprick for another—the two latter were stipulated for—at least did not impede the negociation.—The only difficulty was the pension which was demanded for 21 years, a 3000l. per annum.—This was thought too great and too lavish a profusion of public money—14 years were offered, and rejected—in this stage—a quinsy attacked the Chancellor—alarming symptoms appeared, which soon turned to a mortification, and ended his dissolution.

The late Lord Chancellor has died very rich, worth not less it is said, than 220,000l. Of this by far the greatest part, full 180,000l. was realized in this country—and *every* sixpence of it left Ireland.

Report says that the Attorney General failed for England on last Tuesday night, to push his interest for the seals, on the present vacancy, as far as it will go. If Lord Thurlow continues resolute, and Mr. Pitt cannot procure him the Chancellorship, it is settled that the Duke of Leinster shall be immediately dismissed, and the Attorney General made Master of the Rolls with a Peerage to his family. These are to be the compensations for his disappointment, and the rewards of his unwearied services to Mr. Pitt and the Marquis of Buckingham on the Regency business, and indeed throughout the whole of Mr. Pitt's administration.

Robert Johnston, Esq. member for Hillsborough, is appointed one of his Majesty's Counsel at Law

CURRAGH—SECOND SPRING MEETING.

Saturday, April 25,

CHEROKEE and LOUISA.

A match for one hundred guineas—at starting 4 to 3 against Louisa—as severe a shower as ever fell greatly retarded the running—both very slow—on the flat 6 to 3 on Cherokee; after that a hollow race; Louisa never ran worse, and was beat in a canter.

KING's PLATE, of 100 Guineas,

For three years old, colts 8st. fillies 7st. 11lb. one three miles heat.

Mr. Hamilton's ch. h. Father O'Leary, Mr. Lumm's b. h. Maximen, Mr. Anth. Daly's gr. m. Mr Mannix's Turnip, Mr. Fallon's gr. m. by Friar, and another, assembled at the starting post, and by some unaccountable accident, they all, except Mr. Anth. Daly's rider, set off without the word from the Deputy Ranger. It was in vain to call after them, they went entirely over the course. O'Learly and Maximen ran clear away from the rest—and the race was between them. O'Leary was pushed very hard, and won by near a length. The betts were even at starting—O'Leary against the field—Turnip came in third. The Deputy Ranger was sworn, and deposed that they had started without the word; upon which Mr. B. Daly declared as Ranger, that there was no race—and that for the Plate to be won, they must run over again: it is needless to observe, that this caused much murmuring amongst the gentlemen who had taken O'Leary against the field—they still looked upon their betts to be safe, when on the horses being brought to the post, they found Mr. Lumm's Honest Tom, instead of Maximen—Mr. Lumm declared, that either the former was a race, or no race—if it was a race, why run again? if it was no race, as he had two horses entered, he was certainly entitled to his choice—more vociferation never was caused by any transaction on the turf. Tom being fresh, it was impossible to hedge off a bett. At length they started—an excellent race—Tom kept the lead over the whole course—near the distance post, 3 to 1 against O'Leary—Tom won by a clear length—but Mr. Hamilton disputing the fairness of the race, the matter is referred to the Jockey Club, and the Plate is held over, till their determination shall be known. All betts lie over in the same mannner, except the three to one betts—Tom against O'Leary, in coming up the rails.

LONDONDERRY, April 28.

WITH great pleasure we inform the public, that the Corporation have finally resolved upon the measure of a Bridge, having an agreement for that purpose with Messrs. Cox and Thompson, who are immediately to sail for Boston, in order to prepare the materials. They propose returning here early next spring; and if no accident hapens in crossing and re-crossing the Atlantic Ocean, they expect to complete the structure by the 1st of Nov. 1790.

The Corporation (with a spirit and consistency which reflect the greatest honour on that body of respectable citizens) have determined upon the erecting of the Triumphal Arch at Bishops-gate; and the workmen are soon to begin to pull down the old gate, and clear the ground.—The ornamenting of the other gates will follow in due time.

Last Wednesday the assizes for this city and county were concluded, at which a greater variety of business was transacted, both in the Crown and Civil bill Courts, than on any former occasion that we remember.

At these assizes the following persons were tried and received sentence accordingly, viz.—Dan. Doughterty, for breaking into a house near Claudy with his face blackened, &c. to be hanged on Wednesday the 13th of May.—Charles Stewart, for picking pockets on the stairs of the Court-house on the Saturday of the assizes, to be hanged on Wednesday the 22d of July.—B. M'Alier, for an assault, to be fined 10 marks and imprisoned 12 months.—Thomas Gallaghar for passing bad money, to be pilloried 3 sundry Wednesdays, and imprisoned 6 months.—Several persons, for assaults and petty offences, to be imprisoned three months; and a number ordered to be discharged.

Cha. Conway, charged with the murder of Jn. Murphy near Dungiven, put off his trial by affidavit till next assizes.—John Bell, charged with being an accessary in the murder of a young woman near Moneymore, is ordered to be imprisoned till the 1st of January 1790.—And, James Stephenson (lately transmitted from the goal of Liverpool) charged with house breaking and horse-stealing, to remain in prison till next assizes.

DIED. In the 56th year of his age, Alderman John Coningham. On Thursday morning, his body was carried to the grave in funeral procession attended by all the Aldermen, Sheriffs, &c. in their Corporation gowns, and preceded by the Dean of Derry and the whole of the Established Clergy in the city.—Captain Hugh Wilson of the brig Mary.—In Bogside-street, Mr. Ber. M'Colgan.—At Dunybrewer, Mr. Pat Casey.

SINGULAR INVENTION.

A loom of a new, and very singular nature, has lately been invented, and set to work at Paisley, on the principles of a model constructed some time ago by Dr. Jaffray, with the improvements that have since occurred to him and Mr. Barr. This loom is to be driven by machinery, set in motion by water, steam, &c. and not only takes the cloth from the lay with such regularity, that no part of the web can have more wool driven into it, or be thicker than another; but if a thread in the warp break, the machine instantly stands still. It is said to be capable of weaving all kinds of cloth, from silk to canvas; and if report be true, it is so simple in its construction as not to cost more than double the expence of a common loom, while it is so swift in its motions, and easy to be managed, that one man working a wheel can set five or six of them in motion, and an attentive boy or girl may tie threads and change pirns to three, if not four. The web at present in the loom is a ten hundred muslin. The beauty and regularity of its fabric have given much satisfaction to those gentlemen in Glasgow and Paisley to whom specimens of it have been shewn. And we may venture to say, that nothing hitherto devised to improve and extend the art of weaving, to add new energy to the labour and ingenuity of the country, and to give a decided command of the market, ever demanded a more serious attention from all concerned.

Belfast, *May 5.*

The Brothers, Captain James Jeffreys, from hence to Wilmington in Delaware, sailed on Wednesday noon the 6th inst. with a cargo of linens, glass, printed cottons, &c. &c. and 148 passengers, with a fair wind.

Died last week at Newtownards, Mrs. Echlin, relict of the late Charles Echlin, of Echlin Grove, Esq.

☞ BY Virtue of a Commission from the Court of Prerogative of this Kingdom, ARTHUR DARLEY, of Belfast, was on Saturday last admitted and sworn a *NOTARY PUBLIC.*

On Friday last, Mary White was committed to jail by the Sovereign, for exposing to sale several articles of wearing apparel stolen from the inhabitants of this town.

On Saturday Edward Robinson was committed, being charged with having stolen a double piece of linen out of the bleach yard of Messrs. Corkan and Johnston in Derriaghy.

On Thursday night the green of Mr. James Ferguson, of Woodville was robbed of five webs of cloth——and a few nights ago the green of Mr. James Ferguson, of Belfast, was also robbed of several pieces of Linen.

A few days ago a dispute arose between two women at Nacloghrum, near Castledawson, when one of them struck the other with a griddle, and fractured her scull in such a manner that she died on the spot. The Coroner's inquest sat on the body, and brought in their verdict willful murder. The woman was committed, but, on the road to Derry, was rescued,. Her father and two brothers were sworn against for the rescue; the two latter were taken and lodged in Derry jail, but the father refusing to surrender, received the contents of a musket, loaded with shot, in his head, of which he lies dangerously ill.

Our last paper mentioned, in error, that the Hon. Joseph Hewitt succeeds to the late Lord Chancellors title and estate—The person who does succeeds is the Hon. and Rev Doctor James William Hewitt.

The Lord Donegall, Captain James Mc. Roberts, loaded with linen cloath, bound from this port to London, arrived safe at the Downs the twenty-third ult. after ten days passage.

Died, on Tuesday evening last, the Rev. Hugh Moore of Ballyskeogh, near Newton Ards; a young man whose amiable deportment renders him deservedly lamented by all who knew him.

Ground for Building on.

A Few Lots yet unset in the New Street leading from Peters-hill to Millfield-street, in the Town of Belfast ——Application to be made to John Brown, Esq; Peters-hill, who will give the greatest encouragement to those who take Lots for Building.

Belfast, April 15, 1789.

N. B. He has also to let, his Dwelling-House, &c. in Peters hill, formerly advertised at large in this Paper. Also a quantity of remarkably fine Brick to be sold.

In Banbridge.

SOME Freehold Houses to be set or sold, or fined and the rent reduced for ever, at six per cent. or half the purchase-money left at interest: and if not set or sold by private contract, will be sold by public auction on the premisses, precisely at 12 of the clock, on Monday 11th day of May, 1789.

A Book-case, a Bureau, some Bedsteads, Bedding, and other Things, with many Copper-plate Pictures, a small Library of the most valuable Books, and some Blocks carved in Paris to imitate heads for lectures—they would make exceeding good Wig-blocks.

Notice has been given these ten years past by public advertisement, that no credit be given to Rose Duncan on my account, who has assumed my name: I never will pay any debt or debts she either has or may contract; and as Mr. Mc. Neill's houses have been robbed, he requests no one will buy the booty from her or her accomplices. The robbers that robbed Gillhall Castle are suspected, and if they do not return the goods, they will be prosecuted.

HECTOR Mc. NEILL.

N. B. The Silver Buckles brought from from London, that were feloniously stolen at Banbridge, were seen in the shoes of S——, the he-bawd's hedge whore, &c. &c. &c. Banbridge, 5th May, 1789.

Anno 1789.] Printed by HENRY JOY, and Co. BELFAST.

The BELFAST NEWS-LETTER.

TUESDAY May 12, FRIDAY May 15, 1789.

A VESTRY

WILL be held in the parish Church of Belfast, on Wednesday the 20th instant, at twelve o'clock, to receive the report of the Church Wardens on a case which by a vote of the last Vestry was submitted to Council. May 13th, 1789.

ALL Persons to whom William Todd Jones, Esq; stands indebted by Judgment, Bond, or open Account, are desired to send in the particulars of their respective claims to his Uncle Valentine Jones, Merchant, in Belfast. 14th May, 1789.

THE Revd. Isaac and the Revd. Henry Ashe, who were educated under the late Revd. Dr. Norris of Drogheda, and who have been for many years engaged in the education of youth, intend to open a School in the town of Tanderagee on the first of August 1789.

Their charge for Boarders will be twenty Guineas a year and four entrance;—for day scholars, four Guineas a year and one entrance. No additional charge will be made to boarders for instruction in the French language. Particular attention will be paid to their improvement in History, Geography and Composition at large.—They are determined to pursue uniformly the late Dr. Norris's Plan, and consequently will attend School in the evenings. May 9th, 1789.

Advertisement.

STOLEN or strayed from George Millar of Mullan Crivelough, near Calledon, on Sunday night last, A Black COLT, three years old, a set tail with two nicks, about the breadth of a shilling of white hair above the hoof of the far hind foot, with two stars and a snip in his face, value about eight guineas. One guinea will be paid to the person who returns said horse; or if stolen, two guineas will be paid to the person who will prosecute the thief to conviction in six months, by applying to Mr. Thos. Irwin, Calledon, or George Millar the Proprietor. 7th May, 1789.

To all Persons standing indebted to the Estate of John Dinsmore.

WE the undersigned legal Trustees to the estate of John Dinsmore, do give this publick Notice, That Mr. Robert Hyndman has been appointed by the creditors to collect all debts due to the said Bankrupt at the time of his failure. Every person standing indebted to this estate, are desired to settle with said Mr. Hyndman immediately, or they will be sued for the amount of their different accounts without loss of time.

All persons having claims against their estate, are requested to furnish their accounts, proved by affidavit to Mr. Robert Getty.

ROBERT GETTY, } Trustees.
JOHN BOYLE,   }

TAKEN-UP, on the 14th April, A Black Horse about 12 or 13 hands high, a rowan star in his face, some grey hairs in his tail. Any person proving his property, by paying the expences to Bernard Coyl, in the parish of Aughagallon near Ballinderry, may have the horse.
Brankinstown, May 11th, 1789.

Bachelors Annuity Company.

A Meeting of the Bachelors Annuity Company will be held in the Market-house, Belfast, precisely at twelve o'clock, on Tuesday the second of June next.
Belfast, May 13th, 1789.
HUGH ALLEN, Secretary.

TO be sold for the payment of his Majesty's Duties, by Auction, at the King's Stores, Belfast, several Pipes and Hogsheads of Brandy, Puncheons of Rum, Pipes of Port Wine, and Claret in Hogsheads, on Wednesday the 27th instant. The Auction to begin at twelve o'clock.
Dated the 11th Day of May, 1789.

Pavers wanted,

IN the Town of Monaghan, where there is a large Job to be done.—Proposals will be received by Sir James Hamilton until the 26th instant, at which time the Pavers will be appointed.
Monaghan, 11th May, 1789.

Woollen Drapery, and at prime Cost:

TO be sold, for ready money only, at the Shop of the late Mr. William Kean of Downpatrick, Woollen Draper, the entire Stock of Goods on hand, consisting of an extensive assortment in that line of business, and well worth the attention of the publick.

All persons who stood indebted to the late Mr. Kean at the time of his death, are most earnestly intreated to pay their respective sums due by them without loss of time to his administrators, Miss Margaret Kean of Downpatrick and Mr. William Willey of Killileagh, otherwise it will be unavoidably necessary to take the most effectual and speedy steps for recovery thereof.
Downpatrick, May 14th, 1789.

Train Oil.

JAMES HOLMES is landing a small Parcel of Train Oil from Drontheim, which will be sold on reasonable Terms.
Belfast, 7th May, 1789.

Two Hundred Pounds

WANTED immediately, for which undeniable security will be given.—Application to be made to Mr. Thomas L. Stewart, Attorney at Law Stafford Street, Dublin, or to Mr. Robert Stewart, Belfast.
Belfast, 11th May, 1789.

NEW RED CLOVERS SEED, just landed from England, to be sold reasonable, by
ALEXANDER ORR.
Belfast, 11th May, 1789.

Who has also for sale, Alicant Barilla, Dantzig and American Ashes, Powder Blues, and Dutch Black Soap.

New Dronthon Deals.

CUNNINGHAM GREG is just landing a small Cargo, which he will dispose of on reasonable terms; also a parcel of WELCH SLATES.
Belfast, 11th May, 1789.

THE Partnership between Thomas Mc. Cabe and James Hunter, Watchmakers, is dissolved.
Belfast, 9th May, 1789.
THOs. Mc. CABE,
JAMES HUNTER.

The Business is carried on by Thomas Mc. Cabe, at his Shop, opposite the Exchange, where he will be obliged by the Orders of his Friends and the Publick.
THOs. Mc. CABE.

Wants Employment,

AN active middle-aged Man, capable of acting as House Steward or Butler, in which capacity he has served several families of distinction, from whom he has ample testimonials of his abilities and integrity: He also understands Brewing and Marketing. A line directed to T. F. Castle-Dobbs, Carrickfergus, will be duly attended to.
May 11th, 1789.

Oils and Colours.

ALEXANDER NEILSON has just imported a large Assortment of PAINTS, which with DRUGS of the best Quality, he is selling remarkably cheap for Cash. The strictest attention is paid by Neilson to Apothecary Business.
Belfast, 24th April, 1789.

John Walker,

IS now landing a cargo of Scotch Malting Coal, which on trial proves good—also, Coke for drying Malt, Swansey Coals for Smiths—which, with every article in in the Bleach Stuff line, he has for sale at his Stores on the Bason.
Newry 3d May, 1789.

The Coterie.

WILL be held (as usual) at the Donegall-Arms, on Tuesday next the 19th instant.
Belfast, May 14th, 1789.

Sailor,

WILL stand this season at Mount-Ross, within two miles of Portaferry, and be let to Mares at one Guinea, and half a Crown to the Groom. Any mares that miss to him will be covered gratis next year.
27th April, 1789.

GENERAL,

A Get of the noted Arabian Horse Major, upon a remarkably powerful and fast trotting Mare; he is fine and strong made, sixteen hands high, four years old, nutmeg grey; will stand this season at Henry Garrett's Maragall near Lisburn, at one guinea and half a crown for the season, the money to be paid before service.—Good Grass for Mares at 6½ per night.
2d May, 1789.

Noble Farmer,

GOT by Hugh Horner's Horse Diamond, stands this season also at Hugh Moore's, Crooked-stone, near Killead Meeting-house, and will be let to Mares at so very low a rate as 2s 8d. h. in hand, and 11s. 4d h. for a foal. He is a bay Horse, remarkably strong, well marked, moves fair, and light, full seventeen hands, and has proved remarkably fruitful.
May 5th, 1789.

New Red Clover Seed, Sheet Lead, and English Cyder.

BROWN and OAKMAN are landing a few Bags Red Clover Seed of very excellent quality, Sheet Lead of several Scantlings; and best English Cyder in hampers and hogsheads.
They daily expect a large quantity of Hyson, Congou and Green Teas from the last India sale.
Belfast, 11th May, 1789.
A Parlour, Shop and Store, in a good situation in Waring-street, to be let. Enquire at said Brown and Oakman

GRAZING

TO be Let at Farm Lodge in the Falls.—Enquire at Mr. Bamber.
May 8th, 1789.

DROPPED,

ON the road between Carrickfergus and Belfast, the 7th instant, A plain SILVER WATCH. Whoever finds the same, and leaves it in Mr. Joy's Office, will receive half a Guinea reward.
Belfast, 8th May, 1789.

TO BE LET, During the Summer Season,

A Neat commodious New HOUSE, and Garden, situate in a most convenient place for Bathing, on the Antrim Shore, about six miles from Belfast and two from Carrickfergus.———The House contains a hall, kitchen and parlour on the first floor, and two good sleeping-rooms on the second.—Grazing can be had for two horses and a cow.
Application to be made to John Hughes on the premises, or Mr. Samuel Neilson, Belfast.
11th May, 1789.

NOTICE.

A Meeting of the Custodee Creditors of Roger Mc. Neill, Esq; of Glynvile, is requested at the Donegall-Arms, Belfast, on Friday next the 15th instant, exactly at one o'clock, on business of consequence.
May 11th, 1789.

Welcome-home,

IS to stand this season at Mount-Alexander, near Comber, and to cover Mares as formerly, at half a Guinea and one Shilling.
N. B. The Duke will stand this season at the house of Hugh McMellen, near Comber Course, and to cover Mares at half a Guinea and half a Crown; the half Guinea to be paid when the mare proves with foal.
May 11th, 1789.

AN Adjournment of the Quarter Sessions of the County of Antrim is made to Ballycastle for the 26th instant, for the purpose of registering Freeholders.
May 13th, 1789.

THOs. STEVENSON, Surgeon, Apothecary, and Man-Midwife,

TAKES this opportunity of informing his friends and the publick, that after serving a regular time to the Apothecary Business, and attending two seasons in the University of Edinburgh, he intends remaining in the Shop occupied by his father in Dromore; where he hopes, by his punctuality and attention, to merit their favour.
Dromore, May 14th, 1789.

JOHN SLOAN, Surgeon, Apothecary, and Man-Midwife,

HAVING attended the hospitals in London, and the most eminent teachers in the different branches of the profession for several seasons, has laid in an assortment of fresh Medicines of the best quality, in the Shop lately occupied by Mr. Johnson of Caledon, hopes to merit the approbation of his friends and the public in general, by that care and attention that is requisite in the profession.
May 14th, 1789.

To be sold by publick Auction,

ON Monday 25th May instant, at the house of Mrs. Mc. Caulley's, Curran of Larne, the SLOOP SALLY and JANE, cutter rigg'd, with all her materials, Irish built, five years old, 35 tons and half by the register, now lying in the harbour of Larne—part of the cash may lie in the purchasers hand, giving good security. For further particulars enquire at James Hill, or William Mc. Clelland of Islandmagee.
May the 12th, 1789.

BOTANY BAY.

The settlement at this place has been thought hitherto, by the public, to be intended solely as a receptacle for criminals.

Our Government however was induced to it by political motives, no less advantageous to a great and commercial nation than the punishment and employment of delinquents.

The New-Zealand hemp which was said by the projector to be far superior to the European; and the timber on Norfolk Island, equal in goodness to the English, in regard to ship-building. With these important articles it was intended to supply the East Indies in time of war, when our convoys might be intercepted or delayed.

The situation is also peculiarly fitted to annoy the commerce of Spain, during a war with that power, and during peace, it is well calculated for an intercourse with China and Japan.

However good the intentions of our Ministry might have been, their hopes are now entirely frustrated in regard to all their expectations.

The New-Zealand hemp is not found in any quantities; neither is it a native of the soil.

The timber, which is most excellent on Norfolk Island alone, can never be brought off, on account of the violence of the surf; the settlement itself will undoubtedly be attacked by Spain in case of a rupture—and the trade with China and Japan will excite the jealousy of the East India Company, whose charter it will also infringe.

PRINCESS ROYAL's SUPPER AND BALL.

THE CARDS OF INVITATION,

Were in her Royal Highnesses name to the unmarried Branches of the Nobility and other persons of distinction, who were honoured on this occasion: the married were invited by Lord Aylesbury, in the name of the Queen.

THE COMPANY

consisted mostly of those who were not at the last Gala, which will account for many of the King's particular friends being at the opera on the same night. Among those who were particularized by a second ivitation to Windsor, were the Lord Chancellor and Mr. Pitt, the Duke of Richmond's, Duke of Leed's, Duke of Chandos's, Duke of Marlborough's, Lord Sydney's, Lord Aylesbury's Lord Weymouth's, Lord Aylesford's Lord Waldegrave's, Lord Chatham's, Lord Fauconberg's, General Harcourt's Marquis of Stafford's, and Lord Galloway's families.—These, added to all the foreign Ambassadors and those of the Nobility and Commoners who were foremost in distinguishing themselves as friends to his Majesty, and who had not been at the Queen's Concert, made two hundred and twenty-eight persons, who began to assemble in the ball-room about eight o'clock, which by ten was extremely full.

THE DRESSES

Were the Windsor uniform, with a small distinction between the old and young ladies; the former having a long purple train, the latter without any train at all.

The gown was white tiffany, with a garter blue, or, as it appeared by candle light, a purple body. The sleeves were white, and ornamented, as was the coat, which had three rows of fringe at equal distances from each other, to answer the fringe at the bottom of the gown, which fell only just low enough to appear like another row of fringe over the uppermost of those three, as if there was no separation between the gown and coat.—This gave a neatness, as well as an elegance, to the dress, and, as there was no hoop, made it perfectly convenient for dancing. The gown was laced behind, and, as the reader must perceive, terminated several inches short of the petticoat.

The hair was dressed to suit the colour of the face, extremely light, and in general with not more than two curls on each side. The hind part flowed down in ringlets, which hung over the shoulders, and not being thickened by pomatum, or overloaded by powder, gave no offence to its natural beauty. A large plume of white feathers, either plain or tipped with orange, gave a grandeur to the whole, which had a very fine effect.

Her Majesty and her Daughters did not differ from the general uniform; and, excepting the Princess Mary, whose hair was in curls on her forehead, without powder, their heads were dressed alike.

The King wore the Windsor Uniform, as did all the gentlemen present. He had on his diamond star, which made a most brilliant appearance.

All the ladies wore bandeaus round the front of their head-dress, with the words, "God save the King;" and many of them had beautiful medallions of his Majesty, some plain, some in pearl, and some set in diamonds.

Her Majesty's table was distinguished by gold plates, gold dishes, gold tureens, gold spoons, gold candle-branches, and gold knives and forks.

On the ground works of the Royal Table, were the figures of Peace and Plenty, with the olive branch and cornucopia; the accompaniments, various geniusses weaving wreaths of flowers; the pedesta's presented vases of fruits.

On one of the long tables, the platform was covered with dancing figures—the other had emblematical figures—Hope, Charity, Peace, Plenty, Britannia, &c. &c. which being done on sand, glistened with the reflected light of the candles.

That part of the supper which was hot, consisted of twenty tureens of different soups, roast ducks, turkey pouts, cygnets, green geese, land rails, chickens, asparagus, peas and beans. The cold parts of the collation were the same kind of poultry boned, and swimming or standing in the centre of transparent jellies, where they were supported by paste pillars, not in circumference thicker than a knitting needle. This, with the lights playing from the candles and reflected on by the polish of the plates and dishes, made a most beautiful appearance.

Crayfish pies of all kinds were distributed with great taste, and the hams and brawn in masquerade swimming on the surface of pedestals of jelly, seemingly supported but by the strength of an apparent liquid, called for admiration.

To go further into particulars of this part of the supper, would lead us to a length for which we cannot afford room. We shall therefore only add, it was furnished with all that nature could produce, or art model into what may be called a perfection of variety.

The ornamental parts of the Confectionary, were numurous and splendid; so numerous, that their description in detail would fill our paper: there were temples four feet high, in the different stories of which were sweetmeats. The various orders of Architecture were also done with inimitable taste.

The side tables contained large gold goblets, and a new service of gold and silver plates. In the centre of the latter were embossed that part of the history of the Roman Father, where his daughter is in the pious and filial act of feeding him in prison with her own milk.

THE DESERT

Comprehended all that a hot-house was competent to afford—and indeed more than it was thought art could produce at this season of the year. There was a profusion of pines, straw-berries, of every denomination, peaches, nectarines, apricots, cherries of each kind, from the Kentish to the Morella, plumbs and rasberries, with the best and richest preserved fruits, as well those that are dried as those that are in syrup.

The principal attendants were the King's and Queen's Footmen and Pages, except a few straggling coloured coats that appeared to bustle about as servants—but whether they were in that capacity or not, it is impossible for us to tell. This, however, we may say—they disgraced the uniformity of the room.

DUBLIN, MAY 7.

This morning at 6 o'clock, the remains of Viscount Lifford, late Lord Chancellor of this kingdom, were interred in Christ-church, by his Lordship's special directions given in his will.

The coffin was richly elegant—the hearse very grand, with Rutland plumes, and drawn by six black horses.

DUBLIN, MAY 11.

Friday a Post Assembly was held at the Tholsel, when Alderman Exshaw was chosen Lord Mayor for the ensuing year, in the room of Alderman Sutton who resigned.

DUBLIN, MAY 12.

IRISH HOUSE OF LORDS.

The Regency bill, which has for several weeks past been ready framed by Mr. Pitt, we are well assured, waits only for the prorogation of our houses of parliament the 25th of this month, to be introduced into the British house of commons. The reasons for that artful Minister's, postponing it to that time, are easily guessed at.

The present parliamentary session is now virtually at an end, as no business will be done subsequent to the 25th instant, to which day both houses stand adjourned. The Royal assent will then be given to such bills as have passed both houses, which by that time will have returned from England, and an immediate prorogation will then take place.

TO THE PRINTER.

SIR,

In addition to the various accounts that have lately appeared in your useful paper, of Charitable Schools established in different parts of the kingdom, by giving an early insertion to the following you will much oblige

A CONSTANT READER.

Gilford, May 4th, 1789.

THE free schools of Moyallon and Stramore, which have now been established near half a year, and in each of which about 60 poor children are entered and instructed in English, writing and arithmetick, are supported by the voluntary contributions and subscriptions of the principal inhabitants of those places, provided with proper masters, books, and other requisites, and conducted under salutary regulations.

And, further to extend the utility of this institution, these schools are also opened on Sundays, exclusively for such as have no other means or opportunity of instruction.

What eminently marks the liberality of this establishment is, that no distinction is made between different persuasions, but those of every denomination are equally admitted to participate its benefits.

The rational mind may contemplate with pleasure the effects which this may in time produce—effects, which will not be merely confined to the present race, but may also extend to generations yet unborn. Instead of that uncultivated ignorance, which has too long prevailed among the lower classes of people, and become in a manner hereditary, useful knowledge will thus be transmitted as a blessing and inheritance to their posterity.

On Sunday the 3d inst. about nine in the morning, the scholars of the free school of Moyallon, joining those of Stramore free school, amounting in all to about 170, the Sunday scholars included, proceeded in exact order, under the care of their proper masters, and others appointed for the purpose, to attend divine service at their respective places of worship.—After service they returned in the same orderly manner to their several houses.

The neatness and cleanliness of their appearance, the order and regularity which they observed, and the decency and propriety of their behaviour, deserve to be applauded, as they reflect credit not only on themselves but also on those who are concerned in the management and regulation of these schools.

As this laudable custom of assembling and conducting them to their places of worship is to be regularly continued, it is hoped that the same promptitude of attendance and comely decorum will be observed on future occasions, which so remarkably distinguished this.—Such a spectacle was highly gratifying to all, and infinitely more interesting and intrinsically beautiful than the glitter of empty shew, or the idle pageants of an hour.—To see such a number rescued from hopeless ignorance, instructed in useful knowledge, and trained up in habits of piety and virtue, must warm the hearts of the most indifferent and expand them with benevolence and humanity.

So noble an exertion of charity cannot fail of drawing down the blessing of Heaven on the liberal supporters of this useful institution.—It will afford them a remembrance ever grateful in retrospect, and still more transporting in prospect—it will diffuse a pleasing balm through life, sweeten every domestic comfort, and shed a brighter lustre on their characters, than all the splendour of affluence or worldy grandeur can confer.—Prosperity and peace shall flourish round their habitations, and the fervent prayers of gratitude ascend to Heaven, as sweet memorials of their dignified humanity.

This eulogium is the language of sincerity and truth, and, though unsolicited, cannot be unacceptable to any, except the parties themselves.—Their's, indeed, is the charity that vaunteth not itself, that wishes to confer its blessings unseen, and modestly shuns the public eye.—Nothing, therefore, could have induced the writer of this to offer this public tribute of applause, but a sense of the duty, which, as an individual, he owes to society, and a desire to do justice to such worthy characters, and to stimulate others to imitate so laudable an example.

Belfast.

The Friendship, Capta[illegible]per, for London, is clear to sail, but detained here by contrary winds.

In answer to our correspondent *Julius*, we beg leave to inform him, that we do not at present recollect the reason for which his paper was not inserted; we can only add that it appeared a sufficient one to us at the time.

A detachment of the 69th regiment quartered at Keady four months past, marched to head quarters in Armagh on the 11th. During the time said detachment lay here, they behaved with the greatest regularity, sobriety, and honesty; the inhabitants of the town think it incumbent upon them, in this publick manner to return their commandant Lieut. Hay their thanks for his very polite attention to them; and intreat (if they are to have any of the military quartered here after the Review in Armagh) said detachment may be sent to them again.——Keady, May 11th, 1789.

Belfast. *May 15.*

BRITISH HOUSE OF COMMONS.

CATHOLIC DISSENTERS' PETITION.

MR. VILLIERS informed the house, that he had been desired to present a petition, which he then held in his hand, from the Catholic Dissenters of this kingdom. The object of it was to pray redress of the penal laws which existed against them.—That they conceive these laws were continued by those of a different persuasion, conceiving their tenets and principles inimical to the established church and the state of the country.—And they were assured, when their civil and religious sentiments were really explained and understood, that they (the Catholics) would not be considered as deserving the rigour of laws to which they were in particular rendered amenable.—Leave given.

Friday, May 8.

CORPORATION AND TEST ACTS.

Mr. Beaufoy said, it was unnecessary that he should apoligize to the house for pressing a question which had been before rejected He could not, he said, resist the solicitation which had been made, by a numerous and respectable body of men, the Dissenters of England, to renew his application to Parliament to redress their grievances. It was unnecessary for him to adduce instances of the Legislature, after repeated and ineffectual efforts to carry a particular motion, at length acceding to it.

The principle was a just one, and he hoped in the present instance it would be successful; for he relied on the merits of the case, and had no doubt but the better it was understood the more certainty there was of its being carried. The conduct of other nations in this enlightened period of general toleration, would, he hoped, be an example worthy the emulation of a great and liberal people. There might be, he said, in the great and respectable body of Dissenters, some few intemperate individuals; but it would be cruel and unjust to hold this out as a fit sanction for punishing a numerous and loyal set of men. The house should look to the general character of men, and when it did, there was no doubt but their request would be complied with: for he, from his knowledge could assert, that there were no men had a higher respect for the Constitution, or were more loyal to their Sovereign.

no 1789.]   Printed by HENRY JOY, and Co. BELFAST.

The BELFAST NEWS-LETTER.

TUESDAY May 19,   FRIDAY May 22, 1789.

Freight for *Leghorn*.

A Sloop will be taking in Goods for Leghorn in a few days. For Freight apply to Cunningham Greg.

Belfast, 11th May, 1789.

Cambricks stolen,

OUT of Olivia Tomb's Green at the Whitehouse, on Thursday night the 14th instant, six pieces of fine Cambrick, bleached white, eight or nine yards each, value from 3s. 6d. to 5s per yard.——Five Guineas reward shall be paid to the person who will inform against and prosecute the Thief to conviction, by

Belfast, 18th May, 1789.   OLIVIA TOMB.

Guernsey Cyder.

SAMUEL and ANDREW Mc. CLEAN having purchased the entire cargo of the Sloop Mary, arrived a few days ago from Guernsey—they beg leave to inform their Friends and the Public, that the same will be sold at their Stores in High-street, as so low a price as *Ten Pence* per gallon, by the pipe, hogshead or half hogshead.

This cargo is of a quality superior to any imported here for many years past; and as no other importation is expected from Guernsey this season; those who with to be supplied on terms uncommonly moderate, are requested to give their orders speedily, to prevent disappointment.   Belfast, 18th May, 1789.

Fresh Teas, &c.

TAYLOR, MAXWELL, & Co. are now landing out of the Linen-Hall, Captain Dickson, a parcel of Hyson, Souchong, Congou and Green Teas from the last sale, which, with a general assortment of Groceries and Dyestuffs, they will dispose of on moderate terms.

Belfast, 16th May, 1789.

New Teas, &c.

THOMPSON and OAKMAN have just arrived from London per the Linen Hall, Capt. Dickson, a parcel of fresh Hyson, Bloom, fine and common Congou, Single and Bohea Teas from the last India Sales

They have also received per the Dolphin from Bristol, a parcel of very best English Cyder in hogsheads and hampers, double Gloster Cheese, and a few cases Quarry Glass, which, with an extensive assortment of other Goods in their line, will be sold on moderate terms for good payments.

Belfast, 19th May, 1789.

NEW TEAS.

JONES, TOMB. JOY, & Co. are landing out of the Linen Hall, Captain Dickson, from London, a very large supply of Single, Congo, Bloom and Hyson Teas, from the last India Sales, which they will dispose of on the most reasonable terms.

Belfast, 18th May, 1789.

Leaf Tobacco, Teas, & Rum.

BROWN and OAKMAN are landing for sale about 50 Hogsheads of excellent Virginia Leaf Tobacco of the growth of 1787; also a large quantity of Hyson, Congou, and Green Tea—A few Puncheons of high-flavoured Barbadoes Rum to be sold by Auction at 12 o'clock, on Friday next, at the King's Stores on the Quay.

Belfast, 18th May, 1789.

Samuel Brown & Co.

HAVE received per the Linen Hall, from London, a large assortment of Green and Congou TEAS, purchased at the last East India Sales, which will be sold on the most reasonable terms.

Belfast, 18th May, 1789.

Leaf Tobacco, & New Teas, &c.

HUGH CRAWFORD is now discharging the Brig Sophia, Capt. Thompson, direct from Virginia, with a cargo of best James's River Tobacco.

He is also landing out of the Linen Hall a large parcel of New Teas from the last India Sales in London.

The whole he will sell on the very lowest terms.

Belfast, 18th May, 1789.

Train Oil, Jamaica and Brazil Cotton-Wool, and Dutch Straw Weld—to be sold cheap.

New Dronthon Deals.

CUNNINGHAM GREG is just landing a small Cargo, which he will dispose of on reasonable terms; also a parcel of WELCH SLATES.

Belfast, 11th May, 1789.

POOR HOUSE.

THE Committee of the Belfast Charitable Society hereby give notice that (in consequence of an order of the General Board of the 13th inst.) they are ready to receive proposals for supplying the house. by contract, for one year from the 1st of August next, with the following articles, viz.

Bread, beef, beer, meal, peas, coals, potatoes, barley, soap and candles. A schedule of the quantity of each article, as it will be required weekly through the year, will be had on application to Mr. Alexander at the Poorhouse. The proposals are to be sent (sealed up and directed) to the chairman of the committee which fits every Saturday.

A middle aged woman of good character, without husband or children, is wanted as house-keeper;—none need apply unless well recommended and whose character is unimpeachable—a suitable salary will be given. The election will take place on Wednesday the 3d June next.

N. B. 200 bushels of good potatoes wanted, for which 10d. per bushel will be paid on delivery at the house.

Belfast, 18th May, 1789.

Advertisement

WHEREAS some months past, in the year 1788, an information was given in the public news-papers, that whoever would have given the proper marks, with the number, place, and maker's name of a silver watch dropped in or immediate to Belfast, by applying to the Rev. Father James M'Corry, at either Carrickfergus or Larne, might meet with success, &c.——The public is now to observe if not sure information is given to the said Rev. Father James M'Corry at either of the above places at or before 30 days, from the date hereof, he who found the said dropped watch will consider it as his own.

Dated Carrickfergus, 14th May, 1789.

A Servant,

WHO understands the care of horses, can attend well at table, perform other offices of an inside servant, and is a protestant, who can be well recommended, will hear of a place by applying to the Revd. Francis Johnston at Tullycross, near the four-mile House from Newry.

Wanted also a Postilion, who is a Protestant, and can be well recommended,   May 15th, 1789.

Wanted,

A Helper in a Coach-horse Stable, who can bring a real good discharge, understands his business, and will obey the commands of his coachman. Apply at Mr. Joy's Office.   Belfast, May 18, 1789

New Teas, Kentish Bag Hops, fine Spanish Indigo,

SAMUEL GIBSON has received for sale, an assortment of fresh Teas imported from last India Sales in London, consisting of fine Hysons, fine and common Congous and Singlos, also best Kentish Bag Hops, and very fine Spanish Indigo—all of which, together with his usual assortment of fine and common Scale Sugars, and a general assortment in the Grocery and Dyestuff line, he will dispose of at the most reduced prices.

North-street, Belfast, 19th May, 1789.

William Mc. Clure,

WILL sell by Auction, at his Stores in North-street, about ten Tons of Sicily Barilla Ashes, on account of the Shipper, on Wednesday the 27th instant, at 12 o'clock: Terms, bills or notes at three months on Dublin or Belfast. He also is now landing his Teas from the last India Sales:—And has for Sale,

Fine Scale Sugar,	Ashes.	Wool Cards,
American Pearl,		Liquorice Ball,
Hungarian do.		Glauber Salts,
And Dantzig		Kane Brimstone.

Together with a general assortment of Groceries, will be sold on moderate terms for good payment

Belfast, 19th May, 1789.

Mr. Mc. Grath,

RESPECTFULLY acquaints the Ladies and Gentlemen of Lisburn and its vicinity, that he will do himself the honour to wait upon them, and open his School on Friday the 5th of June next.

Dublin, May the 10th, 1789

The famous Peacock,

WILL cover mares this season, at James Dawson's in Magheragell, near Lisburn, at so low a price as half a guinea, and half a crown to the groom; the money to be paid before service. He will be in Lisburn on Tuesday, and Lurgan on Friday during the season.

No lines or tokens will be taken as payment, nor will any service be done on Sunday.

May 18th, 1789.

Books for Exportation.

WILLIAM MITCHELL,

BOOKSELLER, *North-Street*, BELFAST,

HAS just completed an excellent Assortment of Books suitable to the *American Market*; consisting of Bibles of all kinds, gilt and plain, Testaments, Scotch religious Books, Books of Arithmetick, Spelling Books, &c.

He has also a handsome assortment of PRINTS elegantly executed by our *Native Artists*—with every Article in his line published or sold by any other Bookseller.

He is as usual well stock'd with STATIONARY of every kind, the prices of which it is very unnecessary to mention when he informs the publick, that they may be supplied from him on as low terms as anywhere in the kingdom, *the Capital not excepted.*

A Meeting-House to be built,

AT Lisban near Killinchy. Masons and carpenters are requested to send their proposals before the 27th inst. to Messrs. Joseph Snodden or Robt. Maxwell of Ballyminetha, Samuel Johnston of Lisbarnet, Robt. Minis of Tullynagie, Wm. Shiels or Wm. Sloan of Lisban. Sufficient security, will be expected.

Lisban, May 18th, 1789.

John and Lancelot Watson,

HAVE received per the New Draper from London, a large and fresh supply of

WHITBREAD's PORTER

in hogsheads, barrels, and half-barrels, of a quality equal to any they have hitherto imported, and such as they think will support that character their Porter has already acquired.

They have also a large quantity of Whitbread's Porter in bottle, imported the latter end of last summer, and now in fine order. Being determined to sell only for *ready money*, they beg leave to state their prices, viz.

3l. 8s. 3d. per hhd. and 10s. cask.	These prices for casks must be deposited, if casks of equal value be not returned
2l. 5s. 6d. barrel and 8s. 8d. do.	
1l. 2s. 9d. half-barrel and 5s. 5d. do.	

5s. 6d. per dozen for Porter in common sized bottles—6s. per do. for Porter in quart bottles—Bottles included in the above prices;—if they be returned 2s. per dozen allowed. Hampers made up for the country safely and expeditiously;—charge for a hamper that contains four dozen 1s. 4d.—that which contains five dozen 1s. 8d.—but less than four dozen of Porter they cannot sell.—They have at present a variety of excellent Clarets in high order in bottle—Red Port, vintage 1784, of very fine quality, and old in bottle—Sherry, Malaga, Frontigniac, Champaign and Burgundy. To persons who buy to sell again, and take 10 dozen of wine and upwards, a reasonable allowance will be made.

N. B. They have lately bottled a small parcel of *American Cider*, imported this spring, which they can assure their friends is of high quality and high flavour.

Newry. 18th May, 1789.

THE Committee appointed by the Grand Jury of the county of Down to oversee the building of the Public Gaol for that County, having intrusted me as Architect with the care thereof so far as to receive proposals and to enter into contracts for supplying the works with quarry stones by the perch or load, mountain grit for coins, jaumbs, ashlers and sills by the superficial foot, lime by the statute barrel; sand by the load or perch, masons, smiths, carpenters and slators work, and for all other necessary works relating thereto.

Now I Charles Lilly do hereby give notice, that I will on Saturday the 30th day of this instant May, attend at Downpatrick to receive proposals for the supplying such materials and performance of such works for the purposes aforesaid as any persons desirous to be concerned in undertaking the same shall make to me, and will enter into contracts for the same respectively.

Dublin, 9th May, 1789.   CHARLES LILL.

Irish State Lottery, 1789.

The Tickets, and duly Stampt HALF, QUARTER, EIGHTH and SIXTEENTH Shares, also the FORTUNATE GUINEA TICKETS, are selling on the lowest Terms, at

Mr. NICHOLSON'S

Licensed STATE LOTTERY OFFICES, No. 7, Dame-street, DUBLIN, and Bank-street, Corn-hill, LONDON.

In the LAST IRISH LOTTERY he had the Pleasure to sell to his Customers, the following CAPITAL PRIZES, viz.

No. 23,481 - 20,000l. | No. 17,025, - 10,000l.
      28,322, - 20,000l. | 30,875, - 5,000l.

And in the last ENGLISH LOTTERY,

No. 46,676 - 10,000l.—22,128 - 1000l. as first drawn, besides several of 2,000l.—1,000l.—and 500l. each.

In the PRESENT LOTTERY there are two of 20,000l.—two of 10,000l.—two of 5000l. &c. &c. &c.

PARISIAN INTELLIGENCE.

May 3.

AT length the great political machine is wound up, and put in motion; but it is to be feared that, like other machines, it is too complicated to continue long without being disordered. The cabal that has been long secretly working against Mr. Necker, has at last declared itself openly. At a late meeting of the Noblesse on the subject of the election, one gentleman had the courage to make an harangue again the minister, charging him as the direct author of all the disturbances in the kingdom: and that as a Protestant, he had designedly excited the late tumults to revenge the memorable massacre of St. Bartholomew's Day. A Prince who was present, stopped such a licentious speech, by openly pronouncing it infamous. This occasioned a great disturbance within, and the people, who were assembled from curiosity, having some intelligence of what passed, endeavoured to get in: some of the nobility putting their hands on their swords, declared open war against the Third Estate. Some others, more prudent, called them to order, and happily continued their debate very quietly for the rest of the evening.

Yesterday the Deputies, who are already arrived, were presented in form to his Majesty; the Clergy at eleven o'clock, the Nobility at one, and the Third Estate at four o'clock. To-day a second proclamation is made for the holding the National Assembly. To-morrow his Majesty goes in procession to the two parish churches, and on Tuesday is open the session, at least that is the day fixed; however, it is not improbable that it will be again put off, for the Deputies of Paris are not yet chosen, and it is imagined that the King will rather defer the meeting for a few days longer, than open the assembly without the presence of the Members for the capital of the kingdom; tho' when they will be chosen, seems rather uncertain, from a very important point in dispute between the Nobles and the Third Estate; the former refusing to go to the Assembly at all, unless it be previously determined that they shall deliberate separately from the Commons; the latter equally decided not to elect any member, unless they are assured of deliberating in one common body with the Clergy and the nobility. Our next will probably shew the issue of this dispute.

WESTMINSTER-HALL.

TRIAL OF WARREN HASTINGS, ESQ.

SEVENTH DAY.

Mr. Grey proceeded to read several letters, and shewed by the substance of this correspondence, the opinion Mr. Hastings himself held of the binding tendency of the Acts which relate to the receiving of presents.

Mr. Burke then introduced the charge of Bribery and Corruption. He stated, that in laying out money, no regard had ever been entertained towards seniority of family, which Mr. Hastings had made use of as a pretence to lay out the money improperly, in the family of the Begums.

In proof of this, several papers were produced; to the reading of which Mr. Law objected, as enumerating a great variety of particulars not relating to the charge.

Mr. Burke answered, that they contained a number of material circumstances, amounting to circumstantial proof, the best of all kind of proof; they went to establish the crime charged against Mr. Hastings—it was a crime in Mr. Hastings to make improper payments; it was a crime to make up false accounts of some payments, and conceal the accounts of others; and it was a crime to receive directions from the Company, and say he had conformed to those directions, when, in fact, he never had.

The papers were then read. The next evidence produced, was to prove the salary paid to the Nabob Dowlah; in the account of which, Mr. Hastings had inserted one year's payment more than he had given. Several other papers were read, to prove the false account in this particular; after which the court adjourned.

BRITISH HOUSE OF COMMONS.

Tuesday, May 12.

ABOLITION of the SLAVE TRADE.

Mr. Wilberforce moved the order of the day for the house resolving itself into a Committee of the whole house to take into their consideration the petitions against the slave trade.

The order of the day being read, Mr. Wilberforce moved, "That the report of the Committee of Privy Council be referred to said Committee—That the evidence of the last year on the slave trade be referred to the said Committee—That the acts passed in the islands relative to the slaves be referred to the said Committee—That the petitions last year offered against the slave trade be referred to the said Committee—And that the accounts presented to the house in the last and present year relative to the exports and imports to Africa be referred to the said Committee."

These motions being all agreed to, the house immediately resolved itself into a Committee of the whole house, Sir William Dolben in the Chair.

Mr. Wilberforce then rose, and prefaced a most able and animated speech with a declaration to the Committee, of the magnitude of the subject he had untertaken having created in him the greatest apprehensions, which were occasioned by the motion he intended to make, involving in it not only many interests in this country and its dependencies, but being of considerable importance to the whole world. He said, that as in the progress of the the enquiries he had been under the necessity of making, he had every where been received with that candour that convinced him of his motives being considered in the most favourable view, he had dismissed his apprehensions, and was determined to march forward with a firm step in the cause of justice, of humanity, and freedom. He hoped the house would consider the subject coolly, discard all party motives, and suffer the clear voice of reason to be heard. Much warmth, he said, from the subject having been long in agitation, had been excited on all sides; he wished that heat to be abated, and to enter on the subject calmly; and he challenged a fair and cool discussion of the motion he should have the honour of moving. The motion he meant to offer, though at present it might not be considered a political one, and on that ground might meet much objection, he was convinced, in his own mind, that in the end it would be found serviceable to all parties, and to the best interests of the country. He came not forward to accuse the West India planters; he came not forward to accuse the Liverpool merchants; he came forward to accuse no one; he came forward for the purpose of shewing to that house, that guilt somewhere existed, which ought to be remedied;

LONDON, May 9.

The following petition was presented on Tuesday, the 5th instant, to both Houses of Parliament

The humble Petition of the Persons whose Names are hereunto subscribed, on behalf of themselves and others,

CATHOLIC DISSENTERS of ENGLAND,

Sheweth,

THAT sentiments unfavourable to your petitioners, as citizens and subjects, have been entertained by English Protestants, and that your petitioners are subject to various penal laws, on account of principles which are asserted to be maintained by your petitioners, and other persons of their religion, and which principles are dangerous to society, and totally repugnant to political and civil liberty.

That your petitioners think it a duty which they owe to their country, as well as to themselves, to protest in a formal and solemn manner against doctrines that they condemn, and that constitute no part whatever of their principles, religion, or belief.

That your petitioners are the more anxious to free themselves from such imputations because divers Protestants, who profess themselves to be real friends to liberty of conscience, have nevertheless avowed themselves hostile to your petitioners, on account of the opinions which your petitioners are supposed to hold; and your petitioners do not blame those Protestants for their hostility, if it proceeds, (as your petitioners hope it does) not from an intolerant spirit in matters of religion, but from their being misinformed as to matters of fact.

DUBLIN, May 11.

Our Linen-hall, is now not only the greatest, but also the most eminent market-place in Europe, affording space and all possible accommodation, to both buyer and seller; the several additions to this useful pile of building being arranged with judgment, having an elegant simplicity, beautiful to behold, but devoid of unnecessary expence or ornament, and fitted n t only for the sale of linens, but also of cottons, plain and printed, and every other spec es of mixed manufacture. The Board (whose every effort has been to promote and extend the staple of this country) have also erected, in the centre of the building, a coffee-room, or exchange for negociating business; and the draper, factor, and merchant, are invited to send or deposit there their several letters, foreign or domestic, commercial papers, or other interesting matters, which will be taken charge of, or forwarded as required; and the Board have established adequate salaries to their useful officers, but judiciously prohibited altogether the reception of fees;—an example well worthy the attention of other Boards. In short, every draper or merchant having occasion to resort to this market, must contemplate, with infinite pleasure, the great changes made therein within a very short period; and in order that merit may be allowed its just tribute, it is but meet to acknowledge that the country is indebted, in a very superior degree, for all the advantages that may be naturally expected to result from these improvements, to the persevering and indefatigable exertions of the Right Honourable the Speaker of the House of Commons.

The expence of erecting the magnificent Ionic portico, which is to connect the south front of the Parliament-house with the new west front, exceeds but by 300l. the cost of raising that clumsy, heavy range wall, with which Mr. Gandon chose to join the front in College-green. In this production we are at a loss whether most to admire his taste or *economy*—but of the latter he seems now to have got completely quit, as the new Custom-house amply proves.

Belfast, *May* 19.

THE COTERIE at Ballymoney, which was appointed for Wednesday the 27th inst. is put of 'till Thursday the 28th (next night).

A CARD.

IT having been proposed at the last Vestry to change the usual mode of applotting Parish Taxes in proportion to the supposed wealth and income of each inhabitant—and instead thereof to adopt a new mode to be in proportion to the yearly value of the Houses and Shops occupied by such inhabitants——to the advocates of that measure the following Queries are submitted.

1st. Is it not *equitable* that every inhabitant should be taxed in proportion to their ability to pay, or, which is the same thing, according to their wealth and income?

2d. Cannot the wealth and income of each inhabitant be pretty nearly ascertained by two or more honest neighbours (sworn to do justice) in a town such as Belfast, where almost every person is known to the rest, although the same mode may not be *so* suitable for London, Dublin, or Cork?

3d. Must not the usual mode be deemed legal from its great antiquity, unless it can be clearly proved to be contrary to some act of Parliament?

4th. Are not many Tradesmen and Shopkeepers under the necessity of having houses and Shops (for the convenience of carrying on business) of as great yearly value as the houses of many gentlemen and wealthy merchants, when perhaps the latter may have many times the wealth and income of the former?

5th. Is the yearly value of a house or shop the BEST criterion by which to ascertain the wealth and yearly income of its inhabitant?—If so, were it not equally easy to determine a man's religion by the colour of his coat, and his courage by the cock of his hat?

A. B.

Belfast, the 18th May, 1789.

PORT NEWS.

ARRIVED.

May 11. New Loyalty, Brown, Liverpool, sugar.
13. Sophia, Thompson, New York, tobacco.
14. Mary, Agnew, Guernsey, cyder.
16. Linen-Hall, Dickson, London, tea, porter, &c. Seven colliers.

CLEARED OUT.

May 11. Hope, M'Mullan, Carthagena, porter, &c.
13. Friendship, Lepper, London, cloth, skins, &c.
12. John, Leitch, Glasgow, flour, cloth, &c.
14 Betty, M'Donnell, St. Vincent's, linen cloth, &c.
16 Peggy, M'Ilroy, Liverpool, ditto.

Belfast, *May* 22.

On Wednesday last a Vestry was held at the parish church of Belfast to receive the report of Counsel's opinion on the mode of applotting parish cesses, which has heretofore been done according to the supposed ability of each inhabitant; instead of the estimated value of each dwelling house. It was agreed that for the present the last applotment for lamp and paving cesses be forthwith paid A Committee was then appointed to search for precedents, to consider of the most eligible mode of assesment, and to report at a future day;—after which the Vestry adjourned.

Yesterday morning the St. James, Mark Collins master, sailed from hence for New-Castle and New-York, with 242 passengers.

Passengers in the Triton East Indiaman, Capt. Agnew.

Major James Buchanan.
Lieutenant Colonel Duff.
Captain Robert Gardiner, of the Artillery.
Lieutenant Dandridge, of ditto.
Lieutenant Bruce, Engineers.
Mr. John Laird.
Mr. Charles Laird.
Mr. and Mrs. Wroughton.
Mrs. Colvin.
Mrs. Ferguson, and
Miss Eliza Blunt.

Eighteen children, and 119 servants and charter-party passengers; making in all 148 passengers.

To the PRINTER.

SIR,

HAVING been formed by a brother divine, that the law allows us liberty to receive a Papist into our communion by suffering him to read his recantation either in our own houses, or at church; and doubting somewhat of the truth of this assertion, I therefore wrote to town to be fully ascertained of the fact; and received for answer, from my correspondent, that he had consulted a lawyer upon it, who gave it as his opinion, that we undoub edly had our option therein.

Now, Sir, if you would convey this useful piece of intelligence through the channel of your admirable paper, to the public notice, so that both the Clergy and Laity should be acquainted therewith, I will venture to pronounce, that the afore-mentioned law would operate in nearly a tenfold degree: for, the aversion the Catholics have to recant publicly in the presence of a large congregation, is almost insuperable. I had lately one who read her recantation in my church, whose dread and apprehensions thereof rose to so high a pitch, that she fainted in the seat and was obliged to be brought out into the air, to recover her sufficiently, to enable her to go through the ceremony.—The accounts we have every day, of converts being received in church, fully evinces, that this fact is not generally known either by the Clergy or Laity; and consequently, your rendering it universally so, would greatly benefit the Protestant cause.

I remain,
Your constant reader and well-wisher,
A Protestant Clergyman.

Anno 1789.]   Printed by HENRY JOY, and Co. BELFAST.

The BELFAST NEWS-LETTER.

TUESDAY May 26,   FRIDAY May 29, 1789.

For *LONDON*,

THE THAMES, a constant Trader, JAMES BENNETT, Master, begins to load this day, has 60 tons of her cargo ready to ship, and will clear out the 15th of June, and sail first fair wind after.——For Freight apply to JOHN NEVILL.
Newry, 25th May, 1789.

HARDWARE.

ST JOHN STEWART, adjoining the Market-House, Belfast, being determined to quit the Hardware Business, will sell off his entire Stock in Trade under first Cost. Any person wishing to enter into that line has now an opportunity of getting into as good a situation for business as in town. If no such person offers in a few days, he will then begin and sell by Auction, &c.——Those to whom he is indebted will please furnish their accounts; and he requests that those who are indebted to him will discharge the same.
May 23d, 1789.

Cockfighting,

TO be held between the Gentlemen of the County Antrim and County Down, on the third Monday of June, for fifty Guineas the Main or odd Battle, at Newtownards.
They will be shewn on the 13th of June, and fought the 15th.
May 25th, 1789

To be Let,

From the first of May last, for such Term of Years as may be agreed on,

AN excellent House in Glenarm Town, with a good Garden and Offices, lately occupied by David Mc. Kellep, Esq.—Proposals to be received (in writing) by Phill. Gibbons at Carnlough.
May 22d, 1789.

Advertisement.

THE Methodist Society, (so called) of Lisburn, return their sincere thanks to the Revd. Mr. Craig, the Trustees, and Congregation of Protestant Dissenters, for the use of their Meeting-house.
They likewise return their sincere thanks to the inhabitants of Lisburn and its vicinity, for their assistance in building their house.
Said House will be opened for publick Worship on Sunday 31st May. Service will begin at seven in the evening.
Some of their generous benefactors seeing the expence will much exceed what was expected, proposed that after sermon there should be an opportunity given them; and others, farther to assist towards the expence.—There will be Hymns sung suitable to the occasion.
N. B. The Revd. Mr. Wesley will preach in said House, (God-willing) Saturday 6th June, at six in the evening.
May 21st, 1789.

Advertisement.

THE noted grey Horse DISTILLER, upwards of 15 hands three inches high, will stand this season at Ballywooden, near Downpatrick, the property of Robert Hanna, and will cover mares at 10 low a rate as half a guinea, and half a crown for a foal, and an English shilling in hand.
He was got by Clericus on Cumberland Fanny. The Horse's pedigree may be seen in the hands of the Owner.
May 25th, 1789.

TO BE LET,

IN Skipper's-Lane, that large commodious House, and Shop, formerly occupied by Mr. James Burns, Grocer.——For particulars enquire at David Patton.
Belfast, 21st May, 1789.
N. B. There is a convenient Back-house lofted, and a Yard belonging to the above.

Notice.

IT is requested that the Trustees of the second and third Division of the Turnpike Road from Banbridge to Belfast, will meet on Saturday the 30th instant, at Hastings', in Lisburn.
N. B. All those to whom money has been issued for the repairs of the road, are desired to attend.
By Order,
WM. YOUNGHUSBAND,
Register.

Woollen Warehouse, *Belfast.*

BROWN, GAW, & CO. are this day landing a compleat Assortment of Cloths, Stuffs, Fustians, &c. &c. &c.
26th May, 1789.

Room Paper Hangings.

WM. MAGEE,

At the Book and Stationary Warehouse, Bridge-street, Belfast,

HAS just received, in addition to his former Stock a great variety of new and most fashionable patterns of Room Paper—among which are White, Chintz, Glazed and Painted Papers; finished in a stile of peculiar neatness and elegance—His assortment of

BORDERINGS

is most extensive, consisting of Festoon and Ornamental of every figure, colour and breadth, adapted to suit the taste and please the fancy of every purchaser.

The highest price given by MAGEE for
Light Guineas and Half Guineas
single or by the ounce, and cut in the presence of the seller, agreeable to act of parliament.

Wanted,

By Mr. Hull at Belvedere,

A FOOTMAN, who can produce satisfactory discharges for sobriety, honesty and attention.
May 25th, 1789.

Partnership Dissolved.

THE Publick are hereby desired to take Notice, that the Partnership which formerly subsisted between the late Allen Searson and Robert Scott, under the Firm of Searson and Scott, hath been for a considerable time past dissolved.
Belfast, 23d May, 1789.   ROBERT SCOTT.

THIS is to caution any gentleman from hiring James Dornan, who left my service early in the morning of yesterday, without my knowledge, after having the day before either carelessly or maliciously, materially damaged my carriage by driving it against the corner of some street; also a few evenings since, endangered the lives of part of my family, by putting the coach in a ditch.—He went away with a guinea he got from me under false pretences, and other sums he borrowed from his fellow servants.
As a duty to society, I mean to punish him by law as a warning to his fraternity.
25th May, 1789, Belfast.   G. WEBSTER.

Wanted immediately,

AN HOSTLER, unmarried, whose character is unexceptionable for sobriety and honesty, and skill'd in the business.——Apply to Edward Conolly, Innkeeper.
Downpatrick, 20th May, 1789.

To be sold for Account of the Insurers,

AT the Stores of Clements Gillespie, on the Merchants-Quay, on Tuesday second June, at eleven o'clock, three hundred Bales of Barilla, damaged on board the Sloop Cambria, John Jones, Master, in her passage from Carthagena.
The Lots to consist of 5 or 10 Bales each, as purchasers may incline——Approved bills on Dublin, at 21 or 31 days, on receipt of bill of parcels will be accepted of in payment. The particular terms of sale will be declared on the day thereof.
CLEM. GILLESPIE.
Newry, 24th May, 1789.

Newry Brewery.

THE extensive concern of the Newry Brewery, with all its fixtures, casks, &c. capable of brewing upwards of ten thousand barrels annually, with a large Malthouse and Bakery,—to be sold by public Auction upon the premisses, on Monday the 8th June next, at the hour of one o'clock.—Terms to be declared at time of sale.
Newry, 23d May, 1789.

BOOKS, &c.

Selling under first Cost.

A Valuable Collection of BOOKS, with a great variety of useful and correct Maps, Mezzotintos, Prints, and Copy Books.—Common Prayers of all sizes, gilt and plain,—Bottle Wax,—with a great many other Articles too numerous to particularize—being the remainder of the Stock of the late JOHN HAY, now selling considerably under first cost, *at the Two Bibles, Bridge-street, Belfast,* where Catalogues may be had GRATIS.
May 27th, 1789.

THOMAS MULLAN,

Next Door to the Broker's-Office, High-street, Belfast,

IMPREST with gratitude for the very flattering encouragement he has met with since his commencement in business, returns his sincere thanks to the Ladies and Gentlemen of Belfast and its vicinity, and begs leave to acquaint them, that he is now landing from on board the Neptune, Capt. Miskelly, from Bordeaux:—
A Quantity of best Whitewine Vinegar, Cinamon Water, and a variety of other French cordials, candied citron, preserved ginger, Narbonne honey, and a general assortment of dried and liquid sweetmeats, in boxes and pots; truffles preserved in oil, anchovies, olives, capers and other pickles; virgin oil, peaches, apricots, nectarines and other fruit, preserved in brandy; figs, almonds, prunes and French plumbs; mareschal and other perfumed hair powder, soft and hard pomatum of the best quality, in pots and sticks; sprop of capillaire, and a great variety of scented waters and essences. He has also for sale a quantity of fresh lemons and oranges; which, with his usual assortment of Goods in the Haberdashery and Grocery Line, he is determined to sell at the most moderate prices.
May 28th, 1789.

The INN of STEWARTSTOWN, 24th May, 1789.

SAMUEL Mc. REYNOLDS, having for the purpose of accommodating such travellers and others, as do do him the favour of calling with him, removed to that large commodious House built by the late Doctor Cornwall; he hopes by his punctuality and assiduity in attending to his guests to merit a continuation of the favour of every gentleman that is so kind as to make trial of his accommodations.
May 26th, 1789.

AS the Partnership of Peebles and Love, of Moy, is dissolved, they take this opportunity of returning their sincere thanks to their friends and the publick for the encouragement they have met with since their commencement in business; and in order to enable them to settle their partnership accounts, they request that all those who now stand indebted to them may speedily pay in the same to Nath. Peebles of Moy. Said Peebles intends to carry on the former business on his own account.
May 27th, 1789.

Advertisement.

WILLIAM WEIR has this day opened the long established Inn, in Broughshane, known by the name of the O'Neill's Arms, where gentlemen will meet with good entertainment.
19th May, 1789.

Advertisement.

THE Sub Commissioners of this District, will sit on *Friday the 5th June next,* to hear and determine the Claims of the several Persons interested in the condemnation of the Sally and Beckey, and her Cargo.—Custom-House, Belfast 29 May, 1789.
GEO. MACARTNEY PORTIS,
Collector.

Two Hundred Pounds

WANTED immediately, for which undeniable security will be given.——Application to be made to Mr. Thomas L. Stewart, Attorney at Law, Stafford-street, Dublin, or to Mr. Robert Stewart, Belfast.
Belfast, 11th May, 1789.

Money wanted.

THREE HUNDRED POUNDS on a Mortgage.—Apply to Mr. Joy.
Belfast, 1st May, 1789.

To be lent on approved Security,

THE Sum of SIX HUNDRED POUNDS, the property of the Bachelors Annuity Company of Belfast.——Apply to the Secretary Hugh Allen.
Belfast, May 1, 1789.

To be lent on landed Security,

TWO THOUSAND POUNDS sterling upon the first day of June next.——Application to be made to David Gordon, Attorney at Law, or to Mr. Patrick Connor, at his Office, Belfast.

For *Oporto*,

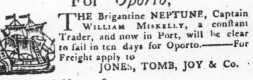

THE Brigantine NEPTUNE, Captain WILLIAM MISKELLY, a constant Trader, and now in Port, will be clear to sail in ten days for Oporto.——For Freight apply to
JONES, TOMB, JOY & Co.
Belfast, 25th May, 1789.

ORIGIN OF THE SLAVE TRADE.

This traffic, so disgraceful to humanity, began in the reign of Queen Elizabeth, about the year 1567.—A Captain John Hawkins, revolving in his mind the situation of the West India islands, then mostly in the hands of the Spaniards and French, was the first who thought of introducing the Africans to assist the inhabitants in cultivating their plantations. He saw in them a people fit to endure labour in such a climate; and considered their situation to be so bad in itself, from climate, rude state of civilization, and continual quarrels and bloodshed amongst themselves, that he thought they certainly would be no losers, if not gainers, by change of country: the only difficulty was, how to get them from one territory to another so remote. This, however, he undertook; and from this arose the famous, or, to speak more correctly, the infamous trade in Negroes.

Projectors are not to be charged with the criminality which often attends their projections in the after-prosecution of them. The intention of Hawkins, at his outset, was not to force, but to persuade the Africans to change their own country for a better. Hawkins having proposed his plan to some friends, a subscription was soon filled up, and three vessels, of about 100 tons burthen each, fitted out for the voyage, with necessary commodities to traffic with the natives.

Having sailed in October, he arrived, without any accident, at Sierra Leona, when he declared his purpose was to traffic, and accordingly exchanged his articles for the best commodities of the country.

During this business, he caused it often to be represented to the people, that he was going from thence to a country more pleasant, fruitful, and happy, in every respect, than theirs: that it was inhabited by such as himself and his company: and that if any of them, tired with their present situation, undoubtedly the most unpleasant spot upon the face of the earth, and of their poor way of living, would embark with him, he would be answerable that, for their services to the people who possessed the country, they should have a share of its many advantages.

This was repeated often; and, by such cajoling, he at length infused a spirit of emigration among them: three hundred of them came to the resolution of trusting themselves with him in this new world, all of full age and strength, and every thing was settled for their departure.

DUBLIN, May 19.

COMMEMORATION of HANDEL.

FIRST DAY.

The Oratorio of the Messiah at St. Thomas's Church on Saturday last, was allowed by all judges to be the most perfect musical performance exhibited in this kingdom.—To do justice to the merits of each person who contributed to this elegant entertainment, would far exceed the bounds of this paper; and though the orchestra was composed chiefly of amateurs, their performance would have done credit to the most experienced professors. Mrs. Ambrose executed her songs in a stile of perfection which left nothing to be desired; her voice, at once powerful, and harmonious, was distinctly heard in every part of the Church, and her manner equally elegant and chaste, is peculiarly adapted to that sort of music. It is but justice to say that the Ladies who so kindly lent their assistance, contributed not a little to the excellence of the choruses; as the brilliancy of their voices (particularly in the semichorus of Lift up your Heads) produced the happiest effect. They were dressed in an elegant white uniform, the simplicity of which accorded admirably with the solemnity of the place, and the display of beauty which the orchestra afforded, was so heightened by the melting sounds which stole upon the ear, "that hearing gave new pleasure to the sight; and thought, to both." It was almost too much for the aching senses to support, and might be said "to snatch the prison'd soul, and wrap it in Elysium." We cannot but lament that their kind intentions of assisting at this festival were not more generally known, as it would doubtless have induced many more to have attended the performance: However they will happily have an opportunity of gratifying themselves on Thursday next, as the second performance is fixed for that day. Mr. Salomon's abilities as a leader are so well known, that it is needless to say more than that he acquitted himself with his usual excellence, and was admirably well supported by Signor Sperati on the Violoncello, who has an uncommon brilliancy of tone, and in his accompaniments of the recitativo's evinced both taste and knowledge of music. The base songs were sung in the very first stile by Dr. Allott and Mr. Weyman; the latter of whom was accompanied in the trumpet-song by Mr. Robertson, who is confessedly the best trumpet we have ever heard. In short, the lovers of harmony were never more highly feasted; and every thing was so well regulated by the unremitting attention of the Arch Bishop of Tuam, and the rest of the Directors, that they merit the warmest acknowledgments from the public.

DUBLIN, May 23.

COMMEMORATION OF HANDEL.

SECOND DAY.

The second day's performance on Thursday last, at St. Thomas's Church, consisted of a most happy selection of music from the works of the justly celebrated Handel, and indeed, all who were present, must have felt the highest delight and satisfaction. The orchestra consisted of about 200 professors and amateurs.——The principals of the professors were Mr. Salamon, Signor Sperati, Mr. Fitzgerald, Mr. Ashe, Mr. Cogan, and Dr. Doyle—and amongst a number of amateurs, we saw the following, Lord Delvin, Right Hon. J. O'Neil, Baron Dillon, Rev. Mr. Quin, Rev. Mr. Austin, Rev. Mr. Sandys, Mr. O'Reilly, Mr. Neal, Mr. Beatty, &c. and about half after 12 the Ladies took their seats in the orchestra, attended by two of the Directors.

The church was very full, and the performance honoured by the first company in the kingdom. At one the Marquis came, and immediately the overture began—it was brilliant and spirited, and the song "Pious Orgies," by Mrs. Ambrose, made a fine contrast—the base duet by the Rev. Dr. Allot and Mr. Weymam, was well sung—in the chorus of "Horse and his Rider," the recitative was excellently performed by Mrs. Ambrose, and the full chorus coming in was grand beyond description—it was *encored* by the Marquis.——The Funeral Anthem was rendered most pathetic by the voices of the Ladies.

Too much praise cannot be given to those amiable ladies who gave their powerful assistance in the cause of charity, namely Lady Piers, Mrs. Saunders, Mrs. Austin, Mrs. Hornidge, Mrs. Jessop, Mrs. Geoghegan, the three Miss Caddles, Miss Crampton, and Miss Wallace.

The Marquis expressed the highest delight and approbation of the performance.——The whole concluded with the Coronation Anthem, which seemed to be felt by all present——it was encored by the Marquis.

Yesterday his Grace the duke of Leinster laid the first stone of the New Club House, on the North side of College-green; several Noblemen and Gentlemen, subscribers—attended also on this occasion.

This building is henceforward to proceed with every possible expedition;—Mr. Latouche, who is banker for the fund, on this occasion is to disburse occasional sums to the undertakers, as wanted.

The ground-work of the New Stamp Office, on an adjoining site, to the Westward, to front into Anglesea-street, proceeds rapidly;—clearances are making with expedition, for erecting the other new buildings to the Eastward, near the Parliament House, and for commencing the ornamental addition of a West-front to that edifice;—so that those works are expected to be in very great forwardness by the next meeting of Parliament.

On Thursday morning, the remains of William O'Dwyer Lyster, Esq; were privately interred in St. George's church. This gentleman, father of the bar, by whom he was universally loved, has been long acknowledged to be one of the first common-law lawyers in this kingdom, and in private life has ever been distinguished for solicial manners, hospitality and the most inflexible integrity. He is the last of the late John Fitzgibbon's cotemporaries, with whom he for many years lived in habits of the strictest friendship.

DUBLIN, May 23.

On Wednesday last, an information was tried in the Court of King's Bench against Nicholas Mahon, merchant, for altering a warrant for the discharge of certain callicoes from 764 yards to 1764 yards, and from the duty thereof of 51, 13, 3, to 10, 13. 3, to defraud his Majesty of the difference between the said duties.

The case was ably supported by the Attorney General, the Prime Serjeant, Solicitor General, and Mr. Berestord, on behalf of the Crown, and defended by Mr. Duquery, Mr. Caldbeck, Mr. Curran, and Mr. Recorder. A verdict was found against Mr. Mahon.

DUBLIN, May 26.

The collection on Sunday last, at the charity sermon preached by the Rev. W. B. Kirwan, at St. Peter's Church, for the benefit of the Lying in-Hospital, amounted to 512l. 9s. 3d.

On Sunday last the Rev. John Collins, a Franciscan Friar, conformed to the Protestant religion, in the cathedral church of Cloyne.

The merchants of Dublin have justly been impressed with alarm on reading in the London prints, that an additional duty on raw or Muscovade sugar will make part of the ministerial budget, shortly to be opened;

LONDON-DERRY, May 26.

On Saturday last, the brig Coningham, Capt. Coningham, with about 300 passengers, sailed for Philedelphia.

MARRIED.] In Butcher-street, Mr. William Gordon to Miss Nelson.—Mr. Wm. Smith, an eminent surgeon in Bishop-street, to Miss Henderson of Ballyshannon.

DIED.] On his passage from the West Indies to Philadelphia, Mr. Clements Church, formerly of this city.

Belfast, *May* 26.

ARTHUR DARLEY, of Belfast, in the County of Antrim, *NOTARY PUBLIC*, is appointed a Commissioner for taking Affidavits in his Majesty's High Court of Chancery——as also—the Courts of King's-Bench, Common Pleas, and Exchequer, in this kingdom.

A few days ago a number of Delegates from the different Corps in the county Armagh met at Clare, and determined to hold a Review in that neighbourhood on the first of August next. They intend to request the attendance of General the Earl of Charlemont. It is with pleasure we hear there were representatives at the above meeting of three Corps which had never been before reviewed.

The mean and unmanly practice that prevails among idle people of shooting RAILS, and other birds that are an ornament to the country, induces the Editor to publish the following abstract of the Law on that subject——in order to remind them of the Penalties to which they wantonly subject themselves.

"Every person who shall wilfully take, kill, or destroy, or who shall sell or expose to sale, or who shall buy or cause to be bought, any moor game, heath game, GROUSE, or any PARTRIDGE, QUAIL, or LAND RAIL, between the tenth day of January in any year and first of September, shall forfeit five pounds. And for every hare bought or sold, or exposed to sale, between the first Monday in November and first Monday in July, five pounds. And also, for destroying any egg or nest of any pheasant, partride, quail, land rail, moor game, heath game, grouse, wild duck, widgeon, plover, or snipe, a further penalty of five pounds."

Married, Mr. James Wilson of this town, to Miss Ellis of Innisrush.

Died, last week at the house of Thomas Foresyth of Achnacloy, Esq. Miss Mary Houlton, daughter of the late Francis Houlton of Armagh, Esq.

PORT NEWS.

ARRIVED.

May 19. Neptune, Miskelly, Bourdeaux, Brandy, Wine, &c.

23. William, Stewart, Liverpool, Sugar and Bale Goods.

Ten Colliers, Coals.

CLEARED OUT.

May 20. St. James, Collins, New-York, Beef, Cloth, &c.

23. Matty, Mc. Donnell, Dantzick, Wine.

Belfast, *May* 29.

The Right Hon. and Hon. the Trustees of the Linen Manufacture have granted to the Person or Company who shall export to Spain, at any one time, and in one cargo, before the 1st day of November next, the greatest quantity of IRISH LINEN, not less in value than 10,000l. a Premium after the rate of 5l. per cent. on the value.

The Claimant must prove the landing of the goods in Spain, and must give a full account of the quality, lengths, breadths, packages, marks, and the mode of making up —and also give every information relative to the same, which may be required by the Board, except as to such matters respecting the sale thereof, as the Claimant may not think proper to disclose.

The frequent instances that occur of injuries received on the roads, in consequence of the improper practice of carmen placing iron and deals across their cars—reflect not a little on the supineness of Magistrates. A proper attention to their duty in this matter, by fining, without reserve, persons guilty of so dangerous a practice, would, in a short time, remove the cause of complaint.

DIED.] On Saturday the 23d inst. the Rev. Thomas Higginson, aged 69 years, Rector of Lead and Vicar of Ballendery, in which last parish he resided above 30 years.—He is deservedly regretted as a father—a friend—and a pastor.

A House in Lurgan.

TO be let and entered upon immediately, the House and Offices, in the Town of Lurgan, now in Possession of James Malcomson;—it is in very good repair, situated in the most central part of the town, and fit for the accommodat on of any gentleman or merchant.

James Malcomson returns his most grateful thanks to his friends and the Public for the favours he has received, and begs to inform, that he continues to carry on his business on a scale more extensive than formerly.

An Apprentice wanted.——Apply as above.

Lurgan, 20th May, 1789.

Anno 1789.]   Printed by HENRY JOY, and Co. BELFAST.

The BELFAST NEWS-LETTER.

TUESDAY June 2,   FRIDAY June 5, 1789.

For Kingston in Jamaica,

THE Brig LOVELY ANN, John Naufdin, Master, 200 tons burthen, will accept of any Freight and Passengers that may offer for Kingston till the 10th June, at which time she will clear out at fartheft; for, freight or paffage apply to Hugh Crawford.

Belfaft, 27th May, 1789.

Said Crawford is now landing out of the above brig from Alicant and Cartagena, a large parcel of Barilla Afhes, and Cane Reeds of the very beft forts.—His friends and the public will find on trial that both prices and qualities will prove agreeable—He is also largely supplied with Dantzig Afhes, firft and second Brands, beft American Pot afhes, firft and second Smalts, fine and common Starch, with every other article for the use of Bleachers, —Likewise a large parcel of New Teas from the laft India Sales. Belfaft, 27th May, 1789.

Gentlemen in the Linen Trade,

WILL pleafe obferve, that MAGEE, No. 9, Bridge ftreet, BELFAST, is now largely supplied with OUTSIDE and INSIDE LAPPING PAPERS, of the beft Fabric.

PRUSSIAN BLUE STRIPES, of such a quality, as can be engaged not to foil the webs—an abatement made on five quires, or upwards.

MARKING LIQUID, warranted to ftand the bleach, at 1s. 7d. halfp. per bottle.

ACCOMPT Books for the Office, or brown Market, of various Rulings and Bindings—or made to any pattern—with every fort of STATIONARY, by Wholefale and Retail.

WEIGHTY GUINEAS,

Given in exchange for light Guineas, at the smalleft discount, according to the late Gold Coin Act of Parliament.

June 5th, 1789.

George Langtry,

WITH the utmoft refpect informs his Friends and the Publick, that he has removed from Donegall-ftreet to the lower end of North-ftreet, a few doors from the Exchange; where he has for sale a large affortment of fresh TEAS, juft landed from the laft India Sales; Confifting of

Fine and common Hyfon,	Real Souchong,
Fine and common Congou,	Singlo and Bloom :

Which, with the under-mentioned Articles, will be fold on good Terms :

Beft French Indigo,	Nail-rod Iron,
Bourdeaux Vinegar,	Kieve and small Hoops,
Cocoa Nuts,	Tin Plates,
Split and boiling Peas,	Hempfeed.

Belfaft, 4th June, 1789

JOHN CRAIG, North-ftreet,

HAS juft imported from London, beft superfine Cloths and Caffemeres, (New Colours.)—He has lately received a fashionable and extenfive Affortment of fine Foreft Cloths, Fancy Waiftcoatings and Buttons,—a few pieces genuine Nankeens—Carpets and Carpetings; with a great variety of Woollen and Cotton Goods suitable to the feafon, which will be fold remarkably low, for Ready Money. Belfaft, 4th June, 1789.

RICHARD Mc. CLELLAND, Surgeon and Druggift,

HAS juft imported a quantity of DRUGS, the quality of which his friends may rely upon.—He has also for sale, a great variety of PAINTS, OILS, &c. all of which will be fold on the moft moderate terms. High-ftreet, 2d June, 1789.

☞ An Apprentice wanted to the Apothecary Bufinefs.

TO BE LET,

For such Term as can be agreed upon,

THE Farm of GLENGIFT, in the Parifh of Dundonald, within three miles of Belfaft, confifting of forty Acres of excellent Land, on which there are a convenient Dwelling-Houfe, Offices, &c. and two Orchards in full bearing.——Apply to John Glenholme.

If agreeable to the Tenant he may have the prefent Crop at a valuation, and be put into immediate poffeffion. Glengift, 4th June, 1789.

Post-Coach.

THE Proprietors of the Belfaft Poft Coaches, return their thanks to the public, for the very great encouragement given them, since their commencement. They are much obliged to Mr. and Mrs. Byrne, of the Globe-Inn, for the accommodation afforded the Paffengers, and for their attention to the coaches.—Seats in future to be taken at Mr. Edward Quillen's, Water-ftreet, Newry, and in Belfaft and Dublin at the ufual places.

His Majefty's Mails will be taken up on the 5th next month, and conveyed in said Coaches between Dublin and Belfaft. Newry, 1ft June, 1789.

Sign of Lord Charlemont, Ann-ftreet, Belfaft.

THOMAS GIHON, Aughalee, who lived some time with Mr. Cunningham, White-Crofs,—begs leave to inform his friends, that he has commenced the Publick Bufinefs in a large commodious House, with Stabling, &c. (in the above ftreet). He hopes, from ftrict attention to his house and ftables, always keeping the beft fpirits and malt liquors, hay, oats, &c. to merit the countenance and protection of his friends and the publick in general.

3d June, 1789.

Flax Premiums 1788,

I HAVE iffued the neceffary papers to the Infpectors of the Counties of Armagh, Donegall and Monaghan, for payment of the Premiums in those Counties : the fundry Claimants are therefore defired to call on the Infpectors at the Markets in their Neighbourhood, where regular attendance will be given ; and the Claimants in the other Counties of the Province will receive like publick Notice, on Orders being iffued to their Infpectors.

Lurgan, 30th May, 1789.

JN. GREER, Infpector General Ulfter.

New Brick.

RICHARD SIMPSON begs leave to inform his Friends and the Public, that he has this day FIRED HIS FIRST KILN, which will be ready for SALE in about TEN DAYS; after which his Cuftomers may rely on being regularly supplied with any quantity they may want during the season.

Brickfield, 3d June, 1789.

N. B. Said Simpson has ftill a few of laft year's Brick remaining for fale.

The Races at Glafslough,

COMMENCE the second week in July :—There will be four, ten, and two twenty Pound Prizes.—Articles at large in a future Advertisement.——Subscriptions will be gratefully received by the Secretary, WM. CROOKSHANK.

May 30th, 1789.

N. B. A Stag Main the same Week.

A Claffical Scholar, of unexceptionable moral character, whose experience as a teacher, will, he prefumes, give fatisfaction, could be ready to engage either in a public or private capacity by the 20th July next; as the young gentlemen under his immediate direction will be then prepared for the different profeffions for which they are intended. As to his character, conduct and abilities, he refers himself to the Revd. Wm. Sturrock, Banbridge, the Revd. Doctor Kennedy, Downe, the Revd. Samuel Burdy, Strangford, or the Revd. Robert Black, Derry. A letter directed to A. C. care of Mr. Burdy aforesaid, will be duly attended to.

N. B. Said person lately prepared for Trinity College a young Gentleman of fifteen, who, at the late examination obtained a very honourable diftinction. 2d June, 1789.

ROBERT CALLWELL has received his Summer Stock of ENGLISH CYDER and PERRY, which he can warrant of a good quality.—Hampers of Cyder, &c. are engaged on delivery free from breakage, and to contain the quantity fpecified.——The

Cheese and Ham Warehouse

is at prefent supplied with forty hundred weight English Cheefe of various kinds, and variety of nice well-cured Hams. No. 11, Bridge-ftreet, 1ft June, 1789.

Those indebted to the late Partnerfhip of R. Callwell & Co. are requefted to pay their accounts soon as poffible to the said Robert Callwell.

John Bafhford,

HAS for Sale a large Parcel JAMAICA RUM in Puncheons, which he will fell on the loweft terms for cafh or good bills.

He alfo has Swedifh Iron, Blifter and German Steel, Kieve Hoops, and Plate Iron, which will be fold on the loweft terms.

St. John's Day,

THE Mafters, Wardens, and Brethren of Lodges Nos. 272—491—550—621—687—of the town of Belfaft, are to meet in their refpective Lodge Rooms on WEDNESDAY the 24th June inft. at ELEVEN O'CLOCK in the forenoon, in order to proceed to Church—where a SERMON suitable to the occafion will be preached by their Brother, the Rev. GEORGE PORTIS—after which a Collection will be made for the benefit of the Poor-houfe and Infirmary.

Such Lodges of the Town or Neighbourhood as chufe to accompany them, will pleafe to attend at that hour, Belfaft, 1ft June, 1789.

I Do hereby acknowledge my very bad behaviour to my late Mafter, G. Webfter, Efq; who in confequence of my making proper fubmiffion; returning his money, and giving ten fhillings to the Poor-Houfe, has ftopt all proceedings againft me—For which lenity, I am much obliged, and it fhall have proper effect upon me. Belfaft, 1ft June, 1789. JAMES DORMAN.

To be Sold,

In Banbridge Fair, the 9th June next,

A Number of fat BULLOCKS :—They are fix years years old, will anfwer butchers or exportation, as they never tafted pot-ale ;—a remarkable good Springer to be fold at fame time, and will be given on a Gentleman's Word.——To be inferted twice. 30th May, 1789.

WE the Jurors impannelled at a Court-Leet held in Ballycarry on the 21ft day of May 1789, and other principal Inhabitants of the Manor of Broad Ifland, take this public method of returning our sincere thanks to Conway Richard Dobbs, Richard Gervas Ker, Marriott Dalway, George Anson Mc. Cleverty, and Edward Kingfmill, Efqrs. and the Gentlemen united with them, for the laudable purpofe of suppreffing Cock-fighting, petty Horfe-racing, and other lawlefs meetings in their refpective neighbourhoods,—Fully fenfible of the many evils arifing from such illegal affemblies, as hoftile to the tranquility of the country as they are deftructive to induftry and good morals; we entirely approve of the wife and promifing means adopted by them for the prevention of practices, which so materially affect the peace of society : And we pledge ourfelves in the moft determined manner, that we will exert our utmoft activity and influence in our feveral families and departments to accomplifh this defirable object.

As Tenants of Richard Jervas Ker, Efq; our grateful acknowledgments are peculiarly due to him for his kind and unremitting attention to the welfare of his tenantry.

JURORS:

James Sillyman, Foreman	Wm. Shaw	Alex. Horfbrough
Samuel Cowan	James Brannion	Thos. Simral
John Loggan	Andrew Downey	Edward Brannon
John Campbell	William Hill	John Brynan
Roger Mc. Kinftry	John Allen	Robert Kneill
Archd. Dick	Andrew Miller	Arch. Dicke, fenr.
Alex. Jordan	Wm. Rabb	John Horfbrough
	Alex. Nelfon	James Beggs

INHABITANTS;

The Revd. John Bankhead	James Steele	Sam. M'Caufland
	Alex. Sillyman	John Mc. Kinley

With upwards of one hundred Inhabitants on said Richard Gervas Ker's eftate of Broadifland, which would take too much room in a News-paper to be inferted.

ALL perfons who intend taking their paffage in the Ship HAPPY RETURN, James Ewing, Mafter, from Londonderry to Newcastle and Philadelphia in America, are requefted to be on board the 12th June. 30th May, 1789.

Strayed or ftolen,

OUT of the Demefne of Newtownards, on the night of Friday the 29th inftant, two Coach Horfes, the property of the Right Hon. Robert Stewart; one of them a dark bay, fix years old, full fifteen hands and a half high, with a forced ftar badly made ; the other a fhade lighter in colour, five years old, fame fize, with a retch and fnip, the off hind foot white, and on that quarter a hand's breadth of the fkin quite bare, from a hurt he had received.——If ftrayed, any perfon giving information where they may be found, fhall be fufficiently rewarded; and if ftolen, Twenty Guineas will be paid by Francis Turnly, Efq; for horses and thief, on profecuting to conviction.

Newtown-Ards, 30th May, 1789.

N. B. On fame night was likewise ftolen or rode off out of a field of Gilbert Jackfon's of Newtownards aforesaid, a bright bay Gelding, with a faddle-mark upon the mounting fide, and a little fpavened in both hind legs, about eight years old.

SLAVE TRADE.

PAPERS submitted to the HOUSE of COMMONS.

The Committee having directed Mr. Chalmers, the first clerk in their office, to prepare estimates of the present value of the slaves in the British West Indies, and also of the whole property in the same; the two following estimates were prepared by him, after conversing with several persons, whom he conceived best able to give him information on the subject.

An estimate of the present value of the British Islands in the West Indies; distinguishing each Island.

	Number of slaves.	Price.	Value.
Jamaica	256,000	at 40l.	10,240,000
Antigua	37,808	ditto	1,512,320
Montserrat	10,000	ditto	400,000
Nevis	8,420	ditto	336,800
St. Christophers	20,435	ditto	817,400
Virgin Islands	9,000	ditto	360,000
Barbadoes	62,115	ditto	2,484,600
Grenadas	23,926	ditto	957,040
St. Vincents	11,853	ditto	474,120
Dominica	14,967	ditto	598,680
Bahamas	2,241	ditto	89,640
Bermudas	4,919	at 45l.	221,355
Total	461,684		18,491,955

N. B. By returns which have been received since this estimate was made up, it appears, that in some of the before-mentioned islands, there are a few more negroes than the foregoing estimate contains, and in some other of the islands a few less.

FRANCE.

No country in modern history has undergone a more rapid change in its system, not excepting even the late revolution in Sweden, than this country during the last twelve months.

In proof of our argument we shall notice three occurrences, which are rendered the more curious by their exact similitude of dates.

REMARKABLE EVENTS.

On the 3d May 1788, the Parliament of Paris made a decree which overturned a system proposed by the King of abolishing the Parliaments, and introducing in their stead a Plenary Court, consisting of only a few Members, chiefly under the controul of the Crown.

On the 3d May 1789, the Nobility for the County and City of Paris, chose their Deputies to the States General of the nation.

On the 5th May 1788, the King's troops invested the Assembly where the Parliament was sitting.

On the 5th May 1789, the opening of the States General by a speech from the Throne.

On the 6th May 1788, M. d'Espremenil, a Counsellor of Parliament was seized in the House of Peers, to be exiled to a state prison in the Island of St. Marguerite.

On the 6th May 1789, M. d'Espremenil was chosen a Deputy from the Nobility of the County of Paris to the States General.

Sic transit gloria Mundi !

DUBLIN, May 30.

An account of the patent for creating our Lord Lieutenant—Duke of Buckingham, is expected to appear in the London Gazette of Tuesday next.

As to the Chancellorship, every thing is still in *statu quo*, except, that according to the London prints, Baron Eyre has declined.

This morning a most magnificent Venetian breakfast was given by the Right Honourable Henry Grattan, to upwards of one hundred and fifty of the Nobility and Gentry, at his seat at Tinnehinch, in the county of Wicklow.

Lieutenant Colonel Lenox, who had the late affair of honour with his Royal Highness the Duke of York, is the son of Lord George Lenox (brother to his Grace the Duke of Richmond) whose bravery war so eminent during the late German war, and who figured particularly at the famous battle of Minden, where Lord George Germaine blasted his laurels.

On Wednesday last, we hear, a gentleman was brought a prisoner to the Castle, from the county of F———, as a state criminal. Some charges of a treasonable nature, it is said, have been exhibited against him, particularly that of promoting the excesses committed by the insurgents who distinguish themselves by the appellation of " Break-of-day Boys, Right Boys, &c." A Privy Council, supposed to be on this business, met at the Castle at two o'clock in the afternoon of Thursday last.—[Dublin Chron.

The ill-fated Father Fay, we hear, has received orders to prepare himself against next week, to be put on board a vessel along with other convicts, in order to be shipped off for transportation.

On Monday next the annual Volunteer review will take place in the Phœnix Park. A guard accordingly this day, does duty at the house of the reviewing General, the Right Hon. the Earl of Charlemont, in Rutland-square.

DUBLIN, May 28.

We have the pleasure of hearing, by a letter from a great mercantile house at Cadiz, that the late extraordinary export of Irish yard-wide linens, has been received at Cadiz, Seville, and St. Lucar, with open arms. The manufacture of that article has been long and successfully carried on in various parts of Spain; but it seems, that the great encouragement given by Philip the Fifth, his son Ferdinand, and the late King Charles, for the cultivation of other branches, particularly silks, velvets, and fine woollen cloths, has rendered the farmers rather indifferent about the rearing of flax; the manufacture of linens of all sorts, however, still goes on, though in a limited degree, and not quite sufficient for general consumption in so extensive a country, doubled in its population within the last seventy years: These favourable circumstances should rouse the diligence of our linen manufacturers, who, whilst they preserve good faith in the fabric, and moderation in the price, will probably enjoy the benefit of the Spanish markets for many years to come.

Amongst the packages of cloth exported from this city to Seville, in the month of March last, fourteen pieces were selected of such extraordinary texture, beauty and colour, as to engage the attention of many of the best judges, who declared them superior to any linens they had ever seen. They were immediately sent to the Duke of Medina, who resides at St. Lucar, near Seville, who purchased the whole for himself and family, at the high price of fourteen reals, or nine shillings and sixpence a yard. These pieces were marked *Antrim*, a town and county long celebrated for some of the best and finest linens manufactured in this or any other country.

The session of Parliament is now finally closed, and one more marked by obnoxious measures, scarcely occurs in the annals of this country. Commencing with a pointed attack on the rights and claims of the Heir Apparent of the Crown, by the English Minister's Agent in this kingdom, the spirit and honour of the nation roused by the emergency of the occasion, resisted and defeated it. But ever since a steady opposition to every popular proposal, and an invariable overthrow of every patriotic scheme, has distinguished the conduct of Administration and its Supporters. An enormous Pension-list, an extravagant; a desperate and ineffectual Police, an increase of needless places and salaries supported; relief of the grievances and distresses of the poor; security to the election franchises of the people, protection to the independance of the House of Commons opposed. But one single, solitary plan of public u ility, the encouragement given to the inland navigation, appears in the dreary waste.

Curious Lists respecting the Prisons of Great Britain and Ireland.

The following is the average number of persons confined at one time in the prisons in Ireland :

Debtors	—	550
Criminals	—	1004
		1554
Supposed omitted	—	20
Total		1574

Account of the number of prisoners in the gaols and prisons of England and Wales, at the last time they were visited in 1787 and 1788 :

Debtors	—	2011
Felons, &c.	—	2052
Petty offenders	—	1412
In the hulks	—	1937
Supposed omitted	—	70
Total		7482

The numbers confined in the London prisons and in the hulks, at the time they were visited in 1788 :

Debtors	—	927
Felons, &c.	—	670
Petty offences	—	538
Total		4135

Which is far more than a half of the number confined in the whole kingdom.

According to an exact calculation presented to the House of Commons, the average number of prisoners ordered for transportation in England in one year, is 960.

Account of the number of prisoners convicted of capital crimes in Scotland, from January 1768, to May 1782:

Condemned	—	76
Pardoned	—	22
Executed	—	54

And the number from January 1783 to August 1787, is

Condemned	—	58
Pardoned	—	15
Executed	—	43

The number executed in London and Middlesex, from Dec. 1787, to Dec. 1788, is 54.

Near eight times as many as in all Scotland, for about the same space of time.

LONDON-DERRY, June 4.

Since our last, sailed for Wilmington in America, the Brig Maria, Capt. Forte, with 220 passengers; also, the Keziah, Capt. Brown, with 180 passengers.

On Saturday, the Rev. John Wesley, now in the 85th year of his age, arrived in this city —He preaches twice every day.—To-morrow he proceeds on his way to Coleraine, &c.

Married.] Mr. James Dysart of Carnamaddy, to Miss Macky of Galliagh.

Died.] Suddenly, Micah Cary, Esq; of Innishowen.—Near No-Limavady, Miss Garraway, daughter of the Rev. James Garraway.—In Bishop street, Mr. Daniel Ganble.

" ☞ The Ship HAPPY RETURN, James Ewing, Master, will positively sail from hence, to Philadelphia the 12th day of June, of which all persons intending to take their passage are desired to take notice."

Derry, 30th May, 1789.

Belfast, June 2.

A correspondent begs leave to remark, that two men who were pillored at Armagh on Monday last, for the second time, were suffered to have their faces covered——which he conceives to be lenity misapplied to such daring offenders.

Died, on Sunday last, in the 87th year of his age, John Gillilan of Holestone, Esq. during which long period of life he enjoyed a good state of health with an upright character. None excel and very few equal him as a man of real virtue, as a good christian, and an honest man. He was charitable to the poor, and a good landlord, and is very deservedly lamented by all who had the pleasure of knowing him.

QUERIES!

Can a Clergyman of the Church of England refuse to administer the Sacrament of our Lord's Supper to any man, who demands it in order to qualify himself for a civil or military office; the clergyman knowing the party to be a professed infidel and openly profligate, and assigning as the cause of his refusal such knowledge, and an unwillingness to prostitute either the ordinance or his own dignity? Would he not be liable to an action—if not, by what statute is a provision made for his relief.

May 26,

LEONIDAS.

Belfast, June 5.

We hear that the Revd. Mr. Wesley intends to preach at the Brown Linen-Hall of this town at six o'clock, on Monday evening next.

Our readers will observe by the Advertisements, that the Mail-Coach is to run daily from the 5th next month.

We are informed that they will take up the Mail so as to leave Dublin at 10 o'clock at night, and arrive at Belfast at seven the next evening in summer, and eight in winter; and will leave Belfast at nine in the morning, reaching Dublin at seven the next evening.—This is 21 hours in summer, and 22 in winter.

The Sale of the Newry Brewery, advertised in the first page of this paper, is postponed to Monday the 29th inst.

PORT NEWS.

ARRIVED.

June 3. Hillsbro', M'Donnell, Liverpool, drapery.
Charlotte, Campbell, London.
Six colliers, coals.

Bleach Green,
(To be Let or Sold)

To be sold by public Auction,

Anno 1789.]   Printed by HENRY JOY, and Co. BELFAST.

The BELFAST NEWS-LETTER.

TUESDAY June 9,   FRIDAY June 12, 1789.

Elizabeth Wilson,

Caſtle-ſtreet, oppoſite the New Inn, Belfaſt,

BEGS leave to inform her Friends and the Publick ſhe has juſt received her uſual ſupply of Goods in the Millinary and Haberdaſhery Line ſuitable to the preſent Seaſon,—among which are a variety of new Ribbands and Gauzes, plain and figured Muſlins and Muſlin Handkerchiefs, Modes, Sarſnets and Perſians, black and white Laces and Edging, ſome white Chip, Dunſtable, and Leghorn Hats, and a parcel of Beaver Hats for women and children, in a variety of colours, with ſome faſhionable Bands for ditto; alſo black and white Feathers, &c. &c.   8th June, 1789.

A Cargo of beſt red and white Deals from Dronton, beſt Polyheny and Erris Kelp, and Oak Barrel Staves,

Are arrived to John Ogle & Sons,

Beſt Alicante Barilla, New-York, Pot Aſhe, Dantzig Weed Aſhe, Pitch, Fir Timber and Planks, Pipe Staves, Laths, Gabbard Maſts, plain and figured Linens, old Claret, and red Port of ſuperior quality, for ſale at their Warehouſes.—They daily expect a Cargo of large Fir Timber.—To be continued three times.

Newry, 8th June, 1789.

New White-Croſs Inn, Pill-lane,
DUBLIN.

DAVID KELLY late of Exchequer-ſtreet, takes the liberty of informing his Friends and the Public in general, that he has juſt opened the above Inn on an improved and extenſive ſcale, and has laid in a large ſtock of the very beſt WINES, SPIRITS, PORTER, HAY, OATS, and every thing neceſſary for the accommodation of all perſons of every deſcription who ſhall pleaſe to honor him with their commands.

☞ Having had the pleaſure of knowing Mr Kelly and all his family for upwards of twenty years, and having frequented his houſe in Exchequer-ſtreet, and no other in Dublin, ſince my arrival here, I beg leave to aſſure my NORTHERN FRIENDS they will have every reaſon to be pleaſed with their treatment and accommodation at the above Inn.   AMYAS GRIFFITH.

Clarendon-ſtreet, June 8th, 1789.

Notice to Creditors,

THAT the major Part of the Commiſſioners named and authoriſed in the different Commiſſions of Bankrupts awarded and iſſued againſt

David Bleakley, of Greenvale, County Armagh, Linen Draper, meet at the Tholſel, Dublin, 24th inſtant, 11 o'clock forenoon.

John Bleakley, of City of Dublin, Factor, meet at the Tholſel, Dublin, 24th inſtant.

David Bleakley the younger, of Ann Vale, County Armagh, Linen Draper, meet at the Tholſel, Dublin, 25th inſtant, 11 o'clock forenoon.

William Bleakley, of Drum, Co. Armagh, Linen Draper, meet at the Tholſel, Dublin, 1ſt July next,

at the hour of eleven o'clock in the forenoon, in order to make a dividend of the different Bankrupts Eſtates and effects, when and where the Creditors who have not already proved their debts, under the different Commiſſions, are deſired to come prepared and prove the ſame, or they will be excluded from the benefit of the different dividends.   June 2d, 1789.

Horſe ſtolen

WHEREAS on the night of the third inſtant, A dark Bay HORSE, ſeven years old, fifteen hands high, with a handſome ſtar, and ſtrip'd by the traces, with a ſhort ſet ſwitch tail, was ſtolen off the Glebe Lands of Armagh, the property of Robert Bleakley:—A Reward of *Twenty Guineas* will be paid to any perſon or perſons who in three calendar months will return ſaid Horſe, and proſecute the thief to conviction.

Mullaloughtan, near Armagh, 6th June, 1789.
ROBERT BLEAKLEY.

A Caution,

THAT no Perſon may hire, harbour, or entertain David Mc. Coy, who was my ſervant, and did laſt Tueſday night break out of my back yard over ſome of my office-houſes, and eloped from my ſervice, taking with him part of my livery clothes, &c.

The ſaid David Mc. Coy is a ſmart little lad, aged about twenty years, was born in Lurgan, and ſerved an apprenticeſhip to Jacob Turner, Eſq; now of Newry, to be a ſervant: He is given to drunkenneſs, and for ſome days after he has been drunk is very idle and incapable to do any buſineſs; this I publiſh that he may not impoſe upon any other perſon as he did on me.——Given under my hand at Moira this 4th day of June, 1789.

MORGAN JELLETT.

THE GLORIOUS MEMORY ORANGE LODGE, Dungannon, No. 689, dine at Mr. James Tracy's, on 24th June inſt. Dinner on the table at 4 o'clock.

The Coterie;

WILL be held (as uſual) at the Donegall-Arms, on Tueſday next, the 16th inſtant.

Belfaſt, June 11th, 1789.

To be ſold at Dundrum,

ON Friday the 19th June 1789—The Sloop James, of Greenock, with all her materials as ſhe lays in the harbour of Dundrum, Britiſh built; burthen about fifty-five tons.

Belfaſt, 11th June, 1789.
ARCHD. M'CALLUM.

Good Bills payable in three months will be taken in payment.

MARY Mc. AULAY,
CORN-MARKET, LISBURN,

RESPECTFULLY informs her Friends and the Public, that ſhe has juſt received her Summer Aſſortment of Millinary and Haberdaſhery Goods, which ſhe flatters herſelf on inſpection muſt pleaſe.—As uſual, every article in the Millinary Line made up on the ſhorteſt notice in the moſt faſhionable manner. By the advice of ſeveral of her friends, ſhe has been induced to lay in a variety of Teas, which ſhe is determined to ſell for the ſmalleſt profits, for *Ready Money*.

June 9th, 1789.

New Brick.

JOHN FERGUSON begs leave to inform his Friends and the Public, that he has new Brick ready for ſale, and his Cuſtomers may depend on being regularly ſupplied with any quantity they may ſtand in need of during the ſeaſon; and as this is his firſt attempt in this line, he has taken care to employ the beſt workmen, in order to have them made equal to any in the country, and will be ſold on reaſonable terms.

Comber, June 10th, 1789.

ALL perſons having Debentures on the ſecond and third Diviſion of the Turnpike Road from Banbridge to Belfaſt, are hereby to take Notice, that the ſecond Diviſion will immediately pay off one year's intereſt, and the third Diviſion one half year's intereſt.

Application to be made to William Younghuſband, Springfield, near Liſburn.

7th June, 1789.

Iriſh State Lottery, 1789.

The Tickets, and duly Stampt HALF, QUARTER, EIGHTH and SIXTEENTH Shares, alſo the FORTUNATE GUINEA TICKETS, are ſelling on the loweſt Terms, at

Mr. NICHOLSON'S

Licenſed STATE LOTTERY OFFICE, No. 7, Dame-ſtreet, DUBLIN; and Bank-ſtreet, Corn-hill, LONDON.

In the LAST IRISH LOTTERY he had the Pleaſure to ſell to his Cuſtomers, the following CAPITAL PRIZES, viz.

No. 23,481 - 20,000l. | No. 17,025, - 10,000l.
28,322, - 20,000l. | 30,875, - 5,000l.

And in the laſt ENGLISH LOTTERY,

No. 46,676 - 10,000l.—22,128 - 1000l. as firſt drawn, beſides ſeveral of 2,000l.—1,000l.—and 500l. each.

In the PRESENT LOTTERY there are two of 20,000l.—two of 10,000l.—two of 5000l. &c. &c. &c.

SCHEMES at large, Gratis.——The full money allowed for Engliſh Prizes in Exchange for Iriſh Tickets and Shares.

Drugs, Paints, Oils, &c.

WILLIAM ANDERSON has on hand at preſent, a very extenſive and general aſſortment of freſh Drugs, Paints, Oils, &c.—which, being lately imported from the beſt Markets, he is enabled and determined to ſell on ſuch reaſonable terms as will ſecure the intereſt of his Friends, and induce others who ſhall make a trial to give him a decided preference, being reſolved not to be underſold in any Article by any perſon, quality, &c. conſidered. A full allowance will alſo be made by him for ready Money.

☞ He will be obliged to thoſe perſons who know they are too long indebted to him, if they pay their accounts as ſoon as poſſible.

Belfaſt, 10th June, 1789.

Dantzig Aſhes.

HUGH MONTGOMERY is juſt landing a Quantity of New Dantzig Aſhes of the beſt quality.

Belfaſt, 12th June, 1789

Belfast White Linen-Hall.

AT the deſire of ſeveral Gentlemen, notice is hereby given to the Linen Drapers in the North of Ireland, that notwithſtanding the former Advertiſement, the *next Market* will actually commence on Thurſday the 18th inſtant;—the ſellers of white Linens are requeſted to attend on that day.

Belfaſt, 6th June, 1789.   JAMES CARSON, Chamberlain.

Jones, Tomb, Joy & Co.

ARE landing out of the Welfare, Captain Landenberg, from Dantzig, choice New Fir Timber, Plank, Pipe Staves, and Weed Aſhes of the beſt brands, which will be ſold on reaſonable terms.

Belfaſt, 8th June, 1789.

A New Edition in Quarto,

Corrected, Improved, and greatly Enlarged, and now publiſhing by ſubſcription in Edinburgh.

Lately imported by W. MAGEE, *Bookſeller, Belfaſt,*

Price HALF-A GUINEA each in blue Boards,

The Three Firſt half Volumes of

ENCYCLOPÆDIA BRITANNICA; or, A Dictionary of Arts, Sciences, and Miſcellaneous Literature, on a plan entirely new, &c. &c. The whole to be illuſtrated with upwards of 360 Copper-Plates, containing many Thouſand Figures, neatly engraved. It is computed that the work will be compriſed in from 24 to 30 half Volumes.

Propoſals at large may be had from MAGEE, who ſhortly expects to receive from Edinburgh three half Volumes more. Thoſe who wiſh to be furniſhed with this work regularly, are requeſted to apply as ſoon as poſſible, as 'tis not intended to import more Copies than what are ſubſcribed for.

London Porter.

TWO hundred and forty Hogſheads of excellent London Porter are juſt arrived to SAMUEL BROWN & Co. by the Britannia, Capt Morgan, which will be ſold on reaſonable terms.

Belfaſt, 8th June, 1789.

Archibald Bankhead,

HAS juſt received a parcel of DRUGS, of a remarkable fine quality, among which he has a quantity of Peruvian Bark, which he will engage to ſell lower than any perſon in the kingdom: He is well ſupplied with every article in his line, which he will diſpoſe of at his uſual reduced prices.

He has on hand Seltzer Water, that is accounted fine by thoſe who are judges, which he will ſell at 12s. per the dozen.

Belfaſt, June 8th, 1789.

New Dantzig Timber.

CUNNINGHAM GREG has juſt received a Cargo of a remarkably fine quality; alſo a quantity of Fir Plank of different ſizes, and Pipe Staves, which he will diſpoſe of on reaſonable terms.

Belfaſt, 8th June, 1789.

New Dantzig Weed Aſhes.

DAVISON and MINISS have imported by the Elizabeth from Dantzig, New Weed Aſhes of different Brands:—They are largely ſupplied with freſh TEAS, and a general aſſortment of Goods in the Grocery Line, which they will ſell low for good payments.

Belfaſt, 8th June, 1789.

New Dantzig Weed Aſhes.

SAMUEL GIBSON has received per the Ship Elizabeth, Capt. Kruſe, from Dantzig, a parcel of New Weed Aſhes; conſiſting of a variety of brands of firſt, ſecond, and third qualities.—He is alſo well ſupplied with Teas, Scale Sugars, Spaniſh Indigo of very beſt quality, Kentiſh Bag Hops, &c.—all of which, together with his uſual aſſortment in the Grocery and Dyeſtuff Line, he will diſpoſe of at the moſt reduced prices.

North ſtreet, Belfaſt, 6th June, 1789.

The Union Aſſembly,

WILL be held at the Rooms (as uſual) on Wedneſday the tenth inſtant.

Belfaſt, 7th June, 1789.

To be ſold by Cant,

At Cultra-Houſe, on Saturday thirteenth June, at twelve o'Clock,

A Conſiderable Quantity of WOOL, belonging to John Kennedy, Eſq; for ready Money, and for which 6d. in the pound will be allowed.

HIS MAJESTY'S BIRTH DAY.

ST. JAMES'S.

At two o'clock, the Poet Laureat's Ode was performed in the Great Council Chamber, at which all the Royal Family, and numbers of the Nobility and Gentry were preſent.

Immediately after the performance of the Ode, the Drawing-Room commenced.

What took from the univerſal joy of the day, was the abſence of the King.

Every eye ſeemed to look for him—every mouth ceaſed not to enquire after him.

Her Majeſty felt this, and with obliging condeſcenſion, ſatisfied all—

"The King wiſhed to ſee his friends, but was fearful that he might be too much affected by the kind expreſſions of loyalty and perſonal reſpect that he would be liable to receive; and on that account, not on the ſcore of ill health, had refuſed himſelf the pleaſure of acknowledging their compliments in perſon."

The Queen was, in an extraordinary degree, well, and animated—her chearfulneſs never flagged for an inſtant. Her dreſs, and addreſs, both became her to admiration; and there can be few ſenſations more exquiſite, than what aroſe at ſight of ſuch a circle as ſurrounded her.

The Drawing-Room was an unequalled aſſemblage of all that conſtitute the nation's glory—the virtue, the wiſdom, the property, the wit and beauty of the kingdom!

LADIES' DRESSES.

The Court in general appeared in Engliſh dreſſes; and from the novelty and elegant variety in the decorations of the Princeſſes, and many of the Nobility, we flatter ourſelves that the improved genius of our preſent artiſts, will ſtill entitle them to the laurel, ſo long uſurped by our formidable rival on the Continent.

The Queen. Her Majeſty's dreſs was one of the moſt ſuperb ever ſeen at Court. It was a lilac ground, covered with crape, embroidered with green, and flounced with five rows of beautiful deep lace. The pockets were laced all over, and ornamented with large diamond bows, to each of which there was a chain of brilliants ornamenting the whole length; about thirty large diamond buttons and taſſels were faſtened on the petticoat—

ODE performed this day at the Caſtle of Dublin, being the Birth-day of his Majeſty GEORGE III.

Proclaim in accents loud and clear,
Proclaim it to the nations round,
Heav'n hath a people's ardent pray'r,
With mercy heard, with kindneſs crown'd.

Late o'er the plains pale Melancholy threw
Her deepeſt robe of ſable hue,
While Malady its baleful influence ſpread,
Around the ſacred, the anointed head.

Soil of freedom, ſoil of peace,
Unannoy'd by foreign foe,
Muſt thy happineſs give place,
To private ſorrow, private woe?

In the Royal Sufferer's ſmart,
Each beholder bears a part;
Rumour gave th' afflicting tale,
In ſighings to the paſſing gale,
That boſoms, never wont to ſigh,
Were clogg'd with ſpeechleſs agony.

When royal boſoms teem with woe,
When royal eyes with tears o'erflow,
Can the private heart refrain
Mingling in the mighty pain?

Contagious Grief, in that afflicting hour
How wide, how gen'ral was thy pow'r!
Sad was each geſture, ev'ry ſtep was ſlow,
Silent each tongue, and ev'ry look was woe;
The ſupplicating eye preſum'd alone
To beg compaſſion at the heav'nly throne.

The King of kings vouchſaf'd a pitying eye
On the worn couch of reſtleſs agony;
Beheld a prince's and a people's grief,
Beheld——and gave relief.

Lo! what ſudden luſtre beams,
And wide around its radiance ſtreams:

O! Royal Matron, weep no more,
See, Deſpair flies far away,
Ceaſe, filial mourners, to deplore,
Hail this more than natal day!

FULL CHORUS.

Hail this more than natal day!
Tune the heart-expanding lay,
GEORGE reſumes the regal ſway. }
Loud be the ſtrain!—our duty's lord,
Our friend, our father is reſtor'd!
Bleſs'd may he reign, and late be call'd away,
To the bright realms of everlaſting day!

D U B L I N, JUNE 5.

The Dublin Packet, which, upwards of twelve months ago, failed from Philadelphia for this port, as being a miſſing ſhip, it was generally thought that ſhe had foundered at ſea:—this morning, however, it is ſaid, ſhe was captured on her paſſage, by the Moors, and brought into Sallee, and the crew immediately ſent into ſlavery, where every communication was precluded:—At length three of the ſailors, (who are thoſe that brought the account) having eſcaped to the ſea ſide, ſeized a boat, and got ſafe to the coaſt of Spain, from which country they are juſt arrived.——A day or two will aſcertain the truth of this account.

Monday evening as Lord Kingſborough was dreſſing in his apartment at his Lordſhip's houſe in Henrietta-ſtreet, a piſtol was fired from the ſtreet. The ball paſſed cloſe to his head, and lodged in the wainſcot near him. The ſervants ran immediately into the ſtreet, in order to diſcover who fired the piſtol, but in vain, as they could perceive no perſon on whom to ground the ſuſpicion of this daring attempt.

We are happy to inform our readers, that the mail coaches will commence running between Dublin and Cork, on Monday next:—They will go three times a week, with paſſengers only, until the 5th of July, from which day they are to convey the mail, and ply ſix times a week.

D U B L I N, JUNE 6.

Several veſſels laden with coals from the colliery at Ballycaſtle are at preſent diſcharging their cargoes at Alton's-quay. It is much to be lamented, that the peculiar ſituation of the coaſt contiguous to theſe pits, makes it unſafe for ſhips, unleſs in the ſummer months, to ride there and take in the lading. If this was not the caſe, a continual ſupply of theſe coals would keep down thoſe we get from Cumberland, &c.

The bounty of 5 per cent. lately appropriated by the Truſtees of the Linen Manufacture, on the exportation of linen to Spain, has already had ſo favourable an operation, that ſome cargoes are preparing to be ſent abroad; and it is expected will make very profitable returns to this country.

D U B L I N, JUNE 9.

Mr. Secretary Hobart is not yet arrived, but he is daily, and by many anxiouſly expected; for it is ſaid that he is to bring over with him all the commiſſions, promotions, and peerages that have been ſo long and ſo ardently looked for. Among the latter we underſtand there are two Marquiſities for the Earls of Tyrone and Hillſborough, ſix Earldoms for the Viſcounts Valentia, Erne, Enniſkillen, Clifden, Lords Carysfort and Loftus, and the dignity of Barons for the Right Hon. Denis Daly, Right Hon. Luke Gardiner, Sir Nicholas Lawleſs, Mr. Henry Gore, Mr. L. H. Harman, and Mr. James Alexander.——*Dub. E. Poſt.*

It is now the general opinion, that Mr. Fitzgibbon will be appointed our Chancellor, and all the private informations from England concur in eſtabliſhing that idea.

Laſt Thurſday the Right Hon. Lord Donoughmore was elected Grand Maſter of Freemaſons in this kingdom, in the room of the Right Hon. Lord Glerawley.

The articles of chief notoriety exported from Ireland in the year ending Lady-day, 1788, conſiſted of

Bacon, in flitches, to the number of	29,587
——— in hams, hundreds weight,	491
Beer, in barrels,	1,251
Beef, dittto,	130,157
Bullocks and cows, in number,	17,609
Bread or biſcuit, hundreds weight,	14,941
Bullion, or ſilver, ounces of	10,338
Butter, hundreds weight,	341,599
Candles, ditto	3,796
Cheeſe dittto	965
Copper ore, tons	143
Barley, barrels	54,045
Malt, ditto	617
Oats, ditto	279,125
Rye, ditto	635
Wheat, ditto	50 157
Oatmeal, hundreds weight,	139,288
Flour, ditto	8,885
Old drapery, yards	7,747
New ditto, ditto	315,111
Herrings, barrels	16,855
Salmon, tons	305
Flannel, yards	61,000
Fuſtians, ditto	16,803
Frize, ditto	4,092
Drinking glaſſes, in number	8,480
Glaſs-ware, in value, pounds ſterling,	[illegible]
Tanned hides, in number,	24,225
Untanned ditto	69,641
Horſes, ditto	2,338
Linen, plain, yards	35,487,691
Ditto, coloured, ditto	157,723
Pork, barrels	111,000
Rape ſeed, quarters	11,785
Shoes, pounds weight	12,682
Yarn, of linen, hundreds weight,	27,275
——— of woollen, ſtones	31,885
——— of worſted, ditto	7,109

Note. The exportation of grain and flour that has taken place this year, is computed almoſt to double the above.

L O N D O N - D E R R Y, JUNE 9.

Thurſday laſt, being the anniverſary of his Majeſty's birth, the ſame was obſerved here with many demonſtrations of joy.

Since our laſt, the ſhip Betſey, Capt. Whitten, with 300 paſſengers, failed for Philadelphia.

This day, the firſt diviſion of the 28th regiment will march into this city from Dublin.

The London Papers ſtate, that a reduction of the duty on Tobacco is to take place from 15d to 8d. per lb. In that caſe, we may alſo expect a reformation of the very impolitic tax on that article in Ireland.

Married.] John Stewart, Eſq; co. Tyrone, to Miſs Archdall, daughter of Col. Archdall—Ralph Babington, Eſq; of Greenfort, to Miſs Scanlan of Ballyſhannon.

Birth.] The Lady of Andrew Ferguſon, jun. Eſq; of a daughter.

Died, on Saturday the 30th ult. at the glebe-houſe of Clondavadock, county Donegall, the Rev. Dr. Bedford.—This gentleman was born at the beginning of the preſent century; on the recommendation of the then Duke of Newcaſtle, he came to Ireland as firſt Chaplain to the Duke of Dorſet, Dr. Stone (afterwards Primate) being the ſecond. Dr. Bedford's mind being above political intrigue or cabal, he was removed to a ſmall living, and the ſecond Chaplain was rapidly advanced to the higheſt dignities of the Church.—When Dr. Bedford returned to England, his uncommon excellence as a preacher acquired him much applauſe, and he was followed by crowds of every rank.—On the appointment of the Duke of Devonſhire to the government of this kingdom, Dr. Bedford again came to Ireland as a Chaplain, but a ſudden change of men and meaſures again blaſted his hopes of preferment; and, diſguſted with the duplicity of political men, he retired from public affairs, and took up his reſidence in a remote pariſh in a neighbouring county, where he continued to reſide till his death, notwithſtanding the acquirement of a large fortune, the ſolicitations of his friends, and the allurements of popularity.—Dr. Bedford obtained 40,000l. by the death of one brother, and 100,000l. by the death of another.—Altho' ſimple and abſtemious in his own manner of living, he employed his ample fortune in the ſervice of his friends and relations; for many years he gave 7,000l. among them in annuities.

Belfaſt, *June 9.*

A correſpondent having noticed a few poſts ago, the circumſtance of two men that were pillored in Armagh having been ſuffered to ſtand with their faces covered—we are deſired in reply to mention that the High Sheriff of the county was, at the time alluded to, in Dublin.

Few inſtances have occurred of ſuch a continuance of tempeſtuous weather, at this ſeaſon of the year, as that which we experienced from Friday to Sunday laſt.

On the 30th ult. Mr. James Nevin, of Ballymacrews in the county of Down, was ſworn and admitted an Attorney of his Majeſty's court of Exchequer.

PORT NEWS.

ARRIVED.

June 3. Alexander, Roche, Alicant, aſhes.
5. Britannia, Moyan, London, ale.
Elizabeth, Kraus, Dantzic, aſhes, timber, &c.
Welfare, Lunderbeg, do. &c. &c.
Four colliers.

ARTHUR DARLEY, of Belfaſt, in the County of Antrim, *NOTARY PUBLIC*, is appointed a Commiſſioner for taking Affidavits in his Majeſty's High Court of Chancery——as alſo—the Courts of King's-Bench, Common Pleas, and Exchequer, in this kingdom.

On Tueſday laſt the Belfaſt Volunteer Company, commanded by Captain Brown, with their Artillery Corps, marched to the Cave-Hill for the purpoſe of exerciſing.

We are informed that the public are to have a volume of Poems, in the courſe of the ſummer, from the Author of the *Patriot Soldier, or Iriſh Volunteer.*

The Friendſhip, Captain Lepper, loaded with linen cloth, from this port for London, arrived ſafe at the Downs the 3d inſt.

The Linen Hall, Hugh Dickſon maſter, for London, is clear to ſail, and will proceed the firſt fair wind.

The Lords Commiſſioners of the Great Seal have been pleaſed to appoint John Craford Gordon, of Florida, Eſq. one of his Majeſty's Juſtices of the Peace for the county of Down.

PORT NEWS.

ARRIVED.

June 8. Speedwell, Read, Drunton, deals.
Adventure, Robertſon, do. do.
Two colliers.

CLEARED OUT.

June 9. Liberty, M'Roberts, Liverpool, butter.

Woollen Drapery, Mens Mercery, and Haberdashery,

RICHARD FULTON has just received, in addition to his former Assortment, a fresh supply of the most fashionable Goods, which will be sold on the lowest terms, for ready money, or to those who take but a short credit.——He continues to confine himself as much as possible to ask but one price for his Goods, which prevents imposition, and adds greatly to the dispatch of business.—Best superfine Cloths, Spanish wool, at Dublin prices, 20s. per yard for cash paid down, and second Cloths at 18s. per do. Lisburn, 5th June, 1789.

Fine English Butter-Salt.

WM. SEED and Co. beg leave to inform their Friends and the Public, they have just landed their usual supply for the season of the very finest and best quality for Butter.—To prevent their Friends being imposed on by ordinary or bad Salt being taken to them at a lower price and passed to them as W. S. and Co. fine English Salt—it is requested that persons in the country may order their carriers to bring tickets which will be signed by
WM. SEED and Co.

OATS,

Are always wanted at Wm. Seed & Co's. Stores, adjoining to the Weigh-house, Belfast, where a fair price is given through the season—and where also Oats are, for the convenience of the public, retailed every day in small quantities.

Gentlemen wanting parcels for export can be served on moderate terms, and on the shortest notice, with good Oats, kiln-dried and skreened, in condition for the longest voyage.

FLOUR,

A constant supply of the different kinds, the produce of their Mills at Biers-Bridge, always to be had at said Stores, where Bran is also retailed.

MESLIN.

A parcel Meslin Meal, of a remarkable fine quality for bread, is now retailing in small quantities at said Stores.
Belfast, June 11th, 1789.

New Dantzig Ashes, &c.

WILLIAM Mc. CLURE is now landing a parcel of different brands; and is well supplied with Hungarian and American Pearl Ashes; Hyson, Green and Congou Teas;—all of which will be sold on moderate terms for good payments.
Belfast, 12th June, 1789.

At Rotterdam,

THE Brig DISPATCH, of Belfast Charles Stewart, Master, is now loading on freight for Belfast. Any persons wishing for Goods from said place, will please send their orders immediately, as she will positively sail from Rotterdam early in july, most of her cargo being already engaged.
Belfast, 11th June, 1789.

A Felony.

WHEREAS James Dunn who served me for upwards of five years as an apprentice and journeyman baker, eloped from my service on Saturday the 6th inst. and carried off with him a considerable sum of money, which he had collected on my account.—Now I do hereby offer a reward of ten guineas to any person or persons who will apprehend and lodge him in any of his Majesty's goals in this kingdom, or give information so as he may be apprehended. He is about 22 years of age, five feet six or seven inches high, black complexion, marked with the small pox; and was bred in the parish of Killileagh. As it is supposed he intends to take a passage to America, should he offer to any vessel for that part, it is requested he may be stopped and notice given.
Downpatrick,   JAMES SWEENY.
11th June, 1789.

LOST,

ON the 28th of May last, on the road leading from Carrickfergus to Island Magee, a small square Trunk, containing Ladies Wearing Apparel, &c.

Whoever has found the same, by returning it to James Glasgow, Tanner, Larne, shall receive three Guineas Reward.
Larne, 6th June, 1789.

Ten Thousand Pounds,

TO be lent on a Mortgage in either of the Counties of Down or Antrim.——Application to be made to Thomas Ludford Stewart, Attorney at Law, Belfast, and in Term Time, in Dublin.
Belfast, 8th June, 1789.

THE Committee for conducting the Ships in the Linen Trade, beg leave to acquaint the Gentlemen Linen Drapers, that the following Vessels are appointed to attend the White Linen Market, and will sail punctually at the time the Shippers may direct:

The Charlotte, Wm. Campbell, Master, for London.
Peggy, James Mc. Ilroy, Master, for Chester Fair Hillsborough, Wm. Mc. Donald, Master, for Liverpool.
Peggy, Angus Lamont, Master, for Greenock.
And the Richard, John Brag, Master, for Whitehaven.
Belfast, 15th June, 1789.

Partnership Commenced.

ROBERT WILSON and GEORGE Mc. CAMON,
RESPECTFULLY inform their Friends and the Public, that they have lately commenced Partnership in the Silk and Haberdashery Business, at the House of Mrs. B. Wilson; under the Firm of

Robert Wilson & Co.

and have laid in from London and Dublin an extensive Assortment of the most fashionable Lustrings, Tabbinets, Modes, Sarcenets, Laces, Jaconet, Decca, Mull and Book Muslins; also New painted and coloured japanned Muslins, Brussels Launs, Calicoes, Muslinets, Dimities, &c. &c.—which they are enabled and determined to dispose of on as moderate terms as any House in the kingdom. Belfast, 15th June, 1789.

N. B. R. WILSON & Co. are always largely assorted with Black Silks, Bombaseens, Bombazet Stuffs, Italian Crapes, Love Ribbons, &c.
Belfast, 13th June, 1789.

Elizabeth Shipboy,

CHURCH-STREET, COLERAIN,

HAS just got home an extensive Assortment of Haberdashery and Millinary Goods, which she has been exceedingly careful in chusing; her Modes, Laces, Calicoes, Muslins, Ribbons, &c. will be found to merit inspection: She has some exceeding good Beaver Hats for Gentlemen and Ladies, Fancy Waistcoat Patterns, and many other Articles not formerly sold in her Shop. As she has laid in her Goods on the best terms, and is determined to sell for a very low profit, she hopes for the continuance of that favour she has so amply experienced, and for which she returns her most grateful thanks.
15th June, 1789.

Robert Bradshaw,

IS now landing two Cargoes of very best Dronthon DEALS:—He immediately expects a Cargo of Dantzig Timber and Ashes.
Belfast, 12th June, 1789.

Damaged Barrilla

TO be Sold by Auction, for account of the Underwriters, at the Stores of Mrs. Ashmore in Waringstreet, and Mr. Alexander Orr's Stores in Linenhallstreet, on Friday the 20th instant, a large parcel now landing from out the Briton, Capt. Greave, from Alicant, lately stranded at Killough. The Sale to commence at Mrs. Ashmore's Stores at 12 o'clock at noon.—To be set up in Lots agreeable to the purchasers;—terms of sale—ready money.
Belfast, 12th June, 1789

Cotton Manufacture & Printing

NICHOLAS GRIMSHAW has for Sale the following Articles—all of which are of the best quality, and will be sold on the most reasonable terms, at the House of

Messrs. Haslet, Strong & Co. Belfast,

Printed Cottons, Calicoes and Muslins of the newest and most fashionable Patterns; Chintz Furniture, Copper-plate ditto; Shawls and Handkerchiefs.

He has likewise at the White-House, double Warps for Corduroys and Thicksets, and Cotton Twist for Stockings, white and mixed, from one to five fold.

WE think it incumbent upon us to acknowledge in this Manner, the lenity we have experienced in having one Guinea from each of us, accepted of to be given to the Poor-House, in lieu of the corporal punishment we had brought ourselves liable to, by breaking into the garden of Mr. Hugh Dunlop in Ballymacarrett, contrary to law. Given under our hand the 11th June 1789.
JOHN SMITH, Pensioner.
JOHN SCOTT. Carman.

Sherry and Lisbon Wines.

CUNNINGHAM GREG has for sale a quantity of each in Pipes, Hogsheads and quarter Casks, old and of an excellent quality, which will be sold for ready money or good Bills on reasonable terms.
Belfast, 15 June, 1789.

Spirit Store, Ann-street

JOHN GRAHAM, at his retail Store, formerly Messrs. John Campbell & Co's. is now largely supplied with a general assortment of excellent Spirits, &c. laid in on the best terms, which he offers to the Publick (for ready money only, or good paper) as imported, or reduced, in such quantities as may suit their convenience, and at such prices as he hopes on trial will merit their future preference.

To those from whom he has met with so liberal encouragement since his commencement in business he returns his most grateful thanks.
Belfast, 13th June, 1789.

New Timber, new Deals.

A Cargo of each is now arrived to WM. and SAM. HANNA, who are also landing a cargo of excellent Barilla, a cargo of strong Whiskey, which, and the Articles they are usually supplied with, will be for sale at their Stores on the Merchants-Quay.
Newry, 11th June, 1789.

N. B. They have a cargo of Sicily Barilla, Cotton Wool, Liquorice Ball, &c. now at quarantine; and their Iron Stores are well supplied with Nail-rod, Shovels, Hoops, &c.

A Cargo of assorted Swedish Iron daily expected.

NOTICE.

THOMAS Mc. CLEMENTS, as heir at law in right of his wife to the estates of the late Mr. John Wallace, Attorney, requests that all his creditors will immediately furnish him, at Castlereagh, with their accounts and demands they may have against the said estates, as he intends to have them put into a mode of payment.——And he also desires that his late clients, and others that stood indebted to him at the time of his death, will hold themselves in readiness to pay the balances that may appear due, at which time their papers will be had and delivered to them.
Castlereagh, 11th June, 1789.
To be inserted three times.

TO BE LET.

And entered upon immediately, either by the Year or for the ensuing Season,

A Neat House in Holywood, lately occupied by the Revd. George Macartney Portis, with Stabling for four Horses.

For Particulars apply to John Mc. Connell, Innkeeper, Holywood.
Holywood, June 11th, 1789.

Wanted,

A Man who will undertake the management of a considerable number of Looms, to be employed in the manufacture of Muslins in Belfast and its vicinity. Any person whose recommendations prove agreeable, will be treated with, by applying to Joseph Hancock of Lisburn.

Weavers and their families may be accommodated with convenient houses at the east end of the Longbridge, or in Lisburn.
Belfast, 6th Mo. 13th, 1789.

John Richardson,

Of Gortin, near Dungannon,

REQUESTS that all those to whom he is indebted by bond, note, or otherwise, may forthwith furnish their accounts, specifying the particulars of their demands to John Roe of Blackwatertown, (who is settling the family accounts) that the most expeditious method may be taken to settle and discharge same.
Gortin, 1st June, 1789.

Bachelors Annuity Co.

THE Members of said Company are desired to take notice, that a Meeting will be held on Saturday the 20th instant, at the Market-House, Belfast, exactly at eleven o'clock, to lend out on such security as they shall approve of, the sum of Six Hundred and Fifty Pounds.

The passengers who intend to go to New-Castle and Philadelphia in the Sophia, Captain Thomson, are desired to be in Belfast on the 26th of June inst. as she will be ready to leave this by that time, wind and weather permitting.

The Linen Hall, Hugh Dickson, master, loaded with linen cloth, sailed for London on Sunday evening last.

Trenton, April 21, 1789

General Waſhington cannot leave this place without expreſſing his acknowledgments to the Matrons and Young Ladies, who received him in ſo novel and grateful a manner at the Triumphal Arch in Trenton, for the exquiſite ſenſations he experienced in that affecting moment.—The aſtoniſhing contraſt between his former and actual ſituation at the ſame ſpot—the elegant taſte with which it was adorned for the preſent occaſion—and the innocent appearance of the white-robed choir who met him with the gratulatory ſong—have made ſuch an impreſſion on his remembrance, as, he aſſures them, will never be effaced.

* As they ſung theſe lines they ſtrewed the flowers before the General, who halted until the Sonata was finiſhed.

SONNET TO JUNE.

By. W. Hamilton Reid.

DELIGHTFUL Seaſon! bounteous now diffuſe
O'er the freſh glebe, as wont, thy ſweeteſt flow'rs,
That ſmiling quaff the rich nectareous ſhow'rs,
And ſpread the veſtment of a thouſand hues.
The woodbine bring, that wears the virgin bluſh,
The King-cup, that the ſunny meadow ſhews,
Thy blue-bells ſtrew beneath each hawthorn buſh:
But let the gardens boaſt the peerleſs roſe,
Th' auricula, the tulip's gaudy ſhine,
The Julian ſtock flower, laviſh of perfume.
Then woodland nymphs in ſong unequall'd join,
And fancy waves her rainbow-tinted plume;
The moſs-clad cells, where mantling ivies twine,
Steal one from life, or ſoothe its anxious gloom.

PARISIAN INTELLIGENCE.

The diſputes between the Three Eſtates are far from being in a train of accommodation. The Nobleſſe, at leaſt at Paris, have reſumed that *hauteur* which we imagined they had been inclined to lay aſide. The Clergy begin to repent of the conceſſions which they made to the *Tiers Etat*, who, on their ſide, are determined to throw down every barrier between the people and the honour of the State, and to aboliſh every odious diſtinction between the various claſſes of citizens.—A *fracas* happened laſt week on the *Pont-Neuf*, which was attended with the moſt ſerious conſequences.—The Count de B——elle riding furiouſly, and without giving notice, in a phaeton and four, over the bridge, ran down ſeveral pedeſtrians. One unfortunate man loſt his life, and ſeveral had their limbs deſperately cruſhed. A general cry of *arretez, arretez, le foutre*, was vociferated from all ſides. In a moment the carriage was ſtopped—the mob dragged from his ſeat the trembling patrician, and, regardleſs of his cries and piteous intreaties, threw him headlong from the bridge, juſt by the equeſtrian ſtatue of *Henri-quatre*. This miſerable martyr to intemperate inſolence, was in an inſtant daſhed to pieces in his fall. Not ſatisfied with this vengeance, the populace proceeded to demoliſh the carriage, which they broke into a thouſand fragments.

An unlucky accident happened at a coffee houſe at Verſailles the beginning of laſt week.—One of the Count d'Artois' guards entered the room, and on ſeeing three or four Members of the Third Claſs, loudly exclaimed "*F— on ne voit que du Tiers!*" ("D——n it, one meets with nothing but men of the Third Claſs!") Not ſatiſfied with this inſulting and untimely apoſtrophe, he addreſſed his converſation to the waiter, and wanted, deſignedly, to entice him to ſpeak as diſreſpectfully as he did of the Third Claſs. The waiter held his tongue. Soon after he called to him and ſaid, "*Tiers*, bring me a diſh of coffee." One of the Deputies then went out, and returned afterwards in his common (the citizens') dreſs, with a ſword: "Sir, ſays he, on entering, your language is abuſive, and the *Tiers* cannot bear an inſult any more than your maſter: I have a few words to ſay to you in private; come behind the church of Notre-Dame: that field ſhall ſhew whether a Deputy of the Third Claſs reſembles your companion, the waiter." Thither the Officer (who is a gentleman) and the Deputy went, and in the duel the *Tiers* happened to be victorious. Joy ſpread from Verſailles to Paris in an inſtant; and were the Officer's wounds mortal, it would ſtill encreaſe.

The following letter, written by the King of France, has been lately circulated in Paris:

Thurſday Night, May 28.

"I have been informed, that the difficulties which have been made relative to the aſcertaining of the powers veſted in the Members of the States General ſtill ſubſiſt, notwithſtanding the care taken by the Commiſſioners choſen by the three States to find out the means of ſettling this point. I cannot ſee without pain, and indeed much uneaſineſs, the National Aſſembly which I have called together to be concerned with me in the new regulation of the kingdom, ſunk into inaction, which, if continued, would cauſe all the hopes which I have formed for the happineſs of my people, and the benefit of the State, to vaniſh away. Under theſe circumſtances, I deſire that the Conciliatory Commiſſioners, already choſen by the three Orders, reſume their conference to-morrow at ſix o'clock in the evening; and for this occaſion, in the preſence of my Guard of Seſſion and Commiſſioners, whom I ſhall join with them in order that I may be more particularly informed of the propoſals for agreement, which ſhall be made, and directly contribute to ſo deſirable and preſſing a ſtate of harmony. I charge the perſon who ſhall exerciſe the office of Preſident, to make known theſe my intentions to the Aſſembly."

COUNT SARSFIELD.

Count Sarsfield, died the 26th ult. at Paris. He was the great grandſon of the gallant General Sarsfield, who ſo greatly diſtinguiſhed himſelf at the ſiege of Limerick, by intercepting the battering artillery and ammunition deſtined to ſupport that ſiege.

He one day left Limerick with a good body of forces, and having ſo directed his march as to make King William think he had no deſign upon his artillery, he ſuddenly croſſed the Shannon, and coming up in the night with the convoy, he cut to pieces the detachment that guarded it; and then charging the great guns with powder up to the muzzles, and burying them and the reſt of the ammunition in the ground, he, by means of a train, ſet fire to the buried powder, and the whole artillery and all, blew up with a dreadful exploſion.

This exploſion was heard at Limerick, and convinced King William that he had loſt his convoy.

This bold enterprize of Sarsfield made William feel that he had then no other chance for taking Limerick but a ſtorm. He accordingly ordered one; but even after his troops had entered the town, they were repulſed with ſuch ſlaughter, that 200 of the braveſt of them were left dead on the ſpot.

William immediately after this raiſed the ſiege; and Sarsfield had the glory of preſerving Ireland to his unfortunate maſter, King James, for another campaign, againſt the ableſt general of the age. He was afterwards created Earl of Lucan, and was ſecond in command at the battle of Aughrim.

Count Sarsfield, who lately died, had been many years a Lieutenant General in the French ſervice, and formerly Colonel of the regiment de Normandie, when that regiment conſiſted of four batalions of 750 men each.

There is ſtill in France a nobleman, deſcended from the great Sarsfield, who bears the title of Earl of Lucan.

OLD BAILEY INTELLIGENCE.

Leonard Wilſon was yeſterday convicted of ſtealing, on the 3d of May laſt, one gold watch, ſet with diamonds and jargoons, and one ſilver ſpoon, the property of Sir George Staunton, Bart. The priſoner is an Iriſhman, who had received his education in the College of Dublin; but being diſappointed in his early purſuits and expectations in life, had wandered in deſpair through many parts of France, with a view of aſſuming the character of a Roman Catholic Prieſt. His claſſical knowledge, particularly of the Latin and Greek languages, was deep and elegant; and, diſguſted with the bigotry and artifices of the Romiſh diſciples, he returned to England, and was recommended by the uſher of a ſchool to Sir George Staunton, as a ſervant and preceptor to his infant ſon. In this capacity he acted with great integrity and ability, until the evening the theft was committed, when the watch and ſpoon being left in the room where his young pupil lay, he was unfortunately tempted to take it. The felonious intention was very clearly proved by his offering it to pawn to Mr. Heither in Long-acre, who, ſuſpecting it to be ſtolen, ſtopped him, and carried him before the magiſtrates in Bow-ſtreet, where, by an extraordinary coincidence of circumſtances, Sir George then was giving information of the robbery. The humanity of the proſecutor, however, has ſaved the priſoner's life, for though the property was ſtolen in the dwelling-houſe, it was only laid in the indictment to be of the value of 39s.

Mr. Recorder addreſſed him:—"You have been convicted by your country of an offence, committed under ſuch circumſtances of aggravation, that had you been indicted capitally, ſo far from recommending you as an object of mercy, I ſhould have given my advice for an immediate execution of your ſentence. His Majeſty, among his other qualities, executes the law with *mercy*; but, at the ſame time, acknowledges the neceſſity of enforcing with *juſtice*. *Mercy*, no doubt, ſtands foremoſt in the human virtues, but what our ſtation in ſociety requires is not to be forgotten; and Sir George Staunton, in this inſtance, has ſacrificed his public duty to his private humanity. He has valued this watch in the indictment at but thirty-nine ſhillings, which muſt be very much below its intrinſic worth: this has ſaved your life, by making your offence only a ſingle felony; an indulgence which you appear by no means to have deſerved: he relieved you in your diſtreſs, received you as a domeſtic, and gave you a ſacred truſt—the management of his child: inſtead of returning this kindneſs, and performing theſe duties in the manner which the education which you appear to have received ſhould have taught you to do, you have abuſed his confidence, and been guilty of ſuch a crime as demands the forfeit of your life, did not the humanity of your proſecutor ſtill extend itſelf towards you. It is my duty, however, to pronounce as ſevere a ſentence as the law admits; which is, that you be tranſported to the Coaſt of Africa for ſeven years."

A few evenings ago, at a ſmall town in Yorkſhire, juſt as the members of an *unlicenſed* company of comedians were beginning to aſtoniſh the eyes and ears of their ruſtic audience with the "life and death of the *Moor of Venice*," they were ſurpriſed with the entrance of a *conſtable* and his *poſſe*; the former of whom bore a written inſtrument which converted all the reſpectable perſonages of the *drama* into *rogues* and *vagabonds!*—*Othello* took the alarm, and leaving his "plain unvarniſh'd tale" unfiniſhed, jumped over the fiddler's head, and made his way into the ſtreet, where, with his *blackened* face, he created great terror amongſt the children. The *ſooty* hero made his eſcape; but the reſt of the *troop* ſurrendered at diſcretion, and are *rehearſing* in the Houſe of Correction the piece they are to *perform* at the next Quarter-ſeſſion.

DUBLIN, June 11.

Tueſday at noon arrived the Right Hon. Robert Hobart, Secretary to his Excellancy the Lord Lieutenant.

Mr. Secretary Hobart has not brought over with him, as was expected, the appointment of our Lord Chancellor.

A few days ago his Majeſty's frigates the Acteon and Chicheſter, of 44 guns each, arrived at Cork from Portſmouth, having on board the 41ſt regiment of foot, which regiment immediately landed and marched into the Barrack; and on Monday the 1ſt inſtant, the 20th and 21ſt regiments embarked at Cork on board theſe frigates for Nova Scotia, for which place they ſailed three days after. The 24th regiment ſome days before embarked on board the Endymion frigate for Canada.

There is now living in Great Peter-ſtreet, Weſtminſter, a man of the Name of Kelly, who fought at the Battle of the Boyne in Ireland, July 1690. He was in King James's army, and ſays that he remembers that King's face as well this day as he did when at the Boyne. He can both read and write now, and walks more than three miles every day.

CURRAGH—JUNE MEETING.

Monday, June 8.

Mr. Hamilton's 3-year old colt, by Lenox, paid half forfeit to Mr. Cook's 3-year old colt, by Fryar, for 100 guineas each, laſt two and a half miles of the courſe.

Same day, Mr. Dennis's h. Cherokee, carrying 8ſt. beat Mr. Savage's h. Douglaſs, late Raſper, carrying 8ſt. 4lb. for 200 guineas each, p. p. one four-mile heat.

At ſtarting three to two on Cherokee; Douglaſs ran reſtive after running the firſt mile.

Same day, Mr. Hamilton's h. Andrew Armſtrong, three years old, carrying 7ſt. beat Mr. Savage's m. Ducheſs of Leinſter, four years old carrying 8ſt. 7lb. for 100 guineas each, p. p. from the top of the Long Hill home.

Three to two on Ducheſs of Leinſter.

Belfaſt, *June* 19.

Whoever regards the free diſcuſſion of political Subjects, muſt obſerve with regret that the Britiſh Miniſter has propoſed an additional tax upon NEWS-PAPERS and ADVERTISEMENTS, in Great Britain. To that freedom of public diſquiſition, by means of the Prints, which has long diſtinguiſhed theſe countries, we are much indebted for any civil liberty we poſſeſs: to remove a ſingle popular check on men and meaſures, or to damp the ſpirit of enquiry, by limiting the circulation of News-papers, cannot therefore be eaſily reconciled to any true principle in politics. At the ſame time that this remark unfavourable to the Premier is made, and that his recent ſentiments reſpecting the religious liberty of Diſſenters cannot be forgotten, the liberality of his conduct in the queſtion now depending before the Parliament of his country reſpecting the Slave Trade—deſerves to be noticed with honour.

On Tueſday laſt the 39th regiment of foot marched in here from Ayr and Stranraer, and remains.

The Thames, Bennet, from Newry for London, clears out the 20th inſtant.

The Newry, Wilſon, from Newry for London, arrived there the 8th inſtant, after a paſſage of ſix days.

The paſſengers who intend to go to New-Caſtle and Philadelphia in the Sophia, Captain Thomſon, are deſired to be in Belfaſt on the 26th of June inſt. as ſhe will be ready to leave this by that time, wind and weather permitting.

Anno 1789.] Printed by HENRY JOY, and Co. BELFAST.

The BELFAST NEWS-LETTER.

TUESDAY June 23, FRIDAY June 26, 1789.

WHEREAS on Wednesday morning the 17th instant, some person or persons broke a pain of a window in my house near Moira, and carried away 14 pair of women's thread stockings marked M. J. and number'd with black silk, and 4 pair of men's ditto, also two large table cloths, and sundry other articles all wet, and lifted the night before off the grass. Any person who will give information so as said articles may be found, shall have one guinea reward, and for prosecuting the thief or thieves to conviction, shall have a reward of 5 guineas, by applying to Mr. Duke Berwick of Belfast, or to me at Moira.

Dated this 22d Day of June, 1789.

JOHN BERWICK.

Wholesale and Retail Haberdashery, Looking-glass & Carpet Warehouse, &c.

JAMES GRAHAM has just added to his former extensive Assortment, an elegant Variety of the very newest and most fashionable

Carpets and Carpetines,

Plaids, &c. Oil Cloths for floors and stairs, Hair Cloth for do. Furniture Cottons, Checks and Damascus, plain stripe and Sattin, Hair Cloth for chairs, Bed-Ticks, British, Lambeg and Dublin Blankets at manufacturers prices, a large and pleasing collection of

ROOM-PAPERS,

of the most brilliant patterns, festoon and other fashionable borders, Silk Handkerchiefs, Sewing Silks, Purse Twist, Ribbons, &c. Silk and Stuff Petticoats, English, Wildboare and common Stuffs, a very extensive assortment of Hosiery; white and coloured sewing Threads, Lace do. Linen and Worsted Tapes, None-so-pretties, Garters, Silk, Cotton and Thread Laces for Stays, black and white Laces and Edgings, Flannels, Plads and Serges; also the most beautiful and extensive variety of

Gilt Pier Looking-glasses & Gerandoles,

with plain and dressing do. to be seen at any House in this kingdom, at London and Dublin Prices; Cotton and Linen Handkerchiefs for neck and pocket, best and common playing Cards, Hat and Cloaths Brushes, Tooth Brushes, Buckle and Comb do. Powder Bags, do. Boxes, shaving do. with the very nicest Naples and Italian Soap, French and English Wash-balls, best French scented soft and hard Pomatum, Perfumes, best, second and common

Hair Powder, Mareschall do.

Warren's Milk of Roses for beautifying the skin, Liquid and vegetable Rouge, Silk and Swanskin Powder-puffs, Powper-knives, very neat Pocket Ink-cases, Glass do. with Sand Bottles, Spectacles, best and common Pencils, Sealing-Wax,

Wax-Candles, do. Tapers, &c.

Callimancoes, Sattinets, and Lastings, Drogheda Linen, &c. **PINS,**

at Pin-makers prices, of the very best quality, on which is allowed the largest discounts, Hair-pins, Ivory, Boxwood, Quillback and Horn-combs, Muslins and Muslin Handkerchiefs, which will be sold very cheap.

German and Irish Black-ball that gives the shoes an elegant polish, prevents the leather from cracking, and is engaged not to soil the stockings, bathing Caps, Bandoes, Silk Purses; also a very neat parcel of most beautiful

Spring Girth-Webs,

Straining Webs for Cabinet-makers, Ladies and Gentlemens Gloves, &c. &c. &c.—all of which will be sold by wholesale and retail at Dublin prices.

Belfast, June 23d, 1789.

To the Freeholders of the four lower Baronies of the County of Antrim.

WE the undersigned taking it into consideration, that there are upwards of twelve hundred Freeholders in the four lower Baronies, and that there has subsisted time immemorial a strong connection among them; do humbly submit it to their consideration, whether it would not be proper for them to join in nominating some one Gentleman, resident among themselves, at the approaching election for Members to serve in Parliament for the County; and we request a meeting of the Freeholders at Ballymoney, on Tuesday the 14th day of July next, at twelve o'clock at noon, to consider who is the properest object, and to concert measures for supporting him accordingly.

Dated this 23d day of June, 1789.

Hugh Boyd,	Henry O'Hara,
Adam Hunter,	Edm Alex M'Naghten,
Geo. Moor,	John Cromie.
James Hamilton,	Arch. Hutchison.

To be sold

AT Gilford, about Twenty Stone of choice WOOL.—Apply to Mr. Richard Robinson.

This to be continued four times.

Belfast Feather Ware house,

SKIPPERS-LANE, JUNE, 18th. 1789.

PATRICK BURKE returns his sincere thanks to the Ladies and Gentlemen of Belfast, and its Vicinity, for the many favours he has received since his commencement in Business; and informs them he is just returned from the Provinces of Connaught and Munster, with a large assortment of different kinds of Feathers, 1st, 2d, and 3d qualities, (which he is enabled to sell on the most reasonable terms). Numbers of Hawkers having frequently imposed on the public, by vending feathers under Burk's name; he entreats no one will purchase from them unless they can produce a certificate signed by him, as he cannot be accountable for any goods but what he inspects himself, which he will change or return the money if on trial they prove not satisfactory.

N. B. He continues to give the highest price to Tanners for Bullock and Cow-tails, likewise to Travellers for Brute hair. ☞ FEATHER BEDS ready made up.

A Caution to the Public;

NOT to purchase the concerns that were mine in the town of Warringstown and townland of Tullyheron, adjacent to said town, in the county of Down, as I have a deed of mortgage on said lands for one thousand five hundred pounds, and not any part of that principal paid to me as yet. Those lands were sold by me to my brother John Ogle then of Falls and county of Antrim, for two thousand five hundred pounds, the second day of November, 1773, seventy-three, for no other motive than to do justice to the legatees of my father's will; for which purpose of paying said debt to the parties concerned, one thousand pounds of the purchase was then appropriated, and releases obtained from the trustees and legatees of said will, viz. Alexander Legg, Esq; deceased, and Mrs. Ann Ogle, deceased, they were the trustees; Eleanor Ogle, John Ogle, and Marcella Ogle, legatees; his bond, the penalty on that bond to the above specified sum, and judgment entered on the bond, and the deed of mortgage, are my securities, and prior to every other security he ever gave, or could give, to any person whatever, as they were perfected and dated the above recited 2d day of November, 1773, seventy-three, the day of sale, and registered in the Record-Office in Dublin at that time.

Malone, June 19th, 1789. WILLIAM OGLE.

N. B. I have great reason to believe there is another mortgage given to another person since that time mentioned in the former part of this advertisement.

Bristol Cyder, remarkably cheap.

SAMUEL and ANDREW Mc. CLEAN are now landing from on board the Peggy and Mary, Capt Jones, and the William, Capt. Hodgin, about fifty tons Bristol Cyder, *of the first quality*; in Pipes, Hogsheads and Barrels.—They are enabled to sell this parcel at *Eleven Pence per Gallon*, which is not more than half the usual Price; and is only one penny per gallon higher than Guernsey Cyder which they had lately on sale.

A general Assortment of every Article in the Spirit Line on reasonable terms.

Belfast, 22d June, 1789.

To be sold by Auction,

BY the Administrator of the late Revd. Hugh Caldwell, at the house of Mr. Thomas Fisher in Newtown-Ards, on Saturday the 27th instant, a valuable Collection of Books, and several Articles of Household Furniture.——The Auction will commence at eleven o'Clock.

Newtown-Ards, 22d June, 1789.

New Dantzig Ashes & Timber.

BROWN and OAKMAN have just imported a Cargo of Dantzig Timber——and Ashes of the best brands, which will be sold cheap.

Belfast, 25th June, 1789.

A good Dwelling-House, adjoining Mr. Beggs, in Castle-street, to be let.——Enquire at said Brown and Oakman.

Belfast Academy.

THE Public Examinations of the Belfast Academy, previous to the Summer Recess, will begin on Wednesday the 8th of July, at 11 o'clock.—It is earnestly requested, that, on this occasion, there may be a full attendance of the Patrons of the Institution, and other Gentlemen, as this circumstance would not fail of proving an incitement to future industry on the part of the Scholars.

For Sale at *Chichester-Quay*,

THE Brig WILLIAM, burthen about 120 tons.——She was built at Newnham, Gloucestershire, and is only four years old. For particulars apply to Robt. and Wm. Simms.

They have just arrived per said Vessel, a quantity of BARK and CYDER; the latter is of an excellent quality, and will be sold very cheap by the puncheon or barrel.

Belfast, 17th June, 1789.

THE Presbyterian Congregation of Killinshy, beg leave to inform an impartial publick, that the Meeting-house now building at Lisbane is not only unnecessary, as the old Meeting-house is abundantly capacious and sufficient to contain the parishioners of Killinshy, Tullynakill and Killmud, but may prove injurious to the dissenting interest. The publick are requested to be cautious with regard to contributing to the abovementioned building. Done at our Meeting-house in Ballow, by the unanimous voice of the congregation, this 21st day of June, 1789.

Signed by the Session-Clerk,

JAMES LOWRY.

THE Presbyterian Congregation of Lisban, beg leave to assure the Public, that they are under an indispensible necessity to build a Meeting-house, as they have not experienced the most useful and pastoral labours amongst them for several years past: They solemnly declare they are the most decided friends to the Protestant Dissenting Interest, as their chief view in erecting a new Meeting-house is to promote the true interests of genuine religion—they therefore trust, that an enlightened and impartial Public will look upon any illiberal caution given to contract their minds and shut their purses—with the contempt it merits.

Done at Lisban this 24th day of June, 1789.

Signed, by the unanimous consent of the Congregation, by ALEXANDER JOHNSON,
Session Clerk.

Woollen, Cotton, Linen, & Haberdashery.

CATHERINE CALLWELL, No. 25, Bridge-street, is at present largely supplied with Superfines, Refines, Forest Cloths, Cassimeres, Fancy Waistcoating, &c. with almost every Article of Mens Mercery.

The Ladies attention is particularly requested to her present assortment of

Callicoes, Cottons, Muslinetts, Dimities, &c.

which are of the most fashionable patterns, suitable to the season.——THREADS of every denomination always on sale, of the same manufacture which has been so long and so universally esteemed for texture and colour.

Stuffs, Shawls, Modes, Lace, with many other Articles—all of which she will dispose of on the most reasonable terms. Belfast, 25th June, 1789.

New Dronthon Deals and Train Oil.

CUNNINGHAM GREG is just landing out of the Brig Success, from Dronthon, a Cargo of Deals of the very first quality; also a few barrels of Train Oil, which he will dispose of on reasonable terms.

Belfast, 24th June, 1789.

TO be let and entered upon from the first day of November next, or the interest in the lease sold, of that large and commodious Dwelling House, with all fixtures compleat, situated in Hercules-lane, and late in the possession of Alexander Sutherland; it is well calculated for a Merchant, or Inn-keeper, having a large back Yard, good Counting-house, Vaults, Ware-houses and Stabbling backwards. There are upwards of eighty years of the Lease unexpired, and is subject to one pound six shillings per annum ground rent. For further particulars application to be made to John Boyle and Co.

Belfast, 22d June 1789.

Strong Brandy, best Vinegar, *&c.*

DAVISON and GRAHAM have lately received by the Neptune, from Bordeaux, a few Pipes very fine flavoured 2-3ds Brandy, and a few Tierces best White-wine Vinegar; with the following Articles, which they are generally well supplied with, they will sell (as imported) only—very cheap, at their Office in Ann-street, lately Messrs. John Campbell & Co.

Strong Jamaica Rum,
Strong 1-half augmented Geneva,
Malaga, }
Port, }
Sherry, } Wines,
Claret, and Frontignac }

Also a few Casks of American Rosin.

FRANCE.

STATES GENERAL.

The following intelligence may be depended on as authentic; it was brought on Monday evening by one of the King's Messengers from the Duke of Dorset, at Paris.

The divisions, which subsist among the three bodies of the representatives of the people, are every day growing more and more alarming. They are now arrived to an open schism, and it is feared that nothing short of the Royal interference, assisted by the military, can quell them.

That every one of our readers may understand the cause of these disputes, which are rather difficult to describe to those unacquainted with the subject, we shall remark, that the three Orders of the State, namely, the Nobility, Clergy, and Third Estate, are each obliged to prove the *verification of their powers*; or, in other words, to prove, first—the right of their electors to send them to Parliament; and secondly, to prove their qualifications of having been duly elected. This again may require some explanation; for as no Assembly of the States General has been held since the year 1614, and as many towns, which are at present in the most populous and flourishing state, did not exist at that distant period, or were then too insignificant to send Deputies to Parliament, these of course now, from their importance, put in a claim for representation, and have accordingly elected Deputies. The only tribunal, which could properly decide on the merits of these petitions, was the Assembly itself, when once formed. This is what the French have termed the *verification of the powers of the elected.*

The first thing to be considered was, in what manner this question should be decided, and who were the proper persons to do it.

It has already been a cause of very serious debate, how these three Orders of Representatives should vote, whether in a body, or in separate Chambers. The Third Estate has violently protested against the latter mode; as in that case, were the Nobility and Clergy to join, it would be two to one against them. This question is not yet decided.

Having briefly, and we hope evidently, explained the nature of these divisions, we shall lay before the public the news of this dispatch.

The Third Estate, finding that public business did not get forward in the manner they wished, and that they were rather losing in their cause, sent a summons the beginning of last week to the Nobility and Clergy, desiring they would meet them in Common Hall, to prove the verification of their powers. The two latter had always objected to this mode, judging that it was the business of each Order to decide separately on the merits of their own Members being properly elected.

This summons of the Third Estate produced a meeting of the whole of their own body in the Common Hall, and a few of each Order of the Nobility and Clergy, who were attached to their cause. As soon as they were assembled, they declared, that the present was a lawful meeting, and that most of the Nobility and Clergy absenting themselves, was no proof of its illegality, as the summons stated that if any Members chose to be absent, they should proceed without them.

The meeting then proceeded on the business of the Elections, and to consider the state of the nation, and passed several resolutions, which they declared to be the voice of the Assembly of the States General; and they were registered accordingly.

Such a proceeding, on the very face of it illegal, has created the utmost consternation throughout the capital; and we have authority to assure the public, that the French Government had dispatched messengers to several parts of the kingdom, ordering a reinforcement of the Military to Paris; and the messenger, on his way to Calais, met several bodies of soldiers marching thither.

LONDON, June 13.

The Royal Tour commences on this day fortnight: before which there will be a Court at St. James's, for the purpose of the nobility taking leave.

The King has no less than seven hundred and eighty thousand pounds of his Hanoverian revenues in the five per cent. consols, the interest of which has been accumulating for several years.

Mr. Pitt's family receives 60,000l. per annum from the nation.

As every instance of his Majesty's returning health must be grateful to his subjects, we have it from *authority* that he now weighs within *twelve pounds* of what he did two years ago, and that he has increased in weight *one stone* since a little before the procession to St. Paul's.

PRINCE OF WALES's TARTAN.

Edinburgh is very proud in the idea, that the Prince of Wales will shortly appear in a Highland dress.

The dress of the 42 Regiment is the pattern.

Mr. Christie of Stirling is the regimental taylor, and now preparing the Caledonian Tartan.

DUBLIN.

It is said, that the Bath waters have been recommended to the Lord Lieutenant by his physicians, if so, his Excellency will quit his government for two months, during which Lords Justices will be appointed.

Several public-spirited country gentlemen are determined at the next assizes to move an address from the Grand Juries in the respective counties to their Representatives in Parliament, to support a bill (which is to be introduced next session) for laying a tax of two shillings in the pound on the estates of absentee landlords.

DUBLIN, June 18.

Amongst the dispatches brought over is the appointment of the Right Hon. John Fitzgibbon, to the office of Lord Chancellor of Ireland.

Yesterday Mr. Fitzgibbon, while pleading in Court, received by one of the Marquis's Aid-de-camps—the King's Letter, appointing him Cancellor of Ireland.

It was expected that, as this day he would be sworn, and by Saturday take his seat on the Bench.

The Trustees of the Linen Manufacture, at their meeting on the 26th ult. adopted several resolutions tending highly to the interest of the staple manufacture of this kingdom, and among others entered into the following, which we impart with the more pleasure, as it is to be hoped so excellent an idea will lead to similar arrangements at other Boards in Great Britain and Ireland.

"Resolved, that if the Chamberlain, or any other officer attending the Linen hall, shall demand, take, or accept of any perquisite, gratuity, fee or reward, from any merchant, draper, or other person attending the said hall, he shall forfeit his said office, and be rendered incapable of holding any office under this Board, pursuant to the provision made by law for that purpose.

"And if, after public notice be given thereof, any merchant, draper, or other person attending the said Hall, shall give or offer, directly or indirectly, any gratuity, fee, or reward, or make any promise of the same, to the said Chamberlain, or other officer attending the Hall, such merchant, draper, or person, shall never after be allowed any room or standing in the buildings at the said Hall, either by himself, or by any factor or other person whatever."

It must afford the highest satisfaction to every wellwisher of Ireland, that the collieries of this kingdom are beginning to be worked with the most sedulous attention; and we have the pleasure to be informed, that several thousand tons of coals have been, within these few weeks, imported into this city, from the colliery of Murlogh, near Cape Fair, in the county of Antrim; those coals are of an extraordinary good quality, and peculiarly adapted for the use of lime-burners, and come so reasonable as at eight pence the hundred weight.

A spirited house at Waterford exported, the middle of last week, thirty-six thousand yards of plain and printed linens and cottons, for Cadiz and Seville, where Irish piece goods of that kind are in great demand. When the prodigious extent of the kingdom of Spain is considered, being above six hundred miles in length, and near five hundred in breadth, divided into many provinces, some of which are equal to a middling kingdom, we may see our interest in cultivating a trade with that people, who are capable of consuming much more than we could possibly manufacture. The ports of Cadiz and Seville alone are marts from whence the large provinces of Andalusia, Murcia, Granada, and New and Old Castile are generally supplied with every species of foreign ware; a tract of country not inferior in extent to the whole kingdom of Ireland.

Saturday last the convicts, 127 in number, were shipped on board the brig Duchess of Leinster, destined for Baltimore, in Maryland. The Rev. Mr. Fay, not being allowed a coach, went in an open machine, called the Kilmainham cart.—The caravan consisted of thirteen carriages, including Cox's berlin and M'Kinley's landau.

DUBLIN June, 20.

One fourth of our Bishops are now Irishmen, a circumstance hitherto unknown since the time of the Reformation.—Our present Lord Chancellor and Solicitor General are also the same.—The Chancellor of the Exchequer, Speaker of the House of Commons, and many others in high office, are also of this country.

A great number of new and important regulations are spoken of with confidence; the chief, it is said are,

The abolition of the office of Vice-Treasurers, by which the national expenditure will be eased of the sum of 10,500l annually.—The establishment of a Board of Excise, separate and distinct from the Board of Customs, with four additional Commissioners at 500l. per annum each.

The separation of the Board of Imprest Accounts from the Commissioners of Stamps.

By all which the expences of the nation will be reduced 5000l. per annum, and sinecure places annihilated.

Belfast, *June* 26.

A Correspondent has requested us to remind the importers, venders and retailers of spirits, that yesterday was the 25th day of June—one of those quarter days on which they are obliged by law to return to the Collector an exact account of all spirits in their possession, on pain of twenty pounds.

We are requested to inform the Publick, that Mr. Cullen, an eminent Dentist, from Dublin, is on his way to this town, and will arrive in two or three days.—His stay will be very short.

Died, on Friday last, at Cumber, much and deservedly lamented, the Rev. William Henry, Minister of the Dissenting Congregation of that place.

PORT NEWS.

ARRIVED.

June 15. Peggy, M'Ilroy, Liverpool, rum and bale goods.
New Draper, M'Nillage, ditto, sugar and bale goods.
17. William, Hodgson, Gloucester and Chepstow, bark and cyder.
Sara Frederica, Steinbock, Dantzick, timber and ashes.
20. Peggy and Mary, Jones, Gloucester, cyder and cheese.
Fourteen colliers.

CLEARED OUT.

June 15. Unity, Boyd, Liverpool, ballast.
Adventure, Robertson, Drunton, ditto.
19. Lovely Ann, Vousden, Jamaica, linen cloth.

Belfast.

With considerable pleasure the Editor of THE BELFAST NEWS-LETTER inserts the following animated Sketch of the Rise, Progress, and Effects of the Volunteer Institution in Ireland; extracted from *Chambers's Irish* Edition of Gutherie's Improved SYSTEM OF MODERN GEOGRAPHY, just published in Dublin by Subscription.

VOLUNTEERS OF IRELAND.

These associations originated in the year 1778, from the acknowledged inability of an ill-regulated government to guard the island, then threatened with invasion; and from the dictatorial necessity of self-defence, imposed on the people by such shameful dereliction on the part of their rulers. It was the pressure of a calamitous war on a country, in which all the joints of the state were loosened, and government itself had become a grievance, rendered still more intolerable by the ruinous effects of an embargo in the south, and the fluctuating fortuitous demand for the staple manufacture in the north, which at length roused the public mind from a numbness that had locked up all its energy. The people, instead of railing with lazy wickedness at providence, endeavoured to help themselves. They did not tumble over the statute book to know by what law they could set themselves in array, but they acted under the law of Nature; and the storm of war that seemed to seek their ruin, was the occasion that proved them strong. Necessity made the people of Ireland take up arms, but many of the most active and noble principles of human nature kept them Volunteers.

Common danger made all ranks of men unite in a common cause; and every rank rose in self-consequence and attained greater elevation in the scale of society. Their coalescence brought men into a closer sphere of attraction. Patriotism became less a speculative sentiment, and more a principle of action; a passionate prepossession that moved within a smaller circle than the empire, but acquired force by the condensation.

1. The Volunteers saved their country in the time of war, and kept it in guarded quiet. If the standing army had remained in the island, the invasion would probably have taken place: for when a mercenary force is the sole instrument of national defence, the nation must fall with it: the inhabitants surrender with the garrison. But when martial spirit was infused into the whole people, the island became encompassed as with a circle of fire.

2. The Volunteers of Ireland promoted civil liberty in the time of peace. They did not lay down their arms when the war was over, but retained them as pledges of peace, whose blessings they could cultivate best by being always prepared for war.

3. The Volunteers promoted religious liberty and liberality in Ireland. They associated, although differing in religious opinions, because they wished to create that union of power, and to cultivate that brotherhood of affection among all the inhabitants of the island, which is the interest as well as duty of all. They were all Irishmen.

4. The Volunteers of Ireland promoted, perhaps created, national liberty. They appeared under the character of soldiers, without any design of relinquishing for a moment, the name or nature of citizens, but with a view of adding constitutional energy to that sacred title, by adopting a new but consistent appellation.

5. The Volunteers endeavoured to promote the internal liberty of the legislature as well as its external independence, by an adequate *reform in the representative body*; such a reform as might utterly destroy the most noxious of national nuisances; which makes bribery and corrupt influence a principal spring of government, from whence it oozes down thro' all the distinctions of rank, and all the classes of venality, till it mixes with and completely vitiates the mass of the multitude. Their endeavours were unsuccessful, but by no means inglorious.

Anno 1789.] Printed by HENRY JOY, and Co. BELFAST.

The BELFAST NEWS-LETTER.

TUESDAY June 30, — FRIDAY July 3, 1789.

Money wanted.

THE Sum of Three Thouſand Pounds Sterl. on a Mortgage of an unincumbered Eſtate, ſituated in the County of Antrim.——Application to be made to James Moore, Attorney at Law, Cloverhill, near Antrim. Dated 27th June, 1789.

A good Coach, and Harneſs for four Harneſs,

TO be ſold by Auction, on Friday next, at twelve o'clock, oppoſite the Donegall-Arms, Belfaſt.

29th June, 1789.

JAMES SHERIDAN.

County of Armagh. } BY virtue of a Precept to me directed, I do hereby require the attendance of the Seneſchals, Coroners, High, Petty, and Sub-Conſtables of ſaid County at a General Quarter Seſſions of the Peace to be held at Lurgan on Thurſday the 16th day of July next.

Dated this 28th day of June, 1789.

JAMES VERNER, Sheriff.

THE Maſters, Wardens, and Brethren of the different Lodges of the town and neighbourhood of Belfaſt, aſſembled on St. John's Day (the 24th inſt) reſpectfully beg leave to return their ſincere thanks to the Rev. George Portis for his excellent diſcourſe delivered before them on the above occaſion.

Belfaſt, 29th June, 1789.

THE Maſter, Wardens, and Brethren, of the Lodge of Unity Donariſk, No. 668, requeſt Lodge No. 479 may accept of their hearty thanks for the attention and politeneſs which they received from them on the 24th June inſt.——They alſo return thanks to the Rev. Jos. Ferguſon, for his excellent diſcourſe delivered before them on the above occaſion.

Signed by order,
Wm. PARK, Sec.

To be Sold,

A Leaſe for ever, of a good Houſe and Offices, and thirty Acres of Land, pleaſantly ſituated near the ſea, within half a mile of the Giants Cauſway.

Application to be made to Mr. Lyle, Colerain.

June 29th, 1789.

WHEREAS Captain Henry Helcraw, (of the Brig Matty of Workington) has been miſſing ſince Monday 22d inſtant. Said Helcraw is a man of about 5 feet 6 inches high, thin faced; had on a brown wig, a blue jacket, and brown ſlip coat. Any perſon that can give any intelligence of him, by applying at the Ballaſt-Office, Belfaſt, ſhall be handſomely rewarded.

Belfaſt, 29th June, 1789.

Hillsborough Races, 1789.

ON Monday the 20th of July, will be run for over the Maze Courſe, the King's Plate for Iriſh bred Horſes not exceeding 6 years old, carrying 12 ſtone, 4 mile heats

On Tueſday the 21ſt, 50 Guineas, given by the Royal Corporation of horſe breeders, for Horſes bred in the County of Down, 4 years old, 8 ſtone, 5 years old, 9 ſtone; 2 mile heats—3lb to Mares.

On Wedneſday the 22d, 60 Guineas, Subſcription Plate, for 6 years old, 8ſt. 7lb. and aged Horſes 9 ſtone, 4 mile heats, 3lb. to Mares.

On Thurſday the 23d, 60 Guineas, Subſcription Plate, for 4 year olds carrying 8 ſtone, 2 mile heats, 3lb. to Mares.

On Friday the 24th, 50 Guineas, given by the Royal Corporation of Horſe-breeders for 5 year olds, carrying 8ſt. 7lb. 3 mile heats, 3lb. to Mares.

Same day, 50 Guineas, Corporation Plate, for 3 year olds, weight 8ſt. heats, the Hillſborough Mile, 3lb. to Mares.

Saturday the 25th, a Sweepſtakes of 20 Guineas each, for Horſes that never ſtarted for any given Prize whatever, weight 12 ſtone, 2 mile heats.

Same day, the King's Plate for 4 year olds, 7ſt. 11lb. and 5 year old 9 ſtone, 2 mile heats, 3. Mares.

Same day, 50 Guineas given by the Governor for 6 year olds, 8ſt. 10lb. and aged Horſes 9 ſtone, 3 mile heats.

To enter on Monday the 13th of July at 4 o'clock, Subſcribers of 2 Guineas or upwards, to pay one Guinea entrance, all others 3 Guineas; or double before 12 o'clock on the day of running —King's Plate articles.— If any diſputes, to be finally determined by the Corporation.—Ordinaries and Balls as uſual.

The Governor requeſts that ſuch Members of the Corporation as have not ſubſcribed, will pleaſe to ſend their Subſcriptions before, or on the firſt day of the meeting.

30th June, 1789. FRANCIS SAVAGE, Governor.

☞ Whereas Francis Buckle, on account of unfair riding was at laſt Curragh Meeting diſqualified from riding for any Plate, Match or Prize at the Curragh for two years from that date. He is therefore hereby diſqualified alſo from riding at the Maze or Downpatrick, for 2 years

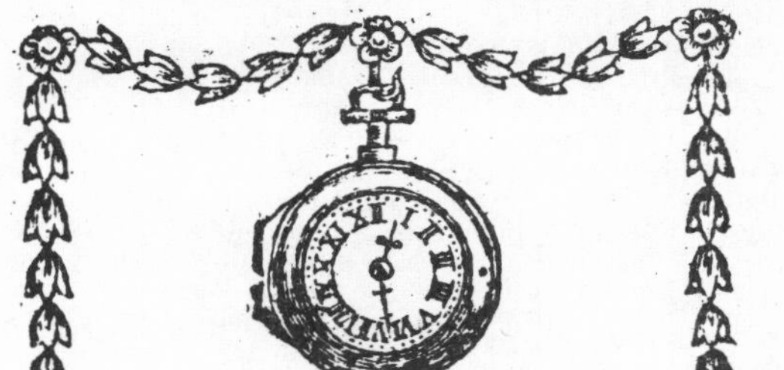

J. KNOX, Watchmaker, &c.

At the GOLD WATCH, High Street,

(Licenſed to buy and ſell Gold and Silver Ware)

RESPECTFULLY informs his Friends, that he has at all times ready for Sale, a variety of Watches in Gold, Silver, and Metal Caſes, on the neweſt Conſtruſtions;—Clocks and every other Article in the above Line.

WHEREAS my Wife Elizabeth Greer, otherwiſe O'Neill, of Morvillan, in the pariſh of Derrinooſe and county of Armagh, has eloped from me and carried away ſeveral Articles of value, my property:— Now I do hereby give notice that I will not pay any debt ſhe may contract, and that I will proſecute any perſon concealing my goods.——Given under my hand this 24th day of June, 1789

ALEXANDER O'NEILL.

Crown Glaſs-Works, Belfaſt.

WANTED,

A Few ſtout Lads of about ſixteen years of age, as Apprentices to the Glaſs Manufacture: They muſt have very good characters and ſufficient ſecurities. Good encouragement will be given them, their wages advancing very conſiderably every year, in proportion to their merit.——Apply to

JOHN SMYLIE & Co.

N. B. Crown Window Glaſs, of a remarkably fine quality, and a great variety of Garden Bell Glaſſes, and Gooſberry Bottles for ſale at ſaid Glaſs-Houſe; where Straw and coarſe Hay for packing is wanted, for which the higheſt price will be given.

July 3d, 1789.

THE Preſbyterians of the Pariſhe of Killinſhy, Tullynakill and Kilmud, who worſhip at Ballow, conceive themſelves now called upon and in duty bound to explain the preſent ſtate of their Congregation to a diſcerning publick, to whom they owe, and for whom they feel the higheſt reſpect.

An Advertiſement of the 18th of May laſt appeared in this Paper, expreſſing that a Meeting-houſe was to be built in Liſban, which is in the pariſh of Tullynakill, and within the bounds of this congregation. In conſequence the Miniſter, Seſſion and Congregation, thinking it neceſſary on this emergency fully to collect the ſenſe of the people, did unanimouſly, on Sabbath the 31ſt of May, publiſh a meeting of the Congregation to be on Tueſday the ſecond day of this inſtant, when accordingly, at a very full meeting after divine ſervice, the preſent ſtate of the congregation, and particularly the efforts of a few individuals to effect an erection at Liſban, came to be conſidered. The cloſe affectionate ſpiritual union between the Miniſter and People manifeſted at this meeting cannot fail to adminiſter pleaſure to every candid good mind. The Preſbyterians have expreſſed their great diſſatisfaction with the attempts now made to divide our ancient congregation. The principal gentlemen in the neighbourhood have been applied to, and have refuſed giving countenance or aid to the erection.

The greater part of the very ſmall number who have declared for it, in all their applications to gentlemen for ground on which to build a Meeting-houſe, ſaid they had no objections againſt the preſent Miniſter of Killinſhy. One, and he a leading man among them, declared he loved him in his heart; another boaſted of the intention of the party to procure him as their Miniſter; and Alexander Johnſon the principal, profeſſed himſelf influenced in this buſineſs not by religion but motives of intereſt, expecting as he expreſſes it, profits from keeping publick entertainment. Beſides, the ſmall party at Liſban has trampled on the government and diſcipline of the Preſbyterian Church, in procuring or admitting a perſon to preach among them who is neither ſubject to, nor has he an appointment from our Synod, nor any Preſbytery in this kingdom; who in his attempts in this place, as is probably ſuppoſed, hath uſed unhandſome devices tending to ſeduce the ſimple and unwary; and who, moreover, hath ſuggeſted an intention of ſettling as an Independent in Liſban.

An enlightened world will judge with what propriety an advertiſement, dated the 24th inſt. ſigned Alexander Johnſon, calls a few individuals in ſuch circumſtances the Preſbyterian Congregation of Liſban. To what Preſbytery do they belong? Of what Seſſion is Alexander Johnſon the Clerk? for we never heard of a Seſſion at Liſban. How many pariſhioners of Tullynakill have joined their ſociety? Where was the man amongſt them to produce a ſingle charge againſt our worthy Paſtor's character on the day appointed for the general meeting?

They were informed that one of his deſigns of calling a meeting was, that he might have an opportunity of vindicating his character if charges appeared.

Mr. Mc. Ewen repeatedly called for ſuch charges, when none appeared; but on the contrary, the moſt honourable teſtimonies to his miniſterial uſefulneſs and fidelity.

The Preſbyterians then of the united pariſhes of Killinſhy, Tullynakill, and Kilmud, beg leave to do juſtice to the publick by aſſuring them, that any contributions for the Meeting-houſe in Liſban, on them at leaſt, do not confer any favour.

Done at our Meeting-houſe in Ballow, after divine ſervice, this 28th June, 1789, and ſigned in the name and by the unanimous order of the Congregation, by

JAMES LOWRY, Seſſion Clerk.

To the Revd. GEORGE M'EWEN,

Reverend and much reſpected Sir,

We, a very great majority of the inhabitants of the pariſh of Tullynakil, have read with aſtoniſhment and abhorrence, a libellous advertiſement dated the 24th inſt. in the Belfaſt News-Letter, and ſigned Alexander Johnſon; in which there is an attempt to engage the publick to aſſiſt in the building a Meeting-houſe in Liſban on the ruins of your amiable character.

From you we have experienced the "moſt uſeful and paſtoral labours," of a Miniſter of Chriſt, who needeth not to be aſhamed, rightly dividing the word of truth. To us, your publick performances have been edifying and agreeable; we know your moral character is pleaſing, and are perſuaded that you have diſcharged the ſacred duties of the paſtoral office with aſſiduity and care.

You, Sir, need not to be informed by us that a malicious perſecution of a faithful Miniſter of Chriſt is no new thing in the Hiſtory of the Church; and that the providence of God can ſo over-rule the wicked purpoſes and paſſions of men, as to make them miniſter to his people's benefit and to his own glory and praiſe.

We derive much pleaſure from bearing teſtimony to your character, when thus publickly and unjuſtly attacked; and in aſſuring you and the publick that we are with duty and eſteem, reſpectfully and ſincerely

Your's

Signed in the name and by order of the inhabitants of Tullynakil in the Meeting-Houſe in Ballow, this 28th June, 1789, by

ROBERT BRENNAN,
ROBERT HAMILTON,
SAMUEL STEWART,
WILLIAM BERRY.

The Preſbyterians of the pariſh of Killinſhy and Kilmud, heartily concur with their brethren of the pariſh of Tullynakill. Signed in their name and by their order, by JAMES LOWRY, Seſſion Clerk.

My Dear Friends,

Accept my warmeſt acknowledgments for the inexpreſſible ſatisfaction, which I have always derived from your kindneſs and zeal in the cauſe of truth; and particularly for the protection and ſupport which your publick teſtimony now gives me in the world. Your approbation and that of the other worthy Members of the Congregation, have made impreſſions on my mind, that cannot be eaſily, or ſoon, effaced. In what manner, as a Miniſter of Chriſt, I have been enabled, through grace, to conduct myſelf among you, it now better becomes you than me to ſay——I am, faithfully & affectionately your's

Roſſvale, June 29, 1789.

G M'EWEN.

THE Proteſtant Congregation of Liſban are ſorry to trouble the Public with diſputes in which they are ſo little intereſted. The tendency of the publications from Killinchy is too obvious to need any comment. The Congregation of Liſban are conſiderably advanced in building a Meeting-houſe, and all they contend for is a privilege they think themſelves intitled to in common with every ſubject of the Britiſh Empire—namely, liberty to worſhip their Maker how and where they pleaſe.—This they confeſs they dare ſcarcely hope for in the neighbourhood of a Clergyman, who, after aſſembling his Congregation in the ſame houſe where he preaches the goſpel of peace, declares his intention of going at their head on the *glorious expedition* of horſe-whipping their Miniſter out of the country.

Signed by order of the Seſſion of Liſban,

ALEXANDER JOHNSTON.

Henderſon and Crawford,

ARE now landing a Cargo of Swediſh Bar Iron: They have alſo for Sale, Bliſter and German Steel, Iron Hoops, beſt Alicante Barilla, Dantzick Weed and Pearl Aſhes, and ſome very good Blanter Oats.

FRANCE.

THE STATES-GENERAL.

VERSAILLES, JUNE 18.

I have been preſent at the three laſt days debates of the Commons, which have indeed been intereſting.—All the principal ſpeakers diſtinguiſhed themſelves.

The Aſſembly on Monday ſat till midnight.

The great queſtion turned on the mode of forming themſelves into an active body, and the title they ſhould aſſume. That of "The National Aſſembly" was at length adopted, after continuing the adjourned debate all Tueſday. Yeſterday morning the powers being all verified, the Commons formally proceeded to vote themſelves the National Aſſembly of France, competent to perform all legiſlative acts conjointly with the King. Their firſt ſtep, in conſequence of this important reſolution, was to declare all the preſent taxes and impoſitions whatſoever NULL and VOID, *de facto*, as not having been granted by the nation; and the next operation to re-eſtabliſh them by the authority of, and until the concluſion of, the National Aſſembly; by this means ſecuring their own exiſtence, unleſs the royal authority, by any violent act of diſſolution, ſhould venture to riſk the conſequences of a refuſal to pay taxes on the part of the nation. They then came to a conditional reſolution to take upon themſelves the national debt, &c. About two o'clock, when theſe important proceedings were at an end, the Preſident was ſent for to receive from the Keeper of the Seals the promiſed anſwer to their juſtificatory addreſs to the King of laſt week, which was read to a very full aſſembly. The galleries of the hall, which are capable of containing near three thouſand people, as well as all the avenues, were completely crouded.

LONDON, *FRIDAY*, JUNE 24.

His Majeſty yeſterday morning breakfaſted at the Biſhop of Wincheſter's Caſtle, at Farnham He arrived at Wincheſter a quarter paſt twelve; at Romſey about two; and at Lyndhurſt, the end of his journey, exactly ten minutes paſt three.

He was received with the uſual ceremony at Lamb's Corner, near Redbridge, by the Lord Warden, Deputy Warden, Verdurers, Gentlemen, Keepers, &c. in a line of proceſſion. They accompanied him to Lyndhurſt.

The Prince of Wales has ſuſpended his intentions of viſiting Ireland this year.

This day ſeveral of the nobility were to take leave of their Majeſties and the Royal Family at Windſor Lodge, previous to their ſetting off on the Summer excurſion.

On the 31ſt of May, his Excellency General Waſhington was unanimouſly inſtalled with the dignity of Chief Magiſtrate of the United States of America.

TRIAL OF WARREN HASTINGS, ESQ.

WESTMINSTER-HALL.

FIFTEENTH DAY.

The Lords came into the Hall at a quarter paſt two.

The Lord Chancellor informed the managers, the Lords were of opinion, that the account offered in evidence ought not to be read.

Lord Portcheſter ſaid, their Lordſhips having formed their deciſion on the opinion of the Judges, he ſhould move that the Judges deliver their opinion in open Court, according to the ancient uſuage of Parliament; that both parties might know the principle on which that opinion was founded. He had two ſhort queſtions to put to the Judges, on which he deſired their opinion might be delivered in this manner.

The Lord Chancellor inſtantly moved to adjourn; and the Lords returned to their own Chamber of Parliament, where they debated on Lord Portcheſter's propoſition, for ſeveral hours, and at ſix o'clock ſent a meſſage to the Commons, that they will proceed farther in the trial on Tueſday next.

DUBLIN JUNE, 25.

Laſt week a company at Dungarven, exported on board the Lively, bound for the Mediterranean, ſix thouſand pieces of ſtamped linen, four thouſand ditto manufactured cotton cloth, ſix hundred and forty-ſix dozen plain and figured cotton ſtockings, chiefly white and dove colour, for the Leghorn market; where goods of thoſe denominations are beginning to be in conſiderable demand.—We are very happy to hear that the above goods were manufactured in the counties of Waterford and Wexford within the laſt ſix months.

Monday evening, arrived from England, Mr. Ryder the celebrated comedian.—Mr. Kelly and Mrs. Crouch are alſo arrived in this city.

BANKRUPT. Nicholas Fitzpatrick, of the city of Kilkenny, chandler, to ſurrender on the 14th and 16th days of July next, and on the 6th of Auguſt following.

A Liſt of the Abſentee Peers of Ireland, with the annual incomes of thoſe who have eſtates in this Kingdom, prefixed to their names; the others have no property here, except ſome that have mortgages on lands, &c.

Earls of	
Clanricarde‡*	£.12,000
Cork and Orrery	7,000
Weſtmeath	3,000
Do. a penſion	800
Deſmond	
Barrymore	10,000
Donegal*	40,000
Cavan,* a penſion only	300
Inchiquin*	10,000
Mountrath	10,000
Waterford and Wexford.	
Athlone	
Fitzwilliam	30,000
Kerry	7,000
Darnley*	12,000
Egmont	6,000
Beſborough	10,000
Verney	2,500
Hillſborough*	15,000
Upper Oſſory	8,000
Shelburne	16,000
Maſſereene	4,000
Louth*	6,000
Fife	
Mornington*	6,000
Ludlow*	6,000
Tyrconnel	
Courtown*	4,000
Mexborough	
Winterton	
Sefton	2,000
Altamont‡*	6,000
Liſburne	1,000
Glandore‡*	4,000
Aldborough‡*	8,000
Clermont*	10,000
Viſcounts.	
Grandiſon of Limeric	2,000
Kilmorey	
Lumley	
Wenman	
Taaffe	800
Fitzwilliam of Merrion	5,000
Cullen	
Tracy	
Bulkely	
Kingſland*	
Cholmondeley	

Viſcounts.	
Downe	
Howe*	
Strabane	£.18,000
Moleſworth	4,000
Middleton	8,000
Grimſton	
Barrington	
Gage	
Palmerſtown*	8,000
Bateman	
Galway	
Aſhbrooke*	5,000
Mountmorres*	3,400
Dungannon*	4,000
Southwell*	5,000
Melbourne	
Cremorne*	8,000
Barons.	
Cahier*	10,000
Digby	4,000
Sherard	
Conway	16,000
Carbery	6,000
Aylmer, a penſion only	400
Forteſcue	1,500
Carysfort*	3,000
Milton	15,000
Liſle*	6,000
Coleraine	
Clive	2,000
Mulgrave	
Arden*	
Macartney*	3,000
Milford	
Newborough	
Lucan*	5,000
Macdonald	
Newhaven*	3,000
Kenſington	3,000
Weſtcote	2,000
Ongley	
Shuldham	1,000
Templetown	4,000
Rokeby*	1,000
Conyngham*	10,000
Sheffield	3,000
Hood	
Delaval	
Muncaſter	
Penryhn	
De Montalt*	8,000

Thoſe marked thus ‡, have lately become Abſentees, owing to their marrying Engliſh ladies.

Thoſe marked thus *, occaſionally viſit Ireland.

DUBLIN, JUNE 30.

This afternoon, the Right Hon. the Lord Chancellor, and the Right Hon. the Speaker of the Houſe of Commons, were ſworn Lords Juſtices of Ireland, at the Caſtle.

Letters received yeſterday morning here from London, contain the very diſagreeable advice, that a capital houſe in the lottery line there had failed for near half a million ſterling.

The Royal Canal, which is on the point of being undertaken, is to form a navigation by a north-weſt line from this city to the great river Shannon, we are credibly informed, it has the happy circumſtance attending it, that in the firſt fourteen miles, from the metropolis, there is one level for nine miles, without the neceſſity of a ſingle lock.

New potatoes have, notwithſtanding the late inclemency of the weather, been ſold in the courſe of laſt week in our markets for four-pence a pound.

Sunday there fell a very heavy ſhower of hail, which is a circumſtance rather uncommon at this ſeaſon of the year.

LONDON-DERRY, JUNE 23.

Since our laſt, the ſhip Nancy, Capt. Crawford, ſailed for Philadelphia, having on board near 300 paſſangers.

DIED.] Mr. John Atchiſon, merchant.—At Caſtlefin, Mr. Henry Darus.—Near Cowthill, in conſequence of a fall from his horſe, Robert Foſter, Eſq; of Coolck.—Buncrana, Dermot Kennedy, a native of Scotland, aged 108 years; he was 8 years old at the famous battle of Killycranky; he came to Ireland, and lived many years at Ballycaſtle, and afterwards took up his reſidence in Iniſhowen; he never could ſpeak any dialect but Erſe, or Iriſh; he married a ſecond wife when between 70 and 80, and has left a daughter now aged about 30 years.

SUMMER ASSIZES.

NORTH-WEST CIRCUIT.

Co. Weſtmeath, at Mullingar,	Thurſday, July	23
Longford, at Longford,	Monday,	27
Cavan, at Cavan,	Thurſday,	30
Fermanagh, at Enniſkillen,	Monday, Aug.	3
Tyrone, at Omagh,	Friday,	7
Donegall, at Liſford,	Friday,	14
City and Co Londonderry, at Derry,	Tueſday,	18

The Right Hon. Lord Earlsfort, } Juſtices.
The Hon. Baron Power }

John Bradſhaw, Eſq; } Regiſters.
Richard Evans, Eſq; }

The Grand Juries of Weſtmeath, Longford, Cavan, and Donegall will be ſworn early on the reſpective Commiſſion days, and all buſineſs will be then proceeded on, and all Records throughout the Circuit are to be entered with the Regiſters on the Commiſſion days before the ſitting of the Court.

Belfaſt, *June* 30.

The Peggy, James M'Ilroy maſter, loaded with linen cloth for Cheſter Fair, ſailed early yeſterday morning, with a fair wind, which ſtill continues.

The Hillſborough, Wm. M'Donald maſter, will ſail for Liverpool on Wedneſday next, with the remainder of the linens for Cheſter Fair.

The London Packet, James Glaſs maſter, now in the port of Newry, will ſail for Cheſter Fair the 1ſt of July next.

On the 4th of June inſt. the party of the 15th regiment of foot quartered at Carrickfergus, commanded by Serjeant John Harper, fired three vollies in honour of the day with the greateſt exactneſs.

PORT NEWS.

ARRIVED.

June 26. Succeſs, Maziere, Drunthon, deals.
Alexander and Hugh, M'Frederick, do. do.
27. Charles, Neil, Gottenburgh, Iron, &c.
Mary, Skelton, Dronton, deals.
Two colliers, coals.

CLEARED OUT.

June 22. Elizabeth, Kraus, Dantzick, Ballaſt.
23. New Loyalty, Brown, Liverpool, butter and ſkins.

Belfaſt, *July* 3.

On Wedneſday laſt, (anniverſary of the Battle of the Boyne) the Lords Hillſborough and Dungannon were ſplendidly entertained by a number of very reſpectable inhabitants of this place.

The Charlotte, William Campbell, maſter for London, is cleared out, and is detained only by contrary winds.

Married, on Monday laſt, Mr. Richard M'Clelland, ſurgeon, to Miſs Tabitha Lewis, daughter to the late James Lewis of the Grove, Eſq.—The Rev. Rich. Babington of Derry to Miſs Boyie of Dungiven.

Died, the Rev. Mr. Adams, Diſſenting Miniſter of the pariſh of Dungiven.

THE Congregation of Liſban, highly ſenſible of the impropriety of Newſpaper altercations, would not upon any account give the publick the trouble of peruſing this, were it not to refute one paragraph, in the Killinſhy Correſpondence of Tueſday laſt——the Seſſion Clerk in his *extraordinary Lucubrations*, repreſents the gentleman called to be their Miniſter as a perſon who, "as it is probably ſuppoſed hath uſed unhandſome devices tending to ſeduce the unwary".—The meaning of this, (as they poſſeſs but ordinary capacities) they confeſs does not appear to them altogether evident; if it has any, they ſuppoſe it implies an inſinuation againſt a perſon who by no means merits it; and they think it incumbent upon them to declare ſolemnly in this public manner, that he neither directly nor indirectly, adviſed or encouraged their ſeparation, but that it was a meaſure long projected and determined upon before they knew he was in exiſtence, and publickly intimated in Killinſhy congregation before he received their call.—The perſon who informed the Seſſion Clerk, that he ſuggeſted an intention of ſettling as an Independent, might have been under the ſame miſtake as he who informed him, that they boaſted of their intentions to make Mr. Mc. Ewen their Miniſter.—The congregation of Liſban congratulate their brethren upon the harmony that ſubſiſts between their paſtor and them; and tho' for the future they are to worſhip in different houſes, they deſire ever to recollect that they worſhip the ſame benevolent Parent, whoſe nature is LOVE, whoſe religion is PEACE.

Signed by the committee in the name of the congregation of LISBAN, the firſt day of July, 1789.

Robert Maxwell,	Joſeph Snoddan,
Samuel Johnſton,	Johas Minis,
Robert Minis,	William Shiels,
William Snoddan,	William Sloan

Anno 1789.] Printed by HENRY JOY, and Co. BELFAST.

The BELFAST NEWS-LETTER.

TUESDAY July 7, FRIDAY July 10, 1789.

Alexander Orr,

HAS just received a large Parcel of Demerera Cotton Wool, and Alicant Barrilla, both of the very best quality, which he will sell on the lowest terms.

Belfast, 10th July, 1789.

N. B. He has also two Casks of remarkably fine English Cyder to dispose of at 11d. per gallon; a few Chests of Hyson and Singlo Teas.

FLOUR.

BROWN and OAKMAN lately landed a quantity of first and second Flour from Dublin, of a good quality, which will be sold cheap, at their Stores in Waring-street.

Belfast, 9th July, 1789.

Cotton Wool.

SEEDS, WELLS, and SEEDS, have imported for Sale a few Bales of the very best *Demerary* Cotton Wool: Also, by the Lord Donegall, Captain Mc. Roberts, from London, a parcel of Kent Hops in Bags, being of the first quality.——Bills on Dublin or Belfast at two and three months date will be taken in payment, or discount allowed for cash.

Belfast, 11th July, 1789.

The Belfast Banks,

OBSERVING inconvenience to have arisen from the General Bankers Holydays being kept by them, have come to the resolution in future to keep Saturday in each Week, Christmas-Day, and Good Friday as Holydays—to which regulation the Publick are requested to attend, as no discounting or other business will in future be transacted at either of the Banks on the days herein mentioned—except on Saturdays during the White Linen Market.

Belfast, 6th July, 1789.

TO BE LET,

From the first of November next,

THAT Farm in Ballyloughan, in the parish of Comber, now in the possession of Mr. Gillespie, held under the Right Hon. Robert Stewart, by a lease for lives, two of which (young men) are in being: The lands are in high condition, containing about 37 acres, of which ten are meadow; the Dwelling-house is fit for the immediate reception of a genteel family, with suitable Offices, an exceeding good Garden, and Orchard of three acres in full bearing; there is also a very fine Ozier Garden, two years old; the whole concern admirably well situated, in a genteel neighbourhood, on the great road leading from Comber to Belfast; there is a sufficient proportion of Moss belonging to the same; the Tenant may be accommodated with any quantity of turf, hay, oats, barley, potatoes, &c. at a valuation.———Application to be made to the Revd. Robert Mortimer, Comber, or the proprietor on the premisses.

July the 2d, 1789.

To be sold by Auction,

On Friday the 4th Day of next September, at the Donegall-Arms, Belfast, at 12 o'Clock,

A Fee Farm Deed of part of the Lands of Ballycloughan, most eligibly situated on the great road leading from Comber to Saintfield, and not more than eight miles from Belfast.—These lands are subject only to 13l. per ann. chief-rent, payable to Daniel Mussenden, Esq; and now yield a clear profit rent of 101l. 2s. 5d. per annum: There is one Farm of 34 acres out of lease, on which there have been erected within these few years, a most comfortable Farm-House and good Offices; another Farm depends on the lives of two old men, at the expiration of which it will rise 20l. per ann.——Ballycloughan is in the middle of a fine sporting country, and well provided with turbary. For the convenience of the purchaser, 1,000l. or 1,500l. of the purchase money may remain in his hands, on giving satisfactory security; the remainder to be paid on perfection of the deeds. Further particulars may be had by applying to the proprietor, Mr. Reid of Ballygowan.

Ballygowan, July 2d, 1789.

NOTICE.

A Letter, directed for Robert Stewart, Esq; near Belfast, was put into the Liverpool Post-Office, which Letter contained a Bill for 300l. accepted by Henry Fairclough & Co. of Liverpool, and payable at the house of Down, Thornton & Free, Bankers in London, and due the 20th instant; and as said Letter nor Bill have never come to hand, it is supposed to have fallen into some improper hands: NOW this is to caution the Publick not to receive or give any value for said Bill, as payment is stopp'd in London.

ROBERT STEWART.

Dated Ballydrain, 1st July, 1789.

A Freehold to be sold in Ballymacarret,

CONSISTING of two Fields, upwards of five Acres, Town Parks, all under Crop: In which are excellent Wheat, Meadow and Oats, most of which was last year highly manured and laid down with Grass Seed—The Lease 41 years or three lives from May 1786.

Apply to William Lowry at the Weigh-house.

Belfast, 3d July, 1789.

Advertisement.

WHEREAS on the 16th of June, a Man of the name of Bumford, left a bay Mare with one white foot, about 13 hands high, in Richard Stitt's of Tynan, which Mare was feloniously taken away by Philip M'Anally, who is now in Gaol for the same.—The Mare is now in said Stitt's custody; and from Bumford not since applying for her, it is supposed she is stolen.

Any person paying the expences and proving their property, may have her.

Dated at Tynan, July 1st, 1789.

Robbery and Reward.

ON the night of the 29th May last, a number of persons assembled at the Kiln of Mr. John Crawford of Duncan, county Antrim, who forcibly entered into and feloniously carried away a quantity of Malt, the property of said Crawford, to a considerable amount: And whereas information has been given that William Mills, John Marshall, and John Clarke of Grange, and James Graffan of Largy, all of the county aforesaid, were actively concerned in said felony.

WE the Subscribers promise to pay the several sums annexed to our names to any person or persons, who will give such further information against the seralready mentioned, or any accomplice or accomplices concerned in said felony, so that they or any of them may thereby be apprehended and prosecuted to conviction:—Or if any of the party concerned in said felony will give information as above, they will not only be entitled to the reward, but application made to procure their pardon. Given under our hands this 6th July, 1789.

	l.	s.	d.		l.	s.	d.
Thos. Morris Jones	5	13	9	John Sheil	2	5	6
Alex M'Manus	5	13	9	Samuel Graves	2	5	6
Jas. & Chas. Dickey	5	13	9	Robt. Crawford	3	8	3
Thos. Adams	3	8	3	James Hamersley	2	5	6
Wm. Adams	3	8	3	Edw. Stewart	1	2	9
John French	3	8	3	John Crawford	3	8	3
Robt. Mc. Gee	2	5	6	Arthur Buttle	3	8	3
John Kerr	3	8	3	Wm. Graves	2	5	6
John Brady	3	8	3	Dawson Downing	3	8	3
Robt. Scott	3	8	3	Robert Mc. Crory	1	2	9
John Mecloskey	3	8	3	John M'Leane	1	2	[illegible]
Sam. Crawford	3	8	3	Hugh Crawford	3	8	3
John Spotswood	3	8	3	John Crawford	5	13	9
Andrew Crawford	3	8	3				

WHEREAS John, Coll, and Charles Mc Donnell of Killmore, parish of Laid, County Antrim, Alexander Mc. Donnell of Ballycastle, with others, the 11th inst. did most outrageously and feloniously fire upon and wound us in a most inhuman and *blood thirsty* manner; we beg and request that all Philanthrophists, (and those that would wish to bring the perpetrators of such horrid and unprecedented barbarity to condign punishment) will exert themselves in lodging the above Mc. Donnell's in any of his Majesty's Gaols, to be dealt with according to law. We return our sincere thanks to Alex M'Auley of Glanvil, Esq; and David Mc. Killop of Glenarm, Esq; for their spirited exertions in attempting to bring the aforesaid Mc. Donnells and assistants to trial.

Randle Mc. Alister,
Alex. Mc. Alister, senr † his Mark.
Nariff, 27th June, 1789. Alex. Mc. Alister, junr ‡ his Mark.
Hugh O'Mulvenan, ‡ his Mark.
Alexander Mc. Vey.

THE Master and Brethren of the Glorious Memory Orange Lodge, No. 689, Dungannon, return their sincere thanks to the Revd. Mr. Armstrong, for the excellent Sermon he preached at their request on last St. John's Day.

27th June, 1789.

GAME.

WHEREAS several Persons, (particularly in the neighbourhood of Castle-Caulfield and Dungannon) have made a practice of taking and killing Game on the Estate of the late Thomas Verner, Esq; in the county of Tyrone, without any authority.—I do hereby give notice, that Gamekeepers are appointed to protect the mountains on said estate, and that I will prosecute any person who shall go on said estate to look for or kill game, pursuant to the Game Acts now in force.

Church-Hill, 30th June, 1789. JAMES VERNER.

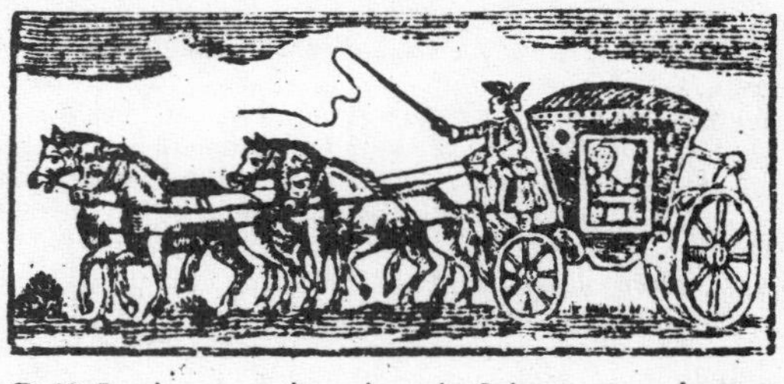

ON Sunday morning the 5th July next, and every succeeding morning, (Saturdays excepted) at the hour of nine o'clock, his Majesty's Mails will be dispatched from the Post-Office of this town in the Mail Coach, under the charge of well-appointed Guards, and will arrive in Dublin at six o'clock every following morning; and, on Saturday night the 4th July next, and every following night, at the hour of eleven o'clock, a Coach with the Mail will also set out from Dublin, and will arrive the following evening in Belfast at 7 o'clock. Passengers to apply for seats in said Coaches at the usual places.—The Coaches upwards will arrive at Newry at a quarter past three o'clock, and set out for Dublin at a quarter past four;—and the Coaches downwards will arrive at Newry forty minutes past eleven o'clock in the morning, and set out from Belfast at forty minutes past twelve.———For the accommodation of passengers, a Coach will set out from Belfast to Dublin every Saturday morning, and from Dublin to Belfast every Sunday night.

Belfast, 30th June, 1789.

THE ensuing Quarter Sessions of the Peace for the County of Antrim, will be held at Antrim on the fifteenth day of July instant, pursuant to precept for that purpose delivered to the Sheriff, where the attendance of the High and Petty Constables is required; and it is hoped for the dispatch of business the Magistrates will send their Examinations and Recognizances, the day before or on that day, to Mr. Heron the Clerk of the Peace at Antrim.

Dated 9th July, 1789.

Private Education.

A Few Pupils are received on moderate Terms at Armagh, by the Revd. W. COKE, A. M. late Fellow of New College in Oxford, and Chaplain to the Marquis of Tweeddale.

Mr. COKE having relinquished his engagements at Armagh School, will endeavour to render his time and labours more immediately serviceable where an early progress is required from such personal attentions as cannot possibly be admitted into the discipline of a public Seminary.

Mr. COKE's number of Pupils will never exceed Twelve: and the only vacation which he allows be always at Midsummer.

Antrim Quarter Sessions.

THE next General Quarter Sessions of the Peace for the County of Antrim will be held at Antrim in and for said County on Thursday the 16th instant, when the attendance of the Coroners, Seneschals, and High Constables will be expected as usual.

Dated 6th July, 1789.

CHARLES CRYMBLE, Sheriff.

The *Sub-Constables* of the Barony of Antrim are desired to attend.

AUCTION

Of Household Furniture, &c.

AT Lisburn, on Monday the 13th July instant, the Household Furniture of Delacherois Crommelin, all in good order, together with a very good full-sized Billiard Table, with Tack, Balls, &c. Also a good Screw and Clips.

N. B. The Auction to begin at 11 o'clock and to continue each day till all are sold.

The House to be set for a term of years, and may be entered upon immediately;——the House, Garden and Offices all in good repair. 6th July, 1789.

☞ Through a typographical error in the former insertion of this advertisement, instead of the house of Delacherois Crommelin, that of Mr. Delacherois was inserted.

Amicable Annuity Company of Newry.

WILL meet at M'Clatchey's tavern on Wednesday the fifth day of August next, to transact the business of the Company and dine together.

All persons wishing to become Members, are desired to apply to the Register 14 days previous to, and appear at the Meeting, otherwise they cannot be balloted for.

JAMES SEARIGHT, Register.

Newry, 2d July, 1789.

PARISIAN INTELLIGENCE.

PARIS, JUNE 25.

The Weather, all on a ſudden, cold, rainy, and damp.

FOR reaſons beſt known to the Miniſtry, his Majeſty did not go to the Aſſembly on Monday, as had been proclaimed in every ſtreet of Verſailles and Paris. The King went from Marly to Verſailles at 11 o'clock, and ſoon after it was whiſpered that the Royal Sitting was poſtponed to the next day. To this report was added an anecdote, that, were it not publicly aſſerted, and contradicted by none, would ſeem hardly credible—That M. Necker, on his return home on Saturday, found a *lettre de cachet*, that deprived him of his charge, and exiled him a certain number of leagues from Verſailles, &c. The worthy Director of the Finances waited on his Majeſty, and, after explaining his conduct on two or three objects that had been miſrepreſented by his enemies (the Nobility) ſoon convinced his Sovereign that ſome evil-minded perſons had impoſed on him. The King immediately tore the unguarded letter, and embracing him, called him his *beſt friend*, and *Protector of the Third Claſs*.

The number of Clergymen who have joined the Commons is upwards of 150: two other Biſhops, Rhodes and Coutances, have ſigned.

The Nobility are more refractory than ever: they came to a reſolution to write a letter to his Majeſty, and 46 members were appointed to wait on him and preſent it. The King received it on Sunday laſt, and did not ſeem diſpleaſed with the contents, to which he returned a favourable anſwer. In this letter the Nobles repreſented the Third Eſtate as actuated by an inordinate ambition, which aimed at depriving the other States, and even the Sovereign, of their privileges and prerogatives.

On Tueſday, at one o'clock in the morning, the Keeper of the Seals intimated to the Preſident of the National Aſſembly, that his Majeſty could not receive the addreſs from the Deputies of the Third Claſs. At nine the Aſſembly doors were opened, and all the Members attended. As ſoon as the Commons were ſeated, they perceived that Linguet, the celebrated lawyer, had been admitted in his bag and ſword. One of the Members immediately roſe, and announced his name to the Aſſembly. Forthwith an univerſal cry of, *out with him*, reſounded through the hall, and he was obliged to quit the premiſſes. He is ſo obnoxious to every body in France for his adviſing his Majeſty, in one of his annals, to become bankrupt, and for having written two treatiſes, one in favour of deſpotiſm, and the other to prove that bread is unwholeſome. *Qu'il ſorte, le gneux!* ſaid loudly one of the Deputies, *il a calomnie juſqu' au pain*. (Out with the ſcoundrel! he has traduced bread itſelf).

REVOLUTION IN FRANCE.

PARIS, JUNE 29.

On Saturday, in conſequence of a letter from the King to the Clergy and Nobility, the members of theſe orders joined the Third Eſtate; and thus happily has terminated the alarming conteſt that has hitherto rendered the meeting of the States nugatory.

This conceſſion of the King was not before it was required, for things here was getting to a moſt alarming height; the army had ſhaken off obedience, and would not have ſtirred a ſtep in ſupport of authority.

It is impoſſible to deſcribe the univerſal joy which this happy event has diffuſed among all ranks of people, as the general opinion now is, that the States will immediately proceed to the great work for which they were aſſembled—the regeneration of credit, and eſtabliſhment of a Conſtitution; the public debt will be conſolidated, and every engagement contracted by the Sovereign fulfilled in the moſt honourable manner.

In the late imminent criſis of public affairs, the dragoons, and all the national troops in the neighbourhood of Paris, loudly declared, that they would neither draw a ſword, nor fire a muſquet againſt their countrymen.

The day after the French Guards refuſed to fire on the people, they were all ordered to be confined to their quarters, both at Paris and Verſailles, except thoſe on duty. They were not, however, to be reſtrained by the orders of their officers, but declaring that they had no intention to be turbulent or deſert, left their barracks, and for the two ſucceeding days amuſed themſelves in walking about the ſtreets, &c. where they were regaled and applauded by their fellow citizens.

Thus one of the moſt important revolutions this country could know, has been happily and almoſt inſtantaneouſly effected without the leaſt bloodſhed!

The body of 150 Clergy, who joined the Third Eſtate, were headed by

The Abp. of Vienna	The Biſhop of Orange
The Abp. of Bourdeaux	The Biſhop of Rhodez, and
The Biſhop of Chartres	The Biſhop of Coutances.

There is a diſtinction paid to the Third Eſtate in France by the other two orders, unknown in this country. At the Royal Seſſion, on the 23d of June, they were received by the Nobles and Clergy, ſtanding and uncovered.

LONDON, JULY 2, and 3.

Monday evening laſt their Majeſties and the three Princeſſes with their ſuite, did Mr. Ballard, of Southampton, the honour of viewing his houſe at Lyndhurſt, which, in point of ſituation, is allowed to command the fineſt and richeſt woodland view in Great Britain. After ſpending near an hour in the colonnade, and amuſing themſelves with excellent teleſcopes, they departed highly pleaſed, and permitted Mr. Ballard to give his charming ſeat the ſtyle of Mount Royal, as a laſting memorial of the very flattering honour he received by ſuch a diſtinguiſhed viſit.

Extract of a Letter from Paris, June 27.

"The troubles of the nation are likely to be increaſed by the great ſcarcity of proviſions in ſome of the Weſtern Provinces, where bread is at ſuch a price as to preclude the poor from purchaſing it, who at preſent ſubſiſt on the fruits of the earth chiefly. This ſcarcity ariſes from the Merchants at Marſeilles having purchaſed ſuch quantities of grain, which they ſhipped for the markets of Italy and the Levant; at which latter it brought a profit of near cent. per cent. Government have at length taken up the conſideration of this matter ſeriouſly."

His Excellency the French Ambaſſador has had an interview with Mr. Pitt at his houſe in Dowing-ſtreet, relative to the wretched ſtate ſome of the French provinces are in for want of bread; and requeſted permiſſion to buy up and export a quantity of flour, to alleviate their diſtreſſes. The Miniſter, we are informed, aſſured his Excellency that every thing ſhould be done, and that immediately, conſiſtent with the ſafety of this country, to afford them ſuch relief as their neceſſities required.

The Queen and Princeſſes, who have never ſeen a fleet of men of war, will make a trip to Portſmouth, and alſo to Spithead and the Iſle of Wight.

When General Waſhington was inſtalled Preſident of the United States, he was dreſſed in a plain brown ſuit; and he rode in a plain carriage.

A few nights ago, a whimſical fellow paraded a great part of the metropolis, in the character of a Bell-man, ſtopping at certain intervals, and exclaiming—

"O yes! O yes! O yes! This is to give notice—that the Summer is put off till the next year.—Paſt twelve o'clock—and a d——d rainy morning!"

Mrs. Siddons, in caſe of any accident to Mr. Colman, has the Royal promiſe for the Hay-market patent.

TRIAL OF WARREN HASTINGS, ESQ.

WESTMINSTER-HALL.

SIXTEENTH DAY.

The uſual ceremonies being over, the Lord Chancellor deſired that the Managers ſhould proceed to make good their charges againſt the priſoner.

Mr. Burke called on the Clerk of the Court to read a letter, dated April 22, 1783, and ſigned by Mr. Goring, conveying the public accounts of that period, in which was included a certain ſum which had been received by Mr. Haſtings, as a preſent from Munny Begum.

The Lord Chancellor made a few obſervations on the inadmiſſibility of this Letter as evidence.

DUBLIN, JULY 2.

The linen market has commenced tolerably briſk; ſeveral Engliſh buyers are arrived, and a conſiderable quantity has already been bought up for the fair of Cheſter, which begins on Monday next.

Belfaſt, *July* 7.

On Sunday morning, the Mail Coach, with the Mail, ſet off from hence for Dublin—and ſame evening the Mail arrived here from Dublin by the ſame mode of conveyance.

The Linen Hall, Hugh Dickſon maſter, arrived ſafe at the Downs the 27th ult.

The Peggy, James M'Ilroy maſter, loaded with Linen Cloth for Cheſter fair, arrived ſafe on Tueſday laſt.

The Charlotte, Wm. Campbell maſter, for London, is ſtill detained here by contrary winds.

☞ The Sale of part of the Lands of Ballyginniff, will be held by the Sheriff of the County Antrim, at the Donegall Arms, on Wedneſday 8th inſt. at 12 o'clock.

DIED.] On ſhip-board, at Garmoyle, (on her return from Briſtol Hot-wells, where ſhe had gone for recovery of her health,) Mrs. Hamilton, wife of John Hamilton, Eſq; of this place—deſervedly regretted by a numerous acquaintance.—At Langford Lodge, on Sunday the 28th ult. Mr. Joſeph Mc. Nielly—who, throughout a long life and in a public ſtation, maintained a character without blemiſh, and poſſeſſed every amiable and reſpectable quality which can do honour to the man and the chriſtian.

⁂ *Prices of grain in our next.*

⁂ Tho' the Editor regrets as much as any perſon, diſputes too frequently prevalent among Proteſtant Diſſenters, yet as he could not inſert an anonymous paper, "in imitation of the Style of the Goſpel," without becoming a party in the controverſy, he muſt beg leave to decline it.

SUMMER ASSIZES.

NORTH-EAST CIRCUIT.

Co. Meath, at Trim,	Wedneſday. July	29
Louth, at Dundalk,	Monday, Auguſt	3
Down, at Downpatrick,	Thurſday,	6
Antrim at Carrickfergus,	Thurſday,	13
Town of Carrickfergus,	Same day,	
Armagh, at Armagh,	Wedneſday,	19
Monaghan, at Monaghan,	Tueſday,	25
Town of Drogheda,	Monday,	31

Hon. Mr. Baron Hamilton, }
Right Hon. Juſtice Kelly, } Juſtices.

Robert Hamilton, Eſq; North Earl-ſt. }
Greg. Dolphin, Eſq; Mary-ſtreet, } Regiſters.

The Grand Jury of the county of Louth will be ſworn on the commiſſion day, preciſely at twelve o'clock, and the records and other buſineſs will on that day be proceeded on; and the records in the other towns will be called on the ſecond day of each aſſizes, and none will be received that ſhall not be entered with the Regiſter previous to the ſitting of the Court that day.

PORT NEWS.

ARRIVED.

June 20. Watts, Aſhridge, Drunthon, deals.
July 4. Watters, Munn, Alicant, aſhes.
Three colliers.

CLEARED OUT.

July 1. Sophia, Thompſon, Philadelphia, Linen Cloth.

Belfaſt, *July* 10.

The reader is referred to the preceding page for General Waſhington's late ſpeech to Congreſs.

In whatever new and untried ſituation this illuſtrious character has been placed, thro' the confidence of A PEOPLE in his wiſdom, moderation and integrity,——his conduct as A FARMER, A GENERAL and A STATESMAN, muſt meet the praiſe of every liberal mind. His prudence and humanity in the field,—his ſervice of his country without the emoluments of office,—and his voluntary reſignation of power without being chargeable with the ſlighteſt abuſe of it, are happily contraſted with the milder virtues of his private life.

The preſent ſeaſon has not been exceeded perhaps by any former one in long continuance of heavy rains and high winds. We find by private and public advices, that it has been at leaſt equally bad over Britain and a conſiderable part of the continent.

The Charlotte, captain Campbell, for London, is ſtill here detained by contrary winds.

Yeſterday oat-meal ſold in our market, from 11s. to 10s. 4d. per cwt.—and wheat at 12s. 2d.

A debate in the Engliſh Houſe of Lords on the 3d inſt reſpecting a bill to prevent vexatious ſuits for TYTHES,—we defer till our next, in order to give it entire.

The lines ſigned H. dated from "Half Land," on the death of a young Lady, are received.—The feelings of relations are ſo often hurt, inſtead of being gratified, by ſuch publications, that in general their inſertion is declined.

FAIRS IN THE ENSUING WEEK.

Monday: Monaghan.—Moy, Tyrone.—N. Livaddy, Derry.—Wheathill, Fermanagh.—*Wedneſday:* Ballycaſtle, Antrim.—*Thurſday:* Randalſtown, Antrim.—*Friday:* Ederneybridge, Ferm.—Rathmelton, Don.—Swatteragh, Derry.

A Caution, dated the 22d inſtant, in the Belfaſt Paper from William Ogle of Lane-Ends, obliges me, reluctantly, to this public reply.——He ſets out with aſſerting, in his very pompous manner, that the ſale of his place aroſe, alone, from a principle of juſtice.—It might, in part, but neceſſity was a ſtrong inducement, as he had got largely in debt on his own account, and which debt was diſcharged by me on getting the concern. His alluſion to a private ſale, is totally unfounded and groundleſs, as neither a private or public ſale of the place ever entered my head: even had it, innumerable bars prevented. He alſo ſays, no part of his demand is paid; to which I anſwer there is, and which ſhall be made appear at a convenient time. His *Nota Bene* if properly explained would ſhew the man in worſe colours than he wantonly attempted to ſhew me, but tenderneſs reſtrains; and the more ſo, as I am led to believe his judgment is impoſed on by the evil inſinuations of ſome in his neighbourhood, beſt known by their ſtrongeſt feature *diſhoneſty*; but let ſuch come forward and openly avow their art, and they may expect a becoming reprimand from the much injured JOHN OGLE.

N. B. I ſhall anſwer no future productions in this way; my perſon and facts are at the ſervice of thoſe who chooſe to enquire for them.

To be Sold,

THE Intereſt in a Farm of Land in Carnon, in the pariſh of Arboe and county of Tyrone, being a Leaſe for three young lives and 28 years unexpired, held under the beſt of Landlords, (James Caulfield and John Staples, Eſqrs.)

Propoſals will be received by Mr. Anthony Mc. Reynolds the proprietor, who will ſhew the premiſſes and the leaſe thereof

UNPLEASING as it is to me to trouble the Publick with my affairs, I am now obliged to do so, in my own vindication. John Ogle afferts in his anfwer to my advertifement, that I had contracted a large debt to the late Mr. Legg of Malone, and after he bought my concern, that he had that debt to pay. I borrowed from Alexander Legg, Efq; four hundred pounds, two hundred pounds of which was to pay to John Ogle, a part of the fum bequeathed to him by my father's will, immediately after his apprenticefhip terminated ; the other two hundred was on my own account, occafioned by the threats of the infurgents in the years feventy-one and feventy-two, who vowed they would burn and deftroy my houfes, moffes, and every production of them, if I did not acquiefce with their terms ; after which I would not confent to fet my mofs to them, who paid me yearly rent for it : That four hundred pounds was included in the thoufand mentioned in my firft advertifement, for the payment of which fum of four hundred pounds, I got every bond and note of mine from the late Mr. Legg, and he confented to be paid by John Ogle out of the 1000l. I appointed by the deed of fale to be appropriated to the purpofe of paying the incumbrance to the legatees, and the debt then due to Mr. Legg. I declare in the moft pofitive manner I had not the leaft intention to injure his character by inferting the former advertifement ; it proceeded entirely from a converfation that paft between me and the perfon he gave the latter mortgage to, who I thought feemed difpofed to take advantage of obtaining the money by a private fale, or by fome method injurious to me as John Ogle was then in England, which I had the greateft reafon to guard againft, as every tranfaction of his relative to his creditors was done fecretly and without my knowledge ; nor did I ever hear the leaft intimation of it until a year elapfed after it happened ; and I fuppofe if that affair is at any time inveftigated in our courts of juftice, they will think they are in fome degree affronted by a regiftered prior judgment, and their decrees upon it, being neglected ; as the Court of Records is always ready to fatisfy thofe who make proper application, but time will beft determine.

Malone, July 12, 1789.   WILLIAM OGLE.

N. B. I do again affert, and can prove the affertion, that I nor any perfon by my order or direction never at any time received any part of the principal fum of one thoufand five hundred pounds, for which fum I have the deed of mortgage on the concerns, except the trifling fum of five fhillings and five pence to afcertain the fale. No perfon in this neighbourhood, nor any other place, ever attempted to influence my mind, or give their advice in regard to the former advertifement, nor faw it until I deliver'd it for infertion. John Ogle fhould have refrained that arrogating infinuation in his anfwer of his having paid for me a large fum to Mr. Legg—my concerns paid it ; that I fold, it was a part of the fum mentioned for the purpofe. The word neceffity might have been left out, as I never experienced it nor dependance of any fort in my life.

Ordinary at Lisburn.

JOHN SHAW, at King's Arms, will have an Ordinary during the enfuing Races. Dinner on the table as foon as Gentlemen can come from the courfe. Private Dinners as ufual—good ftabling, hay and oats, all in the moft comfortable manner.

14th July, 1789.

Stolen or Strayed,

ON the night of the 9th inft. from the lands of John Bolton, in the townland of Ballymote and parifh of Glenavy, a dark bay Horfe, fix years old, with a large reach on his face ftanding to the off fide, which touches on the tail of his far eye, and both hind feet white. Whoever fecures the Horfe and Thief fhall receive one Guinea reward, on profecuting to conviction, by applying to Mr. Francis Logan, Innkeeper, Lifburn, or Mr. Conway Mc. Niece, Glenavy.—If ftrayed, half a Guinea reward will be given for returning the Horfe as above.   13th July, 1789.

Strayed or Stolen,

FROM Newtown-Ards on Saturday night laft, 2 white Ponies, one about 13 hands high, ftrong made aged.—The tail remarkably fhort cut ; the other about 13 h. hands high, ftrong made, eight years old, with a mark of an anchor and harpoon on the near fhoulder, long tail, white fundament, a piece out of his right ear.—Whoever returns them to John M'Cully, or Henry Barr, fhall be handfomely rewarded, or for Ponies and Thief on profecuting them to conviction, fhall receive 10 Guineas.

Newtown-Ards,   JOHN M'CULLY,
13th July, 1789.   HENRY BARR.

Spirits and Wine Stores, Lisburn.

JOHN KENLEY has this day opened for Sale, at his Stores, the following Articles, viz.

Beft Rum,	Red Port,
Rum-D.	Whitewine,
Common Rum,	Geneva,
Brandy,	Englifh Cider in hampers, and
Strong ditto,	
Whitewine Vinegar,	Drontheim Deals.

The quality of the above-mentioned Merchandize there is no doubt will give fatisfaction ; they will be difpofed of on the loweft terms for ready Money ; and he hopes by his attention to the intereft of the publick to merit encouragement, and the friendfhip of his former cuftomers.

Lifburn, 14th July, 1789.

N. B. He fhortly expects a cargo of Dantzig Timber.

Mr. Cullen, Dentist,

RESPECTFULLY informs the Publie, that he is authorized to refer them to the Sovereign of Belfaft, Doctor Haliday, and George Portis, Efq ; for his character and profeffional abilities.——He begs leave to recommend his Tooth-Powder (1s. 1d.), Opiate for the Teeth and Gums (2s. 8d. h.), and his horizontal Brufhes (1s. 1d.)—His hours at home are from eight in the morning till feven in the evening.

☞ He will attend Families at their own Houfes, if required.

Dempfter's, High-ftreet, Belfaft, 12th July, 1789.

BOOKS.

TO be fold by Auction, this and the following Evenings, by JOSHUA LOMAX, at the houfe lately occupied by John Read, in High-ftreet, nearly oppofite the Market-houfe, a collection of BOOKS, confifting of 1500 Volumes, in various branches of literature, all new and in good condition.—Hours of fale from fix till ten every evening—Books fold by hand each day, at auction Price.——A great variety of Copper-plate Prints for fale—likewife fome Boxes.

N. B. The fale will pofitively clofe on Friday next.

Belfaft, Monday 13th July, 1789.

Scythes by Auction.

TO be fold by Auction, for ready money, on Wednefday and Thurfday the 22d and 23d inftant, two hundred Dozen Scythes, at the Warehoufe of Andrew and Hugh Carlile on the Merchants-Quay ; to be put up in lots agreeable to the bidders.

Newry, 13th July, 1789.

By Inch of Candle,

TO be fold at the Cuftom-Houfe, Larne, at twelve o'clock, on Wednefday the 22d inftant, forty-five Mate of very fine Leaf Tobacco.

Cuftom-houfe, Larne, 13th July, 1789.
                    THOMAS LEA, Collector.

John Mc. Coubrey,

SURGEON and ACCOUCHEUR,

RESPECTFULLY acquaints his Friends, that he has opened his new Laboratory in Scotch-ftreet ; where the greateft attention will be given to the calls he is honoured with—would fondly flatter himfelf that his knowledge of the profeffion will not be doubted, having a proper diploma from the College of Edinburgh.

Downpatrick, 15th July, 1789.

To be Let,

From the firft of November next, for 31 Years or three Lives,

THE Lands of Billain, part of the eftate of the Earl of Antrim, fituated in the barony of Glenarm, containing 71 acres of arable ground ; part of the rent to be fined down.—Propofals to be received by Robert Johnfton.   July 16th, 1789.

Farm to be Let,

From the firft of November next,

IN the Corporation of Carrickfergus, Townland Marfhalltown, containing 45 acres, I. plantation meafure : The Land is in good heart, being highly improved with lime, fencing, draining, &c. and will be let for a term not exceeding 21 years ; there is alfo a Dwelling-Houfe, two ftories high, in good repair, with Gardens and Offices fitting either a private Gentleman or Farmer. Apply to Robert Mc. Gowan the proprietor, at Marfhalltown.

Dated this 14th July, 1789.

For Charlestown South Carolina.

THE good Brig JAMES, burthen 160 tons, Englifh built, ROBERT SHUTTER Mafter, will be clear to fail for Charleftown on the 21ft day of Auguft next ; whoever wifh to go as paffengers may depend on the beft ufage, no double births, plenty of water and provifions, Captain Shutter has been long in the paffenger trade, and is remarkable for his attention to the paffengers.—For freight or paffage apply to Mr. James Mooney, Belfaft ; Mr. Robert M'Cracken, Braid ; Mr. Samuel Moore, Broughfhane ; or Mr. Matthew Quin, the owner at the Bank of Larne.

Larne, 6th July, 1789.

WHOLESALE and RETAIL

LINEN SHOP,

At the STAMP-OFFICE, HIGH-STREET, BELFAST.

ALEXANDER BLACKWELL, truly thankful for the very liberal fupport he has received fince his commencement in bufinefs ; begs leave to inform his Friends and the Publick, that they have now an opportunity of fupplying themfelves with almoft every Article in the

LINEN BUSINESS

upon the moft moderate terms.

In addition to his former affortment, he has juft laid in the following :

A great variety of 4 qr wide Linens,	A quantity of Huckaback Towelling,
Do. 7-8 wide do.	Burdy do.
A large quantity of 5-4th do. for Sheeting, from 15d. to 2s. 4d per yard.	A general affortment of Cambricks from 2s. to 12s per yard.
An extenfive Affortment of Diapers, different breadths, from 3-4 to 10.	Dowlas, twilled Linens, Drogheda do. Lawns, Cheques, &c. &c.

As a great part of the above Goods were purchafed by himfelf when brown, he is confequently enabled, and determined, to difpofe of fingle pieces on the fame terms as thofe fold in the Box by Wholefale ; and he can with fafety affure his friends, that his affortment will be found on trial equal in quality and lownefs of terms, to any offered for fale in this country.

Belfaft, July 13th, 1789.

Mrs. Blackwell is (as ufual) well fupplied with a variety of Goods in the Millinary and Haberdafhery Lines, which fhe continues to fell at the moft reduced prices.

James Pinkerton,

IS this day landing from on board the Lord Donegall, Whitbread's beft Porter——The quality of which he will engage fully as good as the laft he imported.

North-ftreet, Belfaft, 16th July, 1789.

WHEREAS John, Coll, and Charles Mc. Donnell of Killmore, parifh of Laid, County Antrim, Alexander Mc. Donnell of Ballycaftle, with others, the 11th inft. did moft outrageoufly and felonioufly fire upon and wound us in a moft inhuman and blood-thirfty manner ; we beg and requeft that all Philanthrophifts, (and thofe that would wifh to bring the perpetrators of fuch horrid and unprecedented barbarity to condign punifhment) will exert themfelves in lodging the above Mc. Donnell's in any of his Majefty's Gaols, to be dealt with according to law. We return our fincere thanks to Alex. M'Auley of Glanvil, Efq ; and David Mc. Killop of Glenarm, Efq ; for their fpirited exertions in attempting to bring the aforefaid Mc. Donnells and affiftants to trial.

	Randle Mc. Alifter,
	Alex. Mc. Alifter, fenr. † his Mark.
Nariff, 27th June, 1789.	Alex. Mc. Alifter, junr. ‖ his Mark.
	Hugh O'Mulvenan, ‡ his Mark.
	Alexander Mc. Vey.

HOSIERY.

THOMAS NEILSON & Co. have received a compleat Affortment of SILK, COTTON, and THREAD STOCKINGS, of the neweft and moft ufeful Kinds, which with their prefent extenfive Affortment of WOOLLEN DRAPERY, LIVERY LACES, &c. they will fell very cheap, for Money.

Belfaft, 9th July, 1789.

Advertisement.

A Meeting of the Truftees of the Turnpike Board, for the road from Lifburn to Belfaft by the County of Down, will be held at the Donegall-Arms, on Saturday the 18th inftant, at one o'clock.

Dated 15th July, 1789.

AMERICA.

New-York, May 18.

LAST Thursday evening his Excellency the Minister of France, gave a ball to the President of the United States, which was uncommonly elegant, in respect both to the company and plan of their entertainment. As a compliment to our alliance with France, there were two sets of Cotillon Dancers, in complete uniforms; one set in that of France, and the other in blue and buff: the ladies were dressed in white with ribands, bouquets, and garlands of flowers, answering to the uniforms of the gentlemen.—The Vice-President, many Members of the Senate, and House of Representatives of the United States, the Governor of this State, the Governor of the Western Territory, and other characters of distinction, were present.

IMPORTANT NEWS FROM FRANCE.

BY the last advices from Paris we learn, that the state of public affairs is materially changed from what appeared as likely to be the result of the present disturbances.

It is certain, that the King is extremely dissatisfied with Mr. Necker for having committed him in the manner he has done, by giving an advice which his Majesty does not now chuse to pursue, and the retraction of which places him in a very awkward situation. The King likewise blames M. Necker very highly for taking so active a part in favour of the Commons, and his resentment prevails so far, that M. Necker will no longer be the Minister that the King finds convenient to his interest.

The measures which his Majesty is now determined to pursue, are evident: he is sorry to have given any kind of assurance to the national assembly, who, whatever their fair pretensions may be, have certainly encroached too far on the Royal prerogative, and forced the King to guard himself in his own defence. What the result may be, no man can possibly determine, but we are assured the King will try his strength, and endeavour to retain that just power which the constitu- has placed in his hands. A civil war in the country appears inevitable, and the question is, which party has the superior force. It depends entirely how far the military will stand by the King.

At Metz, the dearth of flour was such, that the people, driven by hunger and despair, collected in great bodies, and attacked the houses of several persons, whom they suspected of hoarding meal.

The Governor drew out two French regiments; and having furnished them with ammunition, ordered them to act against the mob. They refused.

The Governor ordered them back to their quarters, but without taking from them the ammunition.

Two German regiments were then brought out, which roused the indignation of the national troops, who burst from their quarters, and joined the mob.

A dreadful havock was the consequence!

Upwards of a thousand men on each side were killed, and at length the German regiments were cut to pieces.

The Governor escaped in time from the fury of the populace.

Frenchmen have now to decide whether they will be free or not.

The most gross and indecent caricatures are handed about on the King and Queen, and the most atrocious liberties taken with their characters.

Versailles and Paris, when the last express came away, were both fortified, and exhibited one general scene of the most dreadful confusion. Eight additional regiments had arrived to defend Versailles.

BRITISH HOUSE OF COMMONS.

Tuesday, July 7.

FRENCH FAMINE.

Mr. Pitt, according to his intimation of the day before, presented from the Bar the Minutes of the evidence taken by the Committee of Privy Council, relative to the quantity of flour, &c. now in the kingdom.

Mr. Pitt, after the Minutes had been laid on the table, observed, that the most expeditious mode of determining whether the French request of 20,000 sacks of flour, could, with safety, be complied with, would be by referring the Minutes to a Select Committee. He accordingly moved to that purpose.

The Committee immediately withdrew, and in about three hours came to a decision on the requested exportation.

Mr. Pulteney, the Chairman, brought up the report, which was read at the table as follows:

"The Committee appointed to take into their consideration the minutes of the examination before the Privy Council, have considered the same, and come to the following resolution:

"Resolved, That from a comparative view of the prices of wheat and flour in France and England; that 20,000 sacks of flour ought not to be exported."

DUBLIN, July 9.

Our port is said to be shut against the exportation of wheat and flour; a considerable quantity has, however, been shipped within these few days for Norway.

Yesterday, at one o'clock, Robert Edgeworth was a second time put in the pillory at the front of the Tholsel, for subornation of perjury in the case of Mary Neil, and Anne Molyneux, pursuant to his former sentence. The crowd was immense, and he received so severe a pelting of eggs, potatoes, clods of dirt, and in many instances the throwing of stones, that his life would have paid the forfeit of his crime, if, with the dextrous use of one hand, he had not contrived to guard his face. He was, at two o'clock, delivered from the pillory and taken back to the New prison, in order to undergo his further sentence of six months imprisonment.

A merchant of Alicant has lately acquainted his correspondent in this city, that the Spaniards are very nice in measuring the breadth, as well as whiteness and texture of the linens exported from Ireland. It therefore seems of the utmost importance, that every occasion of complaint should be avoided by the different artists concerned in that staple branch of our trade; not only from motives of prudence, but moral honesty, repeated breaches of which might induce our Spanish customers to decline any further connection in that line. This circumstance is intended as a friendly hint, as a considerable number of pieces sent abroad last April would have been returned, but for the interference of a capital Irish house at St. Lucar, who promised that no such subject of complaint should hereafter arise with respect to his own importation to that market.

The following Resolutions have been agreed to by the Independent Dublin Volunteers.

July 10th, 1789.

Major ROWAN in the Chair.

Resolved, That as Citizens, and Men armed in defence of our Liberties and Properties, we cannot remain unconcerned Spectators of any breach of that Constitution, which is the Glory of this Empire.

Resolved, That the violation of the fundamental laws of these kingdoms, occasioned the melancholy catastrophe of 1648—that the violation of those laws brought on the glorious Revolution of 1688—that we look upon the TRIAL by JURY, with all the privileges annexed to it, to be a most essential part of those laws—that we highly approve of the firm conduct of our worthy Fellow Citizen, on a late transaction, in support of those Rights—to hand down which, whole and unimpaired, to our posterity, we pledge ourselves to co-operate with our Fellow subjects, in every capacity of them.

DUBLIN, July 14.

To the Public in general, and the Friends of this Independent Nation in particular.

In consequence of several extraordinary proceedings lately adopted, and violently pursued, whereby the Constitutional Rights and Privileges of the Subjects of Ireland are essentially endangered, a number of Independent Citizens have united to preserve the same, and to hand them down pure and inviolate to posterity—pledging themselves to each other, and to their Fellow Subjects, to use their best endeavours to oppose, by every legal means, all such attempts and proceedings.

Subscriptions for this laudable purpose will be received by each Member of the Committee, and their Treasurers.

8th July, 1789.

ARCH. HAMILTON ROWAN, Esq.
JAMES NAPPER TANDY, Esq.
HENRY JACKSON, Esq.
SAMUEL GARNER, Esq.

In consequence of an appointment by the Subscribers to the Ballyshannon Canal, the following is Mr. Evan's Report of the practicability of compleating a Navigation for Boats of 35 tons burthen, from Belturbet to Enniskillen, through Lough Erne, to near the town of Belleek, and from thence by a Still-water Navigation to the Tide Water in the Harbour of Ballyshannon:

"He has viewed and examined the lake from Belturbet to Enniskillen, and finds a natural good navigation to near the last mentioned town, but the fall from the upper to the lower lake, being about 8 feet, he proposes to remove this difficulty by a Canal and Locks as marked in the plan; and probably, when the trade encreases, a track-way might be formed along the western banks of the two lakes, for the whole extent; which would render this great extent of navigation both safe and commodious.

"In his report to the Navigation Board in 1784, he laid before them a plan, section, and estimate, of the probable expence of compleating a navigation from the River Shannon, at Letrim, to Lough Skurr, Ballinamore, and Woodford Lakes, to Ballyconnel, by Carrole to Lough Erne.

"Should this great national plan be adopted, it will connect the most distant parts of this kingdom by Inland Navigation; as he finds spirited companies are formed, not only to compleat the navigation of the River Shannon, from Limerick to Lough Allen, but from the Grand Canal to Banagher, to be finished in four years; and also, to execute a new projected line of Inland Navigation, called the Royal Canal, extending from the New Custom-house, Dublin, through Meath, Westmeath, and Longford, towards the Collieries of Lough Allen; together with a branch to Trim and Kells, from whence it is probable, a junction with Lough Erne may be effected, by Lough Rower, Lough Shallin, Lough Gowna, and so on down the River Erne to Belturbet.

"Our present object will form a link of this great chain, and when compleat, will effectually connect the ports of Limerick, Dublin, and Ballyshannon, similar to the ports of Bristol, Hull, and Liverpool, in England; which sufficiently prove the great utility of Inland Navigation, by the rapid encrease of trade, &c. in each of those ports.

"By the completion of this Canal, the whole of the tolls from Lough Erne to the sea, will be collected near the town of Ballyshannon, and will command the most powerful sites for all kinds of manufactures, probably the best adapted of any in his Majesty's dominions, for extensive and ponderous iron works, rolling tin, boaring cannon, turning, Arkwright's machinery in the cotton branch, as well as all others that require a great command of water, having all Lough Erne as a reservoir."

At a meeting of the Subscribers of the Ballyshannon Canal, it was determined to send Richard Evans, Esq. Engineer, to complete the survey and plan for carrying on the work.

N. B. Fifty miles of natural Inland Navigation on Lough Erne, will be obtained by cutting this Canal of only three miles and a half, which must prove uncommonly advantageous to the subcribers.

LONDON-DERRY, July 7.

In consequence of Mail Coaches being established to run from Belfast to Dublin, and from thence to Cork, a new regulation of post hours is immediately to take place here, viz. the Dublin post is to come in at 11 o'clock in the forenoon and is not to set out again on its return till 4 in the afternoon—a regulation that will prove much more convenient to the people of Derry than the former one.

By this new regulation, the coming-in and going out of the Belfast cross posts are altered.—The post from N. Limavady will now arrive here at 6 o'clock in the evenings of Monday, Thursday, and Saturday—and will leave Derry at 10 o'clock in the forenoons of Monday, Wednesday, and Saturday, and is to be at Newtown at half past 1 in the afternoon.

The first Mail Coach was to leave Dublin for Belfast on Saturday night last—that for Cork was to begin as on this night; fare to Cork, two guineas for inside passengers, outside passengers half-price. It is 124 miles from Dublin to Cork.—When this part of the country will be accommodated with Mail Coaches, it is yet very uncertain.

An easy cut of scarcely four miles would open a communication between the Loughs Foyle and Swilly, two of the most capacious and commodious bays in Ireland—every man and merchant confessed its advantages, and was convinced of its practicability—as usual, the thing was *much talked of, and then forgotten!*

Belfast, *July* 17.

On Tuesday the Belfast Volunteer Company, with their Artillery, commanded by Captain Brown, march- to the country to exercise and dine together.

And on Wednesday the Belfast First Volunteer Company, with their Artillery, commanded by Capt. Cunningham, marched to the country for the like purpose.

The Thames, Bennet, from Newry to London, arrived there the 8th inst. after a passage of eight days.

Sunday being the 12th July, the Banbridge Company paraded in uniform, and marched to church, where an excellent sermon, suitable to the occasion, was preached by the Rev. Mr. Sturrock, after their return the company fired three vollies in honor of the day.

So great was the glut of herrings on Wednesday in our market, that they fell from six-pence to two-pence per dozen.

FAIRS IN THE ENSUING WEEK.

Monday, 20, Aghygaults, Don.—Garrison, Ferm.—Killin, Tyr.—Lisbellaw, Ferm.—21. *Tuesday*: Ballyclare, Ant.—Castleshane, Mon.—Killeter, Tyr. Lisburn, Ant.—Mosside, Ant.—23. *Thursday*: Crumlin, Ant.—25. *Saturday*: Glaslough, Mon.——Johnston's-bridge, Arm.——Pettigoe, Don.

PRICES OF GRAIN.

July, 16.

Oatmeal,	9s. 10d. to 10s. 5d.	per. Cwt.
Wheat,	12 00 — 12 2	per. Cwt.
Oats,	00 00 — 6 0	per. Cwt.

Anno 1789.] Printed by HENRY JOY, and Co. BELFAST.

The BELFAST NEWS-LETTER.

TUESDAY July 21, FRIDAY July 24, 1789.

Bloomfield House and Farm, County Down.

TO be let for a few years, (from November next, as can be agreed on, the House and Farm of Bloomfield, containing 25 acres, Cunningham measure, on which is a good Dwelling, together with sufficient Office-houses, a large Orchard in full bearing, and Kitchen Garden; the Farm is highly improved, together with good ditches. The situation is remarkably fine, only one mile from Belfast; this place is very fit for the immediate reception of a gentleman.——Any person who may agree for it shortly, can be accommodated with the crop now on the ground.——For particulars apply to James Mc. Vickar on the premisses.

Bloomfield, 15th July, 1789.

To be Let,

From the first of November next, for 31 Years or three Lives,

THE Lands of Billain, part of the estate of the Earl of Antrim, situated in the barony of Glenarm, containing 71 acres of arable ground; part of the rent to be fined down.—Proposals to be received by Robert Johnston. July 16th, 1789.

WHEREAS an advertisement appeared in the Belfast Paper of the 3d instant, charging John and Coll Mc. Donnell with the commission of several offences; and calling for public assistance to apprehend them.—These Gentlemen think it their duty to mention in this public manner, that they had given bail to submit their case to the decision of the law, previous to the publication of the said advertisement; a circumstance which they humbly presume should have rendered the insertion of their names not only unnecessary but improper.

Moreover, they apprehend that Randal Mc. Allister and his associates were the aggressors in the unhappy riot alluded to; and as several of these persons have been indicted without either being apprehended or giving bail, it is hoped that some of the general philanthropy may be exerted in bringing the said felons to condign punishment.——Kilmore, 16th July, 1789.

JOHN Mc. DONNELL,
COLL Mc. DONNELL.

Stolen or strayed,

STOLEN or strayed off the Lands of Michael Montgomery of Drumenockan, near Hillsborough, on Wednesday night or Thursday morning, being the eighth or ninth of July past, A Black Horse, five years old, about 12 or 13 hands high, without any marks: It is thought he is in the county of Antrim. Whoever returns said Horse to said Montgomery, shall receive one Guinea Reward, or Horse and Thief, three Guineas.

July 16th, 1789.

THE Protestant Congregation of Stewartstown, return the Revd. Mr. Stitt their sincere and hearty thanks for the excellent Sermon he preached unto them the 12th inst. on the opening of their Meeting-house, they flatter themselves Mr. Stitt will be so very obliging as to permit them to publish it.

Classical School, in Lisburn.

ON Wednesday and Thursday last was held the quarterly Examination. The following young Gentlemen obtained Premiums:—Wilson, Andrew Fulton, James Fulton, Campbell, Francis Fulton, Thomas Fulton, Douglass.——For the superior advantages of this institution, Mr. Foley begs to refer the Public to those Ladies and Gentlemen who usually attend on these occasions.——Boarders twenty Guineas a year, and two Guineas entrance. Single beds for such as apply early. School opens the 16th of August.

Charles O'Neill, in Cookstown,

TEACHES English Grammar, Writing, and a complete Course of elementary and practical Mathematics; viz. Arithmetic, Book-keeping, Algebra, Euclid's Elements of Geometry, Trigonometry both plain and spherical, Conic-Sections, Mechanics, Fluxions, Surveying and Levelling, with the Use of the Instruments, Mensuration, Gauging, Navigation, Geography, Dialling, Astronomy, Use of the Globes and Maps, Fortification, Gunnery, &c. in a very regular and comprehensive manner; and he engages to make no demand unless those committed to his care bear a satisfactory examination. July 20th, 1789.

To be Set,

A Double House, in thorough repair, for any term of years that may be agreed upon, formerly inhabited by Delacherois Crommelin, Esq ——Said House is finely situated in Castle-street, Lisburn; with every conveniency fitting for any gentleman, has convenient back buildings, and a good garden, with some wall-fruit.—Enquire as above.

N. B. A Tenant may enter into it immediately.

To the Revd. Mr. BRISTOW.

Revd. Sir,

It is with the sincerest pleasure I take this public manner of offering you my grateful acknowledgment for your very constant and kind attendance for several days in examining the classes of the Belfast Academy. It adds much to my satisfaction, that at the close of the examination you were pleased to express the fullest approbation of the young Gentlemen's proficiency.

I am, with great respect,
Dear Sir,
your most obedient humble servant,
JAMES CROMBIE.

BELFAST ACADEMY,
July 21st, 1789.

Down School.

VACATION having commenced to day, School will open again, and the public Examination will be held, on 31st August.

18th July, 1789.

Two good Hands

WANTED immediately, to work in a FLAX-MILL; who will have constant employment thro' the season, and be accommodated with houses, gardens, and cow's grass.

For particulars apply by letter, or in person, to Mr. Henry Joy, Belfast. July 23, 1789.

John Richards,

HAVING regularly attended three Sessions at College, has opened Shop in Broughshane; where he will act as Surgeon, Accoucheur, &c.——He hopes from attention to business, and the quality of his Medicines, to merit the countenance of the Town and Vicinity of Broughshane. 23d July, 1789.

A Mare stolen.

ON the night of Friday the 17th inst. was stolen on the Farm of widow Mc. Colgan, in the Quarterland of Rish and parish of Dunluce, a Chesnut Mare, about thirteen hands high, lengthy bodied, white mane and tail, a few white hairs in her forehead, eight years old, and about six pounds value. Whoever shall return said Mare to her owner, and prosecutes the thief to conviction, shall receive [illegible] Guineas by applying to me,

ED. ALEX Mc. NAGHTEN.

Beardville,
July 22d, 1789.

If any person has found said Mare and will return her to her owner, he shall receive one Guinea for his trouble.

E. A. Mc. NAGHTEN.

Advertisement.

WHEREAS on Tuesday the 7th inst. a man who calls himself John Johnston, left a Mare, (of a brown black colour, with three white feet, about eight years old) in the neighbourhood of Carnteel, which Mare is now in the possession of James Mason of Mulnahunch; and as he promised to come back and prove his property on the next day and has not since returned, it is supposed the is stolen:—the owner may have her by proving property, and paying the expence, by applying to said James Mason, or Thomas Moore of Baun near Carnteel.——Dated this 11th day of July, 1789.

Swedish Iron & Jamaica Rum.

JOHN BASHFORD is landing a large Cargo well assorted Iron from Gothenburg; also from the Beresford, a parcel strong Jamaica Rum, which, with the following Articles, will be sold on the lowest terms.

Belfast, 24th July, 1789.

Best Blister Steel,	Iron Hoops,
German do.	A Parcel Boxes genuine
Cast do.	Curriers Knives, cheap

To be Sold by Auction,

AT Mr. Tracy's in Dungannon, at one o'clock, on Thursday the 30th instant, the Proprietor's Interest in several Tenements in Irish-street, School-house-lane, and Gallows-hill, in that Town, held by lease renewable for ever, on payment of a small fine.——Mr. William Greer of Dungannon will shew the concerns.

July 20th, 1789.

Cotton Ware-House.

LUKES, OAKMAN, & Co. are now well supplied with the following Articles, ALL OF THEIR OWN MANUFACTURE, which their Friends and Customers may depend on being of a good quality, and will be sold on the most reasonable terms, viz.—Twill'd and plain Cotton Thicksetts, Linen Bottom ditto, double twill'd and plain Cotton Corduroys, Linen Bottom ditto, Jeans, Pillows, Denims, Dimities, Muslinets, printed Cottons, white Cotton Wrappers, &c &c. &c.

Waring-street, Belfast, July 20th, 1789.

THE Volunteer Companies of Belfast, with much respect, request that such neighbouring corps as approve of a Review to be held near that Town, (at a convenient time in the month of August next) may be pleased to send Delegates to a meeting at the Donegall-Arms, at the hour of one o'clock, on Saturday the first of August.

It is thought proper to add, that it is our idea that the ground be free of expence, and so situated that the Corps may march in and return the same day.

STEWART BANKS,	Lieut. Colonel Belfast Bat
W. CUNNINGHAM,	Capt. Belfast 1st Co.
ROBERT WILSON,	Com. Officer of Belfast Volunt. Co. in absence of Capt. Brown.
CHAs. RANKEN,	Capt. of Belfast Troop.

July 18, 1789.

To be Sold,

THE DRUGS and FIXTURES of an Apothecary's Shop.——Apply to Archibald Bankhead.

Belfast, July 21st, 1789.

AT a very respectable and numerous Meeting of the Freeholders of the Four Lower Baronies of the County of Antrim at Ballymoney, on Tuesday the 14th July, 1789, pursuant to notice in the Belfast Paper.

HENRY O'HARA, Esq; in the Chair:

Ezekiel Davis Boyd, Esq; moved, That James Leslie, Esq; be put in nomination as a proper person to be supported by the Freeholders of the four lower Baronies at the next General Election for Members to represent the County; this Motion was seconded by Alex. Mc. Aulay, Esq; and carried *unanimously*.

The following Resolutions were then moved by Edmond Alex. Mc. Naghten, Esq; and seconded by Samuel Allen, Esq; and carried unanimously.

Resolved, That to prevent as much as possible the obvious evil consequences arising from contested elections; We do hereby declare our readiness to unite with the four upper Baronies in supporting their nomination of one Member of this County, provided that they will unite with us in supporting our nomination of one Member, by which means contest will be prevented, every freeholders right of election established, and that harmony so essential to the happiness and prosperity of the county be effectually preserved.

Resolved, That we are determined to unite in supporting, at our own expence, some Gentleman resident in the four lower Baronies at the next election for members to represent the county.

Resolved, That James Leslie, Esq; in consequence of the great services he has rendered this country, and as a man possessing in the most eminent degree, the qualifications necessary for a representative of the people, appears to us to be a man most worthy of our support, and that we are determined to support him accordingly.

Resolved, That a Committee, consisting of the following Gentlemen, (any five of whom to be a quorum) shall meet at such times and places as they shall be called upon by their Chairman so to do, to consider the most proper means of carrying our Resolutions into effect, *viz.* Henry O'Hara, Chairman, Ezekiel Davis Boyd, Edmond Alex. Mc. Naghton, John Cromie, Alex. Thos. Stewart, Hugh Boyd, Archibald Hutcheson, James Hamilton, Adam Hunter, Samuel Allen, Samson Moore, John Cuppage, Thos. Cuppage, Alex. Mc. Aulay, David Mc. Killop, Johnston Henry, Robert Johnston, Robt. Gage, Hugh Lyle, John Dunlop, Wm. Moor, Skeffington Bristow, Archibald Mc. Collum, and John Stewart, Esqrs. the Revd. Robt. Trail, the Revd. Joseph Dowglass of Clough, the Revd. Alex. Marshall, the Revd. Charles Dowglass, the Revd. John Cameron, the Revd. Hugh Mc Clennon, and the Revd. Wm. Linn, Messrs. George Moore, James Wilson of Carncastle, Thos. Caldwell, Henry Clark, Daniel Mc Coy, Alex. Ramage, George Black, Jo. Boyd, Wm O'Toy, Geo. Shaw, Jas. Gamble, and Archibald Mc. Fall.

Resolved, That our Chairman do acquaint Mr. Leslie with our Resolutions.

Resolved, That these Resolutions, together with Mr. Leslie's Answer be published in the Belfast News Paper.

HENRY O'HARA, Chairman.

James Murphy,

TAKES the Liberty to inform his Friends and the Publick, that he has commenced business next door to Brown, Gaw & Co.—and having formed a Partnership with a Gentleman in the Manufacturing Line in England, he is now and will be continually supplied with

Broad and Forest Cloths, Coatings, Bath Rugs, Cords, &c.

to be sold by Wholesale only.——He will pay the utmost attention to have every article on the best terms, and hopes to merit a part of his friends favours.

Baltimore, April 21.

THE Preſident of the United States arrived in this place on his way to Congreſs, on Friday afternoon, the 17th inſt. with Charles Thompſon, Eſq. and Col. Humphries. This great man was met ſome miles from town, by a large body of reſpectable citizens on horſeback, and conducted, under a diſcharge of cannon, to Mr. Grant's Tavern, through crowds of admiring ſpectators. At ſix o'clock, a committee choſen in conſequence of a late notification, to adjuſt the preliminaries for his reception, waited upon him with an addreſs, which, with his anſwer, we are able to give to the public. A great number of citizens were preſented to him, and very graciouſly received.—Having arrived too late for a public dinner, he accepted an invitation to ſupper, from which he retired a little after ten o'clock. The next morning he was in his carriage at half paſt five o'clock, when he left town, under a diſcharge of cannon, and attended as on his entrance, by a body of the citizens on horſeback. Theſe gentlemen accompanied him ſeven miles, when alighting from his carriage, he would not permit them to proceed any further; but took leave of them, after thanking them in an affectionate manner for their politeneſs. We ſhall only add on this occaſion, that thoſe who had often ſeen him before, and thoſe who never had, were equally anxious to ſee him. Such is the rare impreſſion excited by his uncommon character and virtues.

FROM THE LONDON GAZETTE.

Paris, July 12. His Moſt Chriſtian Majeſty has appointed the Baron de Breteuil to be Preſident of the Council of Finances, in the room of M. Neckar; the Duke de la Vauguyon, Secretary of State for the Department of Foreign Affairs, in the room of M. de Montmorin; and the Marſhal de Broglio, to be Miniſter for the War Department.

The following important intelligence was received yeſterday by an extraordinary Meſſenger from Paris —in thirty-ſix hours!

On Sunday morning laſt, Mr. Neckar received his diſmiſſion from the King, as a Comptroller General of the Finances. On receiving this notice, he inſtantly left Paris, and ſet out poſt for Geneva.

Previouſly to this, on the Friday and Saturday, there had been ſuch a commotion in Paris, that one of the ringleaders about the palace was ordered to be taken up; but the perſons, who were ſent with command to arreſt him, were torn to pieces by the mob.

His Majeſty's anſwer to the National Aſſembly, on the ſubject of their repreſentation to diſmiſs the Swiſs troops, was to the following effect:

"That he conſidered them neceſſary for the preſervation of order and tranquillity; that the Aſſembly had no reaſon to be under any conſtraint on their account, and that, if the troops encamped in the neighbourhood of Paris were diſagreeable, his Majeſty would, on a requeſt from the States General, remove their ſittings to Soiſſons or Noyon, in which caſe he would himſelf repair to Compienne, in order to be at hand to correſpond with the States."

The late conceſſions of the Court to the juſt claims of the Tiers Etat, appear to have been a diſſembled acquieſcence!—For while they thus temporized, troops, to the amount of thirty-ſix thouſand, had been ſecretly drawn to the neighbourhood of Paris!—and that ſeveral new appointments had been made in the War-Department, to enable the Marſhal de Broglio to call in, to his aid, ſome field officers, on whoſe compliance he could depend.

The King, from this aſpect of affairs appears to have been entirely under the guidance of his conſort;—and ſo generally was this underſtood, that the Tiers Etat had inſiſted on the baniſhment of the Compte D'Artois;—a ſtop put to the miſcievous and ruinous interference of the Queen, and that her creatures, the Polignacs, ſhould be diſmiſſed!

The Comte de Mirabeau's patriotic endeavours to cauſe the troops to be withdrawn, were in vain:—all he could urge, and other Members, in favour of the People, tended only to encreaſe a ſpirit of reſiſtance to the Court: and it is not exaggeration to ſay, that the moſt dreadful anarchy is on foot!

The foreign regiments, among the forces abovementioned, were ſtationed in ſituations moſt contiguous to the gates of Paris and Verſailles; and they very ſoon proceeded to inſult the people:—riots enſued and a great multitude aſſailed the Palais Royale!—The officer and guard were killed on the ſpot!—The troops advanced into the city, and a continued engagement enſued, in which the people made a ſtand with aſtoniſhing intrepidity.—Before Roſſi, which is the name of the Courier, left Paris, the populace had repeatedly attacked the Comte D'Artois' reſidence, with a view of burning it, and alſo ſome of the Offices of State; and a number of lives on both ſides were loſt in theſe conflicts. A part of the multitude were on their way to Verſailles, and the Palace was threatened to be laid in aſhes.

LONDON, JULY 13, and 14.

THEIR Majeſties live quite a retired, private life, without any officers of ſtate about them, and only two or three belonging to the houſhold, who attend while the Royal Family walk abroad, which is every morning and evening the weather permits. His Majeſty is on horſe moſt days at ten o'clock. Thus the Royal Pair ſpend their time at Weymouth.

The Royal Family receive their proviſions every morning by the Royal mail coach from town. The butter, cream, bread, and even water, are ſent from the Palaces, the latter from a favourite ſpring near the Queen's Lodge, Windſor, which the Queen drinks in preference. The fruit is ſent chiefly from Kew, and the poultry from London.

After the evening walk, his Majeſty generally amuſes himſelf with a game at cards—cribbage is the favourite game, and Lord Cheſterfield has frequently the honour of being the Royal opponent. The ladies amuſe themſelves in the ſame manner.

The morning dreſs of riding habits is changed in the afternoon to undreſs gowns and coats. Her Majeſty for the two laſt evenings has worn a muſlin dreſs with a ſtraw-coloured petticoat. The Princeſſes have all appeared in the ſame dreſſes, dark flowered Geneva chintzes, blue or white ſilk petticoats, with ſmall chip bonnets, covered with half gauze handkerchiefs. Nothing can appear more ſimply neat.

The King will viſit Lulworth Caſtle, the ſeat of the family of the Welds, in which Mrs. Fitzherbert firſt married:—At this caſtle are many of Sir Peter's Lely's beſt portraits, and a beautiful Repoſe, by Claude.

DUBLIN, JULY 16.

There is one particular circumſtance that gives the Dutch a manifeſt advantage over other countries, with reſpect to the mode of carrying on their herring and white fiſheries. They employ buſſes for catching fiſh, and have always quick ſailing veſſels to attend, in order to carry the take to market as ſoon as properly cured, and thereby no delay is occaſioned, and thus alſo they are enabled to ſupply all parts of Europe, in the moſt expeditious manner. This mode is continued till the middle of July, and after that, all taken muſt be brought home, to be repacked, and made fit for winter's keeping. It is computed, that fifty veſſels can diſpatch one of thoſe ſmall craft every day, ſometimes two, from the coaſts of Shetland and the Dogger Bank, in which employment there are above one thouſand veſſels, and forty thouſand ſeamen. Such a regulation might be productive of good conſequences to our Iriſh fiſheries, if adopted, and thereby be enabled to ſupply foreign markets, before too great a quantity of fiſh is ſent off by the Hollanders, and when a good price can be readily procured.

Further accounts, ſince our laſt, from England, ſtate the Marquis of Buckingham's health to be almoſt intirely re-inſtated. He has found benefit in the Bath waters, and if he continues in his amending progreſs, the latter end of Autumn will probably ſee him in Ireland

Every day affords new inſtances of the inefficacy of of Police, and of the diſguſt which that expenſive, and obnoxious eſtabliſhment excites in the public.—To ſpeak of it as a protection to the perſon or property of the citizen, is a downright inſult on common ſenſe too glaring to be endured, for he experiences that it does neither. Daring outrage, and continued depredation infeſt every avenue to the city, whilſt in it, houſe-breaking and robbery have ſeldom ariſen to ſuch a height as of late: they are committed with an audacity that aſtoniſhes, and with an openneſs that deſpiſes concealment. Houſes are ſtripped directly oppoſite the Police ſtations, and Churches are robbed within twenty paces of their principal guard-houſe. Yet the commiſſioners ſleep ſupine, and for their emolument, and to extend the influence of adminiſtration, is this capital taxed to an enormous amount; an amount truly oppreſſive to the lower orders of the people. A general union of the citizens can alone relieve them from this waſteful, this odious inſtitution; though their efforts have recently been blaſted, yet if they perſevere ſome happy day will at length ſurely ſhine propitious on their worthy exertions.

COX *verſus* JOHNSON.

This was an action to recover ſatisfaction, in damages for criminal converſation. It came out in evidence that the plaintiff was 61 years of age, and his wife nineteen. They had been married eight months; and the plaintiff was fond of his wife to a degree of abſurdity; that he was inceſſantly, in the company of his acquaintances, beſtowing encomiums upon her chaſtity, and aſking their opinion of her beauty; that he told the defendant her virtue was invulnerable, and offered to lay him five guineas that ſhe would not permit him to ſalute her, offering at the ſame time to introduce him to her company; that the defendant refuſed to lay wagers, but in three days afterwards he was found in her bed chamber in a ſituation that left no doubt of her virtue. It appeared alſo in evidence, that the lady a ſhort time previous to her marriage, was ſeen at a houſe of ill-fame with a gentleman, late in the evening. The court conſidered the plaintiff's behaviour liable to blame, but no excuſe for that of the defendant's. Verdict for plaintiff, damages forty ſhillings.

LONDON-DERRY, JULY 14.

A ſeries of heavy rains, and a continued coldneſs of the air, have rendered this the moſt inclement ſeaſon that has been known for many years, and has been particularly unfavourable to the cutting of turf.—But we learn that the weather has been rather worſe in England and the continent: In France, to the violent contentions of Deſpotiſm and Liberty, are to be added the miſeries of Famine, cauſed by the failure of both laſt and this year's crops.

Committed to Gaol.——John Divlin and Elizabeth his wife, and a boy, Pat. Divlin, notorious pick-pockets; laſt aſſizes they were diſmiſſed for want of proſecution, and have ſince been in the different fairs held between this and Dungannon. Alſo a woman who ſays her name is Elizabeth Wilſon, and a young man, who calls himſelf Pat. Wilſon, but whoſe real name is believed to be O'Hara, and whoſe connection with ſundry perſons now in the gaols of Derry and Carrickfergus for picking pockets, and for being concerned in the robbery of Mrs. O'Reilly's houſe in the county Longford, give reaſon to ſuppoſe they are part of the gang.

On Saturday laſt, oatmeal ſold from 12d. to 13d. per peck.—Potatoes 4d. and 4d. h. per ſtone.

Same, day, Alderman Fairly ſeized two ſacks of meal from a foreſtaller.

MARRIED. At Nn. Limavady, Mr. William Browſter, the celebrated Grammarian, Arithmetician, and Mathematician, to the beautiful and accompliſhed Miſs Eliza. Starrat.

SHIP NEWS.

ENTERED from
Dantzig, Anna, Panke, weed-aſhes, &c.
Barbadoes, Hibernia, Lithgow, ſugar, &c.
Chriſtianſound, Mary, Stevenſon, deals.
Liverpool, Alexander, James, merchandiſe.
Briſtol, Mary, Fiſhly, do.
Arrived ſeveral veſſels with oats, oatmeal, potatoes, &c.

CLEARED for
Liverpool, Elizabeth, Harward, linen yarn.
Sailed, a number of veſſels in ballaſt.

Belfaſt.

We have received a letter from Banbridge which mentions, that a gentleman of the name of John Fitzpatrick, was on Wedneſday ſtopt in a carriage ſome miles from Newry, by two fellows armed, on which Mr. Fitzpatrick leaped out of the carriage and fired at one of them, but miſſed him. Mr. F. immediately fell, having received a ball from one of the villains, which entered at his neck and paſſed between his ſhoulders; the gentleman was delirious when the letter was ſent off; and being brought into a houſe, his gold watch and 20 guineas were carefully laid paſt ——Mr. Fitzpatrick has of late reſided at L:Derry, and was on his road from Belfaſt to Dublin.

Mr. Geo. Emerſon of this place lays dangerouſly ill, his ſcull having been fractured in two places, by ſtrokes which he received on his return from the races on Monday evening laſt. We think it proper to decline entering into particulars till our next.

The Revd. Mr. John Connor is preſented to the living of Ballenderry by the Earl of Hertford.

As ſome of our mercantile readers may not underſtand the expreſſion uſed by Congreſs, in America, to denote the ſum of duty lately laid on each article of import by that aſſembly, (publiſhed at large in our laſt paper) it is thought proper to explain that what is intended by *Cents*, are ſo many hundredth parts of a Spaniſh Dollar, and not ſo much *per Cent.*

The General Quarter Seſſions of the Peace for the County of Antrim will be held at Belfaſt by adjournment the 30th day of July inſt. for the purpoſe of Regiſtering Freeholders.

Belfaſt, *July* 21.

PORT NEWS.

ARRIVED.

July 14. Charlotte, Hunt, Jamaica, rum and ſugar.
15. Peggy, M'Ilroy, Liverpool, ditto.
Chriſtan, Harris, Memel, timber.
17. Fortitude, Glaſgow, Gottenburgh, Iron.
Two colliers.

CLEARED OUT.

July 14. Milford, Griffith, Rotterdam, flour.
15. Hillſbro', M'Donnell, Liverpool, butter.
16. Agnes, M'Pherſon, Rouen, flour.

The Gentlemen who aſſiſted at public Examinations in Mr. Marrin's School yeſterday, when a month's receſs took place, are unanimouſly of opinion that the majority in each Claſs are, for their knowledge in Greek, Latin, and Engliſh, equally ſo highly entitled to praiſe, that to adjudge a Premium to any one of the number would be a partiality worthy of cenſure.

Newry, 18th July, 1789.

Anno 1789.] Printed by HENRY JOY, and Co. BELFAST.

The BELFAST NEWS-LETTER.

TUESDAY July 28, FRIDAY July 31, 1789.

WE the underſigned Merchants, Traders, and other inhabitants of the Town of Belfaſt, being fully convinced from the experience of other Countries, as well as of different parts of this kingdom, that ſolid and well regulated Banks are ever and muſt be of the utmoſt public Benefit in commercial and manufacturing Countries: And being perfectly ſatisfied of the ſolidity and prudent Management of the two Banks lately eſtabliſhed in this Town, have from the firſt chearfully received their Notes in all payments made to us, and wiſh to the utmoſt of our power to encourage and promote their circulation, convinced that in ſo doing we are rendering an eſſential ſervice to our country; independent of which, for our own eaſe and convenience, we give Notice to all our Friends in Town and Country, that in all payments they may have to make to any of us, we will deem it a particular favor if they will make them in Belfaſt Bank Notes rather than Guineas. They will greatly oblige us by ſo doing, as thereby all trouble reſpecting Light or Bad Money will be totally prevented, and the Buſineſs much more expeditiouſly done.

Belfaſt, 26th July, 1789.

Brown, Gaw & Co.
Hill Wallace
Robt. Scott
George Bradford
James Wilſon
Stewarts, Thomſon & Co.
Joſeph Stevenſon
Hu. Mc. Ilwain,
Wm. Seed & Co.
Edw. M'Cormick
John Cunningham & Co.
Hu. Montgomery
Daviſon & Graham
Val. Smith
Alex. H. Haliday
Will. Jones
Daniel Blow
Wm. Mc. Ilwrath
John Craig
Duke Berwick
And Bankhead
Jas. Graham
David Watſon
A. Barnett
Wm. Anderſon
Jones, Tomb, Joy & Co.
Sam. Brown & Co.
Val. Joyce
Montgomery, Brown, Tennent and Boyle
John Gregg
Alex Orr
James T. Kennedy
John Brown, Peters-hill
Sam. Neilſon & Co.
Hu & Wm. Johnſon
Robt. Thomſon
Sam. & A. M'Clean
Thos. Cavan & Co.
John Boyle & Co.
Rich. M'Clelland
Will. Stevenſon
Mc. Kedy & Stevenſon
John Robinſon
Seeds, Wells, and Seeds
Cunningham Greg
Thomas Greg
Will. Irvin
Will. Burgeſs
Robt. W. M'Clure
James Mooney
Henry Joy, & Co.
Patterſon & Whittle
James Cleland
Daviſon & Miniſs
Robt. Hunter
John Campbell
Geo. Langtry
Sam. Gibſon
David Mc. Tear
Robert Knox
Alex. Watt
John Smylie & Co.
David Tomb
John Martin
John Luke
Narciſſus Batt
Robert Batt
Francis Davis
Fr. Lyle
Sam. Mitchell, ſen.

Sam. Mc. Murray & Co.
Mc. Tear & Henderſon
Wm. Mulrea
James Ferguſon
Haſlett, Strong & Co.
Samuel Hyde
James Holmes
O. Brett
John Alexander & Co.
John H. Houſton
John Reid
Jas. Pinkerton
Jn. Cranſton & Co
Taylor, Maxwell & Co.
Sam. Mc. Tier
Brown & Oakman
Alex. Neilſon
Robert Linn
Wm. Martin
John Galt Smith
Simon M'Creary
Alex. Black
Hugh Crawford
Wm Henderſon
Henderſon and Crawford
Abel Hadſkis
David Dunn
John Hughes
Thos. Saunders
James Patterſon
William Roth
Richd. Callwell
Stewart Banks
Robert Apſley
Hugh Warrin
John Mc. Cracken
John Elliott
John Bankhead
Spears & White
John Cumming
Robt. Herdman
John Gardiner
Wm. Bryſon
Alex. Armſtong
Robt. & William Simms
Thomas Major
Thomas Scott
Chr. Hudſon
Will. Warnick
Mackenzie and Mc. Cleery
James Magee
Wm. Magee
Wm. Callwell
Wm. Blackwell
Orr Reid
Robt. Callwell
James Stewart
Mc. Kain and Sheridan
St. John Stewart
David Bigger
Alex. Sinclaire
John Park
Sam. Woolſey
John Baſhford
John Murdoch
George Monro
John Mc. Clean
Thoburn & Munfoad

Robt. & Alexander Gordon
John Milford
Thos. Sinclaire & Sons
Samuel Ferguſon
Barth. Fuller
John Rainey
Andrew J. Barnett
James Barnett
Thomas Neilſon & Co.
Richard Simpſon
John Taggart
John Smyth
Samuel Shaw
John Johnſon
James Weir
Jas. Cunningham
Benj. Edwards
John Edwards
Gilbert M'Ilveen,
John Mitchell
Jas. Beggs & Co.
Thos. Milliken
Lukes, Oakman & Co.
Thomas Lyons
John Aſhmore
Rainey Maxwell
John Clarke
Row. Oſborne, jun.
James Carſon
William Dawſon
Ann Moor
Jane Kennedy
Arthur Kennedy
James Mc. Kibbin
Samuel Eaddy
Samuel Crothers
Hugh Taylor
Wm. Keenan
David Hunter
Archd. Newbigger
John Hunter
John M'Garragh
John Cuming
Robt. Dempſter
Arthur Buntin
John Vance
Hill Hamilton
Michael Harriſon
John Mc. Tee
James Kyle
Hu. Mc. Cullouch
Sampſon Clark
Hugh Allen
James Martin
Hamilton Neill
John Stewart
James Lowrey
Pat. M'Kinty
Wm. Hutton
James Black
John Fulton
Stewart B. Craig
Robt. Hodgſon
Wm. Mitchell
James M'Maſter
James Scott
Wm. Martin
Mary Torrens
Stewart Beatty
John Lowry
Robert Hilditch
Stewart Lowrey
John Moreland
George Dunbar

Thos. Herdman
Henry Cavart
John Caughey
Robt. Wilſon & Co
John Knox
John Stevenſon
Thompſon & Oakman
Robt. Getty
Wm. Emmerſon
Francis Joy & Co.
Forſyth, Shaw & Co.
Pat. Mc. Maſter
Hugh Wilſon

John Galt Smith & Co.
James Park
Conway Carleton
Robt. Goudy
Robert Orr
Thos. Mc. Cabe
Samuel Robinſon
Robt. Smith
James Murphy
Hugh Quin
David Dinſmore
Jacob Nixon
Alex. Arthur
Thos. Cavan

Robert Cuming
James Mc. Clean
Wm. Spencer
John Forcade
John Armſtrong
Wm. Hendren
Wm. Scott
Andrew Craig
Wm. Ramſey
Robert Hill
Wm. Monear
Matt. Bellew
Thos. Mullan
Iſaac Patton

Advertiſement.

TO be Let from the firſt of November next, in Ballyloran, within a ſhort mile of Larne, two Farms of Land; one of twelve, and one of twenty acres, plantation meaſure, with houſes on the ſame. For further particulars apply to Margaret Ogilvie, who lives on the premiſſes, will receive propoſals, and ſhew the lands.

Ballyloran, July 31ſt, 1789.

To be Sold,

ENGLISH-TOWN—The Houſe and Offices commodious, and all ſlated.—The Farm contains ſixty-four Engliſh acres—in the fineſt heart; a large ſum of money has been expended within theſe eighteen months on the buildings and land. It is held under Lord Cremorn by a toties quoties—The fine aſcertained, being one ſhilling every ſeven years.——It is ſituated four miles from Armagh, three from Kilyleagh, and one from Black Water Town, where Propoſals will be received directed for Mr. M. Anketell.

Engliſh-Town, July 27th, 1789.

Wanted,

A Few STONE CUTTERS, of character and abilities, to work at the Newry Navigation.——Application to be be made to the Revd. William Campbell, Newry. 23d July, 1789.

Two good Hands

WANTED immediately, to work in a FLAX-MILL; who will have conſtant employment thro' the ſeaſon, and be accommodated with houſes, gardens, and cow's graſs.

For particulars apply by letter, or in perſon, to Mr. Henry Joy, Belfaſt. July 23, 1789.

County of Antrim.

THE Secretary of the Grand Jury of the county of Antrim, will open his Office at Carrickfergus, upon MONDAY the 3d of Auguſt next, and ſhut the ſame upon THURSDAY the 6th. The Secretary requeſts, that the Magiſtrates may be pleaſed to cauſe the affidavits which may come before them to be ſworn, to be endorſed with the name of the *Half Barony*, the *number of perches*, and *the amount*, adding thereto, the Overſeer's wages. 13th July, 1789.

THE Inhabitants of the Town of Glaſslough, beg leave to return their ſincere thanks to the Gentlemen who were ſo obliging to officiate as Stewards at the late meeting, and think it incumbent on them in this public manner to acknowledge, its reſpectability was entirely owing to their activity and attention.

Signed by Order,

Glaſslough, July 20th, 1789. WM. CROOKSHANK, Secretary.

WHEREAS on Monday the 13th inſt. (being a fair day in this town) there was a man, who ſaid he came from the County of Antrim, ſold a cheſnut horſe with a white mane and tail, and on the purchaſer's demanding a voucher he abſconded, and has not yet appeared.—Any perſon proving the property and paying the expences of keeping, advertiſing, &c. may have him by applying to William Roſs, Eſq.

N:L:Vady, 25th July, 1789.

To be Sold,

Let for ever, or fined down,

A Very extenſive Bleach-Green, ſituate at Ravenſdale, within three miles of Dundalk, containing thirty acres, capable with its preſent Machinery (which are in compleat order) of finiſhing 12,000 pieces of linen in the year; alſo a Farm adjoining ſaid Green, containing thirty acres: the many and great advantages the above Green poſſeſſes in point of water, cheapneſs of firing, and convenient ſituation for carriage of bleaching ſtuffs are ſo well known they need not be enumerated.—There was a new double Engine erected on the premiſſes laſt year upon the moſt approved plan.

Apply to James Davis, Newry.

27th July, 1789.

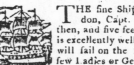

For *New-York*,

THE fine Ship COLWORTH, of London, Capt. Gelſton, 300 tons burthen, and five feet clear between decks—is excellently well fitted for paſſengers, and will ſail on the 15th of Auguſt next. A few Ladies or Gentlemen can be accommodated in the cabin in a ſtate ſuperior to almoſt any ſhip that ever ſailed from Ireland.——For Freight or Paſſage apply to the Captain on board, or

Newry, 27th July, 1789. JOHN NEVILL.

Mr. Millar's School, near Clogher,

OPENS on the 27th inſtant. His his Siſter-in-law, who has reſided with him ſince his commencement in that line, and has been remarkably attentive to the young Gentlemen under his care, will employ her utmoſt efforts to diſcharge the duties of an important department, which is now become vacant by a late melancholy event.

July 26th, 1789.

Belfaſt New Foundery.

THE Partnerſhip of Edwards and Shaw being diſſolved, by Edwards having purchaſed from Shaw, ſaid Edwards requeſts that all accounts due by the ſaid Partnerſhip may be furniſhed, and that he may be enabled to pay off ſuch, he requeſts that all who are indebted to ſaid Partnerſhip, will diſcharge their accounts, for which purpoſe they will be called in.—Said Edwards begs leave to inform that the Foundery Buſineſs is continued in the ſame place as uſual on his own account, and requeſts the protection of his friends and the public, and aſſures them that nothing ſhall be wanting on his part to make his goods acceptable and uſeful.—He is at preſent well ſupplied with a ſtock of good materials, which will enable him to fulfil any orders for Mill-work, and retail Goods at the ſhorteſt notice.

27th July, 1789.

NOTICE.

THE Proprietors of the Belfaſt Mail Coaches want a Coachman in the room of Abraham Dawſon, whom they have diſmiſſed for bad behaviour and inſolence to the paſſengers on Saturday night the 18th day of July inſtant.——None need apply but thoſe who bring good recommendations of their abilities, integrity and ſobriety. Application to be made to Mr John Hutton, Britain-ſtreet, Dublin; Meſſrs. Mc. Kean and Sheridan, Belfaſt; or the Proprietors, in Newry.

Dated the 20th day of July, 1789.

Dromore Summer Fair,

THE Summer Fair of Dromore will be held on Saturday the firſt day of Auguſt next, when there is expected to be a great ſale of Linen at the accuſtomed great Linen Market.

Dromore, July 25, 1789.

The Lurgan Club,

DINE at the BLACK BULL INN, (Saturday being the firſt of Auguſt) on Monday the third. Dinner on the Table at four o'clock. 24th July, 1789.

Signed by Order,

H. Mc. VEAGH, Secretary.

WHEREAS we Daniel Kinny, Alex. Kinny, James Kinny, Daniel Kinny, junr. Bryan Mc. Ilhone, John Stewart, and Archibald Stewart—all of Sheans, in the county of Antrim, Farmers, and Malcom Mc. Donnell of Alterichard and county aforeſaid, yeoman, have been charged with the murder of Shane O'Mullan of Culcoorin in ſaid county, yeoman.—Now, in order to evince to the publick and world at large, our innocence of ſaid crime improperly alledged againſt us, and to ſhew our readineſs to obey and be amenable to the laws of our country, Do hereby give notice to the proſecutors, that we will ſurrender ourſelves to the preſent Sheriff, in order to abide our trials for ſaid alledged offence at the enſuing Aſſizes at Carrickfergus in and for ſaid county.

Dated this 20th day of July, 1789.

GEORGE Mc. COMB, of Killaghies, in the pariſh of Donaghadee and county of Down, having a mind to remove himſelf and family to America, will, on Thurſday the 20th of Auguſt next, ſell by Auction, at his Dwelling-houſe, his Leaſe of ſaid Farm, containing 17A. 2R. 25P. ſubject to 17s. per acre yearly, ſeventeen years unexpired. He will likewiſe ſell at ſame time, another ſmall Farm, containing about twenty acres, ſubject to a yearly rent of 13l. 8s. 6d, ſix years unexpired at November next. One third part of the purchaſe-money to be paid on the day of ſale, and the remainder at four months date. After the ſale of the above two Leaſes, on ſaid day, he will ſell all his Crop on the foot, to wit, about nine acres of Oats, and about three acres of Wheat; three months credit on giving ſecurity.

Dated Killaghies, 20th July, 1789.

PARISIAN INTELLIGENCE.

THE populace hearing of Mr. Neckar's dismissal from the Seals, and apprehending him to be sent to the Bastile, assembled on Saturday the 11th, to the number of 25,000, in the square of Louis XV. from whence they marched, armed with musquets, broad-swords, &c. to the Barriers, at the ends of the town, which being of wood, they destroyed in a few hours: they then took the road to Versailles, and were opposed some miles from Paris, by a number of Swiss guards, whom they dispersed after a conflict, in which many were killed on both sides.——The armed populace returned to town, and seized about forty pieces of cannon, with which, and their small arms, they attacked the King's troops on the Quai du Louvre, between the New and the Royal Bridges, which so terrified the inhabitants, that the shops were shut, and the doors and windows barred, as in a city besieged by a foreign enemy. Skirmishes with cannon and musquetry were continued all Sunday and the ensuing night in various parts of the town, and the streets of St. Eustache, St. Honore, and Monmartre, on one side of the river, and those of Richlieu, Tournon, Dauphine, and all the Quays, from St. Michael's-bridge to the Hospital of Invalids, filled with armed citizens, carrying a fusil and bayonet in one hand, and a lighted torch in the other.

About six on Monday morning, the 13th, strong parties of armed burghers paraded the city, attended by drums, beating to arms, and proclaiming, that from and after that day, no taxes, gabels, excise, or duties whatsoever, were to be paid to the King, at least till the new levies should be voted, and confirmed by the States General then sitting, on pain of military execution being put in force against those who dared to contravene the general municipal order in that behalf.

In consequence of the King's troops encamping ne.r Paris, all house-keepers, with their friends and dependents, capable of bearing arms, have associated in the manner of the IRISH VOLUNTEERS after a solemn oath to protect their liberty, property, wives, children, and other weak persons, to the last extremity, against any power whatsoever. In this state of anarchy and horror, was the once gay any flourishing capital of the French empire involved, on Monday, the 13th instant.

Another account says, that Mr. Neckar, thinking himself in a very dangerous situation, went privately to Versailles, on Friday evening, the 10th instant, where he resigned the seals into the King's own hand, and having sent his lady a day's journey from Paris the day before, got into a post-chaise and joined her, as is supposed, on the road to Franche Comté and Geneva. His fortune has been very wisely and prudently lodged, some weeks past, in the Royal Bank of Turin.

ON TUESDAY

The scene opened in the same violent manner. Fresh troops kept constantly dropping in. Detachments sent out of town on all sides, were continually returning with corn intended for the hostile troops, cannon, powder, &c. &c. Several waggons were intercepted destined for the King, and brought triumphantly into town, each of them drawn by six royal horses.

Before noon a body of 20,000 citizens, headed by the French Guards, now joined by many of their officers, who had previously taken an oath of fidelity, summoned the Hotel des Invalides in form with cannon (the Hotel des Invalides is at 50 yards distance from the Military School, where there now were 4000 hostile troops with a park of artillery); the Governor surrendered, and immediate possession was taken of 52,000 stand of arms, cannon, ammunition, &c. and brought triumphantly into town.

On the other side of the town, the Bastile was summoned by 10 or 12,000 citizens, headed by the grenadiers of the French guards, and on the Governor's holding out a white flag, and opening one of the gates, a party of young citizens, with some soldiers, incautiously entered; the Governor instantly drew up the drawbridge, and his troops, consisting of invalids and some auxiliary Swiss, fired through loop holes, and killed or wounded the whole party. About 30 were killed. Four times he attempted the same stratagem, but not with the same success; at last the fortress was regularly attacked and cannonaded for three hours, and the ditches filled with straw, &c. &c. A breach was effected, and first mounted by a French grenadier; the Governor, the Marquis de Delaune, the Prince de Montbory, the Fort Major, &c. were made prisoners, and all the poor unhappy State prisoners, many of whom had languished for years in this execrable abode, released; among which number was Lord Mazarine, an Irish Nobleman, who had been confined for debt near 20 years.

The great and important scene now followed—The Governor, the Prince, the Fort Major, and officers, were conveyed to the Hotel de Ville, and, after a short trial, M. de Delaune and the Major were executed by first shooting them, and then cutting off their heads. Other officers next underwent the same fate.

WEDNESDAY.

No person is allowed to leave Paris without a previous examination at the Hotel de Ville, and permissions; nor a shilling, or even a silver spoon, to be sent out of it. Large sums have been stopped, intended for the Court. The post, diligences, packets—every thing is examined.

The news of taking the Bastile, and the beheading the Governor, and the Prevot des Marchands, reached Versailles late on Tuesday evening—The effect was easily to be foreseen—this act of firmness made many an exalted neck creek. The King was taken ill—all was alarm at the Court.

The Assembly, early in the morning, adopted vigorous measures; the matter was now come to a point.

Had the King not given way, the Assembly would have joined us at Paris, and he most probably have lost the throne.

In the evening a numerous deputation arrived, bringing his resolution to send off the troops, and his intention to throw himself into the arms of the people.

His answer to the Commons, however, is still worded in indecent and arbitrary language, and exhibits a mixture of despotism and cowardice, worthier of a Stuart than a Bourbon. None of his Ministers were present with him; but, what was as bad, his two unworthy brothers.

The Deputies were received with a discharge of cannon and musquetry at every post and barricade, and by a feu de joye from all the patroles of Citizens, and by applauses that must have touched the most unfeeling heart.

M. Baily, that illustrious philosopher, that eloquent orator, that honest man, was instantly proclaimed by the electors of Paris, assembled at the Hotel de Ville, Mayor of the City of Paris; the title to be assumed in future, in room of the wretched Prevot des Marchands, executed on Tuesday. Thus is this nomination taken out of the King's hands.

THURSDAY.

The first news of yesterday was the retreat of the troops at the Military School, who had stolen off during the night to Versailles, to avoid a siege determined on for the morning; immediate possession was taken of it, and a vast magazine of flour, &c. Things were now got into complete order—batteries established—the streets in the suburbs unpaved, *chevaux de frize* erected, &c. and barricades prepared for the first alarm of the approach of cavalry. Joy and courage was painted on every face.

This morning the whole body of the Militia were under arms, and lined the streets to receive the King and the National Assembly. His Majesty, overcome by fatigue, was too much indisposed to go to Paris; but the National Assembly went, and were received by the citizens under arms; and the *Te Deum* was performed to the most crouded auditory that Paris, in its most religious days, ever witnessed.

When his Majesty excused himself from going to Paris on account of his indisposition, the Parisians sent a dep.tation to say, that his sacred person should be guarded by 12,000 of his faithful citizens. When he still declined, they gave a gentle hint that they should humbly expect his presence in Paris the next day, and 25,000 armed citizens would attend to guard him.

It is expected the King will go in a few days, in state, to the *Hotel de Ville* of Paris, in order to deliver a speech to the *Bourgoisie*—the City. There is no doubt but, on that occasion, he will be received with every demonstration of joy and affection.

The Queen has been at Versailles during the whole time of the tumults. Her reign in the political world has received its death-blow, and the King, will be directed in his future measures by the voice of the National Representatives.

The Swiss Guards have already begun to withdraw from Versailles, and it is believed they will be entirely dismissed. The city of Paris is in future to be guarded solely by the citizens.

The proscriptions against particular persons have ceased, and there is to be an oblivion of all that has passed.

The Duke of Dorset's letter to Government, states the number of persons massacred at the Bastile, in the attempt to take it, to amount only to forty; these had been invited within the draw-bridges, by a presumption that the fortress had surrendered, when they were all treacherously fired on. It was this act, for which the Governor and Deputy Governor afterwards paid forfeit with their lives.

The only State Prisoners, where so many were supposed to have entered—the only prisoners that were forthcoming in the general delivery, amounted to four!

Major White and Lord Mazarine were two out of that number.

LONDON.

Mr. Pitt is not thirty-one years, of age, and yet this is the third attack of the gout.—The two former were only visits of ceremony.

Belfast.

*** The great importance and length of the French news will plead our excuse for omitting an account of the Running at the Maze, till our next, when it shall be given at large.

There is reason to apprehend that the letter received by us last Thursday, bearing the Banbridge post mark, and mentioning that a Mr. John Fitzpatrick had been attacked by two fellows in that neighbourhood—was a fabrication.

The spirit of Liberty in France, long oppressed by the hand of power, received its first spark of returning animation, by the incautious and impolitic assistance afforded to America. The French soldier, on his return from that emancipated continent, told a glorious tale to his countrymen—"That the arms of France had assisted to give Freedom to Thirteen United States, and planted the standard of Liberty on the battlements of New York and Philadelphia!" The idea of such a noble deed became a general object of admiration—the sweets of a similar state were eagerly longed for by all ranks of people, and the *vox populi* had this force of argument—"If France gave freedom to America, why should she not break the arbitrary fetters which bind her own people."

Such, we may venture to say, was the original cause of that important struggle, to the event of which surrounding empires look with impatient anxiety—for the victory of the people must seriously affect the different interests of all Europe.

Extract of a Letter from Armagh, July 22.

"Last Sunday Mr James Scott of this town departed this life, in the sixty-second year of his age, universally regretted by an extensive circle of acquaintances, to whom he was endeared by every tie of social affection.—In his conduct through life he united generosity, humanity, and inflexible justice.—In friendship he was steady, uniform, persevering, and zealous. His heart felt for the distresses of the poor, and his liberal hand was ever ready to alleviate the wretchedness of indigence and the miseries of necessity. In short, having fulfilled his duty as a christian and a man—having finished a well spent life, beneficial to society and exemplary to all—Heaven has been pleased to call him to that seat of bliss where his merits shall be justly weighed and duly rewarded.

DIED.] On Monday the 20th inst. at Comber, Miss MARY GILLESPIE.—She suffered under a severe and lingering illness with admirable piety, serenity, and fortitude;—her virtues have raised an honourable and lasting monument to her memory, in the hearts and affections of her family and friends.——At London-Derry, on the 17th inst. Mrs. Abigail Gardner, a maiden Lady.

The General Quarter Sessions of the Peace for the County of Antrim will be held at Belfast by adjournment the 30th day of July inst. for the purpose of Registering Freeholders.

PORT NEWS.

ARRIVED.

July 21. Dolly, Ross, Gottenburgh, iron.
22. St. Johannes, Mollar, Drontheim, deals, &c.
Eight colliers.

CLEARED OUT.

July 21. Peggy, M'Ilroy, Liverpool, butter, flour, &c.
23. Live Oak, Durham, Rotterdam, flour.

Belfast, *July* 31.

PRICES IN THIS MARKET YESTERDAY.

Oatmeal,	10s.	8d.	to	11s.	0d.	Dried do. 25s. to 26s. per doz
Wheat,	12	2	—	12	6	Rough Tallow, 5s. per st.
Oats,	5	5	—	6	0	Potatoes (new) 3½d. per p.
Barley,	0	0	—	5	6	Eng. coals, 13s. 6d. to 14s.
Butter	48	0	—	0	0	Scotch do. 12s. 6d. to 13s.
C. hides,	32	6	—	34	0	Ex. on London 7 per cent.
Ox ditto,	37	6	—	38	0	Do. on Glasgow 6½ to 7 do.
S.C.skins	40	0	—	42	6	

FAIRS IN THE ENSUING WEEK.

Monday, Aug. 3. Beleek, Arm.—Callaghane, Ferm.—Callowhill, Ferm.—Castledergh, Tyr—Connor, Ant.—Emyvale, Mon.—Orrator, Tyr.—St. Johnston's Bridge, Don. Wednesday 5th. Ballinamallard, Ferm—Pelcoo, Ferm.—Benburbe, Tyr.—Clough, Ant.—Cross, Arm.—Dunfanaghy, Don—Kilmore, Down.—Lurgan, Arm. two days.—Muff, Don.—Newtownbutler, Ferm.—Omagh, Tyr. Thursday 6th. Muff, Der. Friday 7th. Parkgate, Ant.—Sheepbridge, Down. Saturday 8th. Cookstown, Tyr. Middletown, Arm

GAME.

I Do hereby give Notice, that Lord Donegall intends to preserve the Game on his Mountains in the county of Antrim this season; and therefore I hope and request that no person whatever do trespass on his Lordship's Estate:—I do also hereby caution the Game keepers to be vigilant and active in the execution of their duty.
Castle-Office, Belfast, 28th July, 1789.
E. KINGSMILL.

John Davidson,

TAKES the liberty of informing his Friends and the Public, that he has just received a compleat assortment of the following articles, which he is determined to sell, wholesale and retail, at the most reduced prices, viz. plain, striped, and checqued muslins, spaw gawze, lenows, lawns, silk, cotton, and linen handkerchiefs, modes, persians, ribbands, men and women's gloves, white and coloured threads, pins, tapes, garters, paduaserge, pladdings, flannels, &c. &c. with many other articles in the haberdashery and woollen line.
Belfast, 30th July, 1789.

NOTICE.

TO the Tenants of Sir John Blackwood, Bart. Hugh Lyons Montgomery, and Townley Blackwood, Esqrs. that (to save the trouble and expence of light gold) James Savage will take Belfast Bank Notes in payment of rent.
Ballyleedy, 4th August, 1789.

Shane's-Castle.

FRANCIS Mc. CLEAN has just imported a large supply of Memel and Dantzig Timber; also best Deals, Laths, &c. which he will sell on very moderate terms.
5th August, 1789.

MAGEE's LOTTERY OFFICE.

Irish State Lottery 1789.

WM. MAGEE,

BRIDGE-STREET, BELFAST.

HAVING obtained a Licence from the Commissioners appointed by his Majesty for managing the present Lottery, to deal in Lottery Tickets, is now selling

WHOLE TICKETS,
HALVES,	EIGHTHS, &
FOURTHS,	SIXTEENTHS.

Also legal stampt GUINEA TICKETS, which include every Prize in the Wheel.
Prizes in last Irish Lottery taken in exchange without any discount whatever.

Samuel Brown & Co.

HAVE received by the Friendship, from London, their usual assortment of TEAS, purchased at the last East-India Sale; also by the Neptune from Oporto, a few Pipes and Hogsheads of excellent old Red Port.
They have likewise the following Articles, which will be sold on the lowest terms, viz.

Antigua & Jamaica Rum,	Cane Reeds,
Strong Bordeaux Brandy,	Best Alicant Barilla,
Holland Gineva,	Scotch Vitriol,
Claret,	Figs in Casks,
White Port, } Wines in	Muscatel Raisins in small
Sherry, and } wood and	boxes,
Mountain } bottle,	Fine white Powder Sugar,
Bordeaux Vinegar,	Mess Beef,
Bristol Window Glass,	Ditto Pork.

London Porter of an exceeding good quality; and they have yet on hands a very few hogsheads of the much esteemed keeping Porter for bottling.
Belfast, 6th August, 1789

PORT WINE.

CUNNINGHAM GREG, is just landing from on board the Neptune, from Oporto, a few pipes and hogsheads, the quality of which he can assure his friends is of the very best, and will be sold on reasonable terms.
Belfast, 6th August, 1789.

Belfast, 1st August, 1789.

AT a Meeting of Representatives from the following Corps, viz. Belfast first Co. ditto Artillery; Belfast Volunteer Co. ditto Artillery; Belfast Troop of Light Dragoons; Carrickfergus, Killead 1st Co. Whitehouse; Comber and Falls Fuzileers,
The following Resolutions were unanimously agreed to:

1. That a Review be held on Wednesday the 26th August inst. at such a distance from the Town of Belfast that the corps can march to the field and return in one day.
2. That our Chairman in the most respectful manner inform General the Earl of Charlemont of our intention to have a Review on the day appointed, and that his Lordship be requested to appoint a Gentleman to review these corps, and others which may make returns to our Chairman before the 10th August.
3. That Lieut. Col. Banks, Capts. Cunningham, Brown and Ranken, and such other Members of Belfast Corps as are present at this meeting, be a Committee for the purpose of fixing on the ground.
4. That the Plan of Review for last year be adopted for the present year; printed copies of which will immediately be transmitted by our Chairman to each corps here represented.
Signed by Order.
THOs. BROWN, Chairman.

Book Auction,

At BAILIE's Auction ROOMS, Chichester-Quay.

ABOVE 400 Volumes of Books to be sold;—the sale to begin this evening at 7 o'clock, and continue until 1—likewise each succeeding evening untill all are sold.—Catalogues of the Books to be had at the time of sale.　Tuesday, Belfast the 4th August, 1789.
N. B. To-morrow, (Wednesday) there will be sold some Household Furniture, viz Tables, Chairs, Looking-glasses, Feather Beds, &c. &c. &c.
The Sale to begin at 11 o'clock forenoon.

Advertisement.

THE Lord Bishop of Down will hold his annual Visitation at Lisburn, on Wednesday the 12th instant.　August 3d, 1789.

Down Infirmary.

THERE will be a BALL for the Benefit of the IN-FIRMARY at the Market House, on MONDAY the tenth Inst.
Dated the 4th August, 1789.

Wanted,

A LOW PHAETON,

WITH Harness, either for one or two Horses.—It must be clean and in good order—not much the worse for wearing—and it must be sold very low. Any person whom this may suit, will please apply to MAT. SPENCE, Coach-maker, Mill-street, BELFAST.
This to be only once inserted.

Now selling at & under prime Cost, (for Cash or Bills)

AT the Shop of Peter Quinn Kean, a large Assortment of Hardware and Ironmongery, being the entire Stock in Trade of the late Partnership of Mc. Murray and Kean.
Newry, 4th August, 1789.

Lands to be Sold,

THAT Part of the Townland of Ballymenoch, in the County of Down, the property of the late James Hamilton, Esq; to be sold at the Donegall-Arms in Belfast, at Noon, on Monday the 14th of September next, containing the following Denominations:

	Cunningham Measure. A. R. P.	Rent and Duties. l. s. d.	Tenure, lives and yrs. from Nov. next Lvs. Yrs.
William Patton	77 0 0	40 0 0	3 — 28
John Patton	31 2 20	23 4 6	1 — 16
William Patton	31 2 16	37 4 0	3 — 28
Widow Wightman	36 1 34	18 9 9	2 — 1
William Russell	12 0 16	8 12 0	1 — 18
John Lennox	11 3 30	6 18 8	
David Trotter, & } Wid. M'Cutchen }	58 2 0	18 19 6	3
Wid. M'Cutchen	26 0 0	9 11 2	2
Alex. Mc. Clean	26 0 16	8 13 0	3
James Herrot	28 2 20	5 16 9	3
James Reid	31 2 20	12 9 9	3
Demesne.	63 3 8		
Roads	3 2 20		
	439 0 0	189 19 1	

To be Sold,

THE Schooner ANN, Irish register, 71 tons, well found, and calculated for the Straits or Windward Island Trade, at six and nine months credit, at the Hanover-Quay.—Apply to Messrs. Mc. Kedy and Stevenson, who will shew the Inventory.
If not disposed of before the 24th inst. will on that day, at one o'clock in the afternoon, be sold by publick Auction at the Exchange Coffee-room.
Belfast, 3d July, 1789.

J. READ and S. SCOTT,

Successors to the late Nath. Berry, Linen Draper and Haberdasher; No. 34, Pill-lane,

MOST respectfully acquaint their Friends and the Publick, that they have laid into said House a large and elegant assortment of Goods in the above line of business, which they are determined to sell by Wholesale at the most reduced prices; as new beginners, and their strict attention to business hope to merit a continuance of all those who will please to favour them with their commands.
Dublin, 3d August, 1789.

A Cow strayed or stolen;

ON the night of the second inst. out of the townland of Ballymasca, in the parish of Dundonald, A Red Milch Cow, rising 11 years old, about four hundred weight, broad made behind, a hole in one of her horns, white but on her udder. If strayed, a reward of half a Guinea, or, if stolen, two Guineas, upon conviction of the Thief, will be given by me, the owner of said Cow.　ALEX Mc. DONNEL.
Ballymasca, 5th August, 1789.

The Randalstown Knot,

DINE at the King's-Arms, on Monday the 10th instant.——Dinner to be on the Table at four o'Clock.
T. A. S. R. K.
Randalstown, Aug. 6th, 1789.

NOTICE.

WHEREAS I some time ago gave a power of Attorney to Mr. John Coulter to receive my rents of Ballylummon: NOW the tenants are to take notice, that I have reversed said power, and that they are not in future to pay any rents to the said John Coulter, or his order, or I will oblige them to pay it again to myself, as I mean directly to enforce the payment of all rent and arrears due me by said tenants.
Dated at Brokish this 1st day of August. 1789.
JAMES M'LORINAN.

TO BE SET,

FROM November next, ten or twenty acres of Land, in the townland of Knocknagony, situate on the road betwixt Belfast and Holywood, either for a term of years or renewable for ever, well supplied with water, free of tythe, and a beautiful situation.——For particulars apply to John Jackson on the lands.—This to be continued only three times.
Knocknagoney, 7th August, 1789.

A Wherry for Sale by Auction.

TO be sold at Ardglass, on Friday the 14th instant, at the hour of twelve o'clock, by publick sale, for ready money,——A good WHERRY, about two years old, her keel 30 feet in length, beam 14 feet and a half, about 28 tons burthen.——For further information apply to　ALEX. NEEPER, or
JOHN STARKEY.
Ardglass, 1st Aug. 1789.

Advertisement.

A Farm of near forty acres of exceeding good well-enclosed Land in Tullycarnet, within three miles of Belfast, will be let in separate divisions to suitable tenants, or the interest of the grand lease, which is for 39 years and three young lives, sold——For further particulars enquire at William Gelston of Knock, near Belfast.
N. B. Said Farm is free of Tythe.—To be inserted three times.　August 6th, 1789.

NOTICE.

I JOHN Mc. KINSTRY, of the parish of Ballinderry, in the county of Antrim, Farmer, being charged upon oath with having set fire to a turf-stack, the property of John Sillyman, junr. of the parish of Ballinderry aforesaid, will come in, surrender, and take my tryal for the same at the next Assizes to be held at Carrickfergus in and for the said county of Antrim, of which all persons concerned are to take notice.
Ballinderry, 30th July, 1789.　JOHN Mc. KINSTRY.

PARISIAN INTELLIGENCE.

PARIS, JULY 20.

THE tumults of the capital are unluckily renewed in the towns of St. Germain and Poissy.—The populace seized all the Invalids arms, and upwards of 600 men went to the house of one Sauvage, where they found between six or seven hundred sacks of flour. He was a miller, and consequently might have such a quantity in his house. The poor fellow's person was dragged to a convent, where the Friars, after examining him, declared him innocent. Notwithstanding this declaration, the mob led Sauvage to the market-place, where a butcher cut off his head. This they carried about the streets, copying the late transaction of the capital. What enhances their cruelty is, that they insisted on the poor sufferer's son to be present at his father's execution. Sauvage's daughter, unable to bear so horrid a sight, threw herself over a bridge into the water and was drowned. The Deputies of the National Assembly arrived too late to prevent this mischief.

Dreadful have been the excesses committed at Rouen. Many citizens have been killed by the troops, and some have greatly suffered by the populace, who ransack and pillage all the houses they suspect of having any corn concealed. Two vessels have been stripped, and all sorts of carriages attacked and robbed. The Attorney-General of the Province had a narrow escape for his life.

NATIONAL ASSEMBLY, July 19.

Last night the Archbishop of Vienne announced to the National Assembly, that the time of his Presidency was expired, and that he requested them the next morning to chuse a new President.

The Deputies from Dauphiny then communicated to the Assembly news received from their Province, "That the dismission of M. Neckar, and surrounding the National Assembly with a formidable army, had caused a general insurrection; and that this Province was in arms to defend the Liberty of France, and that of its Representatives."

The general result of the scrutiny for a new President was then declared, when it appeared that the Duke de Liancourt was elected by a majority of six hundred out of eight; and on Monday he will enter on his office as President of the National Assembly.

We are happy to hear that the dark clouds of famine and distress, which at present obscure the sprightly atmosphere of France, are likely to be soon dissipated by the arrival of above one hundred vessels from Boston, Philadelphia, Salem, New-Providence, and Charlestown, deeply laden with wheat, flour, and a large quantity of rice. This provision was engaged last April, by Mr. Gerard, the French Envoy to the American States, but could not be shipped till a sufficient number of vessels were procured at the different ports—they are now on their passage, and expected at Nantz, Bourdeaux, Rochelle, and Havre-de-Grace, about the latter end of the present month.

Lord Massarene was confined in the Hotel de la Force. About eighteen months ago he made an attempt to escape with eight others. They had provided rope-ladders and poison, and reached the last wall, when the keeper of the gaol and his servants were awakened by the barking of a large bull-dog, which they had poisoned. They were then secured; and the dog dying immediately after, his body was embalmed, and placed opposite to the room where the prisoners assembled, in order to perpetuate the memory of his fidelity. The noble Lord was transferred to the dungeon of the Conciergerie, for a month's time; and corporeal punishment would have been inflicted for making use of poison, had it not been out of consideration for the *Irish blood*.

LONDON, JULY 25.

The books of the detestable French Police have been seized on by the citizens, and the *respectable* names they contain will be published at large in the course of a few days.

No less than 300 persons are employed in demolishing that once dreadful fortress, the Bastile.

Yesterday M. de Calonne gave a very grand entertainment to their Graces the Duke and Duchess of Luxembourg, and a large party of foreigners of distinction, lately arrived from France.

The Clerical Juggling in France had little weight during the late struggle—and the Pope himself at this moment is like a Conjurer, whose wand is taken away!

WEYMOUTH.

"*Thursday, July* 23. The King mounted his horse about eleven, and the Queen, with the Princess Elizabeth, and two of the Ladies in waiting, got into their carriage, and took an airing till near three o'clock. The Princesses Royal and Augusta walked the Beach, with each a female escort, till one, when they returned to Gloucester House; in the evening the whole of the Royal Family went to the Theatre.

LONDON.

To the great joy of all Scotland, superb preparations are making in Edinburgh for the reception of his Royal Highness the Prince of Wales, who is very soon expected at that place.

The Dukes of York and Clarence are mentioned as intending to accompany him.

Holyrood House, the ancient residence of the Scottish Kings, will appear in greater splendour than it has done since the beautiful but unfortunate Mary swayed the sceptre of that kingdom.

The Nobility and Gentry are crowding from all parts of Scotland to witness the condescension of the Royal Visitor.

Since the year 1745, a period fatal to many in Scotland, none of the Royal Family have honoured this part of the British Empire with their presence.

DUBLIN, JULY 30.

The anniversary of the Prince of Wales's birth-day, which is the 12th of August, will be marked in this country by the most brilliant testimony of universal attachment; several persons of distinction meditate a splendid and tasteful illumination of their houses, on the occasion; and there cannot be a doubt of the promptitude in which every class of the people will manifest their love to a Prince, who is at once the darling and admiration of those realms over which he is born to reign.

Notwithstanding that our ports have been shut for some time past against the exportation of grain, flour, &c. yet we are assured that a considerable quantity of wheat and flour has been lately clandestinely shipped from several of the southern parts of this kingdom, for Bourdeaux and other ports in France.

DUBLIN, AUGUST 1.

Yesterday afternoon Thomas Fitzgerald and Francis Gore were executed opposite the New Prison, pursuant to their sentence.

In the life of Gore, (whose real name it appears was Edward Caulfield) there have been as many singular circumstances as would furnish incidents sufficient to fill a volume, the whole series of which formed a chain of most remarkable deceptions, carried on with amazing artifice. At a very early period he discovered the strongest propensity for the attire of females and their trinkets, he had likewise catched their manners, could imitate all their coynesses, and became intimate with all the secrets of the toilette. About ten years of age, habited in the stolen apparel of a girl, he eloped from Spa Hill, in the county of Carlow, and proceeded to the county of Kilkenny, where, having an handsome recommendatory countenance, he was sheltered by some humane farmer, to whom he had, even thus young, made out a very specious though fallacious story. A few years afterwards he entered on bolder adventures, and having assumed the name of Gore, trumped up a tale of his being respectably connected, of his having forfeited the countenance of his friends by falling in love with an officer, and that his manly habit, (which he now thought proper to take up again) was a disguise to conceal him from his friends and protect him from the insults of the world. By those arts he actually insinuated himself into many respectable families as a distressed young lady, and, strange as it may appear, contrived to remain undiscovered, for a considerable time, in different quarters. At length, however, this singular impostor, having become pretty generally known in the interior parts of the kingdom, and having received a ducking a few years since in a horsepond for some deception at Kilcullen, he came to the metropolis, where his career was finally arrested by the hands of justice, for stealing several articles of plate out of the house of a gentleman in Chancery-lane, after having passed thro' as remarkable a course of impositions as have occurred in this country.

It was the practice of the above extraordinary fellow, when any circumstance arose that produced a determination to examine whether he was of the masculine or feminine gender, to counterfeit fits; by this artifice, at which he was also admirable, he disarmed the curious, and eluded discovery and frequently punishment. In short, from an early imitation and constant habit of personating a female himself, he arrived at a wonderful resemblance of the character, so that his mien, fashion of his apparel, style of his hair, &c. were all studiously calculated and well adapted to carry on his impostures; the gallantry of his own sex, under the idea of assisting an unfortunate female exposed to embarrassment and distress, contributed, in various instances, to support him during the progress of this uncommon species of deception and villainy.

People in the country parts of Dublin, mix one half potatoes, when boiled, with the dough made of coarse flour, perhaps more, and when baked on the griddle, the cakes eat very palatable.

Belfast, *August* 4.

Extract of a Letter from Castlewellan, dated Aug. 2.

"Yesterday part of the Loyal County Down Regiment paraded here, fired three vollies in honour of the day, and partook of an entertainment prepared by their Colonel (Lord Viscount Glerawly) to whom (with a promptitude of spirit which did them much honour) they tendered their service, and declared, they would be ready to a man, on the shortest notice, to aid the civil magistrate to the utmost of their power, in the suppression of mobs, and dispersion of illegal assemblies, without respect to sects or parties. His Lordship politely accepted their offered service, and assured them, he most heartily concurred with them, and should exert his best endeavours to promote and effectuate such laudable intentions."

On Sunday last the Lord Bishop of Down held an ordination in the parish church of Belfast. Mr. William Ravenscourt, Mr. James Skelton, and Mr. Thomas Edward Higginson were ordained Priests—and Mr. Leslie Batterſbea was ordained a Deacon.

The Charlotte, Wm. Campbell master, for London, is safe arrived at the Downs after a passage of eleven days.

The Lord Donegall, James M'Roberts master, is clear to sail, for London and will proceed first fair wind.

The New Draper, from Newry to London, sails next tide with a valuable cargo of linen cloth.

PORT NEWS.

ARRIVED.

July 28. Oroonoko, Fletcher, Antigua, rum and sugar.
New Loyalty, Brown, Chester, bark and drapery.
29. Zufrenheit, Leivertz, Drunthon, deals.
30. Neptune, Miskelly, Oporto, wine.
31. Prosperity, Moatt, Jamaica, rum and sugar.

CLEARED OUT.

July 27. Success, Mazurie, St. Vincent's and Eustatia, pork, &c.
28. Two Friends, Christian, Havre de Grace, flour.
30. Beresford, Horseman, Jamaica, cloth, pork, &c.
New Draper, Kearney, Liverpool, ditto and butter.

☞ MR. CULLEN, Dentist, respectfully informs the Public, that he has moved to commodious Apartments, at Mr. Mooney's, Grocer, High-street, opposite the Crown Tavern, and adjoining Grimes's Entry.—His stay will be about three weeks longer.

Belfast, *August* 7.

The Lord Donegall, James M'Roberts master, for London, is still here detained only by contrary winds.

⁂ The sailing of the ship Irish Volunteer from Larne to Charlestown, (advertised in the first page of this paper) is put off till the first of September next; when it is hoped the passengers will be ready to go on board. Passengers may apply to Mr. Alexander Simpson, Ballynascreen; or Mr. Wm. Mills, in Braid.

Married, Richard Drew, of Dunsilly, Esq. to the amiable Miss Ann Eliza Moore, of Clover-hill.

Died, at Carrickfergus, on Saturday the 1st inst. Mr. John Kirk of that town, a man of exemplary sobriety, universally lamented.

FAIRS IN THE ENSUING WEEK.

Monday, 10th. Castlefin, Don.——Smithsborough, Mon. Wednesday, 12th. Armagh Town—Balenaglera, Ar.—Belfast, Ant.—Castleshane, Mo.—Dervock, Ant.—Enniskillen, Ferm.—Greencastle, Down—Lisane, Der.—Portglenone, Der.—Redcastle, Don.——Strangford, Down——Stronorlane, Don. Thursday, 13th. Machrecregan, Tyr. Friday, 14th. Augher, Tyr.—Jonesborough, Arm.—Keady, Arm.—Killough, Down—Letterkenny, Don. Saturday, 15th. Churchill, Don.—Fivemiletown, Tyr.—Newbliss, Mon.

PRICES IN THIS MARKET YESTERDAY.

Oatmeal,	10s.	8d.	to	11s.	2d.	Dried do. 25s. to 26s. per doz
Wheat,	12	2	—	12	6	Rough Tallow, 5s. per st.
Oats,	5	10	—	6	0	Potatoes (new) $1\frac{1}{2}$d. per p.
Barley,	0	0	—	5	6	Eng. coals, 13s. 6d. to 14s.
Butter,	49	0	—	49	6	Scotch do. 12s. 6d. to 13s.
C. hides,	32	6	—	35	0	Ex [on] London 6 3-4 a 7 per c.
Ox ditto,	37	6	—		0	Do. on Glasgow $6\frac{1}{2}$ do.
S.C.skins	40	0	—	42	6	

ROBERT GETTY,

IS now landing from on board the Friendship from London, a very considerable quantity of New Teas; consisting of fine and common Congous, Singlos, Blooms and Hysons, which will be sold by the Chest at Dub in Prices for Cash or Bills, on Belfast or Dublin. He has also at present arrived, Tobago, St. Vincent's, and Jamaica Cotton Wool, Black and White Pepper, and Martinico Coffee—small barrels.

Belfast, 6th August, 1789.

TO BE LET,

From the first of November, next,

THE House and Fields in Strangford, formerly in the occupation of the late James Aynsworth, Esq; and lately possessed by Mr. Getty.——Application to be made to Mr. Auchinleck, Strangford, or Mr. Crawford, Down.

Anno 1789.]   Printed by HENRY JOY, and Co. BELFAST.

The BELFAST NEWS-LETTER.

TUESDAY August 11,   FRIDAY August 14, 1789.

STOLEN

OFF the lands of Gartnanure, county Fermanagh, on 23d instant, A Black COLT, two years old, with a reach down the face, ringle eyed, four white legs, a white spot under near his navel. Whoever stops said Colt and sends word to Mr. O'Briens, near Clones, shall receive one Guinea reward; and for the Thief, if prosecuted to conviction, two Guineas.
July 31st, 1789.

GAME.

IT is the desire of Arthur Cope and Nicholas Archdall Cope, Esqrs. that every person who shall after this day enter on any of their lands to look for or kill Game, or to fish, without being first legally licenced, may be prosecuted as the law directs; and I request the tenants on said estates to inform me of any person they may see on their respective holdings trespassing as above.
Drumilly, near Armagh, August 3d, 1789.
JACOB TURNER.

Wanted at Drumilly aforesaid, a person properly qualified to act as Gardiner and Land Steward; he must be well recommended.—Apply to Mr. Turner.

A Caution.

WHEREAS my wife Mary Heron, otherwise Stogdel, has eloped from me without any cause whatever:—I do hereby caution the public not to credit her on my account, as I am determined not to pay any debt she may contract. Given under my hand this 1st August, 1789.
SAMUL HEERON, Junr.

To be Set or Sold,
(from the first Day of Nov. next)

ALL that extensive Tenement in Charlemont, lately occupied by Mr. Nathaniel Richardson, deceased: The Dwelling-House, Shop, Offices, Chandling and Soapboiling Houses, with the Utensils, all in good repair, adjoining the river Blackwater, navigable to Loughneagh, and from thence to Newry, &c. The premises would be very suitable for a Distiller and Malster. The tenant or purchaser may be accommodated with very good land and meadow convenient to the premises at a tenantable rent.
Apply to Mr. Richardson on the premises, or Mr. William Cardwell of Tullyelmore, near Armagh.
Charlemont, 1st August, 1789.

Castle-Dawson.

TO be sold by publick Auction, on the first day of October next, the House that Andrew Crawford, Esq; lately lived in near the Bridge; to which there is annexed a Garden, good Office-houses, and a convenient Back-yard, very fit for the accommodation of a gentleman, a publican, a distiller, or a tanner; together with an equal space of ground on the opposite side of the street to build tenements on, at the yearly rent of 1l. for ever, paying 10s. for a renewal at the fall of each life; and also ten English acres of land contiguous to the premises, at 8s. per acre, for a term of years yet unexpired, and three young lives in existence.
N. B. The House and Demesne of Teleriby to be set for 31 years.—Proposals to be received by William Richardson, Esq; on the spot, who will shew the premises. Dated 10th August, 1789.

New Teas,

Strong Jamaica Rum, and fine Scale Sugar; very best white and yellow Cotton Wool, of all Denominations, Pymento. best Crop Madder, and Smalts from No. 1 to No. 4.

A Large Parcel of each is now landing at the Quay from the original Markets, and to be sold on the lowest terms for cash or good bills, by applying to HUGH CRAWFORD.
Belfast, 8th August, 1789.

He is largely supplied with Leaf Tobacco and Train Oil, which will be sold very cheap; also some remarkable fine boiling Pease.

William Mc Clure,

IS now landing from the last India Sales, a parcel of fresh Teas; and is well supplied with Pearl and Dantzig Ashes; together with a general assortment of Groceries, will be sold cheap for good payment.
Belfast, 11th August, 1789.

New Teas & Spanish Indigo.

SAMUEL GIBSON has received for Sale a parcel of Teas imported from last India Sales in London; consisting of fine Hysons, fine and common Congos and Singlos; also Spanish Indigo of the very best quality—all of which will be sold on very low terms.
North-street, Belfast, 8th August, 1789.

Advertisement.

WHEREAS Jane Stewart, otherwise Davidson, my wife, did elope from me without any just cause; also has for some time past behaved herself in a very disorderly manner: Therefore I do hereby give this publick notice, that I will not pay any debts that she may contract. Dated at Ballinahinch 12th of August, 1789.
ALEX. STEWART, § his Mark.

For Baltimore,

THE New Brig DOLLY, Captain Ross, burthen two hundred tons, will be clear to sail for the above Port on Saturday the 15th instant.
For Freight or Passage apply to Hugh Montgomery, or Brown and Oakman.
Belfast, 10th August, 1789.

James Hunter, Watch-maker,

Late Partner and Conductor of the Business under the Firm of Mc. Cabe and Hunter,

HAS commenced Business, (on his own account) and solicits the commands of the Publick, at the corner Shop, Donegall-street, opposite the Exchange, Belfast. He served his apprenticeship with the late Thos. Johnston, Dublin, and afterwards conducted his business for several years:—He will always have ready for sale a variety of

Gold, Silver, and gilt Watches,

horizontal, jewelled and plain ditto of superior quality, also Clocks, all finished under his own immediate inspection. Commands for him left with the following Gentlemen will be forwarded and attended to:—Mr. Wm. Owens, Standing Stone, near Doagh, many years an eminent Watch-maker, now retired; Mr. William Mc. Conchy, Antrim; Mr. John Moore, Ballymena; Mr. Wm. Bell, Templepatrick; Dr. Samuel Faries, Larne; Mr. Alexander Kirk, Carrickfergus; Mr. Alexander Ballyclare; Mr. James Hunter and Mr. James Fitzgerald, Store-House, Ballenderry; Mr. James Mc. Cullem, Lisburn; Revd. Mr. Inch, Hillsborough; Dr. Mc. Carten, Saintfield; Dr. James Fleming, Comber; Mr. William Lowry, Newtown-Ards.——Hunter executes all sorts of Repeating Work, sells new low-priced Watches, and every material that appertains to Watches at Dublin Prices.——He will not put his name on English Watches. August 9th, 1789.

Lately published,

For the Benefit of a SUNDAY SCHOOL to be perpetuated at Lawrence-Town, in the County of Down,

THE first Volume of the Poetic Miscellaneous Works of THOMAS DAWSON LAWRENCE, Esq; dedicated to the Right Revd. Thomas Lord Bishop of Dromore, to be sold at Mr. Marchbank's, No. 11, Dame-street, Dublin; Doctor Crawford's, Banbridge, and the Printers hereof, Price 4s. 4d. bound.

Wanted immediately,

THE Sum of One Hundred Pounds Sterl. for which undeniable security will be given.———Application to be made to Mr. David Smith, Attorney, Dungannon, or Mr. Anthony Mc. Reynolds, Attorney, Stewartstown. August 10th, 1789.

Union Regt. of Volunteers.

I Request a Meeting of the Officers of this Regiment on the 12th instant, at Moira-Castle, to consider of the Time and Place for a General Parade.
Moira-Castle, August 5th, 1789.
WM. SHARMAN.

To be sold together, or separately,

THREE Debentures on the Lagan Navigation, viz. two for 500l. each, and one for 135l. They bear an interest respectively of 5l. per cent. The nature of these securities is so well known, that it is almost unnecessary to add that the interest has been, and must be, punctually paid half-yearly,—that the regular payment of the interest is secured by act of parliament, and that by the same act the principal must be paid at the rate of 500l. per ann. from the 25th of December 1793.
Apply to John Pollock, Jervis-street, Dublin.

New Teas.

BROWN and OAKMAN are landing a quantity of Green, Hyson, and Congou Teas, which were purchased at the last sale. Belfast, 10th August, 1789.

NEW TEAS.

WILLIAM EMERSON is now landing from on board the Friendship, Capt. Lepper, from London,—A Variety of New Teas, purchased at last India Sale.——He is at present well supplied with very fine Roll Tobacco, and his usual assortment of Goods in the Grocery Line, which will be sold on the very lowest terms.
Belfast, 10th August, 1789.

George Langtry,

HAS just imported from the last India Sales, a large Assortment of fresh TEAS; and has for Sale, Clay'd and Scale Sugars of a remarkable good quality, which, with an extensive assortment of Goods in his Line, will be sold on reasonable terms.
North-street, Belfast, 12th August, 1789.

To be Sold,

ABOUT thirty Boles of OATS, of an exceeding good quality.——Apply to Mr. Edwards at the Glass-house.
Belfast, 12th August, 1789.

THE EXCHANGE-ROOMS are to be open every Thursday Evening, from six till ten o'clock, for the reception of Company; where Tea and Cards will be provided.—— Admittance a Shilling British.
August 1st, 1789.

Whitehouse Coterie,

WILL be held at White-Abbey, on the evening of Monday the 17th instant.——Admittance for Ladies, two Shillings—for Gentlemen, three Shillings.—Hour of meeting seven o'clock.
August 14th, 1789.

Wanted,

THE Sum of One Hundred Pounds for six months, on real security; for which a premium of six Guineas will be given.——A Letter addressed to A. B. Belfast, will be received.
Office of Henry Joy & Co.
9th August, 1789.

Belfast Academy.

THE Classes open, after the Summer Vacation, Monday the 17th instant.
Academy, 11th August, 1789.
JAMES CROMBIE.

The next Toome Ball,

WILL be held at Lenox's in Toome, on Tuesday the 18th instant.—No Non-subscribers to be admitted without a Ticket from one of the Managers.
August 11th, 1789.

THE Achnacloy Volunteers, and the Ballymagrane True-Blues, take the earliest opportunity of returning their best thanks to the Citizens of Armagh, for the very polite and hospitable reception they received from them, on their march to and return from the Review on the first of August inst. at Magherdogherty.
Achnacloy, 4th of August, 1789.

Hillsborough Fair

WILL be holden on Wednesday next the 19th instant, when the very extensive Premiums, the same as at the last Fair, will be given.
MICHAEL THOMSON,
Clerk of the Market.
Hillsborough, August 12th, 1789.

N. B. Any Article sold after six o'clock in the afternoon, will not be entitled to the Premium.

Notice is hereby given

TO all Persons holding Bills drawn by Thomas Peden of Achnacloy on John Bleakly of the city of Dublin,—that a meeting will be held at the house of James Richardson in Achnacloy, on Monday the 17th of August inst. to consider of what steps it may be necessary to take, in order to have said bills, charged on the estate of his employer David Bleakly the elder, a Bankrupt.
Dated 6th of August, 1789.

Advertisement.

A Man, who calls himself John Mills, (by trade a Tinker) came to the house of John Boyd of Timpany, near Clogher, in the county of Tyrone, and exchanged a mare with the said Boyd on the 28th day of July last past; and as the said Mills is since fled, the said mare is suspected to be stolen.——She is a chesnut mare with a white mane and tail, about thirteen hands high, lengthy bodied, a few white hairs (or a small star) in her forehead, eight years old, and worth in value about six pounds.——Whoever proves their property may have her by applying to Geo. Gladstanes of Daizy-hill, Esq; or to the said John Boyd, on paying the expences of advertising her and keeping.
JOHN BOYD.

To be continued three times.

BASTILE.

The following description of the BASTILE PRISON in FRANCE, (which has lately been destroyed by the Populace) is extracted from the philanthrophic Mr. HOWARD's STATE of FOREIGN PRISONS, and it is presumed will not be unacceptable to our Readers.

I AM happy (says Mr. Howard) to be able to give some information of the Bastile, by means of a pamphlet written by a person who was long confined in this prison. It is reckoned the best account of this celebrated structure, ever published; and the sale of it being prohibited in France under very severe penalties, it is become extremely scarce.

This Castle is a state prison, consisting of eight very strong towers, surrounded with a *fosse* about 120 feet wide, and a wall of 60 feet high. The entrance is at the end of the street of St. Antoine, by a drawbridge, and great gates into the Court of l'Hotel du Gouvernment; and from thence over another drawbridge to the Corps de Garde, which is separated by a strong barrier constructed with beams plated with iron from the great Court. This Court is about 120 feet by 80. In it, is a fountain; and six of the towers surround it, which are united by walls of free-stone ten feet thick up to the top. At the bottom of this Court is a large modern Corps de Logis, which separate it from the Court du Puits. This Court is 50 feet by 25. Contiguous to it are the other two towers. On the top of the towers is a platform continued in terraces, on which the prisoners are sometimes permitted to walk, attended by a guard. On this platform are 13 cannons mounted, which are discharged on days of rejoicing. —In the Corps de Logis is the Council Chamber, and the kitchen, offices, &c.—above these are rooms for prisoners of distinction: and over the Council Chamber the King's Lieutenant resides. In the Court du Puits, is a large well for the use of the kitchen.

The dungeons of the tower de la Liberte extend under the kitchen, &c. Near that tower is a small chapel on the ground floor. In the wall of it are five nitches or closets, in which prisoners are put one by one to hear mass, where they can neither see nor be seen.

The dungeons at the bottom of the towers exhale the most offensive scents, and are the receptacles of toads, rats, and other kinds of vermin. In the corner of each is a camp bed, made of planks laid on iron bars that are fixed to the walls, and the prisoners are allowed some straw to lay on the beds. These dens are dark, have no windows, but openings into the ditch: They have double doors, the inner ones plated with iron, with large bolts and locks.

PARISIAN INTELLIGENCE.

THE REPORT OF THE COMMITTEE,

Charged with the work of preparing materials for forming the CONSTITUTION, read by Monsieur, MOUNIER, in the NATIONAL ASSEMBLY, the 9th of this Month.

Gentlemen,

YOU have established a Committee for the purpose of presenting you with a plan for the formation of the Constitution of the kingdom. We are now going to lay before you what appears to us to be a convenient one; your wisdom will examine whether it be such as will answer the views which animate you.

ORDER *of* PROCEEDING *proposed by the* COMMITTEE.

Article I. Every Government ought to have the maintenance of the rights of men for its sole end; from whence it follows, that to recal Government to the end proposed, the Constitution ought to commence by the declaration of the natural and unalienable rights of man.

II. The monarchical Government has been chosen by the French nation as a proper one to maintain its rights; it is above all forms the most convenient for a large society; it is necessary to the happiness of France; therefore, a declaration of the principles of this species of Government ought immediately to follow the declaration of the rights of man.

III. It results from the principles of monarchy, that the nation, to secure its own rights, has conceded particular rights to the Monarch. The Constitution, then, ought to declare, in a precise manner, the rights both of the one and the other.

IV. It is necessary to begin by declaring the rights of the French nation, and afterwards to declare the rights of the King.

V. The rights of the King, and of the nation, existing only for the happiness of individuals which compose it, these lead to the examination of the rights of citizens.

VI. The French nation not being capable of assembling together, individually, to exercise all its rights, it ought to be represented: it is, therefore, necessary to declare the mode of its representation, and the rights of its representatives.

VII. The establishment and the execution of the laws must be the result of a concurrence of the powers with which the nation and the King are invested: it is therefore necessary to determine immediately, how the laws shall be established. It will afterwards be examined how the laws shall be executed.

FRENCH ROYAL FAMILY.

Lewis XVI. is now about thirty-three years of age; he ascended the throne of his grandfather about seventeen, and shortly afterwards married the sister of the present Emperor of Germany.

When he was first married, he was thin to a degree of particular observation; but being naturally of a mild, quiescent temper, and indulging in the pleasures of the table, he is now perhaps one of the fattest men in his dominions.

To counteract this in some degree, he rises early, and almost daily takes the diversion of the chase; but from dinner till bed-time, indulges with the intervention of hardly any other business than the signing of dispatches, &c.

He has had four children, two of whom are dead. His present family consists of the Dauphin, (a child about six years old) and a Princess.

The Queen is nearly about the King's age, has much majesty and vivacity in her port, and is on the whole reckoned one of the finest women in France.

Monsieur, the King's next brother, is nearly as fat as the Sovereign, and was in the beginning of the present troubles, rather a favourite of the people.

The Count d'Artois, the King's second brother, is a tall, well-moulded, elegant figure, with much vivacity and decision in his character. He rendered himself unpopular on the first meeting of the Notables, and seems to have increased that unpopularity to a degree of proscription.

The Count's party has, for several years back, been called the Queen's, aided by the Count d'Artois: these two were said to have the most prevailing influence on the King in all his measures.

MARQUIS de la FAYETTE

Is a man of a very ardent enterprising spirit, which seems to proceed from constitution rather than from reflection. The late American war offered a scene for the display of his active disposition, and he quitted the tranquil service of France, for the turbulent scene of America, as we believe, without the leave of the King, or the knowledge of his family. The support of rebellion was then such a favourite measure with the Court of France, that it was ready to pass over such a breach of duty as this, for the sake of the cause which produced it.

DUBLIN, AUGUST 6.

By a gentleman who came yesterday evening from Wexford, we learn, that some barley fields in the neighbourhood of that town were cutting on Monday last, and should the present warm weather continue for a few days longer, a general reaping is expected to take place in that county towards the end of next week.

The fete announced at the seat of Lord Fitzgibbon, for the 12th instant, in honour of the Prince of Wales's birth day—is an early proof of that Nobleman's personal attachment to his Royal Highness.

The Whig Club have fixed for their next meeting, Wednesday next, the 12th of August, being the birthday of his Royal Highness the Prince of Wales.

We hear that the King's letter is arrived for the creation of four Marquisses, two Earls, and one Viscount: the Marquisses are the Earls of Clanricarde, Antrim, Tyrone, and Hillsborough; the Earls, Viscounts Valentia and Enniskillen; and the Viscount Lord Earlsfort. No patents for raising Commoners to the peerage are included in this batch: they must wait with patience for a future day.

Henry Cavendish, Esq; eldest son of the Right Hon. Sir Henry Cavendish, Bart. is immediately to be married to the amiable Miss Butler, with 20,000l. fortune.

A considerable quantity of linens and woollens, particularly flannel, have been shipped in the course of these few days, for Philadelphia.

DUBLIN.

On the 31st July, at Trim assizes, there was tried before the Hon. Mr. Justice Kelly, and a most respectable Jury, composed of many of the principal Gentlemen of the county of Meath, a cause of the utmost importance to the agriculture and corn trade of this country.

This trial was between David Jebb, Esq; plaintiff, and John Finigan, of Moyinet, farmer, defendant, on an action brought by the plaintiff for damages against the defendant, for not delivering 20 barrels of wheat sold by sample at the mills of Slane in December last, which wheat defendant sold again at another mill for an advanced price.

Mr. Jebb proved by his Clerk the sale of the wheat and the delivery of the sample to the satisfaction of the Court and Jury. The Judge pointed out in the most forcible manner the great advantages to agriculture by the establishment of those markets, for the farmer, all over the kingdom, the good effects of which could only be maintained by integrity and punctuality in fulfilling all bargains made there, and charged the Jury accordingly, who found a verdict for Mr. Jebb without quitting the box, with damages and costs.

Belfast, *August* 11.

In consequence of the Resolutions of Deputies to hold a small Review near Belfast on Wednesday 26th instant, we can with certainty inform the several Corps, that General the Earl of Charlemont has been pleased to nominate Lieut. Colonel Banks to represent him by reviewing the companies to be on that day assembled.

Mr. and Mrs. O'Neill, and their family, arrived at Shanescastle on Friday night last.

On Thursday the 30th July, came on to be tried at Wexford assizes, before the Hon. Robert Hellen and a special Jury, a cause wherein Standish Loweay, Esq; was plaintiff and the Earl of Donegall defendant;—and on Wednesday the 5th inst. was tried at Waterford assizes, before the Hon. Wm. Henn and a special Jury, a cause between the same parties.—These were actions brought by the plaintiff for recovery of damages alleged to have been sustained by reason of the defendant having formerly caused him to be arrested and imprisoned for some time in Wexford and Waterford gaols——but in both cases the plaintiff was non suited.

*** The paper signed CANDIDUS, from Derry, would have been inserted had its author given his name.

ROBERT GETTY,

IS now landing from on board the Friendship from London, a very considerable quantity of New Teas; consisting of fine and common Congous, Singlos, Blooms and Hysons, which will be sold by the Chest at Dublin Prices for Cash or Bills, on Belfast or Dublin. He has also at present arrived, Tobago, St. Vincent's, and Jamaica Cotton Wool, Black and White Pepper, and Martinico Coffee—small barrels.

Belfast, 6th August, 1789.

Belfast, *August* 14.

The Members of the North-East Bar of Lawyers met at the Donegall Arms, Belfast, on Wednesday, to celebrate the birth of his Royal Highness the Prince of Wales.

At the Assizes for the county of Down, which ended on Wednesday last, Edward Armstrong was found guilty of the murder of Alexander Armstrong, a child, by administering to him a poison called Corrosive Sublimate. Sentenced to be executed the 15th inst.

Neil Aiken found guilty of stealing a gold watch and three table spoons, the property of George Birch, Esq;—to be transported.

Elizabeth Barlow found guilty of stealing drugget, value 4s. 6d. out of the shop of Mr. Edward Humphrey, Downe, to be transported.

Hugh Lindsey, found guilty of feloniously taking and keeping possession of a dwelling-house at Lisnaward, to be transported.

Peter Morgan, found guilty of riotously assembling with others and assaulting Wm. Parks, sentenced to be imprisoned six months, and to be whipped in Loughbrickland on Saturday the 15th of August, and in Banbridge on the last Monday in October, and to give security to keep the peace for three years.

Pat. M'Keown, found guilty of riotously assembling at Sheepbridge with others, and assaulting Tho. M'Kague, to be imprisoned six months, whipped thro' Banbridge the last Monday in October, and give security to keep the peace for three years.

The important cause respecting the Borough of Dundalk, being tried at the late Assizes for the County of Down (to which it had been removed from Louth) a special verdict was given, by which the facts are merely found, but the questions of law remain for determination in the courts above. At the last summer assizes for the county of Louth, a verdict was found which threw the Borough open by confirming the rights of the Freemen.

DEATHS.] Edward Crmyble, Esq; at Clementshill, near Ballyclare, on Sunday the 9th instant. In early life, this gentleman served abroad in a military capacity, and at the head of a grenadier company, in 1759, assisted in the reduction of Canada; at which time, as well as prior to the expedition for that country, he is known to have possessed the confidence of General Wolfe, and to have been numbered among the more intimate friends of that memorable person.—His last years Capt. Crymble passed chiefly in retirement, acting at particular opportunities, according as an imperfect state of health allowed, as a judicious magistrate, and being at all times happy in the character of an indisputably honest man.——

The 9th inst. at Newgrove, near Ballynahinch, Mrs. Mc. Calla, wife of Robert Mc. Calla, a woman possessed of every virtue.

Anno 1789.]　　Printed by HENRY JOY, and Co. BELFAST.

The BELFAST NEWS-LETTER.

TUESDAY August 18,　　FRIDAY August 21, 1789.

Belfast.

O D E

On the Prince of WALES's Birth-Day. Celebrated August 12th, 1789, by the North-East BAR at Belfast.

I.

HARK! I hear a solemn strain
Of swelling harmony glide o'er the billows of
　the main;
The rude winds lie hush'd on their beds, and hold their
　breaths to hear,
And now, and now, the pealing sounds draw near.
Ierr, or sure from *Cambria's* shore,
Nurse of Bards in times of yore,
Where once, with more than mortal fire,
" Mighty MABOR smote the lyre,"
The strains descend—but no, no more
Shall harmony unfold her store.
" CADWALLO's tongue is cold and dead,"
And URIEN sleeps on his eternal bed.
" Silent is HOEL's harp, LEWELLYN's lay,"
Vocal no more since *Cambria's* fatal day.

IX.

Nor ever let th' auspicious day
That gave this Prince, this hero birth,
Pass without one immortal lay,
To found the theme to all the earth.
Ierne's, Albion's, Cambria's shore,
Shall boast their happiness in store;
Severn and Shannon now shall join,
One object shall all minds combine;
Ierne's Prince, not Cambria's now,
For first we claim the plighted vow.
For now his mind stands first confess'd,
With ev'ry royal virtue bless'd,
Try'd on a late important hour,
Above the common strife for pow'r.
And when his Sire, restor'd so late,
Must yield to the decrees of Fate,
Worthy to fill a virtuous throne,
And make that people's hearts his own.

X.

Join then, ye bards, your vocal pow'rs display,
　And let one glowing strain,
　　Ascend the starry plain,
And to Heav'n's portal the glad song convey;
Hear it—ye tawny sons of Afric's sands;
Hear it—ye feather'd chiefs of Indias' bands,
Great GEORGE was born your fetter'd limbs to free,
And break the bonds of your captivity.
Nor, Britons, now your ARTHUR more bewail,
But hail this godlike youth, this *genuine Briton* hail.

TANDRAGEE SCHOOL,

August the 10th, 1789.

THE Revd. Isaac Ashe, and the Revd. Henry Ashe, who were educated under the late Revd. Dr. Norris of Drogheda, and who have been engaged for many years in the education of youth, have opened a School in the Town of Tandragee. Their charge for Boarders is twenty guineas a year, and four guineas entrance; for Day Scholars, four guineas a year, and one guinea entrance. No additional charge will be made to Boarders for instruction in the French language; and as Mr. and Mrs. Ashe have passed some years in France, the children who are instructed in that language will have an opportunity of speaking it familiarly. Care will be taken to engage proper Masters for those branches of education which do not fall under their own immediate province; and they will *personally* pay particular attention to the improvement of their pupils in the English language.—They are determined to pursue uniformly the late Dr. Norris's plan, and consequently will attend School in the evenings.—Mr. Ashe on leaving College was honoured with the following Certificate, signed by the Senior Fellows.

The Revd. Mr. Ashe passed through his academical course with credit; and is, in our opinion, fully qualified to undertake the education of Youth.

Furniture to be sold.

TO be sold at Thomastown, on Monday the 24th inst. by John Bailie, Auctioneer and sworn Appraiser, *from Belfast*,—Part of the Household Furniture of the late John Echlin, Esq; deceased, consisting of a few articles, such as chairs, beds, tables, and a good many pieces of fashionable plate, a large library of books, a phaeton in good order, a farm, chair, &c.

The sale to begin each day at 11 o'clock, and continue till all are sold.

Woollen Drapery & Hosiery, &c.

JUST arrived to JOHN MONTGOMERY, High-street, a large assortment of Superfine, Refine, and Forest Cloths, printed Ribs, Thicksets and Cords, Fancy Buttons, and a compleat assortment of Stockings for Ladies and Gentlemen, suitable, &c. for the present season, and will be sold under the usual prices.—He takes this opportunity of returning his grateful thanks to his friends and the publick for past favours; and hopes by his care and attention to business to merit their support.
Belfast, 19th August, 1789.

THE Creditors of the estate of Hugh Lyndon, are requested to take notice, that a meeting of them is proposed to be held on Saturday first at nine o'clock in the evening, at James Mc. Kaig's, Ann Street; when proposals will be laid before them, in order that his affairs may be finally settled.
Belfast, 20th Aug. 1789.

147 Cocks of Hay,

WELL-saved and in good order, to be sold by Auction, on Monday next the 24th instant, at Jennymount near Belfast—to begin exactly at twelve o'clock. Dated 19th August, 1789.
ROBERT THOMSON.

A VESTRY will be held in the Parish Church of Belfast, on Tuesday next 25th inst. at 12 o'clock, to receive the Report of a Committee appointed at last Vestry to consider the Town Taxes—and take opinion of Council thereon.
Belfast, 19th August, 1789.

The Belfast Coterie,

WILL be held at the EXCHANGE-ROOMS, on Tuesday next, the 25th instant.
August 21, 1789.

Advertisement.

A Man, who calls himself John Mills, (by trade a Tinker) came to the house of John Boyd of Timpany, near Clogher, in the county of Tyrone, and exchanged a mare with the said Boyd on the 28th day of July last past; and as the said Mills is since fled, the said mare is suspected to be stolen.—She is a chesnut mare with a white mane and tail, about thirteen hands high, lengthy bodied, a few white hairs (or a small star) in her forehead, eight years old, and worth in value about six pounds.——Whoever proves their property may have her by applying to Geo. Gladstanes of Daizy-hill, Esq; or to the said John Boyd, on paying the expences of advertising her and keeping.
JOHN BOYD.

To be continued three times.

Advertisement.

JOHN MILLER, my late father, being seized and possessed of a Farm of Land in Lisnamullan, under the late Charles O'Neill, Esq; for years and lives, devised the same to me and my heirs, and in failure thereof to my two sisters and their heirs. In April 1773, I went to America, where I resided until very lately, and having before my departure borrowed a sum of money from John Millar of Rakeel, I granted a deed of assignment to him of said Farm, together with a power of attorney to receive the issues and profits thereof, and of another Farm, my property, near Connor, to reimburse himself the money so advanced; and at the time of my executing to him the said assignment, he gave me a deed of defeasance whereby he bound himself in the penalty of 200l. to cancel the said assignment, and deliver up to me all the said lands upon being paid the sum of 46l. 12s. 9d. with interest; and the said Millar procured said assignment to be registered, and now threatens to dispose thereof as his own absolute property: I therefore caution the publick against entering into any treaty with said Millar respecting the sale of said premisses, as I have got into possession thereof, and intend to proceed with all expedition to call him to an account for the issues and profits thereof during my absence.
Dated this 8th day of August, 1789.
WILLIAM MILLAR.

STOLEN

OFF the Lands of Finnebrogue, in the county of Down, on Wednesday the 12th instant, a Black Horse, seven years old, fifteen hands high, heavy made, with a bright star in his face, bob tail, never set, a little hollow in the back, and his pasterns shaved with the fetters—value ten guineas:—If strayed, a reward of half a guinea will be paid to the person who returns said Horse; or if stolen, five guineas for Horse and Thief.

Apply at the Office of Mr. Henry Joy & Co.; Messrs. Thomas Nevin and Co. Downpatrick; or to the Owner, Geo. Thompson at Finnebrogue.

From *Dublin*, for *Belfast*,

THE LINEN HALL, HUGH DICKSON, Master, is now at Dublin, and will sail from thence for this Port in ten days. Any person that has a *Quantity* of Goods to ship immediately will be accommodated, and at a much lower freight than is customary from that Port.
Apply to Messrs. Comerford and O'Brien, Dublin, or Mc. Kedy and Stevenson, Belfast.
19th August, 1789.

WHEREAS Mary Gault, (otherwise Burns) wife of William Gault, in the parish of Ballycorr and county of Antrim, hath without any just cause whatsoever eloped from me her said husband, and carried away my property to a considerable amount: These are therefore to give notice to all persons whatsoever neither to credit nor entertain my said wife, as I am determined not to pay any debt she contracts, and to prosecute any person as far as the law directs that will harbour her or any of my Goods aforesaid. Given under my hand this 14th day of August, 1789.
WILLIAM GAULT.

GRAND JURY-ROOM, August 12, 1789.

AT a Meeting of the Sheriff and Grand Jury of the County Down at Summer Assizes 1789, the following Resolutions were by them entered into and agreed to by the Governor of the County:

Resolved, That tho' a riotous disposition does appear to us to have lately crept into a corner of this county, yet we are fully convinced that the state of it in general has been most grossly misrepresented and exaggerated.

Resolved, That we do pledge ourselves to the county and to each other, to use our utmost efforts to suppress rioters of what description or religion soever, they may be, and by every legal means endeavour to bring them to justice.

DOWNSHIRE, GOVERNOR.

J. W. Hull, Sheriff.	12. Pat. Savage,
1 G. Rawdon,	13 John Knox,
2 Edwd. Ward,	14 David Kerr,
3 Richd. Annesley,	15. S. Isaac,
4 Robt. Ward,	16 Ar. Johnston,
5 John Blackwood,	17 Nichs. Price,
6 Richd. Johnston,	18 Savage Hall,
7 Robert Ross,	19 John Slade,
8 John Reilly,	20 James Waddell,
9 Richard Magennis,	21 Daniel Mussenden,
10 Robt. Stewart,	22 Francis Savage,
11 Matt. Ford,	23 Geo. Birch.

Lurgan Brewery.

WILLIAM RICHARDSON respectfully informs his Friends and the Publick, that having compleated his Brewery, and engaged an Englishman of skill and eminence to conduct the business, he requests their countenance and support; and will supply gentlemens families and publicans with fine Ale and Table Beer on the shortest notice. He is also well assorted with Haberdashery Goods, as usual, with Iron, Deals, Hops, &c.
Lurgan, August 8th, 1789.

Dr. Godbold's Vegetable Balsam.

☞ The innumerable Cures, so unquestionably authenticated, performed by the superior Virtues of this Medicine must be convincing proofs to the world of the blessing bestowed on mankind by this providential discovery—the following recent certificate was received a few days since:

Mr. MAGEE.　　　　　　Antrim, Aug. 13, 1789.
SIR,

I Should be wanting in that gratitude which I owe Mr. Godbold, and unjust to the world, did I not acknowledge the astonishing effects of his invaluable Vegetable Balsam.

When I first began the use of his Medicine, I laboured under a severe constant Cough, great difficulty of breathing, often to such a degree as to render it very difficult for me to discharge my duty as Clerk of the Church. Constant pain in my breast, loss of appetite, and every other symptom of a confirmed consumption.—By the use of one Bottle only, purchased at your Shop, my complaints are entirely gone, my appetite better than for some years past, and am so far restored as to be able to follow my usual employment, which I could not do for many months before—and am, dear Sir,
Your's, &c.
JOHN Mc. NIECE.

Reſult of the REPORT made from the Committee of Conſtitution to the National Aſſembly, and read by M. de Clermont Tonnere.

Fundamental Principles of the French Conſtitution, upon which all the Committee are unanimous, and which, therefore, they preſent to the National Aſſembly.

Article 1. The French Government is a monarchical government.

2. The perſon of the King is inviolable and ſacred.

3. The crown is hereditary, from male to male.

4. The King is inveſted with the executive power.

5. The agents of authority are reſponſible.

6. The royal ſanction is neceſſary to the promulgation of laws.

7. The nation makes the laws with the royal ſanction.

8. The national conſent is neceſſary to a loan, or to the impoſition of a tax.

9. No tax can be granted but from one meeting of the States General to another.

10. Property ſhall be ſacred.

11. Perſonal liberty ſhall be ſacred.

From the DUBLIN GAZETTE.

DUBLIN CASTLE, Auguſt 12, 1789.

This Day being the anniverſary of the birth of his Royal Highneſs the Prince of Wales, the flag was diſplayed on Bedford Tower, the great guns at the Salute Battery in his Majeſty's Park the Phœnix were fired three rounds, and anſwered by vollies from the regiments in garriſon, which were drawn up in the Royal Square at the Barracks. In the evening a play was given by their Excellencies the Lords Juſtices to the ladies; and at night there were bonfires, illuminations and every other demonſtration of joy throughout the city.

To Wills, Earl of Hillſborough, and the heirs male of his body, the dignity of Marquis of Downſhire.

To Francis Charles, Viſcount Glerawly, the dignity of Earl Anneſley, of Caſtlewellan, in the county Down, to him and the heirs male of his body, and in default of ſuch iſſue, to his brother, the Honourable Richard Anneſly, and the heirs male of his body.

To William Willoughby, Viſcount Enniſkillen, and the heirs male of his body, the dignity of Earl of Enniſkillen, in the county Fermanagh.

To John, Viſcount Erne, and the Heirs male of his body, the dignity of Earl Erne, of Crumcaſtle, in the county Fermanagh.

DUBLIN, AUGUST 15.

We are aſſured, that the New Cuſtom-Houſe will be opened for buſineſs on the 25th of March, 1790, and not ſooner, in order to give ſufficient time for airing the rooms and drying every part, within and without that extenſive building, for which purpoſe good fires will be kept during the whole of the enſuing winter.

Laſt week a large exportation of wrought bale goods, the product of Iriſh looms, was made by ſome ſpirited merchants of Waterford, for Seville and St. Lucar, where the inhabitants not only of thoſe cities, but of the provinces of Andaluſia, and the Two Sicilies, have expreſſed the higheſt approbation of the former cargoes ſent out in January and March. The trade is certainly beneficial, otherwiſe the knowing ones of that commercial city would not have made three or four valuable conſignments to the Spaniſh ports in a few months.

The interruption of the cotton manufactures in Brittany and other parts of France, occaſioned by the late commotions in that kingdom, will probably ſerve the manufacturers of theſe goods in England and Ireland; ſome orders for thickſets, corduroys, &c. being within theſe eight days arrived from different parts of France at Belfaſt, Limerick, and this city.

Orders we hear have come to Cork, Waterford, and this city from Cadiz, for linens plain and printed, cheques and ſtuffs, deſtined for the next flotilla, which is to ſail from that port for Mexico.

While France is in diſtraction and want, Spain is wiſely purſuing her commerce, and our own kingdom has obtained conſiderable ſhare, as we find the demand for, and the export of linen to be greatly increaſed, particularly ſince the Truſtees of the Linen Manufacture give five per cent. bounty on all linens ſent to Spain.

LONDON-DERRY, AUGUST 11.

At this particular time, it cannot be improper to make known (from an authentic Narrative of the Siege of Derry, which will ſoon be publiſhed) the names of thoſe gallant young men, 13 in number, who firſt ſhut the gates againſt King James's army, viz. Alex. Cuningham, Will. Crookſhanks, Rob. Sherrard, Dan. Sherrard, Henry Campſy, Alex. Irwin, James Stewart, Rob. Morriſon, John Coningham, Sam. Harvey, William Cairns, Samuel Hunt, and James Spike.

PRINCE OF WALES.

BELFAST, 12th Auguſt, 1789.

The anniverſary of his Royal Highneſs's birth-day, was celebrated at the Donegall-Arms, by the gentlemen of the North Eaſt Bar, on which occaſion William Caldbeck, Eſq; preſided, and the following gentlemen acted as ſtewards—

RICHARD SHERIDAN,
TANKERVILLE CHAMBERLANE, } Eſqrs.
and JAMES DAWSON,

The entertainment was magnificent, and in every reſpect ſuited to teſtify the ſtrongeſt attachment to his Royal Highneſs.

After dinner the following patriotic toaſts were drank—and the evening ſpent in the greateſt harmony and conviviality.

His Royal Highneſs the Prince of Wales, and many happy returns of the day——with 3 times 3 cheers.

The King and the true Friends of the Conſtitution—3 times 3.

The Royal Family.

The Duke of York, and may the Military never forget their duty as citizens—3 times 3.

The Duke of Clarence and the Wooden Walls of England—3 times 3.

Proſperity to Ireland—3 times 3.

The Volunteers of Ireland and the Earl of Charlemont—3 times 3.

The Glorious Memory—3 times 3.

The Linen Manufacture.

The town of Belfaſt and the Lord of the Soil—with 3 cheers.

The preſent ſpirit of France all over the World—with 3 times 3.

M. Neckar.

Farmer Waſhington.

The Whig Intereſt of the Empire—with 3 times 3.

[Given by James Dawſon, Eſq; junior ſteward.]

Our much reſpected gueſt, Doctor Halliday.

The North Eaſt Bar.

[Given by Doctor Halliday.]

The Bar Toaſt.

The Lords and Gentlemen, Ambaſſadors from the Lords and Commons of Ireland to the Prince of Wales the 15th of February, 1789.

The Judges of the Circuit.

Our abſent friends of the Bar.

May Great Britain and Ireland be inſeparably united, and enjoy equal liberty—with 3 times 3.

The 15th of June, 1215.

The 26th of February, 1768.

The 1ſt of July, 1690.

The 12th of July, 1691.

The 20th of November, 1759.

The Duke of Portland.

The Duke of Devonſhire, and the hereditary virtues of the Houſe of Cavendiſh.

Richard Brinſley Sheridan, member for Stafford.

Edmond Burke.

Charles James Fox.

Colonel Fitzpatrick.

The Lord Chancellor of Ireland.

Mr. Grattan.

Mr. Forbes.

Belfaſt, *Auguſt* 18.

On Saturday laſt, Edward Armſtrong was execued at Downpatrick, purſuant to his ſentence, for the unnatural murder of his own Infant. This unhappy caſe was rendered ſtill more deplorable by the circumſtance of his Wife having died very ſuddenly and unexpectedly not long before. He declared that poverty was the cauſe.

James Watſon Hull, Eſq; High Sheriff of the county of Down, has been pleaſed to appoint Mr. Robert Garrett of Liſburn to be his Under Sheriff, in the place of Mr. Robert Stewart, who, from bad health, has reſigned; and Mr. Garrett was in conſequence on Wedneſday the 12th inſt. ſworn into office, before the Hon. Baron Hamilton at Downpatrick.

COUNTY OF ARMAGH REVIEW.

On Saturday the firſt of Auguſt, the following corps of Volunteers met at Magherdogherty demeſne, conſiſting of 1062 men.

Armagh Artillery	Ballymagran
1ſt Armagh Volunteers	Clady
Orier Infantry	Clantilew
Orier Grenadiers	Donacloney
Clare Volunteers	Keady
Banbridge	Donamoney
Loughgall	Benburb
Mountnorris	Mullyroden
Teemore & Johnſtown	Armagh Infantry
Liſdrumwhir	Derrycaw
Charlemont	Nappagh
Moy	Callen
Union	Carn Volunteers
Aughnacloy	

General Lord Charlemont being engaged to review the Volunteers in Dublin on the 3d inſt. Capt. Moore was appointed on the ground Reviewing General for the day.

The troops were reviewed in two brigades, each conſiſting of two battalions: they went through the different firings and evolutions with every regularity that could be expected from troops whoſe ſituations ſeldom allow them the advantage of practiſing together. The buſineſs of the day being gone through, much to the ſatisfaction of an immenſe concourſe of ſpectators, the different corps marched home in the moſt regular manner.

The grateful acknowledgements of the meeting were unanimouſly voted to the Right Hon. Sir Capel Molyneux, Bart. for the very polite and friendly manner in which he granted the uſe of his demeſne.

PORT NEWS.

ARRIVED.

Aug. 10. Peggy, M'Ilroy, Liverpool, rum, &c.
14. Jenny, Craigie, Stockholm, iron, &c.
15. Friendſhip, Hughes, Liverpool, ſugar, &c.
Twelve colliers.

CLEARED OUT.

Aug. 13. Hillſbro', M'Donnell, Liverpool, flour, &c.
14 Lord Bulkely, Williams, Beaumorris, cows.
Fanny, ditto, ditto, ditto,
Grizzy, M'Kinlay, Greenock, flour.
Proſperity, Munro, Jamaica, cloth.

Belfaſt, *Auguſt* 21.

At the late Aſſizes for the county of Antrim, held at Carrickfergus, which ended on Monday laſt, Joſeph Blackwood of Belfaſt, butcher, charged with the murder of George Emerſon on his return from Hillſborough Races—was acquitted. In conſequence of an Appeal, by the next of kin, a new trial will be held in the Court of King's Bench, Dublin, on next Michaelmas term, which commences on the 3d day of November next.

At the ſame Aſſizes, Hugh Giffen was found guilty on one indictment of ſtealing three ſheep; and on a ſecond, for ſtealing a firkin of butter, &c.—to be tranſported.

Edward Robinſon and John Knox were indicted for being looſe idle vagrants and vagabonds—to be tranſported purſuant to the ſtatutes, unleſs they give ſecurity within ſix months to be of the peace and keep good behaviour.

James Orr the elder and James Orr the younger, found guilty of ſtealing from Mrs. Margaret Henry, at Ballymoney, one quarter of a hundred of potatoes, value ſixpence, to be privately whipped, impriſoned one week, and to remain in jail until they ſhall give ſecurity before two magiſtrates to be of the peace for three years.

We underſtand that the Proprietors of the Plains near Belfaſt, have generouſly offered the uſe of them for the Review, which is to be held on WEDNESDAY NEXT. The line is to conſiſt of two battalions, and formed on the Plains ſo as the Reviewing General ſhall enter the field at eleven o'clock.

At the inſtance of a correſpondent, we remind thoſe whom it may concern, that there is an adjournment of the Seſſions for the county of Down to Thurſday next, the 27th Auguſt, at Bangor, for the purpoſe of regiſtering Freeholders.

Died, a few days ago, Mr. James Wilſon, of this town, long an eminent clock-maker—a man of a blameleſs character.

The Earl of Maſſareene was at Coleman's theatre on Tueſday ſe'nnight. His Lordſhip was accompanied by a clergyman and another gentleman, and ſeemed wrapt in aſtoniſhment at comparing the buſy ſplendid exhibition of a crowded theatre, with the dreary manſion he ſo lately quitted. He was dreſſed in a plain dark blue frock ſuit of clothes, his hair without powder, and cloſe cropped; his complexion is brown, and his face animated, and on the whole he has very much the appearance of a man of faſhion. His Lordſhip is entering his 48th year.——*Star.*

FAIRS IN THE ENSUING WEEK.

Monday 24. Ballynoſs, Don.—Caſtlecaulfield, Tyr. Churchtown, Der.—*Tueſday* 25. Ballycaſtle, Ant.—Cloghanbegg, Don.—Maghrafelt, Der.—*Wedneſday* 26. Ahogill, Ant.—Banbridge, Down, three days—Benburb, Tyr.—Carlow town,—Carnteel, Tyr.——Donagh, Ferm.—Drogheda town——Lowtherſtown, Ferm.—Monea, Ferm.—Port, Don.——Saintfield, Down.—*Thurſday* 27. Dunymaugh, Tyr.—Raphoe, Don.—*Friday* 28. Kircubben, Down.—*Saturday* 29 Bearagh, Tyr.——Gorten, Tyr.

PRICES IN THIS MARKET YESTERDAY.

Oatmeal,	10s. 6d.	to	10s.	10.		Dried do. 26s. to 27s. od per d
Wheat,	12	0 —	12	6		R. Tallow, 4s 10d. a 5s. per ſt.
Oats,	5	0 —	5	5		Potatoes (new) 2½d. per p.
Barley,	0	0 —	0	0		Eng. coals, 13s. 6d. to 14s.
Butter,	50	0 —	51	0		Scotch do. 13s. to 13s. 6d.
C. hides,	34	0 —	35	0		Ex. on Lond 6 3-4 a 7 per c.
Ox ditto,	38	0 —	40	0		Do. on Glaſgow 6¼.
S.C. ſkins	00	0 —	42	6		

Anno 1789.] Printed by HENRY JOY, and Co. BELFAST.

The BELFAST NEWS-LETTER.

TUESDAY August 25,   FRIDAY August 28, 1789.

TO BE LET,

From the first Day of November next, for such Term as may be agreed on,

THE following Lands, Houses and Tenements, all situated in the town and county of Armagh, viz. Armagh Town, several Houses and Tenements, in different Streets:

Aghrafin,	Ennisfare, together with
Bracknagh,	a Grift Mill,
Ballinagalla,	Farmacailley,
Broghan,	Liffadian, together with
Balleere,	a good Grift Mill,
Ballyfcandell,	Munlurg,
Cuflintrough,	Moncypattock,
Defart, to be let for	Moneyquin,
Town Parks,	Tonagh,
Drumconnell,	Terrafkane,

On the above lands are several remarkable good Sites for Bleach-yards, fituate on the Banks of the noted River Callen. Leafes, toties quoties, will be given with the Bleach-greens, and every reasonable encouragement, to good improving tenants. Proposals to be received by Samuel Faulkner, Efq; until 20th of September next, at his houfe in Armagh, and afterwards at his house, No. 84, Stephen's-Green, Dublin.

August 25th, 1789.

Rum by Auction.

TO be fold by Auction, at the King's Stores on the Hanover-Quay, on Friday the 4th September next, at one o'clock in the forenoon, thirty puncheons well-flavoured Antigua Rum, and ten puncheons old Spirit of excellent quality.——As this Rum will be difpofed of for account of the fhipper, it may be worth the attention of thofe in the trade to attend.——Good bills on Belfaft or Dublin at three months will be taken as payment, or two per cent. allowed for cash.

Belfaft, 26th August, 1789.

Advertifement.

THERE were three pieces Brown Linen taken (fuppofed by miftake) from the houfe of John Haftings Lifburn, marked as follows, No. 937 at 18d. h. per yard 938 at 18d. per and 939 at 18d. h. all marked Jones.—— It is requefted any Gentleman who may have got them will have them returned to faid Haftings.

A meeting of the creditors of Dr. Slone is requefted at the Bear Inn Lifburn on Tuefday next the 1ft September, to infpect into the affairs, and determine on the beft mode of having their accounts paid.

Lifburn, August 28th, 1789.

THE Truftees of the Eftate of Gain Sanderfon, of Ballymena, request all perfons indebted to faid Eftate, to pay their refpective accounts immediately to faid Gain Sanderfon, who is impowered to receive the fame, otherwife the moft fpeedy meafures will be taken to enforce payment.

The creditors of faid Eftate are hereby defired to furnifh their accounts (duly attefted) to faid Gain Sanderfon.

Belfaft, 27th Auguft, 1789.

JACOB FORSYTH
STAFFORD CHURCH ⎫ Truftees.
ROBERT KER ⎬
SAMUEL ROBINSON. ⎭

Whitehoufe Coterie,

WILL be held at White-Abbey on the evening of Monday the 31ft inftant,——Admittance for Ladies two fhillings—for Gentlemen three Shillings —— Hour of meeting feven o'Clock.

August 27, 1789.

In the Matter of James ⎫ TO be fold by Auction, Thomfon, a Bankrupt ⎬ by the Affignees of ⎭ faid Bankrupt, in the Market-Houfe, Belfaft, on Tuefday the 8th of September next, at one o'clock,—A Leafe of a Tenement in North-ftreet, Belfaft, granted by Daniel Muffenden, Efq; to faid Bankrupt for 75 years, (or the life of the Earl of Donegall) from Nov. 1784; yearly rent 6l. fterl. on which are erected two houfes, not yet finifhed. Immediately after the fale of faid leafe, there will be fold a parcel of timber cut up into different fcantlings.

N. B. One third of the purchafe-money to be paid at the time of fale, and the remainder on perfection of the deeds.—Belfaft, 27th Auguft, 1789.

C. GREG, ⎫ Affignees.
ROBT. SCOTT, ⎬

Belfaft Porter Brewery.

JOHN CRANSTON & Co. have now a quantity of Porter in Hogfheads and Barrels, ready for fale, which they hope will pleafe the Publick.

27th Auguft, 1789.

A NOTICE.

THERE being a confiderable outftanding arrear of Rent due to the Earl of Donegall out of his Eftates in the counties of Antrim, Down, and Carrickfergus, I am obliged to give this general Notice to all concerned, that if thofe arrears are not immediately paid at his Lordfhip's Office, I fhall be under the difagreeable necessity of giving directions to his Lordfhip's Law Agent, to proceed in the moft fpeedy and effectual manner, to recover the fame.

Dated Caftle-Office, Belfaft the 24th Auguft, 1789.

ED. KINGSMILL.

A Charity Sermon,

WILL be preached in the Church of Lurgan, on Sunday the 30th of Auguft inft. by the Right Revd. the Lord Bifhop of Dromore, after which a Collection will be made for the purpofe of cloathing the Children of the Free-School eftablifhed there.

August 21ft, 1789.

Fresh Teas, London refined and fine Scale Sugars, French and Spanifh Indigo.

DUKE BERWICK has now landed from on board the Friendfhip from London, the above-mentioned Articles;—thofe, with a very extenfive affortment of Goods in his line, he will difpofe of by wholefale and retail on very low terms.

Belfaft, 24th Auguft, 1789.

Patterfon and Whittle,

HAVE juft received from the different manufacturing Towns, a large and extenfive Affortment of

Hardware and Ironmongery,

which being chofen by one of themfelves, their friends and the publick may depend on being well ferved, at the moft reduced prices.

Belfaft, 24th Auguft, 1789.

Woollen Drapery & Hofiery, &c.

JUST arrived to JOHN MONTGOMERY, High-ftreet, a large Affortment of Superfine, Refine, and Foreft Cloths, printed Velvets, Thickfets and Cords, Fancy Buttons, &c. and a compleat Affortment of Stockings for Ladies and Gentlemen, fuitable for the prefent feafon, and will be fold under the ufual prices.——He takes this opportunity of returning his grateful thanks to his friends and the publick for paft favours; and hopes by his care and attention to bufinefs to merit their fupport.

Belfaft, 19th Auguft, 1789.

New Timber & Afhes, &c.

THOMAS PARKINSON has arrived and is now landing by the Matty, Capt. Mc. Donnell, from Dantzig, Square Timber of the beft quality, Weed Afhes of the firft brands, Oak and Fir Plank of various fcantlings, Crown Pipe Staves, Beech Logs and Clapboards. He is well fupplied with Memel Timber, feafoned Drunthen Deals, flating and cieling Laths, Welch Slates, Teas by the cheft of his own importation; and he daily expects a cargo of Iron, and a frefh fupply of Drunthen Deals. Thofe who are pleafed to favour him with their commands, may rely they will be fupplied on as favourable terms as in his power.

Downpatrick, 24th Auguft, 1789.

Advertifement.

TO be Sold, an Annuity of twenty-five Pounds two Shillings, now fet at double rent; alfo a Leafe at feventeen Pounds ten Shillings yearly—twelve years of faid Leafe unexpired, now fet at twenty-four Pounds eight Shillings yearly; and, together with thefe, a Leafe of twenty-two Pounds eight Shillings yearly, for one life, all the property of the Revd. James Jackfon of Bellyregan, parifh of Dundonnald and county of Down.

Proposals to be taken by Mr. Walter Craford in Belfaft, and by the Proprietor.

August 17th, 1789.

Revd. John Dickfon, ⎫ TO be fold by the She-
Plaintiff. ⎬ riff of the County of
Daniel Manus Murry, of ⎬ Down, on Saturday the
Ravarra, in the County ⎬ 29th day of Auguft inftant,
of Down, ⎬ at the houfe of Edward Co-
Defendant. ⎭ nolly, Innkeeper in Down-
patrick, all the Defendant's right, title, and intereft to a Farm of Land in Ravarra, near Saintfield, containing upwards of forty-four acres, held by article for a term of years, at the rent of 34l. 3s. 2d.——The purchafe-money to be paid at the time of the fale. Dated the 15th day of Auguft, 1789.

Advertifement.

WHEREAS a young man of genteel connections, without any caufe, except an over-hafty defire of trying his fortune in a foreign country, went privately away from Downpatrick, on the morning of Wednefday the 19th inft. and cannot fince be heard of. It is earneftly requefted that the mafters of fhips and other gentlemen in the feaports of this province, from a regard to unexperienced youth and fympathy with his diftreffed parents, may be induftrious to difcover him and to affure him that his parents do heartily forgive this rafh ftep, and anxioufly with his immediate return, in order to fit him out in every refpect fuitable to his ftation for any country he may wifh to vifit. He will be known by the following defcription:—He is feventeen years old, ftraight and tall, has dark brown hair, and a fmall fcar on the left fide of his nofe, near the eye, like a large pockmark; had on when he went away a drab drab coat inclining to wine-ftone, a fpotted jean waiftcoat with green border, and dark olive breeches:—he had alfo with him a black and white ftriped waiftcoat, and nankeen breeches.—A line addreffed to Mr. Joy from himfelf or any perfon that can find him out, is moft earneftly requefted.

August 24th, 1789.

Union Regiment.

THERE will be a Parade of this Regiment and of the Dromore Battalion at Dromore, on Wednefday the fecond of September next, at eleven o'clock.—The Field Exercife to be the Plan of the laft Belfaft Review—of which the feveral Companies are requefted to take notice. The ground will accommodate fuch of the neighbouring Corps as may chufe to honor the Parade with their appearance.

Moira-Caftle, Auguft the 25th, 1789.

WM. SHARMAN.

Muflins and Lawns,

The moft fafhionable for Gowns, Cloaks, Aprons, Cravats, Handkerchiefs, &c.

ROBERT HUNTER has juft received and now on Sale, at the Broker's Office, Belfaft, a great Variety of Tambour'd, Strip'd and Chequed Muflins; Book and Jaconet do. of all breadths—variety of Muflin and Lawn Handkerchiefs and Shawls—Tambour and other Muflin Aprons—Cravat Piece Muflins—Piece Lawns, &c. The above-mentioned Goods will be fold et and under prime Coft, for ready money only.——Ladies and Gentlemen who have occafion to purchafe, will find it much their intereft to view the above Affortment, the fuperior quality of which, added to the very low prices, cannot but recommend them.

Belfaft, 19th Auguft, 1789.

Dealers in the above Articles will find it their intereft to call as above.

THE Inhabitants of Antrim, and neighbouring Gentlemen, take this public manner of returning their fincere thanks to the Revd. Doctor Macartney, for traverfing a prefentment at Lent Affizes, for repairing the Seffion-Houfe in Ballymena, and for his prudent management in conducting the trial of faid traverfe at laft Affizes, by which he has faved this country a very great expence.

Dated at Antrim, in a full meeting in the Seffion-houfe, the 19th of Auguft, 1789.

JOHN RANKEN, Chairman.

To the Revd. Mr. RANKEN, Antrim.

Dear Sir,

I Beg leave to return my warmeft thanks to the Inhabitants of Antrim and Gentlemen of the neighbourhood, for the kind manner in which they have through you their Chairman, publickly teftified their approbation of my conduct in traverfing the prefentment for the repair of the Ballymena Seffion-houfe at laft Lent Affizes.—However reluctant I might have been in giving oppofition to any meafure fanctioned by fo high authority as the Grand Jury of the county of Antrim, yet from a conviction that it was my duty in the inftance alluded to, I was conftrained to act as I did, and was happy to find that my conduct met fo fully with the approbation of the learned Judge and refpectable jury who tried the traverfe, and that it has been approved of by the inhabitants of Antrim, the gentlemen of the neighbourhood, and yourfelf, on whofe favourable opinion I place the higheft value.

I am with very great refpect and efteem, your faithful obedient fervant,

GEO. MACARTNEY.

Antrim, 25th Auguft, 1789.

PARIS, August 17.

THE National Assembly still continue to march forward with gigantic strides, to the total destruction of every species of abuse in the ancient worn out system of Despotism. No Clergyman is to possess two livings, if they jointly exceed 300 livres, or 125l. sterling; nor a Pension and a Living, at the same time, of more than that sum. The present state of the Pension List is to be examined, and measures taken by the Assembly and the King for the retrenchment, or abolition of such as are too considerable, or improper; and a stipulated sum is to be granted the King for that purpose, in future. The salary proposed, though not yet finally agreed to, for the extent of Clerical Livings, is 1500 livres, or about 62l. sterling, for the country Parish Priests; 25l. sterling for their Curates; 100l. sterling, for the City Priests, and 33l. for their Curates. The Bishops, and other beneficed Clergy, to undergo a proportional reduction.

It is intended likewise to abolish the right of Primogeniture, which left younger children destitute of fortune, and of itself produced an aristocracy and irregularity in the State.

The Assembly have come to the following Resolutions:

First—The National Assembly ordain, that in future no money shall be sent to the Court of Rome, to the Vice-Legateship of Avignon, nor to the *Nunciat of Luzern*, for any religious purpose whatever: but the Parishioners shall apply to their Bishop for benefices and dispensations, which shall be granted to them *gratis*, notwithstanding any privilege or exception to the contrary.—All the Churches in France should enjoy the same liberty.

The *Deports*, Rights *de Cote morte depouilles*, *Vacai*, *Droits censaux*, *Peter's Pence*, and other Rights of the same kind, established in favour of Bishops, Archdeacons, Canons, Curates, &c. are hereby utterly abolished, except they should belong to Archdeaconships, or Curacies not sufficiently provided.

Secondly—No person shall in future hold a Benefice, or Benefices, exceeding the annual income of 3000 livres.—No person shall enjoy pensions or benefices to a greater amount than the above sum of 3000 livres.

Thirdly—on the delivery of the Account which shall be laid before the Assembly, of the State of Pensions and Rewards, the Assembly in concert with the King, shall proceed to suppress those that have not been merited, and to reduce such as shall appear excessive, reserving to themselves the power of determining a certain sum which the King shall dispose of in future to such purposes.

Extract of a letter, dated Paris, Aug. 8.

"I am just arrived at Paris, which a few days ago was the scene of horror and despair, but now is gay and chearful as ever. The streets are full of fiddles and fingers. In two words, every body is merry, and in high spirits. Every thing is very quiet at Paris; there are regular patroles day and night, composed of citizens, who maintain good order. The King has again obtained the favour of the nation.

"The Queen will have hard work to be found agreeable. She was spared by the mob, out of respect to the King. On the day the King went to Paris, she requested of him the favour, on her knees, that she might be permitted to accompany him to Paris, which he peremptorily refused.

LONDON, AUG. 19—20—21.

The report, about which so much has been said in one of the morning papers, of a plot against the life of our beloved Sovereign, appears to have had no other foundation than some Letters which were laid before government a considerable time ago.

The Letters had no signature, nor could the person who communicated them give any account by whom they were written.

Wednesday was married, at St. Peter's, Cornhill, Lord Massareene, to the Lady who accompanied him to England. His Lordship had been twice married to this lady in France.

Lord Massereene, like his Grace of Norfolk, studies not exteriors: his hair is short, the colour is almost black, and he wears no powder: his dress is also as much to be remarked for its plainness.

The entrance of the King and Queen into Exeter, as far as it went, was the triumph of truth. All the property and fame of the country, the Church, and the Corporation, all were in waiting to receive them.

Their Majesties occupy the apartment in which King William slept, after his landing at Torbay.

The King of France has been obliged to apply for a resolution of Oblivion for the Queen, in plain English asking their pardon for her; this was thought necessary to keep her in France, to prevent her going to join Artois and his party,

LONDON-DERRY, AUGUST 18.

On Sunday last arrived from Boston the ship Nancy, Capt. G. Mitchel, with a cargo of timber and materials for the new bridge.

We sincerely congratulate the citizens of Derry upon this fortunate circumstance, which gives to them the pleasing prospect, that this important work will soon be commenced.

We copy the following article from the Massachuset's Centenal of the 27th of June last:

"Yesterday arrived in town, from Ireland, Messrs. Cox and Thompson, where they were invited to inspect the building of a Bridge across the river Foyle at London-Derry. These artists were received in that city with every possible mark of joy, and experienced the most polite treatment during their residence there. They are now loading a ship at Sheepscut, with timber for the construction of the Bridge."

On Saturday last, Major Law and his Lady, arrived in this city.—This gentleman, who acquired a large fortune in the East Indies, has lately purchased the fine estate of Castle Cuningham in this neighbourhood, where, we are informed, he intends to build an elegant mansion-house, and where he will principally reside, for the encouragement of his tenantry, and the good of his native country.

At Omagh assizes, Miles Donnelly, for being concerned in the barbarous murder of B. Harvey and his son some time ago near Ballygawly, received sentence to be hanged and beheaded next Thursday.

To the Editor of the BELFAST NEWS-LETTER.

SIR,

THE following letter, which I received a few days ago from Dr. M'Donnell, I request you will publish, to shew the sentiments of that gentleman touching my conduct upon a recent occasion.

I am yours,
JOHN CAMPBELL.

"Dear Sir, Belfast, Aug. 16, 1789.

I am extremely sorry that any thing which fell from me in the course of my examination yesterday should have given you or your friends any offence. It has never been either my principle or inclination to injure any individual wantonly and without reason; and I surely had no foundation to insinuate any thing to your disadvantage. I asserted, that our patient had taken opium on the morning of that day on which his examinations were taken by the magistrate, and I could not deny (when the question was started by the Lawyer) that such remedies have often a tendency (however properly administered) to irritate and inflame the passions of the person who has used them—but I neither asserted (nor insinuated as the Judge at first represented it) that the operation had been imprudently undertaken or improperly performed—on the contrary, I declared then, as I do now, that the operation was undertaken with my consent, and performed with as much dexterity as the nature of the case would admit;—so that I am greatly surprized at your being offended with my evidence, since, in reality, I mentioned nothing which you have not frequently heard me mention on former occasions:—if, however, my words did not convey my opinions, or if these have been misrepresented by the public, in such a manner as to have the least tendency to injure you either as a Citizen or a Surgeon, I am extremely anxious to do you every degree of justice in my power, by giving the most public declaration of my sentiments in your favour, to convince the world, that you have acted with great propriety in this, and indeed every other case, in which I have been consulted with you.

Your's sincerely,
J. M'DONNELL."

To Mr. Campbell.

Belfast, *August* 25.

We have the pleasure of informing the public, that the spirit of Volunteering has revived in Lisburn. A new Corps (the Lisburn Rangers) having within these few days formed, under the command of Captain Robert Bell: their uniform is a green jacket, white half facing, white cape and white edging, a leather cap with green and white feathers, black stock and gaiters—their members are to be admitted by ballot.

The sailing of the Irish Volunteer is put off by desire of the passengers to the 10th September.

Died some time since at Gibraltar, Mr. George Renkin, son to Mr. Michael Renkin of Newtownards, a young man of the most amiable character and whose goodness of heart endeared him to all his acquaintances.

Belfast, *August* 28.

Wednesday the tenth annual Review of Volunteers was held on the Plains near Belfast. By appointment of General the Earl of Charlemont, Lieutenant Colonel Banks acted as Reviewing General. In addition to the corps enumerated in our last Paper, the Downpatrick and Comber Independants attended.

It was remarked with much pleasure, that tho' the Companies had not devoted many hours in preparation for this Review, they acquitted themselves in their marchings, firings, and evolutions, with at least as much regularity and exactness as formerly. It is sincerely to be wished that the military spirit of this country may be maintained by similar meetings on a small scale, through the different parts of the kingdom—whereby the purposes of discipline could be effected without loss of time or considerable expence, and internal peace preserved.

The body reviewed on this occasion regretted much that, in consequence of the number of Regimental Reviews to take place in this neighbourhood, it became improper to request the attendance of their beloved General the Earl of Charlemont. The satisfaction which that illustrious character constantly experiences in the good conduct of the Volunteer Army would, had he been present, have been felt yesterday in its full force; which circumstance, with his Lordship's nomination of a Gentleman to represent him, with the universal wishes of the whole body, were the best compensation the case admitted of for the absence of a Nobleman, whose steadiness, and unalterable attachment to the public weal, gave stability to the Volunteer Institution, and first pointed its attention to the great objects which its arms so happily obtained.

We cannot avoid remarking with much pleasure, as it does honour to a corps so very lately formed, the excellent discipline of the Downpatrick Company.—It is contrary to rule to pay compliments to particular corps—but that corps being so very young, and passing with such credit—oblige us to take this notice of it.

Armagh Assizes commenced the 19th August, 1789, when Mathew M'Aulay, James M'Aulay, Thos. Hand, Bernard Magennis, James Carson, John Clarke, James M'Clave, John Millar, Vance Holmes, Nath. Holmes, Robert Holmes, and William M'Clone, were acquitted of the murder of Hugh Dennis and Cormick Finnegan at Drumlee in November last.

The prisoners were part of a corps of Volunteers, and had, on Sunday the 23d of November, come to Armagh church, and in their return to Benburb, where most of them resided, they were attacked by a party of Defenders, and in defending themselves the said two men were killed.

Daniel Gormly, for the murder of Owen Sally in March, 1788, William Waugh, for the murder of John Clements in May, 1788, Alexander Johnston, John Johnston, the elder, John Johnston, the younger, Arthur Johnston, Robert Johnston, Plobe Johnston, and John M'Clave, for the murder of James Cowry at Tullybrove in May last, were acquitted.—This murder was in consequence of a religious dispute.

Arthur Kinny, for horse-stealing, Thomas John, for petty larceny, John M'Daniel, for picking pockets, Bryan Grogan, indicted on the Chawking Act, Thomas Boyle and James Lowry, for breaking into a shop and taking several articles thereout, William Thomas, for a capital felony, Pat. Hand, for cow-stealing, Alexander and John Johnston, for a felony out of a dwelling-house, Arthur Maginnis, for setting fire to a house by which same was burned, Nicholas Devine, for robbing a bleach-green—all acquitted.

John M'Neale, found guilty of firing, under the Chawking Act, at a Justice of Peace and a party of soldiers who were in search of persons against whom examinations were lodged for various offences.

William Turner, found guilty of a felony at large—William Kean, the like.

Patrick Murran, a capital felony, Neal Nugent alias Nowton, of picking pockets, Francis M'Mahon, for cow-stealing—all found guilty, but sentence not yet passed.

Nicholas Hand, found guilty of procuring a civil bill decree to be obtained at the suit of a fictitious person, altho' no process was served or debt due, and under colour thereof carrying away two cows and selling them.

The sale of the Lands of Ravarra, advertised in the 4th page of this paper, is adjourned till Saturday the 12th of September.

Married, a few days ago, Mr. Robert Young, Jun. to Miss Craig, both of Antrim.

Died, a few days ago, Anthony Hull, Esq. Coast Surveyor, and Stephen Rice, Esq. both of Carrickfergus.

FAIRS IN THE ENSUING WEEK.

Monday 31. Churchill, Ferm. Killygordon, Don. *Tuesday, September* 1. Broughshane, Ant. Castlewellan, Down. *Wednesday* 2.—Ballygawley, Tyr. Clones, Mon. *Thursday* 3.—Fintown, Don. Saintfield, Down, *Friday* 4.—Ballentoy, Ant. Cookstown, Tyr. Cross. Arm. Donegal Town, Emyvale, Mon. Londonderry city, Loughgall, Arm. Seaford, Down; Straid Ant. Trillic, Tyr. *Saturday* 5.—Scarvapass, Down.

To be Let,

FROM the first of November next, part of a Farm in Kylstown, the property of David Heron, held under David Kerr, Esq. of Portavo, for three Lives, all in being. The Lands are well inclosed and watered, with housing on it, containing 20 Acres and upwards, of which four Acres are Meadow, Tythe free. The tenant may be accommodated with Hay, Oats and Potatoes immediately at a valuation, by applying to David Heron on the premisses.

August 25th, 1789.

Anno 1789.]   Printed by HENRY JOY, and Co. BELFAST.

The BELFAST NEWS-LETTER.

TUESDAY September 1,   FRIDAY September 4, 1789.

FOR THE BELFAST NEWS-LETTER.

To the SWALLOW, on its Departure.

FAREWEEL thou bonie bird! full aft
Thou me haft mickle pleasure gi'en,
To fee thee fcud an' wheel, fae daft,
Owre waving fields an' vallies green;

Or where the fportive midgy thrang,
Beneath the warm, mild, evening beam,
Light lead the humming dance alang
The glaffy furface o' the ftream.

Short is the faucy cuckow's ftay,
Her flunkie flyin' i' the rere,
Awhile fhe flaunts frae brae to brae,
An' then flits off—we watna where!

But thou, wi' friendly, fand delay,
Remain'ft our focial haunts to cheer,
Till Autumn's late, contracted day,
An' gloomy Winter's reign draws near.

Fareweel, an' wherefoe'er ye gang,
May peace thy dwelling ay attend!
Whether the lanefome braes amang,
Or cliffs that owre the deep impend;

Or whether owre the fouthern wave,
To warmer climes your courfe ye fteer,
An' Winter's bleak dominions leave,
Till Spring revives the drooping year.

Fareweel!—an' when ye nieft come back,
Ay welcome, in my barn or byer,
Each night thy fonfie lodgin' tak',
Till nature prompts thee to retire.

DROMORE.

To be Sold by Auction,

ON Monday the 7th day of September next, at twelve o'clock at noon, in the *Liberty Market-Houfe*, *A large Quantity of plain and twill'd Corduroys*, being a confignment to John Nevill——Thefe Goods are of a very good quality, having been manufactured with the greateft care; and as they will be peremptorily fold on that day, they are well worth the attention of perfons wanting fuch, to whom the terms of fale will be made as agreeable as poffible.

Newry, 29th Auguft, 1789.

Wanted,

A SOAP-BOILER, who can make Bleachers and Common Soap, and Mold and Dipt Candles. A Perfon properly recommended for fkill and fobriety, will receive handfome wages.——Apply at the Office of Mr. Joy & Co.

Sept. 1ft, 1789.

Land to be Let.

TO be let from November next, either in one or more Farms, about fixty-five acres of very good Land, on which are Farm Houfes, with Offices, &c.—Thefe Lands are fituate in the townland of Dunean, parifh of Drumbo and county of Down, diftant four miles from Belfaft, and about three from Lifburn, Hillfborough and Saintfield. Enquire of Mr. Hunter, Lifburn, or in his abfence of Richard Brifon.

28th Auguft, 1789.

WE, the paffengers, redemptioners, and fervants, in all one hundred and feventy, from Belfaft to America, take this pleafing opportunity of returning our hearty and fincere thanks to James Jefferis, mafter of the brig Brothers, for his unprecedented care and humanity to every perfon on board; likewife for abundance of all forts of provifion diftributed moft liberally. We therefore warmly recommend him to his country for the above, and to our friends in Ireland, as a captain adapted in every degree equal to carry on the paffenger trade.
Signed by order of the Paffengers,

Capt. Henry Hughes,   Chriftopher Love,
William M'Cluney,   Francis Falloon.

Money to be lent.

FOUR HUNDRED POUNDS to be lent. Apply to Alexander Arthur, Attorney.

Belfaft, 3d Sept. 1789.

Advertifement.

THOMAS RANSON, of Downpatrick, Boot and Shoemaker, next door to the late Mr. Kean's Shop, is juft returned from Dublin with an extenfive affortment of every article belonging to the bufinefs for Ladies and Gentlemens Wear, viz. Stained Skins of various colours, Calf and Seal Skins, with Veal, Seal, and Cor de-van Boot Legs of the very beft quality.——The bufinefs to be conducted by William Martin, whofe abilities are fo well known by the firft people in Downpatrick and the furrounding neighbourhood.

A number of Journeymen Shoemakers are immediately wanted, who will meet with good encouragement.

Downpatrick, 17th Auguft, 1789.

ON Monday night laft, at the Coterie, was loft four table-fpoons;—one of them had a creft of an Unicorn—the other three had a Lyon.—Whoever returns them to Edward Darley fhall be handfomely rewarded, and if offered for fale, it is hoped they may be ftopped and information given.

Newtown-ards, Auguft 28th, 1789.

Barley and Wheat, &c. by Auction,

AT John Echlin's of Thomaftown, Efq; on Monday the 14th inft. by John Bailie, auctioneer and fworn appraifer, from Belfaft—to be put up in lots agreeable to the bidders. Approved notes at three months will be taken, or two and an half per cent. for ready money.

Thomaftown, Sept. 1ft, 1789.

J. Bailie requefts thofe indebted to the late fale for books, &c. will be fo kind as to meet him there the firft day of the fale to difcharge their refpective accounts, as a perfon will attend for that purpofe only.

Dwelling-House, Offices, and Fields.

TO be Let from the firft of Nov. next, the Dwelling Houfe and Offices lately occupied by Mr. William Harrifon; they are in complete order, and provided with every neceffary fixture—fituated at the corner of Marlborough-Street, Hanover-Quay—an eligible fituation for a merchant or private gentleman. If more agreeable to thofe who may wifh to treat for this concern, the intereft in the leafe will be fold, and the tenant or purchafer can be accommodated with fields, meadow and pafture grounds) very convenient in Ballymacarrett, of which there is a long leafe, and will be either let or fold along with the above tenement, if required.—For further particulars apply to the poffeffor,   GEORGE WELLS.

Belfaft, July 28th, 1789.

To be Sold

IMMEDIATELY and inftant poffeffion given, with the crop now ftanding, or at the firft of November, the Intereft in a Leafe of the houfe and demefne of Dartrey Lodge, near Blackwater-town, county of Armagh. The demefne confifts of near 148 Englifh Acres in the higheft condition, and the houfe and offices in thorough repair:—27 years of the leafe unexpired from firft of next November, with a claufe of furrender in the year 92 or any year after, giving one year's notice—40 acres referved from being broke up for two years before furrender.

Apply to Captain Waring, Falkland, near Monaghan.

July 18th, 1789.

Room Papers--Essence of Spruce--

Wax Candles, &c. &c.

MAGEE, *Bridge-ftreet*, *Belfaft*, has now on fale, the moft extenfive variety in the North of Ireland, of PAPER HANGINGS and BORDERINGS for Rooms—his affortment of *Glazed Paper*, are executed in a much fuperior ftile to any fold in Belfaft.

Genuine Effence of CANADIAN SPRUCE, in Pots to make thirty Gallons, 6s. 6d. or in Pots to make twenty Gallons, 4s. 10d. h. with printed directions.

WAX CANDLES of various fizes, free from adulteration, and will be fold cheap, as thofe of inferior quality—Wax Taper, Flambeaux, blazing, fuperfine and Bottle Wax of different colours.

Shining Irifh BLACK BALL, fuperior to German, and Patent Blacking Cakes, with directions.

PRUSSIAN BLUE STRIPES, that will not foil the webs, Lapping Papers, and Marking Liquid.

Belfaft, Sept. 1, 1789.

White Oak Staves.

TO be fold by Auction, on Chichefter-Quay, on Saturday next at twelve o'clock,—Twenty Thoufand of White Oak Staves—to be put up in Lots. Terms to be declared at fale.

Belfaft, 3d Sept. 1789.

JOHN BEGG,
Watch and   Clock-maker,
At the GOLD   Figure of TIME,
High-Street,   Belfast,

(Licenfed to buy, fell, and work Gold and Silver)

WITH the utmoft gratitude returns his fincere thanks to his friends, and the public in general, for the encouragement he has met with fince his commencement in bufinefs in this town—begs leave to inform them he has now for fale the following Watches, viz. Repeating, Horizontal, Patent, Seconds, &c. and a variety of others, all of his own manufacturing, which he will fell at as low a price as is fold (of the fame quality) either in London or Dublin.—Any Gentleman or Lady wanting either Clock or Watch of a particular construction, may have it on the fhorteft notice by applying as above.

N. B. Begg fupplies country Watchmakers with ready-made Work, and all Materials in the above line, &c. &c.——Higheft price for old Watches.

Archibald Bankhead,

HAS juft received a parcel of DRUGS, with PAINTS and OILS, of fuch a quality as he hopes will meet the approbation of his FRIENDS, which he will fell on the loweft terms.

WANTED, an Apprentice to the Drug Bufinefs, who can write a good hand. Apply as above.

Belfaft, 31ft Auguft, 1789.

Trinidad Cotton Wool.

JAMES PARK is landing from on board the Lord Charlemont, Capt. Dillon, from Grenada, a parcel of fine Trinidad Cotton, which he will difpofe of on reafonable terms for cafh, or good bills on Belfaft or Dublin.

Belfaft, 28th Auguft, 1789.

H A Y.

A Large Quantity of well-faved Hay to be fold by John Scott at the Falls.

2d September, 1789.

Wanted,

A Middle-aged Man as Butler and Own-Man, who can drefs hair. Such a perfon bringing certificates of fobriety, honefty and good temper, and of having lived in decent families, may apply to Mr. Ranken, Richmond-Lodge.——To be continued four times.

Sept. 1, 1789.

THE Committee of the Belfaft White-Linen-Hall, are requefted to meet in the Donegall Arms, this day, (Friday), exactly at one o'Clock, on bufinefs of importance.

The old Belfast Coterie,

WILL be held on Tuefday next, the 8th inftant, at the New-Rooms, Donegall-Arms, Belfaft.

September 3d, 1789.

American Ashes, Cotton Wool, &c.

JUST arrived to SAMUEL BROWN & Co. a large Quantity of American Pot and Pearl Afhes of the very firft quality—alfo a few Bags of Weft-India Cotton Wool, which, with the following Articles, will be difpofed of on moderate terms, viz.

Antigua & Jamaica Rum,	Beft Alicant Barilla,
Strong Bordeaux Brandy,	Scotch Vitriol,
Holland Gineva,	Train Oil,
London Porter,	Spermaceti Candles in
Red Port,	boxes,
White do. } Wines in	Mefs Beef,
Claret, } wood and	Ditto Pork,
Sherry, & } bottle,	Saint Ubes Salt,
Mountain	White Oak Staves,
Green & Congou Teas,	Cane Reeds,
Figs in Cafks,	A fmall quantity of well-
Mufcatel Raifins in boxes,	cured Cod Fifh.

Belfaft, 3d Sept. 1789.

American Pot and Pearl Ashes.

HUGH MONTGOMERY has juft imported from Bofton per the Schooner Induftry, James Hay, Mafter, a large quantity of Pot and Pearl Afhes, Train Oil, Spermaceti Candles, dried Fifh, and Barrel Staves; all of which he will fell on very reafonable terms for cafh or bills at three months.

SCOTTISH BARD.

The Ayrshire Bard, Mr. Burns, has at his own expence, erected a Monument, or Headstone, in the Canongate Church-yard, Edinburgh, over the grave of the late Mr. Fergusson, with the following inscription:

HERE LIES
ROBERT FERGUSSON, POET,
Born September 5th,
MDCCLI.
Died October 16th,
MDCCLXXIV.

No sculptur'd marble here, nor pompous lay;
No storied Urn, nor animated Bust—
This simple Stone directs pale SCOTIA's way,
To pour her sorrows o'er her POET's dust.

(On the reverse.)

By special Grant of the Managers to ROBERT BURNS who erected this Stone, this Burial Place is to remain for ever sacred to the Memory of
ROBERT FERGUSSON.

The merit of these congenial Poets, whose compositions are chiefly in their own maternal language, is well-known to the public; and their works become an object of greater importance, as they still retain much of the manners and customs, as well as many of the words and expressions, in the ancient Caledonian or Pictish language, now almost obsolete.

DAWN of LIBERTY in SPAIN.

From Madrid we learn, that the people in every province of Spain are beginning to assert their freedom. They insist that the Cortes, the ancient Parliaments of that kingdom, shall be re-established; and they insist upon this point with that firm and intrepid pertinacity which has ever been the character of that noble nation. The court, it seems, mean to employ the Holy Office as an engine to suppress the ardour of liberty. But the Holy Office has lost much of its authority in the minds of the Spaniards, who for some time past have been conversant with the literature of France and England.

In Germany, an excellent and cheap die has been invented by Wogler, adapted to woollen and cotton manufactures.

It consists simply of the seeds of the red trefoil, a plant very common in this country, and employed to feed horses and cattle.

A decoction of these seeds is mixed with different mineral substances, and the dies produced are very beautiful, and of a great variety.

Amongs these are yellows and greens of different shades, as also citron and orange colours.

AMERICA.

Extract of a letter from Wilmington, July 4.

"On Tuesday last arrived here the brig Brothers, Capt. Jefferies, in 45 days from Belfast, with 170 passengers, who informs us, that in lat. 40, long. 53 : 30 they fell in with part of a wreck, which he at the same time picked up, it being some square rigged vessel, fore top-mast, top-sail yard, and cap of the fore-mast, with all the shrouds, back-stays, halliards, chair-plates, dead-eyes, &c. From the appearance, supposes her to be an European."

The following Letter will be an additional proof of the political Foresight of DR. PRICE.

Extract of a letter from Dr. Price, dated Hackney, March 5, 1789.

"A discovery seems to have been made here, since Mr. Pitt came into administration, that the United States are of no use to us.—What a pity it is this discovery was not made before the commencement of the late war, and the shocking waste of blood and treasure it occasioned?

DUBLIN Aug. 25.

The middle price of wheat and flour, having, from the near and flattering prospect we enjoy of a plenteous harvest, fallen under the limited price, Dublin port was yesterday opened for exportation, which will for some time prevent any immediate or considerable fall.

There has not a discovery of greater importance been made these last fifty years in Europe, than the late one of saving flesh meat for ship provisions with so small a portion of salt, that the wholesome and nutritive juices are preserved, and the health of the consumer guarded against the terrible effects salt provisions formerly produced. An adept in this new method is shortly expected to visit this kingdom.

Yesterday being the festival of St. Bartholomew, who, as the proverb has it, "brings in the cold dew," was, on the contrary, close and sultry.

Letters Patent have been passed under the Great Seal of this kingdom, constituting and appointing the Right Hon. Lieut. Gen. William Augustus Pitt, commander in chief of his Majesty's Forces in this kingdom, and the Commander in Chief of his Majesty's said Forces for the time being, together with the Right Hon. James Cuffe, Ponsonby Moore, William Handcock, Robert Langrishe, Esq; Col. David Dundas, Adj. Gen of this kingdom, the Hon. George Jocelyn, Frederic Trench, and the Hon. Henry Pomeroy, to be Commissioners and Overseers of all his Majesty's Barracks in this kingdom.

The disturbances commencing in the South, are but an expected consequence to the operations of the Tythe Proctors—and the disappointment of that legal relief which the poor peasantry were taught to expect in the last Session of Parliament.

The title of Master of the Rolls in this kingdom is entirely changed, and in future the persons who are

DUBLIN, Sept. 1.

It is to be recorded to the honour of Lord Fitzgibbon—that since his Lordship's assumption of the Seals—he has not displaced any of those officers—in the departments of his Court—whose experience and abilities therein rendered them respectively eligible in their appointments. While in the Rolls Office we see—the invidious traits of Back-stair's malevolence, extending to clerks, who have acted for a series of years with unimpeachable propriety.

The National Assembly of France, have in an early instance of their revolutional system, shewn a proper sense of the intollerable burthen of Clerical Tythes on the people, and, they have therefore suppressed them, and allotted to the clergy, in lieu thereof, adequate salaries to support them in temperance, with the becoming decorum and moderation professed in their sacred functions.

The Ballycastle collieries are likely to prove an acquisition of the highest importance to this country.—Upwards of 16,000 tons have been very recently brought to this city, from thence; their quality is so much superior in every respect, to Scots coals, that they have obtained a general preference, and been the means of reducing the latter 2s. per ton.

We are assured that his Majesty's approbation is arrived for Peerages for the following gentlemen; and that their promotions will soon appear in the Gazette.

Mr. Gardiner, Mr. Eden, Sir Sampson Gideon, Mr. Brown of Neal, Chief Justice Carleton, Mr. Robert Stewart, Mr. Gore, and Sir Nicholas Lawless.

MARQUISATES.

This honour, was originally created in this kingdom, being established here so long ago as the year 1385, in the reign of Richard II. by whom his favourite, Robert de Vere, Earl of Oxford, was created Marquis of Dublin.

Since that period we have had many possessors of this dignity.

Ulicke Burke, Earl of Clanrickarde, and Earl of St. Alban's, was created Marquis of Clanrickarde by Charles I. but died without issue male, whereon the title became extinct. The same was the case with the Earl of Antrim, created Marquis of Antrim by Charles I.

James Earl of Ormond, was created Marquis of Ormond in the same reign; and this title became extinct by the attainder of his grandson, James Duke of Ormond, in the year 1715.

Philip Earl of Wharton, was created Marquis of Carlow by George I. which title became extinct by his attainder in the same reign.

James Earl of Kildare, was created Marquis of Kildare, by his present Majesty, in 1761;—which honour is now possessed by his Grace the Duke of Leinster.

Marquis of Clanrickarde, (late Earl of Clanrickarde).
Marquis of Antrim, (late Earl of Antrim.)
Marquis of Waterford, (late Earl of Tyrone.)
Marquis of Downshire, (late Earl of Hillsborough.)

Belfast, *Sept.* 1.

Extract of a Letter from Hillsborough, dated Aug. 29.

"Yesterday a great number of the principal tenants of the Marquis of Downshire gave an elegant entertainment, at the Corporation Arms in this town, to their noble Landlord, to testify the joy they felt on his Lordship's late promotion, and as a grateful testimony to a landlord who may truly be called the father of his people."

A few days ago, a poor man, in consequence of excessive drinking, dropped down dead in this town.

The Lord Donegal, James M'Roberts master, for London, arrived safe at the Downs the 21st ult. after six days passage.

The New Draper, Hughes, from Newry to London, after a long passage of fifteen days, by contrary winds, arrived safe the 21st ult.

The brig Brothers, Capt. Jeffers, from Belfast to Philadelphia, arrived safe there the beginning of July last.

The sailing of the James, from Larne to South Carolina, advertised in the 1st page of this paper, is postponed till the 15th of September.

The Down Independents beg leave to return their grateful thanks to the Inhabitants of Belfast, for the polite attention and hospitable treatment which they received at the late Review.

Married, some days ago, by special licence, Edward Evans, of Mullaghmore in the county Tyrone, Esq. to Miss Kelly of Armagh.

Died, a few days ago, Mr. William Willson, formerly an eminent merchant in this town.

Belfast, *Sept.* 4.

On Tuesday last the Lord Chancellor passed thro' this town in his way to Bangor, on a visit to the Hon. Robert Ward, which place is honoured with the presence of his Lordship, Lady Fitzgibbon, Mr. and Mrs. Richardson, Mrs. St. Leger, Marcus Beresford, Esq. Major Rawdon, and Captain Whaley.

On Sunday last the collection in the church of Lurgan, after a charity sermon preached for the purpose of clothing the children of the free school established there, amounted to 53l. 12s. 4dh. beside which the Governors of the school have received benefactions to the amount of 30 guineas, and 100 Bibles for the use of that most excellent charity.

As some men a few day ago were cutting a drain through Kellynumber moss near Tubermore in the county of Derry, they found a human body, which for some time after it was discovered and raised, appeared not at all decayed, and the hair, which was remarkably long, was entirely perfect and strong, and was cut off by a gentleman of the faculty who was passing near the place, but before interment the body mouldered almost away—there is no recollection of any person lost in this manner in the neighbourhood.

In Mr. Hunter's Advertisement, in the last page of this paper, for Townland of *Dunean* read *Drennan*.

MARRIED. Mr. Hunter Bradford of Laurencetown, Linen-draper, to Miss Dempster of Dempster-hall.

The late Visitation at Armagh was held on Friday last, when a circumstance happened that was worthy of notice.

In the late debates and writings respecting TYTHES, much has been said about "the rights of the Church," to this share of the husbandman's property; and many of its supporters have seemed to consider it as of *divine* origin;—the *equitable* division of it amongst the clergy, it was treason to call in question or propose alterations in.——The particular circumstance alluded to, is a curious proof how ill that distribution agrees with the *divine* principle of *justice*.

A Mr. Gordon, curate of Artrey, in the diocese of Armagh, resigned his cure, which he had held in the same parish for sixty-one years, during which time he performed divine service above 3,000 times—baptized 6,437 children belonging to the parish, and married the greater part of their parents; these and the other duties of his office, he performed with credit and respectability, for which he received an *equitable* share of the church livings amounting to 50l. per annum; and even that pittance this respectable old man is obliged to resign from being *worn out in the service of* HIS MAKER!

Had it been in the service of *his King*, he would have been entitled to a support, which in his 88th year *the Church* cannot afford him. It is true, the present incumbent of the parish (for tho' in one parish he has had many rectors) with a liberality that does him honour, continues him an annuity of 30l. but this is the act of an individual, and therefore he owes the church no obligations for it.

FAIRS IN THE ENSUING WEEK.

Tuesday 8. Roslea, Ferm. *Friday* 11. Middletown, Arm. *Saturday* 12. Wheathill, Ferm.

PRICES IN THIS MARKET YESTERDAY.

Oatmeal,	10s.	2d.	to	11s.	00.	Dried do. 26s. to 00s. od per d
Wheat,	90	0	—	12	9	R. Tallow, 4s 10d. a 5s. per st.
Oats,	0	0	—	6	0	Potatoes 9d. to 10d per b.
Barley,	0	0	—	0	0	Eng. coals, 00s. od. to 14s.
Butter,	51	0	—	52	0	Scotch do. 13s. to 00s. od.
C. hides,	34	0	—	35	0	Ex on Lond 6 3-4 a 0 per c.
Ox ditto,	37	0	—	38	0	Do. on Glasgow 6½.
S.C. skins	00	0	—	42	6	

Land to be Let.

TO be let from November next, either in one or more Farms, about sixty-five acres of very good Land, on which are Farm Houses, with Offices, &c.—These Lands are situate in the townland of Dunean, parish of Drumbo and county of Down, distant four miles from Belfast, and about three from Lisburn, Hillsborough and Saintfield Enquire of Mr. Hunter, Lisburn, or in his absence of Richard Brison.

28th August, 1789.

To be lent on real Security,

SIXTEEN HUNDRED POUNDS.———Apply to Mr. Roger Casement, Attorney.

Ballymena, August 15th, 1789.

Anno 1789.] Printed by HENRY JOY, and Co. BELFAST.

The BELFAST NEWS-LETTER.

TUESDAY September 8, FRIDAY September 11, 1789.

To the Independent Electors of the Borough of Lisburn.

Dublin, September 2d, 1789.

GENTLEMEN,

I SHOULD not have troubled you with an address at this period of parliament, if a canvass had not commenced for your future representation: a measure mutually affecting your interests, and the reputation of the present burgesses.

I have ever expressed myself to you in the language of truth; and as I never SOLD you in the senate, I have held it always unnecessary to attempt to cajole you in your town. Previous to the last dissolution, we were adopted as your representatives, and put in nomination by a general assembly of the electors: and our respect for that measure, I should presume, ought to induce us to await the same honor again, should we be fortunate enough still to retain your good opinions.

You will consider our discharge of your delegated trust; our obedience to your instructions; and your own reiterated approbation of both.—We return to you unbought and unpensioned; and a minute review of the conduct we have pursued in the succession of national questions which have been agitated during a seven years service, will be the best comment upon the propriety of your choice, and upon the evidences of our integrity.—To you we are indebted gratitude for the distinction of your good opinion; and you owe us *protection* for the discharge of our duty. I express myself in the plainness of constitutional language, which will not diminish my weight in your manly minds: with a freedom remote from the vile jargon of polite imposition, and becoming a man born and reared in the midst of you, who in a few weeks will probably become your fellow-resident and *elector* for the remainder of his life.

In the *latter* character, before at present I take my leave, permit to direct your attention towards the gentleman who has also the honour to represent you:—to his unremitted attendance in parliament, and to the vengeance poured upon him by a corrupt administration for SUPPORTING YOUR INSTRUCTIONS:——to his conduct as a volunteer commander of a body of those armed citizens, the voice of whose virtue has awakened *another empire* to the watch-word of liberty, and whose glory, by an imitation of their conduct, is registered in the records of the *French* constitution:——to his public society, uncontaminated by any intercourse with the buyers and sellers of their country's rights—and to the domestic virtues of his private life.——Such, not confined to partial districts, but as general as the island, is the declineation of his character; the unassailableness of which has silenced detraction, and even dried up the printing-ink of defamation.————Is it possible that any bosom among you, not callous to the infamy of a criminal inconsistency, and steeled to the sensations of public gratitude; not careless of the fatal national tendency of *bad example* in the *electors*, and not totally indifferent to the independence of election, *can contemplate that man,* and say, "Like the just Aristides let him be banished from his town; there is another to be found in the kingdom more worthy to assume his chair!—?"——I would to God, there were *three hundred!*—but it remains for your future determinations whether you think there is to be found *one.*

But I know I address men of bosoms of far different sensations, consistent, and independent. And were you to quit your calm retreats of industry, and nearer the scene of political action, contemplate the black cloud of corruption darkening such multitudes of distinguished reprobates, too many of whom have the address to return to their gull'd constituents in a borrowed whiteness, you would nor an instant suffer self-interest to warp, or plausible sophistry to dull the vivacity of your approbation; or throw a languor over the testimonies of your attachment.

Gentlemen, if you wish me to represent you again, I shall with alacrity obey you: and as I formerly express'd myself, undertake the honourable trouble—but the declaration is premature: nobody will have the impudence to obtrude upon your ear in my name, nor the audacity to hazard assertions respecting my determinations, of which he has not received my personal notification.

I remain, Gentlemen,
your obliged and obedient servant,
WILLIAM TODD JONES.

Wanted,

A GAMEKEEPER:——He must be a sober active Man, who can shoot well, and break-in dogs; he will also have the care of woods. He must be well recommended from his last place, for integrity and sobriety.——Application to be made to Mr. Kingsmill, Belfast.

DROPPED,

ON the road between Lisburn and Belfast, a Silver Watch, makers name John Jeffery, Glasgow, with the Letters H L M in place of a Number; whoever found it shall be handsomely rewarded by applying to Mr. James Mc. Clean, Watchmaker, Belfast.

To the Electors of the Borough of Lisburn.

GENTLEMEN,

THE very favourable reception we have experienced on our canvass demands our most grateful acknowledgments, and we are persuaded will justify our resolution of submitting ourselves to your consideration at this period.

The warm and liberal assurances we have received of your support at the General Election, encourage us to look forward with satisfaction to the time when we may hope for the honor of representing your respectable Borough in Parliament; and we beg leave only to add, that it shall be the first object of our ambition to deserve your confidence and good opinion; and we trust our conduct in every situation shall secure the continuance of that kind partiality with which you have been pleased on this occasion to honor us.

We are, with gratitude and respect,
Gentlemen,
your most faithful and obliged servants,
GEORGE HATTON,
JOHN MOORE, junr.

Lisburn, Sept. 7th, 1789.

Burglary.

WHEREAS on the night of Thursday the third, or morning of Friday the 4th instant, the Back Store of Richard Armstrong, in North-street, was feloniously broke open and tann'd Leather taken thereout, to the amount of 20l. or thereabouts. NOW, in order to bring the said felony to light, we whose names are hereunto subscribed, Do promise to pay unto any person or persons who will give information thereof before the next general assize, the sums annexed to our names respectively, when the thief or thieves shall be convicted of said felony.———Given under our hands at Belfast, this 7th September, 1789.

	l.	s.	d.		l.	s.	d.
Richard Armstrong	3	8	3	Mackinzie & M'Clurg	3	8	3
John Harper	3	8	3	Thomas Major	3	8	3
Joseph Smyth	3	8	3	Nath. Main	1	2	9
George Beck	3	8	3	James Humphres	1	2	9
James Martin	3	8	3	Chr. Hudson	3	8	3
Robt. & Wm. Simms	3	8	3	Robt. Wallace	1	2	9
John Ferguson	3	8	3	James Stewart	1	2	9
Sam. Lacy	3	8	3				

Robert Hodgson,

Bookseller, Book-binder, and Stationer, North-street,

RETURNS thanks to his Friends and the Publick for past favours,—has now to advise them, that he has removed to West Side of said Street, opposite the house of Mr. John Robinson, merchant. He continues to do all kind of Book-binding Work in best manner on the shortest notice, and as cheap as any other in town.

Paper-Books

made to any pattern on the shortest notice possible, either ruled or unruled, and bound in Russia Bands, vellum, calf or farrel covers, as may be most agreeable to his customers. Belfast, 10th Sept. 1789.

Valentine Joyce,

HAS just landed out of the *Charles and Margaret,* a large parcel of strong well-flavoured *Jamaica Rum.* He has also received per the *Dispatch,* a quantity of *Holland Gineva*—these, together with his usual Stock of *Spirits,* will be sold at the most reduced prices for Bank Notes, Cash, or Bills.

Belfast, 10th September, 1789.

Hay to be Sold.

ABOUT Fifty Cocks of very well-saved HAY to be sold.—Apply to Cunningham Greg.

Belfast, 10th Sept. 1787.

A Young Man, who can be well recommended, wishes to engage as a Tutor in any genteel Family; he is well versed in the Classics, and several parts of the Mathematics, &c.

Application made at the Office of Mr. Joy & Co. by letter or otherwise, shall be carefully attended to.

September the 8th, 1789.

Old Oats,

SWEET and well saved, to be sold by James Graham of Ballycowan, near Purdysburn.

Sept 6th, 1789.

To be sold immediately,

A HOSIER's FRAME, made by Freebairn, a twenty Gauge, as good as new:——Enquire at John Becket, at the Mile-water; or Mr. Hugh Smith, Hosier, North-street, Belfast.

September 9, 1789.

For Boston,

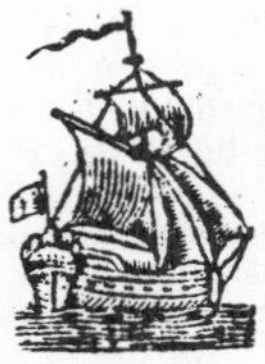

THE Schooner INDUSTRY, JAMES HAY, Master, will be clear for the above port the 12th instant, and sail first fair wind after.

For Freight or Passage apply to Samuel Brown and Co. or Hugh Montgomery.

Belfast, 3d Sept. 1789.

Belfast White Linen Hall.

THE Gentlemen of the Linen Trade in the North of Ireland are respectfully informed, that the next market for the sale of white linens in the Belfast Hall will commence on Friday the 25th instant.

Constant attendance is given to receive and take care of Linens sent to the hall.

Belfast, 7th Sept. 1789. VAL. SMITH, Chamberlain.

American Pot Ashes by Auction.

TO be sold by auction at the stores of Samuel Brown and Co. in High-Street, on Friday the 11th instant, at one o'clock, one hundred barrels of American Pot Ashes of the first quality—to be set up in lots, and terms to be declared at sale.

Belfast, 7th Sept. 1789.

To be Let from the first of Nov. next.

A House in Donegall-Street, opposite the Brown Linen-Hall, at present occupied by Mr. Francis Taggart.—For particulars apply to Abel Hadskis.

Belfast, Sept. 7th, 1789.

Diverney, August 30, 1789.

THIS is to give notice to the Publick, that some time ago I gave my son James Todd a Letter of Attorney to transact for me, which is both disagreeable and unprofitable; therefore I reverse it. Let no man trust him on my account, as I will pay no debts he will contract.——To be continued three times.

JAMES TODD, senr.

The Dromore Battalion

RETURN their warmest thanks to Mr. Stott of Dromore, for his kindness in accommodating the Volunteers with the Review Ground on Wednesday last.

September 7th, 1789.

Wanted,

A Young Man, who can transact the Business of an Apothecary's Shop; his character must bear the strictest scrutiny.———Apply to Mr. Nielson, Druggist, Belfast.

Belfast, Sept. 3d, 1789.

Flats, &c. by Auction.

ON Monday the 14th instant at Noon, will be sold by publick Auction, (for ready money) at the Custom-house Quay,

Three large Flats, with all their Machinery, Anchors, &c. as they were used in deepening the Ford in the River Ban; also one small Boat.

Colerain, 2d Sept. 1789.

TALLOW.

TO be Sold, a few Casks of Tallow of prime quality.——Apply to Cornelius Carleton, Lisburn.

September 4th, 1789.

Wholesale English and Irish Woollen Warehouse,

No. 3, Corn-Market, Dublin.

IMPRESS'D with a deep sense of the obligations I am under to my Friends and the Publick for their distinguished preference since my commencement in business; for which I request they may accept of my most grateful and cordial thanks, and assure them it it shall be my constant study to merit a continuance of the favours I have hitherto so amply experienced.

Take the liberty of informing them, that this day I have imported, from the principal manufacturing towns in England, a large and elegant assortment of Goods in the Woollen and Manchester Line upon such terms and of such qualities as must give general satisfaction to all those who please to make trial——as I only solicit publick favor as long as I continue to merit it, which ever shall be the object in view with the Publick's much obliged and very humble servant,

ROBERT SPENCER.

Sept. 2d, 1789.

☞ An Apprentice of genteel connections wanted.

PARISIAN INTELLIGENCE.

GRAND DEBATE ON RELIGIOUS LIBERTY.

PARIS, AUGUST 27.

THE National Aſſembly having eſtabliſhed Nine Articles of the Declaration of the Rights of the Man and Citizen, on Saturday, a motion was made to adjourn to Monday; but a powerful party, headed by the Clergy, inſiſted on the Aſſembly meeting on the next day, Sunday, to take into conſideration the next Article, relative to Religion; and it is remarkable enough, that this ſhould have been the eve of the Maſſacre of St. Bartholomew.

The article, as propoſed to the Aſſembly, ſtood as follows:—"No Citizen ought to be moleſted, who does not diſturb the eſtabliſhed worſhip."

The Debate was opened by a Biſhop, who pleaded the general cauſe of Religion with dignity and eloquence. "Religion," ſaid he, "is the baſis of Empires; it is eternal reaſon watching over the order of things. You would ſooner build a city in the air, as Plutarch ſays, than found a Republic which had not for its principle the worſhip of the Gods. I wiſh, therefore, to ſee the principles of the French Conſtitution reſt upon Religion, as on an everlaſting baſis."

PARIS, Auguſt 24.

DECLARATION OF RIGHTS.

The Aſſembly proceeded to the diſcuſſion of the 9th Article of the Sixth Bureau, relative to the LIBERTY OF THE PRESS.

The diſcuſſion of the ſubject which follows, being very intereſting to a Free Country, our Correſpondent's exertions muſt amply gratify our readers' curioſity, by the peruſal of M. Robeſpierre's amiable Speech, which breathes all the noble ſpirit and dignified independence of the firſt Britiſh Orator.

M. ROBESPIERRE declared, that on a ſubject of ſuch importance as the Liberty of the Preſs, he conſidered it his duty to ſolicit the attention of the Aſſembly for a few minutes. He entertained a very different opinion from ſome Gentlemen who endeavoured to check the growth of French Freedom, by fettering the Liberty of the Preſs. He hoped, nay, he conjured all preſent, to weigh the dreadful conſequences of ſuch a meaſure. If, ſays he, you pant for Liberty, the glorious reward of your wonderful atchievements—if you wiſh to eſtabliſh that ineſtimable bleſſing on the moſt permanent baſis—if you are anxious for your own honour and glory—let this truth be deeply impreſſed upon your minds, that the Freedom of the Preſs will contribute more to the freedom and happineſs of the people, than all the combined ſtrength of your National Militia.—The ſword or the bayonet may accompliſh ſudden and extraordinary revolutions; but to the arts of civilization, to thoſe manly and exquiſite refinements, to the unlimited exerciſe of our mental faculties—muſt we owe the preſervation of our liberty. To what are we to attribute the affluence and grandeur of Great-Britain? The navy and army of England are deſervedly ſubjects of wonder and applauſe throughout Europe. They now appear equal, perhaps, I may ſay—by the leave of my brave countrymen—ſuperior to any other nation. But to this invincible power alone the generous Engliſh owe not the preſervation of Liberty. They are indebted to their ſalutary laws—to the freedom of ſpeech and of the preſs—which qualities united, direct and command the exertions of the Miniſtry towards their warlike arrangements.

From the LONDON GAZETTE.

PLYMOUTH-DOCK, Auguſt 27.

THIS morning the King, with the Queen and three Princeſſes, left Saltram on their return to Weymouth, after a ſtay of twelve days; during which time their Majeſties, accompanied by the Princeſſes, and attended by the Board of Admiralty, viewed the Dock-yard, the ſhips building and repairing, and thoſe on float; went on board the Impregnable, a guardſhip of 90 guns, and the Royal Sovereign, a new ſhip of 100 guns, in ordinary; and proceeded to ſea in the Southampton frigate (accompanied by the Magnificent, of 74 guns), to review the Squadron of Evolution, under the command of Commodore Goodall, which was cruiſing in the Offing.

WHITEHALL, Auguſt 29.

Notice is hereby given, that the light-houſe at Port Patrick will be finiſhed and lighted on the 20th of September next.

LONDON, AUG. 31—SEPT. 1.

By the French Mails we learn, that the confuſion and diſturbances in the Provinces become every day more alarming; the People every where are diſcontented, and the National Aſſembly ſtill indeciſive in its meaſures.

The City of Guiſe, on the 24th of the laſt month, was viſited by ſeveral brigades of robbers, who committed every poſſible exceſs. They threw ſeveral into the river, and were at length ſubdued by the great activity of the Commandant of the Garriſon.

By the ſame channel we learn, that the Ruſſian and Swediſh fleets had a ſecond action on the 28th and 29th ult. and that the latter afterwards got into Carlſcrone, where it now lies.

The diſorder with which the Emperor of Germany has been ſo long affected, has been pronounced by the Faculty who have attended him, a nervous fever brought on by too intenſe an application to buſineſs. In many ſymptoms it has nearly approached the malady under which our own moſt excellent Sovereign ſome months ſince laboured.

From the preſent diſpoſition of the Swiſs, we may prepare ourſelves to hear of a Revolution in that country. They ſeem not far diſtant to throw off their ariſtocratic Government. The Magiſtrates are become of late extremely condeſcending, and wiſh to prevent the ſtorm by courting popularity.

Mr. Necker is ſaid to be indiſpoſed of a tertian fever.

This is an age in which experience ſeems not only unneceſſary for an Officer of State, but an abſolute diſqualification—thus we find the Premier of thirty, the Speaker of the Houſe of Commons twenty-eight, the Secretary of State twenty-nine, and the grave Divine, whoſe buſineſs it is to perform Divine Service before the Senate of Great-Britain, twenty-three years of age!

Belfaſt, *Sept.* 8.

On Wedneſday laſt the following corps of Volunteers were reviewed by Colonel Sharman on a fine plain near the town of Dromore, Major Patton acting as Exerciſing Officer.

Moira Company,
Ballinahinch ditto, Capt. Armſtrong,
Liſburn Rangers, Capt. Bell,
Ditto Artillery,
Dromore Company, } Capt. Vaughan,
Villa Independents, }

amounting in all to about 300 men. They performed their different manœuvres, &c. with conſiderable exactneſs, but from the wetneſs of the morning had not ſufficient time to go through the whole of the propoſed plan. After the Review a mock attack and defence of the town took place, which afforded great pleaſure to the ſpectators from the judicious and ſpirited manner in which it was conducted. The market-houſe, in the centre of the ſquare, repreſented the citadel, and parties were poſted at all the avenues leading to it; theſe were at the ſame time attacked by different detachments of aſſailants, and a heavy firing for ſome time was heard in every quarter, the defenders retreating as their opponents advanced, till at length, being cloſely preſſed on all ſides, they beat a parley and the citadel ſurrendered.

On Saturday laſt 146 loaves of bread were ſeized by the Sovereign—ſome for deficiency in quality, and ſome for not having the marks preſcribed by law;—which are, for the quality, weight, and baker's name. Till a repeal of the late law for regulating the baking trade takes place, houſekeepers would be prudent in attending to the marks and giving information to the Magiſtrates, where they are wanting or improperly applied.

The Friendſhip, Dalway Lepper maſter, for London, loaded with linen cloth, ſailed the 4th inſt.

At the particular requeſt of an old Subſcriber we inſert the following. The circumſtance on which it turns was immediately after the late Aſſizes there—briefly mentioned in this paper. •

Extract of a Letter from Armagh.

"On Thurſday laſt the Benburb Volunteers were honourably acquitted of the ſuppoſed murder of Patrick Dennis and Peter Finegan, at Drumbee, on the 23d of November laſt. It was fully proved on the defence that thoſe unfortunate men were part of a mob that had aſſembled on the lands of Drumbee, for the avowed purpoſe of attacking the volunteers on their way to the church of Armagh;—that not being fully prepared as the volunteers paſſed in the morning, they only pelted them with a few ſtones;—that when the volunteers came out of church, they were informed that prodigious crowds of armed men were drawn up on the only two roads they had to return;—that in conſequence of this information, they borrowed a few guns in Armagh, for they came abroad with only their ſide arms;—that on their return, when they approached the lands of Drumbee, they ſaw ſeveral hundreds of men armed with guns, and bayonets on the ends of long poles;—that as ſoon as the armed volunteers, who were placed in the front, had paſſed the mob, who were drawn up in a field adjoining the road, the unarmed volunteers were furiouſly attacked with a volley of ſtones which knocked down ſeveral of them, and two ſhots were fired at the front;—that the volunteers were at length obliged to fire to keep the mob at bay until their unarmed and wounded brethren would make their eſcape.

"At the concluſion of the buſineſs the conduct of the volunteers was truly honourable, for when the gang and their leader were arraigned for the aſſault on them, their lawyers were inſtructed to acquaint the court, that if the priſoners would beg pardon for their offence, and promiſe to behave peaceably for the future, they would not be proſecuted;——the poor wretches with the ſtrongeſt marks of contrition in their countenances, acknowledged their crime and their ſorrow for it, and promiſed to behave quietly for the time to come. Such conduct exhibits the volunteers in a moſt honourable point of view, it ſhews they are poſſeſſed of one of the Chriſtian virtues moſt difficult to practice—forgiveneſs of injuries."

On the evening of the 26th ult. at about half paſt nine, a meteor of a high and obtuſe parabolical direction in the zenith of the ſky, and ran in the E. N. E. quarter of the heavens with conſiderable velocity; its nucleus was not ſo large as that which appeared the 18th of Auguſt, 1783, being about ſix times as large as a ſtar of the firſt magnitude, emitting an innumerable multitude of atmoſpheric vapour till it entirely diſſipated; its colour was much brighter than artificial ſtars thrown by balloons in fire-works; it carried after it a long tail, and preſented a beautiful ſpectacle.

Moneymore.

The ſhip Iriſh Volunteer, for Charles-Town in South Carolina, advertiſed in the firſt page of this paper, is now in the harbour of Larne, and will be clear to ſail on the 24th inſt. at which time the owners requeſt the paſſengers may be in readineſs to go on board.

ERRATUM—In the anecdote reſpecting DR. WALLIS (1ſt col. of 4th page in our laſt paper) the ſeventh line was tranſpoſed into the place of the ſixth.

PORT NEWS.

ARRIVED.

Sept. 1. New Draper, Kearny, Liverpool, ſugar, &c.
Induſtry, Griffith, Carmarthen, bark.
Adventure, Robinſon, Drunton, deals.
2. Hillſbro', M'Donald, Liverpool, ſalt, &c.
Brothers, M'Clean, Barbadoes, rum, ſugar, &c.
Induſtry, Hay, Boſton, aſhes, &c.
3. New Loyalty, Brown, Liverpool, rum and ſugar.
Twelve colliers.

CLEARED OUT.

Sept. 4. Friendſhip, Lepper, London, cloth and butter.
5. Brothers, M'Lean, Greenock, ſugar and cotton.

Belfaſt, *Sept.* 11.

The French Aſſembly ſeem to be already adopting ſome of the well known legal maxims of Great Britain and Ireland, and in particular, "that every accuſed perſon ſhall be deemed innocent, until proved guilty." And alſo this principle from Magna Charta, "that no citizen can be ſtopped, detained, accuſed or puniſhed, but in the name and according to forms of law." The words may vary, but the ſpirit and eſſence are the very ſame.

Died, a few days ago, at Granſhaw, near Donaghadee, Mrs. Young; ſhe was a tender wife, and an indulgent parent; her death is greatly lamented by a numerous family and all her acquaintance.

FAIRS IN THE ENSUING WEEK.

Tueſday, Sept. 15, Loughbrickland, Down. Thurſday, 17, Saintfield, Down. Friday, 18, Ballyſhannon, Don. Saturday, 19, Carnteel, Tyr. Drum. Mon. Roſtrevor, Down.

PORT NEWS.

ARRIVED.

Sep. 7. Induſtry, Cragg, Memel, timber.
9. Charles, Neil, Gottenburgh, iron.
Four colliers.

CLEARED OUT.

Sept. 7. New Draper, Kearney, Liverpool, cloth.

PRICES IN THIS MARKET YESTERDAY.

Oatmeal,	10s. 4d.		to	10s. 6d.		Dried do. 25s. to 26s. 0d. per d
Wheat,	00	0	—	12	9	R. Tallow, 4s 10d. a 5s. per ſt.
Oats,	0	0	—	0	0	Potatoes 9d. to 10d. per b.
Barley,	0	0	—	0	0	Eng. coals, 12s. 6d. to 13s.
Butter,	00	0	—	52	0	Scotch do. 12s. 6d. to 13s.
C. hides,	34	0	—	35	0	Ex on Lond 6 3-4 a 0 per c.
Ox ditto,	37	6	—	40	0	Do. on Glaſgow 6½.
S.C. ſkins	40	0	—	42	6	

Anno 1789.] Printed by HENRY JOY, and Co. BELFAST.

The BELFAST NEWS-LETTER.

TUESDAY September 15, FRIDAY September 18, 1789.

THOMAS L. STEWART, the Law Agent choſen and appointed by the cuſtodee and elegit creditors of Roger M. H. Mc. Neill, thinks it neceſſary to inform the ſeveral tenants of the ſaid Roger M. H. Mc. Neill, inhabiting and occupying the manor and lands of Drumbracklin in the county of Down, that notwithſtanding the notice of 8th September inſtant, ſigned Jacob Hancock, junior, the ſaid ſeveral tenants muſt pay their reſpective rents to the creditors as they have hitherto done, the ſaid order appointing Mr. Handcock receiver of ſaid rents having been obtained by ſurprize, and without the knowledge or privity of ſaid creditors, who were previous to the obtaining the ſame legally impowered to receive ſaid rents.

Belfaſt, Sept. 14th, 1789.

FELONY.

WHEREAS on the Night of the 30th of Auguſt laſt, there was feloniouſly taken off the lands of Broghderg (near Gortin, in the County of Tyrone,) one Bullock of a yellow colour, 6 years old, value about 8 guineas, marked on one of the horns I. S. wanted a piece of the top of his horn, and both horns drooping downwards towards his eyes, the property of James Stewart, of Killymoon Esq. And two Heiffers, 3 years old, marked on the horns X. both of them red and white flecked; the property of John Moor, of Cookſtown. As they were fat, it is ſuppoſed they will be ſold to butchers. It is hoped that Butchers and Tanners will be careful to examine ſuch, if offered for ſale.

NOW, in order to bring the perpetrators of ſaid felony to puniſhment, we whoſe names are hereunto ſubſcribed, do promiſe to pay the ſeveral ſums to our names annexed, to the perſon, who ſhall within nine calender months from the date hereof, diſcover upon and proſecute to conviction, all or any of the perſons concerned in ſaid felony. Given under our hands this 5th day of September, 1789.

	l.	s.	d.		l.	s.	d.
William Stewart,	11	7	6	Nat. Alexander,	5	13	9
James Stewart,	11	7	6	F. Trench,	5	13	9
John Cook,	5	13	9	Wm. Magill,	3	8	3
D. Richardſon,	5	13	9	Joſeph Baxter,	2	5	6

I do hereby promiſe to pay the ſum of ten guineas, as a reward to the perſon who ſhall give ſuch private information as ſhall lead to a diſcovery and conviction of the perſons concerned in the aforeſaid felony.

JOHN MOORE.

N. B. Any perſons who can diſcover, or give information, will be duly attended to by letters directed to ſaid John Moore, at Cookſtown.

September 6th, 1789.

To be ſold by Auction,

AT the Dwelling-Houſe of the late Sarah Munro, in Lurgan, ſundry articles of Houſehold Furniture, conſiſting of beds, bedding, chairs, looking-glaſſes, tables, a good mahogany deſk, cheſts of drawers, &c.

The ſale to begin the 21ſt inſtant, at 11 o'clock in the forenoon, and to be continued the following days till all the Goods are diſpoſed of.

Lurgan, Sept. 12th, 1789.

To be Sold,

FOUR Black Coach Geldings, well matched, five and ſix years old—ſound, highly bitted, and fit for immediate uſe.—Application to be made to Mr. Edward Hughes in Killylea, county of Armagh.

11th Sept. 1789.

To be inſerted five times only.

To be ſold by Auction,

At the Market-houſe, Belfaſt, preciſely at 12 o'Clock, on Friday next the 18th September inſtant,

THE Leaſe of a Tenement in Donegall-ſtreet, granted to James Murphy for 25 years from Nov. 1784, provided the Earl of Donegall lives ſo long, (at preſent divided into two Dwelling-Houſes, occupied by Mrs. Armſtrong and Mr. Lemon, Upholder)—the whole ſubject to 31l. 17s. yearly rent; and now yields upwards of 13l. a year profit rent.—For further particulars enquire of JOHN TISDALL.

Belfaſt, 14th Sept. 1789.

☞ At ſame time will be ſold John Mc. Farlane's Leaſe of a new-built Houſe, contiguous to the new Buildings in Ann ſtreet.—Enquire as above.

Bills Loſt,

ON Monday laſt, on the road leading from Ballycaſtle to Ballymoney, viz. one drawn by Mr. Samuel Allan on Meſſrs. Geo. Lang and Co. Dublin, for 100l. dated Larne, Sept. 3d in favour of Mr. Henry Clark, and endorſed by him, payable to Mr. Patrick Deaſe; alſo one drawn by Mr. William Walſh on Meſſrs. Catherine and Ann Walſh, Milliners, Jervis-ſtreet, Dublin, in favour of Mr. Alexander Mc. Neile, and endorſed by him and Henry Clarke for 27l. 15s. 8d. This is to caution the publick not to take either of ſaid Bills, as the payment of both is ſtopt in Dublin.

For Kingſton, Jamaica,

THE Ship CHARLES and MARGARET, Anthony Atkinſon, Maſter, will poſitively ſail the firſt of October, wind and weather permitting — For Freight or paſſage apply to Val Joyce, Mc. Kedy and Stevenſon, or John Reid,—who have for Sale ſtrong Jamaica Rum and Scale Sugar, of the beſt quality.

Belfaſt, 10th Sept. 1789.

County of the Town of Carrickfergus. } I Do hereby give this public notice to the Aldermen and Burgeſſes of this Corporation, that I intend holding an election in the Court-houſe of ſaid Town, on Thurſday the 24th of this inſtant, for the purpoſe of chuſing one Alderman, and three Burgeſſes;—and alſo, on the ſame day, immediately after the ſaid elections, I ſhall hold an Aſſembly of the Aldermen and Burgeſſes, to examine and ſettle the Treaſurer's accompts, and to tranſact any other buſineſs that may come before them, agreeable to an Act of Aſſembly made the 24th day of September 1787 for that purpoſe.

C. Fergus, 10th Sept. 1789. WM. KIRK, Mayor.

Notice to the Tenants of Drumbracklin.

LEST the tenants of the manor of Drumbracklin ſhould be amuſed or deluded by any fallacious repreſentations, in contradiction to my former notice requiring them to pay their rents to me, I think it proper to obſerve in reply to the advertiſement inſerted in yeſterday's paper by the law agent of the cuſtodee and eligit creditors of R. M. H. Mc. Neill, that the order which I have alluded to impowering me to receive their rents was *fairly* obtained and not by any ſtratagem or ſurprize: The ſeveral tenants on ſaid manor well know that they were individually ſerved with an order from the Court of Chancery near ſix months ago, reſtraining them from paying their rents to any perſon till a receiver ſhould be appointed, unleſs cauſe ſhould be ſhewn to the contrary—that to defeat this, a frivolous attempt was made by ſome of the cuſtodee creditors, which was afterwards relinquiſhed, and in conſequence, the order was made abſolute, enjoining the tenants to pay their rents into my hands, as being the receiver appointed by the court—What purpoſe then can it anſwer for the creditors, or their law agent to declare "that the ſaid ſeveral tenants muſt pay their reſpective rents to the creditors as hitherto," when it is preſumed they cannot be ignorant that if they receive a ſingle ſhilling for rent, or paſs a receipt to any tenant, they will unqueſtionably ſubject themſelves to the proceſs of an immediate attachment for contempt of court, and the tenant who pays them to the like proceſs, or to the neceſſity of paying his rent over again? and how can it, under the circumſtances before-mentioned, be aſſerted that the order which I have received was obtained by ſurprize and without the knowledge or privity of the creditors? If it was ſo, does it not appear very extraordinary that ſuch a powerful body of creditors as are engaged in this buſineſs,—in poſſeſſion of the rents of the premiſſes—ſurrounded by a numerous hoſt of very able law agents to defend them, and aſſiſted by the firſt counſel in the land, could be *all taken by ſurprize*—that the High Court of Chancery *could be taken by ſurprize*, and that thoſe *acts of ſurprizal* ſhould all be effected by a ſingle woman?

JACOB HANCOCK, junr.

Liſburn, Sept. 16th, 1789.

Bellville Demeſne

TO BE LETT, near Clough, within four miles of Downpatrick.—Birnie will ſhew the Lands.

And a Farm near Portavo.—For further particulars apply to Mr. Ker at Portavo, Donaghadee.

September 16th, 1789.

THE enſuing General Quarter Seſſions of the Peace for the county of Antrim, will be held at Antrim on the 8th day of October next. Mr. Heron, the Clerk of the Peace, requeſts the Magiſtrates may return their Examinations and Recognizances to him on that day, in Antrim, agreeable to the Reſolutions for that purpoſe entered into by the Magiſtrates for diſpatch of buſineſs. Mr. Heron hath been informed, that at this Seſſions ſeveral Freeholders will have occaſion to regiſter their freeholds; for diſpatch, Heron on being informed in the mean time, by letter or otherwiſe, of the names, places of reſidence, ſituation of freehold, pariſh, and Barony in which ſuch freeholders reſide, &c. will before the Seſſions, prepare the neceſſary affidavits and certificates for ſuch freeholders; he therefore hopes the LORDS and GENTLEMEN of the county will give directions accordingly to their Agents.

Liſburn, 14th Sept. 1789.

SHOOTING.

The SPORTSMAN's MORNING.

The night recedes, and mild Aurora now
Waves her grey banner on the eaſtern brow;
Light float the miſty vapours o'er the ſky,
And dim the blaze of Phœbus' gariſh eye;
The flitting breeze juſt ſtirs the ruſtling brake,
And curls the cryſtal ſurface of the lake;
The eager Sportſmen ſnatch a ſhort repaſt,
And to the field repair with anxious haſte.

The active Pointer, from his thong unbound.
Impatient daſhes o'er the dewy ground,
With glowing eye, and undulating tail,
Ranges the field and ſnuffs the tainted gale;
Yet 'midſt his ardour, ſtill his maſter fears,
And the reſtraining whiſtle careful hears.

See how exact they try the ſtubble o'er,
Quarter the field, and every turn explore;
Now ſudden wheel, and now attentive ſeize
The known advantage of th' oppoſing breeze,
At once they ſtop! yon careful Dog deſcries
Where cloſe and near the lurking Covey lies.
His caution mark, leſt even a breath betray
Th' impending danger of his timid prey;
In various attitudes around him ſtand,
Silent and motionleſs, th' attending band!

They riſe!—they riſe!—Ah yet our fire reſtrain,
Till the 'maiz'd birds ſecurer diſtance gain!
For, thrown too cloſe, the ſhots your hopes elude,
Wide of your aim, and innocent of blood;
But mark with careful eye their leſſening flight,
Your ready gun, obedient to your ſight,
And at the length where frequent trials ſhew
Your fatal weapon gives the ſureſt blow.
Draw quick!—

JUST PUBLISHED,

By WILLIAM GILBERT, Bookſeller, Dublin, and ſold by WILLIAM MAGEE, Belfaſt.

THE ELEMENTS of ENGLISH; being a new method of teaching the whole Art of Reading, both with regard to Pronunciation and Spelling, by THOMAS SHERIDAN, A. M.—author of the pronouncing Dictionary, &c. price 1s. 1.

The *Communicant's Spiritual Companion*, or an Evangelical Preparation for the LORD's SUPPER: in which are ſhewn—the nature of that Ordinance and the diſpoſitions requiſite for a profitable participation thereof—wherein the careleſs Sinner is admoniſhed, the Formaliſt detected and reproved, the Feeble minded comforted, the Doubting relieved, the Sinner aſſiſted and the Faithful confirmed, with ſuitable Meditations and Prayers—by the Rev. THOMAS HAWEIS, price 1s. 7d. h.

Cotton Wool

SEEDS and WELLS have for Sale, at their Stores in Ann-ſtreet, a few Bales of the very beſt *Demerary* Cotton Wool, which they will ſell cheap for Bills on Dublin or Belfaſt, or allow a proper diſcount for caſh.

Belfaſt, 16th Sept. 1789.

The Belfaſt Coterie,

WILL be held at the Exchange-Rooms (as uſual) on Tueſday next the 22d inſtant.

Sept. 19th, 1789.

Lamp and Train Oil.

A Quantity of each in hogſheads and barrels, to be diſpoſed of on reaſonable terms by ROBERT and WILLIAM SIMMS.—They have alſo for ſale, a ſmall quantity of remarkable good Engliſh Stock Brick.

Belfaſt, Sept. 17, 1789.

MR. GORDON, Curate of Artrea, takes this opportunity of expreſſing his entire diſſatisfaction, and informing the publick, that the paragraph in the Belfaſt paper of the fourth inſt. was in general falſe: 'Tis certain Mr. Gordon attended the viſitation at Armagh, and received a liberal contribution from his worthy brethren, to whom he returns his grateful and unfeigned acknowledgements. As to what has been inſerted therein reſpecting Dr. Stokes, Mr. Gordon has every reaſon to expect that Dr. Stokes will appear at the head of the liſt of his beſt friends, which his abſence at that time prevented.

Sept. 16th, 1789.

DUBLIN, Sept. 12.

DUBLIN CASTLE, Sep. 9, 1789.

His Majesty's Royal Letters have been received, granting the dignity of a Baron of this kingdom to the following gentlemen, and the respective heirs male of their bodies lawfully begotten, by the names, stiles and titles undermentioned; and Letters Patent are preparing to be passed under the Great Seal of this kingdom accordingly, viz.

The Right Hon. Hugh Carleton, Chief Justice of his Majesty's Court of Common Pleas, Baron Carleton, of Anner in the co. Tipperary.

The Right Hon. William Eden, Baron Auckland.

The Right Hon. Luke Gardiner, Baron Mountjoy, of Mountjoy, in the co. Tyrone.

The Right Hon. Robert Stewart, Baron Londonderry.

Sir John Browne, Bart. Baron Kilmaine, of the Neale, in the co. Mayo.

Sir Nicholas Lawlets, Bart. Baron of Cloncurry, in the co. Kildare.

Henry Gore, Esq; Baron Annaly, of Tenelick, in the co. Longford.

Sir Sampson Eardley, Bart. Baron Eardley, of Spalding.

We are assured, in a letter from Paris by the last French mail, that the celebrated speech of M. de St. Etienne on Religious Toleration, pronounced lately in the National Assembly, has had such an effect, that not only Protestants of every denomination will, in a few weeks, enjoy every right of denizenship throughout France, but their public worship be permitted, without any controul, in every part of that populous and extensive kingdom, in any chapels they will build for the purpose. At present the religious meetings, or assemblies (as they are stiled) of Protestants in France, are only winked at in seaport towns and other great cities.

SPORTING INTELLIGENCE.
CURRAGH MEETING.

Monday, Sept. 7.

The Northumberland Cup, and 200 gns. each, p. p.

Mr. Dennis's Morgan,	1
Mr. Hamilton's King David,	2
Mr. Daly's Louisa,	3

Louisa fell lame in running, and pulled up going down the Long Hill.

Same day, a match from Lord Gore's Post home, was won by Mr. Savage's Boreas, who beat Mr. Hamilton's Andrew Armstrong, for 50 gns. each.

Wednesday.

King's Plate of 100 guineas, to carry 12st. best of three 4 mile heats.

Mr. Cooper's b h Columbus	1	1
Mr. Daly's c h Tom Turf	2	4
Mr. A. Daly's g h Fryar	5	3
Mr. Savage's g h Hyder Ally	4	2
Mr. Conolly's b h Shot	3	dr.

Same day, a Sweepstakes of 50 gns. each, from the Red Post home, was won by Mr. Daly's Politician, who beat Mr. Cooke's Planet, the rest paid forfeit.

Thursday.

King's Plate of 100 gns. for three year olds, carrying 8st. one 2-mile heat.

Col. Lumm's c f Lady Emily	
Mr. Daly's c c Politician	1
Mr. A Daly's b colt	2
Mr. Lill's b c Jig	3
Mr. Cooke's b c Planet	4
Mr. Savage's b c Boreas	5
Mr. Conolly's b c Bombardier	6
Mr. Edgeworth's c Burk O'More	7
Mr. Smyth's b c Xenophon	8
Mr. Kirwan's c f	9

Same day, a match for 100 gns. each.

Mr. Daly's b h Rutland	1
Mr. Dennis's g h Morgan	2

Same day, a Handy-cap Plate, from the Red Post home.

Mr. Daly's Little Moll	1
Mr. Eyre's Jane Harold	2
Mr. Savage's Duchess of Leinster	3
Mr. Cooper's Columbus	4
Mr. Bell's h Tinker	5

The Curragh Meeting in the course of this week, has been remarkably numerous and splendid; all the sporting nobility and gentry, besides crowds of others attending it.

Dispersed as they were over the extensive space, unmatched for its destination in Europe, they did not immediately fill the eye of a stranger; but to repeated surveys the concourse appeared great.

DUBLIN, Sept. 12.

His Majesty's royal letters patent, it is said, are arrived for granting the following pensions:

500l. per ann. during pleasure, to Lady Viscountess Boyne.

200l. per ann. to Lady Catherine Toole.

200l. per ann. to Lady Catherine Mariay.

The revolution now effecting in the kingdom of France is attended, naturally enough, with a variety of commotions and disorders; some of a tragical, some of an alarming, and some, even of a ludicrous nature; of this last kind we may rank a combination that took place about a fortnight ago, among the valets in Bourdeaux, where this worthy fraternity of the brush and napkin came to some resolutions; the principal of which, we are informed, were, "That as slavery was abolished in France, every badge of it should be abrogated."

"That the wearing of liveries, carrying parcels and lanterns through the streets, were a degradation to freemen, and not to be endured by any Frenchman."

The Magistrates of Bourdeaux (our advices add) immediately put a stop to these proceedings, by committing a dozen of the ringleaders to the Bridewell, (the Maison de Force) where plenty of hard labour, and a scanty portion of maigre diet, soon brought those party-coloured conspirators to their wonted obedience.

The late treaty between Spain and the American States, relative to the cession of considerable tracts of land, and the privilege of settling and cutting logwood at Campechy and the Bay of Honduras, cannot but give umbrage to the British Court, when it is considered, that the most trifling interruption to that branch of Commerce was the original, if not the only cause of the war of 1739, which lasted till the conclusion of the treaty of Madrid, by Sir Benjamin Keene and General Wall, in 1746. How Great Britain may digest this partition of commercial favour, is a point that will soon be determined in the Cabinet.

On Saturday a walking match, of five miles an hour, along the banks of the Canal, between Mr. Whaley and Mr. Ferns, was won rather easy by the latter; his horse performing it some minutes within the time. The bet depending was an hundred guineas.

DIED.] Last Thursday, in Dawson-street, James Forde, Esq; in the 83d year of his age. This worthy man, through the course of a long life, humbly followed the example of his Saviour, who went about continually doing good: he was the father of many charitable institutions, and promoter of every one in this city, a member and director of every Society for the encouragement of industry. The simplicity of his manners, the piety of his heart, and his fair, upright conduct, merited, and obtained the esteem and affection of all those who knew him, and make his death a loss to society.

ORDNANCE OECONOMY.

The Right Hon. the Earl of Carhampton is appointed Lieutenant general of the Ordnance, at a salary of 600l. per annum, in room of General Hale, who goes out on a pension of the same sum, which the M——— has been graciously pleased to have remitted to him from this country as a reward for his never having set his foot in it.

The other Officers of the Ordnance are provided for as follow:

The Hon. Captain Pakenham, Surveyor-general, at a salary of 800l. per ann. which, before was not more than 300l.

Captain Loftus, principal Store-keeper, at a salary of 400l. per ann. for which Mr. Coghlan had only 150l.

Mr. Magennis, Clerk of the Ordnance at 400l. for which Mr. Joseph Keen had only 200l.

And tho' last, not least, Mr. Wynne, at 400l. per annum, as Clerk of the Deliveries.

The new peerages occasion four vacancies in our House of Commons, namely, for the county of Dublin, in the room of Mr. Gardiner, now Lord Mountjoy.

For the county of Longford, in the room of Colonel Gore, now Lord Annaly.

For the borough of Carlow, in the room of Sir John Browne, Bart. now Lord Kilmaine.

For the borough of Lifford, in the room of Sir Nicholas Lawleis, Baronet, now Lord Cloncurry.

Belfast, Sept. 15.

An account of an assault on a Mr. Gordon, on his return from Magillegan, is received, but cannot be inserted; as the author has not given authenticity to it by his signature. As anonymous intelligence can seldom be admitted into this paper, it is hoped that gentlemen who wish to communicate any domestic news thro' this channel, will take the trouble of giving their names.

The sale of the lands of Castleaspie and Tullanakill, &c. advertised in the 4th page of this paper, is postponed till Friday the 2d of October next.

Belfast, Sept. 18.

The badness of the harvest will require every possible care to preserve the corn, particularly wheat and barley, from growing in the stooks. It is recommended that great care should be taken in stooking the corn, so that the hooding sheaves may cover the grain of the standard sheaves from the sun and rain, and that the hooding sheaves be tied together to prevent their being blown off. If a hedge stake could be driven into the ground in the seat of every stook in hilly grounds, it would be of great use in keeping the stook standing in case of high wind.

If the weather should continue showery till the corn is fit for stacking, it is recommended to keep the hood sheaves, with any part of the standard sheaves that may be maltined or weather stained, by themselves, and to thrash it separately. By this means the farmer will obtain a better price, and the malster and miller will not be injured.

A barbarous murder was on the 8th inst ant committed on John Devlin, of Lisnamorra, parish of Artrea, and County Londonderry, by a person, who lived in that neighbourhood. He has since absconded, and a considerable reward is offered for apprehending him. (The advertisement at large will appear in our next.)

The London Packet, from Newry to London, sails first fair wind.

Those who have agreed to take their passage in the ship Irish Volunteer, for Charlestown, South Carolina, advertised in the first page of this paper, are desired to be in Larne on Monday, the 5th day of October, as the vessel will sail the first fair wind afterwards.

FAIRS IN THE ENSUING WEEK.

Tuesday 22 Ballibought, Arm. Mountcharles, Don. Wednesday 23. Newtonards, Down, Rathfriland, Down. Friday 25. Johnston's-bridge, Arm. Saturday 26. Glaslough, Mon.

Anno 1789.]   Printed by HENRY JOY, and Co. BELFAST.

The BELFAST NEWS-LETTER.

TUESDAY September 22,   FRIDAY September 25, 1789.

THE Committee for conducting the Shops in the Linen Trade, beg leave to acquaint the Gentlemen Linen Drapers, that the following Veffels are appointed to attend the White Linen Market, and will fail punctually at the time the Shippers direct:

The Linen-Hall, Hugh Dickfon, Mafter, for London,
The New Loyalty, Hugh Brown, Mafter, for Liverpool,
The Peggy, James Mc. Ilroy, Mafter, for Chefter,
And the Eliza, John Auld, Mafter, for Glafgow.

Belfaft, 21ft Sept. 1989.

A barbarous Murder

WAS committed on the body of John Devlin of Lifnamorra, parifh of Ardtre and county of Londonderry, on Tuefday the 8th inft. by William Louden, his neighbour, for which the faid Louden has fince abfconded.——Now we the under-named Subfcribers, having a juft abhorrence of fo atrocious a crime, do promife to pay the feveral fums to our names annexed, to the perfon or perfons who will within the fpace of twelve months from the date hereof, lodge the faid William Louden in any of his Majefty's Gaols in this kingdom Said Louden is about 5 feet 9 or 10 inches high, fair complexion, a little pitted with the fmall pox, long vifaged, dark brown hair tied, grey eyed, flender made, round-fhouldered, his left arm contracted in confequence of a fracture he formerly received; by trade a weaver

	l. s. d.		l. s. d.
Arthur Tracy	5 13 9	Ninian Steele	1 2 9
John Spotfwood	2 5 6	Andrew Torrens	1 2 9
Wm. Greaves	2 5 6	Richard Dawfon	1 2 9
John Sheil	2 5 6	Samuel Brown	1 2 9
Samuel Greaves	2 5 6	John Buntin	1 2 9
Sam. Crawford	1 2 9	Hu. Glenholme	1 2 9
Andrew Crawford	1 2 9	John Miller	2 5 6
John Mc. Leane	1 2 9	Robt. Maxwell	1 2 9
Robt. Mc. Crory	1 2 9	Jas. Wall	2 5 6
Jas. Hammerfly	1 2 9	Rich. Williams	1 2 9
Guftavus Dickfon	1 2 9	John Walfh	1 2 9
John Mc. Dade	1 2 9	Wm. Given	1 2 9
Thos. Pollock	1 2 9	John Hagen	1 2 9
Edward Doolm	3 8 3	Wm. Buntin, junr.	2 5 6
Jofeph Chambers	1 2 9		

Advertifement.

STRAYED or STOLEN off the lands of William Bailie, of Ballyhalbert in the county Down, upon Wednefday night laft——A light bay Mare, five years old, fet in the tail, a fmall ftar, and a few white hairs like a ratch down her face, with a little curled hair on the near fide between her hip and loin; fhe is about thirteen hands high, value nine guineas. Whoever returns faid mare to John Mc'Cully of Newtownards, or to faid Bailie, fhall receive Half-a-Guinea reward, or for the mare and thief Two Guineas.

Ballyhalbert, Sept. 19, 1789.

DROPPED, 28th ult. on the road between Carrickfergus and Doagh,

A Silver Watch,

Maker's Name John Johnfon, Liverpool, No. 1025.——Whoever returns her to Mr. Thos. Mc. Cabe, Belfaft; Mr. Harper, Antrim; Mr. Gordon, Ballymoney; or Mr. Moor, Randalftown, Watchmakers, fhall have half a Guinea reward.

September 16th, 1789.

MONEY.

FIFTEEN HUNDRED POUNDS to be lent on real fecurity, by James Armftrong, Attorney, Armagh.
19th Sept. 1789.

To be fold by Auction.

FOR ready Money, oppofite to the Donegall-Arms, at noon, on Friday the fecond of October next; a good POST-CHAISE, and Harnefs for a pair.
Belfaft, 21ft Sept. 1789

To be Let,

GLASSDRUMMOND, in the County Fermanagh, from the firft of November next, containing about eighty acres of arable ground, well enclofed and laid out in parks; with a convenient Farm-houfe and Offices, one fhort mile from Swadlingbar Spa; the tenant may have a large quantity of Hay, and Oats if required.
Application to be made to Mr. Laurence Spear on the premiffes.——To be continued four times.
Sept. 19th, 1789

WHEREAS on the night of Tuefday the 22d inft. an attempt was made to break open the Office of Jones, Tomb, Joy & Co. in the Wine-Cellar-Entry.
NOW, in order to difcover the perpetrators, We do hereby promife a reward of Twenty Guineas to any perfon who fhall difcover on and profecute to conviction any one or more of the perfons concerned, within fix calendar months from the date hereof.
Given under our hands, Belfaft the 23d September, 1789.
JONES, TOMB, JOY, & Co.

To the Free and Independent Electors of the County of Armagh.

GENTLEMEN,

AS I am invited by many refpectable Freeholders of your County to offer myfelf as a Candidate to reprefent it at the next General Election, I fhould think myfelf ungrateful, if I did not comply with your defire, after having been thought a proper perfon to fill fo important a truft:——I therefore intend to offer myfelf to your confideration at the next Election, to fhew my inclination to gratify your wifhes; and though I may not be able to canvafs every perfon, yet let me be fo fortunate as to fucceed, or not, your fupport fhall ever be moft gratefully acknowledged by,
Gentlemen,
your moft faithful
and obliged Servant,
JOHN MOORE.

Jamaica Rum, Singlo and Congou Teas,

EACH of a good quality, are now arrived to Wm. and Sam. Hanna, who are landing a cargo of excellent Memel Timber.
Newry, 14th Sept. 1789.

County of Fermanagh.

TO be Sold, the Lands of Strannareagh and Ballyderrymore, fituate in the manor of Mount Sedborough, in faid county, within three miles of the town of Clones, and are at prefent let by leafes, of which two lives are now in being, at the expiration whereof faid lands will rife more than treble the prefent rent: And alfo, the Lands of Coolnemana, and Mount-darby, in faid county, at prefent out of leafe, and capable of great improvement; the whole containing 503A 3R. 3P. Irifh plantation meafure, and yielding at prefent 113l. 5s. yearly, fubject to a quit rent of 2l. 13s. 4s.
Propofals to be made in perfon, or by letter (poft-paid) to the Revd. John Barton, Portron, Rofcommon; Robert Barnes, Efq; Venetian-hall, Dublin; John Mayne, Efq; Freamemount, Coorehill; William Rogers, Efq; Lifburn; and Mr. Richard Crofs, Clones.

American Pot and Pearl Afhes.

HUGH MONTGOMERY has juft imported from Bofton per the Schooner Induftry, James Hay, Mafter, a large quantity of Pot and Pearl Afhes, Train oil, fpermaceti Candles, dried Fifh, and Barrel Staves; all of which he will fell on very reafonable terms for cafh or bills at three months.
Belfaft, 4th Sept. 1789.

A Boat to be Sold;

FOR ready Money, burthen about twelve tons, very ftout built, with all her materials.——Alfo thirty thoufand Laths, for flating, cieling and thatched cabins; they are of the beft Bog and Dantzick Fir. Good encouragement will be given to thofe that buy a quantity.——Apply to John Trevor at Mount-Stewart.
7th September, 1789.

Cuftom-Houfe, Larne, 21ft Sept. 1789.

TO be fold by Inch of Candle, on Tuefday the 29th inftant, four Mats of Tobacco, and eight Kegs of Brandy and Rum.
THOs. LEA, Collector

Robert Kennedy, Land Surveyor

SURVEYS, maps, and divides Land by the moft certain and demonftrable methods; being inftructed therein by the moft eminent Mathematicians and Surveyors in this kingdom.——Letters directed to him at Rathfryland, franked or poft-paid, fhall be duly attended to.——To be continued three times.

In a very eligible Situation in High-ftreet.

TO BE LET, two new Shops, and two Parlours in rere of them.——Enquire at Samuel and Andrew Mc. Clean.
Belfaft, 10th Sept. 1789.

Wanted immediately,

AN Apprentice to the Hat-Making Bufinefs, by Sampfon Clark.
Belfaft, 22d Sept. 1789.
N. B. Said Clark carries on the Hat-making Bufinefs (as ufual) at his Houfe in High-ftreet, oppofite the New Inn; and hopes his punctuality and knowledge of his profeffion will entitle him to a continuation of the countenance of his friends and the publick.

Mr. Cullen, Dentift,

WITH the utmoft refpect informs his Friends and the Public, that his engagements oblige him to be in Derry the third of October, where he will ftay about a month, and then return to this town, on his way to Dublin.——He takes this opportunity of prefenting his beft acknowledgements to his friends for the very flattering reception he has met with in Belfaft, and to the gentlemen of the faculty, for the patronage they have been pleafed to honor him with—which he will be always ambitious to merit.——He purpofes to be here next June, and continue till the laft of September.
Belfaft, Sept. 25, Mooney's, High-ftreet.

Advertifement.

TO be fold at Newry, near the Dublin Bridge, a parcel of choice good Mill-ftones, lately landed from Lough-Eafke, in the county Donegall, equal if not fuperior to any Englifh ones. For further particulars enquire of Roger Magenis, Cabra, or Henry O'Neill, North-ftreet, Newry. Part of the above Mill-ftones will be fent round to Dundrum as foon as a veffel can be procured for that purpofe.
Newry, Sept. 19th, 1789.

Tolls to be Let.

THE Truftees of the Turnpike-Road from Newry to Banbridge, will meet at the Liberty Market-houfe in Newry, on Friday the 2d of October next, at twelve o'clock at noon, to let the Tolls of faid road for three years from the firft of November next; the rent to be paid monthly, for which fufficient fecurity muft be given.
September 19th, 1789.

COUNTY of ARMAGH. } MICHAEL OBINS, John Greer, James Afhmur, and James Harden, Efqrs. Juftices of the Peace, were appointed laft Affizes to attend the next General Quarter Seffions of the Peace for this county at Armagh the 8th day of October next.
The Senefchals,—Hugh, Petty, and Sub-conftables, muft attend to fave their fines.
JOHN Mc. KINSTRY, C. P.
The Magiftrates are requefted to fend their examinations (at leaft a day before the feffions) to the Clerk of the Peace.

Seed Wheat

EARLY White Wheat, the produce of the firft Crop from Seed imported from the county of Kent, to be fold at Greenville, near Belfaft, at 11s. 4d. h. per hundred weight.
A Gardener wanted, whofe character will ftand the ftricteft fcrutiny.

To be Sold or Set from firft November,

THE Dwelling-Houfe, Green, and Farm of Greencaftle, fituate on the road leading from Belfaft to Carrickfergus, about three miles from the former.——Application to be made to Mrs. Ledlie on the premiffes.
This Green is admirably calculated for any perfon in the Cambrick or Muflin Bufinefs. The houfe, which is commodious, would fuit a gentleman for a fummer refidence, and may be fet feparately from the reft of the concern.
Greencaftle, Sept. 22, 1789

In the Matter of James Wc. Cleery, A Bankrupt. } THE Creditors who have proved their debts under a commiffion of Bankrupt awarded and iffued againft James Mc. Cleery, late of Portaferry, in the county Down, a Bankrupt, are defired to meet the Affignee, on Thurfday firft day of October next, at 12 o'clock noon, at the houfe of Mr. Taylor Trevor in Portaferry, in order to affent to, or diffent from the faid Affignee commencing, profecuting, or defending, any fuit or fuits at law or in equity for the recovery of any part of the faid Bankrupt's eftate and effects; as alfo to his compounding, fubmitting to arbitration, or otherwife agreeing any matter or thing relating thereto.
Portaferry, 12th Sept. 1789.
THOMAS MAXWELL, Affignee.

FEMALE FORTITUDE.

When the gallant Sir George, now Lord Rodney, was engaged in the Sandwich, againſt the French Admiral, and before any of his own ſhips were up to ſuſtain him, Sir George thought it neceſſary to viſit the three decks, in order to animate his men, who received him wherever he went with three cheers. To his great ſurpriſe, he found a woman aſſiſting at one of the guns, upon the main deck; upon aſking her what ſhe did there, ſhe replied, "An't pleaſe your honour, my huſband is ſent down to the cockpit wounded, and I an here to ſupply his place. Do you think, your Honour, I am afraid of the French?" After the action, Lord Rodney called her aft, told her ſhe had been guilty of a breach of orders, by being on board, but rewarded her with ten guineas, for ſo gallantly ſupplying the place of her huſband.

Anecdote of Parson Patten.

Parſon Patten was ſo much averſe to the Athanaſian Creed, that he never would read it. Archbiſhop Secker, having been informed of his recuſancy, ſent the Archdeacon to aſk him his reaſon? "I do not *believe it*," ſaid the Prieſt.——"But your Metropolitan *does*," replied the Archdeacon. "It may be ſo," rejoined Mr. Patten, "and he can well afford it. He believes at the rate of *ſeven thouſand pounds a-year*, and I only at *that of fifty*."

Yeſterday between three and four o'clock, the King, Queen, Princeſſes Royal, Auguſta, and Elizabeth, with their ſeveral attendants in a train of four carriages, arrived ſafe at the Queen's Lodge at Windſor, after an abſence of twelve weeks. The King, as ſoon as he got out of his carriage, received the dutiful affections of the three youngeſt Princeſſes. The manifeſtations of joy on this occaſion were beyond deſcription. The bells were ſet ringing, muſic was diſperſed in ſeveral places, and at night there were illuminations at Windſor and Eaton. The Royal Family ſat down to dinner at half paſt four, but being ſomewhat fatigued with their journey, did not leave the Lodge afterwards.

D U B L I N, Sept. 19.

Letters patent have been paſſed under the Great Seal of this kingdom, conſtituting and appointing the undernamed gentlemen to the following offices, viz.

The Hon. T. Packenham, Surveyor General and Aſſiſtant to the Lieut. Gen. of the Ordnance.

Richard Magenis, Eſq; Clerk of the Ordnance.

Thomas Loftus, Eſq; Principal Storekeeper of the Ordnance; and

Robert Wynne, Eſq; Clerk of the Deliveries.

Alſo, their Excellencies the Lords Juſtices have been pleaſed to ſign a warrant, appointing John Armit, Eſq; Secretary to the Board of Ordnance in this kingdom.

It has been ſaid that Mr. Butler of Kilkenny, the repreſentative of the Ormond family, has refuſed a new Dukedom, becauſe he expects to be reſtored to the ancient honours of his houſe; by the repeal of the Act of Attainder, by which the laſt Duke of Ormond forfeited all the hereditary dignities of the Butlers—and the repeal of this act, it has been ſaid, would make Mr. Butler Duke of Ormond, and give him precedency of the Duke of Leinſter.

But this is a miſtake. Though the Act of Attainder were repealed this moment, and the laſt Duke's heirs reſtored in blood, (as in juſtice they ought to have been long ſince) Mr. Butler could not, in conſequence of the repeal, aſſume the title of Duke of Ormond; for the Dukedom never was limited to the breach of the family from which the preſent Mr. Butler is ſprung.

To ſuch a pitch of audacity have the marauders in the vicinity of this capital of late proceeded, that five of them a few nights ago attacked the carriage of the Lord Chancellor, on his Excellency's return from town to his ſeat at Merrion. Meeting with a warmer reception than they expected, and being fired on by the attendants, they retreated without their hoped-for booty.

D U B L I N, Sept. 22.

The Parliament of this kingdom which now ſtands prorogued to Tueſday, the 29th inſtant, is further prorogued to Tueſday, the 1ſt day of December next.

The report of yeſterday was that a noble Lord, high in office in the Ordnance department, had received a letter from a near connection in London, informing him, that the Marquis of Buckingham would certainly not return here as Lord Lieutenant; and that he was to be ſucceeded in that office by his Royal Highneſs the Duke of Glouceſter. The motive for this appointment is ſaid to be a ſcheme of conciliation; as it is ſuppoſed that his Majeſty's brother would be able to reconcile all parties in this country, and to unite them all in ſupport of his adminiſtration.

Bankrupt. Richard Draper, now or late of Waterford, brewer, to ſurrender the 12th and 14th of October, and 3d November, at the Tholſel.

To the EDITOR.

SIR,

IF you think the following worthy of being inſerted in your paper, it is at your ſervice. It comes from one well acquainted with the facts, and whoſe wiſh it is, that a ſimilar ſpirit might be excited in other towns throughout the kingdom.

Lurgan, Sept. 19th, 1789.

Laſt Thurſday this town exhibited a ſpectacle, of all others, the moſt grateful to the eye of humanity.—Above two hundred children, males and females, who are educated in our free-ſchools, paraded and went, attended by their reſpective maſters and miſtreſſes, to the demeſne of the Right Hon. Mr. Brownlow, where a moſt excellent and plentiful dinner was provided for them. Each maſter and miſtreſs had a table for their own ſcholars, at which they ſat and conducted themſelves with a propriety and regularity that might have done credit to perſons educated in a much higher ſphere of life; and though they were not ſo fortunate as to have their new clothes ready for the occaſion, yet in point of neatneſs and cleanlineſs, particularly the girls, their appearance was highly pleaſing. Their excellent hoſts and all their family, even to the leaſt child, attended upon them, not only to ſee that they were properly taken care of, but with their own hands ſupplying them with whatever they wanted. A general ſatisfaction appeared in the countenances of all preſent—and it is hard to ſay whether the entertainers, the gueſts, or the ſpectators were moſt delighted with the entertainment.—Two French-horns played during the time of dinner, which being ended, a chorus of girls and their maſter ſung, God ſave the King, and a ſong adapted to the occaſion;—then, all riſing from their ſeats and hailing their generous benefactors with three cheers, returned to their reſpective ſchools in the ſame good order in which they came.

This moſt excellent inſtitution has now ſubſiſted three years, ſupported by the voluntary ſubſcriptions of the inhabitants. The boys are taught to read and write; the girls to read, ſew, and knit; and ſuch has been their progreſs, that many of them who knew not the letters when they came there, can now acquit themſelves very well in all theſe branches. They are alſo carefully inſtructed in the knowledge of divine truths, and in the principles of morality reſulting from them. Nor, whilſt their patrons are thus attentive to the forming of their minds, are they negligent of their bodies: a charity ſermon is preached yearly for the purpoſe of clothing them, the amount of which, with caſual benefactions, enables the Governors to dreſs in a decent manner, every well behaved boy and girl belonging to the ſchools. Premiums of books are alſo occaſionally given, which has an excellent effect in exciting an emulation among them: and as a further encouragement, the beſt ſpinners among the girls, at appointed times, have a week allowed them to ſpin in ſchool, and wheels are given in premiums for the fineſt and beſt yarn. This has a double effect, exciting them to diligence in ſchool, that they may be admitted to the kemp, and to induſtry at home, that they may be qualified for it. It is much to be wiſhed that this or ſome ſimilar plan was followed in all the towns of the kingdom;—in the great ones it could be carried on to the full extent, in all ſomething might be done.—Here the rich, without any apprehenſion of being impoſed upon, would have an excellent method of diſpoſing of their charity—and the clergy an opportunity of inſtilling religious knowledge into the tender minds, which, at a more advanced period, when ignorance and vice have taken too deep a root, they often find very difficult, if not impracticable. There is no reaſon to apprehend a miſcarriage in the inſtitution, if properly attended to;—the effects, for the ſhort time theſe ſchools have ſubſiſted, are indeed great, the proſpect, as far as human foreſight can reach, of future good to be derived from them ſtill greater.

L O N D O N - D E R R Y, Sept. 15.

Laſt market-day, oatmeal ſold at 13d. per peck, and potatoes at 2½d. per ſtone.

Caution.—Thoſe who buy the above articles in our market, would do well to examine the weights. On Wedneſday laſt, a man was detected ſelling potatoes with weights 3lb. ſhort of the lawful ſtandard.

The brig Coningham, Rob. Coningham, maſter, of this port, arrived ſafe at Newcaſtle in the Delaware the 10th of July, and landed her paſſengers all in good health.

The people of Great Britain, ever inventing new ſchemes of trade and commerce, have lately eſtabliſhed a Fiſhing Company for the improvement and extenſion of the fiſhery on the coaſts of Scotland. In ſeveral of the Scots ports, ice-houſes are already eſtabliſhed for the purpoſe of tranſmitting ſalmon and other fiſh freſh to London. The experiment has been made, and it is found, that fiſh packed in ice will keep 12 days in excellent order.

Married.] John Hamilton, Eſq; to Miſs Bennett.

Died.—At Birdſtown, in the 73d year of his age, William Maxwell, Eſq; a gentlemen who was poſſeſſed of the moſt amiable deportment through life, highly eſteemed by all his acquaintance, and now ſincerely lamented by his family and connections; to ſum up in few words this reſpectable character, he was the kindeſt friend, and the beſt of men.—At Ramelton, Mr. John Patterſon.—At Jamaica, Capt. James Hayes, maſter of the brig Derry Packet.——At Biſhop's-gate, Capt. Wm. Mackey, late maſter of the ſhip Jenny.—On Sunday laſt, in Free-ſchool-lane, after a long and ſevere illneſs, Mrs. Leech, relict of the late Mr. Oliver Leech.

Belfaſt, *Sept.* 22.

We underſtand that a Charity Sermon, for the uſe of the Poor-houſe and Infirmary of this town, will be preached in Doctor Crombie's Meeting-houſe at *two* o'clock on Sunday next. Conſidering the preſent ſtate of the funds of that Charity, and the great number of deſerving objects that receive out of the houſe a very poor allowance (many nothing at all) it behoves not only the inhabitants of the town, but the neighbouring gentlemen, to ſhew their countenance to ſo excellent an inſtitution by liberally contributing to its ſupport.

The Friendſhip, Capt. Lepper maſter, loaded with linen cloth, from this port to London, is ſafe arrived at the Downs after eight days paſſage.

Died.] On Sunday laſt, Mrs. Cunningham, wife to Mr. James Cunningham, of this town. Lately in London, Hugh Johnſton, Eſq. an eminent merchant and an honeſt man.

To the Freeholders of the County Tyrone.

AS a report prevails that the Parliament of Ireland will ſoon be diſſolved, it would be proper to convene pariſh meetings, in ſuch places as may be moſt convenient to the gentlemen of the neighbourhood, and there to deliberate coolly, impartially, and uninfluenced, who are the proper perſons to be Repreſentatives in the enſuing Parliament. That proper perſons be appointed to carry ſaid reſolutions to a general meeting of the county, to be convened ſoon after; and if the freeholders ſhould approve of the conduct of our preſent Repreſentatives, we ought to addreſs them in a grateful manner for their upright behaviour, making it our earneſt requeſt to repreſent us in the enſuing Parliament, and promiſing them a ſteady and faithful ſupport.

Sept. 14th, 1789. A FREEHOLDER of the COUNTY TYRONE.

Belfaſt, *Sept.* 25.

AT the requeſt of the Committee of the Belfaſt Charitable Society of this town,—a CHARITY SERMON will be preached on Sunday the 27th inſt. at Dr. Crombie's Meeting-houſe, for the benefit of that inſtitution, by the Rev. Dr. William Bruce. Divine ſervice will begin at TWO o'clock.

SAM. NEILSON, Chairman.

New Oatmeal ſold in our market yeſterday at 11s. per cwt.

*** Some very humane and judicious remarks on Bull-beating, and other improper amuſements, ſhall appear in our next.

PRICES IN THIS MARKET YESTERDAY.

Oatmeal,	10s.	6d.	to	11s.	od.	Dried do cos. to 26s.od per d
Wheat,	9	6	—	10	6	R.Tallow,os od.a5s. per ſt.
Oats,	5	0	—	5	6	Potatoes od. to 10d per b.
Barley,	5	0	—	5	6	Eng. coals, 13s. to 13s. 6d.
Butter,	50	0	—	51	0	Scotch do. 12s. to 12s. 6d.
C. hides,	00	0	—	35	0	Ex. on Lond 6 3-4 a 7 per c.
Ox ditto,	37	6	—	40	0	Do. on Glaſgow 6½.
S.C.ſkins	00	0	—	42	6	

FAIRS IN THE ENSUING WEEK.

Sept. 28, Monday, Carrickmacroſs, Mon. Tedounet, Mon.—Tueſday 29, Aghygults, Don. Ballytrain, Mon. Dromore, Tyr. Forkhill, Arm. Kilmore, Down,——Wedneſday 30, Benburbe, Tyr.—Thurſday, Oct. 1, Deſertmartin, Der. Mounthill, Ant.——Friday 2, Ballibay, Mon. Ballynahinch, Down. Ballintra, Don. Balneglera, Arm. Caſh, Ferm. Dumfanaghy, Don. Magherevooly, Ferm. Magwire's-bridge, Ferm. Narraw-water, Down. Omagh, Tyr.——Saturday 3, Frederickſtown, Tyr.

To be Sold by Auction,

ON the Premiſſes, the 31ſt day of October next, at the hour of one of the Clock,—A Houſe in the Town of Newtownards, held by leaſe of lives renewable for ever under Lord Londonderry (at preſent occupied by Mr William Pollock). For further particulars apply to Daniel Moore Echlin.

Sept. 25th, 1789.

Anno 1789.] Printed by HENRY JOY, and Co. BELFAST.

The BELFAST NEWS-LETTER.

TUESDAY September 29, FRIDAY October 2, 1789.

Antrim Races.

MONDAY the 26th inst. 30l. for any horse, &c. that never won 50l. at any one time, matches excepted, 3 years old, a feather; 4 years old, 7st. 5 years old, 8st. 6 years old, 8st. 10lb. and aged, 9st.—If a three years old starts, 3 mile heats, if not, 4 mile heats.

Tuesday, 20l for any horse, &c. bred in the County of Antrim, that never won sixpence, matches excepted. Weights the same as Monday's plate;—four mile heats.

Wednesday. 20l for hunters that never started for any thing but a hunter's plate, matches excepted; 4 years old, 10st. 5 years old, 11st. 6 years old, 11st. 10lb. and aged 12st.—4 mile heats.

Thursday. 20l. for any horse, &c. that never won 30l. at any one time; weight for age and inches, 14 hands, aged, 8st. half a stone for each year and each inch, upwards and downwards: 4 mile heats.

Friday. 30l. for any horse, &c.—Weights the same as Monday's plate; the winners of a 50l. plate 3lb. extra for the first, and 2lb. more for every other 50l.—The winner of 100l. plate, 5lb extra, of 2 100l. plates, 8lb. 4 mile heats.

Saturday. A plate for the beaten horses, &c. that save their distance any one day they run.—Weight for age the same as Monday's plate. Half-a-guinea entrance each;—all to go to the winner.—4 mile heats.

Three pounds to mares and geldings. No crossing, &c. Horses to be entered with James Young eight days before their days of running; one shilling in the pound entrance, or double at the post. Judges to be appointed each day. The winner to pay 6d. in the pound for scales and straw; one pound for waste: half an hour for rubbing: to start at 12 o'clock. Nothing will be admitted to qualify horses but a certificate from the breeder, or the oath of a gentleman, if required. Tents half-a-guinea each. Every stand for bread, &c and every hawker of bread, fruit, &c. 2s 8d. h. each, if not a subscriber's.

October 1st, 1789. JAMES YOUNG, C. C.

N. B. These articles to be published every Friday only.

Wants a Place,

A GARDENER, who understands the management of the Kitchen, Fruit, and Flower Garden; also Hot-houses, Green-houses, and Hot-beds: He also understands the propagating and planting of Forest Trees and flowering Shrubs, can write and keep accounts, is a single man, and can be well recommended.——Letters, post-paid, directed to H. M Donaghadee, will be duly attended to.

Donaghadee, Sept. 28th, 1789.

To be Let from the first of Nov. next,

A House in Donlady, two stories high, and in thorough repair, with any quantity of land from ten to thirty acres, for the term of 27 years or three lives, now in possession of William Kirkwood; the tenant to have the nomination of the lives. Also a small House with a slated roof, and in good repair.——Proposals to be received by Robert Mc. Leroth, Esq; Donlady till the 20th October, when the tenants will be declared.

October 1, 1789.

A NOTICE,

ELEANOR GUTTERY, one of the daughters of James Douglass, late of Maralin, Merchant, deceased, thinks it prudent to inform the public, that by a marriage-settlement, duly executed and registered, she is entitled to a proportionable share of the personal estate of which her late Father died possessed, and that the lease under Mr CROOKS, with a clause of renewal of ten acres of land, and the house in which her late Father lived in Maralin, lately occupied by her brother, Richard Dowglass, and the goods in said house, advertised to be sold by Mary Dowglass, on Wednesday the 30th inst. are part: the public are therefore cautioned against purchasing the above farm, or goods, as a bill is preparing to be laid before Council to bring Mary Dowglass to an account for the goods and chattels of the late James Dowglass, which were possessed by Richard Dowglass (in her absence in America) and to set aside voluntary Deeds alledged to have been executed of said farm by James Dowglass and to be decreed to a part of said farm and house.

Dated at Maralin, the 22d Sept. 1789.

Auction.

THE Heirs of the late Rev. Wm. Henry of Cumber will sell by auction, on Tuesday the 13th October, the farm on which he lived. The improvements on the lands are considerable; dwelling-house and offices are in good repair—the situation is pleasant;——the lease was a few years since granted by the late Nicholas Crumlin, Esq. for three lives and forty-one years, the lives are young. The lands are not subject to tythe, and there are other immunities which make the place desirable. The sale will begin at eleven o'clock and continue till all the household furniture, farming utensils, and cattle (the property of the late Mr. Henry) are sold.

University of Glasgow.

IN the University of Glasgow the usual Prelections for the ensuing Season will be given at the following Terms:

I. On the tenth of October.

Natural Philosophy,	Logick and Rhetoric,
Moral Philosophy,	Greek,
	Humanity.

II. On Monday the second of November.

Divinity,	Materia Medica,
Oriental Languages,	Chymistry,
History,	Anatomy,
Law,	Mathematicks,
Medicine, Theory, and Practice,	Modern Languages.

Advertisement.

TO be Sold, the Woods of Dillonstown, in the county of Louth, containing eight thousand five hundred Trees, mostly Oak, Ash and Elm, situated on the sea-coast, from whence the Timber can very conveniently be shipp'd to Dublin or any northern port; one and a half mile from Castlebellingham, three from Dunleer, eight from Dundalk, and nine from Drogheda.—Apply to Acheson Thompson, Newry.

25th Sept. 1789.

On Wednesday last the subjoined Address, signed by the present and late High Sheriffs of the County, by Marriot Dalway, Esq; by William Sharman, Esq; and by upwards of sixteen hundred other Freeholders, was presented to the Honorable Hercules Rowley, at Langford-Lodge, and to the Right Honorable John O'Neill, at Shanescastle, by a number of Freeholders from different parts of this County.

WE whose names are subscribed, FREEHOLDERS OF THE COUNTY OF ANTRIM, take leave to return our warmest thanks to the Knights of the Shire, the Honorable H. ROWLEY and the Right Honorable JOHN O'NEILL, for their having in so faithful and exemplary a manner represented this County in the present parliament;—for their consulting the opinion of the constituent body, and having made that the invariable rule of their conduct;—for their having taken a constitutional test, and for their honorable adherence to its principles.

In consideration of such eminent services, we should deem it inconsistency in our own conduct, and ingratitude to confirmed worth—did we not in the most strenuous manner request the present Representatives of the County of ANTRIM again to offer themselves Candidates for a Trust which they have already given unequivocal testimonies of meriting.

To which ADDRESS the following ANSWERS were returned.

GENTLEMEN,

ACCEPT my most grateful thanks for this very honorable testimony of your approbation of my conduct in Parliament. If any additional inducement was wanting to me to adhere to the same principles which have hitherto guided me, I should find it in the public approbation of so large a body of my Constituents; to whose confidence I am indebted for representing this great, opulent, and I may justly add, spirited, and really independent County. This I have ever considered as the chief honor of my life, and hold myself most happy at this moment in receiving your commands once more to offer myself to your service in a union, I am proud to subscribe to, with my most esteemed Colleague, Mr. O'Neill.

I have the honour to be,
Gentlemen,
your most obliged,
and faithful humble servant,
HERCULES ROWLEY.

Langford-Lodge 23d Sept. 1789.

GENTLEMEN,

THE Address I have had the honour of receiving this day, affords me the greatest satisfaction.—It has been my highest ambition to deserve your good opinion, and it must ever be one of my first objects to merit that reward which you have on this occasion so liberally bestowed.

Encouraged by the good fortune of having obtained your approbation, I feel myself highly honored by your commands, esteeming myself most happy in forming an united interest with my worthy Colleague, Mr Rowley, and in offering myself, in that conjunction, a Candidate for this County, on a future occasion.

I have the honour to be,
Gentlemen,
Your much obliged
And very obedient servant,
JOHN O'NEILL.

Shanescastle, Sept. 23d, 1789.

To be Sold by Auction,

ON Friday, 2d October next, precisely at 12 o'clock, at the Exchange Coffee room, the brigntine Christy, of Greenock, burthen about 110 tons, with all her materials, as she now lies at the Chichester Quay. She is British built, about four years old, and well calculated for the West Indies, fishery, or coasting trade. The inventory to be seen in the hands of the master on board, or at the office of John Boyle and Co.—Approved bills or notes at three and six months date, will be taken in payment.

Belfast, 29th Sept. 1789.

TO BE LET,

ON the first of November next, at Cherryvalley, near Comber, for such Terms as can be agreed on:

One Farm,	containing	16	Acres.
One	do. ———	25	do.
One	do. ———	4	do.
One	do. ———	7½	do.
One	do. ———	5	do.
One	do. ———	2h	do.

The above Lands are all Cunningham Measure, in good order, free of tythe, most of them having turf and marl, all adjoining the town of Comber, and pleasantly situated near Strangford Lough.——Apply to Wm. Mc. Murrin at Cherryvalley.

Sept. 25th, 1789.

MONEY.

TO be lent by the Minister and Church Wardens of the Parish of Carrickfergus, on good personal security, (three in a bond) 300l. the property of the Poor of said Parish.——Application to be made to the Revd. Dean Dobbs.

Carrickfergus, 25th Sept. 1789.

Theatrical Intelligence.

THE Managers of the Comedians now in Downpatrick, takes this method of opening a correspondence with the lovers of the Drama.——He has at present an open for two or three Performers; young men who have an inclination to try their talents on the Stage, may depend on their letters being answered with care and expedition by applying to Mr. G. Jackson, Theatre, Downpatrick. Sept. 25, 1789.

Without the Risk of a Blank!!!

Mr. NICHOLSON,

At his Licensed State Lottery Offices,
No. 7, Dame-street, Dublin; and Bank-street, Cornhill, London;

MOST respectfully acquaints his Friends and the Public, that he is selling the
TICKETS, and DULY STAMPED HALF, QUARTER, EIGHTH, and SIXTEENTH Shares,
In the present Irish State Lottery,
On lower terms than at any other office in Ireland.
*** Schemes, at large, gratis.

Also his much approved Plan of
STAMPT ADVENTURES, at ONE GUINEA
each, without the Risk of a Blank!

Which entitle the bearer to a share of every prize in the Irish Lottery from 10l. to 20,000l. and if a blank, a NEW CHANCE for the ensuing English Lottery. Thus in Mr. Nicholson's Guinea Adventures, after having the chance of ALL the Irish benefits, a blank will produce 1000l. or any of the three hundred and ten additional benefits in the English Lottery, although unfortunate in the first instance.—Elsewhere the blanks yield nothing;—but here they revive, and will produce thousands! And as the Chance given gratis for the Blanks could not be sold for less than Half-a-Guinea, Purchasers of Mr. Nicholson's Guinea Adventures may fairly reckon, that they have them at Half a-Guinea each.

GUINEA ADVENTURE will produce in the Irish Lottery,

£.		£.
2000	if a prize of	20,000
1000	if	10,000
500	—	5000
200	—	2000
100	—	1000
50	—	500
10	—	100
2	—	20
1	—	10

50 if first drawn the 1st, 4th, 10th, 16th, or 22d days of drawing, and 50l. if last drawn.

If the Guinea Adventure is a blank in the Irish Lottery, a new Chance will be given gratis for the next English Lottery, viz.

£.		£.
1000	if a prize of	25,000
800	if	20,000
400	—	10,000
200	—	5000
80	—	2000
40	—	1000
20	—	500
4	—	100
2	—	50

40 if first drawn, and 40 if last drawn.

PARISIAN INTELLIGENCE.

PARIS, Sept. 18.

AT length the long and important Debates on the grand fundamental points of the New Conſtitution of France, which in its conſequences will probably operate a total Revolution in Europe before the middle of the Nineteenth Century, in ſpite of the Pruſſians and Imperial Cordons, and ſpread its contagious influence to the ſhores of the Euxine and the Baltic, in defiance of Royal Repreſentatives, and the deſpotic regimen of Princely Lazarettos, has terminated.

Some of your public Prints ſay, the National Aſſembly has been trifling, yet in two months ſince the moſt glorious Revolution the World has ever witneſſed, this auguſt Body, formed of 1,200 perſons, of all ranks and orders of men, emerging from the moſt profound ſlavery, collected together for the firſt time ſince the days of darkneſs in a popular Aſſembly; an Aſſembly compoſed too of jarring intereſts, and violent animoſities—this auguſt Body, beſides an infinity of troubleſome but urgent diſcuſſions ariſing out of the Revolution, has already produced—a Declaration of Rights, which will form the Catechiſm of Europe—eſtabliſhed the Permanency of the Legiſlative Body—determined the grand Political Problem of the Inſtitution of one or of two Houſes—limited the moſt abſolute Monarch in Europe to a conditional Negative on Legiſlative Acts—decided on the reſponſibility of Miniſters—reſtored the powers of the Purſe irrevocably to the People—brought an army of 200,000 men under fealty to the Nation—overturned the power of the Parliaments—proceeded far in a new Judicial Code—united all the diſcordant Provinces of the Kingdom—deſtroyed the Feudal Syſtem, tripped up the Papal Chair, and brought the whole wealth and power of the Clergy to its feet—and in deſpight of bad examples, the temptations of ambition, and the natural thirſt for power, by a ſolemn act of juſtice and moderation, thrown themſelves and their ſucceſſors into the hands of their fellow-citizens, by limiting the exiſtence of the Legiſlative Body to the ſhorteſt poſſible period conſiſtent with the neceſſity of public affairs in ſuch a country, and with the public ſafety. The writer of this, who has had ſome experience and knowledge of mankind to enable him to appreciate ſuch labours, and who has attended on the wonderful progreſs with reſpect and admiration, leaves it to Philoſophers, Politicians, Legiſlators, and Men of the World, on reviewing this ſummary of its tranſactions, to pronounce how far the charge of trifling can be juſtly imputed to the National Aſſembly of France.

The National aſſembly, before they broke up on Saturday, after ſome Debate, agreed to require the Royal Sanction to all the decrees they have already paſſed, including the celebrated Reſolutions of the 4th of Auguſt, notwithſtanding the prayers and entreaties of Abbe Maury, to grant a reſpite for thoſe concerning the Clergy.

The city of Troyes is in the utmoſt conſternation. On the 9th inſtant a report was ſpread that a quantity of rice was poiſoned. The magiſtrates inſtantly aſſembled to keep the peace. In vain did the Mayor attempt to ſatisfy the furious populace that the report was falſe. A thouſand voices exclaimed at once, "He wiſhed to famiſh us before, and to-day to poiſon us." They mounted the ſteps of the Hotel de Ville, ſeized the unfortunate Mayor, dragged him into the ſtreet, and diſpatched him by a thouſand blows. They then faſtened a rope about the neck of the lifeleſs body and dragged it through an arm of the river, and about the ſtreets. While this tragedy was acting, another party plundered his houſe and razed it to the ground. Thence they proceeded to the houſe of M. Bezançon; but ſome of his neighbours, juſtly alarmed for their own ſafety, repulſed them with muſquetry. This was affected the more eaſily, as the greater number of the rioters was engaged in plundering other houſes. Next day the rice ſuppoſed to be poiſoned was burnt without the city, the populace threatening to burn M. Bezançon along with it, whom they accuſed as the accomplice of the Mayor. The calm that ſucceeded this tumult was hardly leſs alarming than the tumult itſelf, being conſidered as the prelude to a freſh outrage.

Another account ſays, the cruelty ſhewn to the Chief Magiſtrate of Troyes is unparalleled in modern hiſtory, and more ſhocking than the executions in Paris. The Mayor was not only dragged by the mob from the ſeat of juſtice where he was officiating, and a cord tied round his neck, by which he was led through the principal ſtreets, but on coming to the place of execution, he was firſt mutilated, then hung up, and afterwards cut in ſmall pieces. He was eſteemed a moſt worthy man and of excellent character. He was a Deputy of Troyes at the meeting of the States General in 1787, and his only crime was a ſuppoſed attachment to the King.

NATIONAL ASSEMBLY.

PARIS, Sept. 19.

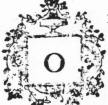

ON Thurſday the National Aſſembly came to a final determination reſpecting the ſucceſſion of the Crown, &c. in the following Reſolution:

"The National Aſſembly recognizes and declares, as the fundamental principle of the French Monarchy,

"That the King's perſon is ſacred and inviolable.

"That the Crown is indiviſible; and,

"That the Crown ſhall be hereditary in the reigning family, from male to male, in the direct order of primogeniture to the perpetual and abſolute excluſion of females and their deſcendants, without meaning to predetermine any thing on the effect of renunciations."

DUBLIN SEPT. 26.

TYTHES.

On this topic, much has already been urged, and the ſubject can never be forgotten to the feelings of humanity, or the principles of ſound policy—ſo long as it continues to harraſs the induſtry of the huſbandman, and abridge the ſcanty ſuſtenance of the vaſſal peaſantry of Ireland.

The celebrated ſpeech of Mr. Grattan in the laſt Seſſion of Parliament, and ſince publiſhed at large in a pamphlet—abounds with information the moſt extenſive, and argument at once the moſt grand, forcible, and ingenious.

The tar obtained from coal, which in England is now uſed for all neceſſary purpoſes of ſhip-building and rigging, is found to anſwer extremely well, as appears by various certificates from maſters of veſſels by whom it has been uſed in paying (as it is termed) their ſhips.—It is found to repel the attacks of worms during long voyages with more efficacy than the tar heretofore uſed, and by a ſuitable proceſs, it has been diſcovered an excellent ſubſtitute for oil in common painting.—By Lord Dundonald's diſcovery, therefore, the introduction of foreign tar will in a great meaſure be ſuperſeded.

Wedneſday night a ſervant woman, after a diſpute, as is reported, with her miſtreſs, proceeded from Bow-ſtreet, to the Old Bridge and precipitated herſelf from the battlements th . The tide being out, ſhe fell on the piles, and her cries having brought ſome perſons to her aſſiſtance, ſhe was taken to an hoſpital, her leg being broke and otherwiſe ſo dangerouſly wounded, as to render little hopes of her recovery.

So great has been the falling off in their exportation of beef lately, that by the returns made to Parliament, for the two laſt years, it appears that the exportation of barrels of beef in the year ending Lady-day, 1787, conſiſted in 153,649 Barrels.

But in the year, ending Lady-day, 1788, it was only 130,857 ditto.

Decreaſed export in one year 22,792 ditto.

An alarming truth this, if it was not known that tillage has encreaſed in much greater proportion than the reduction which the commiſſion trade has ſuffered; and that, however ſome individuals might complain, if there was not a barrel of beef exported, yet the thouſands who ſhould be benefited from the encreaſed agriculture, would drown the clamour of the few.

DIED.] In Anne-ſtreet, after a ſevere and tedious illneſs, which ſhe bore with truly Chriſtian patience, the lady of Doctor Quinan. The ſorrows of her family, and the regret of a numerous acquaintance, are the beſt teſtimony how well ſhe fulfilled the ſeveral duties of life.

Belfaſt, *Sept.* 29.

We underſtand that the Collection at the Charity Sermon, preached on Sunday laſt in Dr. Crombie's Meeting-houſe, by the Rev. Dr. Bruce, amounted to 85l. 5s. 4d.

On the 24th ult. Capt. Thomſon, of the brig Bee, from Jamaica, ſpoke the ſhip Happy Return, Captain Ewing, from Londonderry to Philadelphia, in long. 68, lat. 38, all well.

On the 10th ult. Hector Beatton, maſter of the brig Chance, from Jamaica, ſpoke the ſhip Wincheſter, Capt. Brice, from Jamaica to London, in lat. 29, 31 N. long. 78, 38 W. all well.

The London Packet, Glaſs, from Newry, arrived in the Downs the 20th inſt. after a four days paſſage.

Married, Mr. James Hyndman of this town, to the agreeable Miſs Crawford of Cherryvale, county Monaghan.

Died, on Friday laſt at Ballytweedy, after a ſevere and lingering illneſs, Mr. Robert Stewart of this town, late Sub-ſheriff of the county Down—a young Gentleman poſſeſſed of many amiable qualifications, which not only endeared him to his own relatives, but to a numerous and reſpectable acquaintance.

PORT NEWS.

ARRIVED.

Sept. 21. Fortitude, Glaſgow, Gottenburgh, iron.
Brownlow, Pinkerton, St. Ubes, ſalt and wine.
23. Chance, Beatton, Jamaica, rum, ſugar, &c.
Recovery, Neilſon, St. Vincent, ditto.
Chriſtie, Johnſon, Dominica, do.
25. Peggy, M'Ilroy, Liverpool, bale goods.
Bee, Thompſon, Jamaica, rum and ſugar.
Marianne, Eaſtwood, Waſhington, tar, pitch, &c.
Six colliers.

CLEARED OUT.

Sept. 26. New Loyalty, Brown, Liverpool, butter.

Belfaſt, *October* 2.

On Tueſday the 29th ult. Samuel Black, Eſq. gave an elegant entertainment to a very large company, having that day been ſworn into the office of Sovereign of this Borough, in the room of the Rev. William Briſtow, whoſe eminent ſervices in that capacity for a period of three ſucceſſive years, are too generally known and acknowledged to receive additional luſtre from any eulogium we can here offer.

Method of preſerving Fruit of different kinds in a freſh State, about twelve Months, for which a Premium of Ten Guineas was lately given by the Dublin Society to Signior Ignacio Buonſegna:

IT is neceſſary to pull the fruit two or three days before you begin the proceſs.

Take great care not to bruiſe the fruit, and to pull them before they are quite ripe.

Spread them on a table, over a little clean ſtraw to dry them; this is beſt done on a parlour floor leaving the windows open to admit freſh air, ſo that all moiſture on the ſkin of the fruit may be perfectly dried away.

Pears and apples take three days—ſtrawberries only twenty-four hours—theſe latter ſhould be taken up on a ſilver three-pronged fork, and the ſtalk cut off without touching them, as the leaſt preſſure will cauſe them to rot; take only the largeſt and faireſt fruit: This is the moſt tender and difficult fruit to preſerve: but if done with attention, will keep ſix months: There muſt not be more than one pound in one jar.

Chooſe a common earthen jar with a ſtopper of the ſame which will fit cloſe.

The pears and apples then ſorted as before muſt be wrapped up ſeparately in ſoft wrapping paper, and twiſt it cloſely about the fruit; then lay clean ſtraw at the bottom, and a layer of fruit; then a layer of ſtraw, and ſo on till your veſſel is full; but you muſt not put more than a dozen in each jar; if more, their weight will bruiſe thoſe at the bottom.

Peaches and apricots are beſt ſtored up wrapped each in ſoft paper and fine ſhred paper between the fruit and alſo the layers.—Grapes muſt be ſtored in the jar with fine ſhred paper, which ſhill keep one from touching the other as much as poſſible. Five or ſix bunches are the moſt which ſhould be put into one jar; if they are large, not ſo many; for it is to be underſtood that whenever you open a jar, you muſt uſe that day all the fruit that are in it.

Strawberries as well as Peaches ſhould have fine ſhred paper under and between them in the place of ſtraw, which is only to be uſed for apples and pears. Put in the ſtrawberries, and the paper layer by layer, when the jar is full, put on the ſtopper, and have it well luted round, ſo as perfectly to keep out the air.—A compoſition of roſin or grafting wax is beſt: Let none of it get within ſide the jar, which is to be placed in a temperate cellar, but be ſure to finiſh your proceſs in the laſt quarter of the moon.

Do not preſs the fruit, as any juce running out, would ſpoil all below.

PRICES IN THIS MARKET YESTERDAY.

Oatmeal,	11s. 0d.	to	11s. 3d.		Dried do 00s. to 26s. 0d per d
Wheat,	10 0	—	10 3		R. Tallow, 5s. a 5s. 5d per ſt.
Oats,	5 0	—	5 6		Potatoes 0d. to 10d per b.
Barley,	5 0	—	5 6		Eng. coals, 00s. to 14s. 0d.
Butter,	50 0	—	50 0		Scotch do. 00s. to 13s. 0d.
C. hides,	00 0	—	35 0		Ex on Lond 6½ a 6 3-4 per c
Ox ditto,	37 6	—	40 0		Do. on Glaſgow 6½. a 6 3 4.
S.C. ſkins	00 0	—	42 6		

FAIRS IN THE ENSUING WEEK.

Monday 5th—Caſtlefin, Don. Liſburn, Ant. Mounthamilton, Tyr. Tueſday 6th—Armagh town, Monaghan town, Rathmelton, Don. Trillic, Tyr. Thurſday 8th.—Ardſtranbridge, Tyr. Clones, Mon. Shaneſcaſtle, Ant. Saturday 10th.—Aughnacloy and Cookſtown, Tyr. Donaghadee, Down, Dundrum, Down, Newtownſtewart, Tyr. Norris, Arm. Orrator, Tyr. Stronorlane, Don.

Anno 1789.]   Printed by HENRY JOY, and Co. BELFAST.

The BELFAST NEWS-LETTER.

TUESDAY October 6,   FRIDAY October 9, 1789.

An Auction at Belfaſt;

WILL commence on Monday the 26th day of October inſtant, by order of the Aſſignees of Henry Haſlett, a Bankrupt, (at his late Ware-houſe in Roſemary-lane) the entire Stock of ſaid Bankrupt, conſiſting of the following Goods, viz.

242 Pieces,   } Foreſts, Hunters, and Plains.
74 Half Pieces }
7 Half Pieces 6-4 Cloths.
23 Pieces and half Pieces Coatings.
9 Pieces and half Pieces Naps.
38 Half Pieces printed Velverets.
45 Pieces and half Pieces Thickſets, Cords and other Fuſtian Goods.
200 Bags wove, 180 Bags Legee Buttons.
170 Groſs, plated and Metal Buttons.
640 Squares 4-4 } Black Silk Mode.
260 Yards 3-4   }

A quantity of Sewing Silk, Twiſt, Mohair, Silk Gauze, Waiſtcoating; and many other articles that will be ſpecified in hand-bills at the ſale.

Approved bills on Belfaſt or Dublin, not exceeding 61 days, will be taken in payment of any ſum above 20l.——The ſale to commence at ten o'clock every morning, and continue until the whole are ſold.

Belfaſt, 7th Oct. 1789.
WAD CUNNINGHAM, }
JOHN BOYLD,   } Aſſignees
WM. TENNENT.   }

The Belfaſt Hunt,

DINE at the Donegall-Arms, on Monday the 19th October inſtant——Dinner on the table at four o'clock.

Belfaſt, 8th October, 1789.

Houſhold Furniture, &c.

(AT THE SUIT OF A CREDITOR.)

AT Bailie's auction rooms, Chicheſter Quay, Belfaſt, to-morrow, Saturday the 10th inſt. and Monday the 12th—conſiſting of mahogany dining, card, backgammon, and other tables—do. and other chairs, do. cheſts of drawers, do. knife-caſes, a do. converſation-bed, a do. comode, and a do. writing deſk, bedſteds, feather beds, &c. looking-glaſſes, an eight day clock, a chamber do. a piano-forte, a ſpinet, a guitar, ſome plate, with a variety of other articles too numerous to inſert.

⁎ As the above muſt be ſold for what they will bring, they are well worth attention. The ſale to begin at 11 o'clock each day.

Belfaſt, 9th October, 1789.

Wants a Place,

A Middle-aged ſingle Man, long experienced as a LAND STEWARD and GARDENER in Families of Diſtinction in this Country, from whom he has the warmeſt recommendation.

Apply to Mr. Bradford, Poſt-maſter, Belfaſt, for further particulars.

October 8th, 1789.

Sale by Auction.

TO be ſold by Auction, on Monday the 19th day of October inſtant, and the ſucceeding days, all the Houſhold Furniture in the houſe of Nathaniel Richardſon, late of Charlemont, deceaſed, conſiſting of Mahogany, Oak, Dining and other Tables, half Tallboys, Beds and Bedding, ruſh-bottom and other Chairs, Lookingglaſſes, Delft-ware, China and Glaſſes, Kitchen Furniture, a large aſſortment of Farming, Soap-boiling and Chandling Utenſils, with a variety of other Articles too tedious to mention.

Dated—Charlemont, 2d October, 1789.

Hard-Ware.

EDWARD CREEK, at the Golden Horſe Shoe and Key, Newry, is juſt returned from England, where he has laid in from the different manufacturing Towns, an extenſive aſſortment of Hardware and Ironmongery, which will be ſold as uſual on the loweſt terms.

29th September, 1789.

£. 2,000

Without any Deduction—may be gained at

MAGEE's BELFAST LOTTERY-OFFICE,

BY the Purchaſer of the legal ſtamped; GUINEA SHARE—which entitles to the following very ſuperior Benefits, viz.

£				Prizes of	£.	
2,000	if either of the	2			20,000	
1000	———	2			10,000	
500	———	2			5,000	
200	———	3			2,000	
100	———	5			1,000	
50	———	10			500	
10	———	30			100	

New Dantzig Timber.

SAMUEL HOUSTON has juſt received by the Volunteer, Capt. John Johnſton, a cargo of choice Dantzig Timber:—He is alſo well ſupplied with Memel timber, Dantzig Pipe Staves, Oak and Fir Plank of various Scantling, Beech Logs, red and white Deal-boards, which with every article in the timber line he will ſell on the very loweſt terms.

Larne, 6th Oct. 1789.

N. B. Orders from the Country for timber cut into any ſcantling, will be carefully executed.

Ironmongery and Hardware,

(AT AND BELOW FIRST COST.)

WILL WARNICK being determined to quit ſaid Buſineſs, is now ſelling at and below firſt coſt, his entire ſtock in the above line, conſiſting of an aſſortment which is worth the notice of thoſe that wiſh to buy cheap for ready money. He earneſtly intreats that all perſons indebted to him will diſcharge their accounts immediately.

North-ſtreet, Belfaſt 8th Oct. 1789.

Natural Philoſophy,

THE Claſs for Theoretical and Experimental Philoſophy, in the Belfaſt Academy, will be opened on Tueſday the 3d of Nov. next, and be continued every Tueſday and Thurſday during the Seſſion. Tickets, one Guinea, to be had of Rev. J. Neilſon at the Academy.

About the ſame time, Mr. Neilſon propoſes to begin a Courſe of Experiments in the ſeveral branches of Philoſophy, for Ladies, in a convenient part of the Town.—Tickets, one Guinea, to be had as above.

Belfaſt Academy, 8th Oct. 1789.

Engliſh and Iriſh Woollen Drapery, Haberdaſhery and Hoſiery;

ALEXANDER SINCLARE has juſt laid in an extenſive aſſortment, from the beſt markets, of every article in the above branches, all of which were choſen by himſelf.——He alſo has an elegant variety of the neweſt FANCY WAISTCOAT PATTERNS; which, with every article in his line, he will ſell at the moſt reduced Prices, for ready money only.——With gratitude for paſt favours, he ſolicits a continuation of the liberal encouragement he has experienced from his friends and the public, to merit which ſhall be his conſtant ſtudy.

⁎ He requeſts all thoſe who have accounts with him of ſix months ſtanding to come to an immediate ſettlement. Belfaſt, October 9th, 1789.

Bradberry's Optical Exhibition,

At Mr. Lindon's, in Orr's Entry, High-Street, Belfaſt;

CONTINUES open for the inſpection of the Curious. Nothing can better declare the novelty and ſurprize than the great number who daily reſort to ſee them: Theſe wonderful and ſurprizing effects are beyond the power of words to expreſs, and prove that our ſight is of all other ſenſes the moſt liable to be deceived. He has for ſale Cameras for the purpoſe of Drawing, ſuperior and more portable than any yet invented; likewiſe Spectacles upon a principle that cannot fail aſſiſting the ſight.——Mr. Bradberry is already honoured with 150 Subſcribers for his Lecture on Optics, will be much obliged to the Subſcribers to ſend for their Tickets, which will prevent confuſion at the time of the Lecture, which will be at the Exchange-Rooms, on Wedneſday the 21ſt of this preſent October; to begin preciſely at one o'clock. Tickets to the Lecture 2s. and admittance to the Exhibition 1s. from 11 till 3, and from 7 till 9 in the evening.

October 8th, 1789.

Houſes in Belfaſt to be let,

From the firſt of Nov. next.

THE two Dwelling Houſes lately occupied by John Sutton, Eſq. and Thomas Faris, pleaſantly ſituated at the corner of Hanover-Quay, adjoining the Long-Bridge;—alſo three Houſes in Princes-ſtreet, at preſent inhabited by Edw. Brown, Joſeph M'Creedy, Henry Brown, and Allen Mc. Annaly; with a Lot of encloſed Ground exactly oppoſite the gateway leading into the King's New Store-Houſes, that would anſwer well for a Coal, Timber, or Stone-cutter's Yard. Apply to Francis Turnly, Eſq

Antrim Quarter Seſſions

THE next General Quarter Seſſions of the Peace for the Co. of Antrim will be held at Antrim in and for ſaid county on Thurſday the 8th of October inſtant, when the attendance of the Coroners, Seneſchals, High and Sub Conſtables will be required as uſual. October 1ſt, 1789.

CHARLES CRYMBLE, Sheriff.

Thoſe who have been ſummoned to ſerve as Jurors, and neglect to attend, will moſt certainly be fined by the Court.

The Falls Mill, and ſundry Houſes.

WADDELL CUNNINGHAM, JAMES HOLMES and JOHN HAMILTON, will ſell by public auction in the market houſe, Belfaſt, on Wedneſday the 21ſt inſt. exactly at 12 o'clock, the following Leaſes.

No. 1. The leaſe of two houſes in Carrickfergus-ſtreet, at preſent unoccupied, ſubject to 1l. 11s. 4d. yearly rent, and held by leaſe for three lives or ninety-one years from 1768.

No. 2. The leaſe of three ſmall houſes in Pound-ſtreet, held by leaſe for three lives or ninety years from 1767, at 1l. 3s. 4d. yearly rent. One of thoſe houſes is let to a good tenant at two guineas per year, and the other two unoccupied.

No. 3. The leaſe of a large dwelling-houſe and offices in Warren-ſtreet, next adjoining to Mrs. Elizabeth Wilſon's tenement, held for 41 years, from Nov. 1776, at the yearly rent of 12l.

No. 4. The leaſe from Mr. Daniel Blow of the mill in the Falls, and 9A. 0R. 20P. of land adjoining; lately occupied by Mr. N Wilſon, held for 31 years, from Nov. 1786, with a clauſe for a farther term of 31 years, provided the lives in the original leaſe ſhall ſo long laſt, or provided Mr. Blow ſhall renew with Lord Donegall, Rent 70l. per annum.—Conditions will be declared at the ſale.

Belfaſt, 5th Oct. 1789.
WADDELL CUNNINGHAM,
JAMES HOLMES,
JOHN HAMILTON.

ON Monday the 12th inſt. will be ſold by auction at the Market-Houſe in Belfaſt, by the Sheriff of the county of Antrim, a very extenſive aſſortment of

Woollen and Cotton Goods;

the property of Thomas Gihon. As the quantity is very conſiderable, it will be well worth the notice of all the dealers in theſe articles to attend; and for the accommodation of purchaſers, good bills on Dublin or Belfaſt, at three months date, will be taken in payment of every ſum exceeding ten pounds, or a ſuitable diſcount allowed for caſh.

Belfaſt, 2d Oct. 1789.

Advertiſement.

TO be ſold by Mr. Jackſon of Steeple,—Sixty fat Bullocks and Eighteen Cows.

Steeple, October 3, 1789.

A few Bleachers

WANTED for the enſuing ſeaſon, by John Ruſſel of Edenderry. None need apply that are not well recommended for ſobriety and attention to their buſineſs. They may be accommodated with houſes, gardens and cows graſs if required.

Edenderry, Oct. 5, 1789.

Wants Employment

FOR the enſuing ſeaſon, an experienced Overſeer of a Bleach Green, who is well ſkilled in boiling and bucking, and whoſe character for ſobriety and honeſty will bear the ſtricteſt enquiry. For his knowledge in the bleaching buſineſs, he refers the public to Meſſrs. Handcock's, Liſburn, or Mr. Wakefield, Moyallen. A line directed to John M'Kowen, Liſburn, will be duly attended to.

4th October, 178

Stolen or Strayed,

OUT of the Rev. Dr. Atkinſon's fields near Liſburn, on Tueſday night the 29th of September laſt,—A ſtrong black Coach Gelding, four years old, about 14 hands high, with a ſtar; three white feet, and a ſplint on his near fore leg, a little below the knee. Whoever returns him to the Doctor ſhall receive one Guinea reward—if ſtolen, five Guineas will be paid on returning him and proſecuting the thief to conviction.

Liſburn, 3d October, 1789.

To be ſold by Auction,

ON Friday the 30th day of October, inſt. at the Donegall Arms, Belfaſt,—a Farm of Land in the Townland of Tullygirvin in the county of Down, containing thirty-two acres, Cunningham meaſure, alſo two acres of Moſs immediately adjoining ſaid farm. Theſe lands were granted by the late Robert Kyle, Eſq. to George Gilleſpie, Eſq. deceaſed, for a term of 999 years, at the yearly rent of 6l. and are at preſent ſet at about 30l. a year clear yearly profit rent; about ten years of the leaſes are unexpired, and will riſe conſiderably at the expiration of ſaid term. The lands are remarkably good: there are ſeveral acres of good meadow ground, moſs convenient and plenty of water. This farm is pleaſantly ſituated, within ſeven miles of Belfaſt, three of Cumber, and two of Saintfield. For further particulars enquire of Henry Savage, Gent. Proſpect.

FOREIGN INTELLIGENCE.

Naples, Aug. 11. On the 26th inst. we were very much alarmed by a dreadful storm, during which the lightning fell in many places in the city; Mount Vesuvius was very much disturbed the whole day, and vomited torrents of flames; a great stream of lava was perceived the next evening, which appeared like a mountain of fire; shortly after a fresh eruption was discovered some miles below the old one, between the Greek Tower and that of the Annonciado, near the lands which are inhabited and cultivated, but to which it did no damage.

LONDON, SEPT. 24.

SPANISH KING'S INAUGURATION.

The Cortez of Spain met on Monday last—we wish we could say for the purpose of resuming their constitutional importance in the State, of wresting from the Crown the unconstitutional power with which a successful usurpation of the rights of the subject has armed it from the time of Charles V.

It was for no such glorious purpose that the Spanish Cortez assembled this week.

Retaining nothing of the spirit which formerly animated that body, and made it a model fit for freemen to copy, they met for the purpose of receiving and acknowledging a master.

This body, now the mere shadow of a shade, is always assembled on the accession of a new King—and his Majesty so far compliments it, not on account of what it is, but of what it is was, as to take in its presence an oath, which in other countries might be called a Coronation oath.

The King having taken this oath, framed by himself, received the oath of allegiance sworn by the Cortez, and by the Deputies of such Provinces as had not in days of old any Cortez or National Assemblies of their own.

After this ceremony, the Cortez were, according to annual custom, entertained with a bull feast or fight; according to established etiquette, the Queen sat on the King's right hand, the only time in her whole life, when a Queen of Spain enjoys such an honour.

DUBLIN, OCT. 1.

Of the powerful effect which the establishment and encouragement of manufactures has, in promoting the population, and consequently the wealth of a country, there cannot be a more striking instance than the parish of Halifax, in Yorkshire.

This parish, situated in a wild mountainous part of the country, which Cambden describes as "a sterile soil, where the comforts of life were not to be obtained, and scarcely the indispensable necessaries," was about the beginning of the sixteenth century one of the least populous parts of England. A woollen manufacture, however, being established there about that time, and receiving every encouragement from the proprietors of the soil, it increased in consequence and population so rapidly, that by an accurate survey made in the year 1764, it was found to contain 8244 families, which at only five to a family amounts to 41,220 inhabitants. Thus by the establishment of the woolen manufacture, properly attended to and encouraged, from being an insignificant spot, containing only a few scattered hamlets, it became, in the course of a couple of centuries, the most populous parish perhaps in the universe; it certainly is one of the most important in Britain. What a lesson this for the proprietors of land in Ireland!

We hear with pleasure, that in consequence of a number of œconomical arrangements lately made by the Commissioners of Police, an annual saving to the amount of thirteen hundred pounds is made; which saving, it is said, will be applied to encreasing the number of watchmen.

Wednesday afternoon, Ambrose Leet, Esq; Accountant of the Police Establishment, together with all the second clerks of the Divisional Justices, were by a special order of Government, dismissed from their employments.

We are happy to have it in our power to contradict the report of the death of Mr. William Beeby, merchant, of George's street; that gentleman, who was dangerously ill, being now much better, and it is hoped in a fair way of recovery.

DUBLIN, OCTOBER 6.

Early this morning the Cork Mail-coach, on its way to town, broke down near Kill, and was considerably retarded. None of the passengers received any hurt.

We have authority to announce, that the Marquis of Bath is certainly appointed Lord Lieutenant of Ireland, in place of the Marquis of Buckingham, who comes here no more. His new Excellency is expected to set out for this country by the beginning of the next month.—*Dub. Ev. Post.*

Last Wednesday night, there was the most violent storm ever remembered in Limerick; in town, several houses were totally unroofed; in the country, several trees were torn from their roots, and carried to a very great distance, stacks of corn and hay entirely carried away, and we fear the corn unreaped, has been materially injured; the storm began at eleven, and continued above four hours; several vessels were driven from their moorings in the river, and stranded. On the above account the post did not arrive next day until 12 o'clock.

We hear that two wherries were lost in the storm of Wednesday night last, one of them is said to belong to Skerries, and the other was coming from Holyhead to this port with a cargo of herrings.

Last Thursday a duel was fought in the church-yard of Clonbeg, near Tipperary, between Henry Fitzgerald of the county Limerick, and Thos. Laurence, of Nenagh, Esqrs. wherein the latter was dangerously wounded in the thigh by his antagonist's ball, which was endeavoured (though ineffectually) to be extracted. We hear that the dispute arose in consequence of an altercation which took place between them a few nights ago.

COUNTESS OF DONEGALL.

The death of this amiable Lady is sincerely regretted by all those who had the good fortune to be intimately acquainted with her.

AT a meeting of the Officers of the following Volunteer Corps, reviewed at Dromore, on the 2d Sept. 1789—viz.

Union Regiment.	Union Grenadiers—Captain Moore, Rosevale Loyalists—Major Patten, Aghalee Company—Captain Moore, Ballynahinch Comp.—Captain Armstrong, Moira Company—Lieutenant Dobbin,
Dromore Battalion.	Dromore Company—Captain Vaughan, Villa Independents—Lieutenant Hamilton,
	Lisburn Artillery—Captain Ward, Lisburn Rangers—Captain Bell,

the following Address was unanimously agreed to:

Captain VAUGHAN in the Chair.

To WILLIAM SHARMAN, Esq. Reviewing General.

SIR,

THE Volunteers assembled here are sensible of the honour you have done them this day. They are convinced that your attachment to that association, to which Ireland owes both her freedom and her fame, has been the cool result of steady patriotism, untinctured by vanity or ambition—Nor has your conduct as a Representative of the people in the great assembly of the nation been less meritorious in the eyes of your countrymen; who have beheld with admiration its undeviating rectitude, and marked in your public character, the operation of that principle which has been the uniform rule of your private life.

That the present state of this country should be so unfavourable for the exertion of virtue like yours, is to us matter of deep regret—but we trust the time is not far distant when a portion of that light, whose brilliancy at this instant illuminates a neighbouring kingdom with such distinguished lustre, shall be communicated to us—when corruption shall cease—an inordinate love of power in the *rulers* yield to the interest of the *ruled*—and the rights of this great kingdom be established on the solid foundation of justice and equal liberty. Happy in the esteem of your countrymen—happy in the consciousness of having acted well—may you long live an example to your amiable offspring, of public spirit, and private virtue.

GEORGE VAUGHAN, Chairman.

To the OFFICERS of the different Volunteer Corps reviewed at Dromore on the 2d September, 1789.

GENTLEMEN,

I received the honor of your address; and as I consider it a very strong portrait of a very feint original, I shall keep it before my eyes as a *memento*—not of what I am, but of what I ought, and wish to be.

As you have been pleased to notice me as a Volunteer, and a Representative; and as both you and I may be soon called on as Electors, either to supersede or continue our public servants, according as they have behaved to us; give me leave to say a few words to you on each of those important subjects.

With respect to the duty of a Volunteer—Our right to the possession and use of arms, is one of those original rights of man, which he could not surrender to society, and remain free. It has been handed down to us through all the revolutions of the feudal—common—and statute laws of these kingdoms; and is at this day that very right which is exercised and asserted by the Volunteers of Ireland. The man who does not qualify himself to defend his freedom, has but a bad chance of recovering what he has lost, and runs a great risk of losing what he has. At a time when the other nations of the world are copying our example, it would be inglorious in us to lay down, what we had taken up with so much credit to ourselves, and so much benefit to our country.

With respect to the duties of an Elector and a Representative—I am naturally disposed to pass over in silence those public situations which I despair of counteracting: but the force of your address has compelled me to come forward, and to mention serious truths in a serious stile.

If we compare public with private crimes, as to their causes—their effects—and the punishments which ought to await them; we shall find that the enormity of public criminality so far exceeds any thing of a private nature, that the mind of man has not comprehension sufficient to set bounds to the excess. In the same manner if we compare public with private merits, the effects will be similar. What then has the Elector? What has the Representative to answer for, in the case of a breach of trust? Their duties are the most solemn ones, which a creature can owe to his Creator—which a citizen can owe to the state—or which a man can owe to mankind. They concern the life—liberty—and property of every individual in the community, and whatsoever else is dear to him as a moral or a social being. If either of them is more criminal than the other, as an offender, the Elector is the more guilty of the two: because he is the parent of all that swarm of evils which grow up in the Representative, and lay waste the community.

If the Representative, therefore, to the dishonor both of himself and his Constituents, becomes both the plunderer of a nation and a sharer in its spoils—the Elector of such a Representative is a principal in the guilt. He resembles the man who would send a wolf to take care of his flock, or a common thief to watch over his treasure.

But if the Representative, in obedience to the instructions of his principals, acts for his Constituents, as he thinks they would have acted for themselves, their fellow citizens, and their posterities—— or, if being left to his own discretion, and reflecting that man was not made alone for himself, nor for the spot of earth which he inhabits—nor for the generation which he was born in—he becomes the restorer of an empire—the protector of generations—or the benefactor of the whole human race;—acting as if he was a Representative of the world, with all mankind his Constituents. The Elector of such a Representative, as the parent of his honors, ought to be a sharer in his reward.

Now if we compare such crimes and merits with any thing of a private nature, we shall find, that he who relieves those miseries only which he sees and hears, can claim no kind of competition with the man who feels for sorrows which he could not hear, through portions of the globe which he never saw, and ages of the world which he could not see ——We shall find that the crime of robbing an individual on the high-way, can form no sort of parallel with that of national pilfering—with that of forging the will of a nation to the disherison of its posterity, that the forger himself might become one of the legatees. The mathematical ratio of an unit to millions, gives but a loose calculation of their criminal distance. If death is the penalty of the first—there is nothing to be found in the penal codes of the world commensurate to the enormity of the second. It is a melancholy reflection—that the very law itself may become both an instrument of the plunder, and an asylum for the plunderer: but if there are other tribunals superior to those of man—the culprit in such a case, with all his principals and accessaries, must tremble for their eternity.

The history of the Jews informs us, that there were two sects among them of opposite principles—the Pharisees and Sadducees—the former maintained, whilst the latter denied, the immortality of the soul. If there are such sects as the latter among modern Christians, the public systems and manners of nations may be easily accounted for. The system of such men must be—to live, as they believe they shall die—like the beasts of the forest. As they must consider their existence as a perishable commodity—they will make the best market which they can of it. Scoffing at all religion as a bugbear, they will laugh at you and me, gentlemen, for our idle hopes and fears: but let us leave their titles—places—and pensions to perish with themselves, and teach them this important truth—that whatsoever is the safest road through human life—that road is best. We are not, I hope so far advanced in the fashionable world, as to mortgage our eternity for a freehold, or a few shakes of the hand—or to stake our salvation on a dinner or a bottle of wine. It has always been our Creed, and I trust we shall persevere in it, that—AN HONEST MAN IS THE NOBLEST WORK OF GOD.

These are my principles as a Volunteer—an Elector—and a Representative; and it makes me happy to think that I have so respectable, and so virtuous a body of men as yourselves, and those whom you represent, to sanction such sentiments.

I am, Gentlemen,
with every sentiment of
gratitude and attachment,
your faithful fellow citizen
and servant,
WILLIAM SHARMAN.

LONDON-DERRY, SEPT. 24.

Yesterday Roger Harrison, Esq; was elected a Burgess of the Corporation of this city, in the room of George C. Kennedy, Esq; lately elected an Alderman.

Yesterday the following gentlemen were elected Honorary Freemen of this city, viz. Alderman William Alexander of Dublin, James Ferguson, Esq; of Belfast, Marcus Beresford Esq; and Thos. Newburgh, Esq.

Belfast, *October* 6.

The present Lord Lieutenant of Ireland, to a certainty, meets the Parliament of Ireland in his present capacity, where he will find the interest of Government much stronger both in the House of Commons and House of Lords.

The Peggy, Capt. M'Ilroy, loaded with linen cloth for Chester fair, sailed yesterday the 4th inst.

The New Draper, Capt. Kearney, will sail for Liverpool on Thursday next.

Anno 1789.]　　Printed by HENRY JOY, and Co. BELFAST.

The BELFAST NEWS-LETTER.

TUESDAY October 13,　　FRIDAY October 16, 1789.

The MEDICAL LECTURES,

In the UNIVERSITY of DUBLIN, will commence on Monday the 2d of November next.

DR. Cullen's, on Materia Medica, at nine o'clock.
Dr. Dickson's, on the Institutes of Medicine at twelve.
Dr. Cleghorn's, on Anatomy, at one.
Dr. Percival's, on Chemistry, at two.
Dr. Brereton's, on the Practice of Medicine, at three.
Clinical Lectures will be given twice a week.
Attendance on the Clinical Hospital, every day from eleven to twelve.

Stewart Beatty,

IS just now landing a large parcel of strong Jamaica RUM.—He has also received from Oporto a few Pipes of old Red Port, which will be sold at his Stores in Hercules-Lane on the most reasonable terms, with Brandy, Geneva, old Antigua Spirits, Claret and Red Port in bottles, Mountain and Sherry Wine in quarter casks, and best French Vinegar.
　　　　　　　　　　　Belfast, 12th Oct. 1789.

Cheap Scale Sugar.

STEWARTS, THOMSON, & Co. at the old Sugar-House in Rosemary-lane, Belfast, are now selling finest Scale Sugar, at 8s. 6d.—second quality at 8s.—and third quality at 7s. 6d. per stone.

Those who chuse Scale Sugars will (upon trial) find this parcel of a very superior quality, and such as will give perfect satisfaction.

NOW selling at the New Sugar-House, Waring-street, by Montgomery, Brown, Tennent, and Boyle, fine SCALE SUGAR, at 8s. 6d. per stone—second Scale, 8s.—and third Scale, 7s. 6d.

Wanted at November,

A Careful middle-aged Man, who has been accustomed to attend horses and cars: he must be unmarried, and if he can do a little at attending table when required, he will be the more acceptable.—Enquire at the Office of Messrs. Henry Joy & Co.
　　　　　　　　　　　10th October, 1789.

COUNTY OF ANTRIM. A General Quarter Sessions of the Peace for the County of Antrim, was held at Antrim in and for said county on the 8th day of October, 1789.

Said Sessions are adjourned, and will be held by adjournment at Ballymena, on Saturday the 17th day of October instant.

And said Sessions are further adjourned, and will be held by adjournment at Belfast, on Friday the 23d day of October instant

And said Sessions will be held by further adjournment at Ballymoney, on Thursday the 12th day of November next.

SAM. HERON, Clerk of the Peace.

JOHN O'NEILL,
ALEXANDER McAULAY,
THOMAS THOMPSON,
ALEXANDER Mc. MANUS,
JAMES WHITE.

A stray Cow,

IS now on the Lands of widow Innis, near Purdysburn. Whoever proves property, and pays the expences, may have her by applying as above.
　　　　　　　　　　　13th October, 1789.

A few Bleachers

WANTED for the ensuing season, by John Russel of Edenderry. None need apply that are not well recommended for sobriety and attention to their business. They may be accommodated with houses, gardens and cows grass if required.
　　　　　　　　　　　Edenderry, Oct. 5, 1789.

Lands adjoining Colerain.

TO be Let, or the Interest of the Lease sold, from November, 1789, a compleat small Farm, containing about nine acres, on which there is a neat New House, in which several gentlemen have already liv'd; or would answer very well for a yarn merchant, having fine conveniency for bleaching, and near the market of Colerain and Ballymoney, situate on the bank of the fine Bann-water, and is near enough Ballyaughran shore for bathing. The land is in great heart, by being lately limed, manured, and ditched.—There is 23 years and three young lives (all healthy and well) to come of this lease from November next.—For terms enquire of Mr. Scarlon, King's-Gate, Colerain.

This to be continued three times.

A Bull to be sold.

A Remarkable large fine striped Dutch Bull, imported from Holland about eighteen months ago, to be sold. His age—rising three years. Enquire at Mr. William Irwin.　Belfast, 12th October, 1789.

New China.

GEORGE BRADFORD, at the Post-Office, has just imported per the Charlotte, Captain Campbell, from London, an extensive and elegant assortment of TEA CHINA of the very newest patterns; and as these Goods were purchased at the last India Sales, for ready money, he is enabled and determined to sell for the very smallest profit.　　　　Belfast, 14th Oct. 1789.

To be Let,

From the first of November next, for twenty-one or thirty-one years,

A Farm of Land containing one hundred and eighteen acres, two roods, Irish plantation measure, situated in the town land of Ballybentro, parish of Broad Island, and county of Antrim—distant about 12 miles from Belfast, three from Carrickfergus, and five from Larne. A great part of said land is highly improved;—there are about 12 acres of excellent meadow, and upwards of thirty acres lately limed; the remainder may be improved at a very moderate expence, there being abundance of lime-stone in the farm. Coals can be brought within one mile by water, and there is an excellent lime-kiln lately erected on the premisses.

For particulars apply to Robert Scott, merchant, Belfast.　　　　　　　　　13th October, 1789

N. B. If an eligible tenant does not offer for the whole of the above-mentioned land, it will be divided into three farms of about forty acres each.

MAWHINNEY'S

Latin and French School, with Reading, Writing, Arithmetick, and Book keeping.

ON Monday next 19th inst. he intends to open a Class from 7 to 9 in the Evening, for the conveniency of those who cannot attend his other Classes at an earlier part of the day.
　　　Pottinger's-Entry, Belfast, 16th Oct. 1789.

N. B. He will teach privately if required.

Winter Assortment.

THOMAS NEILSON & Co. are now most extensively supplied with every Article of Woollen Drapery and Mens Mercery which they usually sell, of the most serviceable kinds, and perfectly suitable to the Season.——Their New Fancy Waistcoats, Buttons and Cloths, are of the neatest patterns; and they are determined to dispose of them on the lowest terms.

☞ A large Assortment of Worsted and Yarn Stockings daily expected.
　　　　　　　　　　　Belfast, 15th Oct. 1789.

Sheet Lead.

CUNNINGHAM GREG is just landing a quantity, which will be disposed of on reasonable terms.
　　　　　　　　　　　Belfast, 14th Oct. 1789.

AS several Members of the Belfast Monthly Club were absent from the two last Meetings, it is thought proper to give this general notice, that Wednesday the fourth of November, being the next Club-day, it hath been unanimously resolved that each Member may invite such friends as he chuses, to dine with him at the Club, and commemorate the Birth of our Great Deliverer, and the blessed event of the Glorious Revolution.——October 14th, 1789.

　　　　　　　　　　　A. B. Secretary.

Patrick Mc. Kinty,

HAS imported a large quantity of Earthen Ware, with English Cloths and Corduroys, which he will sell by wholesale and retail on the most reasonable terms.　　　　　　　Belfast, 15th Oct. 1789.

To be Let at Nov. next,

WHITE-ABBEY Green, with the houses on the same, machinery, all in complete condition:—Also seven houses on the farm, and, if required, a part of the land:—Also the dwelling-house and garden, with such quantity of the remainder of the farm as may be required.

Apply to Thomas M'Cabe.
　　　　　　　　　　　Belfast, 15th Oct. 1789.

The Belfast Coterie,

WILL be held at the Exchange-Rooms, on Tuesday next the 20th instant.
　　　　　　　　　　　Oct. 16th, 1789.

Harmonic Fete.

MRS. ARNOLD, first Singer at the Rotunda in Dublin, having been repeatedly flattered that her presence in Belfast would be peculiarly pleasing to the noble, polite, and spirited Inhabitants, most respectfully acquaints them that she has done herself the honour to attend them; and that, on Thursday Evening next, the 22d instant, (for one night only) at the Exchange-Rooms, will be

A Concert of Music, Vocal and Instrumental,

conducted in the most elegant manner: Particulars of which will be expressed in the printed Bills of the Performance.

Admittance, { Gent. 3s. 3d.—Ladies, 2s. 8d. h.—and Children, 1s. 7d. h each.

☞ The Rooms will be superbly illuminated with wax. The Concert begin precisely at Eight o'Clock, and conclude about Ten.

Tickets to be had at Sheridan's Hotel; the Exchange Coffee-house; and of Mrs. Arnold, at Mr. Hendren's, Grocer, in High-street.
　　　　　　　　　　　15th October, 1789.

For SALE,

THE Sloop SUCCESS, Welch built, burthen Forty Tons. She would answer the Coasting Trade very well, particularly for carrying Grain——If not disposed of in eight Days, will be sold by Auction on Saturday the 24th inst. at 12 o'Clock at the Coffee house.

Mc. KEDY & STEVENSON.
Belfast, 13th Oct. 1789.

Wanted,

On the first of November next,

A House-Maid, who can be well recommended for honesty and sobriety.——Apply at Mr. Ranken's, Richmond-Lodge.
　　　　　　　　　　　13th October, 1789.

Cabin Hill.

TO be sold by auction, at the Donegall Arms, on Friday the 6th November, at noon, the three following leases, lying within 2½ miles of Belfast, in Ballycloghan, and county of Down.

No. 1. For the lives of Mr. William Haliday and his son, Samuel, both of Liverpool, contains seventeen acres and fifteen perches, subject to the yearly rent of seventeen pounds. On this there is a very good dwelling-house, with suitable offices and an excellent kitchen garden.

No. 2. For the same lives, contains fourteen acres, subject to the yearly rent of 12l. 5s.—On this there are three cabins.

No. 3. For the same lives, a meadow, distant from No. 1 and 2 about a quarter of a mile, contains 3½ acres, yearly rent seven guineas.

Allen M'Cormick, who lives on the land, will shew the premisses. For further particulars enquire at Samuel M'Tier, at the Ballast-Office. Belfast, 15th Oct. 1789.

A Miller

WANTED to work a Corn-Mill; He must bring a good character, may be accommodated with a house and garden if married.——Apply to Hugh Hamilton, near Ballynahinch.
　　　　　　　　　　　8th October, 1789.

ARTHUR GRUEBER and RANDAL Mc. ALLISTER,

Booksellers, Stationers, and Lottery-Office-Keepers,

No. 59, Dame-street, Dublin,

TAKE the liberty of acquainting the Inhabitants of Belfast, that they are constantly supplied with all New Publications, and a great assortment of Books in most languages;—also a great variety of Stationary of the best quality, which they will sell by wholesale and retail on the most reasonable terms. Country Booksellers and Schools will find their advantage to deal with them for the above articles: They have also on sale, a great variety of Tickets and Shares, which they are selling at the most reduced prices. All commands which they may be honored with shall be attended to with the greatest punctuality.　　　　　　　Oct. 11th, 1789.

Advertisement.

TO be sold by Auction, on Friday 16th instant, at the house of Mr. Getty in Strangford, sundry articles of Household Furniture, consisting of Mohogany and other Chairs and Tables, &c. some farming Utensils, and some young Pigs of a very good kind.
　　　　　　　　　　　8th October, 1789.

PARISIAN INTELLIGENCE.

PARIS, SEPT. 28.

ON Saturday last, the National Assembly adopted Mr. Necker's plan, in consequence of which every citizen of the realm will deposit, within eighteen months, a quarter of his yearly income, once for all. This contribution is to be obligatory, and not voluntary, as it had been supposed; and will be collected agreeably to the owner's simple declaration. This new kind of impost causes some murmurs, but necessity has no law; without this resource, bankruptcy is inevitable.

Caricature-prints begin to be as common in France, as they are in England; one of them struck me as I went by a print shop. The Monarch is represented as indisposed, swallowing a draught, called *French Constitution.* He does it with a steady hand, and after evacuating *despotism,* finds himself quite recovered, and receives the compliments of the nation, who had presented the cup to him.

LONDON, OCT. 2—3.

Great expectations are raised in Rome on the subject of the concealed treasures of the Jesuits. The discovery of this secret was made by a Piedmontese Ecclesiastick, who is permitted to dig at his pleasure, though under the inspection of the Pope's Guards.

FROM THE LONDON GAZETTE.

Mr. Neckar is now in the utmost danger of losing his popularity and his character altogether. He has already failed in two loans; and his project for supplying the public necessities by a tax of 25 per cent. on all personal property, is not likely to be much more successful. If this fails, the bankruptcy of France is certain.

A letter from a gentleman at New-York says, "The constitution is now in full operation. The President shines in every thing, and his great and good example will have an happy influence. His acknowledgments of the Creator on every occasion do him honour, and add an amazing lustre to his character, while the uniform tenor of his conduct shews they are not words intended merely *ad captandum,* but flow from an heart almost overwhelmed (to use his own phrase) with a sense of the divine munificence. His deportment is mild, courteous, and humble, and yet there is a dignity about him that inspires reverential awe."

A letter from Philadelphia, speaks of the rapid advancement of the Americans in all those manufactures which heretofore were chiefly derived from Europe. It appears by the Customhouse books of Philadelphia that they have exported 7000l. worth of tanned leather, the manufacture of the country, to Virginia, during the last year; a Mr. Cabet, of Beverly, in Massachusetts purchased and exported 70,000 pair of womens shoes from that place. In consequence of a premium from the Manufacturing Society, a large volume has been printed on types made in America, and so many paper mills (upwards of 60) exist in Pennsylvania, as almost to supersede the necessity of importing. Glass-houses are established in Albany and Boston, the fabrics of the former vending as cheap as those of Europe. At New York one or more mills are erected for making castor oil from the fruit of the Palma Christi, which thrives there. The nail manufacture has been pushed forward within three years so as to render importation no longer necessary. The coarse linens of New England and Connecticut excel those of Europe of the same quality, which can no longer be sent to any places at least north of Philadelphia. Manufactories for fabricating duck have been set on foot through Connecticut and New England, and in the cotton line two manufactories are already established at Philadelphia and Beverly, and others are intended in Lancaster and in Pennsylvania, Arkwright's machinery having been introduced at Beverly, and their carding machines are made at Philadelphia. The importation of steel is lessened a fourth at Philadelphia, and that of beer has also considerably diminished. In fine, this letter represents the Americans to have most splendid prospects, and states that they are able considerably to undersell the Irish in the provision trade, and actually exported great quantities to the East and West Indies, fifty thousand barrels of salt beef having been made in Connecticut and New England.

Manufactures are not the only line in which they have exerted themselves with success; agriculture and commerce have gone on with equal rapidity, and the new settlements, canals, and other great objects, are advancing amazingly.

DUBLIN, OCTOBER 8.

The Marquis of Bath, our new expected Viceroy, is a *bon vivant* of the first water—his hours of recumbence are from four in the morning till two in the afternoon, the remainder of the four and twenty are devoted to his Lordship's chosen avocations.

It is the intention of a numerous and most respectable part of the citizens of Dublin to request Lord Henry Fitzgerald, and the Right Hon. Henry Grattan, to stand forth as candidates for the city at the next general election. Not a man would think of opposing the re-election of Mr. Hartley, but it is well known that he means to retire from public life at the close of the present Parliament: and a worthier successor to him they could not fix upon than Lord Henry Fitzgerald, the eloquent and spirited offspring of the house of Leinster, so justly dear to the citizens; and whose merits, as their representative, they have experienced in the present most amiable and illustrious head of the family. Mr. Grattan's abilities need no encomium, and his exertions in the public cause have been vigorous and uncommonly successful. Should he be called upon by the citizens, we believe that he would give up the county Wicklow, and rather chuse to represent the capital.

By a private letter from Bourdeaux, we learn, that the vintage has, this year, almost entirely failed in France.

Dangan Castle, the seat of the Earl of Mornington, is now to be set; and if an adequate tenant cannot be got for it, report says, that it is to go to the hammer, his Lordship having determined to remain a constant absentee. This is one of the blessed effects of an English school education.

A humane Senator has pledged himself to introduce a Bill of insolvency in the next session, for the benefit of distressed debtors.

By the last British mail an account has been received here of the death of the Right Hon. Francis Hastings, Earl of Huntingdon, and one of his Majesty's most Honourable Privy Council of Great Britain. By the death of this Nobleman, an estate of 7000l. per ann. devolves upon Lord Rawdon, son to the Earl of Moira, whose consort was sister to the Earl of Huntingdon.

The Earldom of Huntingdon, it is thought is now extinct, by the death of Francis the last Earl, whose demise we have this day announced to our readers;—

PHYSIOGNOMICAL ANECDOTES.

[FROM LAVATER'S ESSAY ON PHYSIOGNOMY.]

NATIONAL CHARACTERS.

[FROM THE SAME]

THE ENGLISHMAN.

THE Englishman is erect in his gait, and generally stands as if a stake were driven through his body. His nerves are strong, and he is the best runner. He is distinguished from all other men by the roundness and smoothness of the muscles of his face. If he neither speak nor move, he seldom declares the capability and mind he possesses in so superior a degree.—His silent eye seeks not to please. His hair, coat, and character, alike are smooth. Not cunning, but on his guard, and perhaps but little colouring is necessary to deceive him, on any occasion. Like the bull dog, he does not bark; but if irritated, rages. As he wishes not for more esteem than he merits, so he detests the false pretensions of his neighbours, who would arrogate excellence they do not possess. Desirous of private happiness, he disregards public opinion, and obtains a character of singularity.

THE GERMAN.

A German thinks it disgraceful not to know every thing, and dreads nothing so much as to be thought a fool. Probity often makes him appear a blockhead. Of nothing is he so proud as of honest, moral understanding. According to modern tactics he is certainly the best soldier, and the teacher of all Europe. He is allowed to be the greatest inventor, and, often, with so little ostentation, that foreigners have, for centuries, unknown to him robbed him of his glory.

LONDON-DERRY, *October* 6

Tuesday the 29th ult. being Michaelmas Day, Wm. Ross. Esq; was sworn in Provost of the Borough of Newtown-Limavady. On this occasion, Mr. Ross gave an elegant entertainment to a polite and numerous company; and great pleasure was testified by the inhabitants of Newtown and its vicinity, on this Gentleman's being chosen, their Chief Magistrate.

For some time past, the weather has been extremely unfavouarble to the harvest, which, in this part of the country, is very late—but, on the night between Wednesday and Thursday last, a most violent storm of wind and rain came on, which continued with little intermission till Saturday. Our accounts from every quarter relate the destruction of vast quantities of grain, hay, and turf by the prodigious overflowing of the rivers; in particular, we learn that the damage on the banks of the Faughan has been immense, where, besides the injury done to the various mills and bleach-greens on that water, a bridge, several horses and cows, and a great number of linen webs, and three men have been swept away by the impetuous flood.

MARRIED.] Alex. Brown, Gent. one of the Attornies of his Majesty's Court of Exchequer, to Miss Anna Maria Maddan.

SHIP NEWS

ARRIVED from
Oporto, Ann, Scott, wine.
London, Nancy, Dedwith, merchandise.
Liverpool, Volunteer, Campbell, do.
Moldieu, Saltam, Reed, deals.

Belfast, *October* 13.

*** Having found by experience that, with the utmost care on our part, mistakes prejudicial to our advertising friends unavoidably arise from the custom of occasionally inserting advertisements ONCE A WEEK—we are obliged to give this notice that they will be henceforth continued twice a week, without intermission, for whatever publications may be ordered. It is respectfully requested that the exact number of times may be expressed.

At a meeting of the Inhabitants of this town, held yesterday, for the purpose of having the town lighted during the winter, it was determined unanimously, that it should be done by a General Subscription, and a Committee was appointed to collect the subscriptions and direct the expenditure.

We have the pleasure of hearing that Sir James Bristow, commander of the Langrishe cruiser, a few days ago took a smuggling cutter with a very valuable cargo of tobacco and spirits. He started her at Red Bay, and run her a-shore at Portpatrick. The smugglers had not time to land any of her cargo.

We are informed that Mrs. ARNOLD, first Singer at the Rotunda in Dublin, arrived here on Sunday evening, and purposes having a *Grand Musical Fete* at the Exchange Rooms in the course of next week.

On Thursday morning last, the fore axle tree of the mail coach, from this town, broke a little beyond the Malone turnpike; the horses run a quarter of a mile before they were stopped, but no accident happened save the coachman being slightly hurt. And on Saturday night last, the coach downwards was delayed upwards of two hours, beyond the usual time, by accidents of a similar nature on the road.

The Porcupine sloop of war arrived in this harbour on Sunday last.

An adjournment of the Quarter Sessions of the county of Downe, will be held at Hillsborough, on Wednesday next, the 14th inst.

PORT NEWS.

ARRIVED.

Oct. 6. Brothers, English, Alicant, barrilla.
8. Betty, Campbell, Glasgow, rum.
Seven Colliers, coals.

CLEARED OUT.

Oct. 3. Peggy, M'llroy, Livepool, cloth.
6. Linen Hall, Dickson, London, do.
8. Lord Charlemont, Dillon, St. Vincents, do.
10. Fortitude, Glasgow, Gibraltar, do.
New Draper, Kearney, Liverpool, do. and butter.

Belfast, *October* 16.

Extract of a Letter from Gibraltar from an Officer of that Garrison, dated the 6th Sept. 1789.

"This garrison is extremely improved since you left us—we are supplied with all kinds of provisions and in the greatest abundance from Barbary.—The Spaniards send in quantities of fruit, and pork in high perfection; but we are in appearance as far as ever from having the communication open. General O'Hara is very much liked by us all, and indeed we are as happy as men in a state of confinement can be."

BIRTH. At Purdisburn, the Lady of the Bishop of Down of a daughter.

Married, a few days ago, Mr. James Caldwell, of Tullyhappy, near Newry, to Miss Dalzell, of Armagh.

FAIRS IN THE ENSUING WEEK.

Monday, Oct. 19. Comber, Down.—Tuesday 20. Castlederg, Tyr. Oldtown, Don. Straid, Ant. Tubermore, Der. Wed. 21. Ballimena, Ant. Bushmills, Ant. Jonesboro', Arm.—Thursday 22. Donaghmore, Down. Oldstone, Ant.—Saturday, 24. Gorten, Tyr.

PRICES IN THIS MARKET YESTERDAY.

Oatmeal,	9s.	6d.	to	10s.	0d.	Dried do. 25s. to 26s. 0d per d
Wheat,	9	0	—	9	6	R. Tallow, 5s. a 5s. 4d. per st.
Oats,	5	0	—	5	4	Potatoes 9d. to 10d per b.
Barley,	5	0	—	5	6	Eng. coals, 00s. to 14s. 0d.
Butter,	51	0	—	52	0	Scotch do. 00s. to 13s. 0d.
C. hides,	00	0	—	35	0	Ex. on Lond 6 3-4 a 7 per c.
Ox ditto,	38	6	—	40	0	Do. on Glasgow 6½.
S.C. skins	00	0	—	42	6	

Anno 1789.] Printed by HENRY JOY, and Co. BELFAST.

The BELFAST NEWS-LETTER.

TUESDAY October 20, FRIDAY October 23, 1789.

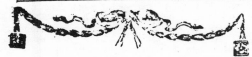

IRREGULAR ODE.

TO THE MOON.

TO thee the ſcreech-owl cries,
The wolf to thee, and all the tribes of prey
That ſhun the honeſt day,
And ſhrink from human eyes.
They call thee not to gild the midnight hour;
They deprecate thy pow'r;
They call thee, with a duſky cloud
Thy beauteous face to ſhroud,
'Till the nightly ſpoil is won,
'Till the feaſt of blood is done,
And deep within his den the glutted ſavage lies.
Nor beaſts alone that prowl for food,
More ſavage men thine influence feel;
Thy virgin preſence daunts
The robber in his haunts;
Th' aſſaſſin ſtays th' uplifted ſteel,
And when he ſees the victim nigh,
And when the poignard thirſts for blood,
Smote by thy ſacred eye,
He feels an icy dart
Transfix his coward heart,
And flies!

LONDON PORTER.

SAMUEL and ANDREW Mc. CLEAN have receiv-ed per the Charlotte, Capt. Campbell, a freſh ſupply of Whitbread's Porter;—and have alſo on hand *five* Puncheons of their laſt Cargo of Engliſh Cyder, which they will ſell cheap.

Belfaſt, 19th Oct. 1789.

Iriſh Woollen Warehouſe,
BELFAST.

SAMUEL NEILSON, and CO. are juſt receiving their *Winter Aſſortment of Iriſh* manufactures, which will be ſold cheap for caſh or bills.

21ſt October, 1789.

☞ The ſame diſcount allowed on *pins* as in Dublin.

New Dantzig and Pearl Aſhes.

DUKE BERWICK has juſt received per the Elizabeth, from Dantzig, a large parcel of new Aſhes, and has now for ſale a conſiderable quantity of Scale Sugars of different qualities, which will be ſold on reaſonable terms.

Belfaſt, 19th Oct. 1789.

New Woollen Warehouſe.

HASLETT, STRONG, and CO. have this day received per the Peggy, from Liverpool, the firſt parcel of their winter aſſortment, conſiſting of Coatings, Naps, Wildbore Stuffs, &c. which, as uſual, they will ſell on the moſt reaſonable terms, for Belfaſt Bank Notes, or good Bills.

Belfaſt, 19th Oct. 1789.

American Pot-Aſhes, &c.

HUGH CRAWFORD is now landing a large parcel of American Pot-Aſhes—the firſt ſort. He is largely ſupplied with Alicant and Carthagena Barilla, beſt and ſecond Dantzig aſhes, a large ſtock of Teas from laſt ſales, white and yellow cotton wool, Jamaica rum and ſugar, with many other articles;—both prices and quality will be found pleaſing to his Cuſtomers and the Public.

He expects a parcel of new Fruit in daily;——he has alſo for ſale 96 hogſheads of very beſt Virginia Leaf Tobacco that will be ſold cheap. Belfaſt, 19th Oct. 1789.

Robert Knox,

HAS juſt arrived a few hogſheads of very fine Virginia Leaf Tobacco, which, with Strong Jamaica Rum, he will ſell by the hogſhead and puncheon on moderate terms;—alſo a quantity of old Cheſhire Cheeſe.

Belfaſt, 19th October, 1789.

A General Half-yearly Meeting of the Belfaſt Annuity Company will be held at the Market Houſe in Belfaſt, on Monday the 2d day of November next, at eleven o'clock in the forenoon, for the purpoſe of electing a Preſident, Secretary and Committee, paying the half-yearly Subſcriptions then due, and to ballot for nine Gentlemen who have propoſed to become Members.

Belfaſt, 16th October, 1789.

HUGH CRAWFORD, Secretary.

THIS DAY WAS PUBLISHED,

BY GRUEBER AND M'ALLISTER,

No. 59, DAME-STREET, DUBLIN——

ADAMS's FLOWERS of antient and modern Hiſtory; comprehending on a new plan, the moſt remarkable Revolutions and Events, as well as the moſt eminent and illuſtrious Characters of antient and modern Times; with a view of the progreſs of Society and Manners, Arts and Sciences, from the earlieſt time to the concluſion of the American War, 2 vols. 6s. 6d.

This Selection of the Beauties of Hiſtory, will be found to merit the title it aſſumes, being truly the moſt elegant FLOWERS that could be culled from the wide field of antient and modern knowledge. A work of this kind, arranged as it is with judgment, muſt not only be conſidered as a valuable addition to the ſchools, but will alſo be found an excellent remembrancer to thoſe who wiſh to refreſh their minds with the moſt intereſting occurrences in hiſtory.

A moſt convenient Town Park and ſeveral Tenements,

TO be ſold by public Auction, on Friday the 30th day of October inſtant, at the Market-houſe in Belfaſt, at 12 o'Clock forenoon,—a Leaſe under Lord Donegall, of which five Years and a half remain from the 1ſt of November next unexpired, conſiſting of three Tenements in Pottinger-Entry, one of which is held by Mrs. Park for the full term, at the yearly rent of 10l. 18s. the other two pay only 3l. 9s. 5d. until November 1791, when the Leaſe will expire and they will riſe very conſiderably; and alſo of a FIELD adjoining the Poor-houſe Concern, in Fiſhers-row, containing three Acres and a half, upon which ſeventeen Cabbins have been built, which is entirely out of Leaſe at the 1ſt of November next; the whole Concern is ſubject to the yearly rent of 10l. 10s.

The Title Deeds may be ſeen and every information given by applying to Mr. Alexander Arthur, Attorney. The one half of the Purchaſe Money to be paid at the time of Sale, the remainder upon the Deeds being perfected.

Belfaſt, October 14th, 1789.

COUNTY OF ARMAGH. } THERE will be an adjournment of the Quarter Seſſions held at Richhill, on Saturday the thirty-firſt day of October inſtant.

Dated this 10th day of October, 1789.

JAMES VERNER, Sheriff.

To be Let,

From the firſt of next November,

THE Houſe in Caſtle-Street, occupied at preſent by Doctor Bell.———For particulars enquire at the Houſe.

October 19th, 1789.

Meſſrs. Reed, and Co. of Portaferry,

RETURN their ſincere thanks to their numerous Friends and Cuſtomers, ſince their commencement in the Brewing Buſineſs, and take this public opportunity of letting them know that the company account is to be ſettled early in November firſt, and requeſt that all indebted to ſaid Company may be prepared to pay off their reſpective debts, as a perſon will be ſent in a few days to collect the ſame.

Portaferry, 21ſt October, 1789.

The Dwelling-houſe, in Roſmary-lane,

OCCUPIED by Val. Jones, is to be let from the firſt of November.

Apply to Mr. Jones or to David Tomb.

Downpatrick School

REVD. RALPH WILD has taken, for the accommodation of Boarders, the houſe at preſent occupied by Mrs. Hurly, and ſhall have it ready for their reception in about a month. It is in an airy part of the town, and very convenient to the country.——Terms; twenty guineas a year, and four guineas entrance.

Downpatrick, 19th Oct. 1789.

Cheap Spirits.

THOMAS DAVISON, near Broughſhane, (at the inſtance of many of his Friends, and for the accommodation of his Cuſtomers in the Whiſky line)—has received a ſupply of foreign Spirits, viz. Rum, Brandy and Geneva, which he will ſell either as imported or reduced, in any quantity not leſs than one gallon, at the Belfaſt Prices

Having formed a connection with a conſiderable importing houſe in Belfaſt in this line—his friends may depend that he will be conſtantly ſupplied with a good aſſortment.——Good bills on Dublin or Belfaſt, not exceeding three months, will be taken in payment, or a diſcount of 1½ per cent. allowed for Guineas or Belfaſt Bank Notes.

Knockboy, 21ſt Oct. 1789.

Burglary & Reward.

WHEREAS the Shop of Hugh and William Johnſon was broke open on the night between the 17th and 18th inſt. and a large quantity of Goods of different kinds carried away.

NOW, in order to bring to puniſhment the perſons guilty of ſaid offence, we do hereby promiſe to pay, in proportion to the ſums to our names reſpectively annexed, a reward of ONE HUNDRED GUINEAS to whomſoever ſhall within ſix months from this date, diſcover or and proſecute to conviction any of the perſons guilty of ſaid Burglary;—and in caſe any perſon concerned ſhall diſcover on his or her accomplices, he or ſhe ſhall, on their conviction, be entitled to the above reward, and to his Majeſty's moſt gracious Pardon.

Belfaſt, 19th October, 1789.

	l.	s.	d.
Sam. Black, Sovn	11	7	6
Wm. Briſtow	11	7	6
Edward Kingſmill	11	7	6
Stewart Banks	11	7	6
John Brown	11	7	6
Ewing, Holmes & Co.	11	7	6
Cunningham, Campbell & Co.	11	7	6
Stewarts, Thompſon & Co.	11	7	6
Montgomery, Brown, Tennent, and Joyle	11	7	6
John Boyle & Co.	11	7	6
Brown & Oakman	11	7	6
Jones, Tomb, Joy & Co.	11	7	6
Narciſſus Batt	11	7	6
Thos. Sinclaire & Sons	11	7	6
Cunningham Greg	11	7	6
Henry Joy & Co.	5	13	9
Robert Apſley	5	13	9
James Ferguſon	5	13	9
Wm. Clark	5	13	9
John Robinſon	5	13	9
Wm. Stevenſon	5	13	9
Robt. & Wm. Simms	5	13	9
Daviſon & Miniſs	5	13	9
M'Kinzie & M'Cleery	5	13	9
Gilbt. Mc. Ilveen, junr.	5	13	9
Sam. Ferguſon	5	13	9
David Mc. Tier	5	13	9
Wm. Irwin	5	13	9
Thos. Milliken	5	13	9
James Stevenſon	5	13	9
John Gregg	5	13	9
Wm. Burgeſs	5	13	9
Robert Bradſhaw	5	13	9
Charles Brett	5	13	9
Thomas Lyle	5	13	9
Thompſon & Oakman	5	13	9
Hugh Crawford	5	13	9
Francis Joy & Co.	5	13	9
Robert Getty	5	13	9
Haſlett, Strong & Co.	5	13	9
Samuel Gibſon	5	13	9
Chriſt Hudſon	5	13	9
John Galt Smith	5	13	9
James Hyndman	5	13	9
Hill Hamilton	5	13	9
Forſyth Shaw & Co.	5	13	9
Robert Willſon & Co.	5	13	9
Joſeph Stevenſon	5	13	9
Robt. & H. Hyndman	5	13	9
Sam. M'Murry & Co.	15	3	9
Henderſon & Crawford	5	13	9
Lukes, Oakman & Co.	5	13	9
Thos. Stewart	5	13	9
Val. Joyce	5	13	9
David Dunn	5	13	9
Daviſon & Graham	5	13	9
Alex. Arthur	5	13	9
Hu. Montgomery	5	13	9
Robert Scott	5	13	9
John Cunningham	5	13	9
Alex Orr	5	13	9
Thos. Neilſon & Co.	5	13	9

	l.	s.	d.
David Biggar	5	13	9
Jas. & A. M'Ilrath	5	13	9
Sam. Brown & Co.	5	13	9
Thos. Andrews	5	13	9
Sam. Neilſon & Co.	5	13	9
William Lemmon	4	11	0
William Bryſon	4	11	0
John Elliott	4	11	0
William Magee	4	11	0
William Anderſon	4	11	0
Sam. and A. M Clean	4	11	0
Francis Davis	4	11	0
James Beggs & Co	3	8	3
Alexander Neilſon	3	8	3
Richard M'Clelland	3	8	3
Patterſon & Whittle	3	8	3
Iſaac Patton	3	8	3
John Daviſon	3	8	3
Thomas Major	3	8	3
George Langtry	3	8	3
William M'Clure	3	8	3
Robert Knox	3	8	3
Duke Berwick	3	8	3
Thomas M'Cabe	3	8	3
John Smyth	3	8	3
John M'Millen	3	8	3
Hugh Willſon	3	8	3
Hugh M'Ilwain	3	8	3
John Craig	3	8	3
Alex. Armſtrong	3	8	3
John Murdoch	3	8	3
Thos. Cavan	3	8	3
John M'Atee	3	8	3
John Bankhead	3	8	3
Wm. Hendren	3	8	3
Wm. Emerſon	3	8	3
Taylor, Maxwell & Co	3	8	3
Alex. Sinclaire	3	8	3
Pat. Gaw	3	8	3
John Martin	2	5	6
Hugh Warren	2	5	6
Wm. Calwell	2	5	6
Orr Reid	2	5	6
Sam. Mitchell	2	5	6
James Graham	2	5	6
Robert Orr	2	5	6
John Hughes	2	5	6
John Aſhmore	2	5	6
Thomas Parker	2	5	6
David Watſon	2	5	6
Robt. W. Mc. Clure	2	5	6
James Clelland	2	5	6
Mc. Kain and Sherridan	2	5	6
George Bradford	2	5	6
Samuel Woolſey	2	5	6
David Dinſmore	2	5	6
Catharine Calwell	2	5	6
John Vance	2	5	6
Robert Dempſter	2	5	6
Hugh Dunlap	2	5	6
John Knox	2	5	6
James Weir	2	5	6
Theburn and Munford	2	5	6
Sam. Robinſon	1	2	9
Alexander Watt	1	2	9
A. Hadſkis	1	2	9
Robert Smyth	1	2	9
Robert Steel	1	2	9
Brown Gaw and Co	17	1	3
Hugh and William Johnſton	22	15	0

☞ *Ten Guineas* will be paid by W. JOHNSON to any perſon who ſhall give the *moſt private information* that may lead to a diſcovery—and the diſcover's name ſhall be kept inviolably ſecret.

PARIS, Oct. 7.

Farther Particulars of the present TUMULTS *in* FRANCE.

The King's government may now be supposed to be at an end. His situation is truly deplorable. When he was at Versailles he did not think his life secure, though he was surrounded by the corps of Life Guards, the 100 Swiss, and the regiment of dragoons called *les Trois Eveches*, from the three bishoprics of Toul, Metz and Verdun, in Lorraine, where it was raised. ——It was resolved, therefore, by the Council, in consequence of his Majesty's wish, that another regiment should be ordered to Versailles, to duty about the King. In the selection of this regiment, which was to be added to the King's guards, the ministers considered principally that which was eminently distinguished for an attachment to his Majesty's person. The regiment du Roi, or the King's own regiment, would therefore have been singled out on this very account; but it consisted of four battalions, and it was feared that the approach of so very numerous a corps would have given umbrage to the people. The well-known attachment of the Marquis de Lusignan to the person of Louis XVI. and the attachment of his regiment to their Colonel, determined the King to order the regiment de Flandre, commanded by that nobleman, to march to Versailles.

The military etiquette of France has established a custom through the service, that when a regiment marches into a town where there are troops in garrison, it is always entertained at the expence of those troops. In consequence of this etiquette, and by no means through design, the officers of the Flanders regiment were invited to dinner by the Life Guards. The dinner was served up on the stage of the Opera House in the Palace, as the most capacious place. When the glass had circulated rather freely, some toasts were given by the Life Guards, strongly expressive of loyalty to the King. The officers of the Flanders regiment shouted approbation when they heared them, and drank them in the English style with loud huzzas. This convinced the Life Guards that their guests and they were all of one mind; and then it was, that the proposal was made for trampling under foot the national cockade, in which all joined most heartily.

The appearance of the King and Queen, with the Dauphin, who entered the place merely to do honour to the guests, encreased the flow of loyalty: but when the music struck up the air of, 'O Richard—O my King,' the allusion to his Majesty's situation, which those who ordered the band to play this tune would have thought to be like that of Richard Cœur de Lion, the situation of a Monarch deprived of his liberty, the officers felt themselves wound up to the highest pitch, and as if animated by one soul, began to sing the words of the song. The King himself was affected; he immediately walked out, unable to speak, and with his handkerchief up to his eyes. The officers then solemnly pledged themselves to one another, that they would stand by their King, release him from the bondage in which he was kept, or perish in the attempt.

These gentlemen, however, were comparatively few in number; and therefore, though they were of approved gallantry, they knew that if they were not backed by their soldiers, they could do nothing. Such of the non commissioned officers and privates as were known to have most influence on their fellow soldiers, were called in and sounded. They declared their readiness to fight for their King, and second their officers in what they called a glorious cause. The officers, thus sure of support, treated the Garde Bourgeoise with sovereign contempt, ridiculed their unmilitary appearance, and insulted their national cockade.

One of the Secretaries then announced a letter from two English Gentlemen, written in the English language, in which these strangers begged leave to compliment the National Assembly, felicitate them on the freedom they had already acquired, and offer up their vows for the future liberty of France.

LONDON.

The Marquis of Buckingham will shortly resign the Viceroyship of Ireland, and only waits for his successor to be named. The Marquis retires from public business on the score of ill health.

It is with much regret we mention, that the Marquis of Buckingham is extremely ill at Stowe, and his physicians fear that he is in a rapid decline. It is solely on this account that his Lordship has never appeared in public since his arrival from Ireland.

His Grace the Duke of Beaufort will probably be the new Viceroy of Ireland.

The Spanish Gazettes are prohibited from giving any account of the Revolution in France.—Some writings are however circulated through the provinces, translated into Spanish, which are read with great avidity.

Russia itself will, before the present century expires, shake off the bear's skin, and become an enlightened people: this progress is advancing fast!

The Rev. Mr. Stockdale is now at Morocco, employed in searching the Emperor's library, with the hopes of recovering the supposed lost books of Livy.

At the public rooms at Brighton, and other watering places, the ladies are dressed in a robe something like the *Chemise*; their shoes are of different coloured sattins; chip hats are beginning to be worn, tied under the chin. The men's dresses are light pepper and salt coats, with green capes, silk waistcoats, different coloured sattin breeches, and large oval buckles; shoe strings are on the wane.

The following are the particulars of the disturbances that have taken place in Corsica:—Viscount de Barin, who had the chief military command at Bastia, hearing of the revolution in France, privately assembled at his house those persons whom he considered as most attached to him and to France. He informed them, that it was his opinion they could not give him a more substantial proof of their friendship to him, than by joining with their friends and relations, and lending him their aid to secure some of the principle inhabitants of the town. This service, he informed them, would be the more valuable and useful to him, as he could place but little reliance on the fidelity of the troops. The persons thus assembled assured the Viscount, that they were ready to do every thing that he could wish to convince him of their attachment. But one of them, more under the influence of patriotism than of private friendship for the Commandant, soon communicated to several people in Bastia the object and result of the meeting at the Viscount's house. The intelligence spread like wildfire; the inhabitants flew to arms, and the Viscount was obliged to take refuge in the Castle, beyond the works of which he did not dare to shew himself. Following the example set them by the different cities in France, the inhabitants of Bastia formed themselves into military companies, some of which patroled the city, whilst others undertook to answer for the preservation of order and tranquillity in the neighbouring villages. The example of Bastia was soon followed by Calvi and Ajaccio. The Bishop of Calvi having secretly embarked a considerable supply of corn for Marseilles, the people got intelligence of it before the vessel sailed, landed the corn, and threatened the Bishop with the effects of their indignation. The prelate not knowing what had happened at Bastia, fled thither for safety. He had the good fortune to get into the Castle; but a message was soon delivered to him there from the people of Calvi, that if he did not immediately return, and take charge of his flock, his temporalities should be seized, and his goods confiscated.

FOR THE BELFAST NEWS-LETTER.

To Mr. JOY.

SIR,

AN Inhabitant of Lisburn, who was present at the last public examination of the scholars in the poor-schools of Lurgan, requests his fellow townsmen to consider whether it might not tend much to the civilization of the lower order of children in Lisburn, many of whom for want of employment are likely to become nuisances to society instead of useful and serviceable members, to change the Sunday School, already established, into a daily school, on the plan of those above-mentioned.—A small addition to the present subscriptions would effect this good purpose, and the writer is persuaded his fellow citizens will not be behind-hand with the towns around them.—Let us, fellow citizens, for once forget our political and religious dissentions;—or if we must have contests amongst us, let it be a contest in endeavouring each to do the most good.—A very small matter from each—a small quarterly or monthly subscription would effect this good work.—Many of the Ladies and Gentlemen would willingly undertake the pleasing task of inspecting the conduct of the school, and I am sure my Lord Bishop of Down would very willingly preach a Charity Sermon in Lisburn Church to obtain a fund to set out upon.—From the amiable character of our Dissenting Minister, I cannot harbour a doubt of his heartily co-operating in the work—and the Quakers were never yet known to withhold their contribution from any charitable undertakings.

If these few hints are of any service, the end is fully answered of one that will immediately become,

A SUBSCRIBER.

LISBURN,
October 5th, 1789.

Belfast, *October* 20.

On Sunday morning one of the most daring robberies that has happened in this place was committed on the shop of Messrs. Hugh and William Johnston in Bridge-street. Tho' in a very populous part of the town, the villains had the audacity to remain till five o'clock, and deliberately carry off a great quantity of different kinds of goods, superfine cloths, cottons, stockings and fancy waistcoats. The greater part of them were afterwards found in a field near the town.

The Freeholders of the County of Antrim, resident in Belfast and its neighbourhood, may save themselves much trouble by registering their votes at the adjournment of the Sessions to this town on Friday next. It is unnecessary to add that no freeholder, possessing less than one hundred pounds a year, can vote at an election after the 25th of March, 1790, unless registered six months previous to the test of the writ.

On Friday last a most sumptuous and elegant entertainment was given at the Donegall Arms by a number of County of Down Freeholders, resident in this town and vicinity, to their worthy representative the Earl of Hillsborough, and to his most noble father the Marquis of Downshire. They were also honoured with the presence of many respectable gentlemen who accompanied both Peers, and by the Officers of the Navy and Army.

DIED.] On Friday last, Mrs. M'Tear, widow of the late Mr. James M'Tear of this town. Her conduct thro' life was truly exemplary, and during a severe and tedious illness she displayed that fortitude and resignation which are ever the characteristics of a sincere Christian. Her death is severely felt by her friends, and lamented by a numerous acquaintance.

PORT NEWS.

ARRIVED.

Oct. 13. Liberty, M'Roberts, Liverpool, salt, tobacco, &c.
15. Dick, Saunders, Chester, bark.
17. Margaret, Griffith, Liverpool, sugar, &c. Eleven colliers.

CLEARED OUT.

Oct. 15. Recovery, Nelson, Cadiz, Lisbon and Malaga, cloth and butter.
16. Walters, Munn, Gibraltar, do.
Chance, Beatton, Alicant, cloth and rum.

Belfast, *October* 23.

About ten o'clock on Monday night last a fire broke out in one of the unfinished houses in Linenhall-street, which, by the timely exertions of the inhabitants, was happily extinguished without doing any material damage. It was supposed to have been occasioned by a spark from a pipe, or a glue pot, falling among shavings.

The Freeholders of the County of Antrim, resident in Belfast and its neighbourhood, may save themselves much trouble by registering their votes at the adjournment of the Sessions to this town this day (Friday). It is unnecessary to add that no freeholder, possessing less than one hundred pounds a year, can vote at an election after the 29th of March, 1790, unless registered six months previous to the test of the writ.

An accurate account of the Heirs to the Titles of the late Earl of Huntingdon.

The Earldom alone is supposed to be extinct; or to descend to very distant branches in the male line—but the Baronies, being of more ancient tenure, descend to heirs female, and now rest in Lady Moira: they are eight—Newark, Hungerford, Hastings, Ashby, Molins, Moel, Peverell, and Bittreux——all of which will descend to Lord Rawdon upon his mother's death.

HUGH and WILLIAM JOHNSTON think it their duty in the most public manner to express their gratitude to SAMUEL BLACK, Esq. Sovereign of Belfast, for his very extraordinary exertions in endeavouring to discover the persons who broke open and robbed their shop on Sunday morning last. They cannot avoid acknowledging the affectionate zeal and activity of a number of other Gentlemen in searching for and recovering their goods.

Belfast, Oct. 22d, 1789.

PRICES IN THIS MARKET YESTERDAY.

Oatmeal,	0s.	0d.	to	10s.	0d.	Dried do. 25s. to 00s. 0d per d
Wheat,	0	0	—	9	6	R. Tallow, 5s. 4d. per st.
Oats,	5	0	—	0	0	Potatoes 9d. to 10d per b.
Barley,	0	0	—	5	4	Eng. coals, 00s. to 14s. 0d.
Butter,	51	0	—	00	0	Scotch do. 00s. to 13s. 0d.
C. hides,	00	0	—	35	0	Ex. on Lond. 7 per cent.
Ox ditto,	00	0	—	40	0	Do. on Glasgow 6½.
S.C. skins	00	0	—	40	6	

FAIRS IN THE ENSUING WEEK.

Monday 26th. Convoy, Down. Culloville, Arm. 2 days. Dungiven, Der. Killeter, Tyr. Market-hill, Arm. Saintfield, Down. Tuesday 27th. Castlereagh, Down. Dervock, Ant. Templepatrick, Ant. Wednesday 28th. Benburbe, Tyr. Connor, Ant. Donegall Town. Thursday 29th. Downpatrick, Down. Fintown, Tyr. Glenarm, Ant. Glenavy, Ant. Greyabby, Down. Maghrafelt, Der. Newry, Down. Newtown Cunningham, Don. Newtownlemivaddy, Der. Saturday 31. Carrigait, Don. Glasslough, Mon. Mahery, Arm. Malin, Don.

Anno 1789.] Printed by HENRY JOY, and Co. BELFAST.

The BELFAST NEWS-LETTER.

TUESDAY October 27, FRIDAY October 30, 1789.

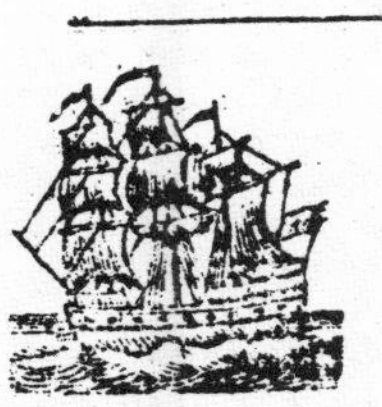

The CHARLOTTE,
WM. CAMPBELL, Maſter,
For *LONDON*,

WILL clear out the firſt of next month, and ſail firſt fair wind after.
Belfaſt, 8th Oct. 1789.

Samuel Hyde, Robt. Thompſon, Samuel Brown, William Sinclaire, Robert Bradſhaw, Jacob Hancock, David Wilſon, Valentine Smith, James Stevenſon.

Second and laſt Concert.

MRS ARNOLD, impreſſed with the moſt lively feelings of gratitude and admiration at the very marked and peculiar attention of the numerous friends who generouſly honoured her Concert on Thurſday Evening with their preſence; begs leave to make them her moſt fervent acknowledgments: and as ſhe is informed that many who could not then conveniently attend, wiſhed to have been preſent; and that ſeveral then preſent will indulge a ſecond attempt with their kind ſupport, ſhe moſt reſpectively acquaints the Ladies and Gentlemen of Belfaſt, and its environs, that (poſitively the laſt Night) on *Friday Evening* next, the 30th October, at the *Exchange-Rooms*, will be a CONCERT of MUSIC, *Vocal* and *Inſtrumental*; to be conducted in the moſt elegant manner.

Half the *Receipts* to be appropriated to the expences of the *Concert*, *the other Half* to be paid the *Charitable Committee*, FOR THE BENEFIT OF THE POOR.

Admittance, {Gentlemen, 3s. 3d.—Ladies, 2s. 8d. h. and Children, 1s. 7d. h. each.

N. B. The Concert will begin preciſely at eight o'clock, and conclude about ten.

Concert and Ball.

AT THE ASSEMBLY-ROOM, ANTRIM,

ON Friday evening next, the 30th October, inſtant, there will be performed a grand CONCERT of MUSICK;—the band to conſiſt of Violins, Tenors, Violincellos, Flutes, Clarrionets, Horns, and a Double Baſs.

Firſt Violin, by Mr. Mahoon, from London.

Principal Flute, by Mr. Aſhe, from Dublin.

Particulars at large in hand bills.—The Performance to begin exactly at ſeven o'clock—and tickets (at 2s. 8d. h. each) to be had of Mr. Robert Young, Antrim; and of Meſſrs. Aſhe and Mahoon, Shanes-Caſtle.

Poor-houſe,

THE Committee of the BELFAST CHARITABLE SOCIETY, hereby give notice, that, (in conſequence of an order of the general Board of the 13th June laſt) they are ready to receive propoſals for ſupplying the Houſe by Contract, for one year from the 1ſt November next, with the following articles, viz—Bread, Beer, Meal, Peas, Coals, Potatoes, Barley, Soap and Candles. A Schedule of the quantity of each Article, as it will be required weekly through the Year will be had on application to Mr. Alexander at the Poorhouſe. The Propoſals are to be ſent (ſealed up and directed) to the Chairman of the Committee which ſits every Saturday.——Belfaſt, Oct. 28, 1789.

A Genteel firſt Floor to let, elegantly furniſhed, for any length of time, with ſtabling for a pair of horſes if required, at John Bailie's, Chicheſter-Quay.
Belfaſt, 29th October, 1789.

N. B. An exceeding good one-horſe Chaiſe, and a Pheaton, with harneſs for each, to be ſold by auction at the Donegall-Arms, on Friday next the 6th of November, at the hour of 12 at noon, by ſaid Bailie.

To be continued three times.

Liquorice-Ball, &c.

CUNNINGHAM GREG is juſt landing out of the Margaret and Jennet, from Leghorn, a parcel of caſes of Liquorice-Ball, a few caſks of Cream Tartar, and bags of Alleppo Galls, which will be diſpoſed of on reaſonable terms at his ſtores in Ann ſtreet.
Belfaſt, 29th Oct. 1789.

BALL.

MR. DUMONT reſpectfully acquaints the Ladies and Gentlemen of Belfaſt and its vicinity, that his Scholars BALL is fixed for Thurſday the fifth November, at the Aſſembly-Rooms, in the Poor-houſe. Cotillons, and a variety of Dances to be performed between the Sets of Country Dances.——Tickets 3s 3d. each (Tea included) to be had at Mr. Forcade's, High-ſtreet.
Belfaſt, Friday 30th October, 1789.

AT a Meeting of the Pariſhioners of Killileagh, on Friday the 16th October, 1789.
Dr. LITTLE in the Chair.

The following Reſolutions were agreed to:

1ſt. That by engaging with the Rector to lay a certain annual ſum on the pariſh for their tythes during his incumbency, (of which each individual who ſigns the deed is only bound for his own proportion) the pariſhioners have preſerved themſelves from tythe-farmers; and by laying this ſum fairly on the pariſh, quantity and quality of the land conſidered, the more ſubſtantial landholders have by taking their full ſhare of the public burthen, manifeſted a laudable attention to the intereſts of their neighbours in lower claſſes, and in this ſet an example worthy to be followed.

2d. That thanks be returned to Sir John Blackwood of Ballyleedy, Bart. and Gawin Hamilton of Killileagh, Eſq; (the latter being abſent) for their kind and polite anſwers to the letters of the pariſhioners on the ſubject of tythes, and for their protection and good offices on all occaſions.

3d. That thanks be returned to Mr. Thos. Oſborne and the Tythe-Committees, both general and particular; to the former for fixing ſo juſtly the relative value of the tythes in the ſeveral townlands; to the latter for ſetting the relative value of the tythes of the ſeveral holdings in each townland, and ſo laying the whole ſum fairly on the pariſh.

Doctor Little having left the Chair, and Mr. James Richardſon having taken it—Reſolved

4thly, That thanks be returned to Doctor Little for the plan of agreement for the tythes, and the exertion of his influence in carrying it generally into effect; for promoting at all times as much as in him lies the intereſts of this pariſh and of his country, and ably diſcharging his profeſſional duties as an honeſt man.

Woollen Drapery, &c.

(At and under prime Coſt.)

TO be ſold at the Shop of the late Mr. Thomas Mc. Quoid of Downpatrick, (for ready money only) the entire Stock of Goods now on hand, conſiſting of ſuperfine and coarſe broad and foreſt cloths, rugs, coatings, thickſets, cords, velverets, ſattinets, florentines, printed cottons and linens, Marſeilles quiltings and dimities, callimancoes and ſerges, wildbores and durants, crapes, gauzes, ſilk and cotton handkerchiefs, flannel and Padua ſerge, checkers, metal, legee and hair buttons, mens hats, gloves, ribbons, &c. &c. with many other articles too tedious to inſert.——Such perſons as are indebted to the late Mr. Mc. Quoid, are deſired immediately to diſcharge the reſpective ſums due by them, otherwiſe the ſpeedieſt method will be taken for recovery thereof.

James Neill is empowered by the executors to receive the debts and diſpoſe of the Goods.
Downpatrick, 21ſt Oct. 1789.

THE Publick are cautioned againſt taking a joint note of James Harrot, ſenr and junr. payable to James Martin and William Whitla, for three pounds, nineteen ſhillings and ſeven pence halfpenny ſterl. as there was no value received.
THOMAS CLARK.

ARMAGH, October 19th, 1789

WHEREAS on Saturday night the 17th inſt. the Coach-houſe of Thomas M'Can, Eſq; chief Magiſtrate of this city, was unlawfully entered by ſome perſon or perſons unknown, who in a moſt wanton and malicious manner cut and almoſt deſtroyed his Poſt-Chaiſe.——Now, in order to put a ſtop (as far as in us lies) to ſuch wicked acts, and in particular to ſhew our deteſtation of the above outrage;—We the undernamed inhabitants of Armagh, do promiſe to pay the ſeveral ſums annexed to our reſpective names, to any perſon who ſhall within twelve kalendar months from this date, diſcover and proſecute to conviction the perpetrators of the above wicked and malicious outrage.

AND whereas there is reaſon to ſuppoſe that the above outrage originated in the malice of ſome who were offended with Mr. M'Can for the diſcharge of his duty as a Magiſtrate. we, duly ſenſible how neceſſary it is to the due execution of the laws, upon which the ſecurity of our lives and properties depends, to preſerve the Magiſtrate free from all apprehenſion of danger or acts of private malice and revenge,—Do hereby engage to ſupport him to the utmoſt of our power in the execution of his office; and we moreover engage to pay the like ſums as are now annexed to our names for the diſcovering and proſecuting to conviction any perſons who ſhall in future feloniouſly injure the property of the chief Magiſtrate or of any of the Subſcribers.

Signed by the principal Inhabitants of Armagh, who have ſubſcribed 188l. 16s. 6d. for the above purpoſe.

NOW ſelling at the New Sugar-Houſe, Waring-ſtreet, by Montgomery, Brown, Tennent, and Boyle, fine SCALE SUGAR, at 8s. 6d. per ſtone—ſecond Scale, 7s. 6d.—and third Scale, 7s.
27th October, 1789.

Wanted immediately,

TWO Servants to take care of horſes, and attend at table occaſionally.——Apply at this Office
Belfaſt, 29th October, 1789.

Cuſtom-houſe, Strangford.

ON Thurſday the 6th of November next, will be ſold by public auction, preciſely at 12 o'clock,
20 Kegs of Brandy,
10 of Rum,
10 of Geneva,
2 Cheſts of Tea in 4lb. bags,
1 Cwt. of Tobacco,
12 Small Rolls of Pigtail Tobacco,
being part of the Seizure ſaved out of the Cutter Swan of Weick, wrecked on the Back Shore
28th October, 1789.

Glaſgow College, Oct. 22, 1789.

THE following Medical Lectures will commence on Tueſday the third of November:

Theory and Practice of Phyſic, at 12 o'clock, by Drs. Stephenſon and Hope.

Materia Medica, at one o'clock, by Dr. Cleghorn.

Anatomy and Surgery, at two o'clock, by Mr. Hamilton.

Chemiſtry, at ſeven o'clock in the evening, by Dr. Hope.

On Monday November 16, at ten o'clock forenoon, Clinical and Caſe Lectures, by Dr. Cleghorn.

On Monday Nov. 23d, at 5 o'clock afternoon, Midwifery, by Mr. Hamilton.

Next May, Botany, by Mr Hamilton.

Land in Dunany, in the Pariſh of Carmoney.

ON Friday the ſixth of November next, will be ſold by auction, at the Market-houſe in Belfaſt—a leaſe of which 19 years are unexpired, of nineteen acres of land in Dunany, held under Thomas Stewart, Eſq; by Mary and John Mc. Neill, at the yearly rent of 20l. 8s. 6d. The land is all arable and meadow, and delightfully ſituated, commanding an extenſive proſpect of Belfaſt harbour and the ſurrounding country The purchaſer to be put in immediate poſſeſſion.——For farther particulars pleaſe apply to Thomas Brown, Belfaſt, or John Mc. Neill on the premiſſes
Belfaſt, 29th October, 1789.

STOLEN,

ON Tueſday night 27th inſt. out of the ſtable of Hugh Gribben, a Black Horſe, ſhort tail'd, with a Star on his forehead.——Whoever returns ſaid horſe to Adam Chriſtie, near the Poor-houſe, ſhall receive one Guinea reward.
Belfaſt, October 29th, 1789.

STOLEN

OUT of a field near Killylea, in the county Armagh, on Saturday night the 24th inſtant, a ſtrong made coarſe Black Horſe, riſing four years old, thirteen hands high, his tail ſet and cut, a ſmall ſtar, ſome white on one of his hind feet, and a few white hairs under the ſaddle.——Whoever returns ſaid horſe to Bernard Mc. Quade of Annagharap, near Killylea, ſhall receive half a guinea reward. or two guineas for the horſe and thief.
Dated 25th October, 1789.
BERNARD Mc. QUADE.

WHEREAS the Bleach-yard of Thomas Stott and Co. was feloniouſly robbed of *Six Pieces of Cambrick*, fully white, on the night of the 21ſt inſtant; we promiſe to pay the ſum of 20l. Sterl. in addition to the above reward of 105l. to any perſon who will give us ſuch information as may lead to a diſcovery and conviction of the perſon or perſons concerned in ſaid robbery.——Dromore, 23d Oct 1789.
THOs. STOTT & Co

Any perſon who will give ſuch information as may lead to a diſcovery, ſhall be handſomely rewarded, and their names kept ſecret.

The Merry Career,

DINE at James Tracey's, Dungannon, on Monday the ſecond of November next; the Club hounds to be on Lowertown-hill, preciſely at eight o'clock, where a Fox is to be unbagg'd.
THOs. RICHARDSON,
Oct. 20th, 1789. Preſident.

Dropped,

THE 2d. inſtant, between Mr. David Mateers corner and the Malt-mill,—a Silver Watch, makers name Stephen Cecil, Dublin, No. 364. Whoever returns her to James Mc. Clean or Robert Getgood, Watch-makers, of Belfaſt, ſhall have half a guinea reward.
October 26th, 1789.

PARIS, October 11.

Speech of M. BAILLY *to the* KING, *on Thursday the 8th instant.*

" SIRE,

"THE Representatives of the Commons of Paris have sent us as Deputies to your Majesty, to convey the tribute of their respect and love. They have charged us to express their consciousness of the honour which you have done Paris with your August Consort and the Prince, who is the hope of the nation. Sire, you have gratified our wishes; but perhaps the extent of those wishes is not perfectly known. We hope never to lose you; we demand that Paris shall be in future your chief residence; you are beloved by all your subjects, they all wish to possess you, you are to all France as dear as all France is to you, but we claim our ancient privilege. It is here, that your illustrious ancestors resided, here the French Empire was founded, and here was it raised to that height of power, which the reign of your Majesty has placed on an unshaken base. Return, Sire, to our fight, stay with us in your Capital, that this illustrious infant, so dear to you, may be educated amongst us. He will learn our sentiments, and always behold unalterable love and fidelity for the King, union and fraternity in all parts of the kingdom. We have no other advantage over the rest of your subjects, than that of living in the centre of the Empire; the centre of the Empire ought always to be the residence of the King; this prerogative was formerly ours, and we again demand it. Sire, you have regretted the circumstance of being removed from the Assembly: you have approved the Decree which renders it inseparable from your person; the Monarch, in fact, is one only with the Nation. At the moment then when liberty is renewed under your auspices, when the National Assembly is about to revive the ancient spirit of the Monarchy; when your Majesty with liberty comes to restore splendour, and perform every act of justice and bounty which is worthy your paternal heart; restore to the Capital her Kings, which contribute to her glory, and above all your presence, which constitutes her happiness!"

The KING'S *Answer.*

" THE new assurances, which you present me of the affection and fidelity of the Commons of my good town of Paris give me the most perfect satisfaction. I trust you will continue your care for the necessary subsistence of the inhabitants, and the security of public order. I voluntarily fix my chief residence in my good town of Paris, in the confidence of once more beholding the reign of peace and tranquillity. I beg leave to repeat to the National Assembly my resolution of seconding the wish it has formed of not separating itself from me. As I knew a place to be fit for the sittings, I have given the necessary orders for its preparation."

DUKE OF ORLEANS.

On Wednesday last the Duke of Orleans left Paris with an intent to come to England by way of Boulogne; but on Friday morning, just as he was going to embark, he was stopped by a body of Fish-women, who discovered his Highness, and would not permit him to go on board the vessel, but obliged him to return to his hotel, where they immediately placed a guard of the Bourgeois Militia over him, with directions not to permit the Duke to go out of the house, as they were determined he should remain in close custody until the return of a deputation they had sent to Paris, to inform the National Assembly of the event!

And these heroines also laid an embargo on every vessel in the port, in order that no person whatever might depart; which embargo was not taken off until Saturday morning.

REVOLUTION IN FLANDERS.

By yesterday's Flanders Mail, the following letter was received from a Gentleman of rank in the Austrian Netherlands, from which it appears that a Revolution in those Provinces is certainly at hand, and that they will shortly be the Theatre of War.

OSTEND, Oct. 9.

By letters just received from Antwerp, we are assured that not fewer than 10,000 men had left that city in the course of a few days.

They directed their march in separate bodies towards Breda, in that part of Brabant which belongs to the Dutch, to join a far more considerable number of Flemings, whom the Republic has not only suffered to assemble on its territory, but also to practise the use of arms, and to learn military discipline.

This army, for from its numbers it is now entitled to that name, has assembled from different quarters, in consequence of underhand invitations from the States of Brabant, whom the Emperor was so injudicious as to suppress by force, but who in their state of suppression are considered by the people as Guardians of their Country's Liberty, and its only legal Representatives.

The object of this patriotic band is to restore the Constitution, but at the same time to change its head.

They have taken a solemn oath that they will perish, or free their country from the tyranny of the House of Austria.

Though strong in their own numbers, and in the concurrence of the whole Flemish nation, the army of Patriots now at Breda, have not been rash enough to rush into a war single-handed against the whole Power of the Austrian Monarchy; they have made sure of the friendship of Holland and Prussia.

DUBLIN,

We are from credible information assured, that no business is proposed to be transacted in the New Custom-house until the end of the summer 1792; as it will be morally impossible to complete the inside work of so great a pile of building, excavate and embank the collateral docks, &c. &c.

The Earl of Westmoreland, just appointed Lord Lieutenant of this kingdom in the room of the Marquis of Buckingham, is a nobleman of between thirty and forty years of age, of an ancient and respectable family. From being of a grave and very silent cast of character, he has made no distinguished figure in the House of Lords since his accession to the honours of his house; but is deemed a man of sense and integrity. Some years ago he married Miss Child, only daughter of Mr. Child, the great banker in London; with whom he got an immense fortune, exceeding half a million sterling: and by whom he has a numerous issue. His Lady shines in the first circles, eminent for gaiety, elegance, and fashion.

Catherine Devereux, found guilty of robbery on Wednesday last, whose male associate had been found guilty likewise, but recommended to mercy, was yesterday brought to Court and pleaded pregnancy. Thirteen females were stopped according to custom, by the peace officers and constables in the street, in order to be on the Jury, one of whom, a very well dressed woman, fainted away, and when she came to herself, declared it was the opinion that she was taken up on a Green Wax Process, which she heard had been issued out, that terrified her so much. Appearing to be big with child, and not recovered from her fright, they humanely let her go away, and stopped another in her stead. After a long examination, the Jury of Matrons gave in the verdict of pregnancy. The prisoner appeared to be a wretched looking creature, without shoe or stocking, and in rags—her sentence of execution was therefore in consequence respited.

Last week, John Roe, a labourer, had his body bruised in a shocking manner, by a fall from a house in Henrietta-street.—Thomas Sullivan, a tailor, had his head cut and otherwise much bruised by bricks falling on him from a building in Dame-street——Thomas Conroy, a boy, was desperately burned from his shoulders down, by falling into a lime-kiln at Raheny.—John Kilchioan, a sawyer, had his skull fractured by a brick falling on him in Great George's-street, Rutland-square.—Margaret Holiday, a poor woman, had her leg broke by a fall down two pair of stairs in Newmarket on the Coombe.—William Brown, a painter, had his head cut desperately, and sunk between his shoulders, by a fall down two pairs of stairs, while painting a staircase in Capel-street; they were all brought to the Charitable Infirmary, Jervis-street.

LONDON-DERRY,

We are sorry to learn, that the effects of the late storm have extended over the greatest part of the kingdom.—the damages done along the banks of the river Roe, Faughan, Finn, Burndale, &c. in this neighbourhood, have been very great, vast quantities of hay, corn, and turf having been swept away by the impetuous torrents; indeed the necessary article of turf is almost totally lost, or rendered useless, in every part of the country, by the continued rains: In short, should the weather be much longer wet or tempestuous, the most serious consequences may be apprehended.

The brig Maria, Capt. Fort, from Derry to Wilmington, was spoke with in the river Delaware on the 27th of July.

The brig Keziah was also spoken with off Cape Henlopen the 28th.

On Thursday last, a most uncommon circumstance happened in the neighbourhood of this city.—As two men were tying corn on a car for the purpose of bringing it home to be stacked, in drawing the cord tight, it broke, and the man above fell down upon the one below; the latter (Matthew Leechman) was so bruised, that he died a few hours after.

Belfast, *October* 27.

The Gentlemen who have at different periods been under the tuition of the late REV. MATHEW GARNET, are reminded that their meeting is to be at the Donegall Arms this day (TUESDAY) at 12 o'clock.

Saturday last Robert Johnson, Esq. one of the representatives of the Borough of Hillsborough, being appointed Recorder by the Most Honourable the Marquis of Downshire, was sworn into office before the Worshipful Arthur Ormsby, Esq. Sovereign of the said borough.

We have the pleasure of mentioning that almost all the goods stolen out of the shop of Messrs. Johnston of this place, have been recovered; two sacks full, besides what was formerly got, having on Monday last been found under a bundle of straw in a garden in this town.

As it might lead to a discovery of the robbers, it is recommended that any persons who have lost sacks may take the trouble of examining these which contained the goods lately found—they are much worn, and one of them is mended in the inside with a small piece of brown cloth. A pitch-fork was found some days ago near the Poor-house with the first parcel of goods that were recovered.

It being a matter of doubt whether the Justices can legally adjourn the Quarter Sessions to more than one market town within the county, and consequently whether Freeholders registered at a second adjournment are entitled to vote,—it is earnestly recommended to the Freeholders of the county of Down not to register at the adjournment to Comber on the 26th of November,—but to attend at Downpatrick the first Tuesday, being the 3d of November, where a registry will be held according to act of Parliament.

The sale of the Lands advertised by Henry Bamber in the fourth page of this paper, is adjourned till Friday the 30th inst. on account of the Sessions being held at Belfast the 23d.

The Linen-hall, Capt. Dickson, loaded with linen cloth from this port to London, arrived safe at the Downs the 18th inst. after a passage of nine days.

The Margaret, Capt. Griffith, for Liverpool, has one half of her cargo on board, and will be clear to sail on Wednesday next the 28th inst. For freight or passage apply to the Captain on board.

DIED.] William Harrison, Esq.—a man of the most unblemished character and amiable dispositions. ——On his passage from America to Ireland, Mr. Edward Peers, of Lisburn; an honest man and useful member to society.

A VESTRY will be held in the Parish Church of Belfast, on Monday the 2d day of November next, at twelve o'clock at noon, for the purpose of taking the opinion of the Inhabitants of the Town in Vestry assembled, respecting the necessity of establishing a Town Watch. Oct. 26th, 1789.

Belfast, *October* 30.

A Sessions, agreeably to Act of Parliament, will be held at Downpatrick on Tuesday next the 3d of November, for the purpose of Registering Freeholders.

The Ann, Capt. Sinclair, which sailed from Larne on the 19th of June last, arrived at Charlestown after a pleasant passage of eight weeks and a few days, with her passengers all in good health.

MARRIED. Mr. Robert Dempster of this town to Miss Jane Mc. Nall of Dundonald.

FAIRS IN THE ENSUING WEEK.

Wednesday, Nov 2.—Aghygaults, Don. Ardara Don. Ballycarry, Ant. Ballimagorey, Tyr. Ballygawly, Tyr. Carrickfergus, Ant. Churchtown, Der. Dromore, Tyr. Newton-Saville, Tyr. Randalstown, Ant. Rostrevor, Down, Stuartstown, Tyr.—Tuesday 3.—Ballycastle, Ant. Beleek, Arm. Convoy, Don. Fintown, Don. Middletown, Arm. Omagh, Tyr. Tullyadonald, Don.—Wednesday 4.—Parkgate, Ant. Raphoe, Don.—Thursday 5—Garvagh, Der. Kilmore, Down. Port, Don. Tendragee, Arm.—Friday 6—Manorcunningham, Don. Sheepbridge, Down, Tullyvallen, Arm.—Saturday 7.—Cookstown, Tyr.

PRICES IN THIS MARKET YESTERDAY.

Oatmeal,	9s.	4d.	to	9s.	8d.	Dried do 25s. to 00s. 0d per d
Wheat,	9	0	—	9	6	R. Tallow, 5s. 4d. per st.
Oats,	5	0	—	0	0	Potatoes 9d. to 10d per b.
Barley,	0	0	—	5	6	Eng. coals, 00s. to 14s. 0d.
Butter,	50	0	—	00	0	Scotch do. 00s. to 13s. 0d.
C. hides,	00	0	—	35	0	Ex on Lond. 7 a 1-4 per c.
Ox ditto,	40	0	—	42	0	Do. on Glasgow 6¼.
S.C. skins	00	0	—	40	6	

Mrs. ARNOLD's LAST CONCERT.

This present Evening (FRIDAY)

FOR THE BENEFIT OF THE POOR.

In order to prevent confusion by receiving money at the doors, such Ladies and Gentlemen as conveniently can, are most respectfully entreated to send for tickets to any of the places mentioned in the printed bills.

A VESTRY will be held in the Parish Church of Belfast, on Monday the 2d day of November next, at twelve o'clock at noon, for the purpose of taking the opinion of the Inhabitants of the Town in Vestry assembled, respecting the necessity of establishing a Town Watch. Oct 26th, 1789.

LOST,

ON Thursday laft, a fmall red Pocket-book, in which there was an accepted Bill, of J. Mc. Cormick's Woodvill, on Meffrs. Curry, Belfaft, at 41 days fight, for 9l. 2s. and fome other papers; alfo two Breaft-pins with fmall Diamond in each. Whoever will return the fame to this office fhall receive half a guinea reward.
Belfaft 2d Nov. 1789.

A Caution,

NOT to hire John Breartou, my Servant. He got leave on the 5th inft. to go to Londonderry to profecute a man at the Quarter Seffions for an affault, and has not returned to his fervice. He carried off with him a new pair of Boots, a blue Cloth Surtout with a fcarlet cape ; he fhews many difcharges, particularly one of Lord Briftol's. Any one hiring him or keeping him after this notice, will be profecuted as the law directs ; and any perfon lodging him in any of his Majefty's gaols fhall be paid two Guineas, by
RICHARD LLOYD.
Tamnamore, near Dungannon,
26th of October, 1789.

To be Let,

A Farm of Land, containing 42 acres, plantation meafure, in the townland of Creaghduff: There is a good Farm Houfe and Offices on the premiffes, and its fituation very convenient, being one mile from Clough and four from Downpatrick, on the great road leading from Caftlewellan to that town.—— For further particulars enquire of James Watfon, Efq; Brookhill.
Brookhill, 28th Oct. 1789.

THE Partnerfhip of Patrick Gaw & Co. having been diffolved by mutual confent on the 3d of November, 1788 ; and, in order to have accounts fettled, their Stock in Trade will be immediately fold off at firft coft for cafh or approved bills, at their Ware-houfe, Donegall-ftreet ; confifting of an excellent affortment of

Printed Cottons and Cali-	Cotton Handkerchiefs,
coes,	Linen do.
Muflinets and Dimities,	Shawls, &c. &c.

And it is requefted that every perfon indebted to faid Partnerfhip do pay off their accounts as foon as poffible to Mr. John Mc Millen ; and alfo that all who have accounts againft the faid Partnerfhip do furnifh the fame to faid Mc. Millen in order to have them difcharged.
Belfaft, 31ft October, 1789.

JOHN CUMING,

Woollen Draper, High-ftreet, Belfaft,

GRATEFUL to his Friends and the Publick for paft favours, informs them that (being determined to quit the Woollen Bufinefs) he is now felling by wholefale and retail, his prefent Stock in Trade, firft coft, for ready money only ;—confifting of a variety of Goods in the Woollen Drapery Line, viz. Superfine and refine broad and narrow Cloths, Coatings and Bath Rugs, Cotton Thickfets and Cords, printed Calicoes, Cottons and Velverets, Fancy Waiftcoats and Stockings, with a great variety of articles in his line too tedious to infert.
Said Cuming requefts all thofe who ftand indebted to him will immediately fettle their refpective accounts, otherwife the readieft method will be taken of recovering them ; and thofe who have accounts againft him will pleafe fend them in that they may be paid as faft as poffible.
Belfaft, November 2d, 1789.

J. NIXON,

RETURNS thanks to his Friends for the liberal fupport he has experienced fince his commencement in bufinefs—begs leave to inform them he has removed from Bridge-ftreet to a more commodious Shop in High-ftreet, adjoining Mr. John Bafhford's ; where he inteuds carrying on bufinefs as ufual—and will conftantly be fupplied with a general affortment of Medicines, Perfumes, &c. &c &c.
N. B. A Lad of good education and genteel connections, will be taken as an Apprentice on moderate terms.
Belfaft, 5th Nov. 1719.

The Map of the Lough and Harbour of Belfaft.

MR. LAWSON begs leave to acquaint his Friends and the Gentlemen who favoured him with their Subfcriptions, that it is now ready for delivery, being neatly executed by an Engraver of eminence. They will be delivered at the Ballaft-Office on the terms formerly propofed. A few Copies to be difpofed of, which may be feen at his Office. Price to non-fubfcribers 6s. 6d.
November 2d, 1789.

Samuel Mc. Murray & Co.

BEG leave to inform their Friends and the Public, that they have received from the feveral places of manufacture in England and Ireland, an elegant affortment of Hofiery, fuperfine *Broad* and *Foreft Cloths, Coatings, Naps,* &c. &c. for the winter trade, which they flatter themfelves will, on infpection, be found equal to any ever offered for fale in this kingdom.—They are likewife fupplied with *Fancy Waiftcoating* and Buttons, the neweft and moft fafhionable patterns.
Belfaft, Oct. 24th, 1789.
N. B. They have conftantly for fale, on commiffion, Chequers, ftript Linens, &c. &c. from one of the firft Manufactories in the kingdom.

Wholefale Woollen Ware-houfe.

BROWN GAW & Co. have lately received, per the Peggy, and this day, per the New Loyalty, a large quantity of Goods, which compleat a very extenfive affortment for the Winter Trade. As they can with confidence affure their friends and the publick, that thofe goods were every piece carefully chofen by one of their Partners, it is hoped they will give general fatisfaction.
Belfaft, 26th October, 1789.

Hemp and Iron.

JOHN GALT SMITH & Co. are landing out of the Ann, Capt. Martin, from St. Peterfburg, a cargo of beft clean Hemp, and old Sable Iron, which they are felling on the moft reafonable terms.
Belfaft, 2d Nov. 1789.

By Defire of the Prefidents,

THE BELFAST COTERIE will be held at the Exchange-Rooms (as ufual) on Tuefday the 17th inftant.
November 2d. 1789.

THE VESTRY held yefterday in the parifh Church of Belfaft for the purpofe of confidering the neceffity of eftablifhing a Town Watch—was adjourned until this day, (Tuefday the 3d inft.) at 12 o'clock at noon.
Nov. 3d, 1789.

To be Sold for ready Money,

A Farm of Land in Gatrofs, parifh of Maralin, and county of Down, the property of Mr. Robert Lylburn, now refiding in New-York, in America—containing 37 acres, Irifh meafure, at the yearly rent of fourteen pounds five fhillings, held by leafe under the Earl of Moira, during the natural life of his prefent Majefty, King George the Third.—Application to be made to Samuel Lylburn at the Freeftone-Quarry, near Moira, who will fhew the premiffes and give every neceffary information to fuch perfons as wifh to propofe for the faid farm.
October 26th 1789.

Malaga Wine.

DAVISON and GRAHAM have on hands a few Quarter Cafks Malaga Wine, which they will fell reafonably.
Belfaft, 2d November, 1789.

WHEREAS fundry perfons, whofe papers are miflaid, and names forgotten, have made propofals to Hill Willfon, Efq; for certain farms in the lands of Magheremourne.—Notice is hereby given, that Mr. Willfon will be at Larne on Monday the 9th inftant, in order to receive propofals for and grant leafes of faid lands.
Belfaft, 2d November, 1789.

Potatoes.

A Few Tons of good Potatoes wanted immediately by ROBERT SCOTT, for which Market Price will be given.
Belfaft, 31ft October, 1789.

Larne, 31ft Oct. 1789.

A Meeting of the Creditors of the late Nathan Moore, junior, of Larne, is requefted at the Houfe of Charles Mc. Garrel, (Antrim's Arms) on Thurfday 5th November, at noon ; to confider of the moft expeditious mode of liquidating the claims of his creditors.
Larne, 31ft Oct. 1789.

THERE will be fold at the Cuftom-houfe of Down, by Inch of Candle, on Saturday the 7th November, a large quantity of extraordinary good Brandy, together with a very large quantity of Leaf and Roll Tobacco of the beft quality—Alfo fome Port Wine.—Great part of the Leaf Tobacco is in large Cafks in good order.
November 2d, 1789.

An Apprentice

WANTED to the Apothecary Bufinefs immediately, by Nathaniel Wilfon, Donaghadee.
November 2d, 1789.

HILLSBOROUGH CONCERT and BALL.

THE Nobility and Gentry of Hillfborough and its Vicinity are moft refpectfully informed, that, ON FRIDAY NEXT, THE 6th INSTANT, NOV. *AT THE ASSEMBLY ROOMS*—WILL BE, A CONCERT OF MUSIC, *VOCAL AND INSTRUMENTAL* ; To be conducted in the moft elegant manner, The Vocal Parts by Mrs. ARNOLD and GENTLEMEN.
After which will be a BALL.
Admittance—Gentlemen, 4s. 4d —Ladies, 3s. 3d. each.
N. B. The CONCERT to begin precifely at Eight o'Clock, and the BALL at Ten.
†§† Tickets to be had of Mrs. Rickards, at the Poft-Office.
BELFAST, 2d Nov. 1789.

Profeffional Concerts.

MR. WARE, (having engaged with Meffrs. *Mahon, Afhe,* and Mrs. *Arnold*) takes the liberty of informing the Ladies and Gentlemen of Belfaft, and its vicinity, that there will be a Grand CONCERT of Vocal and Inftrumental MUSICK, on Thurfday 19th inftant, and continue regularly (the week of Chriftmas excepted) every Thurfday for eight nights ; and after each of which will be a BALL. The Band to be led by Mr. Mahon.
The Concert will confift of two Acts ; in each Mrs. Arnold will perform twice ; alfo a Solo Concerto in each by Meffrs. Mahoon and Afhe ; particulars of which will be publifhed the 12th inftant.
The undertaking being attended with great expence, (and alfo for the convenience of large families) Mr. Ware will give Tickets at a Guinea each (to be paid on delivery) for the eight nights, which will be transferable in a family only.—He requefts thofe who mean to fubfcribe will be fo kind as to fend their names in writing to his houfe as foon as poffible, and fpecifying the number they wifh to fubfcribe for.

Non Subfcribers,	3s. 9d. h. ⎱ each.
Children,	2s. 8d. h. ⎰

Wine and Spirit Stores.

THOMAS MARTIN, who formerly lived with Meffrs. Montgomery, Brown, Tennent and Boyle, at the New Sugar-Houfe, has this day commenced bufinefs next door to Mr. Thomas Brown's, Waring-ftreet ; where he has laid in from the beft Markets, a large quantity of the following Goods—which will be fold very cheap for cafh or good bills, viz.

Strong Jamaica Rum as imported,	Common Rum, Brandy,
Old Antigua Spirit,	Geneva,
Rum Dee,	Porter, wood & bottles,
	Sweet Mountain.

He fhortly expects a quantity of London Porter.
Belfaft, 2d November, 1789.

Banoge Flour-Mills.

READY Money for good WHEAT, and the higheft price giving at Portadown or Moira, will always be given here ; the Farmers about Moira will be paid for the carriage to thefe Mills.
November 3d. 1789.

For Hire,

A CHAISE and Pair of good Horfes any diftance agreed for ——Application to
WM. CROOKSHANK.
Glaflough, 2d Nov. 1789.

WHEREAS the Partnerfhip of Coulter and Byrne was by mutual confent diffolved on the firft day of Auguft laft ; all thofe to whom faid Partnerfhip was then indebted, are requefted to fend their accounts for payment ; and thofe who now ftand indebted to faid Partnerfhip, are requefted to pay off theirs as foon as poffible.
Lurgan, 2d November, 1789.
N. B. The Spirit Bufinefs is now carried on by Wm. Coulter, who has for fale, Rum, Brandy, Gineva, &c. all of excellent quality, at loweft prices.

To be Sold,

BY Publick Auction, at the Market-houfe in Belfaft, on Friday the 13th inft. at one o'Clock, a Tenement in Barrack-ftreet, adjoining the Porter Brewery ; there is a good Houfe on the Premiffes let to Mr. Robert Hamill at 20l. per Year, exclufive of feveral fmall Cabbins, a Tan-yard, &c. the whole fubject to the yearly rent of 3l. 12s. Approved bills on Dublin or Belfaft at three months, will be taken in payment, or one and a half per cent allowed for Cafh.—The Deeds to be feen at John Brians and Co. Caddels-entry.

89

EXTRACT from STATISTICAL TABLES of the PRINCIPAL EMPIRES and STATES of EUROPE.

FRANCE.

POPULATION, &c.

Population and rate per mile.

24,800,000 ſouls, upon a ſurface of 157,924 ſquare miles, being at the rate of 157 perſons to each ſquare mile, diſtributed amongſt 400 cities, 1500 ſmall towns, 100,000 villiages, and 39,142 pariſhes.

Population of Capitals.

Paris 760,000—Lyons 160,000—Toulouſe 100,000 —Bourdeaux 85,000—Marſeilles 81,000—Rouen 72,500—Liſle 65,000—Verſailles 65,000—Nantz 60,000—Straſburgh 46,500—Niſmes 45,000—Amiens 43,500—Caen 33,000—Montpellier 33,000—Troyes 32,500—Breſt 31,000—Rheims 31,000—Toulon 28,000—Tours 25,000—Poitiers 17,500.

Corſica, the whole of the iſland, 124,000.

ARMED FORCE.

ARMY.

On the Liſts, 228,797 men, and 70,000 militia.

Houſehold troops 7996, 81 regiments French infantry, of 1659 men each—25 do. foreign do.—106 regiments of infantry—31 do French and foreign cavalry, of 870 men each—24 do. Dragoons—6 do. Huſſars—6 do. Chaſſeurs—67 do. cavalry—7 do. Artillery, 700 each—9 companies of Artiſans—6 corps of Miners.

Beſides 34 companies of Marechauſſé, garriſon battalions, provincial corps, invalids, &c.

Actual ſervice, 132,030 men, viz.

Infantry	100,000
Cavalry	26,000
Artillery, &c.	6,030

All under one of the Secretaries of State, called Miniſter of War.

RELIGION.

Roman Catholic,

Or, as their writers call it, the Gallican Church, was the only one allowed of ſince the Revocation of the Edict of Nantz; but towards the concluſion of 1787, ſome of the laws againſt Proteſtants (under the name of Non-Catholics) were conſiderably relaxed. There are not however any public places of Proteſtant worſhip except in the province of Alſace, where the Lutheran religion has been allowed of agreeable to the treaty which ceded that province. In the Cevennes there are vaſt numbers of Proteſtants, and the proportion they bear to the Roman Catholics throughout the kingdom, is ſuppoſed, as 1 to 12.—The government of the church is by Biſhops, under whom are 9 *Chambres Eccleſiaſtiques ſuperieures*, beſides which, every Biſhop has his Diocelan Court for inferior matters.

LITERATURE.

There are 6 Academies in Paris, viz. The French, that of Painting and Sculpture, the Belles Lettres, and the Sciences of Architecture and Surgery, and 2 Royal Societies of Agriculture and Phyſic, with about 30 Academical Inſtitutions in various capitals. There are 24 Univerſities: thoſe of Paris, Thoulouſe, and Dijon, the moſt celebrated. The number of eccleſiaſtical perſons, of both ſexes, are near 200,000, enjoying a revenue of about 118 million of livres, near 5,000,000l. ſterling, but ſubject to conſiderable taxes called free gifts. They have Aſſemblies every five years, and oftener if neceſſary, when thoſe free gifts are granted.

REVOLUTION IN SPAIN.

The following account we received laſt night from Paris:

"God be praiſed! the ſacred fire of Liberty has at length ſpread itſelf to the country of the Inquiſition!

"An attempt having been made to prevent the Spaniards from reading our newſpapers, or knowing the cauſes and effects of the Revolution which has happened in this country, the people of that kingdom have begun to ſatisfy their curioſity, by demanding the heads of the Inquiſitors. Six thouſand of the regular troops, which were ſent to Catalonia to quell the inſurgents, have only ſerved to exaſperate them more. Near two thouſand of the troops have joined their fellow-citizens, and the others remain inactive. The inſurrection, in ſhort, is become general in Spain.

D U B L I N, November 3.

Yeſterday his Excellency the Lord Chancellor held his firſt Seal ſitting, in the Court of Chancery. The number of petitions preferred, we hear, amounted to twenty-ſeven.

The Marquis of Buckingham ſtill continues extremely ill; his diſorder is a windy dropſy, and a total want of digeſtion. This is a mere conſtitutional ailment, as it is well known that his Lordſhip is the moſt temperate of men.

The accounts received of the Earl of Weſtmoreland, give the moſt pleaſing impreſſion of his character. He is ſpirited, lively and generous, a character which will highly recommend his Excellency to the Iriſh nation; and as he has lived in the firſt ſtile of elegance, his preſence, as well as that of his Counteſs, muſt draw a great deal of company to town, and we may conſequently expect a ſplendid winter.

Of the Counteſs it is ſaid, that to the charms of beauty, and the utmoſt elegance of external form, ſhe adds theſe accompliſhments which render their impreſſion irreſiſtable.

The troops in garriſon, and the different corps of Volunteers, will parade to-morrow, and pay their uſual compliments to the memory of King William, round his ſtatue in College-green.

We are happy to have it in our power to ſay, from the beſt authority, that Henry Flood, Eſq. that celebrated orator and patriot, who has lately returned from England, means to attend his duty in the Houſe of Commons during the enſuing ſeſſion of Parliament.

His Grace the Primate, has been pleaſed to grant a faculty to the Rev. Thomas Greene, to hold the Prebend and Rectory of Clandehorky in the dioceſe of Raphoe, together with the Vicarage of Glankeen in the dioceſe of Caſhel.

At Longford, on Friday laſt, Sir William Gleadowe was, without oppoſition, elected Knight of the Shire for the county of Longford, in the room of the now Lord Annaly.

Sunday morning a handſome young woman threw herſelf into the river at Aſton's-quay, and was unfortunately drowned. A love affair is ſaid to have been the cauſe of this melancholy cataſtrophe.

A fine boy near Caſtle Malone, in the county of Clare, better than a month ſince playing with a favourite dog, received a bite from the animal. About 12 days ago, he ſhewed ſtrong ſigns of the hydrophobia, from the violence of which it was found requiſite to terminate his exiſtence between two feather beds on Thurſday laſt.

The civil war of 1641 deſolated the kingdom of Ireland to ſuch a degree, that, in 1642, the Treaſury in Dublin was quite exhauſted, ſo as no longer to enable Government to maintain a force to protect either it or the conſtitution. The inhabitants of Dublin, then conſiſting only of about five hundred houſekeepers, rich and poor, brought their plate, to the amount of twelve hundred pounds, to be coined at the public mint, (for then we had a mint of our own). This ſum, when compared to the value of money, wealth, and population of the Iriſh capital at this day, may be fairly eſtimated as if the inhabitants were this winter to devote their plate to the amount of 140,000l. to the public ſervice.

SPORTING INTELLIGENCE.

CURRAGH OCTOBER MEETING.

3lb. To mares, and 4lb. additional weight for every King's Plate, and 2lb. for every 50l. plate won this ſeaſon; alſo 3lb. under for every horſe that has not won a plate this year, (Peeping Tom excepted.)

Monday, 26.

Fifty guineas for 3 years old, 7ſt. 11lb. each.—3 years old courſe, the beſt of heats.

Mr. Connolly's b c Bombardier by Richmond	1	1
Mr. Graydon's b c Peter Pindar, by King Fergus	2	2
Mr. D. B. Daly's g f Caroline, by Lenox	3	3

Bombardier the favourite, a good race.

Tueſday, 27.

Fifty guineas for 4 and five years old—4 years old 7ſt. 7lb. five years old 8ſt—from the red poſt home, the beſt of heats.

Mr. Savage's m Dutcheſs of Leinſter by Cromaboo, 4 years old, 50l. plate, 7ſt. 6lb.	3	1	1
Mr. D.B. Daly's m Little Moll, by Glacus, 5 years old, two 50l. plates, 8ſt. 1lb.	1	3	2
Mr. Lumm's b h Maxamin, by Evergreen, 4 years old, (no plate) 4ſt. 4lb.	2	2	3

At ſtarting, Little Moll the favourite, each heat a great race.

L O N D O N - D E R R Y.

A Correſpondent has favoured us with the following article:—In the Tythe Cauſe of King and King againſt the Revd. Edm. Hamilton (tried at a late Aſſizes in Derry), the defendant gave conſent for judgment being marked againſt him; and that judgment has ſince been made up and entered for the Plaintiffs in the Court of King's Bench, whereby the Pariſhioners of Drumachoſe have eſtabliſhed a modus for the tythe of flax and potatoes. Mr. Hamilton has alſo conſented to reverſe and annul the ſeveral ſentences given in his favour in the Conſiſtory Court of Derry."—We have only to add our ſincere wiſh, that the pariſhioners of Drumachoſe may long continue to cultivate a friendly connection with their truly benevolent and reſpectable Paſtor.

MARRIED.] On Friday laſt, Mr. Wm. Hamilton, an eminent attorney of Stafford ſtreet, Dublin, to Mrs Graham, widow of John Graham, Eſq; late of Summerhill, co. Donegall.

DIED.] In Biſhop ſtreet Alex. Scott, M. D.

Belfaſt, November 3.

In conſequence of intoxication, a woman of the name of Jane Smith died early on Sunday morning laſt in this town. A ſuppoſition of her being murdered having aroſe, the Coroner's Inqueſt was held on the body, who brought in a verdict "that ſhe received her death from falls when in a ſtate of intoxication."

This is one inſtance among many which daily occur, of the caution that ſhould be obſerved by Magiſtrates in granting certificates to Publicans; as moſt murders and other crimes are occaſioned by the great number of perſons at preſent licenced to ſell ſpirituous liquors in this kingdom.

A correſpondent obſerving that the fences in this country are in general very bad, which may in a great meaſure ariſe from the high price of thorn quicks—recommends it to every farmer to ſow a few buſhels of haws;—no crop will pay him better;—an acre of two year old thorns is worth 100l. at 2s. per 1000.—They muſt be buried for a year—or, Mr. Miller ſays, that if put into a caſk and buried in a dung-hill, for a month or ſix weeks, they will grow the firſt year. Hips, the fruit of the wild roſe, if bruiſed and ſowed now, grow the firſt year and make an excellent fence.

PORT NEWS.

ARRIVED.

Oct. 27. New Loyalty, Brown, Liverpool, Drapery and ſalt.
29. Margaret and Janet, M'Mechan, Leghorn, brimſtone.
31. Betty and Molly, Blair, Dantzic, aſhes. Six colliers.

CLEARED OUT.

Oct. 27. Margaret, Griffith, Liverpool, beef.
29. Hawke, Curry, Irwine, luggage.
31. Liberty, M'Donnell, Liverpool, butter.

Belfaſt, November 6.

Monday evening laſt, two young boys were detected cutting holes in bags filled with ſugar on a car loaded for the country. Being taken before the Sovereign, they gave information of three women who uſed to buy the ſugars from them, upon which the whole five were lodged in the county jail, to take their trial at the enſuing aſſizes.—This practice it ſeems has been carried on for a conſiderable time, to the great loſs of poor carmen and country dealers, and would probably have continued much longer had not the vigilance of a gentleman, to whom this town has been indebted on many occaſions, been the means of detecting theſe young villains and their aſſociates.

☞ It may not be deemed unneceſſary to apprize the public, that the *Iriſh Lottery* begins drawing on *Thurſday* firſt, the 12th inſt.—To young adventurers, who may on firſt trial, obtain more in one auſpicious minute from the fickle Goddeſs than in an age—well as to thoſe who are willing to give the gracious deity *Fortune*, an opportunity of re-paying what ſhe may be indebted to them—are now on delivery. *Whole Tickets, Halves, Fourths, Eighths, Sixteenths*, and the *Guinea* Tickets, which include every Prize, and entitle to the capital ſum of £.2,000 ſterling.

State Lottery Office, Bridge-ſtreet, Belfaſt, Nov. 6, 1789.

FAIRS IN THE ENSUING WEEK.

Monday, 9th Nov.—Anadoine, Down; Ballywalter, Down; Balneglera, Arm. Belfaſt, Ant. Clough, Ant. Deſertmartin, Der. Drumquin, Tyr. Letterkenny, Don. Strangford, Down; Tuſkin's paſs, Arm. Wedneſday, 11.—Pomeroy, Tyr. Thurſday, 12.—Antrim Town; Armoy, Ant. Augher, Tyr. Bellaghy, Der. Charlemont, Arm. Dunluce, Ant. Figgvee, Der. Grange, Tyr. Killough, Down; Killybeggs, Don. Loughbrickland, Down; Redcaſtle, Don. Strabane, Tyr. Friday, 13.—Caſtlewellan, Down; Portadown, Arm. Saturday, 14.—Scarvaghpaſs, Down; Trillic, Tyr.

PRICES IN THIS MARKET YESTERDAY.

Oatmeal,	10s.	0d.	to	10s.	4d.	Dried do. 24s. to 25s. 0d. per d
Wheat,	11	0	—	11	8	R. Tallow, 5s. 4d. to 5s. 8d. ſt
Oats,	5	0	—	5	5	Potatoes 8d. to 10d per b.
Barley,	5	0	—	5	8	Eng. coals, 00s. to 14s. 0d.
Butter,	50	0	—	51	0	Scotch do. 00s. to 13s. 0d.
C. hides,	34	0	—	36	0	Ex on Lond. 7 a 1-4 per c.
Ox ditto,	40	0	—	42	0	Do. on Glaſgow $6\frac{1}{2}$.
S.C. ſkins	00	0	—	40	0	

Anno 1789.]   Printed by HENRY JOY, and Co. BELFAST.

The BELFAST NEWS LETTER.

TUESDAY November 10,   FRIDAY November 13, 1789.

EXTRACT from STATISTICAL TABLES of the PRINCIPAL EMPIRES and STATES of EUROPE.

IRELAND.

POPULATION, &c.

POPULATION AND RATE PER MILE.

CONTAINING 3,040,000 inhabitants, upon a surface of 18,699 Irish square miles, or 28,012 English, being at the rate of about 109 persons to each square mile, distributed amongst 2,293 parishes. N. B. The rate of population in Leinster and Ulster is much greater than in the other two provinces.

PRINCIPAL DIVISIONS.

Divided into the Provinces of

ULSTER,

Containing 9 Counties, Antrim, Armagh, Cavan, Down, Donegall, Fermanagh, Londonderry, Monaghan, and Tyrone.

LEINSTER,

12 Counties, Carlow, Dublin, East Meath, Kildare, Kilkenny, King's County, Longford, Louth, Queen's County, West Meath, Wexford, and Wicklow.

CONNAUGHT,

5 Counties, Galway, Leitrim, Mayo, Roscommon, and Sligo.

MUNSTER.

6 Counties, Clare, Cork, Kerry, Limerick, Tipperary, and Waterford.

POPULATION OF CAPITALS.

Dublin 221,000—Cork 87,000—Limerick 32,000—Waterford 18,500—Londonderry 18,000—Belfast 20,500—Newry 9,500—Galway 9,000—Roscommon 8,000.

ARMED FORCE.

ARMY.

(Incorporated with the British Army in the pay of Ireland.)

On the Lists 15,235 men.

Effective about 12,000, viz. 4 regiments of horse, 8 do. Light Dragoons, 20 regts. of Infantry, a corps of Invalids, and a Royal regt. of Artillery.

NAVY.

NONE—This kingdom being protected by that of Great Britain.

For prevention of smuggling, there are some cutters in the pay of Ireland.

STATE OF FINANCES, &c.

ANNUAL REVENUE.

Gross Revenue about 1,500,000l. from whence various deductions on account of drawbacks, premiums, bounties, and management, reduce it to about 1,060,000l. the nett sum applicable to the current expences.

The wages of collecting this revenue amount to about 10 per cent. which with the incidental charges make the total expence of collection 16 per cent.

MILITARY CHARGES.

The Military Charges, Ordinary and Extraordinary.

Average about 630,000l. per annum.

GENERAL EXPENCES.

Total expence, (including charge of interest and annuities 153,695l.) 1,210,000l. Consequently a deficiency in the nett unappropriated revenue, to answer the expences, of 150,000l. per annum.

PUBLIC DEBT.

Debt funded and unfunded, at Lady-Day 1787, 2,179,252l. to which adding the value of Tontines and other annuities 751,000l.—the actual debt is 2,930,252l. whereon is paid for interest and annuities 153,695l. being no less than 5¼ per cent. upon the aggregate.

Wheat, Barley, and Oars.

JAMES HOLMES is constantly purchasing Wheat, Barley and Oats, of good quality.——Apply at his Stores, Donegall-street.

Belfast, 12th Nov. 1789.

A News Carrier

IS immediately wanted to carry this Paper from Belfast to Lurgan.——Apply at this Office.

Belfast, 9th Nov. 1789.

James Kennedy,

HAS for Sale, at his Stores in Rosemary-Lane, a large parcel of high-flavoured old Clarets, imported in May 1787, which will be sold cheap; also the following Articles, viz.

Jamaica and Barbadoes Rum, Brandy, Geneva, Red Port, Sherry, Lisbon	In the Spirit and reduced, In wood and bottle,	Calcavella, Muscatell, Mountain, Frontiniac, Prighiac, and Via de Goute, — In wood and bottle.

He has also PORTER in Bottle, from the Belfast Porter Brewery, the quality of which he can recommend.

Belfast, 9th Nov. 1789.

Six Fat Cows,

WERE found trespassing on my Farm last Friday and sent to the Pound. The owner proving his property and paying expences may have them by applying to

ROBERT THOMSON.

Belfast, 9th Nov. 1789.

THE Executors of the late James Hamilton of Ballymenoch, Esq; request, that if there are any legal demands, by bond, note, or otherwise on them, they may be produced at the Donegall-Arms, on Monday the sixteenth instant, at eleven o'clock, to receive payment.

November the 9th, 1789.

Mr. Metralcourt,

WITH the greatest respect begs leave to inform the Ladies and Gentlemen of Belfast and its vicinity, that for the better accommodation of his Pupils he has taken a large and commodious House in Linenhall-street; where he intends opening his School for Dancing, on Thursday the 12th instant, at twelve o'clock.

Mr. Metralcourt flatters himself, by the strict care and attention he will pay to his Pupils, to gain the approbation of the publick.

Belfast, Nov. 6th, 1789.

WE the Legatees of the late Mr. John French of Randalstown, do think ourselves bound in duty to return thanks to Mr. James Bailie, Auctioneer, of Corn market, Belfast—from whose conduct in our sales at Randalstown we have experienced a considerable advantage.——Randalstown, Nov. 10th, 1789.

ELIZABETH FRENCH,
and other Legatees.

To be Let,

From the first of November 1789, for 21 Years and Lives,

A Farm of Land in the Estate of Sir Robert Bateson Harvey, in the county of Antrim, containing about 30 acres of land, Cunningham measure, situate on the river Bann, and adjoining to Portneal Bridge, lately occupied by Mr. James Henry, the greater part meadow, and the whole very improvable. Proposals in writing, (post paid) will be received by Mr. David Tomb, Belfast.

11th November, 1789.

Four Sheep,

FOUND in the custody of a person driving the same to the Fair of Stewartstown, on Monday the second of November, who being suspected, and on pretence of going for a voucher did not return. The person driving said Sheep called himself Daniel O'Neil, wore a sky-blue coat, was of a fair complexion, about 5 feet 8 inches, and spoke with a Connaught accent.

Any person proving the property, and paying the costs incurred, may have the same on application to Thomas Caulfield, May, or to Wm. Anderson, near Eglish, county Tyrone, in whose custody they are.

WHEREAS on the night of the 10th instant, at or about the hour of 12 o'clock, some malicious person or persons, did break the windows and frames of the King's House, Holywood, together with several stones hove at the door of said house. Now, in order to punish such offenders, I do hereby offer a reward of 20l. to any person or persons that shall discover the such offenders. November 14th, 1789.

JOSEPH DAVIS.

SEVERAL Gentlemen in the Linen Trade having been disappointed in getting their Linens shipp'd on board the Charlotte, Wm. Campbell, Master, for LONDON; we think it proper to send another Vessel at an earlier day than usual——Therefore the Lord Donegall, James Mc. Roberts, Master, will clear out for LONDON the 20th instant, and sail first fair wind after

Belfast, 8th Nov. 1789.

Samuel Hyde,	Jacob Hancock,
Robt. Thompson,	David Wilson,
Samuel Brown,	Valentine Smith,
William Sinclaire,	James Stevenson.
Robert Bradshaw,	

TWO Journeymen Saddlers will meet with good encouragement by applying to HARRISON, Saddler, Belfast.

To be sold by Auction,

At the Market-house, on Saturday the 21st of Nov. inst. at 12 o'Clock.

THE LEASE of one acre of land in Ballymacarret, adjoining Conn's-Water at the New-Bridge, granted to Robert Mc. Crea, for 79 years from Nov. 1783, at the yearly rent of 2l. sterling.——On the premises, fronting the New-Road, are erected several tenements, (particularly two new-built brick houses) which produce a considerable yearly profit rent—and the situation of the ground is the most eligible about Belfast for lime-burning, or a coal-yard, &c. having the great advantage of water carriage to a very populace and improving neighbourhood.——Further particulars may be known by applying to JOHN TISDALL, with whom the Title Deeds lie.

Belfast, 9th Nov. 1789.

E. QUILTON,

Ligonier's-Arms, Water-street, Newry,

RETURNS his sincere acknowledgments to his Friends and the Public, for the very great encouragement and distinguished preference he has experienced since his commencement in business—Begs leave to inform them, that he has now his carriages fitted up in the strongest and genteelest manner for the road with stout cattle, and careful drivers.—A quantity of best hay and oats; a variety of neat wines, spirits, &c. a well furnished larder, and comfortable accommodations for Ladies and Gentlemen.

☞ Seats in his Majesty's Mail-Coach to be engaged at said Inn, where every attention is paid to passengers.

N. B. Dinner ready to put on the table at the arrival of the Coach.

Newry, Nov. 1st, 1789.

Wholesale Woollen Warehouse.

CULLEY and CAMPBELL have just received from England a very large assortment of Goods fit for the Winter Trade; and as every article has been chosen by one of the partners, they are therefore enabled to sell Goods on as good terms as any other House in their line.—Every encouragement will be given to those who purchase for cash or good bills.

Newry, 5th Nov. 1789.

Hillsborough Fair,

WILL be holden on Wednesday next, the 18th instant, when the very extensive Premiums, (the same as at the last Fair) will be given.

Hillsborough,   MICHAEL THOMSON,
Nov. 11th, 1789.   Clerk of the Market.

N. B. Any Article sold after four o'clock in the afternoon will not be entitled to the Premium.

A General half-yearly Meeting of the Bachelor's Annuity Company, will be held at the Market-house in Belfast on Tuesday second day of December next, at 11 o'clock in the forenoon, for the purpose of electing a President, Secretary, and Committee, and paying the half-yearly Subscriptions then due.

Belfast, 14th Nov. 1789.

HUGH ALLEN, Secretary.

Money to be lent.

THE Sum of Three Hundred Pounds to be lent immediately, upon Mortgage of sufficient Freehold or Leasehold Property contiguous to Belfast.——Apply to JOHN TISDALL—who wants some smaller Sums at Interest; and has for Sale a valuable Lease in perpetuity.

Belfast, 12th Nov. 1789.

☞ Letters post-paid can only be attended to.

PARISIAN INTELLIGENCE.

NATIONAL ASSEMBLY, *Thurſday, Oct.* 22.

THE Preſident informed the Aſſembly, that his Majeſty had given the royal ſanction to the riot act.

A deputation from the people of colour in the Weſt India iſlands, being admitted to the bar, preſented an animated and ſtriking picture of the indignities and oppreſſions to which they were expoſed from the abſurd and barbarous prejudices of the whites, which operated with all the force of laws againſt them. They ſtated, That although by the edict of 1685 the deſcendants of free parents ought to be ranked with other citizens, they were ſubjected to all taxes, and yet excluded from public employments and even from the exerciſe of ſeveral mechanic arts; that when the whites aſſembled to chooſe perſons to repreſent them in the National Aſſembly, the people of colour were not invited to attend. But that, rouſed by the voice of reaſon, which, ſpeaking from the boſom of the Aſſembly, called all ranks of citizens to exerciſe that ſovereignty which belongs equally to every member of the body politic, when all aſſemble either perſonally or by repreſentation; and encouraged by the Declaration of the Rights of Men and Citizens; they had met together, drawn up an account of their grievances, and choſen repreſentatives to carry their remonſtrances to the Aſſembly. That, they had, moreover, enjoined there Deputies to depoſit ſix millions of livres on the altar of their country, and to give a fiftieth of their property towards the redemption of the National Debt.

Their repreſentation was received with applauſe, and the Preſident aſſured them it would be taken into conſideration.

A Deputy from the inhabitants of Mount Jura, who were formerly in a ſtate of vaſſalage, was introduced to return thanks to the Aſſembly in the name of his countrymen for the bleſſings of liberty diffuſed among them, by the abolition of the feudal ſyſtem. This venerable repreſentative, 120 years of age, was led into the Hall by his daughter, and ſeated oppoſite to the Preſident. The Aſſembly reſolved to make a contribution for him among its own members, the amount to be placed in the public funds, and the intereſt paid him during his life, with reverſion to his family. This they preferred to granting to his family the reverſion of a penſion of 200 livres, which the King, to whom he was preſented, had been pleaſed to beſtow on him.

PARIS, October 26.

SPEECH of the Preſident to the KING.

" Sire, The National Aſſembly having voted themſelves inſeparable from your auguſt perſon, they are now led by their affection to approach your Majeſty, and offer to you the homage of their immutable affection and reſpect.

" The love of the French people to their Monarch has been unbounded ever ſince that day when the public voice hailed you ' The Reſtorer of Liberty !' It remains only for you, Sire, to acquire the endearing title of ' The beſt Friend to the Nation.'

" Henry IV. obtained that appellation from a city in which he ſpent part of his youth; and we learn from hiſtory, that with an incomparable affability he concluded a letter to them with that expreſſion.

" This, Sire, is alſo your indiſputable claim. The whole nation has ſeen your Majeſty firm and tranquil in the midſt of danger, running every hazard for the good of the State, and ſupporting and encouraging a beloved people by your preſence and your protection.

" We have beheld you for this renouncing eaſe and pleaſure, and in the midſt of an unquiet and turbulent multitude, bringing the promiſe of better days, by reſtoring concord, renewing peace, and rallying the ſcattered ſtrength of the empire.

" While we repeat the thanks of a mighty nation, who join in offering you the tribute of their admiration, allow us, on our own part, to declare our zeal for the execution of the laws, and the maintenance of your tutelary authority.

" Theſe ſentiments are a debt which we owe to your Majeſty: they are thoſe of our conſtituents, they correſpond with the wiſhes of all Europe, and will be ſanctioned by the ſuffrages of poſterity."

His Majeſty's Anſwer.

" I am highly ſatisfied with the attachment which you expreſs toward my perſon; and while I entirely rely on your profeſſions of regard, the recollection of them affects me with the greateſt ſenſibility."

The Martial Law already ſeems to have done more towards the eſtabliſhment of order in the city of Paris, than all the efforts of the Committees of the Hotel de Ville, and the ſixty diſtricts into which the city is divided. Their daily reſolutions, threats, and remonſtrances, had no other effect than that of rendering the people more inſolent and ungovernable; and although a very trifling force would in all caſes have been ſufficient to have diſperſed them, there has not been one inſtance in which any part of the Pariſian army, conſiſting of 30,000 men, has ever oppoſed the lawleſs fury of the mob.

The moſt alarming accounts from all quarters of the kingdom of France daily reach the capital. The army is divided among itſelf, and want of ſubordination and deſertion are the ſmalleſt evils which proceed from it.

At Gibet, the people have been obliged to protect their proviſions by force of arms; at Liſle and Vienne, the inhabitants have riſen on the military, whom they deteſt, without knowing for what reaſon; at Arras, they have ſeized the Comte de Virtemont, Major of the light horſe, and, after carrying him naked about the ſtreets, have thrown him into priſon, without the troops under his command ſhewing him the leaſt protection.

In ſhort, the army is every where in a ſtate of mutiny, and refuſes to obey.

Cherbourg is at preſent in great commotion, and not a day paſſes without ſome expreſs from the National Aſſembly, with orders how to act. The works, notwithſtanding, are carried on with the ſame indefatigable induſtry.

The Governor of Cherbourg is at preſent a priſoner in his own houſe, which is ſurrounded night and day by a ſtrong guard, to prevent his eſcape. It ſeems he has been diſcovered to have held a correſpondence with ſome of the fugitive Nobleſſe, and ſome of their letters have been intercepted. One of them was the means of his houſe being ſearched, when eighty or a hundred barrels of gunpowder were found concealed.

The excuſe he makes is, that they were kept there for the ſafety of the place in caſe of neceſſity—an excuſe by no means deemed ſatisfactory by the people, who are all attached to the National Aſſembly.

No man is allowed to purchaſe more than two or three buſhels of wheat each day (according to the number of his family), and that by an order from the Committee for regulating the prices of bread and other matters.

REVOLUTION IN AUSTRIAN FLANDERS, AND THE *IMPRISONMENT OF THE CHANCELLOR OF BRABANT.*

The embers of rebellion, which have been for ſome months kindling, have at length broke forth into a flame, and the whole of the Emperor's dominions in Brabant are a ſcene of mutiny and civil war. The ſword is drawn, and God knows how many lives may be loſt ere it is ſheathed.

We ſhall ſhortly mention the ſtate of the patriotic force in Brabant, previous to the rebellion becoming in its preſent ſtate of activity. The States General of Holland having tacitly acquieſced in giving protection to the Brabanteſe inſurgents, the latter have for ſome weeks paſt flocked in large numbers towards Dutch Brabant, and had taken up their head quarters at Tillbourg. To this place they invited their countrymen to join them, and promiſed the pay of fourteen ſols daily for their ſupport.

This protection of the States General, and the punctual payment of the prop... daily hire, ſoon brought the Patriots into very conſiderable force; and it is evident from this circumſtance, that they were aſſiſted with very large ſuccours of money and proviſions.

Accordingly, we find that the inſurgents have attacked two forts ſituated between Antwerp and Bergen-op-Zoom, belonging to the Emperor, and made themſelves maſter of them.

They have further ſeized on M. de Crumpepen, Chancellor of Brabant, and impriſoned him as an hoſtage and ſecurity againſt the Emperor's Government ill treating any of their party, for they have ſignified that the firſt man among them who is ſacrificed to the Emperor's authority, ſhall be revenged by the Chancellor's being hung upon the ramparts of one of the forts they have taken.

On the other hand, Count Trautmanſdorf, the Governor at Bruſſels, has iſſued a proclamation, ſetting forth, that whatever villages or habitations ſhall be found to conceal any of the inſurgents, the ſame ſhall be inſtantly ſet fire to, and no quarter given—that although this is much againſt his wiſh, the exigency of the moment demands it.

In the mean time, the Emperor's Government has ſeized Count L'Aunoix, Preſident of the States, the Archbiſhop of Malines, and two other members of the State, who are kept by way of repriſal for the Chancellor, and are threatened to be hanged the inſtant they hear of any hurt offered to him.

General D'Alton, on hearing the news of the two forts being taken, inſtantly marched at the head of 7000 troops, to retake them, iſſuing another proclamation, that he meant to take them by aſſault, and would put every ſoul he found in them to the ſword. It is not known what effect this threat will have.

On Tueſday and Wedneſday laſt, there was a general ſearch made by the military, in all the houſes in Bruſſels, not excepting even the Foreign Miniſters, to find whether any fire-arms or ammunition were concealed in them.

Lord Torrington's hotel was ſearched, and afterwards the Dutch Miniſter's,—who refuſed his permiſſion, but the military inſiſted on it, and broke in.

Belfaſt, *November* 10.

Early on Friday morning laſt, in a gale of wind, the Glory, of Maryport, Capt. M'Cloud, loaded with coals from Air, bound for Dublin, was put on ſhore on the ſouth ſide of Bangor bay: the veſſel was drove to pieces, but fortunately the people on board were all ſaved by the humane exertions of the Hon. Robert Ward, who had his pleaſure boat manned and ſent to their aſſiſtance.

On 29th ult the Brig Chance ſpoke the Recovery of Belfaſt off Dungarvan, bound from Belfaſt for Liſbon, with the Hon. Mrs. O'Neill and Mrs. St. Leger, all well.

☞ It may not be deemed unneceſſary to apprize the public, that the *Iriſh Lottery* begins drawing on *Thurſday* firſt, the 12th inſt.——To young adventurers, who may on firſt trial, obtain more in one auſpicious minute from the fickle Goddeſs than in an age—well as to thoſe who are willing to give the gracious deity *Fortune*, an opportunity of re-paying what ſhe may be indebted to them—are now on delivery. *Whole Tickets, Halves, Fourths, Eighths, Sixteenths*, and the *Guinea* Tickets, which include every Prize, and entitle to the capital ſum of £.2,000 ſterling.

State Lottery-Office, Bridge-ſtreet, Belfaſt, Nov. 6, 1789.

Extract of a Letter from Coleraine.

" On Saturday, the 31ſt ult. died at Jackſon-Hall, near Coleraine, of a ſhort illneſs, the Right Hon. Richard Jackſon, whoſe death, a moſt eminent and important loſs, will be more ſenſibly felt in the proceſs of time, as it is at preſent moſt deſervedly and univerſally lamented by all degrees and ranks of men;—for he was worthily honoured, eſteemed, and reſpected by the community in general.

Belfaſt, *November* 13.

☞ FOUR MAILS DUE.

The ſhip Nancy, Capt. Crawford, which ſailed from Londonderry with paſſengers, arrived ſafe and landed them all healthy and well at Philadelphia, after a pleaſant paſſage of ſeven weeks.

The ſhip Sally, Capt. Millar, is ſafe arrived at Philadelphia after a paſſage of ſeven weeks, and landed all her paſſengers in good health.

Married, on Sunday the 8th inſt. by the Lord Biſhop of Down, James Leſlie, Eſq. of Leſlie-Hill, to Miſs Fleming.

PRICES IN THIS MARKET YESTERDAY.

Oatmeal,	10s.	od. to	10s.	4d.		Dried do oos. to oos. od per d
Wheat,	11	6 —	11	10		R. Tallow, 5s. 6d. to 5s. 8d. ſt.
Oats,	4	10½ —	5	2		Potatoes 9d. to 11d per b.
Barley,	5	0 —	0	0		Eng. coals, oos. to 14s. od.
Butter,	50	0 —	51	0		Scotch do. oos. to 13s. od.
C. hides,	35	0 —	37	6		Ex on Lond. 7 a 1-4 per c.
Ox ditto,	40	0 —	42	0		Do. on Glaſgow 7.
S.C. ſkins	40	0 —	42	6		

PORT NEWS.

ARRIVED.

Nov. 2. Ann, Martin, Peterſburgh, hemp, &c.
6. Jenny, M'Pherſon, Glaſgow, ſtationary, &c.

CLEARED OUT.

Nov. 2. Marianna, Eaſtwood, Charleſtown, cloth.
Charlotte, Campbell, London, ditto.
3. Brownlow, Pinkerton, Antigua, ditto.
Charles and Margaret, Atkinſon, Jamaica, ditto.
7. Dick, Saunders, Cheſter, hides.

FAIRS IN THE ENSUING WEEK.

Monday, 16th Nov. Ardſtradbridge, Tyr. Banbridge, Down. Clady, Tyr. Maghrea, Der. Raſharkin, Ant. Rathmelton, Don.—Tueſday 17. Ballyſhannon, Don. Clady, Der. Dunfanaghy, Don. Scotſtown, Mon. Tullamore, Ant.——Wedneſday 18. Hillſborough, Down. Mountcharles, Don. Orrator, Tyr.—Thurſday 19. Aughnacloy, Tyr. Cloghanbegg, Don. Downpatrick, Down. Dunnelong, Tyr. Killeter, Tyr. Loughill, Ant. Omagh, Tyr. —Friday 20. Armagh Town. Crumlin, Ant.——Saturday 21. Carndonagh, Don. Gilford, Down. Monaghan Town. Ramullan, Don.

Anno 1789.]   Printed by HENRY JOY, and Co. BELFAST.

The BELFAST NEWS-LETTER.

TUESDAY November 17,   FRIDAY November 20, 1789.

New Publications,

Now felling by WM. MAGEE, BELFAST,

AN INTRODUCTION to READING and SPELLING: To which are added PRINCIPLES of ENGLISH GRAMMAR, with other fupplementary Pieces. Price 1s. 7d. h. By WM. SCOTT.

The HIBERNIAN GAZETTEER; being a Defcription of the feveral Provinces, Counties, Towns, Rivers, Lakes, Harbours, Mountains, Bogs, Caftles, Churches, Mines, Collieries, principal Buildings, Mineral Springs, and Roads in IRELAND—alphabetically arranged, exhibiting a compleat view of the Antiquities, natural Curiofities, ftate of parliamentary Reprefentation, and other ufeful and entertaining particulars, with two new and accurate Maps, Price 4s. 4d.—collected from the lateft and beft authorities, by W. W. SEWARD, Efq.

SHERIDAN's ELEMENTS of ENGLISH, Price 1s. 1d

Hawes on the Sacrament. Price 1s 7d. h.

ROBERT GETTY

IS now landing from on board the Lord Donegall, from London, an extenfive parcel of
NEW TEAS;
alfo beft Turkey Coffee.

Belfaft, 16th Nov. 1789.

Madeira Wine

ROBERT SCOTT has for Sale a few Pipes of beft London Particular Madeira Wine, of the vintage of 1785—it went the rounds, and was landed in Jamaica, where it lay fix months —He is alfo largely fupplied with the undermentioned Goods, which he will fell by the Package as imported on reafonable terms:

Jamaica Rum,	Dantzig Weed ditto,
Fine Scale Sugar,	Pimento,
Hyfon, Bloom, Singlo, and	White Ginger,
Congou Teas,	Mahogany,
St. Domingo and Jamaica	Logwood,
Cotton,	Englifh and Ballyhack Mill-
Coffee,	ftones, &c. &c.
Hungarian Pearl Afhes,	

Belfaft, 14th Nov. 1789.

NEW TEAS, Raifins, Figs, Malaga Wine, Black Pepper, | Fine and fuperfine Muftard, And London refined Salt-peter,

juft arrived and will be landed in a few days. Apply to H. Crawford.

Belfaft, 16th Nov. 1789.

∗ He has alfo on fale a large parcel of ftrong Jamaica Rum and fine Scale Sugars, in barrels—and 90 hogfheads of beft wrappery James's River Tobacco.

MR. WARE having not yet received an Anfwer to his Application for the Exchange Rooms, begs his Friends and the Public may be kind enough to excufe his deferring the Concerts for a few days longer.

November 16th, 1789.

A Ball,

THERE will be a Ball at Downpatrick, on Thurfday the 26th November inft. during the Extra Meeting of the Town Hunt.

Nov. 16th, 1789.

Archibald Bankhead,

IS landing for fale, from on board the Lord Donegall, a confiderable quantity of Salt-peter, which he will fell remarkably low.

He has juft received from the beft Markets a large affortment of DRUGS, of the qualities he ufually fells.

Belfaft, Nov. 17th, 1789.

To be Let,

FROM the 1ft of November laft, for the term of 21 Years or the life of the Prince of Wales, the Lands undermentioned.

	A.	R.	P.
One Orchard and one Meadow in Spring- field, containing,	2	1	7
Two Fields in ditto, containing,	6	1	29
Five Fields in ditto, containing,	9	3	27

Apply to James Irvin, who lives on the Premiffes.

16th November, 1789.

THE entire houfhold furniture of Mr. John M'Clure of Drumbo, to be fold by auction, to-morrow, Wendefday, the 18th inftant, and the following days, by JOHN BAILIE, Auctioneer, Chichefter-quay, Belfaft—confifting of bedfteds and bedding, fheets, and table linen, mahogany and other tables, chairs with ftuffed and other feats, looking-glaffes, a monthly clock in a mahogany cafe, a cow in calf, farming utenfils, kitchen furniture, &c. &c.

Sale to begin at 11 o'clock each day and continue until all are fold.

WE, whofe names are hereunto fubfcribed, paffengers in the fhip St. James, from Belfaft to Newcaftle and New-York, impreffed with a deep fenfe of refpect and efteem, which no length of time can efface, take this public manner of returning our moft ardent and fincere thanks to Capt. Mark Collins, for his very kind, humane and generous treatment to us during the whole of our paffage. Our obligations to him are fo great, for his attention and humanity to the fick and aged, that to let pafs this opportunity of expreffing our heartfelt fenfe of his merit and abilities, we fhould confider ourfelves as guilty of the greateft injuftice, as well as ingratitude. But what claims our higheft efteem was his exemplary behaviour, with refpect to fobriety and temperance, in the fulleft fenfe of the words.

Tho' train'd in boifterous elements, his mind
Was yet by foft humanity refin'd;
Each joy of wedded love at home he knew,
Abroad confeft the father of his crew :
Kind, liberal, juft, the calm domeftic fcene
Had o'er his temper breath'd a gay ferene.

Revd John Martin & Son,		William Adams	ditto	
Alex. M'Neight for Self and Family,		William Henry	ditto	
		Ifaac Glafs	ditto	
John Pollock	ditto	Samuel Harbifon	ditto	
Robert Bell	ditto	Thomas Snodden	ditto	
David Bell	ditto	Andrew Thomfon	ditto	
John Brown	ditto	James Harris	ditto	
John Barron	ditto	Alex. Cochran	ditto	
Arch. Watfon	ditto	John Ringan	ditto	
William Lee	ditto	Robert Dunlap	ditto	
John Lowry	ditto	Jane Dalzell	ditto	
John Marfhall	ditto	William Holliday	ditto	
John Mofman fen.	ditto	Samuel Brown and wife,		
John Mofman jun.	ditto	Adam Wilfon and wife,		
Hugh Fairly	ditto	Arch. Ball and wife,		
Samuel Magowan	ditto	John Armftrong and wife,		
James White	ditto	Matthew Malcom & wife,		
Robert Law	ditto	James Hamilton & fifter,		
Jofeph Wilfon	ditto	John Young & fon,		
John Moore	ditto	Samuel Fingey & fon,		

Andrew Fergufon	George Young	Robert Bell
Alex. Williamfon	Robt. M'Illwrath	David Stevenfon
Jane Haney	Robert M'Lean	Daniel M'Ree
Geo. M'Lelland	John M'Caughtry	Wm. M'Alade
James Lowry	Andrew Carr	Henry M'Cullough
James Furgufon	Wm. Dennam	George Ofborne
George Willis	Jas. Summerville	Henry Marcer,
John Barclay	John Lyle	Wm. M'Rillop,
John M'Lean	John M'Fall	John Smith
Eliza Wilfon	Mofes Wright	Jofeph Henry
John Morton	John Lemon	James Whan
Wm. Morton	Wm. Lemon	James Park
Alex. Gordon	Thomas Jardaine	James Nickle
Elizabeth Vance	Mary Stewart	James M'Voigh
James Boyd	Sam, M'Cullough,	Jofeph Martin
Samuel Stott	James Clarke	Pierce Duffey
Hugh Miller	John M'Connell	James Brown
Samuel Wilfon	Samuel Miliken	John Boyd
Edward Purdue	Bernard Burns	Samuel Thompfon
Daniel Sanderfon	Alex. Agnew	Hugh Johnfton
Thomas Shields	Patrick Beatty	Arthur Short
William Smyle	Wm. Gordon	John Mayne
John Smyle	Samuel Irwin,	John Horon
John Hayfe	Sam. M'Caghey	Alex. Hagowan,
Andrew Young	Wm Ramfey	Rainey Boomer.

N. B. Captain Collins of the St. James, intends being in Belfaft with a Cargo of Flaxfeed, and will fail early in Spring, for Newcaftle and New-York.——For Freight or Paffage apply to Jones, Tomb, Joy & Co. who will alfo have another Veffel to fail early in the Spring for Charleftown, South-Carolina.

Belfaft, 19th Nov. 1789.

Wanted,

AS Helper under under a Groom, a Perfon accuftomed to the care of Horfes : He muft produce fatisfactory difcharges as to fobriety, honefty and attention. Apply to James Watfon, Efq; Brookhill, Lifburn.

November 18th, 1789.

To be Let from firft of November, for a Term of Years,

A Farm of Land, containing about 25 acres, contiguous to Ballylefson—This Farm is well circumftanced, one half of it being meadow, and the other half lately limed, and having a road to it from the King's highway ; there are at prefent three cabin houfes upon it, and if a good tenant offers there will be a brick and lime houfe built for him.——Apply to Robert Stewart, Ballyfinlay.

N. B. A pair of good Draft BULLOCKS to be fold ; as alfo a pair of light bay HORSES, well trained for the carriage, young and found.——Apply as above.

October 30th, 1789.

For LONDON,

THE THAMES, JAMES BENNET, Mafter, (a conftant Trader now in port) will be clear the third December next.—For Freight, &c. apply to
ARCH. TAYLOR.

Newry 7th Nov. 1789.

A Caution

WHEREAS Charles Mc. Aree, otherwife King, my apprentice, has eloped from my fervice on Friday the 13th inft. without any Reafon whatever.——As he has often collected money for me, I do hereby caution the publick who may be indebted to me, not to pay any debts to the above Charles Mc. Aree, otherwife King ; and I am determined to put the law in force againft any perfon or perfons who may harbour or employ him after this notice.

Dated at Augher, Nov. 14th, 1789.
ACHESON MOORE.

LOTTERY TICKETS, Warranted undrawn,

ARE now felling at the Belfaft Lottery Office, where the patent lift of blanks and prizes are daily received

Cafh for prizes foon as drawn ;—the higheft price for light guineas, which are cut in prefence of the feller, to prevent farther circulation.

William M'Clure

IS now landing, and has for fale, from the beft markets—

Hyfons,		Patent and	
Real Souchong,	Teas.	Common	Shot,
Green and		Pearl and	Afhes,
Gongou		Dantzig	
Saltpetre,		Roll Brimftone,	
Spanifh Indigo,		Glauber Salts,	
Allum,		Sulphur,	
New-Hops,			

The above, with his ufual affortment of groceries, will be fold cheap for good payments.

Belfaft, 20th Nov. 1789.

N. B. He expects new fruit, lintfeed and olive oil in a few days.

NEW TEAS.

DAVISON and MINISS have received from the laft Eaft India fales, in London, by the Lord Donegall, a parcel of frefh Teas, confifting of bohea, plain green, fine and common congo, blooms, and hyfons. They are well fupplied with beft French and fine Spanifh Indigo, black pepper, ginger, fine and fuperfine muftard, and a general affortment of groceries and dyeftuffs, which they will fell on low terms for good payments.

Belfaft, 18th Nov 1789.

Robert Hill,

HAS in his Stores, in Anne-ftreet, Jamaica and Antigua Rum, old Jamaica and Antigua Rum, Rum-D, common Rum, Brandy, Gineva, Cherry and Rafpberry Brandy, Rafpberry Rum ; Red Port, Sherry and Mountain in wood and bottles.

The above articles will be found good and reafonable.

Belfaft, 19th November, 1789.

John Alexander, and Co.

ARE giving the higheft prices for wheat, barley, and oats, at the Belfaft mills.

19th Nov. 1789.

Soapboiling and Chandling

JOHN POLLOCK refpectfully informs his friends and the public, that he has commenced the above bufinefs, and has ready for fale, at the fhop formerly occupied by Mr. William Watfon, two doors above the Broker's office, corner of Forreft-lane, High-ftreet—beft and common foap, mould and dip'd candles—the quality of which he trufts will give fatisfaction ;—and as he means to fell on the very loweft terms, retailers and others will find it their intereft to deal with him. Belfaft, 18th Nov. 1789.

§||§ Two front rooms, furnifhed, to be let—enquire as above.

John Hamilton Corbitt,

HAVING removed from Banbridge to Belfaft, where he is carrying on the Soapboiling and Chandling Bufinefs extenfively, in all its branches—hopes, from his attention and the excellent quality of his goods, to merit the commands of his friends and the public.

Ann-ftreet, Nov. 20th, 1789.

PARISIAN INTELLIGENCE.

National Assembly, *Thursday, Oct.* 29.

THIS day a letter was read from a Nun to the Committee of Reports, which will in all human probability, occasion the abolition of Convents, Monasteries, and all religious houses of that kind, by prohibiting the administration of vows.

This Lady informed the Assembly, that being a member of the Council convoked by her Abbess, she had it in her power, and thought it her duty to relate the tyranny of their community, as two Novices were at present about to be forced to take the veil, a circumstance which she hoped their august body would immediately prevent, if they intended to annihilate religious institutions of this kind.

This appeal to their justice, was received by all the members, with all those transports of joy, which it was possible for the defenders of liberty to evince. All were flattered to testify to the European world, how odious, tyrannical, and barbarous the most enlightened Assembly on earth was pleased to think these absurd institutions, which Oriental superstition had introduced among us.

A Bishop, and two other Ecclesiastics, made some feeble efforts, in order to prevent a prohibition, but in vain; for the following arret was immediately agreed to:

"The National Assembly having heard the report of the Committee, adjourn the question concerning monastic vows; but in the mean time order, that no vows whatever shall be made in future, in any monastery belonging to either sex.

Troubles in Brabant.

Hague, Oct. 29. Letters from brabant, dated the 27th, mention, that the troubles in those parts, far from diminishing, increase more and more, especially at Antwerp, where the garrison has retired into the Citadel, not thinking themselves safe in the town. It is added, that the Brabantine Army, which consists of 40,000 men, have made themselves masters of the Forts of Lillo and Liefkenshoek, where they have torn down all the Imperial Arms.

EDINBURGH, Oct. 31.

It is with much satisfaction that we are able to announce the completion of the operations upon the old works of the Forth and Clyde navigation, by which an additional foot of water has been acquired; an improvement which cannot fail to prove extremely beneficial to the coasting trade of the country, as vessels drawing eight feet water may now pass from Grangemouth to Glasgow, and in the course of six months, if the season should be favourable, there is every reason to expect that this great inland navigation will be open from sea to sea.

DUBLIN, November 12.

Mr. John Magee of College-green was this day brought up to the Court of King's-Bench in order to receive judgment on the information at the suit of Mr. Higgins; when he was remanded to the custody of the Sheriffs, to be again brought up on Tuesday next, in order to assign error.

The best ox beef was lately selling at Cork, Youghal, and Waterford, for three halfpence, and middling cow do for one penny a pound. From hence it appears, that the slaughter business has dwindled in those parts of the kingdom which were looked on as the grand emporium of the provision trade. The consequence must certainly be a proportionable increase of tillage, which, with the judicious bounty on the exportation of corn, meal and flour, will, with God's blessing on our harvests, ensure wealth and plenty.

Since the resolution entered into for encouraging the slaughtering of cattle in Limerick, beef of every weight has risen 1s. 6d. per cwt. in Cork.

Persons of every denomination in the provinces bordering on the Ocean and Mediterranean, in Spain and Portugal, are very desirous of our linens, fustians, plain and figured velverets, calimancoes, poplins, and other mixed goods; a manufacture of black, blue, silver grey, or chocolate coloured velverets, spotted with small stars of gold, seems the reigning taste for winter amongst persons of quality; and if such were made in Ireland, they would find an excellent market at Cadiz, Malaga, Valencia, Barcelona, Seville, St. Lucar, and in general throughout the opulent provinces of Spain and Portugal.

DUBLIN, Nov. 14.

Thursday, in the Court of King's Bench, the Attorney General, on the part of the Crown, moved for a conditional rule for an attachment to issue against John Magee, for two publications of the 15th and 17th of September last, in a paper called the Dublin Evening Post, of which the said John Magee is proprietor, for misrepresenting the proceedings of the Court of King's-Bench, and reflecting on the Judge who presided. Rule granted unless cause in four days.—*Dub. Chron.*

On the business respecting J. Magee's situation, we say nothing while that business is at issue—we have only to say, he is now a prisoner in Newgate—and that Tuesday next is fixed for the determination of the Court of King's Bench, upon the business of a celebrated trial at *Nisi Prius* at the conclusion of last term. *D. E. Post.*

Should the report, prevalent here for some days, prove well founded, of an open and determined rupture having taken place in England between Mr. Pitt and Lord Thurlow, it may probably prove the means of preventing the Earl of Westmorland from assuming the Viceroyship of this country: For the Earl is confessedly an *eleve* of Mr. Pitt's, and should he, in consequence of this rupture, be forced from the ministry, his personal connections will certainly retire with him. *D. E. Post.*

In order to diffuse the spirit of liberty as extensively as possible through this kingdom, various clubs are forming, in the different country towns, on the same plan and principles with the Whig Club in this city.—These being composed of the most spirited individuals in their respective districts, mean to open a correspondence with the club in the capital, and to co-operate with it in those manly measures which its members have engaged to pursue for the promotion of the public good, and the resistance of despotic authority.

A writ for a Member to serve in Parliament for the County of Dublin, was announced in this day's Gazette, by the Right Hon. the Speaker, in the room of the Right Hon. Luke Gardiner, now Lord Mountjoy.

DUBLIN, Nov. 14.

Yesterday, and during the whole of last night, it blew a perfect hurricane, so that great apprehensions are entertained for the shipping which happened to be cruising between the Irish and English coasts.

Houses, in different parts of the city, were stripped last night of part of their slates, from the violence of the storm, which raged for upwards of twenty-four hours, so that it was exceedingly dangerous to walk the streets. A woman in Thomas-street is said to have had her skull fractured by the fall of a large brick, that was blown from the top of a chimney; and it is to be feared that many similar accidents befel unfortunate passengers in other parts of the town.

Among the disasters occasioned by the storm of wind abovementioned, we are sorry to tell the falling of two old houses in Upper Kevin-street. These tottering mansions, it seems, were inhabited, as from under their ruins two men were afterwas dug, whole mangled bodies, with scarce any appearance of life, were carried to the county infirmary.

The Rev. M. James Willson, of Stockport, in Cheshire, has some time ago invented a method of bleaching cotton and linen goods, in a safe and much more expeditious manner than has been hitherto known or practised. Cotton is perfectly bleached in the course of a few hours, and linen in one-third the usual time. The Lancashire bleachers have for some time past employed his method with much satisfaction.

Bankrupts, George O'Maley, of Castlebar, in the county of Mayo, merchant tanner, dealer and chapman, to surrender the 26th and 28th days of November, and 26th of December.——James Smith, late of the city of Dublin, linen-draper dealer and chapman, to surrender the 26th and 27th days of November, and 26th of December.

DUBLIN Nov. 17.

Extract of a letter from the county of Fermanagh, November 12, 1789.

"I am certain you will be pleased to hear that Laurence Peebles, of Lisnaskea, in this county, against whom examinations have been lodged, as aiding and assisting his brother, John Peebles, in several robberies, and particularly in a late daring attempt to break into the house of Mr. Clark, in the county Cavan, was apprehended on Tuesday last.

"Two of the sons of Major Brooke having taken the hounds as far as Lisnaskea, a gentleman of the party, who knew Peebles, saw him at work in a potatoe field, with a gun by his side, on which the whole party went to the house of a neighbouring gentleman, and there furnished themselves with arms, returned to the field in full gallop with the huntsman, and hounds at their head, and coming up to Peebles, desired him to surrender, which he refused, at same time endeavouring to escape, by leaping over two large quickset ditches, over which he was directly followed by one of the Mr. Brookes', by him overtaken, and kept at bay, until the rest of the gentlemen came round; when surrounded, he presented his gun, and fortunately missed fire; upon which he was fired on by Mr. John King, of Droomgoon, and instantly after by both the Mr. Brookes', by which shots he was severely wounded; he was then seized by Mr. John Balfour, of Drumcrue, and being properly secured, was immediately taken to, and lodged in the gaol of Enniskillen."

BOROUGH of SWORDS.

In this borough, of notorious fame in the annals of bribery and corruption, the right of election is vested in the Protestant inhabitants six months residence previous to the election: and from their tender regard to their personal interests, the weightiest purse is, commonly, here successful.

The Bolton, the Cobbe, and the Hatch families have, successively and conjointly, been supposed to possess a decisive influence over the voters: but they have, before now, been defeated by money scriveners from England, and parchment scribblers of our own.

General Massey, some time since, cast a longing eye on this borough, which he considered as a common open to any occupant: and to secure the command of it to himself, he began to take and build tenements within its precincts, in which he placed many veteran soldiers, who having served under him in war, were firmly attached to their antient leader.

Belfast, *November* 20.

☞ ONE MAIL DUE.

On Wednesday night there were several very loud peals of thunder and vivid flashes of lightning, such as we seldom experience in this climate at so late a season.

On Sunday last the Lord Bishop of Down preached in the Church of Lisburn, when a collection was made for the Sunday Schools within the parish, which with the subscriptions from the inhabitants of the town for the present year, amounted to 65l.

The Committee for managing the Schools, desire to return thanks to his Lordship for the support which the institution has received from his excellent sermon, and from his liberal donation to it.

We have the satisfaction to mention, that this benevolent institution in the town of Lisburn, has been supported by the contributions and the attention of all denominations of Christians.

The enameled Watch, advertised in the first page of this paper, was dropped at Belvoir, near Belfast, on Saturday the 14th inst. A reward of three Guineas will be paid by James M'Clean for the Watch, or to any person giving information so as it may be found.

Extract of a Letter from Edinburgh, dated Nov 11.

"At the annual meeting of the American Physical Society, in Surgeons-square, assembled for the purpose of electing Presidents for the ensuing year, the following four were, by majority, elected.

Charles Bankhead, Carrickfergus, Ireland.
Peter Ward, Charlestown, South Carolina.
John Muir, Island of Antigua, West-Indies.
Robert Cunningham, Dunbar, Scotland."

Extract of a Letter from Edinburgh, dated Nov. 16.

"This day the Foundation Stone of the New College was laid with great solemnity by the Right Hon. Francis Lord Napier, Grand Master Mason of Scotland, in presence of the Right Hon. the Lord Provost, Magistrates, and Town Council, of the City of Edinburgh, with the principal professors, and Students, of the University of Edinburgh, a number of Nobility and Gentry, and the Masters, Officers, and Brethren, of all the Lodges of Free Masons in this city and neighbourhood, besides an innumerable crowd of spectators.

Belfast, *November* 17.

☞ TWO MAILS DUE.

The Nancy of P. Glasgow, laden with linen cloth, hides and butter, bound for Greenock, sailed from this port on Saturday morning and put into Larne that day. In the night, the anchor being foul, the master and two men (which were all the crew) having gone out in the boat to clear it, were drowned, the three bodies being found on the beach next morning. Mr. M'Neile of Larne has taken charge of the vessel and cargo.

Married, at Bangor, last Saturday, Samuel Richard Perry, Esq. to Miss Elizabeth Clewlow.

FAIRS IN THE ENSUING WEEK.

Monday, Nov. 23. Bangor, Down. Castlefin, Don. Clough, Down. Curran, Der. Fivemile-town, Tyr.—Tuesday 24. Ballybought, Arm. Ballyclare, Ant. Dungannon, Tyr. Macrecrigan, Tyr. —Wednesday 25th. Benburbe, Tyr. Johnston's-bridge, Arm. Roccorry, Mon. St. Johnston's, Don. —Thursday 26, Carnteel, Tyr. Lifane, Der. Saintfield, Down.—Friday, 27. Dunymanagh, Tyr.—— Saturday 28. Donegall Town. Glaslough, Mon. Kircubbin, Down. Middleton, Arm.

Anno 1789.] Printed by HENRY JOY, and Co. BELFAST.

The BELFAST NEWS-LETTER.

TUESDAY November 24,   FRIDAY November 27, 1789.

OLD WINE VAULTS,
AND
LONDON PORTER STORES,

No. 6, LOWER JERVIS STREET, DUBLIN.

CHARLES CARROTHERS and WILLIAM BOYD,

WITH much respect inform their Friends and the Public, that they have entered into Partnership, under the firm of *Carrothers and Boyd*.

Their joint Stock of *Wines* forms an extensive assortment, particularly CLARETS of *high growths, twelve to twenty-four months in bottle*.

They have also several tuns of *old Red Port*, and *White Wines* in wood and bottle, of very superior quality, all which they will sell at a very moderate profit, for *ready money only*.

They have renewed a contract which the House has had for many years with S. *Whitbread, Esq.* for an ample and regular supply of LONDON PORTER, the *best produce* of his famous Brewery, of which they have now on hand, a large quantity in wood and bottle, fit for immediate use.

GLOBE INN, NEWRY.
ETIENNE MORTEGUITTE,

BEGS leave to inform the nobility, gentry, and public in general, that he has taken the noted Globe Inn of Newry, lately kept by Christopher Byrne, which he has fitted up in a superior style of convenience, having provided the very best beds and bedding, and is determined to have his larder constantly supplied with the best articles in season, and his cellar well stocked with best genuine spirits and choice wines, and hopes by his care, attention, and moderate charges, to merit the approbation of such as are pleased to favour him in his business.

☞ He has provided a number of new post chaises, with able horses and careful drivers, also saddle horses, which will always be ready at a moment's notice—together with a large stock of good hay and a quantity of good old oats, for the accommodation of all travellers.

A Classical Scholar,

WHOSE experience, as a teacher, would, he presumes, give satisfaction, will be ready to engage either in a public or private capacity first January next; as the young gentlemen, under his immediate direction, will be then prepared for the different professions for which they are intended. As to his moral character, conduct and abilities, he refers to the Reverend Mr. Sturrock, Banbridge; Revd. Mr. Kennedy, Downe; Revd. Mr. Burdy, Strangford; or the Revd. Mr. Black, Derry. A few lines, directed to A. C. care of Mr. Burdy aforesaid, will be duly attended to.

N. B. Said person lately prepared for Trinity College, a young gentleman of sixteen, who, by good answering at Examinations, obtained very honorable distinctions.

. Said person will also engage to teach English Grammar, &c. with the greatest accuracy

12th November, 1789.

£1,000

TO be lent on real security in the county of Antrim or Down.—Application to Messrs. Heron and Kennedy, Attornies, (postage free) to Mr. Heron now at Lisburn, or to Mr. Kennedy now in Dublin, No. 10, Peter-street.

Dated this 26th day of Nov. 1789.

Apprentices for Sea.

MC. KEDY and STEVENSON want a few young Men to go Apprentices in the London and Liverpool Traders.—Those who are well recommended and give security, will meet with great encouragement.

Belfast, 26th Nov. 1789.

The old Belfast Coterie,

WILL be held (as usual) at the Donegall-Arms, on Tuesday Night, the first December next.

Belfast, 26th November, 1789.

To be sold by Auction,

OPPOSITE the Donegall-Arms, an elegant fine Horse and Mare, on Friday the 4th of December next.

Belfast, 26th November, 1789.

A Stray Bullock.

ANY Person proving the Bullock to be his property, and paying the cost incurred, may have him, on application to James Davison.

Nowhead, 25th Nov. 1789.

£500 or £600

TO be lent from the first day of December next, on approved security.—Application to be made to Samuel Mc. Tier at the Ballast Office.

Belfast, 23d Nov. 1789.

James Pinkerton,

IS this day landing *Whitbread's best London Porter*, in Hogsheads and Barrels;—it will be found of the finest quality, and will be sold at his usual prices, for cash only.

North-street, Belfast 21st Nov. 1789.

Strong Brandy, Vinegar, &c.

DAVISON and GRAHAM have on board the Neptune, Capt. Miskelly, from Bordeaux, (who is arrived in Newry, and will be here in a day or two) a few pipes and hogsheads of the very best 2-3 augmented Brandy, and a few tons of the best Whitewine Vinegar, which they will sell (as imported only) for a very moderate profit.

Belfast, 20th Nov. 1789.

. They have also on hand about twenty Quarter Casks Malaga Wine of a superior quality, which (to close sales) they will sell cheap.

THE Noblemen, and Gentlemen of the Counties of Antrim, Down, and Counties adjacent, are respectfully informed that J. WILLIAMSON, Land Surveyor, and Draughtsman, has removed from Ballymena to Belfast, for the greater convenience of attending the commands of his respectable employers, and the public in general.——Having had the honour of being instructed in Drawing for some years in the Dublin Society's Academy—and from an extensive practice in his profession—flatters himself his Surveys and Maps, will ensure him a continuance of that share of publick favor which he has experienced for ten years past, and claims his most grateful thanks

Large Books of Maps,

elegantly drawn, wrote, ornamented, &c. with references, shewing the quantity, quality, &c. of each tenant's denomination:—likewise will be delineated, all arable, meadow and boggy grounds, hills roads, rivers and houses, or whatever may be remarkable on the lands.

Small Pocket Books of Maps,

drawn out, and elegantly embellished—tho' reduced to the the size of 8 by 7 inches—will contain every particular above-mentioned, making an useful and elegant Pocket Companion for any gentleman of landed property when bound in red Morocco and gilt.

Gentlemen's Demesnes,

surveyed and drawn on a large scale, exhibiting at first view, a correct and picturesque Map in miniature of the land—framed and glazed if required.——Lands divided, and small Maps drawn plain to annex to leafes.

MAPS of every denomination, copied, enlarged, or reduced, either ornamented or done plain—and printed Maps, coloured, mounted on linen, with rollers, cut for the pocket

He intends to keep constantly in Ballymena, surveying Instruments for the convenience of paying immediate attention to the commands of his employers in that part of the country.——Specimens of his Maps may be seen in the Grand Jury-Room, Carrickfergus, or at his house in Princes-street.

November 17th, 1789.

Castle-Bellingham Ale

FRANCIS AICKIN has for Sale, at his Stores in Lurgan a constant supply of Castle-Bellingham Ale, remarkably good,—which, with his usual assortment of Rum Brandy, Geneva, Whiskey, Port and White Wines, will be sold on the lowest terms.

He is well assorted with spun Cotton, both reel'd and in Caps, which will be sold reasonably, and engaged to be of the very best quality.

Lurgan. Nov. 18, 1789.

William Johnson,

Nursery and Seedsman, Lisburn,

HAS now for sale at his Nurseries, a good assortment of Fruit and Forest Trees, Ever-greens and Flowering Shrubs, Thorn and Crab Quicks, &c—all of which he will sell on reasonable terms—in particular he has a large stock of four year-old Scotch Firs, the most approved age for planting, remarkable strong, healthy plants, about 18 inches high, and a great deal of good Oaks, which he will sell very cheap.

Lisburn, 24th Nov. 1789.

A House to be Let,

IN Donegall street, with every Fixture compleat.—Apply to John Elliott.

Belfast, 27th Nov. 1789.

N. B. Immediate possession will be given

The Capital Prizes

YET in the Wheel—and *Seven thousand, nine hundred and twenty five Blanks drawn.*

STATE of the PRIZES in the Wheel at the close of the ninth Day of Drawing:

2	Prizes of	£ 20,000	78	——	£ 20
1	——	10,000	7659	——	10
1	——	5,000	First drawn 10th day,		500
3	——	2,000	First do. 16th,		500
4	——	1,000	First do. 22d,		500
10	——	500	Last drawn,		500
22	——	100			

A few TICKETS of different Kinds, received by last post, are now selling at MAGEE's, which he can with certainty WARRANT UNDRAWN, being daily supplied with the Managers List of Blanks and Prizes.

Tickets already drawn Prizes, taken in exchange at full value

Hu. and Wm. Johnson,

HAVE received their Winter Assortment of superfine Broad and Yard-wide Cloths, Coatings, new Fancy Waistcoating and Buttons, Cassameres, Thicksets, Worsted and Cotton Cords, Dimities, Musslinets, Marseilles Quilting, Marseilles Quilts, Counterpanes, Moreens, &c. &c.

Belfast, 24th Nov. 1789.

Eloped,

MARY Mc. ALIES otherwise Rainey my Wife—I do hereby caution the Publick, not to trust her on my account, as I will not pay any Debt she may hereafter contract.

SIMON Mc. ALIES, ‡ his mark.

Falls, Nov. 19th 1789

NOTICE.

ALL those to whom the late Mr. John Reid stands indebted, will please furnish their accounts to his Executors, *James Ferguson, Valentine Joyce,* and *James Stevenson*; and those who are indebted to him, are requested to pay their respective accounts to said Executors—who will sell by public auction, on Friday the fourth of December next, exactly at one o'clock, opposite the Donegall-Arms, a very beautiful high-bred *English Mare,* the property of the deceased

Belfast, 25th Nov. 1789.

To be Sold by Auction,

AT Mr. Charles Mc. Garry's in Points-Pass, on Saturday the 5th of December, A Lease of five Storehouses in Scarva, adjoining the Canal. The Houses are new and in good repair; and the lease is for four young lives, or thirty years. Mr. Keenan, of Scarva, will shew the premisses.

November 23d, 1789.

Linen Cloth mislaid.

ABOUT four months since there was left at the house of Thomas Mackey in Belfast, (by some person unknown) two pieces of Brown Linen Cloth.

Whoever can prove property may have them by applying as above, and paying the expences.

Belfast, 23d Nov. 1789.

N. B. To be continued three times.

PROFESSIONAL CONCERTS.

On MONDAY Evening the 30th inst. (at the Exchange Rooms, B-Hall, will be performed a GRAND CONCERT of Vocal and Instrumental Music. First Violin Mr. MAHOON, from London.

ACT Ist.

Overture, PICHLL.

Song (I route the game) Mrs. ARNOLD.
Concerto Harpsichord, Mr. BUNTING.
Song (Hush every breeze) Mrs. ARNOLD.
Concerto Flute, composed by Mr. Ashe, in which will be introduced " Robin Gray," Mr. ASHE.

To be Sold,

A Pair of cocked tail black Geldings, well matched, with small stars, sound, highly bitted and fit for immediate use. They will be in the Fair of Killelea (county of Armagh) on Friday the 27th instant; as also some fat Bullocks, seven years old, and spayed Heifers. Apply to Mr. Edward Hughes.

November 25th, 1789.

A Young Man, who understands the Apothecary Business, will hear of employment by applying to James Moore Walker.

N. B. An Apprentice is also wanted.

Lisburn, Nov. 24th, 1789.

95

LONDON, Nov. 14—16.

The following appointments have been made in the Diplomatic department: Earl Gower goes ambaſſador to France; Lord Auckland goes ambaſſador to the Hague, and takes Lord Henry Spencer, the ſon of the Duke of Marlborough, with him as ſecretary to to the Embaſſy; and Mr. Fitzherbert goes to Madrid.

The King on Monday laſt fixed a pin money annuity of 2000l. per annum, payable quarterly out of his own privy purſe, on the princeſs Auguſta at her Royal Highneſs's coming of age. The Queen has alſo preſented the Princeſs with jewels of value on the occaſion.

The Marquis de la Fayette's ſituation is by no means pleaſant at this moment:—As, by a Gentleman who left Paris on Wedneſday laſt, we learn, that a very powerful faction, among the lower order, prevailed againſt him—and his life was thought to be in danger.

The Houſe of Repreſentatives, in America, have fixed the Salary for the Preſident at 25,000 dollars *per annum*, including all expences; for the Vice Preſident 5000 *per annum*; and for each of the Secretaries and Repreſentatives ſix dollars per day.

The Flemiſh Patriots have taken not only Lillo and Liefkenſbourgh, but alſo Fort Frederic Henry on the Scheldt.

DUBLIN Nov. 21.

Laſt night about 12 o'clock, a fire was diſcovered in the Firſt Commiſſioner's apartments in the New Cuſtom-houſe, which communicating with other parts of the weſt building, raged with great violence, and before any aſſiſtance could be procured, the furniture was conſumed. From the exertions of the water-engines and the military, it is hoped the damage will not be very conſiderable.—The progreſs of the flames had been nearly prevented from communicating to the other parts of that extenſive building when this paper went to preſs.

Letters lately received from Maryland adviſe, that the demand for bread and corn thoſe two years paſt from Portugal and France, has entirely revived the ſpirit of the planters or tillage farmers in that province, where the growing of corn had conſiderably declined ſince the kingdom of Ireland, from its increaſed agriculture, and prohibitory laws, no longer afforded a vent for American ſuperfluity.

Lord Weſtmoreland is expected to arrive about the 17th of December next to take upon him the Government of this country. Major Hobart, will certainly retain his ſituation of Lord Lieutenant's Secretary.

The WHIG CLUB.

THIS patriotic body dined together at Ryan's in Fownes's-ſtreet on Wedneſday. The meeting was numerous, and moſt reſpectable—the members were in uniform—blue coats, edged buff, with buff waiſtcoats and breeches, and an elegant fancy button. ſtruck on purpoſe—device the Imperial Crown and Harp, with the title of Whig Club in a garter.

The Clerical Members, and there are many of the dignified clergy of the number, wear at their breaſts a garter blue ribbon, edged buff—and ornamented with an impreſſion in gold, of the Imperial Iriſh Crown and Harp, with the title of Whig Club in a garter.

In the abſence of Mr. Conolly, Mr. D. B. Daly acted as Secretary, *pro tempore*.

The acceſſion of patriotic ſupport to this Society was rapid and reputable, even while their ſpeculative principles were but partially known; but now that they have announced in the public prints the grand objects of their aſſociation, we doubt not their cauſe will meet warm and univerſal ſupport throughout the kingdom.

Though this Club, as to its parliamentary members, will be ſelected by ballot, yet we underſtand it is intended their public days will be very ſhortly arranged on the ſame principle on which the Whig Club in Weſtminſter conduct theirs. Their meetings on thoſe days will be open for the acceſs of every gentleman, whether Senator or not, introduced by a member.

This regulation will be productive of the happieſt effect in promoting harmony and mutual confidence between the reſpectable citizen, the ſpirited freeholder, and the patriotic branch of the repreſentative body, and will, we truſt, very much tend to ſtrengthen the Whig cauſe throughout the kingdom, and lead to the eſtabliſhment of ſubordinate aſſociations of the ſame kind through every county in Ireland.

Now that we are at the eve of a general election, when every engine of Government is ſet in motion, to procure a majority in the new Parliament—when honours are ſold, and the price applied to the purchaſe of ſeats—ſalaries encreaſed, obſolete offices revived, and uſeleſs ones created—all for the purpoſe of enabling the Miniſter of England to ſwindle away our freedom; ſurely, ſimilar inſtitutions, on a ſmaller ſcale, ſhould be eſtabliſhed in the country parts of the kingdom, to ſupport the election of men, whoſe integrity and attachment to the Conſtitution, have diſtinguiſhed them as its real friends.

We have ſet forth the great principles and objects of the Whig Club; and we have formed this Society, becauſe we apprehend ſome of thoſe objects are in danger.

The Rights of the People of Ireland have been publicly and miniſterially queſtioned by the preſent Chief Governor.

A right in the Parliament of another country to make laws for this kingdom in the caſe of a Regency, has been by the Miniſters of the Crown in Ireland, advanced and defended.

The competency of the two Houſes of the Iriſh Parliament on a late occaſion has been denied.

The legiſlative capacity of the King of Ireland has been denied, and the Great ſeal of another country held up as a ſubſtitute for the Imperial Crown of this Realm.

The undue influence of the Crown over both Houſes of Parliament has been of late beyond all example encreaſed.

A penſion bill has been rejected by the influence of the preſent Miniſters of Ireland.

A place bill has been rejected by the *ſame* influence.

A bill for the better ſecuring the freedom of election, by diſqualifying Revenue Officers from voting for Members to ſerve in Parliament, has been rejected by the *ſame* influence.

The preſent extravagant, ineffectual and unconſtitutional Police of the city of Dublin, has been continued and patronized by the *ſame* influence.

All proceedings in Parliament to remove the grievance, or cenſure the abuſe, have been reſiſted and defeated, by the *ſame* influence.

The expediency of combating by corruption, a conſtitutional majority in Parliament, has been *publicly* avowed, and the principle ſo avowed has been in part carried into execution.

Honours, as we apprehend, have been ſold, and the money depoſited for the purpoſe of purchaſing ſeats in the Commons, for the dependants of Adminiſtration, in order to procure for the Miniſter a majority in Parliament. For the ſame corrupt purpoſe uſeleſs offices have been created or revived.

The foundation ſtone of the New Cuſtom houſe was laid on the 13th of March, 1781.

The fire at the New Cuſtom-houſe afforded on Saturday laſt a plentiful harveſt to the light fingered gentry, ſeveral perſons having to regret on that occaſion the loſs of their purſes, and pocket handkerchiefs.

Further Particulars.

The cauſe which gave riſe to the fire at the New Cuſtom-houſe has not yet been diſcovered; but the general opinion is inclined to put it down to the premeditated malice of ſome incendiary. But a rigid inquiry is making into this affair, and if poſſible, the real truth will be inveſtigated.

The damages are ſuppoſed at about four thouſand pounds, but the repairs will be immediately proceeded on, and finiſhed without any kind of intermiſſion.

Had the cielings of the rooms been lined with ſheet iron, in the manner invented by Lord Dundonald, the flames could not penetrate to the roof, but have gone through the windows. All public buildings ſhould be guarded in this manner, eſpecially, as conſidering the utility, compared to the expence, it exceeds every degree of conſideration.

The military guard, horſe and foot, did not return from the New Cuſtom-houſe, until Sunday morning, when every trace of the fire was extinguiſhed. Luckily the fire did not communicate to the lower ſtores, which contained a great deal of oil and ſpirits.

It is imagined, had not the army ſpeedily attended at the New Cuſtom-houſe, after the late dreadful fire commenced, that far greater injury, from an irruption of the ſurrounding mob, would have been ſuſtained, than what was experienced from the devouring flames.—*Freeman's Journal.*

Good beef is ſelling in the country parts from twelve to thirteen ſhillings the hundred; but here, in town, an artificial ſcarcity is held up, and in ſome of our markets, three-pence and three-pence halfpenny a pound is demanded. This, among a thouſand other inſtances which could be adduced, proves, that until the time may arrive when the principal manufactures are executed in the country, we ſhall not be able to hold any competition with the Engliſh at even our own market.

At a meeting of the Subſcribers of the Royal Canal in Dawſon-ſtreet, Mr. Davis, architect, laid before them the drawing of a paſſage-boat, to be wrought without the aſſiſtance of men or horſes. This he ſaid he would build at his own expence, and ſhould carry eighty tons, to go with a velocity equal to the draft of four horſes. This moſt uſeful piece of mechaniſm will be of the firſt conſequence, not only to this uſeful undertaking but to Canals in general.

Mr. Grattan is fully determined to bring on the buſineſs of tythes in the enſuing ſeſſion. How dear does this attention to the welfare of the country parts of Ireland make this character to the people, eſpecially when they reflect that the idea originated with him, and that our neighbours on the Continent have ſince taken it up. Mr. Grattan's principles are ſuch, as when he eſteems any thing to be a grievance to the kingdom, he is not to be intimidated by apparent difficulties or miniſterial menaces, but exerts himſelf with inceſſant labour, till he has redreſs'd the wrongs ſo loudly complained of.

Laſt week, a young girl, daughter to a reſpectable citizen, was decoyed by a maid ſervant to a houſe in Mary's-lane, where is kept one of theſe kind of dancing ſchools, called a nightly-hop. The young lady was introduced to a waiter, as a partner, who found means to detain her until it was late; when the fellow, with ſome of his ruffian aſſociates, forced her into a coach, and ſhe has not ſince been heard of.

Herſchell's amazing teleſcope, which promiſes to ſhew us the man in the moon, is perhaps the largeſt machine ever erected in this or any other country.——

Belfaſt, *November* 24.

On Sunday evening the Earl and Counteſs of MASSEREENE, Mr. and Mrs. Bircier, her Ladyſhip's brother and ſiſter, the Marquis of Pelleport, Mr. De la Tour, Mr. Vernon, and Doctor Macartney, arrived here from London on their way to his Lordſhip's ſeat at Maſſereene Caſtle.

The long abſence of Lord Maſſereene, from ſo early a period of his youth, and the peculiar circumſtances attending it—render his return to his native country a ſubject of univerſal exultation to a numerous and reſpectable tenantry.

By the lateſt accounts from Dublin, it appears that the fire in the New Cuſtom-houſe was not extinguiſhed when the letters were ſent off at night.

MARRIED.] Mr. Samuel Ferres of Larne, ſurgeon, to Miſs Dorothea Biers of Ballymoney.

DIED. In this town, on Friday laſt, Mr. John Reid, merchant, ſincerely and deſervedly lamented.—At Newtownards, on Thurſday laſt, after a tedious illneſs, Mr. William Pollock, merchant; a man poſſeſſed of every amiable quality, and whoſe death is ſincerely regretted by a numerous and reſpectable acquaintance.

PORT NEWS.

ARRIVED.

Nov. 16. Lord Donegall, M'Roberts, London, tea, rum, &c.

17. Simpſon, Knulf, Dantzick, timber.

20. Liberty, M'Donnell, Liverpool, bale goods. New Draper, Kearney, ditto, ſugar, & ditto. Eight Colliers.

CLEARED OUT.

Nov. 17. Elizabeth, Krews, Dantzick, ballaſt.

18. Marcella, Cargey, Leghorn, cloth.

Belfaſt, *November* 27.

The Charlotte, Wm. Campbell maſter, loaded with linen cloth from this port for London, put into Millford the 15th inſt. all well. Captain Campbell writes, that his ſhip and cargo received no damage during the late tempeſtuous weather.

We underſtand that a Regiſtry of Freeholders of the County of Down is to be held in Down on *Tueſday the firſt of December.*

The 21ſt inſt. Morgan Jellett, jun. the ſon of Morgan Jellett, Eſq. of Moira, was ſworn an Attorney in his Majeſty's Court of Common Pleas in Dublin.

MARRIED. A few days ago, Doctor Dickſon, of Dungannon, to Miſs Ann Shaw, of Caſtlecaulfield.

DIED. On Friday night laſt, at her houſe in Earl-ſtreet, Dublin, univerſally lamented, Mrs. Elizabeth-Maria Johnſton, Siſter to Nicholas Johnſton, of Wood-Park, co. Armagh, Eſq.

FAIRS IN THE ENSUING WEEK.

Monday, 30th Nov. Ballintra, Don. Ballynaſs, Don. Bearagh, Tyr. Caſtlecaulfield, Tyr. Drumadoon, Ant. Gorten, Tyr. Newbliſs, Mon. Warrenpoint, Down.——Tueſday, 1ſt Dec. Ballycaſtle, Ant. Killygordon, Don. Larne, Ant.——Wedneſday 2. Convoy, Don. Knockboy, Mon. Tullydonald, Don.——Thurſday 3. Caſtlederg, Tyr. Donaghy, Tyr. Jonesbro' Arm. Swatragh, Der.——Friday 4. Toome, Ant.

PRICES IN THIS MARKET YESTERDAY.

Oatmeal,	00s.	0d. to	11s.	4½.		Dried do 25s. to 00s. 0d. per d
Wheat,	12	0 —	13	0		R. Tallow, 6s. 0d. to 6s. 4d. ſt.
Oats,	5	0 —	5	6		Petatoes 9d. to 11d. per b.
Barley,	5	8 —	6	0		Eng. coals. 00s. to 14s. 0d.
Butter,	51	6 —	52	0		Scotch do. 00s. to 13s. 6d.
C. hides,	35	0 —	38	0		Ex. on Lond. 7 a 7-4 per c.
Ox ditto,	37	6 —	40	0		Do. on Glaſgow 6½.
S. C. ſkins	40	0 —	00	0		

Anno 1789.]   Printed by HENRY JOY, and Co. BELFAST.

The BELFAST NEWS-LETTER.

TUESDAY December 1,   FRIDAY December 4, 1789.

Advertisement.

WE, the antient journeymen Taylors of Belfast, take this method of acquainting the Gentlemen of said town, as also the inhabitants in general, that our former Employers are endeavouring to persuade their customers that their journeymen are advancing their wages to 15s. per week, and will not work, which is as false as the authors of said representation, as we only want our former wages that we have received for near two years, and which the said Employers are endeavouring to pull down, by reducing our wages to 9s. per week. Its well known by their customers that the masters' bills are from 11s. 4d.¼ to 13s. per suit—but allowing 11s. 4d. h. per suit, which a man can make well in three days and a half, the man's wages come to 5s. 10d. per suit, the master's profit being 5s 6d. h. which any reasonable person will allow is sufficient to support their over-grown pride—ambition—and grandeur. We likewise request that no gentlemen or ladies will give the smallest credit to what these false accusers set forth, as we are all willing to appear before our most worthy Sovereign and vindicate what we set forth to be the truth;—but our Employers' design, by all appearance, is to employ young boys from the country for about five or six shillings per week, which of course cannot avoid spoiling gentlemen's clothes.

Belfast, 29th Nov. 1789.

This is to give Notice,

THAT any person that has lost a bay Mare may have her by proving property, and paying the expences, on making application to Samuel Hall, Greens-Barns, near Belfast.

November 27th, 1789.

Dromore Winter Fair and Linen Market.

THE WINTER FAIR will be held at Dromore on Saturday the twelfth day of December next, when there is expected to be a great Sale of Linen at the accustomed Linen Market.

Dromore, Nov. 30th, 1789.

THIS is to caution the Public not to credit Mary Mc. Murry, formerly Thomas, of Aughaskeough, any debts or demands, as she is now eloped from her husband without a lawful cause. Given under my hand, this 29th of November, 1789.

JOHN Mc. MURRY.

This is to give Notice,

THAT there is a stray Black BULLOCK in Connor Pound. Any person that can prove their property, and pay the expences, may have him. Dated this 23d November, 1789.

JOHN Mc. CULLOUCH.

William Hunter,

SURGEON and Man-midwife, has opened shop in the town of Moy, and intends to sell Drugs wholesale and retail on the most moderate terms—likewise Oils and Colours of all sorts. He flatters himself that from his assiduity and abilities he will merit the attention of the inhabitants of Moy and vicinity.

Nov. 28th, 1789.

To be sold by Auction,

ON the Premisses, on Saturday the 12th day of Dec. next,—the interest in a Lease of 39 Acres of Land, situated within one quarter of a mile of Richhill, in the County of Armagh, held by Edward Kennedy under Wm. Richardson, Esq. for three Lives or 31 Years from Nov. 1786, at the yearly rent of 33l.——There is a good dwelling House, Offices, and Orchard on the Premisses, and there is six Acres of the Farm sown with Wheat.

Same Day will be sold a quantity of Hay, Oats, Barley and Wheat, all in stack; also Horses and Cows, Cars, Plow, Harrow, &c. all for ready Money.—The sale to begin at 11 o'Clock.   Nov. 27th, 1789.

Jas Fitzsimons, Taylor, &c.

RETURNS his most sincere thanks to the Ladies and Gentlemen of Belfast and its vicinity for past favours, hopes, by his care and strict attention to business, to merit a continuance of his Friends and the Public in general. Said Fitzsimons is supplied with the very best workmen in town, at their usual wages. Ladies and Gentlemen may depend on their commands being executed with the utmost care and dispatch by applying as above, at his former prices.

Mitchel's-Entry, Belfast, 28th Nov. 1789.

Wanted,

A BUTLER, in a Family where a Pantry-boy is under him.—He must be well recommended for honesty and sobriety.—Enquiry to be made at this Office.

December 1st, 1789

To the Public

THE principal Master Taylors of Belfast, having observed with surprize in the last Belfast News-Letter, an Advertisement wherein several charges are exhibited against them by a disorderly set of men, who stile themselves the ancient Journeymen Taylors of Belfast, think it necessary to inform the Public, that the said charges are not only false but malicious, as can be proved upon oath: They also declare, that the said Journeymen for a considerable time past have by their combinations prevented strange Journeymen from coming to town, having made it a practice to extort from them large sums of money, before they would permit them to work; and have also obliged their employers to give to the most indifferent workmen the same wages that is paid to men of the first abilities in their profession, the consequence of which has been, that they (the said Journeymen) have of late become factious, inattentive to business, and intolerably insolent——it is therefore hoped and requested that the candid Public will pay no attention to the malevolent assertions of the said " Ancient Journeymen Taylors of Belfast."

A number of sober good workmen in the Tayloring Business, will find immediate and constant employ, with suitable wages, by applying to any of the underfigned persons, at their respective places of abode.

Belfast, Nov. 30th, 1789.

William Corbett,	John Wilson,
Cornelius Brennan,	James Wilson,
Joseph Cuthbert,	Hugh Fullerton,
Francis Norton,	John Hannah,
Thomas Hood,	Robert Mc. Coan.
Joseph Wilson,	

A Labourer wanted.

STEWARTS, THOMSON, & Co. at the Old Sugar-House, Belfast, want a stout young Man to work in the House—where he will have constant pay all weathers. None need apply without good recommendations for honesty and sobriety—he must be a married man—this to be only twice inserted.——They are largely supplied with every kind of Refined Sugar and Molosses, which they continue to sell at the lowest prices.—They sell Scale Sugars at the following rates—The finest kind at 8s. 6d. per stone—Second at 7s. 6d. and Third at 7s.—The quality of each will, upon trial, be found such as will give content to the consumer.

FLOUR.

WILLIAM SEED & Co. have now ready for Sale, at their Stores adjoining the Weigh-House, First, Second, Third, Fourth, and Fifth Flour; and are daily receiving fresh supplies from their Mills, the quality they expect will give satisfaction.

At said Stores they are constantly retailing Oatmeal, Meslin Meal, and Oats, even in so small quantities as three pounds and a half, which they intend continuing to do through the season.

They always give the highest price for Wheat, Barley and Oats, delivered either at their Stores in Town, or at their Mills at Bier's-Bridge.

Belfast, 30th November, 1789.

Hugh Montgomery,

HAS for Sale, at his Stores in the back of Linenhall-street, nearly opposite Mr. Buntin's Calendar, a few Bags NEW KENTISH HOPS, of the very best Quality.

N. B. The Brigantine Ann, James Martin, Master, will be ready to sail in a few days for Norfolk in America.——For freight or passage apply to said Montgomery, who wants a few tons good Potatoes.

Belfast, 28th Nov. 1789.

NOTICE.

ALL who are indebted to the Estate of Thomas Gihon, are requested to pay their respective accounts to William Auchinleck in the course of this month, that the Trustees may be enabled to settle with the creditors. The Trustees are convinced that no person concerned who is indebted will need any further application.

Belfast, 30th November, 1789.

TAKEN out of the Stable of Alexander Wright of Ballygreney, parish of Bangor, county Down, a black Mare, 4 years old, about 14 hands high, with a star, and an eye-sore on her far hind foot, weighty bodied, her tail not set, but long and round cut. Said mare was taken on Tuesday night, 24th of Nov. 1789.—Whoever returns said mare to Alex Wright, as above, shall be sufficiently rewarded—and for thief and mare, if prosecuted to conviction, a reward of 3l. 8s. 3d. Apply to Alex. Wright as above.   Dated 29th Nov. 1789.

Choice old Wines.

THIS Day, Friday the 4th of December, exactly at twelve o'clock, will be sold by auction, for approved notes at three months, under the Exchange, in single Casks, eleven Hogsheads Claret, two Hogsheads Frontigniac, and two Hogsheads Vin du Greve.—The Wines are very old and of excellent quality.—importers as well as consumers will find their interest to attend, as they will certainly go far under their cost.

Robert Wilson & Co.

Have received their Winter Assortment of

Half Tabbinets, Cloak Sattins,

Modes, Peelings, Sarcnets, Persians, Florentines, Florinets, Ribbons, Silk Handkerchiefs, black and white Laces and Edgings, Tambour, japanned Jacconet, Decca, Book, striped and checked Muslins, Jacconet, Decca and Book Muslin Handkerchiefs,

Hosiery of all Kinds,

Muslinets, Dimities, Marseilles Quilting, Calicoes, Cottons of the most fashionable patterns, Yorkshire, Glasgow, Stirling and Kilmarnock Carpets and Carpetings,

Furniture Checks and Ticks,

Blankets, Worsted and Yarn Flannels, Plaiddings, Padua Serges, Sattinets, Lastings, Durants,

Fancy Waistcoating,

Thicksets, Cotton Cords, Sewing Silks, Townspun Threads, Shoe Tapes, &c. &c.

All which will be sold by *Wholesale* or Retail at reduced prices, for ready money only.

Belfast, Dec. 3d, 1789.

☞ R. WILSON & Co. are always largely assorted with black Silks, Bombazeens, Bombazet, undressed and glazed Stuffs for Mourning

Samuel & Andrew Mc. Clean,

ARE receiving from on board the Neptune, a few Pipes best Bordeaux Brandy, which, together with a Parcel of strong Jamaica Rum and other Spirits, Wines, &c. they will sell very reasonably.

Belfast, 3d Dec. 1789.

On Wednesday the 7th Day of December will be published,

WATSON's ALMANACK, for the YEAR 1790 To be had of WILLIAM MAGEE, Bookseller in Belfast, and all the Booksellers in Ireland.

Extracts from the Mails published in London on Saturday Evening last, dated Nov. 28.

We are very happy to find that the convulsion which threatened Paris, and the lives of its citizens, by the recall of the King's body guard, has not had the mischievous consequences that were apprehended when the advices which were received last Monday from Paris left that place.

His Majesty never having seen the public buildings in Paris, and having been long in confinement, was asked by the Marquis de la Fayette to go and view them. His Majesty replied, that he would rather decline it for the present, as he should feel himself uncomfortable in appearing in public without his body guards, who had always been accustomed to attend on him. The Marquis mentioned this to the municipality at the Hotel de Ville, who immediately passed a resolution to request his Majesty to recall his guards.

This created very great jealousies and murmurings, which became so alarming, that a riot was apprehended, and the districts were on Friday last summoned to assemble by beat of drums, and the ringing of bells. This occasioned the news we have before mentioned from General Dalrymple, which was further confirmed by the resolution passed on Friday morning by the Magistracy of Paris, which is as follows:

Hotel de Ville, Nov. 20.

"It is resolved, That in case of any alarm or surprise, three pieces of cannon should be fired from the square of Henry the IVth; that on this signal being given, every battalion should instantly assemble armed at their appointed place of rendezvous, and there wait the orders of the Commandant General."

It is now rather doubtful whether the King's body guards will be recalled. The Marquis de la Fayette has taken every precaution to stop any tumult, and on Thursday reviewed each battalion of the Paris Militia, cautioning them at the same time to be vigilant and active.

The King's popularity regains a degree of vigour in the provinces. The whole body of the cavalry in France is decidedly in the King's interest. The garrison of Metz has declared that it will support the late decree of their Parliament, which has brought on them a severe censure from the National Assembly. The States of Cambray have followed the Parliaments of Rouen and Metz, and have threatened to absent themselves if the National Assembly invade on their privileges. In short, there seems to be a very general discontent, which only wants a sufficient protection to shew itself in full force.

The parliament of Britany would fain have followed the example of those of Metz, Rouen, and Cambray, in opposing the decree of the National Assembly for placing them in vacation; but the militia guard of Rennes hearing of their intention, thought proper to oppose their meeting.

The Baron de Besenval's trial is begun. He is accused by the city in the name of the King's Attorney General. In his answers he appeared firm and collected.

A proclamation was published, dated November 5, offering 2s. 6d. per quintal bounty on all wheat or wheat flour imported into France, and a proportional bounty on all other grain.

REVOLUTION IN AUSTRIAN FLANDERS.

By the Flanders mail, which arrived yesterday, we have received the following intelligence through a private channel, which may be depended on.

The Emperor has recalled General Dalton from his command, and has left Count Trautmansdorf with full powers to act as he thinks fit, with the liberty of granting every thing to the Patriots which they may ask. He has offered to restore them the full powers of their ancient Constitution.

General Schroeder, after being shot through the thigh at the battle of Turnhout, died a few days afterwards of his wounds.

At Ostend, the Patriots have issued an ordinance, that all persons should, within twenty-four hours, wear in their hats a large cockade of yellow, pink, and black, under the penalty of 30l. Flemish, or imprisonment;—the Merchants at Ostend all do duty night and day to protect their property, complying with every thing the Patriots have requested.—Great quantities of goods are shipping for safety to England and Holland, as the States of Brabant are collecting all their force to repel any attack that may be made against them.

Near 1000 soldiers enlisted at Bruges on Wednesday, for three years, in the service of the States, who have thrown off all allegiance to the Emperor; and, it is generally believed, that England and Prussia are favourable to their views.

The triumph of the Patriots is complete; for in the Brussels Gazette there is a declaration from the Emperor, dated the 20th instant, which, after a number of professions of paternal tenderness, holds out a general amnesty to all who shall return to their duty within a month, excepting only the leaders of the revolt, and stating that the most positive orders had been given, that no person should be arrested on any account whatever, otherwise than as the fundamental laws of the country prescribe. The alternative is curious.—It is, "that should he, for the time, be obliged to abandon the country, he will, at a future moment, come in full force to crush them!"

During the contest at Ghent, a detachment of 1000 men arrived from Bruges, to the assistance of the Insurgents. The whole Province of Flanders is, at the present moment, in their hands—the Black Eagle every where trampled under foot.

DUBLIN Nov. 28.

M. Buffon, a relation of the celebrated natural philosopher of that name, arrived on Friday night last in this city. He formed an intimate connection with Mr. D'Arcy, of the county of Galway, on the Continent, some years since, and has set off for that gentleman's seat. His purpose is to reside in this kingdom until the present troubles subside in France, where he possesses a very handsome estate.

It is now given out by those, who from their stations ought to know, that his Excellency of Westmoreland will not arrive at the Castle, to take on him the government of this kingdom, till the 10th of January. In the mean time the whole burden of State affairs rests on the shoulders of our modern Atlas, Mr. Secretary Hobart; and from the commotions naturally to be expected next session among the higher powers, we hardly think that he will readily meet with a Hercules to ease his load. The Attorney General may be very willing: but when his predecessor in office ascended into the upper regions, he dropt but a moderate share of his political spirit on his official successor.

The naked state of Ireland in general, for want of trees, is the surprise as well as the observation of every foreigner that travels into its internal parts. And could any of its inhabitants, of the beginning of the last century, take a peep from the grave, and view, in the above respect, the nakedness of their land, they would be still more surprised, as Ireland, about 160 years ago, was one of the most wooded countries in Europe. The present impoverished state of the face of the country, is considerably to be attributed to the extravagance of estated men, who lived beyond their income, and were necessitated, on the first pressing emergency, to level, not only their forests, but even the trees of the avenues to their seats.

Should the Solicitor General be shortly raised to the bench, as report states such a rise to be in contemplation, Mr. Serjeant Duquery is generally looked upon as the person most likely to be his successor. In the able Serjeant, legal abilities and amiable manners unite to form the accomplished barrister.

Letters patent have passed the Great Seal, granting to John Pollock, Esq; the office of Transcriptor and Foreign Apposer in Ireland.

Mr. George Booth Maxwell, a young gentleman of Jamaica, was tried on the 31st of August last, before the Supreme Court of Judicature at Kingston, on a charge of a novel nature, burglary with an intent to ravish. It appeared in evidence, that the lady of an eminent Barrister at Spanish Town, young—beautiful—and of strict virtue, had made an impression on the heart of the unhappy youth:—the propriety of the lady's conduct gave him no room to hope that he should succeed in seducing her from her husband; in his absence, therefore, he secreted himself in the house and broke into Mrs. ———'s chamber, after she had retired to rest. Awakened and alarmed by the intrusion, the lady demanded who he was, and screamed for help; he replied, Maxwell! and behaved in a manner the most insulting and outrageous, but from her reiterated cries, he thought it prudent to desist, and make his escape. The indictment was laid capitally, and he was found guilty, but recommended to mercy by the jury.

DUBLIN Nov. 28.

Thursday, in the Court of King's Bench, the Attorney General, on behalf of the Crown, moved the Court for liberty to file an information against Amyas Griffith, printer and publisher of a newspaper called the Phenix, or Griffith's New Morning Post, for inserting a paragraph in said newspaper of Friday the 20th inst. November, and continuing it in said newspaper of Wednesday the 25th instant, of a tendency dangerous to the good order and peace of society, and in some degree reflecting on the Privy Council of this kingdom. In the course of the reading of the paragraph, the Attorney General was stopped by the Court, who observed that the part of the paragraph which had been already read, was sufficient to ground an information on. The Attorney General commented on the heinous tendency of the paragraph; the Court here observed, that he had it in his power to file the information, and they never would interfere where his Majesty's Attorney General had it in his power to file an information.

Tuesday, in the Court of King's Bench, the Attorney General, on behalf of the Crown, moved the Court, that the conditional rule granted on the 12th of November, inst. for an attachment against John Magee, for certain publications in the Dublin Evening Post, of the 25th and 27th of September last, reflecting on the Court, and the proceedings in the case of the King against Magee, should be made absolute.

WHEREAS on Saturday night the 17th inst. the Coach-house of Thomas M'Can, Esq; chief Magistrate of the city of Armagh, was broke into by some person or persons unknown; who, in a most wanton manner cut and almost destroyed his Post-Chaise.—And whereas a large sum of money has been very properly offered by the respectable inhabitants of said place, to any person who shall discover and prosecute to conviction the perpetrators of this daring outrage.——Now we, the High Sheriff and Magistrates of the county of Armagh, fully sensible how necessary it is to the due execution of the laws, to support the magistrate, not only against all acts of private malice and revenge, but also to preserve him free from the apprehension of danger; do think it necessary in this public manner, to express our approbation of Mr. M'Can's conduct as a Magistrate, and to declare that his spirited exertions in that station are highly honourable to himself, and justly entitle him to the esteem and support of all good members of the community.

James Verner, Sheriff	Savage Hall,	Francis Obre
Gosford	John Maxwell,	Thomas Clarke
Capel Mollyneux, Bart.	John Moore,	Joshua M'Geough
	Mered. Workman	Arthur Noble
	Francis Tippin	John Eastwood
Richard Johnston, Bart.	J. Jones, Rector of Mullabrack	James Forde
		John Ogle
Wm. Brownlow	Robert Maxwell	John Greer
Wm. Richardson	M. Close,	James Ashmur
J. Alexander	Walter Synnot	James Harden
John Reilly	Jacob Turner	Ben. Bell
J. Godley	Acheson Thomson	John Courtney
Art. Molesworth	E. Rudson, Rector of Forkhill	Richard Eustace
Alex. T. Stewart		David Bell
Michael Obins	Hugh Stewart, Rector of Tynan	William Barker
Roger Hall		

Belfast, *December* 1.

On Sunday morning last, a young woman of the name of Elizabeth Kincaid, daughter to Mr. James Kincaid, shoemaker, in North-street, dropped down whilst lacing her stays, and almost instantly expired.

The Lord Donegall, James M'Roberts, master, for London, is detained here by contrary winds.

Sir William Temple was remarkably happy at description. There never, perhaps, was more conveyed in a few words, than, in what he observes of Holland.

"It is a country," says Sir William, "where the earth is better than the air, and profit more in request than honour; where there is more sense than wit, more good nature than good humour, and more wealth than pleasure. Where a man would chuse rather to travel than to live, shall find more things to observe than to desire, and more persons to esteem than to love."

The Dutch were formerly infected by a violent *Tulippomania*, insomuch that their richest merchants were in danger of being ruined by the excessive price they paid for tulips of uncommon colours. It was not unusual to give a sum equal to twenty pounds sterling for a rare tulip flower, and fifty pounds for a bulb which had produced a flower of a very singular kind.

Belfast, *December* 4.

On the 4th of November, the brigantine Recovery, Capt. Neilson, arrived at Lisbon with the Hon. Mrs. O'Neill, Hon. Mr. and Mrs. St. Leger on board, after a pleasant passage of six days from Cape Clear.

The first of Mr. Ware's weekly CONCERTS, which was held on Monday last, gave general Satisfaction to a very polite company, in which there were several Ladies and Gentlemen of distinguished musical talents. The performance of Doctor Arne's celebrated air *Sweet Echo*, on the Clarionet and Flute, has in point of tone, cadence, and execution, been seldom excelled. We are concerned to hear that Mr. Ware's receipts did not do much more than defray expences. Considering how much Music, that delightful science, has been neglected in this country, and particularly in this town, such exhibitions as those of Messrs. Ashe and Mahoon should be encouraged, as the best mean of cultivating musical taste.

PRICES IN THIS MARKET YESTERDAY.

Oatmeal, 11s. 4½. to 12s. od.	Dried do oos. to oos. od. per d
Wheat, 13 0 — 13 3	R. Tallow, 6s. od. to 6s. 4d. st.
Oats, 5 0 — 5 3	Potatoes 9d. to 12d per b.
Barley, 5 0 — 5 8	Eng. coals, 14s. to 15s. od.
Butter, 52 0 — 52 6	Scotch do. oos. to 13s. od.
C. hides, 35 0 — 38 0	Ex on Lond. 7 a 7 1-4 per c.
Ox ditto, 37 0 — 40 0	Do. on Glasgow 6½.
S.C. skins 40 0 — 00 0	

Anno 1789.]   Printed by HENRY JOY, and Co. BELFAST.

The BELFAST NEWS-LETTER.

TUESDAY December 8,   FRIDAY December 11, 1789.

Wanted immediately,

A Person to carry this Paper from AUGHER to FN-NISKILLEN.—Apply to Mr. Thomas Irwin, Enniskillen, or Mr. Samuel Mc. Dowell, Augher.
Belfast, Dec. 9, 1789.

SAMUEL ROBINSON,

Seedsman and Grocer, Waring-street,

BEGS leave to inform his Friends and the Publick that he has just received per the Matty, Capt. Mc Donald, from Bourdeaux,—best Olives, Anchovies, Capers, Sallad Oil, and best Whitewine Vinegar;—also per the Friendship, Capt. Lepper, from London, a Variety of Flour Roots, suitable for planting at this Season—with a Quantity early Peas—Hemp, Rape and Canary Seeds:—all which his Friends and the Public may rely being of the very best Qualities.
Belfast, Dec 10, 1789.

LONDON PORTER.

SAMUEL and ANDREW Mc. CLEAN are this day receiving from on board the Friendship, Capt. Lepper,—a parcel of Whitbread's Porter, which their Friends may depend on being fresh and of good quality.
Belfast, 9th December, 1789.

Valentine Joyce,

IS now landing out of the Matty from Bordeaux, and Friendship from London, a large parcel strong Brandy, and Whitbread's Porter, of a superior Quality.
Belfast, 8th Dec. 1789.

NEW TEAS.

JONES, TOMB, JOY & Co. are landing out of the Friendship, Capt. Lepper from London, an Assortment of Single, Congo, Bloom, and Hyson Teas; also a few Bales Pepper, which will be sold on the most reasonable Terms.
Belfast, 10th Dec. 1789.

George Langtry,

HAS imported from the last INDIA SALES,

Fine and common Hyson, fine and common Congou, real Souchong, Bloom, Single, and Bohea	Teas.	And has on Sale, Best Spanish Flora and French Indigo, Clay'd and Scale Sugars, Cream of Tartar, Liquorice Ball, Boiling Peas, Tin Plates,
From Dantzig, fresh Ashes, 1st, 2d, and 3d brands.		Barrel and Kieve Hoops, Kentish Bag Hops, Figs, Raisins & Currants,

which, with a general assortment of Dyestuffs, will be sold reasonable for cash or bills.
Belfast, 30th November, 1789.

N. B. He has a few small casks of best Bleachers Smalts, which will be sold considerably under the usual prices.

Robert Getty,

IS at present landing from on board the Friendship from London, a second supply of New Teas from the late India Sale—of excellent quality; and from different other Markets—new Prunes, French Plumbs, Walnuts, and Shell Almonds—Black Pepper, Durham Mustard, best fresh Miserable and Turpentine Oil.
Belfast, 7th Dec. 1789.

Alex. Neilson,

IS just landing a very extensive assortment of DRUGS and PAINTS, of the best qualities, which he will dispose of on very moderate Terms.
A few Casks refined SALTPETRE and LINSEED OIL, remarkably cheap, for ready money.
Belfast, 9th Dec. 1789.

Jamison & Galt, of Doagh,

GIVE ready Money for OATS, delivered there at the Granary.
10th December, 1789.

James Tuff,

BEGS leave to acquaint his Friends and the Publick, that he has for sale, at the Blue Anchor in Princes-street, a quantity of Buck and Doe Skins, which he will sell very cheap, for ready money or good bills on Dublin or Belfast at three months.
Belfast, 7th Dec. 1789.

Mr. Metralcourt,

HAVING removed from Linen-all-street to the house lately occupied by Mrs. Hutton on the Parade—begs leave to inform the Ladies and Gentlemen of Belfast and its Vicinity, that he proposes opening a Subscription Cotillion Ball, to commence on Friday the 18th inst. and continue every second Friday for ten Nights. Subscribers to pay one Guinea each, and no other person to be admitted: This he flatters himself will tend to improve such Ladies and Gentlemen as have been taught to dance in that manner. As he proposes having the first Ball at the time above mentioned, he begs that such Ladies and Gentlemen as wish to subscribe, will send in their Subscriptions immediately.

. His present Terms of Teaching are as follow: For two days in the week, viz Every Thursday and Saturday, at twelve o'clock at noon—One Guinea Entrance, and three half Guineas a Quarter
Gentlemen are taught to fence on the same Terms.
Belfast, Dec. 11th, 1789.

LANDS.

TO be Sold, at the Donegall-Arms in Belfast, on Wednesday the 21st day of April next, at twelve o'clock.—The Townland of Killinchey, the Woods in the parish of Killileagh and barony of Castlereagh, and contains 671 acres of Land and 40 acres of Moss; pays 73l. 7s. 9d. chief rent. Rent-Roll in a short time may be had at this Office. Samuel Dunn, who lives three miles from Killileagh on the road to Saintfield, will shew the lands.
December 7th, 1789.

Barony of Lecale, County of Down.

TO be Let, the Houses of Lismore, ready for the reception of a Tenant, with any number of acres from 18 to 100 of excellent land, for any term. The houses contain every necessary accommodation, having been lately much improved: the rent may be fined down.
Lismore is situate in the cheapest and most plentiful part of Ireland, and a fine sporting dry country.
Also to be Set the Water Corn-mill of Tyrella, and the Wind-Mill of Ballydargan, with a very large succoon—and a sufficient Farm with the former on which is a good corn-kiln and other conveniencies;—a good tenant shall meet all reasonable encouragement—Apply to Mr. Hamilton, Custom-house, Downe.—He has also to set, five small Farms, which may be immediately entered upon.
December 10th, 1789.

THE Towns and Lands of Stockestown and White Hills, part of the estate of the Right Hon. Lord Henry Fitzgerald, to be let and entered upon immediately.—These lands lie near the towns of Strangford, Killough and Downe, and on them are good farm houses, and many other conveniencies.——Proposals to be sent to Mr. Hamilton, Custom-house, Downe.
Mr. Clancy, of Strangford, will shew the lands, &c. in the two foregoing advertisements.
December 10th, 1789.

Flour-Mills.

TO be sold by publick Auction, on Thursday the 24th instant, at 12 o'clock, at the House of Mr. Archibald Mc. Clewer, North-street, Belfast.—A Lease of 15 acres, Scotch Cunningham measure, during the life of the Bishop of Osnaburgh, and 16 years from November last unexpired; on which is erected a Flour-Mill with two pair of stones, and machinery in good repair, a fall for a Bleach-mill, on which is erected good houses for the same, a neat cabin and orchard, also three tenements for labourers, all possessed by the late William Thompson of Cyder Court, in the parish of Glenavy and county of Antrim: Those Mills are well watered, being situated half a mile below Crumlin Flour-mills, on the same water, in the heart of a good wheat country. Any person wishing to become a purchaser by private sale, may apply to Mr. Conway, Mc. Niece of Pigeontown nigh Glenavy, or James Sloane, who lives on the premisses, who will shew the same.
Cyder Court, Dec. 9th, 1789.
To be inserted three times.

Horse Stolen,

OUT of the Street of Glaslough, on Saturday night the 22d November last A Black GELDING, rising six years old, bald face, all feet white, with a wart over the right eye, and a small lump in the saddle mark on the back, a set square tail, carries well, about 14 and a half hands high, value about eight guineas, the property of Patrick Hughes. One Guinea reward for the Horse, or two Guineas for Horse and Thief, on prosecuting to conviction. Apply to Mr. William Crookshank, Glaslough, near Tynan.
9th December, 1789.

For New-York,

And to sail 25th inst Wind and Weather permitting,

THE good Ship ANN and SUSAN, burthen 305 tons, William Adams, Master.—For freight or passage enquire of Messrs. Patrick & Co. Abbey-street, or of the Captain, at No. 18, George's-Quay, Dublin.

N. B. As the Ann and Susan will positively proceed the 25th inst. she will take such Goods on board as may offer on very moderate terms; and as she is American property, and navigated by seamen belonging to the United States, the Goods which she carries to New-York will only be subject to half the duty payable on Goods imported by a British Vessel.

. Messrs. Patrick & Co. have for sale a large quantity of American Pot Ashes of first, and some of second quality, which will be sold on reasonable terms at six months credit by bills on Dublin.
Also finest Spanish Flora Indigo, in Serons and half Serons, imported direct from Spain, which will be sold cheaper than it can be imported from London—and St. Domingo Cotton Wool.

Hugh Crawford,

IS landing from on board the Matty, Capt. M'Donnell, from Bourdeaux, pruens in small barrels, best vinegar, and black rozen:—And per the Lilley, new raisins, figs, and Malaga Wine—together with a large stock of new teas, Jamaica rum, &c. will be sold on the lowest terms for good payment.
Belfast, 7th Dec. 1789.

☞ A few bags of ginger and allspice to be sold cheap.

Archd. Bankhead,

HAS just landed for sale, from on board the Neptune, from Bourdeaux, a considerable quantity of Turpentine Oil and Verdigrise which he will sell by the package on good terms.
Belfast, Dec. 7th, 1789.

Watson's Almanack and Exshaw's English Registry, for the Year 1790,

ARE this day published by WM. MITCHELL, Bookseller, North-street—where every new Almanack may be had as soon as printed.
Belfast, 7th Dec. 1789.

☞ An Apprentice wanted to the Book-binding business.

PINS by WHOLESALE.

WILLIAM MITCHELL, North-Street, has lately received a large quantity, engaged of the best quality manufactured in this kingdom—on which he can allow the largest discount.
He is (as usual) well assorted in Books, Stationary, Musick, Prints, and every new Publication.
Belfast, 7th Dec. 1789

To be Set,

AND entered upon immediately, or from the 1st of February 1790—that large and commodious Inn, the sign of the Earl of Charlemont, in Ann-street.—The tenant will not have six-pence to lay out, as it is in thorough repair—and has a large yard and stabling for a number of horses.
N. B. The tenant may be supplied with a large quantity of well saved hay of an excellent quality.
Belfast, Dec. 7th, 1789.

Kilkenny Coals.

A Cargo is now discharging at Chichester-quay——a few tons will be sold out of the vessel this week at 35s. per ton. Apply to
WM. SEED & Co.
Belfast, Dec. 8th, 1789.

NOTWITHSTANDING the former Notice, I find that a practice is continued by gentlemens servants and others, of exercising horses on the walk leading from Castle-street to the Mall, and in the front of the Linen-Hall, and the street leading thereto, to the annoyance of the inhabitants, and very great danger of people on foot passing that way:——I earnestly intreat all persons who keep horses, to give positive orders to their servants to discontinue exercising horses on any of the before-mentioned places in future, to prevent the daily complaints received from the inhabitants of the risque and danger they have been daily exposed to; and I do hope this address will have the desired effect, and make it unnecessary to take any other measure.
Belfast, 30th Nov. 1789.
ED. KINGSMILL.

PARISIAN INTELLIGENCE.

PARIS, Nov. 26.

His Majeſty fearing that the return of his body guards would be productive of very fatal conſequences, in the preſent temper of the times, has thought proper to wave the offer of M. de la Fayette, and content himſelf without them for the preſent. The Queen has written a very flattering letter to the Marquis for his kind intentions in this buſineſs. Their Majeſties will therefore remain immured in the Thuilleries, till ſome happier moment preſents itſelf.

It is nearly decided, that the people of colour in the Weſt India iſlands, ſhall be repreſented in the National Aſſembly. Their claims are ſtrong, and the public voice is with them.

NATIONAL ASSEMBLY.

Of all the addreſſes preſented this morning, the moſt remarkable was one from the merchants and other inhabitants of the city of Nantz, ſupplicating the National Aſſembly to reject every motion for the Abolition of the Slave Trade, as the reſtriction of this commerce would expoſe France and her Colonies to the moſt afflicting calamities.

Another independent State is juſt ariſen: The Corſicans, after having overpowered the ſmall French garriſon in Baſtia and Corte, declared themſelves independent on the 11th of laſt month.

It is reported that General Paoli is among them.

Government has received an expreſs from Madrid, containing, as we underſtand, very important intelligence. We have not yet heard all the particulars; but we learn that the King, dreading the effects of the ſpirit of liberty, which all his art and power have not been able to ſtifle in the kingdom, has countermanded the proclamation for the aſſembling of the Cortez.

OSTEND, Nov. 28.

Bruſſels is preparing for a moſt vigourous reſiſtance, and though the recall of General d'Alton was moſt confidently reported, it turns out to be a manœuvre, as he ſtill holds the command. He has entrenched the city as ſtrong as the time allowed him for it will permit, and the fine park at the top of the town is converted into a camp. On the other hand, the Brabantine Patriots are determined to beſiege it, and from their ardour and courage in the attack of Ghent, the conflict, whenever the two armies meet, muſt be dreadful. It is to be feared that Bruſſels will be reduced to aſhes, whichever party gains the day. Hitherto every thing has remained quiet there, excepting that every one is making the beſt of his way out of it with his property. The majority of the Engliſh there have lodged their moſt valuable effects in Lord Torrington's Hotel, though we fear it will afford little protection in caſe the town is pillaged.

The capture of Ghent has thrown a great damp on the Imperialiſts, and has conſiderably weakened the Emperor's cauſe. Perhaps there is no inſtance in modern hiſtory of ſo dreadful a carnage as took place in the attack of that city. The returns of killed and wounded prove far greater than were at firſt known, and moderate people reckon them at 5000 men, other accounts ſay 12,000. One hundred and twenty capital houſes were burnt to the ground or otherwiſe dedeſtroyed. Since the town has been in the poſſeſſion of the Patriots, they have promiſed to indemnify the inhabitants for all their loſſes. How far their finances will hold good to fulfil this promiſe is another matter; but at preſent they have abundance of money, and pay for every thing punctually. They have offered rewards of 30 guilders for every priſoner taken, and three for every gun taken from the enemy. As ſoon as things were a little ſettled, the inhabitants all took an oath of allegiance to their new maſters.

LONDON, Nov. 28.

The King did not take his uſual airing on horſeback yeſterday; the hardneſs of the ground inclined his Majeſty to prefer a pedeſtrian excurſion. He viſited his farm in the Little Park, and inſpected ſome ſheep which had been lately ſent up from the Iſle of Portland.

The Tea Sales will commence at the Eaſt India Houſe on Wedneſday next; which are expected to be very long, on account of the quantity to be put up.

In Brittany, the people, not the mob, have, without violence or inſurrection, over-ruled the attempts of the Ariſtocracy, and brought about a peaceable ſubmiſſion to the decrees of the National Aſſembly.

Geneva is threatened with a revolution, and the troops of Savoy are in motion. Some important news may be expected from this quarter.

DUBLIN, December 3.

On Saturday laſt letters were diſpatched to the Collectors of all the ports of the kingdom, with inſtructions to lay an embargo on all veſſels laden with flour or grain of any kind, and ſtop ſuch exportation.

On Friday night, a little after nine o'clock, four Bloods, fluſhed with the grape, ſtumbled into the Lottery-office of Nicholſon and Co. the corner of Palace ſtreet, and without any other kind of provocation than the civil remonſtrance of a young man, clerk in the office—they knocked him down, kicked and beat him in a barbarous and unmerciful manner, and blackened both his eyes.

Two of thoſe worthy gentlemen—to the honour of the *ſurplice* be it ſpoken, were of the Church.

Among the many improvements which a lover of this country would wiſh to ſee introduced into the preſent ſyſtem of its agriculture, there is none that deſerves greater attention than the more general uſe of oxen in the room of horſes. The advantages that reſult from the uſe of ſuch animals in thoſe rural operations in which horſes are commonly employed, are ſo many and ſo obvious, that it is really wonderful they have not been more generally ſubſtituted.

In the firſt inſtance, they are kept at much leſs expence; as in the winter they need only ſtraw, turnips, &c. or in defect of thoſe, bran, of which one peck per day will ſuffice an ox while at conſtant labour.—Upon the whole, the annual expence of difference between keeping an horſe and an ox cannot be leſs than four pounds ſterl.

When an ox is caſt for labour, it may be fatted and ſold for more than the firſt purchaſe; whereas an horſe in the ſame ſituation is good for nothing.

The Whig Club, juſt eſtabliſhed in Ireland, is gaining great ſtrength, by the addition of ſome of the moſt reſpectable names in the kingdom, ſo that the new Lord Lieutenant is likely to meet with a much ſtiffer oppoſition than even his predeceſſor.

Sunday morning two large wherries belonging to Drogheda, ſailed for the herring fiſhery, which is become very abundant on the Weſt coaſt of Scotland. They were followed on Monday by ſeveral more, from Ruſh, Skerries, Howth and Malahide; all ſtout boats, victualled for a month, and contained not leſs than from twenty to thirty tons. They are new adventurers in ſuch an undertaking, in which it is hoped, they will be imitated by many more, the next and following ſeaſons.

DUBLIN Dec. 5.

The Counteſs of Weſtmorland was brought to-bed of a dead child, on the 30th of laſt month; her Ladyſhip is, however, very well, and will, we hope, ſoon be able to ſet out for this metropolis. This is the ſecond ſucceſſive unfortunate accident of the ſame nature, that has occurred to this accompliſhed lady—her laſt child but one being ſtill-born alſo.

The value of the corn exported for this laſt year, ending 25th of March, amounts to more than 1,600,000l. the bounty paid on corn exported for that period, is upwards of 200,000l. the bounty for the year before amounted to little more than 50,000l.—The great increaſe is owing to the very plentiful harveſt of 1787—than which a more or ſo plentiful a one is not remembered.

Galway, Nov. 26. At the laſt adjournment of the October Quarter Seſſions of this town, the Magiſtrates taking into conſideration the high price of proviſions, and the appearance of a hard ſeaſon, raiſed the labour of journeymen carpenters, maſons, ſlaters, taylors, ſmiths, and all other handicraft men, to two-pence per day, over and above the wages formerly allowed, and have advanced two-pence extraordinary a pair upon all ſhoes, and ſix-pence a pair to the journeymen ſhoe makers upon boots; one ſhilling and four pence for every ton of coal within the town; to labouring men ten-pence per day without victuals, and eight pence per day with victuals, being two-pence a day advance; all wages and labour to be paid in money—all thoſe prices to be continued until next April Quarter Seſſions.

Limerick, Nov. 26. We have great pleaſure in informing the public, that there is now a certainty of that great and intereſting work the Canal from Rhebogue to the deep water above Killaloe, being completed in a very few years.——The ſum of 16,600l. which is to be paid into the National Bank, on the 25th of December next, by new ſubſcribers, is nearly completed, at which time the Company is entitled to receive from Government in addition to their fund 8,300l.

Belfaſt, *December* 8.

☞ ONE MAIL DUE.

The election of Annual Preſidents came on at the Hall of the Hibernian Medical Society, at Edinburgh, when the following gentlemen were declared duly elected:

Mr. Adair Blackwell, Belfaſt, Ireland;
Mr. Edward Collis-Barrow, Ireland;
Mr. John James Erſkine, St. James's, Jamaica; and
Mr. James Elliot, Edinburgh.

WATSON'S ALMANACK for 1790, is now to be had at this Office.

MARRIED.] Mr. Alexander Douglaſs, ſurgeon, to Miſs Jane M'Key, both of Killrea.

DIED.] At Colerain, after an illneſs of a few days, Mr. John Searſon, ſuperintendant of the Free School of that place:—a man much lamented by as many as knew him, but in particular by the inhabitants of Coleraine, as his general liberality and well-known benevolence, was ever ready to promote public good.

PORT NEWS.

ARRIVED.

Dec. 2. Matty, M'Donnell, Bourdeaux, brandy. Four Colliers.

CLEARED OUT.

Dec. 2. Lord Donegall, M'Roberts, London, linen cloth.

Belfaſt, *December* 11.

☞ TWO MAIL DUE.

A few days ago a fire broke out in the Cotton Works of Mr. Grimſhaw near this town, which was happily extinguiſhed without any material damage.

As the ſeaſon has been remarkably wet, and many of the Farmers have not been able to get their wheat into the ground,—they are reminded that there is a ſpecies of early white wheat which may be ſown in February or March as the weather permits. They would therefore do well to provide ſuch ſeed in time.

The following appears in the Dublin Prints:

At a Meeting of the Mount-Mellick Volunteers, 1ſt Dec. 1789, the following Reſolutions were unanimouſly agreed to:

That beholding with regret that Spirit which lately animated the different Volunteer Corps of this kingdom almoſt extinct, we are Reſolved, that as we were *the firſt Corps who ſtood forth in defence of our Country and Conſtitution*, we ſhall be the laſt to give up a Cauſe by which ſuch manifeſt advantages have been derived to this kingdom.

Reſolved, That at all times we ſhall be ready to aſſiſt the Civil Magiſtracy, as far as in our power lies, to preſerve the internal peace of the country; for which purpoſe we have reſolved, that each Member ſhall appear on Parade the 1ſt of January next, fully accoutred, the uniform as formerly.

The Charlotte, Wm. Campbell maſter, loaded with linen cloth, from this port, is ſafe arrived at London.

James Wallace, of Saintfield, county Down, Gent. is ſworn and admitted an Attorney of the Court of King's Bench.

DIED. On the 26th ult. Mrs. Houſton, widow of the late Francis Houſton, of Armagh, Eſq.

FAIRS IN THE ENSUING WEEK.

Monday, Dec. 14. Buſhmills, Ant.——Tueſday 15. Caſtleſhane, Mon. Port, Don. Rathmelton, Don.—Thurſday, 17. Machrecregan, Tyr.——Friday 18. Killin, Tyr.

☞ Meſſrs Ware, Mahoon, and Aſhe, from the failure of the ſubſcription to their Profeſſional Concerts, are under the neceſſity of informing the public that it is not in their power to continue them—and take this opportunity of returning their ſincere thanks to thoſe Ladies and Gentlemen who have hitherto honoured their Concerts with their preſence, and the Subſcribers in particular, who are requeſted to take the trouble of ſending the remainder of their tickets to Mr. Ware, who will return them a proportionable part of their ſubſcription, deducting only an eighth of a guinea for each ticket made uſe of.

By particular Deſire,

For the Benefit of Mr. ASHE, on next Wedneſday Evening, Dec. 16th, at the Exchange-Rooms, Belfaſt, will be performed a *GRAND CONCERT* of Vocal and Inſtrumental Muſic—in courſe of which Meſſrs. Aſhe and Mahoon will perform ſeveral favourite Pieces on the Flute and Clarionett—particularly "*Sweet Echo*,"—a favourite Solo on the Violin; and, *for that night only*, Mr Aſhe will perform a Double Concerto on *Two Flutes*.—The Concert will conſiſt entirely of Select Pieces, particulars of which will be expreſſed in Hand-bills.—The Orcheſtra will be conſiderably enlarged by a number of *Gentlemen Amateurs*, who have kindly conſented to give their aſſiſtance on the above night.—After the Concert, will be a BALL.

Tickets at 3s. 9d. halfp. to be had at Mr. Magee's, and of Mr Aſhe, at Mrs. Stockman's, High ſtreet.

Anno 1789.] Printed by HENRY JOY, and Co. BELFAST.

The BELFAST NEWS-LETTER.

TUESDAY December 15,   FRIDAY December 18, 1789.

Champaigne & Burgundy.

JONES, TOMB, JOY & Co. have just received a supply of Champaigne and Burgundy, which they can assure their Friends is equal to any ever imported here.

They are largely supplied with the following Articles, at their Stores, the lower end of Waring-street, and in the Wine-Cellar-Entry; and they daily expect the arrival of a cargo of New Alicant, and another of Sicilian Barilla,——Viz.

Claret in wood & bottles,	Black Soap,
Red & White Port,	Smalts of different qualities
Sherry, Lisbon, Calcavella,	Hyson, Congo, Singlo and
Mountain, Hock, Tent,	Bloom Teas,
Champaigne, still and spark-	Black Pepper,
ling—Burgundy,	Timber, Deals, Oak and
Brandy, Rum and Gineva	Fir Plank, Laths, Oars,
in pipes and hogsheads as	Spars, Beech Logs,
imported,	Milled Sheet Lead,
Barilla, American, and	Swedish Iron of best qua-
Dantzick Ashes,	lity,
James River Leaf Tobacco,	Steel.

Belfast, 16th Dec. 1789.

WM. MAGEE,

Printer and Stationer, Belfast,

ENTREATS the Nobility, Gentry, and Public in general, will take notice, that they may now supply themselves and families, with every article of

Stationary,

the best quality, and on terms most moderate, when a quantity is taken.

ACCOUNT-BOOKS, fitted for the Compting-house, Counter or Pocket—or made to any pattern, on short notice.

WAX-CANDLES, free from adulteration, of various sizes—Playing Cards, Wax Taper, Flambeaux, &c.

PATENT MEDICINES and COSMETICKS, of the most approved kinds, now in estimation.

⁎ Circular Letters, Addresses, Hand-bills, and every other species of PRINTING-WORK done with neatness and expedition.

Woollen and Cotton Goods.

TO be sold by auction, at the Market-house, on Monday next the 21st instant, at eleven o'clock, a variety of Broad and Forest Cloths, Stuffs, &c. &c. As the whole will be sold without reserve, it will be well worth the notice of all who want such Goods to attend.

Belfast, 17th Dec. 1789.

To be let immediately,

IN the parish of Maghragall, about 30 acres of land, part of Thornhedge Farm, lately occupied by James Reid Esq; with the House and garden belonging to said farm. Proposals will be received by James Watson, Esq; of Brookhill.

This Advertisement to be continued three times.

Brookhill, Dec. 14th, 1789.

Sale of Lands--County of Down.

THE Sale of the Lands of BALLY-EDMOND, and of the Lodge of EDMOND-HILL, in Killoan, near Rostrevor, lately advertised in the Dublin Evening-Post as to be held at Newry on Monday the 21st instant, IS DEFERRED until Monday the 4th of January, when it will be held at Mrs. Bennet's Tavern in Newry, at one o'clock in the afternoon.—For particulars of the lands, &c. see the said advertisement in the Evening-Post, the apply as therein directed. Terms of sale, as to deposit, &c. to be declared at the time of sale.

December 12th, 1789.

Moneymore Brewery.

JOHN MILLER & Co. beg leave to inform their Friends and the Public, that they have this day commenced Business, and in a few days will be able to supply those who are so kind to deal with them, with the best Strong and Small Beer; and as they have laid in every material of the very first qualities, hope to give general satisfaction.

Moneymore, 25th Dec. 1789

Wanted,

A Very good Woman Cook, to whom good Wages will be given.——Apply at this Office.

December 23d, 1789.

To the Freeholders of the County of ANTRIM.

GENTLEMEN,

A Junction of Interest between two Gentlemen of this County, for the purpose of effecting the Representation of it, being publickly avowed :

Those Friends who think us not unworthy of that honor, have called upon us, to form a similar junction to give effect to their wishes.

We have therefore united; are determined mutually to support each other, as far as you, Gentlemen, will by your favor, enable us so to do—and we now jointly solicit that Representation.

We presume with confidence to assure you, that, if you will be pleased to confer this honor upon us, we shall neither fail in gratitude to you, nor in the faithful and upright discharge of the trust reposed in us.

We are, Gentlemen,
your obedient and
devoted Servants,
Dec. 1789.   CHICHESTER.
JAMES LESLIE.

To the Freeholders of the County of ANTRIM.

GENTLEMEN,

WE think ourselves called upon to intrude once more on your attention, as an Address has lately appeared wherein we see that a junction has been formed, in opposition to us, who have had the honor of your unanimous choice at the last General Election, and who have been invited by a very respectable Body of Freeholders to offer ourselves a second time to your consideration.

We feel no reluctance in submitting our conduct in parliament to your judgment, and we do not entertain a doubt of our being honoured with your effectual support—We conceive that the approbation of the constituent body, and the hopes of the continuation of their confidence, are the great incentives to virtuous exertions.—That the destruction of this principle must lead to every species of political depravity :—and we cannot suppose that THE COUNTY OF ANTRIM, whose character stands so high in the publick opinion, would, by its example, risk this dangerous position,—THAT NO HONORABLE TIES EXIST BETWEEN ELECTORS AND THEIR REPRESENTATIVES.

We have the Honor to be,
Gentlemen,
your devoted
and obedient Servants,
HER. ROWLEY,
JOHN O'NEILL.

MR. ROWLEY and Mr. O'NEILL, having addressed themselves to the Freeholders of this County by Circular Letters, hope that in case of any omissions, they will not be imputed to a want of attention in them, but to the great difficulty of so extensive a delivery.

December 15th, 1789.

GALLWAY, Fencing-Master,

RETURNS his sincere thanks to the Gentlemen of Belfast, for the repeated instances of encouragement he has met with since his commencement as Fencing-Master in this town—that having from a series of years practice, acquired a perfect knowledge of that noble Science, which has been deemed in the present enlightened age, the master-piece of art—and having had the honour of teaching Gentlemen of the first consequence in the country, who can vouch for his abilities, still solicits for a continuance of their favour—Gentlemen initiated in the Science for half a guinea a month, and half a guinea entrance. Six lessons to be given in the week, from twelve to one each day.

P. S. Any Gentleman residing within a few miles of Belfast, who would wish to be taught Fencing, GALLWAY shall be very punctual in his attendance on them.

Belfast, 15th Dec. 1789.

Advertisement.

STOLEN out of the Stable of Alexander Johnston upon Saturday last, being the 12th instant, a dark bay Mare, about 15 years old, with a star in her forehead, set in the tail, switch tailed when taken away, about 15 hands high, in foal when taken away. Any person or persons that will give notice to said Alexander Johnston, in the parish of Bangor and townland of Conligg, or John Jackson, Innkeeper in Newton-Ards, shall have a handsome reward.

December 14th, 1789.

For LONDON,

THE NEW DRAPER, John Hughes, Master, will positively be ready for sea the first next month.
For Freight apply to
ARCH. TAYLOR.

Newry, 5th Dec. 1789.

Wants Employment,

A LAND STEWARD: He understands his Business in all its different branches, and has lived in that station for several years both in England and Ireland in the first families, can be well recommended. Any gentleman wanting such a person, by directing a letter to A. B. Lurgan, will be waited on.

December 4th, 1789.

STOLEN,

OUT of the Stable of John Kerr of Drumnaseamph, near Banbridge, on Thursday night the 19th instant, a Black Mare, five years old, bald-face, both fore feet white, strong made, value fifteen Guineas. Whoever returns said Mare to John Kerr, or Thomas Dawson Lawrence, Esq; Lawrence-town, shall receive two Guineas Reward.   December 12th, 1789.

LINEN STOLEN.

WHEREAS my green was robbed on Monday night, the 7th instant, and 23 pieces of Linen carried away :—I promise to pay Twenty Guineas over and above the rewards promised in the under Association, to the person who will give such information as will convict the same.

ALEXANDER OGILBY.

Stealing Cloth out of Bleach-Greens, or receiving Cloth stolen.

WE, whose names are hereunto subscribed, do hereby promise and jointly bind ourselves to pay the following rewards :

1st—10l. sterling for the discovery and prosecuting to conviction the person guilty of stealing Cloth out of any of our bleach-greens.

2d—50l. sterling for the discovery and conviction of the receiver of any Cloth stolen out of our bleach-greens.

3d—20l. sterling for such private information as will enable us to convict either the thief or the receiver, and the name of the informer concealed, if required.

And whereas the practice of selling cloth which has received damage in bleaching, without sealing it with the name of the bleacher, encourages theft, by making it easy to sell stolen cloth under this cover :—We are determined to put the law in force, which subjects all persons exposing to sale, or having in their possession, half-bleached or white linen not being duly sealed, to a fine of five pounds for every piece :—And all hawkers and petty dealers in linen are required to take notice, that we will pay a reward of five pounds to the person who will inform on and convict them of having unsealed linen in their possession—that we will rigorously enforce the fine in the first instance, and unless they can clearly shew that they bought such linen from a bleacher, they shall be prosecuted as accomplices in the felony, and the reward, Fifty Pounds, as above, paid for their conviction.

9th Dec. 1789.

Alexander and Bond,
James Atcheton,
H. Thompson,
Alexander Ogilby,
James Ross.

John Ash.

No. 8, Capel-Street, Dublin,

TAKES the earliest opportunity of informing the Nobility, his Friends, and the Public, that he is just returned from London, and the principal manufacturing towns in England—and has imported an elegant assortment of articles in the jewellery, plate and plated line—watches of all kinds—and gold enamelled, plain gold, and gilt mounted toothpick cases—smelling bottles and pocket books.——As he flatters himself that his conduct, during many years service to Clements, (of Parliament-street) was such as will merit the approbation of the public—and as he has entered into partnership with one of the first houses in London, they may be assured he will be supplied with every article of the newest fashion, and at the most reduced prices for ready money only—their profits being so small as not to allow them to sell upon any other terms.

Downpatrick School.

VACATION having commenced To-day, School will open again, and the publick Examination will be held on the 25th January.

19th December, 1789.

PARISIAN INTELLIGENCE.

PARIS, NOV. 28.

NATIONAL ASSEMBLY.

M. GUILLOTIN called the attention of the Aſſembly to ſome amendments which he conceived highly neceſſary to be added to the proviſional reform of criminal juriſprudence. Theſe were the ſame penalties for criminals of all ranks and conditions; the ſame puniſhment for all capital offences; a decapitation by a machine conſtructed for the purpoſe, inſtead of an executioner; and the proſcription of the abſurd prejudice which extends the infamy of a criminal to his family. It was agreed to conſider them on Tueſday next.

NATIONAL ASSEMBLY.

PARIS, DEC. 4.

A Letter was read from the proprietors of Weſt India eſtates reſident in France; and an Addreſs from the Deputies of Commerce, and the Maritime Cities, both ſtating—that an inſurrection had broken out among the Negroes in Martinique and Guadaloupe, which had been the occaſion of much bloodſhed, and that there was great reaſon to fear the flame would ſpread to St. Domingo. This brought on a long debate on the eſtabliſhment of a Colonial Committee, which was at length adjourned till Thurſday evening.

The diſturbances in Martinique were of two ſorts—between the Coloniſts and the Count de Viomeſnil, the General, about wearing the National Cockade—and between the Negroes and their Maſters.

The former was appeaſed by permitting the National Cockade to be worn; and the latter was quelled by inflicting the moſt dreadful puniſhment on the ringleaders.

The inſurrection of the Negroes was preceded by the following letter, ſent on the 31ſt of Auguſt to the General, the Intendant and Commandant-General of St. Pierre.

"We know that the King has made us free; we expect to be ſo. If giving us our Liberty be oppoſed, we will ſpread fire and blood through all the Colony. Nothing in it ſhall be ſpared but the public buildings, and the religious houſes.

(Signed)
"ALL THE NEGROES."

FROM THE LONDON GAZETTE.

ESCURIAL, Nov. 9.

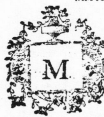

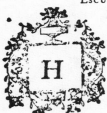

HIS Catholic Majeſty went on Thurſday laſt to Madrid to diſmiſs the Cortes, according to the uſual forms.

Nov. 16.——His Catholic Majeſty was pleaſed to declare on the 12th inſt. the civil promotions made on the occaſion of his Coronation, the publication of which was deferred till the Cortes had finiſhed their deliberations.

Each of the members of that aſſembly, which conſiſted of ſeventy-four perſons, has received a mark of the Catholic King's favour, according to his rank.

Amongſt other numerous promotions, are, the creation of eight Grandees of Spain, nine Honorary Grandees, five Knights of the Golden Fleece, one of whom is M. de Nor∙hna, the Portugueſe Ambaſſador here, ten Knights of the Great Croſs of Charles III. two Counſellors, and four Honorary Counſellors of State, and twenty-two Chamberlains.

An order has juſt been iſſued by this government, to allow the importation, but ſolely for the purpoſe of re-exportation to Spaniſh America, of foreign thread, thread tape, white and coloured, and coarſe thread ſtockings, provided that the ſhippers import to America an equal quantity of the ſame articles of the manufacture of this country.

LONDON, DEC. 4—5.

On Thurſday the city and ſuburbs of London were overſpread with the thickeſt fog almoſt ever remembered by the oldeſt inhabitant. Several of the ſtages travelling between the metropolis and the ſurrounding villages were by five in the afternoon, obliged to be preceded by men with torches or lanterns; others were quitted by the paſſengers, who walked to their reſpective homes; and the horſes of many were led at a very ſlow pace by people on foot; one in particular from Wandſworth to Fleet-ſtreet. A gentleman, in his way to the Surry-ſide, miſtook the road of Black-friars-bridge, and fell down the ſteps to the landing-place, by which he was much hurt. Two perſons going over the Quays below London-bridge had nearly ſtepped into the river, but were ſtopped by a watchman then on duty there.

STAMPS.

An accurate ſtatement of the number of Stamps, for Receipts, Bills, Newſpapers, and Book and Sheet Almanacks, iſſued from the Stamp Office betwixt the 2d day of Auguſt 1788, and the ſame day of the preſent year. The productiveneſs of theſe impoſts is greater than our readers can poſſibly conceive, as they will ſee by the calculation annexed.

		£.	s.	d.
1,673,332	two-penny ſtamps for Receipts, —	13 944	8	8
669,516	four-penny ditto for ditto,	11,158	12	0
277,407	three-penny ditto for Bills,	3,467	11	9
1,004,531	ſix-penny ditto for ditto,	25,113	5	6
368,890	one-ſhilling ditto for ditto,	18,444	10	0
13,392,103	three-halfpenny ditto for Newſpapers, —	83,700	12	11
381,501	four-penny ditto for Book-Almanacks, —	6,358	7	0
245,233	four-penny ditto for Sheet-Almanacks, —	4,087	4	4
18,012,513	Stamps iſſued. Sums rec.	166,274	12	2

DUBLIN, December 10.

A writ for a Member to ſerve in Parliament for the borough of Coleraine, in the room of the Right Hon. Richard Jackſon, deceaſed is iſſued by his Excellency the Speaker.

The aſſertion of the Caſtle now is that the Earl of Weſtmoreland will arrive here by the 22d of this month; the Counteſs having lain in, and recovering with muſt celerity. She does not accompany, but is to follow him.

DUBLIN DEC. 12.

The eſtabliſhment of a mint in this kingdom, is an object highly deſirable, and indeed highly neceſſary.—The whole of the current gold coin of this country is called in as bullion, for want of weight, every fourth year on an average, at a very conſiderable loſs to the public; the whole advantage of recoinage ſettling with the Britiſh mint.

Another very conſiderable loſs which the public ſuſtain is the refuſal of all the offices of Revenue to accept ſtanding beam gold as current weight, though all the offices of his Majeſty's Revenue in England accept them without ſcruple.

Thoſe offices too refuſed them for a very conſiderable time, until the queſtion was brought to the teſt by the ſpirit and perſeverance of a few individuals, who not only convinced the Officers of Revenue that equipoiſe with the ſtandard weights—conſtituted legal currency—but that any perſon refuſing to accept ſuch coin as legal payment, was liable to be committed to priſon by the next Magiſtrate.

In Dublin, the Bank and Revenue offices give law to the currency of gold, and will juſt pay and accept ſuch ſort of coin as they chuſe without appeal.

The Bullion-office ſwallows every guinea in circulation that is not down weight—and the caſh-office iſſues continually guineas that ſcarcely ſtand the teſt of any ſcales but their own—and if the receiver is not extremely cautious, he will have the neceſſity of diſpoſing of a part of the money he receives in *front* of a certain building at a loſs of five per cent. in the *rear*.

The Whig Club held yeſterday their eighth meeting, and dined at Ryan's, Fowns's-ſtreet.

Belfaſt, *December* 15.

☞ ONE MAIL DUE.

It is with much concern that every perſon deſirous to ſee the morals of the lower claſſes improved by education, obſerves the total inattention of the inhabitants of this wealthy, generous and humane town, to the SUNDAY SCHOOL. As long as a few Ladies and Gentlemen attended, that valuable inſtitution continued to improve: now that they have totally abſented themſelves, it is going ſo faſt to decay, that, in a ſhort time we ſhall not retain even the name of one. When the many good effects of ſuch a ſchool are conſidered, our neglect of it, muſt be confeſſed to be indecent and unaccountable. The ſingle town of Mancheſter, which had a weekly aſſemblage of five thouſand of formerly neglected children, for the purpoſe of education, affords a noble example to other places.——The Maſters, who uſed to be paid for attending the Belfaſt Sunday School, from a conſciouſneſs of the good reſulting from it, have attended without receiving any gratuity for their ſervices; the fund for its ſupport being long ſince expended.

The Treaſurer of the County of Antrim Infirmary acknowledges to have received from Mr. Sampſon Robſon of Grange, *Forty Pounds Nineteen Shillings ſterling*, which ſum was given to ſaid Mr. Robſon, for the benefit of that charitable inſtitution, by a friend lately deceaſed, and who at the ſame time earneſtly requeſted, that his name might be concealed from the public.

We take this opportunity of contradicting a falſe, and, we fear, malicious account of the death of Mr. John Searſon of Colerain, which appeared in this paper a few days ſince.

PORT NEWS.

ARRIVED.

Dec. 7. Friendſhip, Lepper, London, drugs, tea, ale, &c.

12. Peggy, M'Ilroy, Liverpool, rum, ſugar, &c.

CLEARED OUT.

Dec. 8. Mary, Corry, Jamaica, linen cloth.

9. Ann, Martin, Norfolk, cloth, glaſs, &c.

10. New Draper, Kearney, Liverpool, butter.

By particular Deſire,

For the Benefit of Mr. ASHE, on next Wedneſday Evening, Dec. 16th, at the Exchange-Rooms, Belfaſt, will be performed a *GRAND CONCERT* of Vocal and Inſtrumental Muſic—in courſe of which Meſſrs. Aſhe and Mahoon will perform ſeveral favourite Pieces on the Flute and Clarionett—particularly "*Sweet Echo,*"—a favourite Solo on the Violin; and, *for that night only*, Mr. Aſhe will perform a Double Concerto on *Two Flutes*.—The Concert will conſiſt entirely of Select Pieces, particulars of which will be expreſſed in Hand-bills.—The Orcheſtra will be conſiderably enlarged by a number of *Gentlemen Amateurs*, who have kindly conſented to give their aſſiſtance on the above night.—After the Concert, will be a BALL.

Tickets at 3s. 9d. halfp. to be had at Mr. Magee's, and of Mr Aſhe, at Mrs. Stockman's, High ſtreet.

Belfaſt, *December* 18.

☞ ONE MAIL DUE.

Joſeph Fulton, of Liſburn, is appointed a Commiſſioner to take SPECIAL BAIL and AFFIDAVITS in his Majeſty's Court of Exchequer.

The Editor acknowleges receipt of a Card from a Gentleman who ſigns himſelf "A Subſcriber." In conſequence of it, he has made particular enquiry into the circumſtance on which the card turns, and is happy to inform its author, that he is authoriſed to aſſert that the very point to which he alludes has always been attended to by the gentlemen concerned.

The paper ſigned J. L. with Magherafelt poſt mark, is received. With all poſſible reſpect for its author and his excellent principles, we muſt, at this early period of the buſineſs which is the ſubject of his letter, decline the inſertion of anonymous publications; as it would open ſuch a door for recrimination as would not perhaps ſerve that intereſt which every unbiaſſed mind feels a concern in. The author will find his arguments anticipated in a late paper, and ſtated with ſuch energy and truth, as perhaps no ſubſequent publication can improve.

DIED.] Mrs. Scott, wife of Mr. Archibald Scott, of this place.——A few days ago in North-ſtreet, Mr. Wm Stewart.——In Anne-ſtreet, Mrs. Gihon, wife of Mr. Thomas Gihon, vintner.———A few days ago at Grange, John Brady, Eſq. much regretted by a numerous acquaintance.

FAIRS IN THE ENSUING WEEK.

Monday, Dec. 21. Roccorry, Mon. Tueſday 22. Ardatra, Don. Benburbe, Tyr. Caſtlewellan, Down. Wedneſday 23. Bailytrain, Mon. Thurſday 24. Ballyboffey, Don. Friday 25. Armoy, Ant. Saturday 26. Glaſslough, Mon.

PRICES IN THIS MARKET YESTERDAY.

Oatmeal,	11s.	$4\frac{1}{2}$.	to	00s.	od.	Dried do 00s. to 00s.od.per d
Wheat,	13	3	—	00	0	R.Tallow,6s.od.to 6s.4d. ſt.
Oats,	5	6	—	5	10	Potatoes 10d. to 11d per b.
Barley,	5	10	—	0	0	Eng. coals, 00s. to 17s. 4d.
Butter,	55	0	—	00	0	Scotch do. 00s. to 17s. 4d.
C. hides,	34	0	—	37	0	Ex on Lond. 7 a 7 1-4 per c.
Ox ditto,	37	6	—	40	0	Do. on Glaſgow $6\frac{1}{2}$.
S.C.ſkins	40	0	—	00	0	

Concert and Ball.

MR. MAHOON with the utmoſt reſpect begs leave to inform the Ladies and Gentlemen of Belfaſt and its environs, that his Concert (by particular deſire) is fixed for Wedneſday the 30th inſtant, when he hopes to meet with their countenance and ſupport.

In the courſe of the Concert there will be ſeveral new Pieces, with a variety of favourite Airs for the Flute, Clarionet and Violin; in particular, a new Echo Piece in imitation of Birds, &c. for the Flute and Clarionet, compoſed for the above Night by Mr. Mahoon.

December 17th, 1789.

*** Particulars will be given in Hand-bills.—Tickets to be had of Mr. Mahoon, as Mr. Stockman's, at 3s. 9d. halfp. each.

Anno 1789.]　　Printed by HENRY JOY, and Co. BELFAST.

The BELFAST NEWS-LETTER.

TUESDAY December 22,　　FRIDAY December 25, 1789.

To the NOBILITY, CLERGY, and GENTRY of the County of DOWN.

THE MEMORIAL AND REPRESENTATION OF THE DEAN AND CHAPTER OF DOWN.

THE ruinous state of the Cathedral Church of Down has for many years been an object of real concern, and reflected a degree of disgrace and of scandal upon the Bishop and Clergy of the diocese, and upon the Nobility, Gentlemen, and inhabitants, residing within it, who have frequently lamented that some method could not be fallen upon to repair and restore it to such an appearance of decency and dignity as would become a diocese of its distinction and importance.

The great obstacle that seemed for many years to render the attainment of this desirable purpose impracticable, was the total annihilation and loss of the fund for the Œconomy belonging to the Dean and Chapter, for the support and repair of their Cathedral, and for defraying the expences attending publick worship therein, which has been one of the melancholy effects of the great confusion which from time to time have afflicted this kingdom.

The Hon. and Rev. Mr. Annesley, the present Dean of Down, being very desirous to restore and render permanent such a future establishment, for the support of the same, has proposed to give, and the Chapter have agreed to accept the sum of three hundred pounds a year to be allotted out of the tythes of his deanery, during his incumbency, and to petition Parliament to pass an act to perpetuate and secure the same from him and his successors Deans of Down, for the support of the Cathedral Church and of Divine worship to be performed therein—and for ever after to be the Œconomy of the same, and to be applied in the following manner, viz.

For the salary of a chaplain	£.50
Two vicars choral, 25l. each,	50
Organist,	40
Eight choristers, 4l. each,	32
Schoolmaster,	10
Verger,	8
Organ-blower,	5
House-keeper,	5
For repairs of the church, elements, surplices, and other extraordinaries,	100
	300

The patronage of all the said employments to be in the disposal of the Dean, for the time being, and the government and regulation thereof to be in the Dean and Chapter—and the Bishop to be Visitor of the whole.

The Dean having by his proposal removed the chief obstacle that remained to the general wish, for the restoration of the Cathedral of Down—the Dean and Chapter have thought fit to have a plan made and drawn for the repair of the Cathedral Church, and an estimate made for the expences of the same, by an able architect, amounting to the sum of Six Thousand Pounds; and as the only method to raise such sum for carrying the same into execution must be by subscription, they presume to lay before the Nobility, Clergy, and Gentry of the diocese, and the other Inhabitants of the County of Down, this their Memorial and Representation, humbly hoping from their assistance, to be able to compleat the work—and they hereto subjoin a list of such persons as have already informed them of their intention to subscribe the sums annexed to their names, together with certain Resolutions that were entered into with the Bishop, at the last meeting of their Chapter.

The publick wish for the reparation and re-establishment of the Cathedral Church of Down, having reached the King's ear, his Majesty has been graciously pleased to signify his Royal intention to give towards the completion of a fund for re-building the same, the sum of One Thousand Pounds, by King's Letter, so soon as his Majesty shall have been certified that such a subscription shall have been made, as shall, in addition to his Majesty's bounty, be equal to the object proposed—and their Excellencies, the Lords Justices, have been pleased to signify his Majesty's commands to the Governor of the County of Down, publickly to declare to the Nobility, Clergy, and Gentry, of the Diocese of Down, his Majesty's most gracious intentions upon this occasion. And in addition to his Majesty's said Royal Bounty, it is expected, and no doubt entertained, but that the Board of First Fruits will contribute towards the repair of the Cathedral, at least the sum of Five Hundred Pounds.

His Grace the Lord Primate,	£.113 15	0
The Lord Bishop of Down and Connor,	113 15	0
The Most Honourable the Marquiss of Downshire,	568 15	0
Earl Annesley,	113 15	0
Earl of Hillsborough,	341 5	0
Lord Viscount Dungannon,	113 15	0
Lord Bishop of Dromore,	22 15	0
Right Honourable Lord De Clifford,	300 0	0
James W. Hull, Esq. High Sheriff,	56 17	6
The Honourable Richard Annesley, Esq.	113 15	0
Hon. Robert Ward, Esq.	56 17	6
Cromwell Price, Esq.	113 15	0
Sir Richard Johnston, Bart.	56 17	6
Richard Magenis, Esq.	56 17	6
William Montgomery, Esq.	56 17	6
John Reilly, Esq.	56 17	6
Robert Johnston, Esq.	56 17	6
The Reverend Dr. Leslie, Archdeacon of Down,	20 0	0
Rev. William Sturrock, Chancellor,	9 2	0
Rev. Lucas Waring, Treasurer,	20 0	0
Rev. Charles Aare, Precentor,	11 7	6
Rev. Robert Trail, Prebendary St. Andrews,	11 7	6
Rev. John Dickson, Prebendary of Dunsport,	22 15	0
Rev. Ham. Trail, Vicar General of Down,	22 15	0
John Brett, Register of the Diocese of Down,	50 0	0
Mrs. Trotter, Down,	11 7	6
Southwell Trotter, Esq.	22 15	0
William Trotter, Esq.	11 7	6
John Slade, Esq.	22 15	0
George Hamilton, Esq.	17 1	3
Cornelius Lascelles, Esq.	22 15	0
Samuel Cowan, Esq.	11 7	6
Steel Hawthorn, Esq.	11 7	6
C. S. Hawthorn, Esq.	11 7	6

At a meeting of the Dean and Chapter the 18th day of July, 1789, it was resolved,

That books for subscriptions be forthwith opened by the Rev. Lucas Waring, Treasurer of the Chapter, and by John Brett, Actuary or Secretary; in which all sums already subscribed, or to be subscribed, shall be entered, not only for the inspection of the said Bishop, Dean, and Chapter, but the Subscribers and publick in general.

Resolved, that the said John Brett be and is hereby appointed Receiver, to collect the several subscriptions—and that for the faithful performance of his duty, he shall enter into sufficient security to the said Bishop, Dean, and Chapter, to be accountable to them from time to time, and as often as required, for all money he shall receive on their account, for this purpose; and that he shall return to the said Lucas Waring, the last day of every month, duplicates or copies of the entries so to be made in his book.

Resolved, that all those who have sent their names as Subscribers, shall pay the amount of their subscription into the hands of the said Receiver, on or before the first day of next Lent Assizes, and afterwards every Subscriber shall pay the money engaged for by him at the time of such his subscription, and which money so deposited, shall be returned to the owner, unless it be applied to the intended use, without any unnecessary delay.

Resolved, that these Resolutions be entered in the Chapter book.

Resolved, that the Memorial and Representation of the said Dean and Chapter be published three times in the Belfast Newspaper, and printed copies thereof sent by the actuary to the Nobility, Clergy, and Gentry, within the said Diocese and County of Down.

Resolved, that the names of the additional Subscribers who shall subscribe after the publication of the said Memorial and Representation, be published in the Belfast Paper, once in every month.

Signed by order
of the Bishop, Dean, and Chapter,
JOHN BRETT,
Actuary and Secretary.

The Chapter Book containing the names of the Subscribers, and the plan and estimate relating to this work, may be seen in the hands of the Actuary at Downpatrick.

Advertisement,

THAT the Fair of Ballynahinch, will be held on the first Thursday in January, (as usual) being the 7th day of the month.
Ballynahinch, 24th Dec. 1789.

WHEREAS my Wife Ann Mc Cartney, otherwise Gillas, (from Ballymacarret, near Belfast) has eloped from me without any just cause: Now this is to give notice, that I am determined not to pay any debt she may contract; and am determined to prosecute any person who may harbour her.
Moira, Dec. 21. 1789.
JOHN McCARTNEY.

Wanted,

A WHIPPER-IN, by Nicholas Price of Saintfield, County of Down: he must be a light weight, and good horseman. None need apply except one who can be well recommended for his good behaviour in every particular.
Saintfield, Dec. 15, 1789.

THE five following articles of the new penal code for France have been submitted to the discussion of the National Assembly, and exhibit a humane and enlightened policy, worthy of the imitation of all European nations.

" The same crimes shall be punished by the same species of execution, let the rank or condition of the offender be what it may.

" In every case where the law pronounces the sentence of death, the execution shall be the same; whatever may be the nature of the offence, the criminal shall be beheaded.

" The crime being personal, the punishment shall reflect no dishonour on the relatives of the criminal, who shall be equally admissible to all sorts of professions and employments.

" No man shall reproach another with the punishment of any of his relations: whoever shall dare to do so, shall be publicly reprimanded.

" The confiscation of the fortunes of the condemned shall in no case be permitted.

" The body of the criminal, after execution, shall be delivered over to his family, if they require it; and in every case, the deceased shall be allowed sepulchral rights, nor shall the register make any mention of the cause of his death."

LONDON, DEC. 11.

On Saturday night last two ladies of distinction, *seemingly* foreigners, in a stage-box of Covent-Garden, sported two of the most extraordinary fans perhaps ever seen in this country. The mounting was of a green colour, and when unfurled they spread in so extraordinary a manner, that the fan which Peter carries before the nurse in Romeo and Juliet was but a type of their magnitude.

DUBLIN

COMMISSION INTELLIGENCE.

December 14.

Yesterday came on at an adjournment of a Commission of Oyer and Terminer, before Lord Carleton, the trial of Robert Kindillan, Esq; Lieutenant in one of his Majesty's regiments of Dragoons, indicted for committing a rape on Miss Elizabeth Egan.

Ann Carrol was also indicted for being feloniously present, and aiding and abetting the said Robert Kindillan, to perpetrate the felony aforesaid.

The first witness produced was Miss Elizabeth Egan—on her coming into Court, and seeing the prisoner at the Bar, she appeared exceedingly agitated, she fainted, and it was some time before she recovered herself—her situation seemed to affect every person present.

She underwent a very long and minute cross-examination by Mr. Curran, by which it appeared, that she reluctantly came forward to prosecute; and that she was induced to prosecute at the instance of her friends, in order to do herself justice; and in the course of her cross-examination, she said God forbid that any thing she would say should hurt his life; but on the whole it appeared, that she was induced to go off with Kindillan, and to continue with him for the time she did, under the impression of his marrying her. In the course of giving her testimony, she was at various times exceedingly affected; and if we may judge from the feelings of a very crowded Court, her unfortunate situation seemed to make very forcibly impressions on every person present.

The examination of witnesses being gone through, his Lordship summed up the evidence with very great accuracy and precision, and having in his charge to the Jury, made some very excellent and judicious observations on the evidence that had been adduced in the course of the trial.

The Jury after retiring for about ten minutes, brought in their verdict that the prisoners at the bar were NOT GUILTY.

*** The readers of the Belfast News-Letter will excuse our not entering further into particulars that might offend delicacy without answering any good purpose.

Accounts from the north-west coast are very favourable to the prospect of the herring fishery, which had been rather indifferent in that quarter for three years last past. Several salt-works are erected in the new town of Rutland, and smoking-houses, built in the manner of those of Yarmouth, for making red herrings. It is now allowed, that if the take of fish continues abundant, the preparations made at Rutland will turn out as one of the first national and commercial advantages of this country.

The extent and perfection to which the English have brought their cotton fabrics, (callicoes and muslins in particular) are justly the subject of wonder. By a late exhibition of British muslins at the General Hall in Bishopsgate-street, London, it appeared that they can manufacture them very little inferior in delicacy of texture to the best kinds imported from India. In the finer fabrics, and especially in the muslins, the value of the finished goods arises almost from labour alone; for the raw material bears no sort of proportion, when it is considered that a single pound of cotton, worth five shillings, may be raised in value so as to draw from foreign countries or retain at home a sum of at least from five to twenty guineas, and in some instances more money.

To give our readers some idea how great a source of wealth those manufactures produce to the sister kingdom, and what an abundant harvest of employment they furnish for a multitude of men, women, and children engaged in the various branches, we shall present the following accurate statement of the quantity of cotton imported and retained for consumption in Great Britain for the years hereafter mentioned:

Namely,		Pounds.	Value in manufactured Goods. l.
	1773	2,559.819	1. 880,000 0
	1783	9,546,179	3,000,000 0
	1784	11,280,238	3,150,000 0
	1785	17,992,888	6,000,000 0
	1786	19,151,867	6,500,000 0
	1787	22,638,944	7,000,000 0
	1788	20,606,848	6,000,000 0
	1789	23,000,000	7,000,000 0

In consequence of the Westerly winds continuing in one point, coals have risen to one pound eight shillings the ton; but the public coal-yards being open for the poor, they cannot feel any inconvenience. The wind having shifted to the North yesterday, we have soon to hope for the arrival of the Christmas fleet of colliers.

DUBLIN DEC. 22.

By a letter from a gentleman at Charanters, near Paris, we learn that Mr. Necker, the French financier, declared to the National Assembly, the 8th of this month, that the voluntary contributions and adventitious aids that had come into the Royal Treasury that day, would enable the government to make good all its engagements to the 20th of May next:—by which time it was expected the regular receipts of the newly equalized taxes (without reckoning the produce of the Church lands) would be sufficient to answer all the exigencies of the state. The writer adds, that the declaration has spread an universal joy among all ranks of people, particularly the monied ones, who, it is said, when the troubles attendant on this great revolution broke out, locked up and buried vast sums of money, that will in all probability be once more in circulation.

A truce it is confidently asserted has been agreed to between the Government of Brussels and the Patriots; but during the period of two months, for which it is to last, neither parties will be inactive in making preparations for engaging with redoubled vigour, should the negociations prove of no effect, which seems to be the prevailing opinion.—It must answer one grand purpose at any rate, to the Patriotic party in both Flanders and the Netherlands, that it will afford them an opportunity of disciplining their troops, and consequently enable them to enter the field much more formidable to their arbitrary opposers, as three fourths of them are as yet unfit for action against the regulars.

As several families in this city frequently give soup at this season to the poor, the following receipt for making a cheap mess of pauper soup is recommended:

" Take eight pounds of coarse gravy beef, to which put four gallons of water, a bunch of turnips and carrots, some whole onions, pepper and salt; let them stew gently for five hours; to these add all the pieces of stale bread collected in your family during the week, also the bones of cold meat broken in pieces. This bread and meat should be carefully put in separate dishes daily."—The gentleman who recommended this, (which he calls Pauper soup) says, " As I always have some of this soup at my own table, and my family partake of it, I can depend on its being good; and as a proof of it, I have known this soup to be preferred to that made from the best beef. Some split peas, rice, or barley, may be added to advantage.

EXPENCE.			s.	d.
8lb. of beef at 2¼ per lb.	—		1	8
Turnips and carrots	— —		0	2
Onions, Pepper, and salt	—		0	2
			2	0

The industrious poor, and distressed working manufacturers, feel the most pinching want at this rigorous season of the year—coals retailed at 30s. per ton—their common food, potatoes, kept up at an enormous price—the assize of bread extremely small—and a species of pestilential cold prevailing among numbers of them, are grievous calamities.—Let therefore all those whom Providence has blessed with riches, affluence and abundance, step forward to relieve the wants and alleviate the necessities of their fellow creatures pining under the pressure of extreme indigence. Hoarded treasure, and the goods of this world, can be of no use the other side of the grave.

We feel no small satisfaction in the mentioning, that very prime ox beef sold in the different shambles of this city, on Saturday last, at eighteen shillings the hundred weight.

DIED. At Primrose-hill, in the county of Dublin, in the 86th year of his age, the Hon. John Butler, grand-uncle to the Earl of Lanesborough.

BANKRUPT.] William Long, of Ballina, in the county of Mayo, merchant, to surrender on the 30th instant, and on the 2d and 30th of Jan. next.

Belfast, *December 22.*

☞ FOUR MAILS DUE.

The Market-day of this Town will be held on Thursday the 24th inst.—as Christmas day happens to fall on Friday.

The Treasurer of the Belfast Charitable Society acknowledges to have received by the hands of the Rev. William Brittow from Mr. Sampson Robson, of Grange, FORTY POUNDS NINETEEN SHILLINGS sterling, which sum was given to said Mr. Robson for the benefit of that charitable institution by a friend lately deceased, who at same time requested that his name might be concealed from the public.

The average prices of provisions, in the market at Plymouth, England, are as follow:

BUTCHER'S MEAT.

Beef, from 3d to 3d h. per lb.
Pork, from 2d 3 f. to 3d f. do.
Veal, from 3d to 3d h. do.
Mutton, from 3d f. to 3d 3 f. do.

POULTRY.

Good fowls, from 20d to 2s per couple.
Geese, from 2s 3d to 2s 9d each.
Ducks, from 2s to 2s 6d per couple.
Turkeys from 3s to 3s 6d each
Woodcocks *only* 4s and 4s 6d per couple.

FISH.

Turbots, from 4d to 6d per lb.
Fresh Cod and Ling, from 3 f. to 1d do.
Wet Salt Fish, 2d do.
Other Fish in proportion.

Butter, 10d per lb. of 18oz.
And other articles proportionate.

Belfast, *December 25.*

On Saturday last was taken up in this town, and remains in custody, a man who calls himself William Callwell, about 5 feet 8 inches high, slender made, and wore a brown surtout coat. There were found with him seven pieces of seven-eight wide linen, apparently fit for rubbing, and rather in a wet state——says he bought them at Ferney, in the county of Tyrone, and received what bleaching they have got at same place: says he is well known to Sir John Hamilton, and is tenant to Lord Bristol, from whom he holds a considerable farm: was not bred to any business or trade: ends of the linen all cut off; some of the pieces tied up with the ends, on which a small part of the marks with liquid remains. He rode a grey mare, about thirteen and a half hands high, cock tail, in low condition.

The Lord Donegall, Capt. M'Roberts, bound from this port to London, put into Dublin the 19th inst. all well.

The New Draper, Captain Kearney, arrived safe at Liverpool the 18th inst.

FAIRS IN THE ENSUING WEEK.

Monday, Dec. 28. Cross, Arm. Desertmartin, Der.—Tuesday 29. Stranocum, Ant. Trillic, Tyr. Wednesday 30. Benburbe, Tyr. Stewartstown, Tyr. Thursday 31. Clones, Mon. Saintfield, Down.——Friday, Jan. 1. Ballybay, Mon. Ballynahinch, Down. Castledawson, Der. Castlederg, Tyr. Emyvale, Mon. Letterkenny, Don. Lifane, Der. Loughgall, Arm. Redcastle, Don.—Saturday 2. Cookstown, Tyr.

PRICES IN THIS MARKET YESTERDAY.

Oatmeal, 11s. 5d. to 00s. 0d.		Dried do 00s. to 00s. 0d. per d		
Wheat, 13 0 — 00 0		R. Tallow, 6s. 0d. to 0s. 0d. st		
Oats, 5 6 — 00 0		Potatoes 10d. to 11d. per b.		
Barley, 6 0 — 00 0		Eng. coals, 20s. to 00s. 0d.		
Butter, 55 0 — 00 0		Scotch do. 00s. to 90s. 0d.		
C. hides, 34 0 — 35 0		Ex on l ond. 7 a 7 1-4 per c.		
Ox ditto, 37 6 — 40 0		Do. on Glasgow 6¾		
S. C. skins 40 0 — 00 0				

Anno 1789.]   Printed by HENRY JOY, and Co. BELFAST.

The BELFAST NEWS-LETTER.

TUESDAY December 28

James Hamill,

HAS just received per the Friendship, from London, a fresh supply of New Teas and Muftard;—and also per the Matty, from Bordeaux, new Prunes, French Plumbs, Almonds and Walnuts—which with new Raisins, Figs, Currants, Spices, and different forts of Dyeftuffs he will fell on the moft reafonable terms.

Belfaft, 12th Dec. 1789.

Stewart Beatty,

IS now landing out of the Neptune from Bordeaux, and the Friendfhip from London, a parcel ftrong BRANDY, and Whitbread's PORTER, which he will fell on the moft reafonable Terms.

Belfaft, 15th December, 1789.

Almanacks for 1790,

Selling by WM. MAGEE, BELFAST.

MAGEE's Miniature Almanack, Price 2s. 2d.
Magee's Irifh Herald, or Parliamentary Regifter, Price 8d.
Magee's Univerfal Sheet Almanack, Price 5d.
——Belfaft Almanack, Price 4d.
Stuart's IRISH MERLIN, containing befides the ufual Information, a Schedule of Stamp Duties, Extracts from the parliamentary Records of laft Seffion, Dublin Society's Premiums, &c. Price 1s. 1d.
Ditto with REGISTRY for Ireland, England, Scotland and America—with a compleat lift of the Judges, Barrifters and Attornies of Ireland—nett Duties on Imports and Exports, &c. Price 2s. 2d.
Watfon's Gentleman's and Citizen's Almanack, 1s. 1d.
Do. with Englifh Regiftry, 2s. 2d.
Lady's Memorandum Book, Price 1s. 7d. h.
Watfon's and Jackfon's Kalendar, Price 6d. h.

To be Sold,

ONE undivided third of the lands of Doe, containing in the whole 2867 Coningham acres, be the fame more or lefs, fituate near the fea, between Sheephaven and Dunfanaghy; the lands are very improvable and well circumftanced, being convenient to the fisheries, and to abundance of limeftone and fea manure: they are now held at will, and fubject to a moderate rent; a divifion of them may be had when defired A map, furvey, and rent-roll may be feen in the hands of the Revd. John Dubourdieu, Anahilt; Revd. Geo. Sampfon, Londonderry; Thos. Seeds, Surgeon, Belfaft, who with Daniel Chambers, Efq; Rockhill, will receive propofals for faid lands, and upon agreement a clear title fball be made out.

Dated this 28th Dec. 1789.

THE Committee who fuperintend the Sunday Scool of Colerain, beg leave to prefent their beft thanks to Mrs. Richardfon, for her attention to the profperity of that inftitution, which fhe lately manifefted by diftributing twenty gowns, amongft thofe of the girls who had diftinguifhed themfelves by good behaviour and proficiency in learning.——They likewife embrace with pleafure this opportunity of publickly acknowledging their obligations to the young Ladies of the town who have condefcended to attend the School, and affift in the inftruction of the children; and of declaring that to their affiduity the pupils improvement in external appearance and behaviour, as well as advancement in learning, is chiefly owing.
The Committee have not been difappointed hitherto in their expectations; they have the fatisfaction to behold the School ftill flourifhing, and the Children improving not in reading only, but in that kind of learning which is more peculiarly the object of a Sunday School; and while there is fuch inftructors and fuch rewarders of merit, they look forward with pleafure to the happy confequences which may refult from this and fimilar inftitutions.—Colerain, 23d Dec. 1789.

Defertion and Robbery.

DESERTED on the evening of the 15th inft. from his Majefty's 39th regiment of foot, quartered at Belfaft, (having firft robbed one of the Officers) Henry Bloomer, mufician, aged twenty-fix years, fwarthy complexion, black hair, hazle eyes, round vifage, marked with the fmall pox, and has a large cut on his right hand, at the back of the joint of the little finger—had on a brown furtout coat, regimental white jacket, waiftcoat, and breeches, and long black cloth gaiters, with white plain buttons.
Whoever will apprehend the above-mentioned deferter and lodge him in any of his Majefty's jails or guard-houfes, fhall receive two guineas reward, over and above the twenty fhillings allowed by act of Parliament, by applying to the Commanding Officer of the regiment, at the barracks.

Barrack, Dec. 17th, 1789.

POTATOES.

MC. KEDY and STEVENSON want a quantity of right good White Potatoes, for which they will give market Price, at their Stores on Chichefter-Quay.

Belfaft, 28th Dec. 1789.

New Alicante Barilla.

A Cargo of beft quality, is juft arrived to JAMES HOLMES, which, with every other article in the Bleaching Line, he has for fale;—as alfo Sicily Barilla for Soapboilers, Ruffian and Dublin rendered Tallow.

Belfaft, Dec. 28th, 1789

COTERIE.

THERE will be a Coterie at Newtown-Ards, on Thurfday 7th of January next.

28th December, 1789.

THE next HOLYWOOD COTERIE will be held on Thurfday December 31ft.

Holywood, December 27, 1789.

Wanted,

A Middle-aged Man, as Butler, in the Country, where a Pantry Boy is kept. Such an one, bringing certificates of fobriety, &c. may apply at this Office.

Belfaft, Dec 28th, 1789.

To be auctioned or fold,

ON Friday the firft January, 1790, at Hugh Lyndon's, High-ftreet:
A BILLIARD-TABLE, almoft new.——For further particulars enquire at faid Lyndon, who will treat with any perfon for it.

Belfaft, 24th Dec. 1789.

WE the underfigned Cotton Manufacturers of Belfaft and its neighbourhood, beg leave to return our moft fincere thanks to Samuel Black, Efq; Sovereign of faid Town, for his fpirited and zealous exertions in detecting and bringing to juftice, Jofeph Mc. Mechan, for receiving and purchafing a bafket of cotton weft, containing fix pounds, the property of Mr. Nicholas Grimfhaw, of Whitehoufe, the fame being feloniously obtained.

Belfaft, 28th December, 1789.

Nich. Grimfhaw,	Robert Hillditch,
Francis Joy & Co.	Robert Armftrong,
Lukes, Oakman & Co.	William Mulrea,
Samuel Mc. Crum,	John Rofs
Nichs. Mercer,	

ALL thofe to whom Henry Bamber ftands indebted, are requefted to furnifh their accounts, fettled up to the firft of January, to Mr. Alexander Arthur, Attorney, Belfaft.

Falls, December 28th, 1789.

MARKET Price given for good WHEAT every Monday by THOs. BAMBER, at his Stores in Ballynahinch, two doors from Mr. James Armftrong's Inn.

December 28th, 1789.

Lurgan Club,

DINE at the Black Bull Inn, on Monday the 4th of January next.—Dinner on the Table at four o'clock.

Signed by Order,

THOs. BOWEN, Secretary.

December 22d, 1789.

Notice is hereby given,

THAT a Petition will be prefented next Seffion of Parliament to the Hon. the Houfe of Commons in this Kingdom, on behalf of Lord Charles Fitzgerald and George Hamilton, of Tyrrella, in the county of Down, Efq; praying aid to erect a Pier for the improvement of the harbour of Ardglafs, in the barony of Lecale in the faid county of Down.

18th December, 1789.

To be fold by Auction,

ON Wednefday the 13th of January next, A Deed for ever of a large Houfe and Garden, in High-ftreet, in Donaghadee, wherein Doctor Mc. Minn now lives, with two fmall houfes on the eaft fide of the fame. The fituation is efteemed as pleafant as any in the town; the whole fubject to a chief-rent of only 2l. 3s 6d yearly. Mr. Adams, who is empowered to fell the fame, will fatisfy the purchafer with refpect to the title.
N. B. One third of the purchafe-money to be paid on the fale, the remainder on perfecting the deed.

Wheat, Rye, Barley, and Oars.

JAMES HOLMES is conftantly purchafing Wheat, Barley and Oats, of good quality.——Apply at his Stores, Donegall-ftreet.

Now loading in Dublin,

FOR BELFAST,

THE Brigantine RICHARD, of Belfaft, John Mc. Kibbin, Mafter—She will pofitively fail from Dublin in about ten or twelve days ——Thofe who have any Goods to fhip, will do well to give their orders in time.

26th December, 1789.

Juft publifhed,

And to fold by the Bookfellers in Belfaft, Price 6d. halfp.

AN ADDRESS to the Freeho'ders of the County of Antrim, refpecting the Choice of Reprefentatives to ferve in the enfuing Parliament.

December 28th, 1789.

French and Englifh Boarding-School.

MRS. BEAUCHAMP begs leave to inform the Nobility and Gentry, that fhe will open her School in ARMAGH on the 18th day of January next. She has fitted up a commodious houfe for the reception of young Ladies; where they will be carefully inftructed in French, Englifh, Embroidery, Tambour, and plain Work. The beft Mafters will be employed for Mufic, Dancing, Writing, Arithmetic, &c.
As Mrs. Beauchamp has had the honour of teaching in families of the firft rank in this kingdom, fuch parents as are pleafed to commit the education of their children to her care, may depend the ftricteft care will be paid to their health, morals and improvement.
Her terms are twenty Pounds a year, and two Guineas entrance.
Day Scholars taught French, Englifh, &c.—a Guinea a quarter, and a Guinea entrance; Englifh, &c. half a Guinea a quarter, and a Guinea entrance.

Armagh, Dec. 20, 1789.

WHEREAS Anthony Cochran of Lifown, in the county of Down, on Saturday the 19th inftant, bought a Mare in the town of Downpatrick from a perfon who called himfelf Neal Donnelly.
And whereas the faid Cochran fince fufpects that the faid mare was ftolen—Said mare is a dark Bay, with a fmall ftar, about four years old, and of a low fize.
Whoever proves their property in faid mare, may have her by applying to faid Cochran, on paying the expence of keeping, advertifing, &c.

Lifown, 26th December, 1789.

Sale by the Candle.

FORTY Puncheons of choice, old, high-flavoured RUM, nearly two years in ftore, and a quantity of manufactured TOBACCO, to be fold at the Cuftom-Houfe of Ballyrain, on Friday the firft day of January next.   Letterkenny, 15th Dec. 1789.

The Morning Herald,

AT the particular defire of fome of the firft Nobility and Gentry in his kingdom, as well as Merchants, Brokers, Traders, Country Gentlemen, the Public in general—and by the advice of one of the moft diftinguifhed characters of the age, tho' humble enough to ftile himfelf a Cobler—the Proprietor of the Evening Herald, with great refpect for that generous Public to whom he feels himfelf fo much indebted, defires to notify in every refpectable Paper in the kingdom that in order to acquiefce with the fenfe of the nation, to have a public Print of general Poft Days, truly impartial, conveying every article of Intelligence, the Debates of Lords and Commons of both kingdoms, Price of Stocks, Provifions, Grain, &c. with other ufeful Tables highly beneficial to the Public, will change the title of faid Paper to the Morning Herald, and publifh the fame every Tuefday, Thurfday, and Saturday Mornings at feven o'clock—commencing on Tuefday the 29th of December inftant.

Concert and Ball.

MR. MAHOON with the utmoft refpect begs leave to inform the Ladies and Gentlemen of Belfaft and its environs, that his Concert (by particular defire) is fixed for Wednefday the 30th inftant, when he hopes to meet with their countenance and fupport.
The firft Act will chiefly confift of feveral new Pieces, with a variety of favourite Airs for the Flute, Clarionet and Violin; in particular, a new Echo Piece in imitation of Birds, &c. for the Flute and Clarionet compofed for the above Night by Mr. Mahoon.
The fecond Act—The celebrated Siege of Gibraltar.
Mr. Sharp will perform on the Double Bafs on the above night; and feveral Amateurs have kindly promifed their affiftance.

December 17th, 1789.

⁂ Particulars will be given in Hand-bills.—Tickets to be had of Mr. Mahoon, as Mr. Stockman's, at 3s. 9d. halfp. each.

ADVICE

To the Gentlemen who have paſſed the age of fifty, and are alarmed by the many inſtances, which now occur, of apoplexies.

Sudden death is the worſt of all deaths. So the compilers of our Liturgy thought; from battle, murder, and from ſudden death, &c. and ſo the ſurviving friends and relations always think.

To ſuch gentlemen, who, from connections, or inclination, may be much in convivial parties, I would ſay in words like the following:

Eat only when appetite prompts, and eat no more than ſatisfies nature. You muſt know what agrees with you; adhere to that alone, and it will adhere to you, but do not vitiate your appetite by variety. Variety in eating is highly pernicious; for it is a friend to nothing but diſeaſe.

Avoid late ſuppers; ſuppers altogether, if poſſible, and meat ſuppers moſt of all.

"After dinner ſit a while." The firſt, which is the principal ſtage of digeſtion, requires reſt. "After ſupper walk a mile," ſays the proverb; but that proverb was made when ſuppers were uſed at ſeven or eight o'clock.—I ſay again, the leſs ſupper the better. Reflect how you feel in the morning, after having eat a hearty ſupper, and having gone to bed without any ſupper.

As to drinking—Every exceſs is poiſon, the effects of which your conſtitution does not recover, although your head may, for many days. Drink moderately at all times—wine in preference to any other liquor; but no diluted ſpirituous liquors. Conſider, that if you drink diluted liquors in large quantities, you may keep ſober, but that is a trifle—you are filling your body and veins with a quantity of ſuperfluous liquor, which you have no powers, and, it may be, no exerciſe to carry off.

Always remember, for it is a ſolmn truth, that you, or your friends will one day repent, when it is too late, that when the powers of nature are decayed by age, when the digeſting faculties ſhould be tenderly nurſed inſtead of being forced; and when the ſecreting veſſels have loſt their ſenſibility to mild foods and common medicines, then is the time to ſtudy nature only, to live temperately, and always proportion your meat and drink to the means which you can uſe to promote digeſtion by exerciſe, air, &c. &c.

A TRIP TO GRETNA GREEN.

On Monday laſt Miſs P———, of T———ll, in Yorkſhire, a young lady of exquiſite beauty and ſenſibility, with a fortune of thirty thouſand pounds, eloped to Gretna-green with Mr. C. linen-draper, of D————, in the ſame county, a gentleman, allowed by all ſtatuaries, who have had the pleaſure of ſeeing him, to be the beſt proportioned and fineſt figure of a man in the kingdom, being upwards of ſix feet high, and of the exacteſt ſymmetry.

There is a very remarkable circumſtance attending the marriage.

Mr. C——— was to have been united to Miſs G—, of Wakefield, and Miſs P——— to Mr. G—, brother to Miſs G—, the ſame day being appointed for both weddings; but, what is melancholy to relate, Mr. and Miſs G— both died a few days previous to the time fixed for their ſolemnization. It was at the funeral of their reſpective Lovers that this preſent couple firſt met; there being a ſimilarity in their caſes, a ſympathizing attachment immediately took place, and they were married within the month.

The monks of the Eſcurial, in Spain, have formerly pronounced the Emperor of Germany "an imperious, turbulent, pragmatical heretic, diſturbing the Holy Church by innovation and maintaining erroneous doctrines by a ſpirit of faction, obſtinacy, and hypocriſy!

The Eſcurial uſed to be called one of the ſeven wonders of the world. It has eleven thouſand windows, fourteen thouſand doors, eighteen hundred pillars, twenty-two courts, and ſeventeen piazzas. It has three libraries, conſiſting of eighteen thouſand volumes, and three thouſand Arabian manuſcripts.—Here the King and Queen have apartments, and the reſt of this ſuperb palace is inhabited by monks. The plan of the building is in the form of a gridiron.

Lorenzo, a famous Spaniſh Saint, was broiled on a gridiron! Philip II. built the Eſcurial in memory of this Saint, and the battle of St. Quintin. At the late Royal promotion by the King, Lorenzo was invoked by the monks to ſhower down bleſſings on the new Grandees.

The Spaniſh gentry are very numerous, and their families ancient; the cauſe of this is, all landed eſtates are entailed, and cannot be alienated but in failure of iſſue, and then not without great expence, which occaſions land to be ſo very dear there; it is worth forty years purchaſe. At the late Royal promotion, each new made Grandee was obliged to produce proof of his being clear, by four generations, of the blood of a Jew!

DUBLIN, December 24.

The brig Two Brothers, from Philadelphia, to this port is put into the river Kenmare, after a paſſage of 25 days.

The following letter from Griffith, Foſter and Co. dated Liverpool, Dec. 17, is filed at the Royal Exchange Coffee-houſe:

"On Monday, the 14th inſtant, ſailed from this port, bound for Dublin, the Three Brothers, John Corkran, maſter, (a conſtant trader) who was this day put back, having met a heavy gale of wind at N. W. in which ſhe received a ſea, which cauſed her to make ſome water. Her cargo, conſiſting of ſugars, bale goods, and ſundry other articles of merchandiſe, are now re-landing into the Company's ware-houſe, where they are to remain (if free of damage) until ſhe can be got ready to proceed to ſea, which it is expected will be in the courſe of three or four days."

At Liverpool, ſince the ports have been opened, 285 bags, 10,080 buſhels, 1089 quarters of wheat, 300 barrels of wheat flour, and 572 quarters of barley, have been imported.

As the Britiſh Miniſtry continues abſolutely to deny a reciprocity of trade between this country and Great Britain, unleſs we conſent to throw ourſelves once more under a ſubjection to the Parliament of England, it is high time for us indignantly to reject our ſlaviſh acquieſcence to the Weſt India monopoly, which for near ten years we have ſuffered by a tax of additional duties on ſugars, to the amount of one hundred and fifty thouſand pounds a year; for which tax

We Get, liberty, to rival Birmingham and Sheffield, by ſending hardware from hence to the Britiſh Weſt Indies.

We Get, the liberty of purchaſing our ſugars in return for the above hardware, (which by the bye we can never ſend there) at only forty per cent. dearer than we could import them from France, Spain or Portugal, who in return are willing to take any manufactured goods we can furniſh.

We Get, the liberty of importing ſugars and all other produce of America, circuitouſly from Great Britain, in the teeth of the act of navigation, in virtue of which act any veſſel from Ireland, attempting to land ſuch produce in England, would inſtantly be ſeized.

Theſe are the brilliant advantages of the Sugar Bill, that taxes us 150,000l. per annum; and which ſeſſion after ſeſſion our Members of Parliament reenact with their eyes open. We challenge the whole miniſterial phalanx to controvert, in the ſmalleſt inſtance, the above facts; or in the leaſt gloſs over ſo glaring an impoſition on the underſtandings of the Iriſh nation!

It muſt be humiliating to thoſe who conſider the tonnage of Ireland, to contraſt it with England.—In 1786, it was aſſerted in the Britiſh Commons, by a Member high in office, that the tonnage of their ſhipping, in the year 1778, amounted to upwards of one million and ſixty-eight thouſand, which exceeded that of 1774 by near 241,000 tons, and continued increaſing. The tonnage employed in the Iriſh trade is but 286,594, of which 236,654 is Britiſh, and 16,528 foreign veſſels. Our trade is ſuppoſed to have increaſed within theſe fifty years one third at leaſt, though the tonnage of Iriſh veſſels has diminiſhed ſince that period very conſiderably. Theſe circumſtances, with which the intereſts of Ireland are intimately concerned, ſhould ſtimulate an Iriſh Legiſlature to inveſtigate the cauſes and endeavour to obtain a remedy.

By the public accounts it appears, that the bounty on the inland carriage of corn and flour to this city, for the year 1787, amounted to 46,990l. 13s. 2d. and the bounty on corn and flour brought coaſtways to this city for the ſame year, amounted to 18,362l. 3s. 7d. h. ſo that the bounty paid for corn and flour brought to this city that year, by inland carriage, and coaſtways, amounted to the ſum of 65,352l. 5s. 9d. h. ſterling.

The bounty on corn and flour exported that year, from the different ports in this kingdom, amounted to 50,865l. 19s. 8d. h. ſo that the whole amount of bounty paid on corn and flour for that year, was 116,218l. 5s. 6d. ſterling.

Average of the yearly Sales of Brown Linens in Ireland:

Antrim	£. 263,200
Armagh	291,900
Cavan	68,200
Down	152,960
Donegall	16,040
Fermanagh	4,100
Derry	116,720
Monaghan	104,000
Tyrone	334,744
Total	1,351,864

At a ſeaſon when coals have riſen to a price ſo far beyond the capacity of the poor, it is pleaſing to reflect on the relief which they receive from the inſtitution of our public yards. Within a few days not leſs than 1200 neceſſitous perſons have received the benefit of thoſe humane eſtabliſhments.

LONDON-DERRY, September 22.

Friday laſt, being the anniverſary of the ſhutting the gte of Derry, againſt King James's army, at 12 o'cloc, the Apprentice Boys' Company, commanded by Cpt. Bennet, paraded and went thro' the uſual ceremony of ſhutting the gates, &c.

At 1 o'clock, the L:Derry Independent Volunteers paradd in their new uniform, and fired 3 vollies in the Damond. At 3 o'clock they again aſſembled, and marced to the New Inn, where they ſat down to a moſt xcellent dinner. After drinking many loyal and patriotic toaſts, in the evening they proceeded to the new Theatre, where, at their deſire, were repreſented th comedy of He would be a Soldier, and the farce of the Agreeable Surpriſe.—Upon this occaſion, the muſter of the Volunteers was numerous; they looked remarkably well, and fired the vollies with great ſteadineſs.

Belfaſt, *December* 29.

☞ THREE MAILS DUE.

Extract of a letter from Ayr in Scotland, dated December 16, 1789.

"Yeſterday morning 12 veſſels (moſtly colliers) ſailed out of this port, which are all on ſhore. One Engliſh brig ſunk, and the whole crew loſt. It is ſaid, there are eight corpſes floated on ſhore: the gale was exceedingly heavy, and is not yet much abated."

Sunday the Rev. Mr. Sampſon, ſo remarkable for extempore eloquence, delivered at the church of Belfaſt a diſcourſe applicable to the ſeaſon.

On Sunday laſt a boat overſet with four young boys near the firſt perch; one of them named Burdy was unfortunately drowned.

Birth.] The lady of Francis Hardy, Eſq. of a daughter.

PORT NEWS.

ARRIVED.

Dec. 28. Ducheſs of Buccleugh, Stevenſon, Cadiz, barilla, almonds, raiſins, cane reeds, &c.

LINEN TRADE.

MR. PRINTER,

THE practice of robbing Bleach-Greens is become an evil of very great magnitude, and of the moſt alarming tendency. The means of preventing the commiſſion of a crime ſo injurious to this country, ought to occupy much of the attention of a good citizen.

The reſult of ſome conſideration on this ſubject is a conviction, that *Retailers of Linen*, who ſwarm in this country, are the *Inciters and Protectors of Linen Thieves.*

They render the diſpoſal of Stolen Linen eaſy to the thief, and his conviction almoſt impoſſible. From the nature of the bleaching buſineſs it cannot be effectually guarded from theft. To ſteal linen from a bleach-green muſt continue eaſy, but to diſpoſe of it, when ſtolen, *may, and ought to be rendered moſt difficult and dangerous.*

Here, in my opinion, is the defect of the laws.—The regulations annexed are an eſſay towards a remedy.

They are offered to the public for the purpoſe of exciting attention to this truly important ſubject; and, in the hope that ſomething more effectual may be offered by perſons of more experience and ability than the writer of this letter.

Dery. A BLEACHER.

PROPOSED REGULATIONS.

All perſons ſelling linen by retail, to regiſter their names and places of abode with the County Inſpector.

Inſpector to give a certificate and licence, and receive——— for the ſame.

Any perſon ſelling or expoſing to ſale any linen cloth without certificate and licence, on conviction, to forfeit to the Informer 5l. and be publicly whipped.

Any retailer, who ſhall expoſe to ſale, or have in their poſſeſſion any half-bleached or white linen, not having thereon the bleacher's ſeal, or the water mark, ſhall, on conviction, for the firſt offence, be fined ———; for the ſecond, be thrice publicly whipped; for the third forfeit his goods and chattles, and be tranſported for life.

Any perſon in whoſe poſſeſſion unſealed linen may be found, ſhall prove, by teſtimony of two or more credible witneſſes, that ſuch linen ſo found was manufactured and whitened by themſelves, or bought from a regiſtered bleacher, or a licenced retailer, on pain of ſimilar penalties.

Perſons ſelling leſs than twenty yards in one piece, retailers.

Index

NAME INDEX

ALEXANDER, JOHN: 93
ANDERSON, WILLIAM: 47
ARMSTRONG, ALEXANDER: 1
ARMSTRONG, ROBERT: 105
ARNOLD, MRS.: 87
ASHE, MR.: 102
ATCHESON, JAMES: 101
ATKINS, MR.: 9, 33

BAMBER, HENRY: 105
BAMBER, THOMAS: 105
BANKHEAD, JOHN: 7
BANKHEAD, JOHN & ARCHIBALD:
 3, 47, 71, 93, 99
BARCLAY, JOHN: 29
BASHFORD, JOHN: 7, 45, 59, 63
BATT, NARCISSUS: 1, 21
BEATTY, STEWART: 83, 105
BEAUCHAMP, MRS.: 105
BERRY, NATH.: 83
BERWICK, DUKE: 69, 85
BLACKWELL, ALEX.,: 57
BLEAKLY, WILLIAM: 29
BOWEN, THOMAS: 105
BOYLE, JOHN: 4, 15, 17, 81, 103
BRADFORD, GEORGE: 43
BRADSHAW, ROBERT: 49
BRENNAN, CORNELIUS: 97
BRISTOW, SAMUEL: 19
BROWN, GAW & CO.: 1, 33, 43, 89
BROWN & OAKMAN: 29, 39, 41, 51, 55,
 65
BROWN, SAMUEL & CO.: 5, 41, 47, 63,
 71
BURNS, ROBERT: 72
BYRNE, MR.: 22

CALLWELL, CATHERINE: 51
CALLWELL, ROBERT & CO.: 35, 45
CARLILE, ANDREW & HUGH: 17, 57
CARMICHAEL, JOHN: 35
CHALMERS, MR.: 22
CHALMERS, MRS.: 11
COAN, ROBERT M.: 97
COILE, BERNARD: 15
COKE, WILLIAM: 55, 63
CONNOR, MARY: 1
CORBITT, JOHN HAMILTON: 93
CORBITT, WILLIAM: 97
CRAIG, JOHN: 65
CRANSTON, JOHN & CO.: 69
CRAWFORD, HUGH: 13, 31, 41, 65, 85,
 99
CROMBIE, JAMES: 59, 65
CULLEN, MR.: 57, 63, 77
CUMING, JOHN: 89
CUNNINGHAM, GREG: 33, 39, 41, 47,
 49, 51, 63, 83, 87
CUNNINGHAM, JAMES: 21
CUNNINGHAM, WADDELL: 4, 31, 81,
 103
CUTHBERT, JOSEPH: 97

DAVIDSON, JOHN: 63
DAVIDSON & MINNIS: 47, 93
DAVISON & GRAHAM: 51, 67, 89
DAVISON, THOMAS: 85
DICKSON, CONNINGHAM: 11
DUMONT, MR.: 87

EADDY, SAMUEL: 7
EDWARDS, JOHN: 21
EDWARDS & SHAW: 61
EMMERSON, GEORGE: 65
EWING, JOHN: 31

FERGUSON, SAMUEL: 29
FITZSIMONS, JAMES: 97
FORSYTH, SHAW & CO.: 1
FREEMAN, MR.: 17
FREEMAN, MRS.: 9, 11
FULLERTON, HUGH: 97

GALWAY, WILLIAM: 19
GAW, PATRICK & CO.: 89
GEEHAN, ANDREW: 11
GEORGE III, KING: 4, 6, 8, 10, 12, 16,
 20, 22, 24, 26, 28, 30, 34, 36, 40, 44, 48,
 52, 54, 60, 64, 68, 70, 72, 76, 78, 100
GETTY, JOHN: 1
GETTY, ROBERT: 1, 11, 93, 99
GIBSON, SAMUEL: 21, 29, 41, 47, 65
GILLESPIE, CLEMENTS: 1, 43
GORDON, ROBERT & ALEXANDER:
 6, 33
GRAHAM, HAMILTON: 19
GRAHAM, JAMES: 17, 49, 51
GRATTAN, HENRY: 13
GREER, JAMES: 15
GRIMSHAW, NICH.:
GRUEBER, ARTHUR &
McALLISTER, RANDAL: 83, 85

HADSKIS, ABEL: 15
HAMILL, JAMES: 105
HAMILTON, JOHN: 81
HANNA, JOHN: 97
HANNA, WILLIAM & SAMUEL: 3, 49,
 77
HASLETT, STRONG & CO.: 33, 49, 85
HASTINGS, WARREN: 36, 42, 56
HENDERSON & CRAWFORD: 53
HENDREN, WILLIAM: 1, 21, 35
HERRON, HUGH: 15
HERVEY, JOHN: 15
HEWITT, SAMUEL & JAMES: 15
HILL, ROBERT: 3, 7, 93
HILLDITCH, ROBERT: 105
HOLMES, JAMES: 23, 39, 81, 105
HOLMES, JOHN: 3, 31
HOOD, THOMAS: 97
HOSKIN, MISS: 15
HULL, MR.: 31, 44
HUMPHRIES, THOMAS: 33
HUNTER, JAMES: 39, 65
HUNTER, JOHN: 29
HUNTER, ROBERT: 69
HUNTER, WILLIAM: 97
HUTCHESON, JAMES: 23
HYNDMAN, HUGH: 7

JAMESON & GALT: 99
JOHNSON, HUGH & WILLIAM: 1, 33,
 97
JOHNSON, WILLIAM: 95
JOHNSTON & HENRY, ALEXANDER:
 29
JONES, TOMB, JOY & CO.: 7, 13, 21, 31,
 41, 47, 77, 99, 101
JOY, FRANCIS & CO.: 105
JOY, MR.: 23, 29, 33, 59, 61, 71, 73, 83, 85,
 103
JOYCE, VALENTINE: 73, 99

KEEN, WILLIAM: 39
KELLY, JOHN: 57
KENNEDY, JAMES T.: 17, 91
KENNEDY, ROBERT: 77
KING, MR.: 9, 17
KINGSMILL, EDWARD: 99
KNOX, JOHN: 33, 53
KNOX, ROBERT: 21, 85

LANGTRY, GEORGE: 1, 9, 21, 45, 65, 99
LINDON, MR.: 81
LINN, JANE: 29
LOMAX, JOSHUA: 57
LOUIS XVI, KING: 50, 56, 58, 60, 62, 66,
 80, 86, 88, 92, 98, 100, 102
LUKES, OAKMAN & CO.: 59
LYDON, HUGH: 67
LYNCH, MR.: 15, 20, 22
LYNCH, MRS.: 29

MAGEE, JAMES & WILLIAM: 3, 7
MAGEE, WILLIAM: 5, 43, 45, 47, 101,
 105
MAGEE'S LOTTERY OFFICE: 5, 7, 10,
 13, 15, 17, 63, 67, 71, 81, 83, 95
MAHOON, MR.: 102, 105
MAWHINNEY, MR.: 83
McAULAY, MARY: 47
McCABE, THOMAS: 3, 7, 9, 13, 39
McCARTNEY, G.: 43
McCLEAN, SAMUEL & ANDREW: 5,
 15, 23, 41, 52, 77, 85, 97, 99
McCLELLAND, RICHARD: 45
McCLURE, WILLIAM: 41, 49, 65, 93
McCONCHY, WILLIAM: 33
McCOUBREY, JOHN: 57
McCRUM, SAMUEL: 105
McGRATH, MR.: 41
McKEDY & STEVENSON: 21, 105
McKINSTY, PATRICK: 83
McMINN, DR.: 105
McMURRAY, SAMUEL & CO.: 89
McQUOID, THOMAS: 87
McREYNOLDS, SAMUEL: 43
McTEAR & HENDERSON: 11
MERCER, NICH.: 105
METRALCOURT, MR.: 91, 99
MILLER, JOHN: 67, 101
MILLER, MR.: 61
MITCHELL, WILLIAM: 3, 41, 99
MONTGOMERY, HUGH: 71, 97
MONTGOMERY, JOHN: 67, 69
MOONEY, JAMES: 35, 103
MORTEGUITTE, EIRENNE: 95
MULLAN, THOMAS: 29, 43
MULREA, WILLIAM: 105
MUNRO, GEORGE: 1, 3
MURPHY, JAMES: 59
MURRAY, DR. WILLIAM: 9

NEILSON, ALEXANDER: 39, 99
NEILSON, SAMUEL: 33, 85
NEILSON, THOMAS: 1, 35, 57, 83
NICHOLSON, MR.: 47, 79
NICHOLSON'S LOTTERY: 41
NIXON, JOHN: 89
NORTON, FRANCIS: 97

OGILBY, ALEXANDER: 101
OGLE, HENRY: 19
OGLE, JOHN: 47
OGLE, WILLIAM: 51, 57
O'HANLON, HUGH: 17
ORR, ALEXANDER: 39, 55

PARK, JAMES: 71
PARKINSON, THOMAS: 69
PATTERSON & FLETCHER: 15
PATTERSON & WHITTLE: 69
PINKERTON, JAMES: 57, 95
PITT, WILLIAM: 6, 10, 52, 62, 72
POLLOCK, JOHN: 93
PRENTICE, THOMAS: 17, 21
PRINCE OF WALES: 4, 6, 10, 16, 20, 22,
 26, 52, 54, 64, 68
PYE, MR.: 13

View of Belfast from Joy's paper mill, 1805.

PLACE INDEX

*Donegall Street, 1831, showing the Brown Linen Market on the right and Commercial Buildings in the distance.
Drawn by T. M. Baynes and engraved by W. Miller*

SHIPS ADVERTISED IN THE TEXT

Select Glossary

Barilla: the ashes of marine plants, e.g. glasswort, which thrives on salt marshes and muddy sea shores, especially in the Mediterranean area, the Spanish east coast, Sicily and the Canary Islands. After sun drying, the plants were burned in small piles and their ashes collected. These produced a rich source of alkali for both glass production and linen bleaching.

Cambric: a fine, plain-woven linen.

Coterie: small, exclusive group of people who shared similar views.

Danzig Ashes: weed ashes produced around the port of Danzig (now Gdansk, Poland). Increasingly imported into Belfast after 1760 to replace disrupted American sources. Like Barilla used as a source of alkali.

Indigo: deep blue dye obtained from the indigo plant.

Kelp: the ash of sea weed or sea wrack. Burned and collected like barilla but contained a much lower alkaline content.

Phaeton: a light, four-wheeled, open carriage.

Train oil: oil obtained by heating whale or seal blubber. Used for lubrication, lighting, leather processing and in soap making.

Volunteers: created in the spring of 1778 as a local defence force against the possibility of local unrest or French invasion. Belfast's paramilitary body was very democratic in structure with elected officers and a stout resistance to government control.

Acknowledgements

We are grateful to Mrs Valerie Fawcett for typing the introduction and index. Mr Roy Dixon from Belfast Central Library kindly gave this project his assistance for which we are most grateful. The views of High Street on the first page, Joy's mill and the Williamson map came from John Anderson's *History of the Linen Hall Library* (Belfast, 1888). The other view of High Street and Donegall Street were taken from G. N. Wright, *Ireland illustrated* (London, 1831). The drawing of the corporation bellman on the final page was found in R. M. Young's *Historical notices of old Belfast* (Belfast, 1896). The Ulster Museum provided the cover picture of Belfast, engraved by John Nixon, *c.* 1790.

THE CORPORATION BELLMAN OF BELFAST.